1 MONTH OF
FREE
READING

at
www.ForgottenBooks.com

By purchasing this book you are eligible for one month membership to ForgottenBooks.com, giving you unlimited access to our entire collection of over 1,000,000 titles via our web site and mobile apps.

To claim your free month visit:
www.forgottenbooks.com/free876780

ISBN 978-0-266-65987-7
PIBN 10876780

PANOPLIST,

AND

MISSIONARY MAGAZINE,

FOR THE YEAR 1814.

VOL. X.

BOSTON:

PUBLISHED BY SAMUEL T. ARMSTRONG,

NO. 50, CORNHILL:

Of whom any or all of the preceding volumes may be had. Also of him may be had a general assortment of Religious and Miscellaneous Publications. Dr. Scott's Family Bible, at various prices, from $19 to $35 on hand.

1814.

PREFACE.

IT is generally the design of a preface to make the reader acquainted with something, which it will be useful for him to know, before he commences the perusal of the work itself. But this cannot be the design of a preface to a volume, which has been published and read before the preface was written. The Editors of periodical publications naturally fall into the habit of writing *postcripts*, though they are placed at the beginning of volumes, and usurp the name of *prefaces*. It will not be unprecedented, therefore, if we cast our eyes back for a moment, on the volume which is now closed, and which, as we are willing to believe, has been read with candor by our patrons generally.

Though we could wish our pages had been more worthy of perusal, and though we are by no means blind to their imperfections, yet it is a consoling thought, that the tendency and the effect of the Panoplist, are, as our friends encourage us to hope, decidedly beneficial. There is the more reason for expressing this opinion of our work, as we could not be justified in publishing it, were its utility doubtful in our own view, and as a large proportion of the original matter is furnished by men, whose deliberate reflections are certainly entitled to an attentive consideration. On looking over the numbers, which compose this volume, as we have been obliged to do in compiling an index, the vast importance of a religious magazine, conducted with even tolerable propriety, has been very deeply impressed on our mind.

One most cheering characteristic of the present times, is an enlarged and still increasing benevolence. Efforts to meliorate the condition of man are now made by a greater number of enlightened individuals, and on a grander scale, than ever before. It is of infinite importance to the world. that these efforts should not be slackened; that the zeal, which is now so happily excited, should not languish; and that the number of persons, who labor and pray for the prosperity of Zion, should be multiplied. Though these desirable results can only be secured by the divine blessing. yet it is to be received as an undoubted maxim, that this blessing is not to be expected, unless in the use of the means which God has kindly furnished, and which have often been honored with sure tokens of his approbation. Let the friends of the Redeemer see to it, then, that no vantage ground be abandoned; and that no temporary inconvenience be suffered to impede the progress of that cause, the success of which is infinitely more valuable than any temporal interests.

These considerations should induce all publishers of religious works, and all writers in them. to look forward with a steady eye, and an unwavering faith, to that blessed consummation, when truth and virtue shall become triumphant on earth. and when the Lord Jesus shall be universally received as the Savior of sinners That we may act under the influence of these high and commanding motives, and that our readers may be interested in the blessings of that *covenant, which is ordered in all things and sure,* is our earnest supplication to God.

Boston, December, 1814.

INDEX,

INDEX TO THE POETRY.

INDEX TO THE PRINCIPAL TEXTS OF SCRIPTURE.

INDEX TO THE SIGNATURES.

THE

PANOPLIST,

AND

MISSIONARY MAGAZINE.

No. 1.   JANUARY, 1814.   VOL. X.

ADDRESS TO THE PUBLIC.

AT the commencement of a new volume, it is proper that we avail ourselves of the common practice of Editors, and lay before our readers several considerations, which are naturally suggested by the occasion. Every editor of a periodical work must feel, if he has the real good of mankind at heart, that a very important and interesting relation subsists between himself and his patrons. While the duties, which this relation imposes upon him, will not be forgotten; and while he will cultivate an enlarged good will toward all men, and indulge in particular good wishes toward his readers; he will hope and expect to receive from them correspondent kindness, encouragement, and support. With these impressions, we design to state some principal reasons of the great utility of religious magazines, and to close with such reflections as shall promise to be seasonable and useful.

In considering the advantages, which the Christian community may derive from religious periodical works, we shall necessarily be brief.

1. Works of the kind here specified are extremely beneficial, as they produce and extend a taste for religious reading. By the variety which they contain, and the intelligence which they communicate, they present the reader with much that is both new and interesting. Thus they allure many to commence inquiries on the most important of all subjects. They are peculiarly fitted to excite attention in the young. When curiosity is roused, and the mind is awakened to the pursuit of any great object, it will of course take pleasure in such a pursuit, and will gain knowledge faster, and turn it to a better account, than could in other circumstances be expected. Whatever directs curiosity to a noble object, and tends to restrain the wayward steps of the young, and to lead them into the path of life, must be highly important in itself, and entitled to the countenance of all Christians.

2. The present state and prospects of the Church are particularly worthy of the attention of every person, who feels interested in her prosperity. The revivals of religion with which God has blessed many parts of the Christian world; the increased fervor, animation and zeal of the real disciples of Christ; the rapidly increasing activity of the benevolent and pious;—all these things impart a peculiar interest

to every occurrence, which respects the state and progress of religion. Who does not feel desirous to hear of the success of missionaries, and of great and most encouraging accessions to our churches at home? Who does not rejoice with holy exultation at the great efforts which are making to extend the influence of the Gospel in every direction? If any, who profess the religion of Christ, are insensible to its triumphs, and regardless of its interests, they have too much reason to fear that their profession is vain.

3. The establishment and success of societies for the reformation of morals in this country, form a new and irresistible argument in favor of supporting publications, in which the proceedings of these societies can be regularly detailed, their beneficial tendency stated, and the duty of supporting them urged. Christians of the present day are trying the efficacy of combinations to do good and to prevent evil; and they are astonished at the greatness of their success. But the good work is only just begun; though it is begun on a large scale, and under favorable auspices. The regular and general diffusion of intelligence is as necessary to any great public-spirited and united exertions, as the free circulation of the blood to the health of the human frame. While this truth is acknowledged in relation to all other subjects, it is surprising that any person should doubt or hesitate in regard to its application to religious and charitable enterprises. While newspapers are daily sent forth in vast numbers, and penetrate into the obscurest corners of society, it is strange, that efficient and abundant support should be withheld by professing Christians from a class of publications, which have a direct reference to religion, and the tendency of which is undeniably salutary in a very high degree. Is it too much to expect, that among the improvements of the present day will be numbered a just regard to the diffusion of religious and moral intelligence, and, consequently, a liberal support of those publications, in which such intelligence is communicated?

Nearly connected with the last mentioned topic is the support of Christian missions. As missions are supported only by voluntary contributions, and these contributions are made by numerous individuals far remote from each other, it is almost impossible, that any great efforts should be made in this cause without a publication of the kind in question.

4. Religious magazines, if conducted only with a tolerable share of skill and talent, exert a powerful influence in promoting the circulation of other new and useful works. Thus they multiply and perpetuate the means of usefulness, and indirectly, as well as directly, subserve the best interests of society. In many different ways they are important auxiliaries in the cause of truth and virtue. It is so ordered by the all-wise God, that every benevolent exertion affords assistance to other similar exertions, and receives assistance from them.

5. The Christian finds in a religious magazine many things to quicken his languid steps, to revive his fainting zeal, to enlarge

his religious views, and to stimulate him to greater activity in the service of his divine Master. He is furnished with new weapons for the spiritual conflict, and with the occasion of brightening and using those which he already possesses. As he is often led to admire the triumphs of the cross, his own interest in the Gospel appears more precious, and his hope more inestimable.

6. A judicious work of the kind here kept in view will of course strengthen and confirm impressions made on the mind, by the stated labors of the clergy. The minister of the Gospel will gain a more ready attention and will preach to better effect, if his people are in the habit of reading and reflecting upon religious subjects; and in no other way can such a habit be so easily formed, as by feeling an interest in a religious periodical publication. Most persons have not the means of possessing or consulting large libraries; but few are so careless as not to be capable of taking an interest in the most important concerns, if furnished with the requisite information.

7. It is highly desirable, that there should exist periodical publications, of known established character, whose decisions shall be worthy of attentive consideration in questions of morals and religion. And it is obvious, that the more extensively such publications can be circulated, the more beneficial will be their tendency and effects. Whether, in short, the promotion of religious knowledge and sound learning, or the defence of the truth, or the extension of the Gospel, be regarded as an object of great value, a multitude of arguments can be adduced in favor of religious magazines.

Though the preceding observations may be familiar to some of our readers, yet a large portion even of the religious community seem not to have justly appreciated the importance of the subject. While we ardently wish that our work were more worthy of the cause in which it is employed—the great cause of religious and moral truth, and of human happiness—and while we shall sedulously labor that it may become so, we commend it to the blessing of God, and the patronage of good men.

We now turn to subjects, in which our readers will probably feel a more direct interest, and seize this opportunity to offer a few exhortations to the minds of all.

Let each one reflect, that it is through the unmerited goodness of God, and for wise and holy purposes, that he is brought to see the commencement of another year. An unusual number of persons, of all ages and descriptions, have gone down to the grave the year past. Sudden deaths of persons in vigorous health have been astonishingly frequent, in many parts of our country. Ministers of the Gospel, magistrates, and other men of great influence and worth, have been removed from the world in rapid succession. Those, who are still spared, should ponder well the distinguishing providence of God. They should consider and inquire, whether they are spared as blessings to mankind, as highly favored in being permitted to serve God and their generation through a longer period, or as instances of increasing stupidity under increasing light and privileges. The year, upon which they have now entered, will soon be numbered with its predecessors, and will have departed forever with all its opportunities and means of usefulness. To every individual it is inconceivably important, that the passing months should bear a good report, and that the closing year should present a happy memorial of time well employed, and duties faithfully performed. Though the year will pass rapidly away, it will, nevertheless, furnish many opportunities of doing good, and numerous motives to improve in piety and virtue.

It has pleased God, within a few years past, to erect his standard of victory over the hosts of Satan, and to bestow distinguished success on the champions of the cross. He has already given an earnest of what he is soon to accomplish, in hastening the permanent increase, security, and glory of his Church. Let all, who profess to be his friends, justly appreciate the value of their time, their influence, and example. Let them openly, zealously, constantly, encourage all beneficent plans, and engage heartily in the cause of God and mankind. Let no advantage already gained ever be yielded to the enemy. Let all the pious be united by the strong bands of love; and each endeavor to promote the peace and happiness of the whole. Let every good institution find a ready and cheerful patronage, every benevolent plan a speedy adoption,

and all charitable labors that perseverance which will ensure success. Let the devout inquiry ascend from every pious heart, *Lord, what wilt thou have me to do?*

The various attempts which are now making, in many parts of New England, to reform the morals of the community, and render vice shameful as well as odious, should receive the energetic support of all friends of their country, especially of all Christians. The vice of intemperate drinking has received a shock from which, as there is reason to hope, it will never recover. The vice of Sabbath-breaking is viewed in its true light by a large portion of the people, and efforts to suppress this evil also are made with hopeful prospects. Let reformation proceed in its course, aided by all who have it in their power to give their countenance, or offer a petition for the divine blessing. Numerous societies must be formed, sermons must be preached, tracts must be distributed, till the community shall be thoroughly apprised of their dangers and their duties; till the virtuous shall raise their courage and activity, in some good proportion to the excellence of their cause, and the vicious shall be confounded and dismayed. Union in a good cause, faith in the promises of God, and perseverance in well-doing, will unquestionably triumph.

There is one class of persons, who ought to feel a peculiar responsibility in relation to these remarks. We refer to those, whom Providence has endued with the talent of writing for the instruction of the public. Though this class of persons is, in all countries, comparatively small, and though the favored few may be diffident of their powers, yet the people of this country know, and should gratefully acknowledge, that there are those among us, who can write ably, and with decisive effect, on the most important subjects. Some individuals of this class can hardly be ignorant of the character and reputation of their writings. Others have yet to learn the full measure and extent of their responsibility, when they shall have engaged more extensively in this great labor of love. To all, who have the talent of writing for the benefit of mankind, we take the liberty of addressing, in the language of earnest intreaty, an admonition not to suffer that talent to lie buried and useless. We beseech them to consider the amazing importance of seizing present opportunities, of securing present advantages, and of bringing every possible accession of strength to the righteous cause, in the mighty conflict which now exists in the world. Let them duly estimate the value of the talent here referred to, and remember, that, though unnoticed and unknown on earth, every one, who shall *convert a sinner from the error of his way*, will *save a soul from death, and hide a multitude of sins.*

For the encouragement of the benevolent it is to be steadily kept in view, that probably no period has existed since the creation of the world, when it was so easy to do good, on a large scale, as at the present day. This observation is meant to apply to those beneficent attempts only, which are made with a prayerful reliance on God. If the observation is correct, and we appeal to every competent judge that it is so, what an unusual weight of responsibility rests upon all who have wealth, influence, or mental endowments? With what energy and activity should the thought inspire all, whom their duty invites to study, or to public labors.

Finally; let every reader look to the state of his own soul, and examine on which side of the grand controversy he now stands. In relation to this controversy there can be no neutrals; and it is vastly important to every individual not to be found in the ranks of rebellion against God, and hostility to the best interests of man. The truth, as it respects the state and character of each person, will be known hereafter, and at no distant period. The character of each will soon be fixed for eternity. Are any of our readers losing opportunities of serving God? How amazing the loss! Let them become truly wise, and embrace the Gospel. Then happy will be their dismission from the body, though they should not live through the year which is now commencing, and unspeakably glorious their reward in heaven.

vine person, would not Jesus have defined or explained the question, before he took the oath? Would he not have declared it, had he not in fact been the Son of God, in the strict, or peculiar sense of that term? Especially so, when he did explain, and define the sense of the question put to him by Pilate, *whether he was the King of the Jews,* before he gave answer. Would he not have done it when he was under an oath, which was too sacred and important, not to be strictly regarded? With such expressions before him, can any one mistake the intention of Jesus to be acknowledged as divine? Let them be uttered by any other person, and see if any doubt would arise, whether he meant to ascribe divinity to himself. The Jews, who were cotemporary with Jesus did understand him as claiming divine honors; a satisfactory proof, that his language in that day appeared to them, as it now does to us, to assert this claim. *He hath spoken* blasphemy, said Caiaphas, and then passed sentence of death upon him; Mat. xxvi, 65. *Art thou greater than Abraham and the prophets? Whom makest thou thyself?* said the Jews, and took up stones to stone him; John viii, 53. The Jews eagerly sought after him to kill him, because he made himself equal to God; John v, 18. *For blasphemy,* said they, *will we stone thee, and because that thou, being a man, makest thyself God;* John x, 33.

In the answer of Jesus, to this expression of the malice of the Jews toward him, which answer was intended to defend and vindicate himself, many suppose a disclosure is made, which shews that all his exalted expressions concerning himself amount merely to the cold position, that *he was a teacher sent from God.* It is somewhat peculiar, to be sure, that a single passage, and of this kind, should outweigh a multitude of other passages, and confine the sense of them. But as this passage is often urged, as an irrefutable argument against Trinitarians, and is much cried up as putting an end to the controversy in question, it may be proper to dwell with some degree of particularity upon it.

The answer of Jesus is as follows: *Is it not written in your law, I said, Ye are gods? If he called them gods, unto whom the word of God came, (and the Scripture cannot be broken;) Say ye of him, whom the Father hath sanctified and sent into the world, Thou blasphemest, because I said, I am the Son of God?* John x, 34—36. According to our Anti-Trinitarians, the meaning of this is as follows: 'In the Mosaic law, they are called gods, to whom a revelation was given by God, and whom he chose and commissioned as the extraordinary teachers of mankind; consequently, I, who am an extraordinary teacher endowed with more exalted and divine illumination, may lawfully call myself God, and the Son of God.' Now, in order to determine whether this be the meaning of the passage in question, let the following considerations be first duly weighed.

1. If Jesus attached to his expressions, which were judged to be blasphemy worthy of death,

only the assertion, that he was a divine teacher, did he not afford reason for the accusation to his face, that he denied his own clear, and express words? and must he not have expected it to be made? The controversy did not here respect the appellation of *God,* or *Son of God,* but the phrases, *I give,* (not I barely procure, but) *I give to my followers eternal life; I and the Father are one.*

2. Jesus shewed plainly, and quite intelligibly to his opposers, that he did not at all explain away the exalted meaning of his previous assertions, nor limit the elevated rank, which he had ascribed to himself, to the dignity of a person divinely commissioned, but still a mere man; for after this explanation of his meaning, as some will have it, the Jews still sought to take and kill him; John x, 39. Jesus does not say, *To me the word of God has come;* but, *The Father hath sanctified me*—distinguished me with peculiar dignity—constituted and exhibited me as one more exalted, more holy, more worthy of respect than others—and *sent me into the world.* He adds, (v. 37, 38,) *If I do not the works of my Father, then believe me not: but if I do, though ye believe not me, believe the works, that ye may know and believe, that the Father is in me, and I in him.* These are words, which neither Moses, nor any other prophet, ever ventured to utter, or ever could venture to utter, respecting himself; much less to say, that nothing more was meant, than to assert, that he was a divinely commissioned teacher.

3. If any one insists on translating the words of Jesus, thus; *If then, he calls those gods, whom God honored with his Revelations,* &c. then he ascribes to him a palpable untruth; for Moses hath not called prophets *gods.* This might, indeed, pass without being discovered by the New Theologians of our day, many of whom have not studied the Mosaic revelation so much as to know, whether the passage in question be in it or not. Among the Jews, however, to whom the writings of Moses were all familiar, this circumstance could not have passed unnoticed.

Ex. iv, 16, *Aaron shall be instead of a mouth to thee, and thou shall be to him instead of God,* does not constitute a proof to the contrary of what I have asserted. Here is a comparison of the connexion in which Moses and Aaron were mutually to stand, with the connexion of which one is reminded, with regard to a prophecy, between the Divinity who gives the prophecy, and the man who delivers it. Moses is likened unto God, not because he was a prophet, (for in comparison with Moses, this character was rather to be ascribed to Aaron,) but because he sent a man, who served under him, as a prophet serves God, by whom he is sent.

Still less does Moses use the word, *gods,* in the sense pretended, in those passages, Ex. xxi, 6; xxii, 28; which are the passages referred to in Ps. lxxxii, 6, from which last passage our Savior makes his quotation. For in these passages, not teachers, but magistrates, are called

Elohim, gods, i. e. worthy of honor, entitled to reverence.

To translate, then, the verses in question, thus: "In the law, they are called gods, to whom the divine Revelations were made," is undoubtedly an error, and expresses what is contrary to the true state of the fact. Those are called gods in the law, who are intended in the passage now in question, or to whom the words, *Ye are gods* are addressed, in the 82d Psalm; i. e. magistrates. The meaning of the passage may be rendered unequivocal, by translating it thus; *If he called them gods, to whom this word or command of God came;* i. e. if those are called gods, who are addressed in the passage cited from the Old Testament, *Say ye of him, whom the Father hath sanctified, &c?*

4. The design of Jesus was, plainly, to convince his Jewish hearers at that time in a brief manner, that his assertion, which had been so offensive to them, gave them no right to take away his life. The occasion did not permit his adducing formal proof, that he was truly God. Had he replied, 'I am equal with God, and, that this is the case, I will now produce the evidence;' they would have put him to death, if they had acted agreeably to the frame of mind in which they then were, before he could have finished his reply. If ever a reply *ad hominem*, a contradiction of opposers on principles avowed and maintained by themselves, be allowable, it certainly may be, in such a case as this. Every person, who proclaimed to the Jews any other God, except Jehovah, was

guilty of a capital offence: such was the law of Moses. Jesus did, in fact, proclaim no other God; but he appeared to the Jews to be guilty of this crime. On the mere appearance of this guilt, the Jews charged him with blaspheming God, and sought to kill him on the spot, without even a trial. Appropriately to the occasion, Jesus answers, 'I have done no evil, which deserves death. Whether I am in fact a blasphemer of God, on whom the law pronounces sentence of death, is a question which should be seriously investigated, and not decided hastily from mere appearances: otherwise ye must adjudge Moses himself to be guilty of a like crime, for he calls magistrates *Elohim, gods;* not indeed with a design to proclaim strange gods, but you must admit that it has this appearance. A sentence of death hastily pronounced on me, would be as unjust as against Moses. Do you not inquire why he calls magistrates *Elohim?* And whether he does in fact oppose the unity of God? Inquire then, in like manner, with respect to my expressions before you pass and execute your sentence.'

5. The kind of reasoning, which Jesus employs in opposition to his enemies, is very apparent. 'If the law styles those *gods*, to whom it says, *Ye are gods*, why should I be accused of blasphemy, because I said I am the Son of God? Because *I* said this, whom the *Father hath sanctified, and sent into the world?*'——A conclusion, evidently, *a minori ad majus*, from the less to the greater! A kind of reasoning, which they must

entirely overlook, who suppose that Jesus intends to shew, that he is no greater than those who are addressed in the law. When Jesus says, 'If God adorns the flowers of the field, and feeds the meanest fowls of the air, will he not feed and clothe you, who are his children?' he surely does not mean to say, that pious men are of no more value in the sight of God, and have no more title to his care, than plants, and animals! No—the very object of the comparison is to set in a striking point of view, the superior worth of the children of God, and the consequent certainty that they will be provided for.

So Christ, in the passage in question, and in the conclusion which it contains, does not affirm that he is only equal to the persons, whom Moses calls *gods*, but that he is far superior to them—"*one whom the Father hath sanctified and sent into the world;*" an expression never applied to magistrates.

6. A critic, who well understands the Old Testament, will easily perceive, that Jesus does in fact introduce a very obnoxious proof, that he had lawfully affirmed, what he had said respecting himself. He calls himself the person, *whom the Father had sanctified, and sent into the world:* and this is a mere translation of יהוה קדוש *the sanctified of the Lord,* and מלאך יהוה, *the angel, the sent of Jehovah.* The former, according to the opinion of the Jews at that time, was the name of the Messiah; see Ps. xvi, 10, and the Messiah was, in the opinion of many Jews then living, to be a divine person The latter was the appellation of an exalted person-

age, who, agreeably to all which is said of him, was undeniably divine. Under this name, he often appeared to the Patriarchs, and manifested himself as Jehovah, the God of Israel. Jehovah says to Moses, '*I send mine angel* (ואלך) *before thee, and my name is in him,* i. e. agreeably to the Hebrew idiom; *I am in him:* Jesus says, The *Father is in me, and I in him.* How exactly the two descriptions agree!

With respect to objections drawn from other passages, where Jesus appears to represent himself as inferior, or subordinate to the Father. our difficulties may more briefly, and more easily be removed. One has only to remember, that our Savior was really man as well as God, and take care not to apply what he says of himself as man, to his divine nature. Thus, John xiv, 28, *The Father is greater than I.* In the context immediately preceding, he says, *I go to the Father;* and this he evidently spake of his human nature, for his Godhead was every where present; his human nature, then, was the subject of his consideration, when he made the expression in question.

Thus also the address, *Why callest thou me good? There is none good but one, that is God;* Matt. xix, 17. By this answer, Jesus does not deny that he is God; but rather inquires of the young ruler who addressed him, whether he had sufficiently considered the meaning of his address; whether he was willing to affirm, what his words strictly taken, imported; and whether he did acknowledge him as perfectly good, or as divine.

So also the following; *That they may know thee the only true God, and Jesus Christ whom thou hast sent;* John xvii, 3. This appears, as if proper divinity were ascribed only to the Father, and that Christ is not the true God, in the same sense as the Father is. The force of the objection, however, lies only in the erroneous translation of the word αληθης, which here, as often elsewhere, does not mean true in the sense of *real, very,* but *veracious,* i. e. the God who fulfils his promises. In the same sense John uses this word, iv, 37, and xix, 35; and this sense only agrees with the context; for Jesus is speaking of the happiness, which his appearance on earth and the accomplishment of his work, procure for his followers. 'Eternal life,' says he, 'is connected with this, that they, whom thou hast given me, may now know that thou art the true God, the only God whose promises do not fail; the God, who hath performed, and will perform that most great and difficult promise, the redemption of men: and not only know this, but know him, by whom this promise is fulfilled, whom thou hast promised to send, and hast actually sent; may know, or acknowledge me, Jesus, as the Christ, the true Messiah.' This was the eternal life, obtained by Jesus for those, and only those, whom the Father had given him; John, xvii, 2. On the contrary, the knowledge that Jehovah was the true, i. e. the real God, was possessed by the unbelieving Jews, of whom Jesus makes no mention in his prayer, and for whom, according to verse 9th, he does not ask any thing.

Thus far the testimony of Jesus respecting himself: and now, what say his disciples and apostles?

(To be continued.)

ON THE DIVINE DECREES AND FREE AGENCY.

The following paper contains the substance of a letter, from an aged minister of the Gospel to a gentleman, who felt it difficult to reconcile free agency with the decrees of God.

Very dear Sir,

Upon my return home, I became possessed of your requests, and rejoiced in the proposal of them —partly as they would stimulate my mind to action; but especially as they afforded an opportunity to express my gratitude for your respect and friendship, and to hope that I might confer some spiritual benefit for the hospitality of your house—but as the observations "upon motives," to myself were familiar and accidental, and the conversation was soon interrupted, and succeeded by a variety of questions upon other subjects, I fear I cannot recollect them to my own satisfaction, nor answerable to your desire and expectation. As far, however, as is practicable, I will effect it—requesting you, Sir, who probably possess the observations more distinctly, to retain them in mind; and when an opportunity presents, I will verbally supply deficiencies.

The conversation commenced with remarks upon Dr. H.'s sermon occasioning the question, *How can we reconcile the moral agency of man with the decrees of God?*

Upon this it was observed,

that we have the evidence of these doctrines from different sources. We have conclusive evidence of an established, universal system of divine government from reason and revelation. This is an object of faith. We believe it, or receive it as true, from the evidence of it addressed to our understandings. We have the knowledge of our moral agency, not from evidence externally exhibited—but from internal perception and reflection—from a consciousness that we think, compare subjects, form conclusions, choose and reject: and this evidence is direct and infallible. We are as conscious of those exercises in which moral agency consists, as we are of our senses, or our existence.— What if we cannot investigate the consistency between God's eternal counsels, decrees, election and reprobation, and our moral agency? Is this a justifiable reason why we should reject either? Or shall this subject embarrass us, when we admit others, without hesitation, as intricate and embarrassing? How do our eyes see, or our ears hear? Does it distress us, that we see with our eyes and hear with our ears? Yet the *mode* of seeing and hearing is as incomprehensible, as the consistency between the decrees of God, and the moral agency of man—and when one person shall explain the *how* we see and hear, another will reconcile the moral agency of man with the absolute government of God.

Will you, Sir, permit it be to remarked, that God's counsels are not the objects about which moral agency is properly exerted. They are without our province

or sphere of action. *Secret things belong to the Lord our God; but the things which he hath revealed to us and our children.* The former are not the standard of moral action, nor shall we be judged by them. In effecting his eternal counsels, or decrees, God has created the heavens and earth, formed an endless variety of objects, and produced natural and moral good and evil. He hath given us natural and moral existence, and subjected us to moral obligation and responsibility. He hath set life and death before us, referred them to our option, and suspended our eternal interests upon our spontaneous election; and these objects involve the great motives to moral action. Moral agency consists in spontaneous volition, or unrestrained choice. In the execution of his counsels, God exhibits the object, or motive, and we make our choice, and in making our election, do we not possess and exercise as perfect rational liberty, or moral agency, as can possibly exist? and this in perfect consistency with the absolute government of God? Has not this effected a reconciliation between these important, and supposed to be, discordant subjects? Will it be said, The choice of the object, or compliance with the motive, was decreed, and this destroyed the morality of it? It may be replied: True; the choice was decreed, and it was involved in the decree, that it should be the spontaneous choice of a responsible, moral agent, and was so far from destroying moral agency, and the morality of the choice, that it positively confirmed them. Decrees are not motives, and can excite no acts of the will; and as the decree is secret, and not perceived by the mind, it can have no influence upon the act, or choice, of the agent. The agent, consequently, is as free and moral with the decree, as he could have been if no decree had existed. Add even to this: The decree is God's act, and the choice the act of the agent; and the act of God in eternity, can never be the act of an agent in time. The decree undoubtedly respected the act, or choice, of the agent, and without it would have been ineffectual and abortive, and the agent, by his voluntary act, has given efficacy, or effect, to the decree of God.

When objects are represented as motives exciting volition, or an act of the will, it is to be particularly remarked, that this should not be understood of objects abstractly, or simply considered, but in connexion with the state of the heart. External objects simply exhibited have no attractive influence to excite the choice of the will. *They derive their influence, or efficacy, from their congeniality, or consent, to THE DISPOSITION OF THE HEART.* Hence the same object, presented to persons of different and opposite inclinations and characters, will make different impressions, and produce opposite effects. That *moral* object, which irresistibly attracts one, infallibly repels the other. Propose attending a scene of worldly amusement, the theatre for instance, to an heavenly-minded saint, and he revolts from it with disgust; to an awakened sinner, and he reflects upon the scene with horror; to a vain, gay youth, and the prospect enraptures his

soul; and if there be mirth, music, and good action, the place is a sensual paradise. Propose attending public worship to a profligate sinner, and he instantly complains, *What a weariness is it;* to an awakened sinner, inquiring what he shall do to be saved, and he complies with avidity, in the hope of deriving relief and comfort; to a devout saint, and he immediately responds, *I was glad when they said unto me, Let us go up to the house of the Lord.* If an avaricious person, with prospects of accumulating property, be unexpectedly disconcerted, he becomes inconsolable. Suggest that it may be for his spiritual benefit, and you are a miserable comforter. Inform him how he may retrieve his disappointment, you are wise and good as an angel. If the outward circumstances of a saint be prosperous, and he be denied the gracious presence of God, his spirits sink, and he goes mourning all the day. Propose his affluence for his support; he replies, *This avails me nothing;* but if his circumstances be embarrassing and his prospects gloomy and dark as midnight, and Christ only whispers, *Thou art mine,* it is morning with his soul.

Of what avail, my dear Sir, are speculations, if they be not applied to the all-important subjects of religion? If moral objects derive their influence, and become stimulating motives, exciting the choice of the will according to *the disposition of the heart,* and this disposition is naturally, altogether corrupted and vitiated, it is infallibly certain, that for a heart with such a disposition, spiritual objects, a holy God, Christ, religion and heaven, will have no attractions; they will be objects of its extreme disgust and aversion; and sinful objects will excite its choice, will be preferred, and embraced with complacency, even at the hazard and in the view of interminable perdition. This exhibits the basis and propriety of Christ's solemn assertion of the absolute necessity of being *born again*—of having a spiritual and holy disposition formed in the heart; preparing us to prefer, choose, delight and rejoice in, a holy God, Christ, and heaven. This change must be effected immediately by the power and grace of God.

If the extension and amplification of the subject be offensive, I pray you, Sir, pardon the error—for truly, the request suggested a series of subjects, so grateful to the mind, that (especially when attended with the hope of explaining and relieving doctrines which perplex and confound many to their destruction) the pleasure of pursuing it could not be resisted nor abandoned.

This effort was commenced in the hope, and has been completed, and is now conveyed with desires and prayers, that God would sanctify and bless it, to preserve you from stumbling at the word; that he would reveal and form Christ, the hope of glory, in your soul; and make you wise to salvation.

I am, very dear Sir, your affectionate friend, ***.

ON THE CAUSES OF ERROR.

To the Editor of the Panoplist.

Sir,
h the following remarks should be judged worthy a place in your useful publica-

tion, you are requested to insert them. Should you approve of the piece in the main, while some sentences or expressions seem objectionable, you are at liberty to correct them. Wishing success to your labors in the cause of Christ,

I am yours, &c. A. D.

THOUGH man is the only terrestrial being, that is endued with reason, and a capacity of perceiving truth, yet we find by observation, that he is more attached to error than to truth. Reason, which was given him that he might find out and maintain truth, is degraded, enlisted in the cause of error, and made use of in framing many absurdities disgraceful to human nature, and pernicious to the best interests of mankind. Man was formed *upright, but he has sought out many inventions.* Errors of various kinds have abounded in all preceding ages, and they abound in the present. If we look around upon the world, how few do we behold, who embrace the truth! What a vast multitude of erroneous opinions are entertained by men! Opinions shocking not only to piety, but to common sense and humanity! If we consider, further, that all these erroneous opinions necessarily produce erroneous conduct; as necessarily as causes produce effects, and trees produce fruits of their own kind, will it not be well to inquire briefly into the causes of error, and learn by what means men are thus deluded,—and made to embrace foolish, absurd and impious doctrines. By so doing only can we remedy the evil; for the fountain must first be cleansed in order to sweeten the streams. Let us then briefly inquire into the causes of error.

1. An innate aversion to the

truth is one great and indeed the principal cause of error. There is in the hearts of all men this innate aversion to the truth. Mankind naturally love error. The glorious and salutary truths, revealed in the word of God, are so opposed to the corrupt and vicious inclinations of men, that they are naturally hostile to these truths and inclined to substitute some other doctrines more congenial to their sinful dispositions.

Men will easily believe almost any thing but the truth. It is certain, that there is no opinion too absurd, or too impious, for them to believe. Any thing that will allow them to gratify *the lust of the flesh, the lust of the eyes, and the pride of life,* will do better than the truth. Why is it that men choose to worship gods of wood and stone rather than the true and living God? Is it not that they think that these gods will let them live as they list, while the character of Jehovah forbids iniquity of all kinds? I cannot believe that idolatry is to be imputed in all cases to ignorance. It must be imputed, sometimes at least, to the aversion of men to the character of God. Averse to this, they form to themselves such gods as their imaginations have devised; such gods as will favor their vices and abominations. For the same reason, men reject the truths of the Gospel. These truths are unpalatable; therefore they are often wholly rejected, or new modelled and metamorphosed till the disgusting features are removed, and the doctrines assume a form more agreeable to the wicked heart.

2. Pride of reasoning is anoth-

er cause of error. Men a willing to be indebted to th *ther of lights* for their (They imagine this or that trine to be unreasonable, be they cannot comprehen(They make their dark and guided minds the standa truth. By this they try th(trines of the Bible; and or explain away, those, whi(not agreeable to it. This sumption is not confined learned; it is found among t literate? They, also, are of their understanding; and often believe nothing whic! are not able to compre Yet it is true, that the le are more liable to err fro(cause than the ignorant. *I edge puffeth up;* and the ed, having contracted hab reasoning, are more ex to reason themselves int(ror. Metaphysical reas(on religious subjects are introduced with caution. man who employs them danger of being so much up with deducing conseque and drawing inferences, depart from the spirit (Gospel, and leave its simp sublime truths for those whi more philosophical and int(

3. An over curious spi inquiry is a third cause of There are some minds, are not content with plain t but are forever prying into hidden and abstruse su To such persons there is danger of running into While they imagine that are improving the Christi(tem, they may involve selves in error, and intr tenets inconsistent with the pel. The great truths of

tianity are simple; and have been understood in all ages of the church, when holiness has prevailed over iniquity. They, therefore, who in the present day, undertake to alter the essential doctrines of the Gospel, and change the creed of the faithful martyrs of God, who have testified to the truth, at the expense of their blood, introduce innovations dangerous to the peace of the church and the welfare of immortal souls. A pride of discovery may help on such inquiries, and make them more daring and more dangerous. Such is the disposition of man, that he will be proud of being called the father of something new, though it should be branded with infamy by all the faithful followers of the Lamb.

4. The introduction of worldly wisdom into religious discussions has been another source of error. The wisdom of men is foolishness with God; and men must become fools before they can be truly wise. Some men with hearts unsubdued by divine grace have taken upon themselves to write upon the doctrines of Christianity. It is to be expected that such persons will pervert the truth; and, when aided by genius and learning, that their works will be specious and delusive, so that num-

bers will be led away by these wolves in sheep's clothing. The errors which have been introduced by the Pelagian, Arminian and Socinian writings prove this. Professions of a candid inquiry after truth, subtle arguments, and ambiguous expressions, have been found by the enemy of souls, powerful weapons in the subversion of truth, and the introduction of false doctrines. This secret, but effectual method of spreading error has of late infected all branches of knowledge. Treatises on the arts, on geology, geography, astronomy, biography, &c. have been employed in disseminating the fatal poison.

These are some of the causes of error, and they should be carefully guarded against. The present is a critical period; the enemies of the truth are peculiarly vigilant; they are employing every species of art and cunning to beguile the souls of men, and lead them in the path to ruin. Shall the friends of truth be asleep while these things are done? Shall they not be vigilant in the glorious cause of the Gospel? Shall they not use their best endeavors to promote the extension and final triumph of the kingdom of our Lord and Savior Jesus Christ?

A. D.

MISCELLANEOUS.

For the Panoplist.

CONNECTICUT SOCIETY FOR THE PROMOTION OF GOOD MORALS.

THE first semi-annual meeting of the *Connecticut Society for the Promotion of good Morals*, was

holden, as the Constitution directs, at the court house in New Haven, Wednesday, Oct. 20, 1813.

At 6 o'clock, P. M. a large number of members attended.

The President was present and took the chair.

It may be recollected, that the Constitution recommends and invites the formation of Branch Societies—one in every parish of the state. A slight inspection of the plan is sufficient to show, that the hopes of those who were friendly to the reformation and preservation of morals, were especially fixed on the efficiency of these Branch Societies An inquiry concerning the progress which had been made in the formation of such essential auxiliaries, was, of course, the first business of the meeting.

At an hour previously assigned, the Society attended in the place of public worship, where, according to an appointment made at their first annual meeting, a sermon was delivered by the Rev. Lyman Beecher. Text, *The Sabbath was made for man.*

After divine service, the Society again assembled in the court house.

The Hon. Simeon Baldwin, Asa Chapman, Esq. and the Rev. Samuel Merwin, were appointed a committee to "present the thanks of the Society to the Rev. Mr. Beecher, for his sermon delivered this evening, and to request a copy of the same; that it may be printed."

The inquiry on the establishment of Branch Societies was resumed: After attending to a few reports, the meeting was adjourned till the next evening, then to be holden in the same place. The session of that evening was closed with prayer by the Rev. Mr. Merwin.

Thursday, Oct. 21st. The Society met according to adjourn-

ment. The unfinished in of the preceding session completed.

About thirty Branch Soci were reported, as having formed and organized in va parts of the state. Their pective constitutions, with resolutions and plans of p dure, for the suppression of and the encouragement of morals, were, some of t communicated. Information likewise received of sundry or Branches, from which members were present, at whose proceedings, there no specific reports were ex ed.

In consequence of applica from a few of the Branch S ties, for advice relative to most efficient mode of oper the following resolutions passed.

Resolved, That, in the op of the general Society, Branch Society is compete decide for itself, on the measures to be adopted, w its own limits, for promotin great object of the institutio

Resolved, That it be re mended to the Branch Soci that in May, annually, the port to the committee, the of their organization; the n and numbers of their mem the measures they have ado and the effects produced.

Vacancies among the of of the general Society were ed by the following elect Asa Chapman, Esq Vice P dent, in the place of the Jonathan Ingersol; Mr. Jere Day, Professor in Yale Col Corresponding Secretary, i place of Charles Denison, and General Garrit Smith, (

mittee, in the place of Charles Sigourney.

The Hon. Simeon Baldwin, and the Rev. Messrs. Lyman Beecher and Nathaniel W. Taylor, were chosen a committee to confer with such gentlemen as might be appointed by the Convention of the Medical Society, on the means of promoting the object of this Association.

Ichabod L. Skinner, Stephen Twining, and James Morris, Esquires, were appointed a committee to devise means of defraying the incidental expenses of the general Society.

The Rev. Calvin Chapin was appointed to deliver a sermon at the second annual meeting, to be holden in May next; and the Rev. Heman Humphrey was appointed his substitute.

"Voted, That 500 copies of the Constitution be printed and distributed by Mr. Increase Cooke."

The Rev. Calvin Chapin and Thomas Day, Esq. were requested to prepare a statement of the proceedings, at this meeting, and transmit the same to the editor of the Panoplist for publication. The meeting was concluded with prayer by the Rev. Mr. Taylor.

Numerous details of operation were not to be expected, in this early period of the institution. The prospects, however, presented by the reports, and by the unanimity of sentiment manifested in favor of the Society's purposes, were pleasant and animating. To the object of the institution an attention, of great respectability and weight, had evidently been excited through the state.

In a few places only, had the Branch Societies commenced their operations. In these few, measures honorable to the Christian name, and worthy of citizens enlightened by the moral precepts of the Gospel, had been adopted, and firmly and effectually pursued. The results had, in their nature, been such precisely as every friend to the human family could wish. Much had been done to restrain the bold profanation of God's name and day—much to discourage the deadly use of strong drink. The same happy results will unquestionably follow the same exertions wherever made.

It should not be forgotten, that nothing valuable can ever be accomplished without action and energy. Whatever evils the slothful man may desire to see suppressed, his hand must be drawn from his bosom, if he would not hang as a dead weight upon a good cause. Even the limited experience of a few months furnishes ample encouragement. No insuperable difficulties can be discovered in the suggestions of indolence, or of fear; or of that unparalleled thirst for ungodly gain which now so extensively bids defiance to every moral principle. Only let all, that behold and lament the desolation of abounding licentiousness, lay aside their cold, calculating cautiousness—their groundless timidity—their inordinate avarice—and no *lion will be seen in the way* of putting notorious vice to shame.

It is no irrational expectation which the numerous friends of this institution indulge. In pursuance of the united exertions recommended and urged by the system of the general Society, certainly much may be done for the well being of families, of neighborhoods, of our country, and the world.

At the same time, it is perfectly evident, that the effects of the system thus happily commenced, must, under a merciful Providence, depend, from year to year, on the discreet, but faithful, persevering, and zealous, efforts of such as feel the indispensable bearings of morality upon the best interests of mankind. Nor, when the great body of considerate people shall be led to a serious view of its immense importance, can the want of such efforts be apprehended for a moment.

Through this and similar institutions, then, the friends of social and moral order have a right to look forward with hope. They *do* thus look forward. It is impossible to behold those numerous citizens, who are reputable for sobriety, intelligence, and integrity, combined in active measures for the suppression of vice and the promotion of good morals, without the strong and lively anticipation of effects in which every good man's heart exults. To the moral influence of such a union, guided by such principles, for the accomplishment of such ends, the just mind will not turn itself in vain, to see the widely extended practice of that *righteousness which exalteth a nation;* and the stamp of public infamy fixed upon those *sins which are the reproach of any people.*

CALVIN CHAPIN, } Committee.
THOMAS DAY, }

ON CHARITY LIBRARIES.

For the Panoplist.

C. A. "*On the distribution of religious tracts*,"[*] closes his communication thus: "From perusing these observations, perhaps some person may be induced to turn his thoughts to this subject, and offer to the public some improvement of the above plan. In such a case I shall be much gratified."

Induced by this communication of C. A. I offer the following communication. Whether it contains an improvement of C. A.'s plan, the public must determine.

In new and destitute settlements, where it is thought proper to distribute books and tracts, let small libraries be formed, to consist altogether of religious books. In each of these libraries, and under the care of a 'librarian and assistants, place ten, twenty, thirty, forty volumes, or more, according to circumstances, and as many tracts, stitched in small volumes, as you please, to be drawn and returned according to certain rules. In this manner, both the books and the tracts will be preserved with care, and circulated among the inhabitants to great advantage.

Let the rules for regulating these libraries be as simple as possible: but, by all means, let one of them be an exhortation *to remember the Sabbath day and keep it holy.* As it is certain, that the books will be of little service, unless they are read; and as they cannot be read without time; if time cannot be afforded on the Sabbath, it is cer-

*See Pan. for Sept. (part II.) 1813, p. 251.

tain that it will not be on any
other day. Perhaps, also, it
would be useful to require, that
persons, in order to receive the
benefit of the library, should refrain from profane swearing, and
the intemperate use of ardent
spirits. That a family may enjoy the benefit of the library, let
the head of it be required to subscribe the constitution and laws.

To complete the system, and
render it more efficient, and productive of greater good, let each
library, so formed, be the property of some Missionary Society, in the first instance, and under their inspection and control,
and removable at their pleasure:
and let that Society, as often at
least as once a year, send a missionary to each of the places,
where such a library is established, with a commission to inspect the library and make report; so that, if it be neglected,
or abused, it may be removed to
some other place.

It may also be stipulated, that
whenever the people, in any one
of those settlements, feel able,
they may purchase the library of
the Missionary Society, at a moderate estimate of its value. Then
it will be their own, and the money may be devoted to establish
a library in some other destitute
settlement.

It is believed that charity libraries, thus established, will be
very useful: for they will not
only furnish the means of instruction to many, who are destitute, but they will operate directly to restrain vice and promote virtue; they will strength-
en the hands of the pious, and
of those, who wish to support
order, by combining their influence, and giving them the influ-

ence of missionaries and the
Missionary Society; they will
furnish employment to the rising generation, and an opportunity of improving their minds;
and they will add to the good influence of missionaries. To
these things we may add, that
these libraries will bear standing
testimony, which cannot be resisted, that the friends of religion are willing to sacrifice a
portion of their property to do
good to the souls of men.

That this is not mere theory
will appear from the following
facts, with which the writer is
personally acquainted.

On the last of May, 1813, two
ministers, (one of them a missionary) moved by the cry from
the wilderness, *Come over into
Macedonia, and help us*, undertook to procure books for, at
least, *one or two* charitable libraries, to consist of Scott's Family Bible, bound in 18 volumes,
and other practical and experimental works, so as to make 25
or 30 volumes for each library.
They had no funds, and therefore depended on the success,
which Divine Providence might
give, by opening the hearts of
the pious and the liberal. Subscription papers were drawn and
circulated: and *through the good
hand of God upon them*, they had
the pleasure of seeing collected,
within 5 months, no less than 350
volumes of new, bound books,
including 10 sets of Scott, each
in 18 volumes, besides many
tracts and pamphlets. They had
also subscriptions, in money and
books, to a considerable amount,
still remaining.

These books were sufficient
for 10 libraries on the plan proposed. Six have been already

established to the joy of many destitute people, and returns of them have been made to the Berkshire and Columbia Missionary Society, whose property they now are, and under whose inspection and control they are placed. The remaining books, and as many more as can be procured, will be formed into libraries, as soon as the necessary preparation can be made in new settlements; and it is hoped that, under the divine blessing, they may be instrumental of much good.

The libraries, already established, are in the counties of Montgomery and Saratoga, in the northern part of the state of New York.

On the same plan, if the means were furnished, charity libraries might be established to a great extent. It would be desirable to have them in all our new settlements. There appears to be need of them along the borders of the wilderness through Maine, New Hampshire, Vermont, New York, Ohio, and the country south and west of Ohio, as far as our territories extend.

If such libraries should be established in those places, they would be so many posts and fortifications for the establishment of the Gospel, where missionaries might consider themselves as at home, and would serve as a rallying point for all the friends of truth and virtue.

It would be easy to enlarge, but the writer fears, that he has occupied too much space on the pages of the Panoplist for a stranger, and therefore will close by observing, that, if it should be thought desirable, he will forward for publication the Consti-

tution and Laws, which been framed for those libraries, which have b ready established.

Φιλο---

STUBBORN FACTS.

To the Editor of the P---

Sir,

THE annexed statemen made, in the year 1803 gentleman of unquestion---racity and accuracy. lately found among his le pers; and, by his consen now forwarded to you for tion in the Panoplist. Th alluded to, is not on the se but in the interior of Ma setts. Its inhabitants ar cipally, husbandmen ar chanics, who have neve considered as peculiarly ed to intemperance; but contrary, have had as high utation for industry and of manners as, perhaps, a ple in New England.

The statement is thus "In this town, we annu taxes for the following pu and nearly the following viz.

For schools -
For support of the poor
State and County taxes
For support of two Mini
ters - -
For making and mendin
highways
Allow for incidental ch
ges - -

Amount,
It is found by exact that, within one year,

*Each minister is partly sup
a parsonage.

lowing quantities of ardent spirits have been retailed in this town.

Eighty hogsheads of New England rum, which at 61 cents per gallon, amount to $6,240
Fifty hogsheads, West India do. at $1 per gal.   5,900
Twelve hogsheads of brandy, at $1 50 per gal.   2,250
Six hogsheads of gin, at $1 50 per gal. $1,170

Amounting to the enormous sum of $15,560."
The paper adds a single reflection—"The money which is paid for schools, for the maintenance of the poor, for the support of the Ministry, and for repairing highways, is expended in the *town*, and again circulates among us; and for it we receive an equivalent, in the preaching of the Gospel, in the education of our children, in convenient roads, and in the administration of good government. But the money paid for ardent spirits, all goes *out of the town*. Fifteen thousand, five hundred and sixty dollars, carried out of town yearly—and for what!"

Now, Mr. Editor, among all the glaring statements on this subject, which have been contained in your pages, I have seen nothing that surpasses this. The population of the town, to which this sketch applies, was at the time about 3000:—so that the expense of ardent spirits was $5,25, to each man, woman, and child, for one year: or about $30 to each family. I forbear to follow out the train of reflections suggested by these facts. Let every plain man sit down to the computation for himself. By the use of a few figures, he may

see, that *more than twenty* missionaries in India might have been supported by one town, with the same money that was employed to procure poverty, poison, and death to its inhabitants! Admitting what I have supposed, that the people of this town are not peculiarly addicted to spirits, it is certain that, within the same year, the inhabitants of Massachusetts and Maine, must have paid, for the same deadly poison, at least *three millions, sixteen thousand, four hundred and sixty one dollars*. Happily, the progress of this evil has been partially arrested by the recent circumstances of the country, and the efforts of good men. We look back and exclaim,—"Verily we have been dreaming on the brink of a tremendous gulf! Our institutions, our liberties, our existence as a people, have been in jeopardy. Still we are but half awakened from our dream, if we suffer the work of reformation to languish, and shrink from the labor of finishing what has been so auspiciously begun."

P.

CAUTION TO YOUNG MEN.

PERHAPS no opinion has been more prevalent, than that a moderate, daily use of ardent spirits is harmless; though *intemperance* is universally considered as fatal to health and life. This opinion has ruined multitudes. It is by this *harmless, moderate* use of spirits that habit fastens its iron fetters on its thousand victims. Especially is this the fact with a certain class of invalids; and with those day laborers, who expect to receive spirits at stated times, from their employers. Dr. H——, one of the most eminent physicians that New England has produced, used to say, that a man of vigorous constitution might be intoxicated once a month, and yet, if he abstained from spirits in the intervals, might perhaps live to old age: but that no young man, who habitually drinks spirits every day, especially before breakfast, has any considerable prospect of reaching the age of forty. P.

FABLE OF GUNPOWDER AND BRANDY.

Extracted from Berkley's Minute Philosopher, p. 104, New Haven ed. 1803.

"THE government of the north being once upon a time vacant, the prince of the power of the air convened a council; wherein, upon competition between two demons of rank, it was determined they should both make trial of their abilities, and he should succeed, who did most mischief. One made his appearance in the shape of gunpowder, the other in that of brandy: The former was a declared enemy, and roared with a terrible noise, which made folks afraid, and put them on their guard: the other passed as a friend and physician through the world, disguised himself with sweets, and perfumes, and drugs, made his way into the ladies' cabinets, and the apothecaries' shops, and, under the notion of helping digestion, comforting the spirits, and cheering the heart, produced direct contrary effects; and, having insensibly thrown great numbers of human kind into a fatal decay, was found to people hell and the grave so fast, as to merit the government, which he still possesses."

REVIEW.

LVI. *The Columbiad.*

(Continued from vol. ix. p. 505.)

THAT the barbarous diction of Mr. Barlow's poem is not justly chargeable upon America, it is happily in our power to prove beyond the possibility of a doubt. The *Vision of Columbus*, which is written in a very pure style, was composed and published before the author had left his native country. It is greatly superior to the poem, which we are now reviewing, and was highly creditable to the author. During the interval of about twenty years, which elapsed from the publication of the Vision of Columbus to that of the Columbiad, the poet resided at Algiers, Paris, London, and other places in the eastern world. In the latter work, numerous marks of the residence at Paris are discernible; and, perhaps, if every place through which the writer passed were to put in its claims, all the new words and phrases might easily be accounted for without recurring to America in a single instance.

It is proper to remark, in this place, that English and Scotch Reviewers have discovered a hy-

percritical petulance, on the subject of *Americanisms*, not very
compatible with their high pretensions to the character of dignified and impartial critics.
Without denying that our countrymen may have insensibly
formed a few phrases, which vary in a slight degree from the
best use in England; and that
they may also have introduced a
few words, not before sanctioned
in our language, by deriving
nouns from verbs, verbs from
nouns, &c.; yet we can prove
undeniably, that in nearly all the
instances which we have seen
noticed, the words in question
were not Americanisms; i. e.
they were neither first used in
this country, nor are they in any
sense peculiar to our writers.

The word *advocate*, for example, used as a verb, has been
called an Americanism by the
Anthology critics, if not by English reviewers. It is not justly
so called, as it is sanctioned by
respectable English authority.

But no other word has furnished so much employment for
wits and critics, as the verb *to
improve*, and its derivatives.
The first and most proper sense
of this word, is, *to make better,
to advance a thing toward perfection*. Another sense, in which
the word is constantly used a-
mong us, is, *to make a good use
of, to employ to advantage*. When
used in this sense, the word is
called an Americanism. Dr.
Franklin began the charge many years ago; and it has been a
thousand times repeated. The
flippant English traveller,[*] when

he first arrives among us, cannot
understand the good minister,
who exhorts the young to *improve* their time, and who regularly comes to the *improvement*
of his sermon. He affects, also,
to be nonplussed, when he hears
the *clearing and tilling of lands
in a new country* styled *improvements;* which, by the way, is taking the word in its strictest and
most proper sense, and simply
applying it to a new object; for
the clearing of land is undoubtedly an *improvement*, as it makes
the land *more valuable*. The
question, whether the second
use of the word originated in
this country, is easily settled.
To a person, who is even mod-
erately conversant with English
books, it cannot be a matter of
doubt, that from a period, antecedent to the settlement of this
country, to the present day, the
word has been used in this sense,
without the smallest intermission, by very respectable writers, who never saw America. It
is so used by Baxter, Beveridge,
and their cotemporaries, by
Watts, Doddridge, and their cotemporaries, and by Mrs. More,
Mr. Wilberforce, Mr. Scott, the
writers in the Christian Observer, and a multitude of other
popular authors, who are now
living. This use of the word is
much more common in religious
books, than within the circle of
polite literature: yet a friend of
ours, who is observant of such
matters, has assured us, that, in
the course of his reading, he has
remarked more than twenty instances of the same use of the

---

[*]We here refer to a class of empty,
idle, ignorant travellers, with which this
country has been much infested. They
make great books, on returning to Europe, and effectually mislead and deceive
multitudes of readers.

word in Addison, Goldsmith, Thomson, and other English classics. So much for this *Americanism*. After all, we wish a good substitute could be found for the word in this sense; but, unless such a substitute *is* found, the old use will continue, wherever the English language is written or spoken.

There is another use of the word, which is so contrary to all propriety, that we cannot but notice it. It is no less, than to *make a bad use of*; as when a person is said to have *improved his youth in sin and folly.* This cannot be said to be a general use; but it is too frequent. It is not confined to the western side of the Atlantic. M'Crie, in his life of Knox, has it more than once.

Another use still, not so utterly perverted as the last mentioned, but still quite improper, is common on both sides of the water. It takes place when *to improve* is intended to convey the same meaning as *to employ,* or *to use.*

Many other Americanisms, if particularly examined, would turn out, like the above, to be Anglicisms of several centuries. In regard to the introduction of new words, while we are far from attempting to excuse Mr. Barlow, we cannot but think, that much very superficial criticism has been displayed on this subject; especially by some of our American reviewers. They would gladly interdict the use of every word not found in Johnson's dictionary. Happily for mankind their wishes are as impotent, as their scheme is visionary and ridiculous. It would be as practicable to build a permanent dam across the Mississippi, with willow twigs, as for critics to prevent all changes and improvements in language, by the interposition of their authority. Several hundred new words have become good English since the days of Johnson, and are used without scruple by *all* the Reviewers themselves, and by nearly all speakers and writers. Many hundreds of words, which hold a place in the latest editions of Johnson's dictionary, are not good English now, and probably never will be, whatever they may have been centuries ago. We mean, that they are not written or spoken now, and probably never will be, by any judicious writer or speaker of our language. How absurd to plead for an unalterable vocabulary, when commerce, the arts and sciences, politics, and all things beneath the sun, are in a state of perpetual change? Who hesitates to use *revolutionize, demoralize*, and perhaps fifty other verbs of the same termination, which are not found in Johnson's dictionary? Nothing is more probable, than that many other verbs, of the same termination, will be added to our language hereafter Verbs will be formed from nouns, and nouns from verbs, and adjectives and adverbs from both, while men think and talk. Many words now in use will be dropped, and many others introduced from other languages. In short, as Mr. Webster argues with irresistible force, whenever the written language becomes fixed, it becomes, or will soon become, a *dead* language; for the great mass of mankind would not hesitate to express new ideas by new words, and new combinations, though the comparatively small number of writers should hesitate to follow them.

Let it not be thought, that we are the advocates of rash innovations in language. We only insist, that such changes as are recommended by utility, necessity, or general practice, should be tolerated in language, as in other things. Critics and reviewers may, for ought we care, lash as severely as they please all pedantic, affected, unnecessary introduction of new terms, and new phrases; but let them not impede that course of improvement, of which our noble and copious language is still susceptible—not less susceptible than any other earthly possession. Above all, let their doctrine and practice agree better than they do, while they attempt to confine others to Johnson's dictionary, and yet boldly avail themselves of a more modern vocabulary.

Should it be asked, when may a writer use a word, which has not been sanctioned by any considerable printed authority? we answer, a good taste is the only proper guide. As a general rule the spoken language should precede the written. When a word is extensively used by well educated persons, in mixed companies, in the hall of legislation, and in the pulpit, where can be the presumption of putting it into a book?

It is to be observed, that at a period when the whole face of the civilized world is changing, we might reasonably expect, that there would be many changes in language; and doubtless greater changes, in all respects, are still to take place, than any which our eyes have witnessed, great and momentous as these have been. Among the many causes, to which the introduction of new words into our language, is to be attributed, no other is so universally operative, as the immense circulation of English reviews, and the avidity with which they are read. In these works, there is a constant propensity to naturalize French words; to introduce new scientific terms into the common dialect; and to form a new style by new combinations. And yet some of these very works appear to be strenuous advocates of the immutability of the English language, and haughty censors of those who venture a step beyond certain limits, by which our tongue was imagined to be circumscribed a few years ago.

But we must return to the poem of Mr. Barlow. The following picture of war contains bombast enough, and at least *one* vulgar image:

"His head is hung with clouds; his giant hand
Flings a blue flame far flickering to the land;
His blood-stain'd limbs *drip carnage* as he strides
And taint with gory grume the staggering tides;
Like two red suns his quivering eye-balls glare,
His mouth disgorges all the stores of war,
Pikes, muskets, mortars, guns, and globes of fire
And lighted bombs that fusing trails expire."   B. v. l. 477—484.

Nearly related to war is cruelty; and we think the family likeness is discernible in the following description:

"She comes, the fiend! her grinning jaws expand,
Her brazen eyes cast lightning o'er the strand,

Her wings like thunder-clouds the welkin
      sweep,
Brush the tall spires and shade the shud-
      dering deep;
She gains the deck, displays her wonted
      store,
Her cords and scourges wet with prison-
      ers' gore;
Gripes, pincers, thumb-screws spread
      beneath her feet,
Now poisonous drugs and *loads of putrid
      meat;*
Disease hangs *drizzling from her slimy
      locks,*
And hot contagion issues from her box."
                    B. vi, l. 45—54.

As instances of low or disgusting expressions, we cite also the
following:

——"The freemen *quit their farms,*
Seize their tried muskets, name their
      chiefs to lead,
Indorse their knapsacks and to vengeance
      speed."   B. vi. l. 302—304
"*Warm dripping streams* from every
      lifted sword
Stain the thin carnaged corps;"
                    B. vii, l. 360, 361.
"His *hissing hell-dogs* o'er the shudder-
      ing tide."   l. 500.
"The shoulder'd rock——
Galls, *grinds them sore,* along the ram-
      part led—" B. viii, l. 243—245.

But the most remarkable instance of the bathos remains yet
to be mentioned. Atlas makes
a long speech, in the eighth book,
on the wrongs which his children, the people of Africa, had
experienced from slavery and
the slave trade. Towards the
close of it, he threatens mankind,
that, unless they desist from such
horrible injustice and oppression, the whole race of men shall
be destroyed by a vast subterranean explosion, which, bursting
from the centre of the earth,
shall throw all the surface of the
globe, in massy fragments, high
into the atmosphere; and the
fragments, returning toward
each other by the power of grav-
itation, shall sink in the rising

waves, leaving only some single
pinnacle of a mountain elevated
above the ocean. So vast an
explosion is certainly a sublime
idea; but Mr. Barlow destroys
the effect of it by several unhappy images, and finally by one of
the meanest, which could be selected from the furniture and
operations of the dairy-room.

——"Far sunk from day,
It crumbles, rolls, it *churns* the settling
      sea,
Turns up each prominence,——"
                         l. 289—291.

The poet talks of '*pumping* the
pearly tear,' of '*tapping* the re-
dundant lakes,' &c. &c.
Of the many passages, which
have no meaning that we can
discover, we cite several:

"His eye bent forward, ardent and sub-
      lime,
Seem'd *piercing nature and evolving
      time;*"   B. iv. l. 253, 254.
"Like sires of unborn states they move
      sublime,
*Look empires thro' and span the breadth
      of time,*——"   l. 429, 430.
"All rights that Britons know they here
      transfuse,
Their sense invigorate and expand their
      views,
Dare every *height of human soul to scan,*
Find, fathom, scope *the moral breadth of
      man,*
Learn how his *social powers may still di-
      late*
And tone their tension to a stronger state."
                         B. v. l. 117—122.
"From all his guileful plots the veil they
      drew,
With eye retortive look'd creation thro,
*Traced moral nature through her total
      plan,*
Marks all the steps of liberty and man;"—
                         l. 465—468.
"Macdougal, Clinton, guardians of the
      state,
Stretch the nerved arm *to pierce the
      depth of fate;*"   l. 621, 622.
"Mold a fair model for the realms of
      earth,
Call *moral nature to a second birth,*
Reach, renovate the world's *great social
      plan*
And here commence *the sober sense of
      man.*"   B. viii. l. 151—154.

"Equality of Right is nature's plan;
And following nature is the march of
  man." 1. 363, 364.
"Nature herself (whose grasp of time
  and place
Deals out duration and impalme all
  space)
Moves in progressive march; but where
  to tend,
What course to compass, how the march
  must end,
Her sons decide not,"—
              B. ix, l. 41—45.

These passages, with some
others which we shall cite presently. when examining the birth
and history of the universe, will
serve as sufficient specimens of
the modern philosophical method of uttering nonsense.

We ought in fairness to present our readers with some of
the best passages of this elaborate poem; and we do so with
pleasure. The following apos-
trophe to false glory is spirited
and poetical; and, though the
author might have improved it,
we have reason to be pleased
with it, on the whole.

"Frazer in quest of glory seeks the field;—
False glare of glory, what hast thou to
  yield?
How long, deluding phantom, wilt thou
  blind,
Mislead, debase, unhumanize mankind?
Bid the bold youth, his headlong sword
  who draws,
Heed not the object nor inquire the
  cause,
But seek, adventuring like an errant
  knight,
Wars not his own, gratuitous in fight,
Greet the gored field, then plunging thro'
  the fire,
Mow down his men, with stupid pride
  expire,
Shed from his closing eyes the finisht
  flame
And ask, for all his crimes, a deathless
  name!
And when shall solid glory pure and bright
Alone inspire us and our deeds requite?
When shall the applause of men their
  chiefs pursue,
In just proportion to the good they do,
On virtue's base erect the shrine of fame,
Define her empire and her code pro-
  claim!"   B. vi. l. 395—412.

The Hymn to Peace, which is
enlarged and altered for the
worse from the Vision of Columbus, is still worthy of particular praise.

"Hail, holy Peace, from thy sublime
  abode
Mid circling saints that grace the throne
  of God.
Before his arm around our embryon
  earth,
Stretcht the dim void and gave to nature
  birth,
Ere morning stars his glowing chambers
  hung,
Or songs of gladness woke an angel's
  tongue,
Veil'd in the splendors of his beamful
  mind,
In blest repose thy placid form reclined,
Lived in his life, his inward sapience
  caught,
And traced and toned his universe of
  thought.
Borne thro the expanse with his creating
  voice,
Thy presence bade the unfolding worlds
  rejoice,
Led forth the systems on their bright
  career,
Shaped all their curves and fashion'd every
  sphere,
Spaced out their suns, and round each
  radiant goul,
Orb over orb, compell'd their train to
  roll,
Bade heaven's own harmony their force
  combine,
Taught all their host symphonious strains
  to join,
Gave to seraphic harps their sounding
  lays,
Their joys to angels and to men their
  praise."   B. viii. l. 1—20.

Toward the close of the last
book, there is a comparison between the delegates of all nations, who will hereafter assemble in Egypt to legislate for the
world; and the general convention of the guardian angels, that
have in charge the planetary
systems. who will meet to give
an account of their several commissions to the Creator. The
simile is noble.

"As the blest guardian guides to whom
  was given
To light the suns and steer the stars of
  heaven,
(When one great *cosmogyre* has proved
  their spheres,
And time well taught them how to wind
  their years,)
Shall meet in general council;" &c. &c.
                B. x. l. 569—573.

Mr Barlow alludes to Moses, to 'the seer of Patmos,' to the arrival of a saint in heaven, to "departed shades," to Luther as an example of intrepid courage; but in all these instances, as in the passages above quoted, poetical embellishment is evidently the only object he has in view. He refers to the common ideas of God and heaven, because they are truly sublime; and, whenever he does so, he rises above himself. When he talks, however, as a philosopher, as a moral instructor of mankind, he explodes all religion whatever; but would tolerate *the worship of the sun*, as the best religion which has yet existed upon earth, and as, on the whole, a pleasing object. ·

The Eclectic Reviewers have said,* that they could not tell what religion Hesper, or Mr. Barlow, was of; but we think our readers will have no great hesitation in saying, before we have done, that, whatever may have been the creed of Hesper, Mr. Barlow was of *no* religion. Before we enter upon this part of our plan, it will be well to advert to the professed and real object of the poet.

Had Mr. Barlow said nothing of his object, it would have been perfectly evident. He does not write like Southey, merely

* Ec. Rev. for May 1810, p. 411.

to please his readers w
fictions that present ther
to his imagination, and
please himself; he neve
the philosopher in the p
never forgets his syste
main principles of whi
these: That the greatest
man is political liberty
this liberty, under the di
of nature and sober sens
finally banish from the e
slavery, cruelty, oppress
justice, and especially
that man ought to seek h
piness in this life, and not
himself about a future
that all religion, (unle
would except the worshi
sun,) must have sprung f
norance and delusion, fr
silly fears of unenlig
men;—and that the *march*
is toward a state of ter
perfection, when his life
prolonged to a most extra
ry date by improvements i
icine, and he will be fina
cued from superstition, fe
error.

But Mr. B. has not lef
conjecture what his obj
He has stated to us, 't
real object of the poem i
culcate the love of rationa
ty:—to show that on the
the republican principle a
morals, as well as goo
ernment and hopes of
nent peace must be fo
He dwells upon the respo
ty which rests upon a poe
instructor of mankind
thinks that an ancient
which should have disco
war, and inculcated pea
justice, a sort of pacific
would have performed w
in the world, and renovate
kind. A year or two al

the publication of the Columbiad, Mr. B. found occasion to give his opinion concerning the moral tendency of his poem; and pronounced it to excel, in this respect, all the writings of *seventy five* of the most illustrious Christian worthies, whom bishop Gregoire was able to enumerate, comprising Bacon, Barrow, Berkley, &c. &c. But our readers shall have his opinion in his own words:

"On the contrary," says Mr. Barlow, "I believe, and you have compelled me on this occasion to express my belief, that the Columbiad, taken in all its parts of text and notes and preface, is more favorable to sound and rigid morals, more friendly to virtue, more clear and unequivocal in pointing out the road to national dignity and individual happiness, more energetic in its denunciations of tyranny and oppression in every shape, injustice and wickedness in all their forms, and consequently more consonant to what you acknowledge to be the spirit of the Gospel, than all the writings of all that list of Christian authors of the three last ages, whom you have cited as the glory of Christendom, and strung them on the alphabet, from Addison down to Winkelman."

For remarks on this passage, the reader is referred to the Panoplist for September, 1810, p. 176. We have cited it here to prove, that whatever the poet has taught, he has taught deliberately and systematically.

From Mr. Barlow's code of morals, all religious belief and all religious duties are utterly excluded. Man owes nothing, according to him, to any other being except himself and his fellow creatures. As to the theology of this poem a few quotations may be acceptable. Hesper seems, at times, to be the god of our universe at least. The poet introduces him as the great revealer of truth to Columbus. Of himself Hesper says:

"This arm, *that leads the stellar host of even,*
That stretcht o'er yon rude ridge the western heaven,
That heal'd the wounded earth when from her side
The moon burst forth and left the South Sea tide,
That calm'd these elements," &c. &c.
B. iv. l. 343—347.

He also punishes nations with volcanoes:

"There lava waits my late reluctant call,
To roar aloft and shake some guilty wall;"—
B. i. l. 283, 284.

He inspired Columbus:

"For this my guardian care thy youth inspired,
To virtue rear'd thee and with glory fired."
B. ii. l. 383, 384.

It seems that Nature and God were united in creating the earth:

"For here great nature, with a bolder hand,
Roll'd the broad stream and heaved the lifted land;
And here from finisht earth, triumphant trod
The last ascending steps of her creating God." B. i. l. 357—360.

Yet Nature seems to have had the honor of creating man without assistance:

"Prove plain and clear how nature's hand of old
Cast all men equal in her human mold!"
B. viii. l. 225, 226.

And she seems to have begun the work of creation:

"When erst her hand the crust of Chaos
    thirl'd
And forc'd from his black breast the burst-
    ing world;"   B. ix. l. 47, 48.

Freedom seems to be entitled
to divine worship, at least from
the poet:

"Almighty Freedom! give my venturous
    song,
The force, the charm that to thy voice
    belong;   .
Tis thine to shape my course, to light my
    way,
To nerve my country with the patriot
    lay,
To teach all men where all their interest
    lies,
How rulers may be just and nations wise."
              B. i. l. 23—28.

According to the following
passages, Freedom seems to be
worthy of the divine worship of
all men:

"Sun of the moral world! effulgent
    source
Of man's best wisdom and his steadiest
    force,
Soul searching Freedom! here assume
    they stand
And radiate hence to every distant
    land;"—   B. iv. l. 487—490.
"Yes, righteous Freedom, heaven and
    earth and sea
Yield or withhold their various gifts for
    thee;"—   l. 499, 500.

Mr. Barlow has the frankness
to hold up religion to detesta-
tion under its own proper name,
and not under the mask of superstition, bigotry, enthusiasm,
fanaticism, &c. as is common
with his brethren. The two classes of men, who experience the
full measure of his vengeance,
are *kings* and *priests*, without
exception or discrimination.

"Religion here, that *universal name*,
Man's proudest passion, most ungovern'd
    flame,
Erects her altars on the same bright base,
That dazzled erst and still deludes the
    race;"—   B. iv. l. 5—8.

"Let the poor guardless nativ
    feel
The *flamen's fraud*, the soldie
    steel;"—   l. 8
"Some cloke, some color all the
    may plead;
Tis avarice, passion, *blind
    de'd*;"   B. vi. l.
"No Bovadilla seize the temptin
No dark Ovando, no *religious* B
              B. ii. l. 30
"Sad field of contemplation! l
    great,
Kings, priests of God, and m
    state,
Review your system here! b
    scan
Your own fair deeds, your benefi
You will not leave him to his na
To tame these elements and till t

    ———   ———   ———
You choose to check his toil and
    eyes,
To *all that's honest* and to *all the
Lure with false fame, *false m
    false lore*,
To barter fields of corn for
    gore,"—   B. vii. l. 66

But the most remarka
sage is found in the las
where, at the introductio
grand political millenniu
voys from all parts of th
are introduced as bringi
symbols of the various s
of delusion, and casting
into a heap. The thou
doubtless taken from Ad
mountain of miseries.

"Beneath the footstool all d
    things,
The *mask of priesthood* and the
    kings,
Lie trampled in the dust; for he
Fraud, folly, error all their emble
Each envoy here unloads his wea
Of some old idol from his native
One flings a pagod on the ming
One lays a crescent, one *a cross
Swords, sceptres, mitres, cro
    globes, and stars,
Codes of false fame and stimulant

* *The person here intended is
ed in the notes as a bloody, fana
pish priest.*

Sink in the settling mass; since guile
began,
These are the agents of the woes of man.'
B. x. l. 599—610.

It will be recollected by many of our readers, that bishop Gregoire complained of a certain engraving in the Columbiad, which as he understood it, reflected on the Christian religion by representing the *cross* as a symbol of falsehood, and classing it with idols, the crescent, &c. To this complaint Mr. Barlow made two pleas: First, that the engraving was made without his knowledge, or consent: Secondly, that he considered the cross as a badge of the Roman Catholic religion only, and that he, being a puritan, had not been accustomed to view the cross with veneration. The fallacy of both these pleas was examined, and we think exposed, in the Pano-

plist for September 1810, p. 172. We did not then look at the passage, from which the engraving was made, and which is quoted above. Had we done so, we should have remarked, that no person but a modern infidel would, after publishing these lines, have had the impudence to evade the charge of disrespect to Christianity, by intimating that the supposed disrespect *was all chargeable upon the engraver.* The *cross* is here plainly classed with *all destructive things;* with the *emblems of fraud, folly and error;* with *some old idol, a pagod, a crescent, codes of false fame,* and *stimulants to wars.* A person unversed in the quibbles of modern philosophy would think this passage a very plain one.

(To be continued.)

RELIGIOUS INTELLIGENCE.

INTERESTING LETTER.

The following letter was written by a gentleman in London to his friend in this country, and communicated to the Rev. Dr. Morse by a gentleman in Princeton, (N. J.) to be handed to the editor of the Panoplist for publication.

FACTS, COMMUNICATED BY DR. NAUDI TO SOME PERSONS IN LONDON, EXTRACTED FROM A LETTER DATED
LONDON, 29th JUNE, 1813.

"THE very important commercial situation of Malta renders it peculiarly favorable to the diffusion of Christian instruction through many places in Asia, Africa, and Europe. A liberal medical education, and a mind emancipated from the shackles of Romish bigotry, and filled with the spirit of pure benevolence, have qualified Dr. Naudi to be highly useful in the promotion of this great, and most noble design. Dr N. was educated a Roman Catholic, but had, probably, never bestowed any very close thought on religious subjects,

till he rather accidentally met with some religious books from England: since then, he has been an increasingly thoughtful character.

"He had successfully practised as a physician in Malta for some years, when, about eleven months ago, the governor requested him to select one of his most suitable pupils, to send to England minutely to investigate the plan of Hospitals, as well as to inspect schools, and other benevolent institutions. and to bring back any information, which might be useful in improving, or forming such establishments in Malta. Naudi, pleased with the idea of visiting the country, where the Bible Society had originated, immediately offered *himself* for this appointment, and arrived in England last July. His account of the religious state of the Continent is highly interesting. The dreadful political earthquakes which have torn kingdoms asunder, and made humanity weep at the misery of men, have no less rent the mental veil, which has so long overspread that part of the world.

"The following relation is nearly in Dr. Naudi's own words: any imperfect English will be easily excused, when it is remembered, that eleven months ago, Dr. N. was totally ignorant of the language.

"In the city of Naples, peopled by about 700,000 inhabitants, several convents and monasteries, containing infinite numbers of friars and monks, have been suppressed by Bonaparte, whose motive doubtless was his own aggrandizement, but I think we may observe the hand of Providence in it, overthrowing one of the obstacles to the ispersion of the Word in those fine countries. I add, as a further exemplification, that, in the same city, since the year 1805, there has been instituted a society of pious Christians, devoted to do good to their fellow creatures, as well in temporal, as in spiritual wants, and this society, eleven months ago, was composed of 5000 people. These meet, on Sundays, in different churches, read the Bible, and sing hymns and psalms to the Most High, to whom they confide their wants, and whose assistance they implore There is another society of the same kind, in one of the most important islands of the Mediterranean sea, in which about 140 persons are united for no other purpose, than that of promoting the spiritual good of their fellow creatures. [Another letter says, a poor man was the means of gathering them.] They meet on Sundays, begin by reading the Bible, when one, or more of them present, explains a text *extempore*, in a very simple manner; they pray together, and then make reflections on various subjects, which can promote Christianity, not only in their own country, but also among strangers, and those of other islands.

"At Mount Lebanon, which must not be considered as one single mountain, but a very populous, and extensive mountain country, there are Bishops, and an Archbishop; but all so poor, they can scarcely be distinguished from the rest of the people; and so ignorant, they can hardly support their character We have sent twenty Arabic Bibles to Archbishop Paleologos. This gentleman distributed them to the bishops, and some other characters. To our great pleasure the archbishop wrote me, that these bishops, and the others, collect the people every Sunday, and read the Bible in the language they can understand What satisfaction has it proved to my friends at Malta, to know, that, by these twenty Bibles more than 150,000 persons of these very countries have begun to hear the word of God, and to praise the Most High in the language of the sacred Bible

"Some months ago, I met with Haw Gellule, first minister of the Bey of Turns, who was appointed by his court to reside

some time at Malta. He w
years of age, and much respe
the Mahometans. On my be
prescribe for one of his follow
proached Gellule, I perceived
ployed in reading an Arabic
quiring respecting it, h answe
particularly fond of reading, wh
get Arabic books. I told him
happy to give him a book, by
of which he might derive g
He desired me to do so. The
ing I sent him a Bible, which
ately began to read with gr
ness. A few days after, I
him, and found him reading th
to all his followers. I stopp
minutes to observe him rea
teenth chapter of Luke, with
est, and 24 Turks listening
the greatest attention. I w
having desired me to sit down
ued his reading, at the conclus
verse, saying, "Alla' Alla' it
true" After he had fini hed
me, "I am very much obliged
am reading your book with gre
and explaining it to these my
In a few days after, he told m
to be convinced, that Jesus C
prophet of the same character
et, and in no way inferior to
miracles were true. This was
cession; for, though the Turk
admit Jesus Christ to have been
they consider him very infer
homet, whom they believe to
the only messenger from Go
give the law, and rule of life to
miracles of Christ were what
lule's mind the most, and,
these particulars, he wanted t
ed. I had much conversation
different times, and found him
posed to be persuaded of the
fore I left Malta, he said of his
that the best proof of the tr
miracles of Christ was, that
wrought them in the presence
ple. This is a particularly s
servation from a people of
who performed all *his* miracles
and proves, that the grace of G
the reading of the holy Scrip
already growing in his heart
first inquires, on returning to
be respecting Haw Gellule. I
fail to let my English frien
whether the work of conversio
pleted in him or not

"The prince Caramanali, o
the Pashaw of Caramanali, of
capital of Georgia, in the Pers
yy, was a young man of a bad
end, having quarrelled with his
obliged to quit the neighborho

Caspian sea, and retire to Scandinari, where my friend, Mr. Marali, lived. On observing some modern Greek Testaments at Marali's house, Caramanali said, that he had already seen one at his father's; the book was exactly the same, and he had begun to find satisfaction in reading it. Marali perceived, that it was then a good opportunity to give him a Testament. This gentleman was indefatigable in reading, and considering the Holy Book, in which he very often desired Marali to be with him. At length, Caramanali was converted to Christianity, and now lives at St. Jean d'Acre, on a pension assigned him by his father, who no longer fears the effects o' his once turbulent spirit. Here he is desiring Bibles from the society, and, living, as he does, amidst the greatest bigotry, and superstition, he may be eminently useful in distributing them. The other account says the young Prince goes about with the Bible in his hand to persuade.

"A Jew, by the name of Murthim, being about four years ago, much indisposed, was advised to leave Africa, and visit Malta for change of air, and medical advice. Some days after his arrival, he was introduced to me as a physician. After my having prescribed for him, he noticed some tracts on my table, published by *the Society for propagating Christianity among the Jews*. Murthim took up one of the pamphlets, which contained an explanation of the prophecy of Isaiah, relating to the coming of the Messiah, in Hebrew, and in English; he asked me what it was. I related to him the history of the Society, from which I had these pamphlets; he answered very coldly, saying; "if this Society succeed in converting any of the Jews in England, or on the Continent, it will be quite useless with the Syrian Jews, particularly those of Jerusalem." He was a native of this place, and, as they are much more zealous in strictly adhering to their Mosaic ritual, they look down with contempt on] their more loose European brethren. I, at length, however, succeeded in persuading him to take this tract home with him to read at his leisure. Two days afterwards, he called again, and when I had prescribed for him, I asked him, what he thought of the little book. He answered it was of no use to him, as it was a portion of the Scriptures, which he always kept with him; but that he found it very well written, and was surprised to find the Christians in England so careful in keeping to the original; then he said — "It is just the same as in our Scriptures." I then gave him some other pamphlets from the same Society. After a few days, when he called again, he said, without my asking him, that he was glad to

have read the others, but sorry not to be able to understand the English. As this consisted, in general, of portions from the New Testament, I sent him a Testament, and the Tracts in explanation of the prophecies, printed at Rome. He called again upon me, sooner than would have been necessary on a medical account, to ask a solution of some of the difficulties, which he had found in reading the Testament, and the Tracts. I now perceived, that the grace of God had begun to work in his heart, and that further opportunities of conversation with him, on the subject of religion, would be successful. Upon this I introduced him to Mr Annotte, who, though a poor man, earning his living by the trade of a barber, had applied himself with so much assiduity to the study of the Oriental languages, that he was a more complete master of them, than any other person in Malta; he was besides a very pious character.

"They frequently met, and the result of their conferences, and his visits to me, was his complete conversion to Christianity, just three months after his arrival in Malta. The Jews very much opposed his connexion with the Christians, wondering what could induce this good man to leave their ancient religion to join himself to this sect. Instead of being alarmed by opposition, he used his utmost exertions, from the time he embraced Christianity, to convert his brethren the Jews, because, as he said in a letter from *Tripoli, "always remembering the great Christian charity, which you, and your friends have shewn, in converting me to the true faith and religion of Jesus Christ, I think I can never do enough in promoting the religious interests of my fellow creatures, and, especially, of my former brethren the Jews, whom I see to be obstinate in unbelief." In his last letter, before I left Malta, he asked us to send the largest number of Testaments we possibly could, as he had it in his power to do great good with them, in many ways. Being unable, at that time, to send him any copy of the Scriptures, this worthy gentleman sat up whole nights to transcribe the Gospel of St Luke into modern Arabic, and Greek, with his own hand.

"The Bible Society is now printing another edition of the modern Greek Testament, of a smaller size than the former, and *the Society for propagating Chris-*

After he had resided three months in Malta, he returned to Tripoli on account of his business, which is so extensive, that he has four counting houses—at Tripoli, Smyrna, Scanderoon, and Barbary, in each of which twenty-four clerks are employed.

tianity among the Jews has promised to assist, as much as possible, this so zealous an advocate, and so attached a friend of the Christian faith.

"Mr. Kako, who remained a long time with me in Malta, is a caravansera merchant, a man of considerable property, and consequence; but so pious, and persevering in his exertion to promote the knowledge of the Gospel, in the different parts, where he happens to be, that his undertakings will be sufficient to form a publication of themselves. His journey is, in general, from the east coast of the Mediterranean, nearly to the borders of China, passing through Syria, Persia, and all the populous cities in those parts. Wherever he goes, it is his custom to collect the people, particularly the nominal Christians whom he can meet with, and preach to them in public, and to give them Bibles, or other religious books. He informed me, in one of his very interesting letters, that, in his passage from Santorini to Cyprus, he was obliged to stay some time in Rhodes, where he endeavored to do some spiritual good, and to spread the Gospel of Jesus Christ, in that island, which exhibits a sad scene of religious, and moral desolation. On his arrival, being with Turks and Greeks, in a kind of market, he gathered some of them about him, and began to speak of his voyage, to gain their attention, as they are very ignorant. He then introduced discourse on religion, and on the glorious Gospel. He was heard with pleasure, and the people began to increase so much, that, in a few days, the Bashaw sent for Kako, to ask him, why the people crowded around him, and to inquire of him, what that amusing book was, which he was reading to them, saying, that he had been informed, it was against God, and therefore against Mahomet, and contrary to the Turkish Government. Such an inquiry from the Bashaw would, in general, have been considered, under this despotic government, almost like sentence of death; but Kako had often met with similar difficulties, and said, that he always found, on these occasions, great assistance from Heaven. It is remarkable, that he usually had a presentiment of such trials; he therefore courageously answered the Bashaw: "The book is the Bible, which is the Holy Book, containing the immutable law of our common Creator, and therefore cannot be in any way contrary to God, or his holy will: and as for Mahomet, he is never mentioned, from the beginning to the end of the book; for it was inspired and written before Mahomet was born. In the third place, there is nothing against the Government; so far from it, if the subjects of the Grand Seignior will carefully read this Sacred

book, and attend to its prece[pts] will not only be more happy, b[ut] life, and the future one, but the[y] more faithful to the Ottoman P[ower] the same time, he presented th[e] with the Bible, that he might [read] more at his leisure, after havin[g] out to him various passages on t[he] of obedience due to the Sove[reign] submission to the *powers that* [be] was enough; the Bashaw acc[epted] book, and proved that he wa[s] saying, "Go on, go on," which during his remaining residenc[e] island, collecting, every day, lar[ge] gations of people. We have dozen of Bibles, which were rec[eived] eagerness, and distributed by a Turkish monk, according to the left by Kako. In the same letter Kako writes that this Dervise i[s] very good character, and has read the Bible with the hope of [find]ing the true religion."

The above was sent from En[gland] very respectable gentleman [to one in New] York.

Princeton, (N. J.) Dec. 15, 1[8..]

EDITORIAL REMAR[KS]

THE preceding letter, w[hich ap]pears to us uncommon[ly inter]esting, may properly be [accom]panied by a few [remarks.] Though the following [reflec]tions should appear ob[vious to] many readers, yet we t[rust] all will be happy to dw[ell a] few moments upon many [use]ful subjects of conten[t] which here rush upon th[e mind.]

It should be premised, [that Dr.] *Naudi* has the perfect co[nfidence] of the leading religious [charac]ters in London, and his [repre]sentations may therefor[e be re]lied on without scruple [or hesi]tation. He has engage[d to ac]company a clergyman i[n a mis]sionary voyage to the [Levant,] under the auspices of th[e Socie]ty *for Missions to Afr[ica and]* *the East*, of which Lord [Gambier] is president, and Mr. [

force, Mr. Henry Thornton, &c. principal members.* He has been an agent for the British and Foreign Bible Society, for several years, if we remember aright, and has sent the word of life from Malta into various distant regions. He is mentioned in a letter from a Roman Catholic deacon at Scandinari,† as having made an acceptable communication of intelligence to the friend of the writer, and is probably the "true friend in the Lord," to whom *Georgio Kako* addressed a letter, which has been published in our pages.‡ We proceed to observe,

1. Dr. N. appears to have become religious in consequence of meeting with religious books from England. This instance, among thousands of others, teaches us the utility and wisdom of an enlarged and diffusive benevolence. Religious books, including Bibles and various kinds of tracts, should be sent wherever there is any prospect of their becoming instruments of good under the direction of Providence. It is our duty to sow the seed; we know not which shall spring up, whether this, or that; but we know that God can give an abundant increase, even in an unpromising soil. Dr. N. may be, through many years, a vigorous and faithful agent in the great business of evangelizing the world, and may be the instrument of raising up many other agents like himself

2. The Bible Society in England evidently has a strong hold upon Dr. N.'s affections. He

wanted to visit the country, *where the Bible Society was formed.* By forming and patronizing this Society, the religious part of the English nation have rendered themselves peculiarly dear to the pious in every part of the globe. Thus a letter from St. Petersburgh styles that Society "*the wonder of the nineteenth century,*" "*the only adequate means that ever was devised for civilizing and evangelizing the world:*" And Prince Galitzin, one of the Russian ministers of state, says, that the Society is engaged "*in the noblest undertaking which can dignify the efforts of man.*"*

3. Dr. N. states the population of Naples to be 700,000. He may include certain contiguous districts. Dr. Morse, in the last edition of his Geography, vol. ii. p. 398, says, "The population of the city, in 1789, was 4,2,489." It is possible that the population has increased since that time, as that of London, and some other large cities, certainly has.

4 That a society of 5,000 praying people has been formed, in a few years, in the midst of this profligate city, is one of the most encouraging facts, which the present wonderful era has brought to view. It throws great light on the designs of Providence, and shews us how easily and insensibly and rapidly God can introduce the Millennium, whenever he sees fit, into Roman Catholic countries. These pious people hold just such meetings, as are usually called prayer-meetings in this country. How delightful and

* See Pan. for Dec. 1813, part II. p. 572.
† See Christian Observer for July, 1813, p. 457.
‡ See Pan. for Oct. 1813, part II, p. 377.

* See Ch. Ob. for July 1813, p. 468,469.

not public service; small groups assembling one night in one part of the city and another night in another.—Several of the members of the church also interest themselves greatly in distributing the Scriptures and scripture tracts among their neighbors, their servants, and the strangers from various parts of India with which Calcutta abounds. For the sake of accommodating these friends, a meeting has been held in the vestry during the greater part of the last year on the first Monday in the month, prior to the meeting for prayer, when such as are desirous, come and supply themselves gratis with the Scriptures in the Bengalee, Sungskrit, Hindee, Orissa, and Persian languages, and, for the sake of strengthening each other's hands, mention the opportunities which the preceding month has afforded them of distributing the Scriptures in any of these languages. Several of the younger members of the church have also applied to the study of the Bengalee, Nagree, and Persian characters, to enable them to read the New Testament to their servants and neighbors. We would fain hope that this will at length raise something like a missionary flame in the minds of some of these young men.—The native brethren, Krishna and Sebuk-ram have found their sphere of action much enlarged in the course of the past year, and their labors have been greatly owned. In addition to these the Lord has been pleased to stir up several other brethren to labor for the souls of others; of these, two have been already mentioned, the brethren D'Cruz and Petruse, the former assisting brother Mardon, the latter with brother Carapiet; two others labor in Calcutta with great diligence, viz. our young brother Thompson, whose correspondence in the Circular Letters plainly discovers the spirit which actuates his mind; and our brother Debrun, baptized about two years ago; who seems to labor among his heathen neighbors with very general acceptance, making known the word as occasion offers in Bengalee, Hindoostʼhanee, and Portuguese. By means of the labors of these brethren, although our stated congregation at the chapel is much below three hundred, more than a thousand of various nations have the word of life constantly ministered to them.

The Benevolent Institution for the instruction of the Indigent has been much encouraged the past year. We have been enabled by the liberality of the public to extend it also to the other sex. A school has been added for Girls in which, at the close of the year, sixty were instructed, who, in all probability, would otherwise have been growing up in ignorance and vice. This however has not lessened the

other branch; on the contrary, that at the close of the year contained 242 boys; so that although we began the year with less than a hundred children, we closed it with somewhat more than three hundred; and, which will excite equal surprise and pleasure, the debt which at the close of the last year amounted to nearly 2000 rupees, at the close of this was almost annihilated. This is owing partly to the liberality of the public, and partly to the new arrangements introduced in teaching on Lancaster's plan, by means of which brother Leonard, whose very soul seems in the work, instructs these 240 boys with greater ease than he, in the last year, instructed a hundred with two assistants. Unwilling to throw too great a burden on the public, we have erected at our own expense an airy and spacious school room in the heart of the town, which will contain nearly 800 children. This we shall for the present, let to the public at a moderate rent. It is not improbable that the number of poor children there taught to read the sacred Scriptures in English and Bengalee and instructed in writing and arithmetic, will by the end of this year, amount to five hundred. Should the Lord be pleased to give that blessing on this institution which is so earnestly desired, its effects in disseminating the Gospel in India, may possibly exceed our expectations.

THE BURMAN MISSION.

In this mission the progress made relates principally to translating the Scriptures. Our young brother F. Carey has at length succeeded in getting an able assistant in the Maguda language, and has been enabled to proceed with increased satisfaction in translating the Scriptures into the Burman language. He has revised the Gospel by St. Matthew and prepared it for the press, and has by this time finished Mark, and probably another of the Gospels. He has changed his condition in life and married a young woman born at Rangoon of Christian parents, whom he describes as being exceedingly attentive to the word of God, which she can read both in the Burman and Portuguese languages, and very desirous of being instructed in the nature of true religion. Should the Lord be pleased fully to enlighten her mind herein, she may be highly useful in the future concerns of the mission, acquainted as she is with the language, and the habits and ideas of the people. Her brother, a steady and diligent lad about 13, is pursuing his studies at Serampore.

Brother Chater, whom we mentioned in our last review as being at Serampore, printing a small volume of scripture-extracts in Burman, after returning to Rangoon and remaining there about two

ng little prospect of security
ster and his family in the dis-
of affairs there, and fearing
 late might not ultimately be
ster Chater's health, return-
...ed is now with us waiting
,new scene of labor in some
th he hopes will be more fa-
a health of sister Chater and
to wished indeed to wait here
by was once more in a state
l, the brethren fearing this
a a delay of years to no pur-
ded to their proposal of fixing
other scene of labor. His
...et on Columbo, where we
that there is any missionary
if where a multitude of in-
aid to amount to 270,000
the island) who bear the
...e, but are almost destitute
scriptures and of spiritual in-
...se to open a field sufficient
...g ministers of the Gospel.
...the New Testament in the
language we are now printing
...ry Bible Society. We hope
...to send a brother to Ran-
t...brother F. Carey there, in
...brother Chater The next
...e is the mission in

HINDOOST'HAN.

...the course of the last year
...that we have on behalf of the
...ed a house at Digah, a few
...atna with a view to its form-
...hool and a permanent mis-
...and in the course of the year
sister Rowe have proceeded
...t brother and sister Moore,
...f the latter of whom, we are
...l, seems much better than at
the former year. Brother
...es the situation at Digah as
advantages for missionary ex-
...ly exceeded by any situation
...cutta excepted We are a-
thither a native brother born
...d acquainted both with the
Persian languages, and intend
...us one of our brethren who
...the Gospel at Calcutta as
...fix on one suited to that
labor. Our brethren at Dig-
...to form themselves into a
...h we pray that the Lord may
...ake the mother of a multi-
...bes around them.
...ere our brethren and sisters
...day, after a journey of four
...was pleased to raise up some
...eceived them with great kind-
...loor seems opened for them
...n the Gospel. Many of our
...in the Fort there seem already

to welcome the glad news of salvation; and
we trust that the word will ere long have
an entrance among the ignorant heathen
around them. Their prospects relative to
a school, too, greatly exceed any thing they
expected; and bid fair to enable them,
while training up children, the future inhabitants of the country, in the nurture
and admonition of the Lord, to contribute
something towards their own support and
the unavoidable expenses attending a missionary station. Brother Chamberlain has
been again plunged into the depth of affliction since his arrival there, by the loss of
his two daughters, Hannah and Mary, the
latter the eldest daughter of our present
sister Chamberlain; and the former rendered peculiarly dear to him on account of
her mother, of whom he was bereaved at
Cutwa about seven years ago. It gives us
pleasure to observe, however, that these
afflictions although heavily felt by our bereaved brother, neither discourage him in
the work of God, nor diminish his activity
therein. He has succeeded in getting a
pundit to assist him in the Brij-Bhasa, in
which language, varying in some degree
from the Hindee, he hopes ultimately to
complete a grammar, a dictionary, and a
version of the Scriptures.

Our brother Peacock has also applied to
the language with much assiduity and success. He is particularly useful in the
school, and his heart seems increasingly
set on the work of God.

ORISSA MISSION.

In the course of the past year, our brother John Peter has been enabled to acquire
the language in a considerable degree, and
to circulate pretty widely the Orissa Scriptures. The fruit of this however must
not be expected immediately; it is sometimes a long time after the seed is cast into the ground before it makes its appearance, and a much longer before it brings
forth fruit. The case is not greatly dis-
similar with the word of God. Seven have
been added by baptism this year to the
church in Orissa; few or none of them however are natives of Orissa; yet we doubt
not but the time will come (nor do we
think it far distant) when multitudes of
these shall obey the word of God and live.
Meanwhile we rejoice in the conversion
of others, as they may be made the honored instruments of spreading the word of
life among the heathen around them. In
this way indeed several members of this
church seem likely to be useful. Some of
them stationed at Cuttack, have in the
course of the year labored greatly to diffuse the knowledge of Christ among the
heathen there, as will appear from several
letters which brethren Greece and Smith
have occasionally sent to their pastor at

Balasore. In a journey to visit these, brother Peter had an opportunity of communicating the news of salvation to many; and the readiness manifested, both to hear the word of life and to obtain the Scriptures, was truly encouraging. Of the church in Orissa eleven members are at present at Cuttack, among whom are the brethren Smith and Greene. Should a blessing accompany their endeavors to make known the Gospel, a church may in some future time be raised there also. The other part of the church, fifteen in number, including brother Peter and brother Krishna-das, is at Balasore; so that the word of life is now made known in Orissa in two places more than a hundred miles distant from each other.

MISSION TO BOOTAN.

The circumstances which have attended this proposed mission have been exceedingly discouraging. Our brethren Robinson and Cornish had arrived at Burbaree only a few days, when their house was attacked by a desperate gang of robbers to the amount of fifty or more, who killing two or three of the servants, pillaged the house of every thing they were able to carry away. The loss thus sustained by the mission was computed by our brethren to be little less than 2000 rupees. Discouraged by this afflicting circumstance, brother Cornish requested leave to return to Serampore. Brother Robinson after some time took another journey to the confines of Bootan; but on making application for permission to enter the country, it was answered, that this would not be permitted. On which, thinking it useless to make any further attempt, he requested that some other field of labor might be assigned him. On four or five being pointed out, he fixed on Java, whither he has obtained the permission of government to proceed. The Mission to Bootan must therefore be conducted in another way: the most practicable seems to be, that of getting natives of the country to assist in translating the New Testament, which when printed, (and the forming of a fount of types from the various copies of the alphabet in our possession is not difficult,) can be easily carried into the country by some of our native brethren, who can enter it at pleasure; as the Bengalee language is spoken by many in Bootan.

THE MAHRATTA COUNTRY.

In our last review we mentioned the opportunity afforded us through the medium of a friend, of introducing the Gospel into this country. From letters received from him in the course of the year, it will appear that the willingness of the inhabitants near

him to receive and read the word is very great. He mentions several as having read the New Testament through, others as applying for it with great eagerness; and three or four as apparently determine to make an open profession of faith in Christ. The youths in his little school too, continue to study the Scriptures and to improve in the knowledge of the Mahratta and Hindee languages. In a word, the seed sown there seems to afford ground for encouragement and hope. We infer from the manner in which the Scriptures are read and apparently relished, that the style and language must be well understood. This affords encouragement to persevere in other translations where the door may not be immediately open for the dissemination of the word.

ISLE OF FRANCE.

Here are stationed our brethren in the 22d regiment, under the pastoral care of brother Forder. A letter we have lately received from him intimates, that there has been a considerable falling off; but does not particularize those who appeared now in that state. Among others however the life of religion seems greatly to flourish. One has been added to them by baptism, and they have hopes of several others. The brethren who seem to take the most lively interest in the cause of God, are stationed in three different parts of the island. Amidst every discouragement, there seems much reason to hope that the Lord will be with them and make them a blessing. For this let our prayers be constantly offered.

JAVA.

Our brethren in the 14th regiment who formed a part of the church at Calcutta, are now stationed at *Samarang* in this island. We rejoice to hear that to the three brethren there, five have since been added, thus forming a little church under the care of our brethren Baird and Russel. A letter which we lately received from them breathes a most pleasing spirit. At Walleredon near Batavia is our brother Brown, baptised at Calcutta about three years ago. When brother Robinson goes, therefore, another little church may be raised there if the Lord be pleased to smile on our efforts.

The increase of the various infant churches as far as we have been able to ascertain, was last year as follows: Added 97; dead 6; excluded, (so far as known) 1; clear increase 90.

It may not be improper to add a list of the brethren who are laboring throughout the various Missions this year:—

ACTUALLY EMPLOYED.
In Hindoost'han.
Agra, Brethren Chamberlain and Peacock.
Digah, Brethren Moore and Rowe.
In Bengal.
Dinagepore, Brother Fernandez.
Goamalty, Brethren Mardon and D'Cruz.
Cutwa, Brethren W. Carey, Jun. and Kangalee.
Jessore, Brethren Carapiet, Petruse, Seeta-ram, Manik-sha, Man-ika, Pran-krishna and Punchanun.
Near Dacca, Brother Bhagvat.
Serampore and Calcutta, Brethrer Carey, Marshman, Ward, Krishna and Se-buk-ram.

In Orissa.
Brethren John Peter and Krishna-das.
In the Burman Empire.
Brother F. Carey.
In the Isle of France.
Brother Forder and Joplin.
In Java.
Brethren Baird and Russel.
Waiting to proceed to their destination.
Brother Robinson to Java.
Brother Chater; station not fixed.
Brethren laboring occasionally.
Proceeding to Digah, Brother Hedut-alla.
Serampore, Brethren Kanta, Kanace, Deep-chund and Vykanta.
Calcutta, Brethren Leonard, Thomson, Debruin and Jahans.
Near Dacca, Brother Cornish.
Orissa, Brethren Greene and Smith.

From this sketch it will appear that the various missions contain twelve missionary stations, ten infant churches, thirty brethren actually employed, (of whom fifteen are Europeans and fifteen natives of Asia;) and twelve who labor occasionally. A retrospect of the whole suggests two considerations: *Ground for gratitude.* Who that recollects the state of things among us thirteen years ago, can avoid perceiving this? Then we were one small church containing only eleven members; now at least ten infant churches cheer our eyes, and one of them contains little less than a hundred and fifty members. Then we were only five brethren, confined to one spot, with not a single native to assist us in making known the word of life; now we are enabled to number thirty brethren who labor according to their ability in six different languages; while no less than twelve others stand ready to devote themselves to the work as far as they have opportunity. What reason then have we to bow in humble gratitude, and cry. "Not unto us, not unto us, O Lord, but unto thy name. be the glory, for thy mercy and truth's sake."

Matter of encouragement.. Scarcely an objection that unbelief has started remains unrefuted; scarcely an obstacle, which the God of grace has not in some degree removed. Was it said that Hindoos would never forsake their cast and the customs of their ancestors? Hindoos have forsaken all; and joyfully make known the glad tidings of salvation to their countrymen. Were Musulmans, once deemed impenetrable to the Gospel? Musulmans have not only received it, but preach a crucified Savior to their former fellow Musulmans. Was the disposition of the inhabitants once deemed such that divine grace could scarcely renew them effectually? Notwithstanding some have fallen, others have adorned the Gospel by their lives; and glorified it even in death. Were the languages of India deemed almost impracticable? In no less than six of them is the word of life now preached. Did circumstances seem to render certain countries and stations unapproachable? Access has in most instances been obtained beyond expectation, which ought fully to encourage us respecting the rest. Were the climate, &c. deemed insupportable to European constitutions? A degree of health has been granted to almost every individual equal to what was formerly enjoyed in our native land. In a word, the Lord has been pleased to set before us an open door, and to shew us that there is no blessing we need for his work, which he is not both able and willing to grant. This plainly points out both our duty and our highest interest; let us walk humbly before him, seeking to please him in all things, and to abound therein more and more, recollecting that memorable declaration of the prophet to Asa and the men of Judah, *"The Lord is with you, while ye are with him."* Let us abound in prayer;—for grace to preserve the life of religion in our own souls, without which we can do little in a right manner in the work of God and for the souls of others;—for our native brethren, who have more to combat than even we ourselves, while their acquaintance with divine things must necessarily be more limited; —for the infant churches; these unless watered by the dews of divine grace, cannot increase, but will on the contrary become extinct,—and for the heathen around, that the number brought in this year may exceed any thing yet seen by us. Let us endeavor to abound in the work of the Lord, and diligently watch for opportunities to make known his glorious Gospel. To this the Lord is particularly calling us by thus setting before us an open door: let us then give proof that we possess the genuine spirit of adoption by following where our heavenly Father leads, and improving every opportunity to call in those, his "other sheep" whom he will surely bring in, and unite with the rest under the same shepherd. Finally, let us expect from him this year and onwards a *still more abundant blessing.* His work is perfect; and what we see him begin, we may be assured he will complete. All we have hitherto seen, though worthy of our praise in itself, derives its principal value from its appearing to be a preparation for still greater things. And is not the residue of the spirit with Him? Must not the knowledge of the Lord our Redeemer cover the whole earth? the stone cut out without hands become an unmeasurable mountain? the mountain of the Lord's house be established on the top of the mountains for all nations to flow unto it? And when must all these things be accomplished, but in these 'last days,' of which however above seventeen hundred years are already gone. Let us not then measure what is to come by what has been already, but rather look forward to brighter things, as men in the dawn of the morning expect, not the return of the midnight shades, but the appearance of the rising sun. Thus let us look forward to the rising of the Sun of righteousness on the benighted lands around us, and on the whole world. Even so, come Lord Jesus, come quickly. We are, &c.

         W. CAREY,
         J. MARSHMAN,
         W. WARD.

DONATIONS TO SUPPORT MISSIONS AND TRANSLATIONS.

Jan. 7, 1814. From Mr Joel Beecher of Farmington, (Conn.) by the Hon John Treadwell, Esq $5 00
In a letter with the Salem postmark*   -   -   10 00
From a subscriber to the Panoplist, for the translations†   -   5 00

     Carried forward, $20 00

This letter, which appears to be in the hand-writing of a female, is as follows: "Sir, In humble imitation of your correspondent, "A Subscriber," (Pan for Nov. 1813, p 178.) I again enclose ten dollars for Foreign Missions,
         Yours respectfully,—"

†*This sum was enclosed in the following letter:*

         "Dec. 1813.

"To the Editor of the Panoplist.

It has been my desire to aid the transla-

     Brought forward, $20 00
From Mrs. Sarah Stone, wife of the Rev. Mr. Stone of Brookfield   2 00
From Dea. Reuben Leighton, of Westford   -   -   2 00
From the following persons in Easton, by Col. Shepherd Leach: viz.
— From Col Leach himself $50
——— Lincoln S———   -   2
——— Andrew Blesdell   -   2
——— Cephas Leach   -   10
——— Jason Leach   -   2
——— Sally Bonney   -   2
——— Betsey Torrey   -   2
——— Caroline Torrey   -   1
——— Lucinda Hodges   -   2
——— Betsey Belcher   -   1
——— Solomon Belcher   -   1
——— Charles Hayden   -   5
——— Alpheus Johnson   -   3
——— Ichabod Macomber   -   5
——— Rezer Keith   -   2
——— Howard Lathrop   -   5
——— A friend to missions   5—100 00
From the Rev. Bancroft Fowler of Windsor, (Ver)   -   3 00
From the Female Charitable Society in the east parish of Windsor, by the Rev B Fowler   20 00
10 From several societies and individuals, by Mr. Henry Hudson, of Hartford, viz
From the Foreign Missionary

     Carried forward, $147 00

tions of the Scriptures—have found it difficult to obtain the means.—The exhortation 'to lay by on the first day of the week as God hath prospered,' has lately come with force to my mind. Having been abundantly prospered some weeks—was led to inquire, whether I had rendered to the Lord his portion. As I doubted whether it was duty, under existing circumstances, to add to my annual stipend, which I enclosed last month—I was thinking whether some new plan might not be adopted, and the sum necessary saved. At this time I was absent from home, and had not communicated my thoughts on the subject. On my return, I found verified the truth of that passage, *A prudent wife is from the Lord*—for my wife in my absence had contrived a plan, by which we shall save at least twenty dollars a year—and although our tea and coffee are less sweet than before, yet when I reflect, that it is for his sake, who being rich, became poor, and was willing to eat barley bread for our sakes,—I do not regret it.—Feeling it my duty to promote the faith I once destroyed, and desiring that God may be glorified in me—I enclose five dollars for the translations, and mean to give more when I can,—   A SUBSCRIBER."

Brought forward, $147 00
Society in Glastenbury,
(Con.) - $13 02
From a female religious
society in the same town 8 00
From sundry ladies in do. 3 00
From Tolland county Aux-
iliary Foreign Missiona-
ry Society - 100 00
From the Foreign Mission-
ary Society in the west-
ern district of Fairfield
county, viz. for transla-
lations - - 68 00
——— for missions 82 00—274 02
11. From the Female Foreign
Missionary Society in Tyring-
ham, by the Rev. Joseph Warren Dow - - - 19 00
14. From the Foreign Missionary
Society of Springfield and the
neighboring towns, by the Hon.
George Bliss, Esq. Treasurer 67 00
15. From the Foreign Mission
Society of Boston and the Vicinity - - 325 06
20. From the Religious Charitable
Society in the county of Worcester, by the Rev. Joseph Goffe,
the Treasurer - 112 75
21. From the Foreign Mission
Society of Brunswick and Topsham, by the Hon. Jacob Abbot,
Esq. the Treasurer - 34 00
From Deacon Bradley, of Stockbridge, by the Rev. Ephraim G.
Swift - - - 10 00
From the Foreign Mission Society
of Middletown, (Con.) by Mr.
Samuel Gill, the Treasurer 150 00
22. From Mr. Robert Porter, of
Pulteney, Steuben county, (N.Y.) 10 40
25. From Mr. Solomon Goodell,
of Jamaica, (Ver) to aid the
translations of the Scriptures, by
the Rev. Dr Lyman - 465 00
From the Foreign Mission Society
in Ware, by the same hands 27 00
27. From the family of John Ba-
chup, Esq. of Barnet, (Ver.) to
aid the translations, by the Rev.
Leonard Worcester - 200 00
————————
$1,841 23

FOREIGN MISSION SOCIETIES.

*The Foreign Mission Society of Boston
and the Vicinity* held its third annual meeting at the hall of the Massachusetts Bank,
on Wednesday the 12th inst. The report
of the Treasurer, by which it appeared
that $1,323 72 had been paid into the
Treasury of the American Board of Commissioners for Foreign Missions by this

Society, during the year past, was exhibit-
ed as certified by the Auditor, and was ac-
cepted. That part of the above sum,
which was appropriated by the donors to
aid the translations, had been remitted to
India for that purpose. The following
gentlemen were re-elected officers of the
Society for the ensuing year
His Honor WILLIAM PHILLIPS, Esq. *Pres.*
SAMUEL SALISBURY, Esq. *Vice Pres.*
The Rev. JOSHUA HUNTINGTON, *Sec.*
JEREMIAH EVARTS, Esq. *Treas*
BENJAMIN GREENE, Esq. *Audit.*

In the evening of the same day, the annual sermon was delivered before the Society by the Rev. WILLIAM GREENOUGH,
of Newtown from James v, 20. *Let him
know, that he which converteth a sinner
from the error of his way, shall save a
soul from death, and shall hide a multitude of sins:* After the sermon, which was
pertinent and interesting, and of which a
copy was requested for the press, a contribution was made to the funds of the
Society.

*The Merrimac Branch of the Foreign
Missionary Society* held its annual meet-
ing at Newburyport, on Monday the 10th
inst. The Treasurer being absent, no re-
port was made of the state of the funds.
The following gentlemen were re-elected
officers of the Society for the ensuing year.
viz.
THOMAS M. CLARK, Esq. *Pres.*
JOHN PEARSON, Esq. *V. Pres*
Mr. SAMUEL TENNEY, *Sec.*
Mr. RICHARD BARTLET, *Treas.*
Rev. DANIEL DANA, *Aud.*

*The Foreign Mission Society of Bruns-
wick and Topsham* held its annual meeting in the present month, when the following gentlemen were chosen officers for
the ensuing year; viz.
The Rev. WINTHROP BAILEY, *Pres.*
JOHN PERRY, Esq. *Sec.*
Hon. JACOB ABBOT, Esq. *Treas.*
DAVID STANWOOD, Esq. *Collector.*

N. B. The Secretary of each Foreign
Mission Society is respectfully requested
to forward to the Editor of the Panoplist
an account of the last annual meeting of
the Society, with the names of the officers
then chosen, if such account has not already appeared in the Panoplist.

MERRIMACK BIBLE SOCIETY.

THE Managers of the Merrimack Bible
Society in conformity to the 8th Article
of the constitution, submit to the members
the following report of their doings the
past year.

They have in the course of the year distributed ninety-nine Bibles and twenty Testaments.

The permanent fund of the Society is One Thousand Dollars.

The balance now in the hands of the Treasurer, due to the Society is $281 21 cts.

By the foregoing statement it appears, that there has been an increased activity in the distribution of Bibles; and from this circumstance conclusive evidence may be derived in favor of the growing usefulness and importance of the institution. The poor are gratuitously supplied with the bread of life; others, who are able to furnish themselves are reminded by the zeal of Bible Societies of the duty of possessing the sacred volume, and a general disposition to read and examine the Scriptures, which are able to make us wise unto salvation, may be reasonably presumed to be the happy consequence. Bible Societies have already been the happy instruments of diffusing incalculable benefits to a large portion of the human race; and the undeniable evidence of their utility has encouraged the formation of a large number in various parts of the world. But it is found by experience, that however numerous the institutions and liberal the means furnished by them, they are far from being competent to the objects, yet to be accomplished. The boundaries of this new field of benevolence expand as the laborers advance. The unity of design exhibited by the various Bible Societies in the United States not only promises a rich harvest of the Christian graces, love and charity, but their mutual correspondence gives rise to many useful projects; and a union of their counsels and efforts must give greater vigor and effect to their designs. In this view, a recent communication from the Bible Society at New York has been received with pleasure by the Managers of this Society, announcing their determination to print and disseminate the Bible in French among the inhabitants of Louisania; where they have discovered a deplorable scarcity of Bibles and a disposition to receive them with gratitude. The work is in considerable forwardness; and the undertaking being expensive, the aid of similar institutions in this country has been solicited. The Managers of this Society have therefore voted to remit One Hundred Dollars to the New York Bible Society to aid in this laudable object. The Managers report with satisfaction the generous donations of individuals to this institution. One Hundred Bibles have been presented by Mr. PEARLY TINNEY, and the sum of One Hundred Dollars has been received from a person whose name is not known to this board;—These pious donations will command the gratitude and respect of each member of the institution.

The Managers voted also to furnish One Hundred Bibles towards replacing certain others which had been captured by an American privateer from a British vessel and had been destined for distribution among the destitute; but they were happy to learn that a sum of money, more than sufficient, had already been raised in Boston for the same purpose.

The statement exhibited this day by the Managers of their doings must establish the importance of the Merrimack Bible Society and excite in the members a new and lively interest in its welfare. A call for the Bible is one which a believer in its truth must find it difficult to resist; and even amid our present distress, an appropriation of a small portion of that substance which will soon perish, in favor of so laudable an object, must appear reasonable, especially in view of the hope, that 'it may be regarded, as a *"treasure in heaven."* But an immediate excitement must be derived to all from the reflection, that when circulating the Bible, they are diffusing the best antidote to those crimes, which bring down the judgments of an angry God; that they are taking the readiest means of removing present calamities; that they are promoting the cause of civilization, literature and humanity, and subserving the temporal and eternal interests of man. The Managers cannot conclude therefore without earnestly recommending to the members renewed exertions in the great cause, in which they have so laudably, and hitherto so successfully embarked.

(Signed)
SAMUEL SPRING, President.
Newburyport, January 5, 1814.

CHARITABLE ASSOCIATION.

THE citizens of the town of Newburyport will recollect the call which was made on their charitable feelings the early part of last winter, by an association, formed for the purpose of affording temporary assistance to poor and distressed families in this town and vicinity. The following extract from the report of the Trustees of that association, and the subjoined communication from the *Female Benevolent Society,* now published by request of the Trustees, will give the benevolent donors a correct view of the manner in which their bounty has been disposed of.

Extract from a Report of the Trustees of the Charitable Society, March 11,

"The whole amount of
subscription, $1119 31
Of which the Treasurer
has received $940 31
Received by assistant
treasurers, in provis-
ions,   162 00
Uncollected   17 00—1119 31

The board of Trustees began their supplies on the 1st of January, (1813) and
have continued them weekly to the present time; during which period applications
have been received from *two hundred and
fifty-nine* families. Of that number *fifty*
have been referred to other sources for
supplies, or have been found on inquiry
not to be so necessitous as to require the
attention of the Board. *Two hundred
and nine* families have received partial
or constant supplies from the Board.
The average number supplied weekly by
the Board, has been about *one hundred
and fifty* families containing from 4 to
500 persons.

The sums appropriated for ten weeks
amount to *Five hundred and fifty-eight
dollars and seventy-seven cents*, exclusive
of wood; of which about fifteen cords
have been distributed.

The Board have also entrusted to the
Female Benevolent Society for distribution, in cash and goods, $153 31 cts. and
have also placed under their direction an
additional sum of $100 for the purchase
of materials for spinning, &c. which last
sum is to be accounted for hereafter to this
Board. So far as the Board have been
under advantages to judge, the amount entrusted to that Society has been very judiciously appropriated

There remains now in the Treasury
one hundred and sixty-three dollars and
forty-seven cents, and there also remains
uncollected $17, which sum it is expected
will enable the Board to continue their
supplies until the first week in April, at
which time, unless further subscriptions
are received, the supplies must cease."

After the date of the above report the
balance then on hand was distributed in
the same manner as therein stated. And
within a few days past the Society have
received the following communication
from the *Female Benevolent Society*,
giving an account of the monies entrusted
to their care:—

"*To the Secretary of the Charitable Association, formed in Newburyport for
the relief of the poor—*

Sir,
When the liberal donations from
Society were put into the hands

Ladies of the Benevolent Society, it was
requested that at the end of the year
some account of the manner in which it
was distributed might be given you. We
therefore take the liberty to present to
you the following statement.

The first *hundred dollars* which was
given us in clothing, was distributed according to the best judgment of our committee in those families which appeared
to them the most destitute. The *fifty
dollars*, given in money, "to be disposed
of at the discretion of the Society," was
appropriated in the following manner,
viz. *Ten dollars* to each of our committee,
(four in number;) with which they clothed poor children to go to school and to
meeting The remaining *ten dollars* was
retained for the use of the sick.

The *hundred dollars* given for stock,
has also been improved in the following
manner: *One hundred and sixty-one*
spinners have been employed, and *four
thousand four hundred and eighteen*
skeins of yarn have been spun. *Twenty-
eight* weavers have woven *one thousand
eight hundred and sixty-seven* yards,
of cloth. Sixteen pair of hose have been
knit One hundred and fifty garments
and *five* pair of cotton cards have been
distributed in pay for spinning and weaving. The stock now on hand is valued
at one hundred dollars.

As it may not be unpleasant to you
to know what the Society have done otherwise, we take the liberty of adding the
following schedule.

(*To be continued*)

POETRY.

For the Panoplist.

JESUS WALKING ON THE SEA MATT. xiv,
24, &c.

I

WILLOW on life, my gliding bark
    Serenely cut its sportive way:
No blast to rough, no cloud to dark,
    The waveless calm, the cheerful day.

Yet I forgot the Mighty One,
    That walked the flood in form unseen;
Whose hand rolled bare the clouding sun;
    And spread the waving sea serene.
* * * * * * * *

II.

Once,—lowered the sky;—the tempest

III.

My way was down the gaping tide:—
  Foundering upon the yawning brink—
Whelming in endless night—I cried;
  'Save, Lord,—or I forever sink!'

Then on the bounding waves I saw—
  O bless'd relief!—the Son of God.
His mandate struck the winds with awe;
  The waves bowed prostrate at his nod.

'Weakling of faith, why didst thou fear"—
  He said—'or doubt my powerful arm'
Didst thou not see thy Savior near?
  Can I not guide thee safe from harm?'
*   *   *   *   *   *

IV.

I never saw his watery path;—
  Nor thought I that he could attend;—
Till mercy, in the guise of wrath,
  Taught me to own my Heavenly Friend.

Lord, I in thee henceforth confide!
  My bark, no more by tempests driven,
Safe wilt thou through the ocean guide,
  And waft me to the shore of Heaven!'
             O. F.

TO CORRESPONDENTS.

Φιλοψυχος is requested to forward the constitution and laws of the charity libraries, to which he refers, that they may be published either in whole, or in an abridged state. He is informed that ten sets of the three first volumes of the Minor Panoplist, in boards, will be delivered to his order, for the use of these libraries, on application to the Publisher of the Panoplist.

Several communications are on hand, which will be mentioned more particularly hereafter.

After consulting with several friends of the Panoplist, as to the utility and propriety of the measure, we have concluded to offer the following premiums for original communications to be inserted in the current volume of our work: viz.

One of *Twenty Five Dollars* to the writer of the best composition in prose; the rule of judging to be *the tendency of the piece to do good:*

One of *Fifteen Dollars* to the writer of the best piece of poetry: and

One of *Ten Dollars* to the writer of the second best composition in prose

The persons, according to whose decision the premiums shall be distributed, will be entitled to respect and deference.

All original communications contained in the current volume, with the exception of those written by the editor and the judges, will be taken into consideration, without any request or intimation on the part of the writers. There is no necessity, that the writers should be known to the editor. It is always convenient, however, that original communications should have signatures.

It is to be remembered, that the preceding offer is not to be construed as limiting, or in any way affecting, the power of the editor over communications.

Our correspondents, who may be influenced by the preceding offer, will bear in mind, that the sooner communications are made, the greater will be the probability that they will be inserted in the current volume, as there may be a press of matter toward the close of the year.

Whether a similar offer will be made another year must depend upon the result of the present offer

Though the value of the premiums may appear small, yet it is as great as that of some of the premiums offered for original compositions, in the English Universities.

TO SUBSCRIBERS.

Our distant subscribers ought to be informed, that the irregularity and delay, experienced in the receipt of our numbers by mail, are not chargeable to us; but must be laid to the crowded state of the mails In several instances, the Panoplist has remained for weeks in the Boston post-office. Hence it has happened, that *later* numbers are sometimes received by our subscribers before *earlier* ones. The postmaster at Boston has declared his disposition to forward our work, with as little delay as possible, not only for the sake of obliging us and our subscribers, but for his own convenience. He conceives himself obliged by law, however, to send all the newspapers, though pamphlets should be delayed. Very probably delays, similar to the one described at Boston, have occurred in other offices on the road. As we have fully stated the complaints of our subscribers to the postmaster, and as we have now returned to our former practice of printing but one number in a month, we hope that there will be less occasion for complaint hereafter.

Subscribers are informed, that a few deficient numbers can be supplied at present, for twenty cents each; and, whenever deficiencies shall probably have arisen from mistake or negligence on our part, they shall be supplied without expense. The fact is, however, that we incur a disadvantage by supplying deficient numbers at the price above stated, as broken volumes may be left on hand in consequence of it.

THE
PANOPLIST,
AND
MISSIONARY MAGAZINE.

| No. 2. | FEBRUARY, 1814. | VOL. X. |

RELIGIOUS COMMUNICATIONS.

For the Panoplist.

SINNERS, IN A SPIRITUAL SENSE, BLIND AND DEAF.

Hear, ye deaf; and look, ye blind, that ye may see....Is. xlii, 18.

If we consider these words as prophetic, they have reference to the period of our Savior's advent, when the Gentiles should be brought into the holy family of God; and, thus received, they are an earnest expostulation with the Gentiles to forsake their idolatry, and receive the illumination of the Gospel. The prophet, however, addressed himself immediately to the Jews, and designed to reprove them for their unbelief and rejection of the truth. His language is strong and impressive; and, as the persons addressed were favored with the natural organs of sight and hearing, no candid mind will be liable to mistake his meaning. He here exhibits, with affecting emphasis, the moral state of all men, while unrenewed by the Holy Ghost; and, by his example, he furnishes us with divine authority, as to the manner in which the impenitent should be addressed. At this time I would direct the reader's attention to the solemn truth, that

Impenitent sinners are, in a spiritual sense, deaf and blind.

A person, who has always been destitute of the bodily organ of sight, is unable to form just conceptions of external objects. The sun may shine in the glory of a cloudless sky, while to him all is total darkness. Describe to him, in the most lively colors, the beauties of creation, and you fail to give him any suitable ideas of these objects, because he never *saw* them.

Moral and religious truths are as distinct objects of vision to the mind, as the earth, the sun, or any material substance, is to the eye. The holy character of God, for instance, may be discerned with perfect clearness; and it abideth forever, an object of delightful contemplation. The same holds true of the character of Christ as Mediator. The loveliness of truth is, likewise, an object of distinct vision; and may be seen and contemplated with as much fixedness and certainty, as any material object.

Holiness and sin, in their true character, are other objects of distinct vision. So also is the divine law. Its beauty and excellence are viewed with un-utterable delight, by all who love its precepts, and are properly awed by its sanctions But the holy character of God,—the complete, perfect character of Christ,—the loveliness of truth,—holiness and sin.—with the glories of the divine law, are objects, which the natural eye seeth not. These are spiritual objects, and can be discerned on-ly by a spiritual vision. This spiritual vision, exists in those only, who have a temper and disposition harmonizing with the divine law, and pleased with the perfect character of Jeho-vah. When this temper and disposition are possessed, *the things of the Spirit of God* are received; the person enjoys spiritual light; and *the secret of the Lord is with him.*

I make these observations, for the purpose of leading you, my readers, to just views, on this important and essential point in theology, and of making a proper distinction between that discernment, which arises from a well-informed under-standing, and the discernment, which accompanies a temper and disposition harmonizing with the divine law. The latter is a *spiritual* discernment, and com-prises all that is intended by spiritual knowledge.

Unless, my readers, your views are correct on this point, you are novices in religion, and are not prepared to reap the best advantage from attention to the subject now under considera-tion. The persons addressed by the prophet are blind, but their blindness is of a peculiar charac-ter—the destitution of spiritual discernment. They know not the true character of God. They discern not the loveliness of truth. And, in addition to this dreadful and universal mal-ady, they are *deaf:*—deaf to the calls of hope;—deaf to the invi-tations of mercy;—deaf to the threatenings of the divine law;—deaf to the intreaties of com-passion.

Can it be necessary to go into an elaborate proof, that this is the deplorable and affecting con-dition of all the impenitent? One might well suppose that the evidence, which is constant-ly exhibited, of this fact, would banish every doubt from the mind, and fasten an unshaken conviction upon it.

Had the sinner *just* views of the divine law, could he feel in-different towards it, and know-ingly transgress it? Did he dis-cern the glory of the divine character; could he be silent, un-grateful, and rebellious? But in his present state he finds fault with the divine dispensations; contends with God as partial and unjust; gives the reins to his selfish appetites, and habitually disobeys. Nor does he perceive the beauty of holiness, or the nature of sin. The former nev-er excites his desires; the latter never excites his disgust, in it-self considered. Its delusive objects he pursues, with all the intenseness of an eager, insati-ate appetite: and this too, when assured by God himself, that the *end of these things is death* Nor does he perceive the loveliness of truth, and therefore rejects it. His dislike will be great, in proportion to the clearness and force with which the truths of the Gospel are exhibited. Hence sinners often denounce, as false and unintelligible, some of the plain, essential truths of the Bible; those precious truths, which delight and support the humble believer They may professedly receive the Gospel as a system of truths, that are correct and obligatory; but the system, in their hands, becomes so garbled, that it loses its divine form, and loveliest features. The habitual disregard of these truths, as manifested in their lives, proves them to be insensible to the excellence of revelation. How uniformly do they neglect to study the Scriptures But why neglect them? All, who discern the excellency of the doctrines, which the Sacred Volume contains, delight to examine the word of God; and they dwell, with joyful particularity, upon its sublime, ennobling, consoling discoveries.

How palpably absurd would it be to imagine, that the person, who beholds and relishes the beauties and sublimities of the material creation, should yet never contemplate them, and never speak of them. Such a course could be pursued by him only, who was born blind, or who, with the loss of his eyes, had also lost all recollection of what he once beheld. Nor can any one rationally doubt, that all are in total spiritual darkness, who do not feel a peculiar interest in the Gospel, delight its lovely truths, and glory in its institutions. The language of *facts* must be the language of conviction. And what the sinner's habitual conduct declares to be true respecting himself, it is madness to deny.

Equally striking and affecting is the evidence, that the spiritually blind are, likewise, spiritu-

ally deaf. God calls them to the belief and practice of the truth;—he invites them in the most endearing and moving strains;—he sets before them, and proffers as their portion, all the happiness of which they are susceptible; but they remain unmoved, and will not obey He admonishes them, reproves them, and threatens them, with all the terrors of Omnipotence in anger, but they still remain unmoved, and refuse to obey. In his Providence, by frowns and smiles, he solemnly enforces the calls, instructions, and invitations of his word; but they regard Him not. Why? If all this does not move them, what can effect the object? Ah! they are *deaf.* They have not heard. *Their ears have they closed.*

The language of Scripture is explicit on this subject. The passage at the head of this paper is full and plain. *Hear, ye deaf; and look, ye blind, that ye may see.* The same truth is stated in the 16th verse of the same chapter. *I will bring the blind by a way that they knew not.* Also verse 6, 7, *I the Lord have called thee to open the blind eyes.* The passage from the prophet is quoted by St. Luke. *The Spirit of the Lord is upon me, because he hath anointed me to preach the Gospel to the poor, and recovering of sight to the blind.* Our Savior, indeed, restored sight to those who were naturally blind. But this constituted a very small portion of the great work, which he came to accomplish. He gave himself a sacrifice, that such as are *spiritually* blind might receive their sight and be saved. 1 Cor. ii, 14. *The natural man receiveth not* the things of the Spirit of God; for they are foolishness unto him; neither can he know them, because they are spiritually discerned. As this blindness is seated in an evil heart, all those passages, which declare the heart to be destitute of holiness, prove the existence of the malady in question. We are taught it by the apostle, when he says; *The carnal mind is enmity against God. You hath he quickened, who were dead in trespasses and sins.*

This blindness to moral beauty, and deafness to the invitations of mercy, are universal. No son or daughter of Adam is naturally exempt from them. Unless renewed by the Spirit of God, we are now, and ever have been, acting under their influence; and our conduct in a moral view, is fitly represented by the prophet. Is. lix, 10. *We grope for the wall like the blind, and we grope as if we had no eyes; we stumble at noon day as in the night.* Hence trifles have been magnified in our estimation into objects of great moment; and things of infinite value have been considered as dross.

We gain little by attending to this subject, unless we realize the truth, in relation to ourselves. I shall have accomplished little, indeed, by exhibiting the moral blindness of sinners, if the reader barely assents to the truth, without any reference to his own situation. Let each one be intreated to realize, that if impenitent, he is enveloped in total moral darkness; blind to the beauty of holiness, to the loveliness of truth, to the nature of sin, and to the true character of

Jehovah. Although he has eyes, he sees not; though he has ears, he hears not. And were he to be translated to heaven, and set down before the throne of God and the Lamb, the same darkness would cover him, unless his heart were changed. No object would meet his eye, which could afford him pleasure. All the glories of the heavenly state would be hid from his view, because they are spiritually discerned. Such is the deplorable state of man while unrenewed: such the alarming state of all, who have not received Christ by faith, and chosen him as their friend and portion.

ALPHA.

For the Panoplist.

ON KEEPING SATURDAY EVENING AS A PART OF HOLY TIME.

OUR venerable ancestors transmitted to us, in their rich legacy of habits and institutions, the strict conscientious observance of Saturday evening. Whether this period is more properly considered as a part of holy time, than Sabbath evening, I shall not now inquire. Every serious man will admit, that the one or the other ought, as a part of the Sabbath, to be consecrated to the service of God. Every such man, likewise, will observe with alarm the general disregard, if not with self-reproach his individual neglect, of this solemn season. Let us look, for the proof of this disregard, into our families and our hearts. The business of the week is urged with redoubled vigor, as the shades of Saturday evening begin to fall. How rarely do any of us find every secular employment ended on that day, with the setting sun. The farmer, the mechanic, the merchant, the mistress of a family, has still to finish some arrangements, which encroach on the time of their Maker. When the business of the day is at length brought to a close, instead of that elevated devotion, with which we should ever approach our glorious Creator, Redeemer, and Sanctifier, how often do we present before him the unworthy offering of a wearied, distracted attention, cold and languid affections, the lifeless service of a heart still clinging to the world.

Many, who are generally conscientious, are apt, I fear, to consider Saturday evening as an introduction to the Sabbath, rather than as a part of it. They are willing to withdraw themselves gradually from worldly thoughts and employments. Lest the transition should be too abrupt, they take for their evening reading some sober history, perhaps Miss Adams's History of the Jews; or the Miscellany, Reviews, or Literary and Philosophical Intelligence of the Christian Observer, or the Panoplist. The student examines, perhaps, the merits of Middleton on the Article, the Dissertations annexed to Magee on Atonement, or takes up some knotty point of polemical theology or biblical criticism. To those, who thus misapply this valuable portion of time, I would say, are your affections, then, so lively, that you fear too rapid and too high a flight? Is your mind so heavenly, that it needs to be bound down to earth? Are

you already too apt to walk by faith and not by sight? Do you fear to become too holy, too much weaned from the world, too much devoted to your God, so that you give to secular pursuits, those hours which He has called his own? so that standing on holy ground, you still look back, with a longing eye, toward the cares and employments of the world?

Six days shalt thou labor and do all thy work; but the seventh day is the Sabbath of the Lord thy God: in it thou shalt not do any work. From even unto even shall ye celebrate your Sabbaths. God has taken to himself the full space of one natural day. It is therefore no longer ours. If we spend any part of it, unnecessarily, in worldly thoughts, or worldly employments, we rob God of that which He has taken as his own. What is this but sacrilege? We rob ourselves. We squander part of the golden season consecrated to the attainment of eternal life; when God is peculiarly on the mercy seat, waiting to be gracious; when, according to the concurrent testimony of all Christians, the strivings of the Holy Spirit are most efficacious; when the heart is most open to His influence; when the means of grace are most effectual. We tempt his patience; we, in a manner, solicit him to give us up to hardness of heart; or, at least, to withdraw from us the light of his countenance.

The neglect, of which I speak, is extensive, is increasing. Wherever I go, I find it prevalent to an alarming degree. It is difficult for a traveller to spend Saturday night, even in the house of a religious friend, as his duty demands. Before I am accused of exaggeration, let me beg the reader to look into his own practice. Is it not time for pious masters of families, who are anxious for their children's salvation, and their own progress in holiness, to ponder these things deeply, and apply the remedy? CLIO.

For the Panoplist.

ON COMING LATE TO PUBLIC WORSHIP.

Mr. Editor,

I HAVE long thought of troubling you with a few remarks upon the habit of coming late to public worship. I say the *habit*, because I have observed, in a considerable number of congregations, that some persons rarely come in, till after the service has commenced.

Whether this is to be attributed to sloth, or design, I shall not presume to determine. I strongly suspect, however, that in many cases, it is owing to the former, and in some, at least, to the latter.

If people rise at a late hour, as it cannot be denied that many do, on the Sabbath morning, it is almost a matter of course, that they should be late in every thing, through the day.

The suspicion may perhaps be deemed uncharitable; but a long course of observation has led me to think, that the desire of being particularly noticed, when they enter the house of God, induces some to enter it late.

It is certain, at any rate, that more than a few seem to derive more satisfaction from the stare of a full house, as they march through the aisles to their pews, making a full display of their persons and costly attire, than from the prayers, praises, and instructions of the sanctuary.

But whatever may be the cause, or causes, of the habit in question, I am sure you will agree with me, Sir, that it is highly reprehensible. I am aware, that occasional hindrances are unavoidable; but those persons who are always, or usually, or very frequently, among the last at public worship, can by no means be excused for their tardiness.

If it is our duty to assemble with the people of God, in his house upon the Sabbath, then it is our duty to be there, in season, that we may unite in the introductory prayer, hear the Scriptures read, and join in the first singing. Surely that man must be a stranger to the spiritual delights of public worship, who feels no desire to be present at its commencement. What would be thought of a son, or a servant, who should cast such practical contempt upon the appointments of his father, or master. *If God*, then, *be a father, where is his honor? If he be a master, where is his fear?*

Further, it should be always, and solemnly, remembered, that no religious ordinances can be of the least avail, without the divine blessing: and what reason, let me ask, has any one to expect such a blessing upon the latter part of the public service, if he carelessly, or intentionally, absents himself at the beginning. The personal loss of the loiterer, in this case, though it may be infinite, involving nothing less than the loss of his soul, is not the only evil resulting from the habit under consideration.

He injures others, as well as himself. His example, especially if he be a person of consequence in the parish, is likely to be copied by a crowd of humble imitators. If he be a master of a family, his children and domestics will naturally walk in his steps. Nor is this all. By entering the assembly after the exercises are begun, he disturbs almost the whole congregation. I have been pained exceedingly, at the noise and bustle, by which a large part of those, who wish to worship God without distraction, have evidently been prevented from hearing the voice of the speaker. This, as it strikes me, is at once a violation of an invaluable religious privilege, and an outrage upon one of the first rules of good breeding.

If my neighbor makes it a point to be early at worship, that he may unite with his brethren in the first exercises, what right have I to disturb him in his devotions? or what right has another to disturb me in the same circumstances?

I shall conclude for the present, with an anecdote, which I have some where met with, and which I think worthy of being universally known and remembered. An aged and pious lady, who lived some miles from the place of public worship, was observed to be always among the first at meeting. Being asked how it was possible for her, considering her age and the distance, to be there so early, she made this short but memorable reply: *"It is a part of my religion, not to disturb others in theirs."* MIKROS.

LETTER FROM A YOUNG LADY IN B—— TO HER FRIEND IN N——.

To the Editor of the Panoplist.

Sir,
The enclosed letter, from a young lady in B—— to her friend in this town, was handed to me a few days since, with a request, that it might be forwarded to you, and (if you think it expedient) inserted in the Panoplist. Yours, &c.

"MAN, my dear cousin, born with faculties which look forward into the depths of futurity, and with powers which are destined to flourish beyond the boundaries of time, is yet prone to fix his heart and affections on this passing world, as though it were *an abiding place*, or could confer permanent satisfaction. With delight he clings to this barren soil; and, groveling among the insects of a day, here concentrates all his cares, desires and enjoyments. He builds his visionary Babel of future greatness; lays out schemes for the acquirement of honors and emoluments; and flies from one object to another, in search of happiness; but it constantly eludes his grasp. He finds by sad and reiterated disappointments, that *vanity and vexation of spirit* is the proper inscription upon all things beneath the sun. Yes, my dear cousin, transient and unsatisfying are all the pleasures of time and sense, and utterly undeserving our supreme attachment. O that we may be enabled to rise above their fascinations, and drink copiously of those pure and heavenly joys, which flow from that river, which is *clear as crystal, and which proceedeth out of the throne of God and the Lamb.* Durable riches and righteousness, consummate blessedness and glory, are offered in the Gospel, *without money and without price.* How sublimely glorious are the prospects of a Christian! The theme is too divinely grand for the dialect of mortals; it needs an angel's eloquence to display its glories. Yonder is his *home*, his peaceful happy home; a region of cloudless day and everlasting light, never to be disturbed by a rising storm; where seraphim and cherubim and redeemed spirits strike their golden lyres to Immanuel's praise, and all heaven resounds with the delightful symphony;—where joys increase in number and in transport, and rivers of perennial pleasure flow, immense as the cravings of the deathless soul, and lasting as the ages of eternity! O the wonders of sovereign grace and redeeming love! If but one sinful soul were renewed and exalted to this vast, boundless happiness, to this unrivalled glory and honor, how great and immeasurable would be the salvation! But when countless myriads are redeemed out of every nation, and kindred, and tongue, snatched from the opening abyss of immediate ruin, and raised to the fruition of all this amazing glory, *which eye hath not seen, nor ear heard. nor the heart of man conceived*—O how unparalleled, how amazing, how ineffably great must be the compassion and grace of Christ. What prodigies of infinite love and power will the redeemed be, and how sweetly will they extol, and magnify, their great Deliverer, and vie with angels, in the loudest notes of adoration and praise,

"O, my cousin, how aggravated and dreadful will be our condemnation *if* we neglect *so great salvation!* Our Savior invites us to accept this salvation. Can we refuse? Can we pass by the mount of Calvary, and not lift our eyes to its summit? Can we slight that Love, which, in the person of our Lord, suffered and bled to save our guilty souls? If we can, we shall not surely do it with impunity. Christ is now upon his mediatorial throne; but he leaves it soon for his dread tribunal; and then all his incorrigible opposers, who would not bow to his golden sceptre, shall feel the awful indignation of the *Lion of the tribe of Judah,* seizing on his prey. O that you, my friend, may now in time listen to the voice of the Charmer, and feel the powerful attractions of that cross, "where Christ, my Savior, lov'd and died." O that you may join the little band of pilgrims marching to the rest of Canaan, and walk, with alacrity, in the path which conducts to the summit of Zion. Though it is a *straight and narrow* road, strewed with briars and thorns, yet here and there a cluster of the grapes of Eshcol refresh the traveller, and the heavenly glories of Tabor shine on his path, as a proof *that the ways of wisdom are ways of pleasantness, and all her paths peace.* Sweet, exquisitely sweet, is that rest, with which Jesus refreshes the weary, and superlatively happy is that man, that woman, that child, whose God is Jehovah.

"This, my dear cousin, is what I want. Earth has no charms for me. Its trifling toys, and inapid pleasures, I have long since viewed with indifference; and have directed my eyes to the world above, where holiness and felicity *forever, ever, reign.* Infinitely rather would I reside in some obscure hut, graced with the *beauties of holiness and the fruits of the Spirit,* and favored with the presence of the King of kings, than in the grandest earthly palace, swaying a sceptre over obedient nations, and possessed of all the joys and pleasures of this nether world;—*but without a God.* O, may we never seek our portion here. Rather let us ascertain our title to a mansion in that celestial world, where the storms of adversity, and the billows of temptation, never arise;—"where time and pain and chance and death expire." Let us be solicitous to build upon a foundation, which the united assaults of earth and hell shall not shake—even the Rock of ages, the illustrious Corner-stone. Fixed upon this immoveable basis, we might meet with composure the greatest worldly calamities, smile at the approach of death, and look forward to the august scenes of the last great day, without dismay or apprehension How inconceivably important is it, that Christ should be formed in us, *the hope of glory!* And if the concerns of our souls are of infinite moment, do they not demand *immediate* attention? Defer them not, my dear N——. for *now is the accepted time, and now is the day of salvation.* Your time is on the wing; your days are taking their flight; and, when you have witnessed a few more rising and setting suns, you will be conversant with dis-

embodied spirits and with all the tremendous realities of eternity. Rest not, then, till you are sheltered in the ark of safety; till you are prepared to meet your God. When you repose on your pillow, apply this question to your inmost soul; *Am I prepared to die?* For your eyes, instead of saluting the splendor of the next rising sun, may open in the eternal world. Did we know what was passing this instant in eternity would it not rouse to energy all our dormant faculties, and awaken to activity our drowsy souls. Should we not exert every nerve to secure the bliss, which some are enjoying, and avoid the agonies and torments, under which others are despairing? O, how highly should we appreciate every passing moment; how indignantly should we scorn the trifles of a day; and how should we value our immortal souls, and the precious atonement of the Lamb of God, who saves from hell, and raises to heaven.

If these things are true, they are of momentous importance; and, however we may evade their force now, the time is not remote, when we shall feel them in all their tremendous emphasis, solemnity and power. O that we may now feel their salutary influence to the saving of our souls. O why, why, are we so supinely careless, when all that is interesting in heaven, or hell, hangs suspended on this *inch* of time, this flying now. O, my dear N——, let me intreat you to live under a deep and habitual sense of eternal things. Realize the unutterable interests of a dying hour, the ineffable preciousness of your immortal soul, and the amazing solemnities of the dread tribunal. Ponder on the word *eternity;* a word, which our language is too poor to explain; which our minds are too contracted to comprehend; but of which we shall ere long *experience* the meaning, in all its *awful import.* I cannot but feel tenderly anxious for your future well being; I cannot but long that you should be a *Christian.* As a proof of my ardent affection, receive this from your affectionate   F."

June 10, 1813.

ON THE DUTY OF CHRISTIAN ZEAL AND IMPORTUNITY.

To the Editor of the Panoplist.

Sir,

THE enclosed essay is with diffidence submitted to you, either to publish or suppress, as you shall judge proper. I would wish here to observe to you, that the Christian Church in general, within the circle of the writer's acquaintance, and probably much further, suffers greatly for want of practical piety, and a diligent and spirited exertion of its members for the prosperity of Zion. The love and cares of this world appear to engross their principal attention. Although doctrinal knowledge is, in many instances, very imperfect, yet it far exceeds a personal obedience to the plain commands of Scripture. If this piece should not be thought worthy of insertion, it is highly probable, that another piece, on a subject of a similar nature, might be the mean of exciting many readers of the Panoplist to a more diligent and zealous attention to eternal things.

Dec. 10, 1813.

BY Christian zeal and importunity are here meant an ardent affection for the Christian religion, and a constant solicitude, (expressed by words and actions,) for the advancement of the Redeemer's kingdom in the world. The object of this zeal and importunity is not the promotion of any secular interest, but the extension of evangelical truth. These active principles are necessary both for the advancement of individual piety, and the progress of religion in general. As these exercises of the mind proceed from a cordial love to God, and a deep sense of the reality and importance of eternal things, they may justly be considered 'as an evidence of Christian piety. The Christian graces are active principles; and, when once implanted in the heart, are to be cherished and improved, only by a lively exercise in a course of godliness. Though the mind should ever be impressed with the fact, that success in spiritual as well as temporal concerns, is only from God, it would yet be extreme folly and presumption, to expect success in the neglect of the established means.

Mankind are by nature formed for active employment; and it is ordained by infinite wisdom, that all the attainments of men, shall be made by means of their own exertions. When these cease to be made, in a proper degree, we are not warranted by experience to expect success in any pursuit. Christians are commanded to love God with all the heart, soul, strength and mind; and to manifest this love by living in actual obedience to his commands. The Holy Scriptures clearly shew the nature and situation of man to be such, as to require his constant and most vigorous efforts, in order to make progress in the Christian life. The natural depravity of the human heart, the vanities and allurements of the world, and the various temptations to which all are exposed, place them in a continual state of warfare. They have to contend not only *with flesh and blood*, but *against principalities and powers, against the rulers of the darkness of this world, against spiritual wickedness in high places.* Scripture examples, and precepts, so plainly enforce the duty and necessity of Christian zeal and importunity, that whoever expects to advance in religion, by a life of neglect and indifference must be ignorant of the bible, and a stranger to the nature of Christianity.

The human heart is naturally so opposed to the doctrines and practice of true religion, and so deaf to the calls and invitations of the Gospel; and the adversary of souls is so busily engaged in effecting their destruction, that the minds of the unregenerate are little excited to attend to religion, by the example of those, who manifest a careless and indifferent attention to divine things. Besides, the duties of the Christian religion imply such a course of self-denial, and are so contrary to our natural inclinations, that the performance of them requires, at all times, a cordial love to God, and earnest supplications at the throne of grace for divine assistance. The Holy Scriptures render it abundantly evident, that all such as would enjoy the divine favor, must seek it with zeal and importunity. All those, who have been the most remarkable for their human attainments, have been equally distinguished for their perseverance and incessant exertions. The annals of the Christian religion shew, that persons, who have been the most eminently useful in the Church, have, at the same time, been the most zealous and importunate. Those who live in the exercise of this zeal, are incessantly engaged, after the example of our Savior, *in doing good.* They strive for growth in grace, not only for their own good, but that they may become the more useful in the cause of religion.

Believers are styled, *God's husbandry, and workers together with Him.* They are commanded *to grow in grace; to give diligence to make their calling and election sure; and to let their light so shine before men, that others, beholding their good works, may glorify their Father who is in heaven.* If the word of God requires believers to be zealous and importunate in the concerns of religion, success is not to be expected, without a practical obedience to his commands. The following words of the prophet *Isaiah*, among other passages of Scripture, very strikingly enforce the duty of Christian zeal and importunity: *I have set watchmen upon thy walls, O Jerusalem, which shall never hold their peace day nor night. Ye, that make mention of the Lord, keep not silence, and give Him no rest, till he establish and till he make Jerusalem a praise in the earth.*

Ministers of the Gospel, and all who name the name of Christ, are here commanded to exert themselves incessantly for the enlargement of Christ's kingdom. That this command is not more generally obeyed, in no degree diminishes its force. Although professors of religion, through slothfulness and the love of this world, yield a very imperfect obedience to many of the divine commands; yet their practical obedience *ought* to increase in proportion to the advancement of scriptural light and knowledge. If it is now ascertained to be a Gospel command. to afford pecuniary aid for missionary purposes, it is then a duty equally incumbent on the people of God, to labor incessantly, and zealously, in every other way, for their own spiritual welfare and that of others. The attention of the bulk of mankind, at the present time, is remarkably diverted from the concerns of religion, by the love of this world, and by the extraordinary commotions existing among the nations of the earth. This neglect of religion, at the same time that the Lord is punishing the inhabitants of the world for sin, loudly calls for the most strenuous efforts of the friends of Zion, in the cause of truth and righteousness. *When the enemy comes in like a flood, the Spirit of the Lord shall lift up a standard against him.*

Although it is true, that *Paul may plant, and Apollos water, but God alone gives the increase;* it is nevertheless, usually found to be a fact, that the prosperity of religion in any place, is in some proportion to the spiritual diligence and zeal of its ministers and professors. The prince of darkness is not disturbed by a mere outward profession of religion; neither is he displeased with a speculative belief of the doctrines of the Gospel, and a cold formal round of religious duties, provided professors of religion are not conformed, in their lives and conversation, to the temper and disposition which the Gospel requires. But when, from an ardent love to God, they are diligently and zealously engaged in the concerns of religion. the powers of darkness are dismayed; the wicked are constrained to acknowledge the reality and importance of religion; their consciences become alarmed; and many, in consequence of beholding the good works of others, are induced to glorify their Father who is in heaven. When the careless and secure find Christians in earnest, and see that they make much of eternal things, they are in a degree restrained from gross sins; and, by perceiving Christians not ashamed of *the cross of Christ*, they become less reserved in their inquiries on the subject of religion.

Although ministers of the Gospel, possessed of the best natural and acquired abilities, preach good orthodox sermons every Sabbath; and although professors of religion lead apparently moral lives, and attend regularly on the ordinances of the Gospel; yet if they remain silent and indifferent as to eternal things, at all other times, and do not evince the sincerity of their profession by a zealous and importunate pursuit of religion, the work of the Lord will seldom prosper with them. Those, who live in the lively exercise of the Christian graces, and are diligently and zealously engaged in the cause of Christ, embrace every opportunity to advance the spiritual good of others. They not only urge the wicked to attend to religion by the example of a holy life and conversation; but are incessant in endeavoring to excite them to attend to the various means of grace. This Christian zeal embraces the various missionary objects of the present day. Those, who have this spirit in exercise, not only feel it a duty incumbent on them, to extend the knowledge of the Gospel to heathen countries, but likewise find numerous occasions at all times of performing or supporting missionary labors themselves, within the sphere of their own acquaintance. Ministers, and Christians in gereral, who neglect on week-days to use all the means in their power, for the spiritual good of their fellow creatures, lose their greatest opportunities of doing good. There are numbers, in every Christian society, almost as ignorant of the Gospel, as the heathen in Africa.

The discountenancing and suppressing of vice; the instruction of the ignorant, in moral and religious knowledge; and the distribution of the various religious tracts and publications of the present time, furnish ample scope for the benevolent exertions of every well disposed person. Considering the feeble and limited efforts of most Christians, for the advancement of religion, there is no wonder that it is not more flourishing. If the Lord's watchmen, and people were more universally and earnestly zealous in the best of causes, there is encouragement to expect, that He would appear, and more generally revive and extend it. The Scriptures assert, that lukewarmness and indiffer-

ence in spiritual concerns, are highly displeasing to God. Therefore, Christian professors, who remain idle and indifferent spectators in this enlightened and eventful period, not discerning the signs of the times, have reason to apply to themselves the denunciation to the church of the Laodiceans: *I know thy works that thou art neither cold nor hot: I would thou wert cold or hot. So, then, because thou art lukewarm, and neither cold nor hot, I will spue thee out of my mouth.*

T. Θ.

For the Panoplist

ON THE EVIL OF SIN.

Sin is defined, in the Westminster Catechism, to be the "want of conformity to, or transgression of, the law of God." I think no important exceptions can be taken to this definition. It is clear and comprises much, in concise terms.

The existence of law, is implied in the existence of sin. *Where there is no law, there is no transgression.* Were there rational beings in the universe destitute of law, they must be free from guilt. Had not Pagans a law in their own consciences, transcribed there by the finger of God, they must be acquitted in the day of judgment. Such as have in their hands the Scriptures, will be judged by the Scriptures; and their demerits will be estimated, according to the standard there established.

Hence, in estimating the evil of sin. we are bound in duty to ourselves, and in gratitude to heaven for *the lively Oracles*, to form no other rule, than that, which will regulate the decisions of the *last day*. Consulting our own happiness, and the honor of God, we shall unquestionably limit or extend our views of the heinousness of sin according to the testimony that *cannot lie.*

1. Regard the character of the lawgiver. *God is good.* He is, essentially, Love. He allows to every creature, not only the good things claimed in virtue of a divine promise, and the privileges held in virtue of his rank among other creatures, but he bestows countless favors, that are unsolicited, and unpromised, as well as undeserved. He pursues one grand object, in all his works;—the highest happiness of the Universe. *He is wise in heart.* He adopts the best possible means to secure his object, and cannot be deceived. *He is just.* The precepts and penalties of his laws are equably poised. *Justice and judgment are the habitation of his throne.* He will inflict no more punishment, in any instance, than is deserved; and will deprive no one of any promised or deserved good. He is independent. No motives of interest, terror, or partiality, can sway him from rectitude. His authority being underived, is stable beyond the possibility of being shaken. He has power to enforce his laws No being can resist him; no successful opposition can be made. Now, if these perfections belong to God, he is perfectly qualified to be a lawgiver. And let it be remembered, that they *do* belong to him, in an unlimited sense. He is *infinite* in benevolence, wisdom, justice, and power. Who then will question his right to impose laws, at his pleasure, on beings of yesterday? And what finite mind can calculate the enormous guilt of violating those laws. But

2. Consider the obligations under which men lie to God. *They live, move, and have their being in Him.* Man is formed with noble powers. He looks above, around, below, and, in all things, discerns the majesty of GOD. He looks back on years long since gone, forward on years to come. He lifts the curtain that hides the eternal world, and converses with invisible spirits. He knows what God expects from him: he knows the doom that awaits him if impenitent, and the inheritance he is heir to, if a believer. Day after day he is upheld; year rolls on after year; and each revolving sun brings to light new pleasures, opens new prospects, and enlarges the sphere of enjoyment. True, he is not perfectly happy; but his very sorrows are medicinal, and his trials are so accommodated to his circumstances, as to evince rather the solicitude of a parent, than the severity of a master. Now if the earth pours forth her treasures; if the eternal God reveals his justice, his mercy and his truth; if all heaven urges man to be happy; must not the sin of disregarding the obligations, thus imposed, be incalculably great?

3. Consider, further, the qualities of the law which sin violates. It is perfect. It neither requires too much, nor too little. Its penalties are neither too rigorous, nor too mild. The punishments it threatens, are exact-

ly proportioned to the crimes it forbids, and the promises it implies are worthy of God. It is therefore *holy just and good.* It is an *eternal* law. If I mistake not, we are apt to consider the moral law, as issuing from the arbitrary will of the lawgiver, and consequently as liable to be revoked at his pleasure. If so, we place it exactly on a footing with the ceremonial law, and all the other temporary ordinances that God has appointed for the benefit of his church. Herein we err. The moral law, or the great law of love; is no more dependent on the divine will, than Omnipotence, or any other divine attribute, is so dependent. It is the necessary result of infinite perfection, and of course is coeval with the existence of God. It is not eternal as to its publication, because creatures have not existed eternally; but, whenever and wherever moral created beings have existed, this law has been made known, and carried into operation. Therefore, it is an *universal* law. Does it bind man? It binds the angel and the fiend of darkness too. God himself its author, its supporter, and its end, regulates his conduct by the same principles of love that he inculcates on us. This law binds together all worlds; and controls all operations in the natural, intellectual, and moral systems of the universe. Let it be annihilated, and confusion pervades every corner of God's dominions. Nature returns to her primitive nothing. The fire of intellect is extinguished. Moral affection expires. The throne of God is mingled in the general ruin. Such is the *tendency* of sin; and if its evil may be estimated by its tendency, human language is not expressive enough to describe it adequately.

4. Again; sin produces actual suffering incalculably great. It blots out eternal happiness. It creates eternal misery. That spark of immortality, kindled in the human breast by the Spirit of God; that living principle, which is destined to survive a burning world, and to blaze forth a radiant star in the courts above, or to gleam a baleful wandering meteor through regions of eternal darkness;—this it is, which sin makes its victim; this is the object, which it drags from celestial glory down to regions of never-ending horror. Before we conclude, that the demerit of sin can be estimated by a finite mind, we ought to pause, and distinctly view its consequences. These are defined, certain, and irretrievable. We do not calculate the severity of an affliction by its magnitude merely, but by its continuance. A momentary pang, however excruciating, is quickly forgotten, if it be followed by uninterrupted quiet; but let pains follow pains, for years and ages without intermission, would not the evil be considered as proportionate to its duration? Suppose, then, that the sinner is given up to be food for a worm that *never* dies; fuel for fire that *never* shall be quenched;—suppose that misery strictly *eternal* is allotted to him for his portion, and this as *the wages of sin;* must not the *cause* of such suffering be an evil so great as to baffle all calculation? But on

the authority of God's word, we pronounce these to be the legitimate and unavoidable consequences of sin, unless the sinner become penitent.

I am sensible, that it is sometimes said, that punishment will be eternal for no other reason, than that men, if they die impenitent, will continue to sin forever. I am much mistaken if a passage can be found in Scripture to warrant such an opinion. We are authorized to affirm, that at the day of judgment every man will be tried, and acquitted, or condemned, *according to the deeds done in the body;* not according to his deeds between death and the resurrection, nor according to his deeds after the judgment. His conduct and feelings in this world, and these *alone*, are matters on which he will be tried and sentenced. In that solemn day the universe assembles—for what? To learn that sinners will continue to sin in hell, and *therefore* be punished forever? No; but to learn how they have regarded the law of God and the Gospel of Christ, while on earth; and to learn, that contempt for the law, and rejection of the Gospel, deserve everlasting misery.

The evil of sin appears from the obligations which it violates. We are bound to love, and honor any being, in proportion to his rank and excellence. We are under greater obligations to love a *good* man, than a *bad* one; and under greater obligations to love a good man in authority, than a good man *without* authority. This is the dictate of that wisdom that is *without partiality.* Now, if God is infinite in excellence, our obligations to love him supremely are infinitely great. If we fail in rendering him his due, we violate these infinite obligations; and this violation is a sin, which none but the Infinite Mind can fully estimate.

Finally, the demerit of sin may be learned, from the cross of Christ. To see the Son of God willingly led as a sheep to the slaughter; to see the second person of the adorable Trinity, in the character of the Messiah, giving up his life as a sacrifice to make atonement for sin, and to magnify and honor the law which sin had violated; to see one, who was infinitely rich, become poor, that we through his poverty might be rich; to look at this scene, and then turn away coolly to affirm, that the occasion of his sufferings is not an infinite evil, argues a state of mind that few Christians will wish their own.

May the writer of this article, and his readers, be preserved by the grace of God, from limiting the magnitude of that evil and bitter thing which God's soul hates, according to the conceptions of our darkened understandings. May we cheerfully submit this, and every other subject connected with our immortal interests, to the infallible decision of Him, whose lips shall pronounce the final doom of the impenitent:—*Depart, ye cursed, into everlasting fire prepared for the devil and his angels.*

S. S.

For the Panoplist.

ON THE HAPPINESS OF THE DYING CHRISTIAN.

INFIDELITY is not totally blind to the advantages of religion. A heart, abandoned to every virtuous principle, sometimes pays homage to truth, by the acknowledgment of its transcendent excellence. No situation, in which piety is exhibited on this side of the grave, is more favorable to its triumph over prejudice, and its honor in view of the world, than the death-bed. The dying Christian has extorted from many unsanctified hearts the prayer of Baalam; *Let me die the death of the righteous, and let my last end be like his.*

If we consider the character, the state, and the prospects of the good man, at the closing scene of life, we may be sensible that his situation is a happy one.

He has, then, peculiarly enlarged and correct notions of the nature of sin. The diseases and dissolution of the body, form but a subordinate part of the curse originally laid on disobedience; but even these serve to illustrate its demerit. The revoltings of nature in prospect of the last struggle; the anguish of the separation between soul and body; and the farewells, that are given to surviving friends, teach lessons of repentance, which are to be learnt no where else. It is in such circumstances, that the love of Christ, and the voluntary sufferings that were the fruit of it, appear most illustrious; and, of course, the guilty infatuation of despising

the Gospel is most deeply deplored. The sorrow thus produced is holy, and inseparably connected with joy of the purest kind.

He has confidence in the power and compassion of his Savior. He falls asleep—not to lose the pleasures of faith,—but that faith may be absorbed in vision. If he has doubts, they flow only from imperfection, and continue but for a moment. His faith is unconquerable. His eye is fixed immovably on Jesus. The glories of Immanuel absorb his meditations; and he exclaims, "It is enough; I go to dwell with my Redeemer."

He is humble. He has not the labor of looking over past life to collect his good deeds, and arrange his virtues, against his appearance before his Judge. He cheerfully acknowledges, "I am less than the least of all saints;" and instead of valuing himself on the integrity he has preserved, the alms he has dispersed, or the external duties of religion, he rests all his hopes on sovereign mercy, and ascribes glory to Him only, to whom it is due.

He is patient. If excess of pain extort a groan, he answers only the demand of nature. But while he laments his imperfection, at a time when infidelity vents its complaints in imprecations, he struggles against a repining spirit, and quietly endures, *as seeing Him that is invisible.*

He is resigned. *Not my will but thine be done,* is the language of his heart. He submits to death, not because he is tired of life; not because oppressed with anguish; nor because he may now die with honor; but because the choice of his heavenly Father is his own.

Consider his state. He is at peace with himself. His accounts are made up. His passions are composed. His days of mourning are at an end. No imaginary rectitude of life; no persuasion of his innocence; no review of a long catalogue of charities forms the basis of his tranquillity; but while conscience summons before him his multiplied sins, it is that he may perceive the efficacy of grace, and hear a voice saying to him, *Son, be of good cheer; thy sins are forgiven thee.*

He is at peace with the world. His name rises above reproach. His character is delivered from the pollution attached to it, by the calumnies of the envious and malicious. No impoverished family rejoices in his exit; no oppressed widow, no orphans feel their sorrows passing away, with the hearse that conveys him to the tomb. Involuntary tears declare the common estimation of his worth; and the grave proves a sanctuary to protect his reputation from the assaults of malice.

He is at peace with God. Compared with this, what are all the delights of life and health to one whose heart is at war with his conscience, and who keeps on his steady course to destruction in despite of the Spirit of God. I repeat it, the believer is at peace with God. His sins are forgiven; the blood of Jesus washes away his guilt; and he is entitled through grace, and the sanctification of the Spirit, to ineffable joys. Once he was an *alien*

from the commonwealth of el; a servant of the pri darkness. The wrath of l hung suspended over him. sword of justice glistened afar, and as it appro threatened instant and death. He had no hiding —no defence—no hope. cy intervened, and staye pending vengeance. A ti respite was allowed him broke his covenant with d annulled his agreement hell,—and bound himself service of God. Now h in peace on the bed of He bids defiance to the powerful enmity, which c ist against him. He lea the arm of the Lord, and zes the truth of the decla *Thou wilt keep him in 1 peace, whose mind is sta thee.*

Consider his prospects passes from a state of tri state of enjoyment; from tre of war to a region of Before him is deliverance all the broils and fierce c tions of this nether world; all the dangers and mi that crowd the path of How often are we oblig weep over the treache friends—or the uncertai friendship! How often gayest visions of fancy formed into the sad reali woe! How often have dreamed of new fountai pleasure, and awaked to the bitter waters of disap ment! The grave exen good man from farther pa tion in these evils. A di body will no longer embit intellectual pleasures, nor tion of spirit mingle its g the cup of his joys. Fear will no more drive him to the verge of despair, nor hope hold out an almost extinguished taper to light him through the dreary apartments of his prison.

He is about to be delivered from a greater evil still; from sin—the prolific parent of all the misery in the universe. Sin though often foiled, and partially subdued; though meeting with decided and persevering opposition; is still the constant disturber of his breast while he lives on earth. He is obliged to see it in various situations, and contend with it under every variety of shape. It lurks in every corner, and fills his way to heaven with impediments. He earnestly longs for deliverance, and death delivers him.

His victory is complete. The last words, that vibrate on his tongue, declare him conqueror over all his enemies. *O death where is thy sting; O grave where is thy victory.* Not only victory, but triumph awaits him. He shall wear a crown that never fades. He shall be enthroned at the right hand of Jesus. He shall sit in judgment on those that have traduced him, and fought against the Church; and, when the Judge of quick and dead shall say to them *Depart,* he shall respond, *Alleluia, the Lord God omnipotent reigneth.* S. S.

REVIEWS.

LVII. *The Columbiad.*

(Concluded from p. 33.)

We shall now present our readers with the theory of Mr. Barlow respecting the origin of the universe, of our world, and of the human race;—a theory, which was not invented by him, but which has been received by modern Atheists generally, as the best scheme, on the whole, which they have been able to patch up. In the early parts of the Columbiad, there are several very intelligible hints of the poet's views on this great subject; but the full developement of them is reserved for the ninth book, as introductory to that great display of light, which is to pervade the earth in the political millennium. A part of the argument of this book is as follows:

"Columbus inquires the reason of the slow progress of science, and its frequent interruptions. Hesper answers, that all things in the physical, as well as the moral and intellectual world, are progressive in like manner. He traces their progress from the birth of the universe to the present state of the earth and its inhabitants; asserts the future advancement of society, till perpetual peace shall be established."

From this account of the book we were led to expect an infidel cosmogony, at full length; nor were we disappointed. Any person who is desirous of comparing the silly dreams of modern Atheists with the sublime and authoritative account of the creation, as written by Moses, may here have as good an opportunity as could be wished. Columbus closes his first inquiry, as to the state and progress of man, in these lines:

"Why did not bounteous nature at their birth
Give all their science to these sons of earth,

Pour on their reasoning powers pellucid
   day,
Their arts, their interests clear as light
   display?
That error, madness, and sectarian strife
Might find no place to havoc human life."
              B. ix. l. 29—34.

The answer to this inquiry
embraces the great revelation
from Hesper; a revelation, which
anticipated all the boasted discoveries of modern philosophy.
It begins thus:

"To whom the guardian Power: To
   thee is given
To hold high converse and inquire of
   heaven,
To mark untraversed ages and to trace
Whate'er improves and what impedes
   thy race
Know then, progressive are the paths
   we go
In worlds above thee, as in thine below.
Nature herself (whose grasp of time and
   place
Deals out duration and impalms all space)
Moves in progressive march;" &c. &c
              l. 35—43.

Thus Nature is exalted to the
rank of Creator and Upholder of
the universe. We quote the
beginning of her creation as a
great curiosity. It will answer
several purposes; and will be
useful, particularly, as a specimen of the "crude and crass"
style, in which a great part of
this poem is written. The
"hand" mentioned in the first of
the following lines, is the hand
of Nature:

"When erst her hand the crust of Cha-
   os thirl'd
And forced from his black breast the
   bursting world,
High swell'd the huge existence crude
   and crass,
A formless hard impermeated mass;
No light nor heat nor cold nor moist nor
   dry,
But all concocting in their causes lie.
Millions of periods, such as these her
   spheres
Learn since to measure and to call their
   years,

She broods the mass; then into motion
   brings
And seeks and sorts the principles of
   things,
Pours in the attractive and repulsive
   force,
Whirls forth her globes in cosmogyral
   course,
By myriads and by millions, scaled sub-
   lime,
To scoop their skies, and curve the
   rounds of time.
She groups their systems, lots to each his
   place,
Strow'd through immensity and drown'd
   in space,
All yet unseen; till light at last begun,
And every system found a centred sun,
Call'd to his neighbor and exchanged
   from far
His infant gleams with every social star;
Rays thwarting rays and skies o'erarching
   skies
Robed their dim planets with commin-
   gling dies,
Hung o'er each heaven their living lamps
   serene
And tinged with blue the frore expanse
   between:
Then joyous Nature hail'd the golden
   morn,
Drank the young beam, beheld her em-
   pire born."   l. 47—72.

A paragraph on the immensity of Nature's creation which
displays an excursive fancy,
closes thus:

"Nor can a ray from her remotest sun,
Shot forth when first their splendid morn
   begun,
Borne straight, continuous through the
   void of space,
Doubling each thousand years its rapid
   pace
And hither posting, yet have reacht this
   earth,
To bring the tidings of its master's birth."
             l. 85—90.

We have not yet arrived to
the origin of the earth, which is
quite a young member of the
planetary family. Our readers
must feel a peculiar interest in
the history of this portion of the
universe, and in the production
of the first men. The following
passage will probably open their

ayes to quite a new exhibition of the subject.

"And mark thy native orb! though later
    born,
Though still unstored with light her silver
    horn,
As seen from sister planets, who repay
Far more than she their borrow'd streams
    of day,
Yet what an age her shell-rock ribs attest!
Her sparry spines, her coal-incumber'd
    breast!
Millions of generations toil'd and died
To crust with coral and to salt her tide,
And millions more, ere yet her soil began,
Ere yet she form'd or could have nurs'd
    her man.
    Then rose the proud phenomenon, the
        birth
Most richly wrought, the favorite child of
    earth;
But frail at first his frame, with nerves
    ill-strung,
Unform'd his footsteps, long untoned his
    tongue,
Unhappy, unassociate, unrefined,
Unfledged the pinions of his lofty mind,
He wander'd wild, to every beast a prey,
More prest with wants, and feebler far
    than they;
For countless ages forced from place to
    place;
Just reproduced but scarce preserved his
    race.
At last, a soil more fixt and streams more
    sweet
Inform the wretched migrant where to
    seat;
Euphrates' flowery banks begin to smile,
Fruits fringe the Ganges, gardens grace
    the Nile;
Nile, ribb'd with dikes, a length of coast
    creates,
And giant Thebes begins her hundred
    gates,
Mammoth of human works! her gran-
    deur known
These thousand lustres by its wrecks
    alone;" &c.   l. 91—118.

After adverting to Memphis, Mr. Barlow pays one of the handsomest compliments to Homer, which we remember to have seen:

"Belus and Brama tame their vagrant
    throngs,
And Homer, with his monumental songs,
Builds far more durable his splendid
    throne,
Than all the Pharaohs with their hills of
    stone."

The poet proceeds:

"High roll'd the round of years that hung
    sublime
These wondrous beacons in the night of
    time;
Studs of renown! that to thine eyes attest
The waste of ages that beyond them rest;
Ages how fill'd with toils! how gloom'd
    with woes!
Trod with all steps that man's long march
    compose,
Dim drear disastrous; ere his foot could
    gain
A height so brilliant o'er the bestial train.
    "In those blank periods, where no
        man can trace
The gleams of thought that first illumed
    his race,
His errors, twined with science, took
    their birth
And forged their fetters for this child of
    earth."   l. 125—140.

Mr. Barlow holds, that fear is the parent of all religion, in accordance with the old atheistical maxim, *Primus in orbe timor fecit Deos.* As man is exposed to the elements, which appear to be under some unknown influence, he endows them with intellect, and calls them Gods. So reasons the philosopher:

"Hence rose his gods, that mystic mon-
    strous lore
Of blood-stain'd altars and of priestly
    power,
Hence blind credulity on all dark things,
False morals hence and hence the yoke
    of kings."   l. 157—160.
"Accustom'd thus to bow the suppliant
    head
And reverence powers that shake his
    heart with dread,
His pliant faith extends with easy ken
From heavenly hosts to heaven-anointed
    men;
The sword, the tripod join their mutual
    aids
To film his eyes with more impervious
    shades."   l. 175—180.

"Two settled slaveries thus the race con-
    trol,
Engross their labors and debase their soul;
Till creeds and crimes and feuds and fears
    compose
The seeds of war and all its kindred
    woes ?   l. 185—188.

The conclusion of this whole description, supported by reference to many kinds of religion, is as follows:

"Man is an infant still; and slow and late
Must form and fix his adolescent state,
Mature his manhood and at last behold
His reason ripen and his force unfold.
From that bright eminence he then shall cast
A look of wonder on his wanderings past,
Congratulate himself, and o'er the earth
Firm the full reign of peace predestined
    at his birth."   l. 301—308.

It may be well to refer, in this place, to the second book for further illustration of the scheme, which has been developed in the preceding quotations. In the argument of that book, we are told, that

"Columbus demands the cause of the dissimilarity of men in different countries. Hesper replies, That the human body is composed of a due proportion of the elements suited to the place of its first formation; that these elements, differently proportioned, produce all the changes of health, sickness, growth and decay; and may likewise produce any other changes which occasion the diversity of men; that these elemental proportions are varied, not more by climate than temperature and other local circumstances; that the mind likewise is in a state of change, and will take its physical character from the body and from external objects."

These doctrines are discussed at large in the course of the book.

"From earth's own elements thy race
    at first
Rose into life, the children of the dust;
These kindred elements, by various use,
Nourish the growth and every change
    produce;
In each ascending stage the man sustain,
His breath, his food, his physic, and his
    bane.
In due proportions where these atoms lie,
A certain form their equal aids supply;
And while unchanged the efficient causes
    reign,
Age following age the certain form main-
    tain.

But where crude atoms disproportion'd
    rise,
And cast their sickening vapors round the
    skies,
Unlike that harmony of human frame,
That moulded first and reproduced the
    same,
The tribes ill formed, attempering to the
    clime,
Still vary downward with the years of
    time;
More perfect some, and some less perfect
    yield
Their reproductions in this wondrous
    field;
Till fixt at last their characters abide,
And local likeness feeds their local pride.
The soul too varying with the change of
    clime,
Feeble or fierce, or groveling or sublime,
Forms with the body to a kindred plan,
And lives the same, a nation or a man."
    B. ii. l. 71—94.

Columbus is thus admonished, in a subsequent passage:

"But think not thou, in all the range of
    man,
That different pairs *each* different cast
    began."   l. 135, 136.

From these passages compared together, it appears to have been the poet's opinion, that *every* variation in the human frame, and complexion, does not prove the existence of different pairs at first; but that the great diversities originated in the different proportions, in which the elements were moulded in different places. We suppose, that men crept out of the mud of the Nile, the Euphrates, the Ganges, the Niger, the Senegal; but not from the banks of every petty stream.

Our readers will observe a breach of grammar, in making *age* agree with *maintain*. Several similar instances occur in different parts of the poem; as *"league after league,"--"land after land,"* with plural verbs.

The metaphysical abstraction

discoverable in some passages exceeds any thing of the kind, which we have ever observed. In the last long quotation, a certain *harmony* of the human frame, is represented as having *first moulded* the very *frame*, of which it was the harmony; and then as having *reproduced the same.* A wonderful harmony, indeed, this must be, which formed a human frame antecedently to its own existence. But this harmony, wonderful as it is, sinks into nothing, when compared with certain abstract *generations*, millions of which *toiled and died* in the laborious operation of salting the ocean and forming its coral, long before any beings existed of which *generations* were predicable.

But let us return to a consideration of the progress of man, after he had learnt to speak and walk. In a note on l. 287 of the second book, we have the following disquisition:

"One consequence of the invention of alphabetical writing seems to have been to throw into oblivion all previous historical facts; and it has thus left an immense void, which the imagination knows not how to fill, in contemplating the progress of our race. How many important discoveries, which still remain to our use, must have taken their origin in that space of time which is thus left a void to us! A vast succession of ages, and ages of improvement, must have preceded (for example) the invention of the wheel. The wheel must have been in common use, we know not how long, before alphabetical writing; because we find its image employed in painting ideas, during the first stage of the graphic art above described. The wheel was likewise in use before the mysteries of Ceres or those of Isis were established, as is evident from its being imagined as an instrument of punishment in hell, in the case of Ixion, as represented in those mysteries. The taming of the ox and the horse, the use of the sickle and the bow and arrow, a considerable knowledge of astronomy, and its applica-

tion to the purposes of agriculture and navigation, with many other circumstances, which show a prodigious improvement, must evidently have preceded the date of the zodiac; a date fixed by *Dupuis*, with a great degree of probability, at about *seventeen thousand* years from our time. This epoch would doubtless carry us back many thousand years beyond that of the alphabet; the invention of which was sufficient of itself to obliterate the details of previous history, as the event has proved."

What do our readers suppose to have been the "source of that ancient, vast, and variegated system of false religion, with all its host of errors and miseries, which has so long and so grievously weighed upon the character of human nature?" It is no other, if the conjecture of Mr. Barlow is to be received, than the invention of the alphabet, which brought the hieroglyphic art into disuse. This era was seized, as a good opportunity for introducing priestcraft, by making the study of hieroglyphics a mysterious business. 'A profitable function or profession was, therefore, established, in the practice of which a certain portion of men of the brightest talents could make a reputable living; taking care not to initiate more than a limited number of professors; no more than the people could maintain as priests.'

Unfortunately for the schemes of Mr. Barlow, they are too numerous, and not a little contradictory. In more than one passage, he ascribes all religion to an ignorant and superstitious fear of the elements.

"On the supposition," says he, "that Greece and Western Asia, regions whose early traditions are best known to us, derived their first theological ideas from Egypt, it is curious to observe how the pure heliosebia of Egypt degenerated in those climates in proportion as other visible agents seemed to exert their influence in human affairs."

"The difference in the moral cast of religion in Peru and Mexico, as well as Egypt and Greece, must have been greatly owing to climate. Indeed in what else should it be found? Since the origin of religious ideas *must have been* in the energies of those visible agents which form the distinctive character of climates." Note. B. ii, l. 421.

The poet takes occasion, from the imagined antiquity of the Chinese, to teach us, that the inhabitants of Western Asia and Europe may be much more ancient, than they had supposed themselves to be. Take his own words:

"As the Chinese have not adopted an alphabet, but have adhered to an invariable state of the graphic art, which is probably more ancient by *several thousand years* than our present method, may we not venture to conjecture that the traces of their very ancient history have been, for that reason, better preserved? And that their pretensions to a very high antiquity, which we have been used to think extravagant and ridiculous, are really not without foundation? If so, we might then allow a little more latitude to ourselves, and conclude that we are in fact as old as they, and might have been as sensible of it, if we had adhered to our ancient method of writing; and not changed it for a new one which, while it has facilitated the progress of our science, has humbled our pride of antiquity, by obliterating the dates of those labors and improvements of our early progenitors, to which we are indebted for more of the rudiments of our sciences and our arts than we usually imagine." Note. B. ii, l. 287.

Now all which is said here, and throughout this long note, on the subject of the Chinese manner of writing, happens to be incorrect; as has been lately proved by Dr. Marshman, in his work on the Chinese language. As to the pretended antiquity of Chinese history, Mr. Morrison, who has had much intercourse with the Chinese, declares, that

the learned and intelligent a them have no confidence i of their histories, which back more than three thou years. Who ever imag that the inhabitants of E were *not* as old as the Chi Their ancestors and ours descendants of Noah; their children of Shem, and ou Japhet.

The poet institutes a pa lar comparison between the and political systems of M Lycurgus, Mahomet, Capad Peter the Great; the resu which is, that Moses is p quite in the back ground, th he has the whole credit of l the founder of the Jewish not the slightest hint being en, that he had any superna assistance, and many thing ing said which imply the trary. Moses and Lycurgu treated with equal respect; are considered as having r exclusively on their own po and with respect to their i it is at last said;

"These systems appear to have formed with an express design to p future improvement in knowledge largement of the human mind, and those nations in a state of ignoran barbarism. To vindicate their a from an imputation of weakness o tention in this particular, it may be that they were each of them surro by nations more powerful than thei it was therefore perhaps impossib them to commence an establishmen any other plan." Dissertation on F

Of Mahomet we are gr told, that "the first object of islation, [i. e. as had been viously stated, that the sy should be capable of redu the greatest number of mer der one jurisdiction,] appe have been better understood by him, than by either of the preceding sages." Again; "Like Moses, he convinced his people that he acted as the vicegerent of God; but with this advantage, adapting his religion to the natural feelings and propensities of mankind, he multiplied his followers by the allurements of pleasure and the promise of a sensual paradise."

Capac is quite a favorite of our poet. Of him it is said that, "by availing himself of this popular sentiment [the adoration of the sun] he appeared, like Moses and Mahomet, in the character of a divine legislator endowed with supernatural powers." After delineating the institutions of Capac, Mr. Barlow delivers the following judgment upon them:

"In the traits of character which distinguish this institution we may discern all the great principles of each of the legislators above mentioned. The pretensions of Capac to divine authority were as artfully contrived and as effectual in their consequences as those of Mahomet, his exploding the worship of evil beings and objects of terror, forbidding human sacrifices and accommodating the rites of worship to a god of justice and benevolence, produced a greater change in the national character of his people than the laws of Moses did in his; like Peter he provided for the future improvement of society, while his actions were never measured on the contracted scale which limited the genius of Lycurgus."

Mr. Barlow treats the Jews with the most undisguised contempt, in declaring, that "their national character was a compound of servility, ignorance, filthiness, and cruelty" And yet we are afterwards told, that

"Perhaps no single criterion can be given which will determine more accu-

rately the state of society in any age or nation than their general ideas concerning the nature and attributes of deity In the most enlightened periods of antiquity, only a few of their philosophers, a Socrates, Tully or Confucius, ever formed a rational idea on the subject, or described a god of purity, justice, or benevolence."

From these passages and many others, it is perfectly evident to our minds, that Mr. Barlow felt the most inveterate hostility to the Bible; and especially to the character of Jehovah as there revealed. This enmity is not the less manifest, from the care with which every direct expression of it is smothered

The *solar* religion is repeatedly brought forward as worthy of the admiration of the reader, and as the purest and most beneficent system, which the world has yet seen. Mr Barlow laments over its corruptions with heart-felt anguish, and at considerable length He says of Capac and his subjects,

"With cheerful rites their *pure devotions* pay
To the bright orb that gives the changing day." B. ii, l. 421, 422.

After representing Capac as having feigned a descent from the sun, and instituted a system of worship to be offered to that luminary, Mr. Barlow says; "A system so just and benevolent, as might be expected, was attended with success." It is true, that this *solar religion* was not very highly esteemed by Moses, who thus charged the Israelites: *Take ye therefore good heed unto yourselves.—lest ye corrupt yourselves—and lest thou lift up thine eyes unto heaven, and when thou seest the sun, and the moon, and the stars, even all the host of heaven, shouldest be driven to worship them, and serve them*—Deut. iv, 15—19. But it cannot be expected, that the decision of Moses should have much weight with the enlightened men among whom the poet doubtless wished to be ranked. We have always been of opinion, that latitudinarianism in religion leads to infidelity; infidelity to atheism; atheism to idolatry; idolatry to the most debasing superstitions and to universal profligacy of manners. We have a full belief, that, if God should withhold from men the renewing and sanctifying influence of the Holy Spirit, the progress to idolatry in religion, and despotism in government, would be rapid and irresistible, notwithstanding all the boasted improvements of the present times. We did not expect, however, to see so complete a developement of a part of this progress, as we find in the work before us.

As if to disparage the very idea of a divine revelation, Mr. Barlow gives a particular account of the introduction of a new religion among the Peruvians, by means of pretended miracles; and though this achievement was accomplished by a series of the grossest falsehoods, yet the design and the result receive the unqualified eulogium of the poet. To crown the whole, he informs us, in sober prose, that, in the story of Capac and Oella, he 'has given what may be supposed a *probable* narrative of their *real origin and actions.*' The story was briefly stated in a preceding part of this review; and is more at large, as follows:

Capac, a young warrio those regions of South Am which lie to the north of formed the design of beco a great benefactor of man He was then a savage, clothed with the skins of beasts, or not clothed at all. project was, to migrate t milder climate of Peru, an himself up for a civilizer o natives; but he knew not h leave his beloved Oella. I pened, just at this time, tha had invented the spinning weaving of cotton, and had ried these arts to such pe tion, that she easily form splendid white robe for he er and another for herself. made her wheel, her cards distaff, her loom, her shuttl &c. the poet does not say; it material. Furnished these white robes, they el from their parents, trav ten days to the south, exhi themselves to the natives, declared themselves to be children of the sun, and they were commissioned b god, as instructors in the religion.

"The work begins; they preach to band
The well form'd fiction, and their demand,
With various miracles their powe play,
To prove their lineage and confirm sway." B. ii, l. 627—
"The astonisht tribes believe, witl surprise,
The gods descended from the fa skies,
Adore their persons robed in white,
Receive their laws and leave each rite,
Build with assisting hands the throne
And hail and bless the sceptre o Sun." l. 641—

The plan so auspiciously begun continued to succeed, and civilization was rapidly introduced. For twenty years the progress was uninterrupted, till the government of Capac was assailed by the eastern savages. He sends his oldest son, Rocha, as an embassador to them, and he performs a miracle, as has been before stated, by setting dried leaves on fire with the aid of a concave mirror.

"This method of procuring fire," says Mr. Barlow, "directly from the sun, to burn a sacrifice, must have appeared so miraculous to the savages who could not understand it, that it doubtless had a powerful effect in converting them to the solar religion and to the Incan government." Note. B. iii, l. 273.

The thirteenth descendant of Capac, to Mr. Barlow's great grief, broke over one of the fundamental laws of the empire of Peru, and destroyed the mighty fabric of four centuries. This disregard of institutions held sacred is pointedly condemned in the following remark, which our readers are requested to bear in mind for the purpose of applying it to Mr. Barlow himself: "For he who disregards *any part* of institutions deemed sacred, teaches his people to consider *the whole as an imposture.*" This sentence contains an important truth, and proves, that the writer's attempts to undermine many *parts* of Divine Revelation, were calculated, in his opinion, to subvert the whole.

The story of Capac, which was intended to convince the reader that it is very easy to introduce a new religion among savages, is so monstrously incredible that it must utterly fail to produce that effect. Let some of our modern infidels, who are for ever prating about their benevolence, undertake a mission to the tenants of our western wilderness; let them preach the *solar religion,* if they see fit, and support their preaching by all the false miracles which they can invent; let them take with them an abundant supply of white robes, and allege that they descended from the sun; let them talk largely of the beauty of virtue, of industry, humanity, civilization and peace, not forgetting to inveigh bitterly against *creeds,* in order to prove their own consistency: and we shall then see, peradventure, a great, civilized, opulent, happy empire rise up under their hands. If the solar religion, as preached and practised by an Atheist, is sufficient to convert the savage into a wise, intelligent, peaceful, enlightened philosopher, and to transform a desert into a cultivated and populous country, we shall then know it. But till the experiment is made, and the result well authenticated, we must continue incredulous.

The notion that savages are easily led to embrace any new and wonderful system of religion, is wholly unsupported by fact. It was justly observed by a very able writer in our pages, that "not credulity, but incredulity, is the predominant characteristic of uncivilized man, with regard to every thing of a religious nature."[*] Of the justness of this opinion we have long been convinced, and we chal-

[*] See Lecture XV, on the Evidences o. Divine Revelation. Pan. for June 1813, p. 10.

lenge a refutation of it, should it be thought capable of being refuted.

Among many passages which clash with the Bible, the following is not the least remarkable. After alluding to the scriptural history of the dispersion at Babel, which the poet calls "the tale of Babel," he proceeds thus:

"For that fine apologue, with mystic
    strain,
Gave like the rest a golden age to man,
Ascribed perfection to his infant state,
Science unsought and all his arts innate;
Supposed the experience of the growing
    race
Must lead him retrograde and cramp his
    pace,
Obscure his vision as his lights increased,
And sink him from an angel to a beast.
"'Tis thus the teachers of despotic sway
Strive in all times to blot the beams of
    day
To keep him curb'd nor let him lift his
    eyes
To see where happiness, where misery
    lies.
They lead him blind," &c. &c.

"Long have they reign'd; till now the
    race at last
Shake off their manacles, their blinders
    cast," &c.   B. x. l. 393—414.

Lest this passage should not be sufficiently clear, Mr. Barlow pursues the same train of thought in a long note, very artfully directing all his shafts against the idea of a *golden age;* but evidently discrediting the fact, that man was originally perfect and happy.

We are informed, in a note on B. iii, l. 135, that 'from the religion of the Egyptians *all* the early theological systems of Asia and Europe, as far as they have come to our knowledge, were evidently derived.'

In the fourth book we have some glimmerings of the light which was to burst out toward the close of the poem:

"When first the staggering globe its
    breach repair'd
And this bold hemisphere its shoulders
    rear'd,
Back to those heights, &c." B. iv, l. 359.
"When first his form arose erect on
    earth,
Parturient nature hail'd the wondrous
    birth,
With fairest limbs, and finest fibres
    wrought,
And fram'd for vast and various toils of
    thought.
To aid his promised powers with loftier
    flight,
And stretch his views beyond corporeal
    sight,
Prometheus came, and from the floods of
    day
Sunn'd his clear soul with heaven's inter-
    nal ray;"   l. 443—450.

Having detailed a particular account of the labors of the human race hitherto, Hesper arrives at the following conclusion:

        "The proud Titanian ray
O'er *physic nature* sheds indeed its day;
Yet leaves the *moral* in chaotic jars,
The spoil of violence, the sport of wars,
Presents contrasted parts of one great
    plan,
Earth, heaven subdued, but man at swords
    with man;
His wars, his errors into science grown
And the great *cause of all his ills* un-
    known."   l. 463—470.

From these ills, whatever they may be, Freedom, the *Sun of the moral world,* is to deliver him.

Mr. Barlow has deliberately and solemnly declared his poem to be "more favorable to sound and rigid morals, more friendly to virtue, &c. &c. than all the writings of all that list of Christian authors &c. &c. whom you [Bishop Gregoire] have cited as the glory of Christendom, &c." Now we have been very anxious to understand, and become fully acquainted with this excellent code of morals. What must be our surprise to find, that this illustrious poem con-

of morals at all.
en here collected,
of morals, is alto-
gative kind; and
rised under the
us.

of accountability
Being is to be ex-
cluded.

ence to a future
hee is to be ex-
men shall have ar-
te of perfection.
s to that state, it
mplied, in several
n accommodating
are to be tolerated.
ets must take spe-
gard all sorts of
ually good; and,
may have different
one must regard
creed with as
picy as his own.
any thing which
positive morality,
fore us, the sub-
sists in hatred to
ests, and love of
a system. Even
e of all adequate
We have looked
great motives to
d the whole sys-
y destitute of ev-
ch can interest the
or any length of
easant song of lib-
ity may amuse for
ut to rely upon
instrument of rew-
rld is childish in

In addition to
already quoted,
are the chief
ch we have been
respecting moral-
. Atlas threaten-
with a convulsion,
ready stood, en-

less the grievances of the people
of Africa were speedily redress-
ed. His speech is followed by
a speech of the poet, who, in
his proper person, as the argument teaches us, addresses the
American Congress on the same
subject. Lest his distinguished
countrymen should take Atlas
to be in earnest; in other words,
lest they should suppose the poet to be so superstitious as to
urge the possibility of a divine
judgment, he takes care to guard
against any conclusion of that
sort.

"Fathers and friends, I know the bold
her fears,
Of many hundred of vanished years,
And act only the years whose change
through shadowy nature looks with an-
For whom she wrote the homage of her
and hate
Strikes from Jove's hand the branded
bolt of fate
Gives each chief his own indubious merit,
Divides her moral from her physic heir,
Shows where the virtues find their la-
turing food,
And men their motives to be just and
good." B. vii. l. 500—512.

In like manner, when Columbus supposes the glorious reign
of Christ, as he had read of it in
the Apocalypse, to be approaching, Hesper repels such an
opinion.

"Such views, the Saint expluse, too
sense too bright;
Would god thy vision's steemd aight,
Men cannot see no myriad years firmy
The mystic house of truth to curled day,
Enough for them, that thy deliphued mind
Should trace the sovereign prince of thy
kind, &c. B. i. l. 515—526.

In those happy times, when
universal peace and philosoph-
phy shall have assumed the
nation of the World, Columbidw
will be a Pantheon

of those days is represented as of that description:

"Soaring with science then he learns to string
Her highest harp and brace her broadest wing,
With her own force to fray the paths untrod,
With her own glance to ken *the total God*," &c.   l. 269—272.

But

"The *Sage* with *steadier lights* directs his ken,
Through twofold nature leads the walks of men,
Remoulds her *moral* and *material* frames,
Their mutual aids, their sister laws proclaims.
Disease before him with its causes flies
And boasts no more of sickly soils and skies;
His well proved codes the healing science aid,
Its base establish and its blessing spread,
With long wrought life to teach the race to glow,
And vigorous nerves to grace the looks of snow.
    "From every shape that varying matter gives,
That rests or ripens, vegetates or lives,
His chymic powers new combinations plan,
Yield new creations, finer forms to man,
High springs of health for mind and body trace,
Add force and beauty to the joyous race,
Arm with new engines his adventurous hand,
Stretch o'er these elements his wide command,
Lay the proud storm submissive at his feet,
Change, temper, tame, all subterranean heat,
Probe laboring earth and drag from her dark side
The mute volcano, ere its force be tried;
Walk under ocean, ride the buoyant air,
Brew the soft shower, the labor'd land repair,
A fruitful soil o'er sandy deserts spread,
And clothe with culture every mountain's head."   l. 277—302.

These are some of the principal traits in the character of the political millennium. There remains a passage in the poet's

address   to   his   cou
which, in our opinion,
a direct insult to the
religion.   Whether it
signed, or not, to be
the reader will judge.

"EQUALITY, your first fir
    stand;
Then FREE ELECTION; then
    ERAL BAND;
This *holy Triad* should forev
The great compendium of a
    vine,
Creed of all schools, whence
    millions draw
Their themes of right, *their a
    law;*
Till men shall wonder (in
    inured)
How wars were made, how t
    endured."   B. viii. L

The office of a religi
er, who will be suite
progressive state of m
the days of perfectibi
have arrived, is thus d

"Here fired by virtue's anim
The   preacher's task pers
    claim,
To mould religion to the mor
In bonds of peace to harmoni
To life, to light, to promised j
The soften'd soul with arde
    move."   B. viii. L

It is afterwards said
preachers.

"Though different creeds th
    robes denote,
Their orders various and the
    mote,
Yet one their voice, their lal
    bined,
Lights of the world and frien
    kind."   l.

But after the general
shall have met in Egyp
delegates shall have
one heap all the symb
ligion, there is no m
preaching.   Mankind
have become too wise

instruction in any thing but politics. The *republican principle* will have been discovered to be the foundation of all morality, and will supersede all religion. As a preparation for that event the author seems peculiarly fond of the project of an universal empire; and even holds, that modern wars will help forward the work of civilization till, in the French phraseology, a general peace shall be conquered.

It is curious to observe on what slender foundations philosophers are compelled to erect the vast superstructure of human happiness. We have seen, that political liberty is to supply a foundation for this superstructure; but, in some places, the poet seems to build on other foundations. At one time, *the spirit of commerce* is to answer the mighty purpose of civilizing the world; at another, a pacific Iliad is to produce a pacific disposition in all readers. As to the spirit of commerce, we are told, that

"This leading principle, in its remoter consequences, will produce advantages in favor of free government, give patriotism the character of philanthrophy, induce all men to regard each other as brethren and friends, and teach them the benefits of peace and harmony among the nations.

"I conceive it no objection to this theory that the progress has hitherto been slow; when we consider the magnitude of the object, the obstructions that were to be removed, and the length of time taken to accomplish it. The future progress will probably be more rapid than the past. Since the invention of printing, the application of the properties of the magnet, and the knowledge of the structure of the solar system, it is difficult to conceive of a cause that can produce a new state of barbarism; unless it be some great convulsion in the physical world, so extensive as to change the face of the earth or a considerable part of it. This indeed may have been the case already more than once, since the earth was first peopled with men, and antecedent to our histories. But such events have nothing to do with the present argument." Note. B. ix. l. 499.

On this passage we may perhaps remark hereafter.

Mr. Barlow laments greatly, that 'Homer, instead of the Iliad, had not given us a work of equal splendor founded on an opposite principle;' and thinks, that 'mankind, enriched with such a work at that early period, would have given a useful turn to their ambition through all succeeding ages.' Note. B. x. l. 261.

He must be a novice in morals, who does not know, that the influence, which the Iliad has exerted in favor of war, has been solely in consequence of the adaptation of that poem to the natural state of the human heart. To argue that a poem of an opposite character would produce correspondent opposite effects, or even immensely greater effects, is not less absurd than to say, that because fire thrown upon gunpowder produces a tremendous explosion, *therefore* water, at the temperature of the human body, if thrown upon the same combustible, will produce a mild and genial heat.

But let us examine this supposed transforming energy of a pacific Iliad. Can a single fact be selected from the whole history of our race, which warrants the expectation, that mankind will become peaceful, virtuous, and happy, merely by contemplating the excellence of peace, virtue, and happiness? Is it not high time, that such a fact should have existed, if it can ever be expected to exist? The worst that Mr. Barlow and his brethren would probably say of the New Testament, in their sober moments, would be, that it is a *fiction.*[*] It stands on as high ground, therefore, in their own estimation, as any pacific Iliad could do, so far as its authority is concerned. Why does not the New Testament produce, in the hearts of those who believe it to be a fiction, all those pacific dispositions, and in their lives all that pacific conduct, of which the world certainly stands in need? If we are compelled, for the sake of argument, to regard this book as a fiction, we have a right to say, that no man, who has a particle of taste or sense remaining, can deny, that it is the most interesting and the most sublime book in the world; that it is uniformly, and in the highest degree, favorable to peace, justice, temperance, kindness, charity, benevolence, and the happiness of mankind; and that it condemns all those ambitious, revengeful, and implacable dispositions whence wars proceed.

But we will not, for any length of time, consider this holy book as a fiction. It has God for its Author, a God of holiness and purity, who will not regard it as a light offence to exalt the beneficial tendency of a mere effort of human genius above the benign influence of the Gospel which He has given to perishing man.

The contemptuous manner, in which Mr. Barlow is accustomed to speak of the scriptural

history of the Old T(
is observable in the (
sentence:

"The manner in which the
set at work to constitute their
proves that they were convin
they must have a king, he mu
them from God, and receive (
consecration which should e
authority on the same divine (
was common to other nations (
they borrowed the principle."
vii. l. 39.

We have said that k
priests were exhibited,
poem, as the great au(
human misery. After a
tion of anarchy or chao(
natural world, and of sub
order, we read;

"So *kings* convulse the m(
the base
Of all the codes that can accord
And so from their broad grasp, (
ly ban,
'Tis yours to snatch this earth
regenerate man."

"These were the arts that nu
qual sway,
That *priests* would pamper and
would pay," &c. B. ix. l.

Creeds are not less o(
Mr. Barlow's view, th(
are in the view of latitud
in religion:

"The cares that agitate, the c(
blind."   B. (

But we learn, after a
his objections, like theirs
so much against creeds
selves, as against a *fra
kind* of creeds. Both
they are willing enough (
creeds of their own fo
His creed, if drawn out
length, would be much
mysterious and much
than any which has been

---

[*] Mr. B. did say, on a certain occasion, that the Christian religion was a "*damnable mummery;*" but he was probably writing under the influence of violent malice, which took away all appearance of sobriety.

from the Bible, and would require a most marvellous stretch of credulity. Let us illustrate this subject by adverting to the account of the formation of the universe, which has been already given in the words of the poet, and we shall see that there must be in his scheme the materials of a voluminous creed. For the sake of perspicuity we will divide this account into distinct periods.

1. In the beginning of the poet's creation, so far as he thought proper to reveal it, Nature and Chaos existed together. Which was the oldest we are not told; and it would probably take many a learned disquisition to settle the point.

2. Nature broke the crust of Chaos, and *"thirled"* forth the materials of the universe. These materials were then in the most singular state imaginable. There was

"No light nor heat nor cold nor moist
  nor dry,
But all concocting in their causes lie."

3. These materials lay in that state for millions of years. Nature, in the mean time, had the hard task of *brooding the mass* during all that vast period. It is a great wonder that she had not given up the experiment in despair.

4. Nature then *seeks and sorts the principles of things*, puts the whole mass in motion, and *whirls forth her globes by myriads and by millions.*

5. After these globes had been well sorted and placed by Nature, and had proceeded in their *cosmogyral courses*, light begun to appear. At this she

seems to have been surprised; but she hailed the light with joy.

6. At some later period, which appears to have been a very remote one, the earth was born. It seems to be implied, that the sun is the father of our earth, and that the earth is the mother of the moon; which seems to have been extracted by the Cæsarian operation; for Hesper

——"healed the *wounded* earth *when
    from her side*
The moon burst forth and left the South
    Sea tide."

7. Millions of generations *toiled and died*, while coral was forming in the ocean, and its waters were becoming salt: i. e. as we suppose, as much time elapsed as would be occupied by millions of successive generations of men. A generation is never reckoned to be less than thirty years; sixty millions of years at least must have elapsed, therefore, while the earth was undergoing this process.

8. At least sixty millions of years more elapsed while a soil was forming on the earth, before the said earth could form or nurse her *man*. Nature appears to have retired before this time, and left the earth to produce such beings as she could sustain.

9. At some unknown period after the soil was formed, man *rose from the earth*. We are not to understand, however, that man was at first erect; for we read that his *footsteps* were *unformed*, and his *tongue untoned*, and that he continued in that pitiable state for *countless ages.*

These were the times, beyond controversy, of which Lord Monboddo spake; when man was a quadruped, and was furnished with an appendage very necessary to brush away the flies withal. Our miserable race were then exposed to wild beasts, and, considering the extreme weakness of our ancestors, it cannot be sufficiently admired, that any of them should have survived all their enemies. Yet so it was; and for countless ages, which can hardly be less than millions of generations, or sixty millions of years, they continued in this wretched and disconsolate state.

10. After man had learnt to speak and walk, he wandered for a while, and then begun to make regular settlements. A *vast succession of ages of improvement* then came on, and, at the end of these, man invented the *wheel.* The exact time allotted to this progress, is not stated. Perhaps when we become acquainted with Chinese history, for which Mr. Barlow has a profound respect, and which reaches back, we believe, some millions of years, we shall be better able to fix these dates. Some other inventions which were quite as late as the wheel, preceded the invention of the zodiac.

11. The date of the zodiac is fixed by *Dupuis,* at seventeen thousand years from our time. Though considerable progress has been made in science, yet *"man is an infant still."* His future progress is not marked out with precision; but, if we regard the immense changes which are to take place, and *the means with which they are to be brought about,* we should have

reason to think our post well off, could it be foreseen the grand congress will in Egypt, and establish an i lable peace, within a hur millions of years from the ent day. It is questionable, whether even the Colun will reach that period. If progress of philosophy, fo last fifty years is to be take a part of the converging towards perfectibility, we confident that the above p is by far too short. And an unlucky thing it will just as the political millen has arrived, and the world become peaceful, populous, happy—just as the men of days have delivered thems from all superstitious fears, mastered earth, air, and sea have, by the aid of medi learned to become immortal below;—what a cruel disapp ment it will be, if another should burst from the *A Sea tide,* and should take all the northern parts of Eu Asia, and America. Such avulsion must destroy ever man being, as the ocean w rise with a tremendous s and sweep the tops of the est mountains. Who ca certain, that this is not a p Nature's plan? Even the does not venture to insure world against such a cala He shrewdly hints, that event of a similar character have taken place more once already. In that case, will be the issue we are not enough to tell. Perhaps race will creep out of the under better auspices, and learn to speak and stand to build and plant, to write philosophize, in a less time than our wretched progenitors spent in making these acquirements.

But the scheme, which we have been detailing, should receive more serious treatment. Mr. Barlow, in his letter to Gregoire, offered a challenge which is thus expressed:

"I defy you, and all the critics of the English language, to point out a passage, if taken in its natural unavoidable meaning, which militates against the genuine principles, practice, faith, and hope of the Christian system, as inculcated in the Gospels, and explained by the Apostles, whose writings accompany the Gospels in the volume of the New Testament."

This passage relates to the very poem from the text and notes of which we have selected passages, by which we can substantiate the following charges: That the author explodes the idea of a superintending Providence; that he ridicules and speaks in opprobrious terms of the Jewish theocracy; that he utterly rejects the idea of a Divine Revelation; that his scheme contradicts, in the most palpable manner, the whole Mosaic history; that he casts contempt on the Gospel, by relying on his own miserable inventions for the production of human happiness; that he never implies, for a moment, the truth of the Gospel; that all the morality of his system, if it can be said to have any morality about it, is entirely adverse to the morality of the Gospel in its character, its end, and its sanctions; that he systematically excludes religion from having any influence in human affairs, so far as his instructions shall be regarded; and that he never implies the existence of a God with moral attributes,

but would make his pupils at one time Atheists, at another Pantheists, at another worshippers of the Sun, and at another worshippers of Nature. We refer to the preceding parts of this review, and to the poem itself, for the support of these charges; and we will not insult our readers by undertaking to *prove*, after having made such ample quotations, that the poem 'militates against the principles, practice, faith, and hope of the Christian system.'

It is proper to observe here, that the pretence of *Dupuis*, that the zodiac was invented 17,000 years ago, has been refuted and ridiculed, even at Paris. If a writer in the Christian Instructor, a respectable magazine printed at Edinburgh, is to be credited, La Place has lately undertaken to prove, that this earth cannot be more than *three thousand* years old! La Place is one of the greatest astronomers living, a much greater man than Mr. Barlow ever was, and quite as much of an infidel. What would the poet say, to have his countless ages, his millions of generations, his illustrious Chinese histories, all cut down by a brother philosopher to three thousand years!

In regard to the contempt which Mr. Barlow evidently felt for the Jewish nation and for the Mosaic history, we should take no further notice of it, but for the sake of introducing the testimony of Mr. Ames to the sublimity and divine original of the Jewish Scriptures. A friend and intimate acquaintance of that distinguished man gives the following account of his opinions on this subject.

"He has been heard to say, that it appeared to him impossible for any man of a fair mind, to read the Old Testament, and meditate on its contents, without a conviction of its truth and inspiration. The sublime and correct ideas, which the Jewish Scriptures convey of God, connected with the fact that all other nations, many of them superior to the Jews in civilization and general improvement, remained in darkness and error on this fundamental subject, was in his view a conclusive argument. After reading, on a particular occasion, the book of Deuteronomy, he expressed his astonishment, that any man versed in antiquities could have the hardihood to say, that that book was the production of human ingenuity. Marks of divinity, he said, were instamped upon it." See Pan. for July 1808, p. 93.

It is surprising to us, that infidels and Atheists are not overwhelmed with melancholy, when they contemplate their own schemes for the melioration of the human race. They confine all their labors, their motives, their hopes and expectations to this life. Seeing the world full of injustice, oppression, violence and war, they predict a future more auspicious period, when reason and philosophy shall subdue all these evils, and men shall live in peace and make great improvements in science and in social order. But what have they to offer adequate to the desires of the human soul? Literally nothing. Man is nothing, according to them, but a reasoning animal, a moving vegetable. He appears for a short time, *reproduces his kind*, falls into the earth, rots like the most noxious weed, and is no more for ever! He may derive consolation, as modern philosophers have taught him to do, in reflecting, that his body may hereafter make excellent manure; that he may blossom in the rose, ripen in corn, sprout in grass, be eaten

by oxen, and perhaps be food for his descendants. thought of such distingu usefulness must abound in fort, to be sure! Accordin philosopher was greatly pl with the consideration, tha lions of mosquetoes originate from the bodi French and Austrian sol scattered over the plains of many, in the course of the consequent upon the F revolution; and who coul but these mosquetoes have as much happiness tributed among them, a soldiers had, from whose b they derived nourishment! would take the liberty of gesting to infidels of this whether they ought not rect, in their last wills and taments, that their bodies be deposited forthwith in a of compost, so that their v may immediately conduce good of the public, and n suffered to lie useless, for lions of generations perhap feet beneath the surface o globe. Without stopping patiate on the horrible glo Atheism, it is sufficient t claim, in the forcible word late writer, 'If the Eye o universe be extinguished, *great is the darkness!'*

The miserable success fidels in their latest and extended efforts to pro their favorite reign of pe liberty and peace, accomp by the emancipation of the man race from all error, an ligion, may well cover with confusion and sh Most of them have been co ced already, that their sch are impracticable, and fror preachers of lawless freedom have become patrons and promoters of unlimited despotism. Some continue to promulgate the doctrine of philosophical perfectibility, as we must call it, for want of a better name. Their confidence, however, seems abated; and their proselytes are too few to encourage their exertions. We may venture to predict, that the poem, which we are reviewing, is one of the last elaborate works of this class.

The following anecdotes will show, that leading infidels soon begun to suspect the issue of their attempts.

When the late chief justice Ellsworth was in France, in 1800, he happened one morning to meet with Volney, who had been taking an airing on horseback for his health, and who therefore took occasion to observe that *his horse* was *his Providence*. They fell into conversation on political subjects, and, among other things, upon the infidel scheme of perfectibility, in which Volney, who was as thorough a philosopher as our poet, appeared to confide. At last Mr. Ellsworth proposed this question: How will you subdue or restrain the gigantic passions of avarice and ambition? "*There's the devil of it,*" said the philosopher, and instantly put spurs to his horse, and bade the chief justice good morning.

The great revolutionist Danton made some confessions, just before his execution, which are worthy to be considered by our readers. He was the author of the revolutionary tribunal, and was himself brought to the scaffold by its decision, at 'what the Robespierrians called the second weeding of the republican garden.' He professed to be a *Theist.*

"When he was asked his name at the bar, he replied, 'I am Danton, well known in the revolution; my home will shortly be annihilation, but my name will · live in the pantheon of history.' Like every other victim of that accursed tribunal, which he had instituted, he was treated with equal insolence and injustice; but his trial was shortened by a manoeuvre, and he was executed the same day before measures could be taken by his friends for raising an insurrection in his behalf. Legendre was at that time wholly employed by fear for himself; otherwise, had he exerted the same spirit as on the day of Robespierre's overthrow, the tyrant might then have perished instead of Danton. When he was taken back to the Conciergerie, he exclaimed, 'It is the anniversary of the day on which I caused the institution of the revolutionary tribunal, for which I implore pardon of God and man! I leave every thing in dreadful confusion;—*there is not one among them who understands any thing of government.* After all, *they are such brethren as Cain:* Brissot would have had me guillotined, even as Robespierre has me guillotined.' It was true that Brissot would have condemned him,—not as Robespierre did; he would have condemned him not as an Orleanist,—not as a royalist,—not for a mock conspiracy,—but for his share in those massacres, of which it appears almost certain that he was the prime mover." See Quarterly Review for June 1812. pp. 424, 425.

Danton certainly declared two solemn truths;—that his brethren knew nothing of government, and that they were such brethren as Cain; from which we infer, that his confidence in his theoretical schemes had begun to shake. Our readers will not infer, however, that Danton was an Abel; for, as there were no Abels in the family, the Cains were under the sad necessity of cutting the throats of each other.

In the course of our remarks on the Columbiad, we have been often struck with several points of resemblance between the methed of reasoning adopted by Mr. Barlow, and that into which latitudinarians in religion are prone to fall. In no particular is this resemblance more striking, than in the use of the little word *must;* a word which proves to be not only an auxiliary verb as heretofore, but to be capable of containing the seeds of a thousand auxiliary arguments. Thus, if an assertion is apparently hard to be proved, Mr. Barlow declares very gravely it *must* be so; and this puts an end to the controversy at once. "The origin of religious ideas," says he, "*must have been* in the energies of those visible agents which form the distinctive character of climates." In like manner, the editors of the Improved Version say, concerning the narrative of the miraculous conception, "If the genealogy be genuine," as they admit it to be, "this narrative *must be spurious.*" If a thing *must* be so, of what avail is it to oppose either testimony or argument? Mr. Barlow somewhere speaks of the great improvements which are hereafter to be made, when the contents of a whole volume are to be expressed by a *single word.* Probably he had his eye on this same word *must;* and we are free to confess, that by its aid he has settled points, which it would take more than one volume to prove.

Mr. Barlow was once a professed Christian, a candidate for the ministry, a chaplain in the army, and a versifier of the psalms which Dr. Watts had omitted. In versifying these psalms he expressed many solemn religious truths, which he afterwards abjured and vilified. His edition of the psalms was at one time quite popular, and contains some happy efforts of poetry. His 137th, which it is strange that Dr. Watts should have omitted, as it is justly pronounced by Chateaubriand to be the "finest of all canticles on the love of country," begins as follows:

"Along the banks where Babel's current
    flows
  Our captive bands in deep despondence
    stray'd,
While Zion's fall in sad remembrance
    rose,
  Her friends, her children mingled with
    the dead.

"The tuneless harp, that once with joy we
    strung,
  When praise employ'd and mirth inspir'd the lay,
In mournful silence on the willows hung
  And growing grief prolong'd the tedious day."

These stanzas are worthy of particular praise. It is a sorrowful reflection, that talents which might have been a credit to any good cause, and any country, should have been utterly perverted and abused; and that a man, born and educated under favorable circumstances, where the true God is known, the Bible is understood, and pure worship offered, should have apostatized from the religion which he once preached, and plunged into the gulf of Atheism.

The Edinburgh Review is very tender of Mr. Barlow's religious reputation. On the word *cross,* in the passage which has been the subject of our animadversion, the Reviewers have the following singular note.

"We have put this word in Italics, not to insinuate any charge of impiety against Mr. Barlow, but to guard him against that imputation. From the whole strain of his poem, in which he speaks with

bation of reformed Christian-
ies the purity an ' evan.gelical
the priesthood as one of the
ings of his millennium,—and
into a holy rapture on the
the coming of the Redeem-
r satisfied that he here speaks
a merely as the emblem of the
rsecuting superstition of the
papists, and other sectaries,
the crucifix an object of idola-
ation." Ed. Rev. No. XXIX.

pity that these Review-
iot referred to the pas-
which they venture to
: above assertions. Had
ie so, we should have
assages before our read-
each one might judge
elf. As they have not,
inly give a general de-
heir general assertions.
efore say, that from the
train of his poem we
judge the writer to be
iat; that he no where
with approbation of
iity in any form; (we
:member that he speaks
tianity, or the Gospel,
that he speaks of no
od in his millennium;
ie the slightest hint of
ion existing at that time;
he does not admit the
that Christ is to come.
ia, indeed, when the
the millennium is rising
breaks out into rapture
ospect of the coming of
but Hesper, who always
he opinions of the poet,
checks this rapture,
a Columbus to confine
ghts to the *temporal* af-
iis race.
Eclectic Reviewers are
raid, that the Columbiad
the standard of imitation
ountry, and a stumbling
o genius for ages to

come.' And "this," as the Reviewers inform us very kindly,
"is not *a random speculation.*"[*]
We thank these gentlemen for
their concern on account of the
perverse taste of our countrymen; and, in our turn, condole
with them, on the prospect that
Blackmore's Eliza will become
a standard of imitation in Great
Britain, and a stumbling-block
to genius. This is not a random
speculation of ours; for the two
poems certainly resemble each
other in the important article of
falling *dead born from the press.*
The Columbiad, to be sure, has
been re printed in a smaller
form; not because the first edition was sold, but because it
would not sell. We have never
heard that the poem has had a
single admirer in this country;
and it is not sufficiently known
to have any considerable number
of enemies.

Lest the Reviewers should
suppose, that the people of this
country have no taste for poetry,
as they seem to consider Americans as a stupid, ignorant, mercenary set of creatures, we very
respectfully inform them, that
Milton, Dryden, Pope, Young,
Watts, Cowper, Campbell. Montgomery, Scott, have their many
thousands of readers and admir-
ers; and that we should think it
very proper for candid and liberal Reviewers not to undertake
to give a national character,
when they know nothing about it.

To conclude: It may be objected, perhaps, that there is no
occasion for taking notice of a
work, which is so little likely
to be read as the Columbiad.
Our object has not been to coun-

* Ec. Rev. for May 1810. p. 403, 404.

teract the influence of this poem; for it is not likely to have any influence. But we have wished to expose the wretched, odious system, on which it is built, and which it was intended to promote. To the defence and propagation of this system the author sacrificed the years, during which he moulded and fashioned, pared, and patched, and chisseled, this very elaborate work;—a work by which he plainly expected to lead his countrymen in the path of infidelity, and to be known to all future times, as a great instructor of mankind in their true interests. While we can easily pardon the self-complacency with which authors sometimes regard their own works, we hold that no peculiar tenderness is due to any person, who sets himself up as an opposer of all religion, and attempts to undermine and subvert the blessed Gospel. Such a person declares an impious war against his Maker, and his fellow men; becomes an enemy of all that is good and desirable; and should be held forth to public condemnation, as an example to be shunned. The baseless schemes of infidelity need only to be stated, that their absurdity and folly may be manifest.

The volume before us is allowed to be as splendid a specimen of printing, as any country can produce. We have discovered but four typographical errors, which, considering the size of the work, is an extremely small number.

LVIII. *Fragments, being illustrations of the manners, incidents, and phraseology, of*
Holy Scripture; principally selected from the most esteemed and authentic voyages and travels into the East; with additional remarks, observations, and plates, intended as a continued appendix to Calmet's Great Dictionary of the Holy Bible. In four volumes. Charlestown; Samuel Etheridge, jun. 1813. 4to.

It has afforded us much satisfaction to see this very valuable book republished in our country, and in an improved form, with the correction of numerous errors. The work has already been stamped with the public approbation, (especially the approbation of all, who are devoted to the study of sacred literature, and the interpretation of the Scriptures,) so as not to need the recommendation of Reviewers. The third and fourth volumes afford more aid for the illustration of the very numerous passages of Scripture, the explication of which depends on oriental, or local manners, customs, laws, ceremonies, civil or religious, geography, zoology, architecture, arts and manufactures, and other like things, than any other books in the English language, within the same compass. The reader of the Scriptures, who has not been accustomed to seek the explanation of difficult passages, which contain *technical* words, or others of *limited* and *appropriate signification*, will be very agreeably surprised, as well as greatly instructed by the perusal of these volumes. What adds exceedingly to their value, is the great number, (more than 120,) of well executed illustration of the various subjects of inquiry. Every reflecting reader well knows, that ideas, acquired by means of the eye, make a much more deep and lasting impression on the mind and memory, than those which are acquired by reading, or hearing, a description of the objects. The original compilers of these volumes well understood this principle, and have, to the great profit and delight of their readers, accompanied every illustration, depending on visible objects, with an appropriate drawing, which has been faithfully and beautifully copied by American artists.

It should be made known to the public, also, that the American edition is not only much more correct than the English, but cast into a much better form, and provided with good indexes. The third volume, for instance, of the English editions, contains 400 Illustrations, or Essays, which were originally published by centuries, and the index added after each; and, in all the copies that we have seen, bound up in the same manner. This intermixture makes it excessively difficult to find any particular subject, unless a person is intimately conversant with the whole volume. The index moreover is very imperfect, and entirely destitute of a regular account of *texts* illustrated, which is a deficiency very important. The American Editor has been at the pains and expense of casting the whole index into a regular form, at the end of the book, and making it complete. The numerous incorrect references to scriptural passages, in

the English edition, have likewise been corrected.

We cannot but express our sincere wish, that, for the interests of sacred literature, the aid of biblical interpretation, and the literary honor of our country, such an important publication may not want patrons. The expenses of it, on account of the very numerous engravings, must have been great; and we understand, that booksellers have not hitherto given much encouragement to the Editor, under the apprehension that the expense of the book would, in a great measure, prevent its sale; and because it is a book, but little known as yet to our religious public. With regard to the first particular; the execution of the work is in a style much superior to that of the English edition, and the price much less. The second reason is at present well founded; but we hope it will not long be so. Certainly clergymen, whose occupation it is to expound the Word of Life, will be anxious to obtain possession of every possible mean within their power to aid them in this great business; and we t.ust there are many laymen, who feel sufficient interest in such a subject, to patronize, and to read, the volumes in question.

If our information be correct, (as we fear it is,) the editor of this work has not as yet been able to sell a sufficient number of copies, to defray the original expense of the edition It would be matter of regret, if an individual, enterprising in so good a cause, should be left to suffer a loss, through the want of patronage. It would afford too much evidence of the truth of what ill-disposed foreigners reproach us with, that America can patron-iz nothing, by which no money is to be made!

The sale of the work may be slow; but we do believe it will be sure; and that, when the merits of it are known, there are patrons enough in this country, not only to purchase one edition, but demand a second.

RELIGIOUS INTELLIGENCE.

ORDINATIONS.

ORDAINED, July 7, 1813, the Rev. BENJAMIN RICE, over the first church in Marcellus and Skaneateles Religious Society, (N. Y.) Sermon by the Rev. Hezekiah Woodruff, from 2 Cor. v, 20.

At Boston, on the 9th inst. the Rev. EDWARD EVERETT, over the Religious Society, which worship at the Church in Brattle Street. Sermon by the Rev. Dr. Kirkland.

At Pawtucket, (R. I.) the Rev. Mr. HOUGH as an Evangelist.

At Billerica, (Mass.) on the 26th ult. the Rev. NATHANIEL WHITMAN, as colleague with the Rev. Dr. CUMMINGS. Sermon by the Rev. Mr Flint, of Bridgewater, from Col. i, 7, 28.

Dec. 7, 1813, at Cazenovia, Madison County (N. Y.) the Rev. JOHN BROWN, lately a tutor in Dartmouth University, as Pastor over the first Presbyterian Church and congregation in that place.

At Cambridgeport, on the 19th ult. the Rev. THOMAS BRATTLE GANNETT, as pastor over th Congregational Church at that place Sermon by the Rev. Dr. Holmes, from 1 Cor. ix, 22.

INSTALLATIONS.

INSTALLED on the 19th ult. the Rev. JOHN BASCOM, over the church of Christ in Smithfield, (Penn.) Sermon by the Rev. William Wisner, from Acts xx, 28.

On the 21st ult. the Rev. WILLIAM WISNER, over the church of Christ in Athens, (Penn.) Sermon by the Rev. Samuel Parker, from Luke x, 1.

On the 26th ult. the Rev. WARREN FAY, over the Congregational church and society in Harvard, (Mass.) An appropriate and evangelical sermon was preached by the Rev. Dr. Puffer, of Berlin, from John vii, 46. *Never man spake like this man.* The audience was unusually large and attentive for the occasion; and the music was grave and devotional.

DEDICATION.

A NEW meeting-house, belonging to the Congregational church and society in Wilmington, (Mass.) was solemnly dedicated to Almighty God, on Tuesday, the 14th of Dec. last.

MISSIONARY ZEAL IN GREAT BRITAIN.

THE following letter was lately received by the Treasurer of the American Board of Commissioners for Foreign Missions from Junius Smith, Esq.

"London, Nov. 29, 1813.

"Dear Sir,

I have the pleasure to acknowledge the receipt of your favor of Sept. 18th, covering exchange on Baring, Brothers, and Co. for £100, which shall be remitted to India agreeably to your instructions.*

"I shall forward to you some interesting accounts of the progress of the missionaries in Africa, by the first opportunity. Although the Bible Society has taken the highest ground and the most extensive range, yet I am happy to say, that the Society for the support of Missionaries is rapidly advancing, and has already received the most flattering support from Auxiliary Societies, established in some of the most wealthy parts of the country.

The zeal manifested by all ranks of people in this kingdom is wonderful beyond description, and distinctly points more happy and glorious days, than as yet dawned upon this fallen world."

DONATIONS TO SUPPORT FO EIGN MISSIONS AND TRAN LATIONS.

Feb. 7, 1814. From the Berkshire and Columbia Missionary

* *This sum was a donation from Hon. Elias Boudinot, Esq. of Burten. (N. J.)*

Society, by Henry Brown, Esq.
the Treasurer $120 00

9. From a young female in Steuben county, (N. Y.) for the translations*   5 00

Carried forward $125 00

* This donation was enclosed in the following letter to the Treasurer of the Board:

Jan. 30, 1814.

"SIR,

Enclosed I send you five dollars as a donation to the American Board of Commissioners for Foreign Missions, to be applied to the translations. This small sum I have kept for some time in order to send to you; but as no opportunity offers I have concluded to send it by the mail If I find that it reaches you, I shall be encouraged to send more." I have ever felt a lively interest in the Missionary cause. I have read with emotions, which I cannot describe, all that has been said on the subject in the Panoplist; and in particular I have been very anxious for the welfare and success of your Society and the Missionaries whom you have sent to Asia. But is there nothing to be done for the heathens in our own country? I see the poor Indians almost daily; I gaze at them with pity; I sigh for them; and wonder that Christians, who enjoy the blessings of the Gospel, and so highly prize them, can bear to see these poor creatures, who have souls as precious, and immortal as their own, live and die utterly ignorant of the great Redeemer. Christians all acknowledge, that one soul is of infinitely more value than all the treasures of the earth. Oh then why do not many devote all that they possess, and their whole lives, to the great work of evangelizing the heathens? Why do they not learn their language, and go to their huts, if there is no other way, and tell them that a Redeemer has died to save poor lost wretched men. Cannot something more be said on this subject in the Panoplist? Cannot Christians be aroused to do something more? If they cannot, how little do they deserve the name!

A YOUNG FEMALE IN STEUBEN
COUNTY, N. Y."

* It is proper to state, that no intimation has ever been received, that any money remitted to the Treasurer has failed of its destination. The donations are copied from the Treasurer's books every month, and not a cent received in donations has been omitted in these monthly publications.   ED.

Brought forward $125 00

12. From Mrs. Florella M. Ripley, of Cornish, (N. H.) by Mr. Newton Whittelsey†   5 00

14. From Mr. Francis Brown, of Boston, by Mr. S. T. Armstrong   1 00

From an unknown person, by the same hands   1 00

From the Foreign Mission Society of Hallowell, Augusta, and the Vicinity, by Mr. John Sewall, the Treasurer   77 00

From the Female Religious Society in Augusta, by the same hands   23 00

15. From the Female Cent Society in Rowley, (Mass.) by the Rev. J. W. Tucker   18 74

From two friends of missions   2 00

17. From Mrs. Catherine Freeman, of the state of Georgia, by Mr. James Clap   10 00

From the Rev. Thomas Worcester, of Salisbury, (N. H)   5 00

24. From a lady in New Ipswich, (N. H.) by the Rev. Richard Hall   10 00

$277 74

SALEM FOREIGN MISSION SOCIETY.

THE *Foreign Mission Society of Salem and the Vicinity* held its third annual meeting, Jan. 5, 1814. The following gentlemen were chosen officers for the current year, viz.

EBENEZER BECKFORD, Esq. *Pres.*
The Rev. RUFUS ANDERSON, and
The Rev. SAMUEL WORCESTER, D. D.
     Vice Presidents.
The Rev. SAMUEL WALKER, *Secretary.*
Mr. JOHN JANES, *Treasurer.*
Mr. ELIPHALET KIMBALL, *Auditor.*

From the report of the Auditor it appeared, that the sum of *three hundred and eighty-four dollars* had been received into the treasury of the Society in the course of the last year, one hundred and forty-three dollars more than was received the preceding year: And that *three hundred and twenty-eight dollars, fifty-six cents* had been transmitted to the treasury of the Parent Institution.

At 2 o'clock, P. M. an appropriate discourse was delivered before the Society by the Rev. Joseph Emerson, of Beverly, from Matt. vi. 10. *Thy kingdom come.*

† This lady sent also $5 to be expended in sending Bibles to Louisiana.

From the number of persons, who attended the meeting, and the unanimity with which all the business of the Society was transacted; as well as from the state of the treasury; it was evident that there was no abatement of the zeal of its members in promoting the benevolent object of the Institution. On the contrary, it is believed it may be safely affirmed, that within the limits of the Society, the missionary cause is viewed generally in a more favorable light, and that the people more readily contribute to aid the great and good work now, than at any former period. Christians are waking up to the interests of Zion and becoming more and more alive to the case of the perishing heathen; and it is devoutly to be hoped that a conviction is spreading in all directions of the obligation upon all to aid by their influence, wealth and prayers, in the diffusion of Christian light.

CHARITABLE ASSOCIATION.

(Concluded from p. 47.)

The Society have expended *two hundred and forty-three dollars and thirty cents* in the last year, have relieved about *one hundred and forty-three* families; distributed *four hundred and forty-six* garments, and *ten and a half* yards of cloth; *eight pair of shoes*; and to the sick *fifteen dollars and forty-two cents.*

The Gentlemen will give us leave to add, That in visiting the chambers of the sick, and the hovels of the poor, the hearts of our committee are ready to despond, and to shrink from their office, when they find their means so inadequate to relieving the distresses they are called to witness. But we encourage ourselves with the hope, that the Gentlemen will find it consistent with their many other calls, to afford us some further aid, which together with the unremitting exertions of the benevolent of our own Society, may enable us to meet the calls of the present winter, with less painful sensations.

Per Order of the Society,
　　L. Frothingham *Scribe."*
January 6, 1814.

EXTRACT FROM THE REV. MR. KOHLOFF'S LETTER.

In the Appendix to the first annual report of the Calcutta Auxiliary Bible Society, a very interesting letter from the Rev. Mr. Kohloff, missionary on the Coromandel coast, is published. The design of the writer was to return thanks for the Bibles, which had been received from the friends of religion in Bengal, and to exhibit the great need of Bibles, in which numbers of native Christians still remained. The following extract contains the applications of several individuals to Mr. Kohloff for the word of God.

1. *Samuel Njanaperagasam* says, he considers the word of God as shewing unto men the way of salvation, calling them to eternal life, and adorning them with the robes of the righteousness of Jesus Christ; he therefore craves a Bible, and thanks God for his mercy to this poor man, who has put it into the hearts of the Bible Society at Calcutta to bestow the book.

2. *Njanaperagasam Mutter*, Schoolmaster, is very desirous of reading the Old Testament, wishes to keep every word of God in his heart in order to get rest to his soul; says, he is too poor to buy, but if it be given to him he will never sell it under any necessity whatever, but will read it day and night.

3. *Twarlay* requests the Holy Scriptures, as being necessary for the salvation of her own soul, and the souls of her household and people, and renders a thousand thanks to God, and to the honorable Society at Calcutta.

4. *Wodimutter*, Catechist, says, the Old and New Testament, which a merciful God has granted by his divine servants through the incitement of the Holy Ghost, are living words; but he has never had them his own property; several times he has borrowed them from other people, that he might have the comfort of reading them, being unable to purchase them. Now the merciful God, having illuminated the hearts of the Bible Society to place the Scriptures for charity without price, he prays to God for the Society on account of this beneficial act, and to Mr. Kohloff to get for him the heavenly blessing.

5. *Dewoptrayer Njonamutter* says, the divine word is more precious than riches, gold, silver or gems; but he has never had the book which shews the good way; asks for a New Testament, which he will hold as a lamp to his feet and a light to his path all the days of his life, and will read and study it, and walk according to the manner which it directs.

6. *Njanamutter Arulopen*, Catechist, represents, that when his father was a Catechist he received from the Reverend Mr. Swartz a Bible, but his house being afterwards burnt down, it was lost; therefore requests to be favored with an Old and New Testament.

don *Arulopen* says, the
awaken every one to piety
s; he is athirst for them.
hem he shall pray the Lord
ie Society according to his
words of his prophet Dan-
y that be wise shall shine
ess of the firmament, and
*many to righteousness as
wer and ever.*"

Sundupen, Assistant Cat-
rough the paternal com-
. Kohlhoff he has been pla-
yard, which the living God
this country; but can a vine,
g water upon it grow in a
aner so as to give ripened
possible; therefore the pe-
th very much for the spir-
if the Holy Bible so very
lvation, and he prays for all
ings on the honorable Bible

represents that being at
pery, or a Roman Catholic,
rom his own Romish minis-

ter a New Testament, which was appointed by the Savior Jesus Christ for his
salvation. He therefore petitions for a
New Testament for to save his soul, and
he promises to use it for that purpose, and
will take the utmost care of it.

10. The Address of 75 children of the
Free-School of Kanandagudi. After thankful acknowledgments for the benefits derived from the institution, they add: Moreover, worthy Father, your petitioners are
much rejoiced by the benevolence of the
gentlemen of the Calcutta Bible Society,
who have granted them the ripened spiritual fruits, namely, six Old Testaments,
and five books, each containing the Four
Gospels. These books they will use as the
weapons of the Savior for the destruction
of Satan's kingdom; and they pray that
God may fulfil the promise which he has
made in the Gospel to these charitable
gentlemen, viz. "Whosoever shall give to
drink unto one of these little ones a cup
of cold water only in the name of a disciple, verily I say unto you, he shall in no
wise lose his reward."

OBITUARY.

Haven, in Dec. last, Mrs.
WOOLSEY, wife of *William*
Esq. a lady of uncommon
lamented by a numerous
s.

ton, (Ver.) the Hon. SAM-
CK, Esq. aged 59. He was
triet Judge for the state of
subsequently a Judge of the
of the United States.

7th to the 27th of Nov. last,
died of the spotted fever, at
(Ver.) within the distance

gh, (Penn) Lt JOSEPH E.
S. navy, aged 27.

ro', (N. H) on the 13th of
JAMES TOLBURT, aged 26,
children;—all of the spotted
were sick only from 8 to 10

on, (Ken.) Major LEVI HU-
. army.

n, in Fairfax county, (Vir.)
of Nov. last, Mr. PHILIP
l 115 He was a native of
d removed to this country in
as remarkably active and
ne day of his decease. His
m he had nine children, lived
101.

sburg, (Md.) on the 17th of
. BENJAMIN STODDART, Esq.

aged 62. He was formerly Secretary of
the navy.

At Brownville, (N. Y.) three children
of a Mr. BARTLETT perished in his house,
which was consumed by fire.

At Adams, (Mass.) two children of Mr.
A. CARPENTER perished in the same
manner.

At Marietta, (Ohio,) DAVID EVERETT,
Esq. formerly of Boston.

The deaths in Hartford, (Conn.) during the year 1813, were 122, of which 10
were of U. S. soldiers.

At Burlington, (Ver.) Capt. JOHN
JONES, of Newark, Upper Canada, a prisoner of war.

At New Orleans, WILLIAM DONALD-
SON, Esq. formerly President of the Louisiana Bank.

At Norwich, (Con.) ELISHA HYDE,
Esq. Mayor of that city, aged 63.

At Philadelphia, Col. PATTEN, the post-
master.

At Boston, Deacon DAVID TILDEN,
aged 72.

At New Haven, (Con.) Mrs. REBECCA
HILLHOUSE, wife of the Hon. *James Hillhouse*, Esq. aged 50,—a lady greatly respected and beloved.

The deaths in New Haven, during the
year 1813, were 228;—a very unusual, if
not an unparalleled number.

In England, Lt. Gen. Sir HARRY BUR-RARD.

At St. Christophers, Lt. Gen. RICHARD HARKSHAW LOSACK, aged 83.

At Wrightstown, (Penn.) four children lately fell through the ice, while sliding on a mill-pond, and were drowned.

At Monmouth, (N. J.) the Rev. WILLIAM MILLS, aged 70.

At Springfield, (Mass.) on the 8th ult. Miss MARY HORTON, aged 92; and, on the 9th, Miss MARGARET HORTON, aged 90. These maiden sisters had slept together ninety years, and one survived the other only eleven hours. They were both buried in one grave.

At Roxbury, (Mass.) on the 24th ult. the Hon. WILLIAM HEATH, Esq. aged 77, —the only surviving Major General of the United States revolutionary army.

At Copenhagen, in Sept. last, the eminent Jewish banker, MEYER, immensely rich.

In North Carolina, the Rev. JOHN NOWELL.

In the poor house and hospital of Savannah, (Georgia,) during the year 1813. the deaths were 31 The expenses of the institution were $6143—208 persons having been admitted, of whom 30 were from New England, and 16 from New York

Near Buffaloe, (N. Y.) by a cannon ball from an invading enemy, Major WILLIAM C. DUDLEY, of Canandaigua.

At Baltimore, WILLIAM HAYWARD, a minister of the Society of Friends, aged 77.

At Philadelphia, Gen. IRA ALLEN, of Colchester, (Ver.)

At Pomfret, (Conn.) the Rev. AARON PUTNAM, aged 80.

At the French Mills, Capt. JEREMIAH CHAPMAN, of U. S. army.

At Claremont, (N. H.) two brothers of the name of PUTNAM, aged 27 and 19,—suffocated by placing a kettle of coals in their chamber.

At Stamford, (Conn.) Mrs. SARAH BISHOP, in her 100th year.

Also, Mrs. MARY WHITNEY, wife of Mr. *Eliasaph Whitney*, aged 91. Mr. Whitney is now 97.

At Barre, (Mass.) Mrs. EUNICE BROAD, aged 96. Her descendants are 214.

At Black Rock, (N. Y.) killed in the battle of Dec 30th, Lt. Colonel SEYMOUR BORSHTON, aged 44.

Near Richmond, (Vir.) the Rev. JOHN TURNER.

In England, the Hon. DAVID HARTLEY, Esq. aged 82; the minister, who, on the part of Great Britain, signed the treaty of peace with the U. S.

At Cape May, (Vir.) the Rev. DAVID EDWARDS,

At Weston, (Mass.) the Rev. SAMUEL KENDALL, D D. pastor of the Congregational church in that town, aged 62.

At Wenham, (Mass.) the Rev. RUFUS ANDERSON, pastor of the Congregational church in that town.

In England, Nov. 16, WILLIAM FRANKLIN, Esq. formerly British Governor of New Jersey, aged 82.

In Virginia, Dr. JAMES CRAIK, formerly Physician General to the armies of the United States.

At Lunenburg, (Mass.) on the 17th inst. ZABDIEL B. ADAMS, Esq. counsellor at law, aged 44.

At Lower Dublin, (Penn.) the Rev. SAMUEL JONES, D. D. a native of Scotland, aged 79.

At Hudson, (N Y.) STEPHEN PADDOCK, Esq. late President of the Bank of Columbia.

At Windsor, (Conn.) the Hon. ROGER NEWBERRY, Esq. aged 78, formerly a member of the Council of that state.

At Lyme, (Conn.) Mrs. ABIGAIL LESTER, aged 93, leaving 235 descendants.

At Granby, (Conn.) Gen. CHAUNCEY PETTIBONE, aged 52.

The deaths in Boston, during the year 1813, were 786; males 452; females 334. Under 20 years of age 330; above that age 456. Above 70 years of age 61; above 90 years, 5. Of consumption, 193; of apoplexy, 15; indigestion, 16; drowned, 15; fevers, 101; infantile diseases, 206; dropsy, 17; still born, 36; old age, 48; sudden, 11; convulsions, 11; of various other diseases, 78; diseases not mentioned, 39.

At Charlestown, on the 23d inst. ABNER ROGERS, Esq. Counsellor at Law, aged 37. This gentleman was graduated at Harvard College; afterwards held the office of rein that university, and was appointed tutor, which appointment he declined accepting.

POETRY.

HYMN.

Jer. xxxi. 18. *Thou hast chastised me, and I was chastised, as a bullock unaccustomed to the yoke: turn thou me, and I shall be turned; for thou art the Lord my God.*

YES, gracious Lord, I yield me now,
  Thy child, no rebel as before;
I feel—I cannot tell thee how—
  I feel, that I will stray no more.

I was a steerling, young and wild,
  That would not stoop to wear the yoke:

For sin's enticing fields beguil'd—
But I have felt thy chastening stroke.

How oft that angry scourge was sent,
To tame my proud, rebellious will!
Alas, what pain I underwent!
And yet I madly wander'd still.

But now, I yield to thy command,
Reclaim'd and soften'd by thy love:
A child may guide me with its hand,
In silken chains, a little dove.
URANIUS.

ON DEATH.

If death indeed were endless sleep'
And nought disturb'd the grave's repose,
O why should they, who live to weep,
Whose days are full of cares and woes,
So dread in death's embrace to lie?
Why should the wretched dread to die?

Why should the man, whose deeds of shame
Have robb'd him of the world's respect,
Consent to bear a blasted name,
And suffer long, deserv'd, neglect?
Ye sons of infamy and scorn,
If death were peace could life be borne?

The guilty fair one—would she live,
A faded flower, unsought, unblest,
To years of grief compell'd to give
Her heart, with poignant woe opprest,
Unless she fear'd a heavier doom,
Eternal shame beyond the tomb?

But no—our greatest hope and fear
Beyond our mortal being roam,
Both tell us man's a stranger here,
And that ETERNITY's his home:
Tis that makes cowards of the brave;
That makes them tremble at the grave.

For all that ranks us great or fair,
This side the precincts of the tomb,
Avails our spirits nothing there,
When they have pierc'd its darkest gloom;
Since with our dying bodies die
The strength to dare—the speed to fly.

The dread of judgment after death
Disturbs the proud and checks the vain;
Hence they prolong their mortal breath,
And back recoil from endless pain:
And hence, when all is woe and strife,
The wretched fondly cling to life.

And is there then no ray of hope
The dying hour of man to cheer?
At that sad moment must he grope,
In dread and darkness, doubt and fear!

Is there no arm that's strong to save?
Is there no joy beyond the grave?

Yes,—there's an arm of boundless might,
And hope and joy beyond the tomb;
A world of unalloy'd delight,
Where flowers of bliss perpetual bloom.
But who shall drink without alloy
The living stream of perfect joy.

Not they, whose only pleasures grow,
In vales of vice, in fields of sin:
Their joys begin and end below,
Nor can they heavenly pleasures win:
But they, who love the Lord, are blest
To see his face, t' enjoy his rest.

Tis ours to choose—if heaven has charms
To touch our hearts, we gain the prize;
For Jesus stands, with open arms,
To take us to the upper skies,
From care and trouble, grief and pain,
With Him to live, with Him to reign.

But if we pant for earth-born toys,
And spurn the offers of His love,
Earth is the limit of our joys;
We have no share or lot above:
Our mad, deluded, souls must go
To realms of everlasting woe.

And shall we sleep our lives away,
Careless of time's eventful flight?
Neglect, abuse, the precious day,
And rush to shades of endless night?
May He, whose glory fills the sky,
Wake us to thought before we die!
OLNEY.

New Hampshire, 1814.

PRECAUTIONS AGAINST FIRE.

The liability of all persons to suffer by the calamity of fire, should induce a habit of unceasing caution against it. The following directions should be remembered and practised by all.

1 When about to leave your fire, make your calculations to have no more fire than you can leave with safety.

2 Never leave a stick of wood upon another stick, nor upon the andirons, nor standing in the corner, nor in any manner except *perfectly flat*, so that it cannot *fall*, in any direct on whatever.

3. Examine your brush, or broom, after sweeping a hearth, especially if about to leave the room.

4. Never place hot ashes, so that they can come into contact with wood.

5. Never leave papers, or linen, or cotton, near the fire.

6. Never read in bed by candle-light.

7. Never suffer a candle, unless well secured by a lantern, to be carried into a

garret, a barn, a stable, or any other out-house.

8. In case of fire, act with presence of mind. Many destructive fires might have been easily extinguished by a small share of courage and judgment.

9. Never suffer a fire to be increased by any needless opening of doors or windows.

10. Should the fire have made such progress as to prevent your escape by a staircase, and should the distance be too great to leap from a window, endeavor to descend by your bed-cord, or by tying your bed-clothes together.

11. If safety does not appear probable in this way, wrap yourself in a blanket, hold your breath, and rush through the fire.

12. Do not resort to this last expedient, till you are sure there is a clear passage; as you will perish, if obliged to stop to remove obstructions.

13. When unable to escape, keep the door of your chamber shut, and it will probably protect you till ladders can be brought to your relief.

NEW WORKS.

Two Sermons on Infidelity, delivered Oct. 24, 1813. By William Ellery Channing, Minister of the church in Federal Street, Boston. Boston: Cummings & Hilliard. pp. 36.

A Sermon, delivered Oct. 27, 1813, at the dedication of the Meeting-House in the third society in Abington. By Jonathan Strong, A. M. pastor of the church in Randolph, (Mass.) Boston; Samuel T. Armstrong.

An Explanation of the Principal Types, the Prophecies of Daniel and Hosea, the Revelation, and other Symbolical Passages of the Holy Scriptures. By Aaron Kinne, A. M. Minister of the Gospel. Boston; S. T. Armstrong. 1814. pp 389. 8vo.

A Key to the Figurative Language found in the Sacred Scriptures, in the form of questions and answers. By Ethan Smith, A. M. Minister in Hopkinton, (N. H.) Author of the Dissertation on the Prophecies. Exeter; C. Norris and Co. 1814.

A Sermon, preached Oct. 20, 1813, at Sandwich, (Mass.) at the dedication of the Meeting House, recently erected for the use of the Calvinistic Congregational Society in that town. By Edward D. Griffin, D. D pastor of Park Street Church, Boston Published by request. Boston; N. Willis.

A Sermon preached at the installation of the Rev. Samuel Wood Colburn, to the pastoral care of the third church and society in Abington, Oct. 27, 1813. By Otis Thomson, A. M. pastor of the congregational church in Rehoboth. Boston, S. T. Armstrong.

The Clergyman's Almanac, No. VI. for 1814.

TO CORRESPONDENTS.

We have doubted, whether it is advisable, or not, to take any notice of the book which our correspondent Clio has reviewed. Some publications should be suffered to sink quietly into the gulf of oblivion. Should we hereafter determine to review the work now referred to, it would be examined in connexion with certain other works. Clio, and all our other correspondents, will please to remember, that no reviews, biographical notices, or statements of facts not generally known, can be inserted in the Panoplist, unless the persons who make the communications are known to us, or we are assured of the accuracy of the statements, in some other manner. The same reasons do not apply to the writers of other communications; such as expositions of Scripture, essays, &c. &c as these can be judged of without reference to any external means of information. Clio is entitled to a respectful notice on account of the ability displayed in his communication.

The communication of Titus, though obviously well-intended, and as it seems to us, in most things correct, would yet appear, in the apprehension of many readers, to be a mere dispute about words. Certain it is, that many, if not most, who apply the word *supernatural* to regeneration, do not use the term in the sense which our correspondent opposes.

Several communications from O. E. have been received, and will be considered hereafter

E. O. in answer to O. E. will be inserted.

Candidus, a short sermon, F. J., Frank, F, N°, L. C., Observer, and other pieces, are on our files.

We thank V. for his version of the 126th and the 137th psalms. They shall appear

D., *on the Sabbath*, is respectfully informed, that we are in expectation of a series of papers on that most interesting subject, in which there will be a very extended discussion of it The thoughts of D. may however be of use to us at some future time.

THE
PANOPLIST,
AND
MISSIONARY MAGAZINE.

| No. 3. | MARCH, 1814. | VOL. X. |

RELIGIOUS COMMUNICATIONS.

ON RULES OF PRUDENCE IN POLEMIC THEOLOGY.

The following rules are translated for the Panoplist, by an obliging correspondent, from Stapfer's Theologia Elenchtica. In the original, the composition is divided into sections, the numbers of which we have thought it unnecessary to print. This extract is taken from chapter 2, sect. 141 to 265. It is probable that the whole work may be translated, and printed in a volume, should the public call for it. Stapfer is said to have been much read and admired by the great President Edwards; which will doubtless be considered as no ordinary recommendation. ED.

THE necessity of prudential rules, in Polemic Theology, has already been demonstrated.

That, which relates to the glory of God, to the eternal salvation of man, to the defence of essential truth, and to the refutation of essential error, cannot be treated with too much caution.

The appropriate ends of Polemic Theology, are the demonstration of truth, and the refutation of error. In this science, therefore, every thing should be so arranged, as that nothing may be omitted which may conduce to the attainment of its end; and, on the contrary, every thing should be avoided, which may impede the attainment of its end: hence true *prudence* consists in using the best means in the best manner

These prudential rules relate either to the *disputant*, or to the mode of *disputation*.

A wise man will surely propose to himself the best end; which, in Polemic Theology, whether divine truth is to be demonstrated, or error refuted, or an errorist convinced, is no other than a *love of truth;* for all these aim at truth, that the purity of the divine word, which is truth itself, may be preserved and vindicated.

Therefore the FIRST rule of prudence is this:

Let a person, who is disposed to undertake a controversy, scrutinize himself; let him examine the end and design of his undertaking, whether it be a sincere love of truth, or whether it be ambition, or a censorious spirit, or some other sinful passion.

For if a sincere love of truth possessed the minds of all who hold the sacred office, most controversies would immediately terminate of their own accord, and that peace, so ardently desired, would be restored to the Church. But if erudition is preferred to piety, and religion becomes an art, the natural and only effects are discord and debate.

But no one can convince another of the truth, who, being tinctured with false notions, has no certainty of the truth himself.

For he, who demonstrates any principle, becomes convinced of its truth by his own demonstration; but if he doubts that principle, it must be that the demonstration was not sufficiently evident to himself: he cannot, therefore, by that demonstration, hope or expect to convince another of the truth of principle.

Wherefore the SECOND rule of prudence is this:

Let no one commence a controversy on a principle in religion, unless, having laid aside all his preconceived opinions, he has acquired a certainty of the truth, founded on demonstration.[*]

It is the special duty of a wise man to employ no means, which do not conduce to the end proposed: hence he, who undertakes a controversy, ought for his own sake to beware of every thing, in his understanding, or in his heart, which may obstruct the attainment of the end.

The human mind, on account of its extreme imbecility and depravation, is so deeply imbued with false notions and prejudices, and is so distracted by them, that it often mistakes the truth and defends error.

For preconceived notions,

arising from heedlessness, or from perverse education, or from rash judgment, or from authority, have such control over many persons, that even those, who esteem themselves learned, frequently assent to the truth for no other reason, than because human authority has given it influence over their minds.

Indeed any one, who does not derive the truth from the very fountain of truth, and does not studiously labor to arrive at certainty, is guided only by prejudices of authority; and then he esteems any proposition true, either because he has heard it from some man in high repute, or because it is extant in the writings of some celebrated character, or because it is found in mystical books.

Superstition *only* can arise from blind assent. He, who is thus hurried forward by blind assent, never discerns the connexion and harmony of truth, however it may flow from his own principles; nor is able to demonstrate it to the conviction of another. Nor can he know the importance of defending a truth, unless he has an intimate and correct apprehension of its connexion with fundamental principles: whence arise many unimportant disputes, which ultimately terminate in a mere strife of words.

As the preservation of pure truth is the ultimate end of Polemic Theology, every thing which is hostile to truth should be laid aside.

Whence arises this THIRD rule:

Since the depraved affections of the heart, especially ambition,

[*] On this and the two succeeding rules, the very Rev. and celebrated Praffius should be read. *In Primitiis, Tubing. Dissert. De Præjud. Theol.* p. 17. seq.

a spirit of persecution, and attachment to sects, are very hostile to the truth, we should, therefore, entirely divest ourselves. of them before we enter upon a religious controversy.

On the part of the will, it must surely be granted, that such depraved affections, as ambition, a spirit of persecution, and partiality for sects, are extremely injurious to the truth.

For he, who is inflated with ambition, seeks not truth, but applause: hence those unhappy religious contests, (these are the words of the celebrated Praffius,) in which no one will yield to another, lest he should appear to have been in an error; hence so many logomachies, or disputes about words; hence the seeds of new disputes; hence a fondness for contradiction, and pertinacity in the defence of error; hence, also, truth is lightly esteemed, while celebrity alone is sought.

Thus some, alienated from the love of truth, are influenced only by a fondness ' for disputation, which flows from a spirit of persecution. He who is imbued with this spirit, cannot tolerate those who dissent from him, but regards their every word with suspicion; and, by exaggerating their errors, infers heresy from any thing, although the system of truth is not affected: Hence new disputes originate. How much the progress of truth is thus obstructed, scarcely admits of computation. In this way, the mind is exasperated rather than convinced.

Most men are so attached to that religion in which they were educated, that they defend opin-ions, derived from that source, without ever examining their truth for themselves. Thus they confide more in human, than in divine, authority; whence arises such a blind zeal and fondness for sects, that we condemn those who do not entertain the same sentiments on controverted subjects with ourselves.

We ought to conduct our inquiries after truth, as if we had not yet discovered it; and to manage our controversies, as if we were inclined to no sect.

These are special rules, or cautions, which respect the person who undertakes a controversy; but even in the controversy itself, or in the mode of conducting it, rules of prudence are no less necessary, lest there should be an aberration from the end proposed.

Two things are sought in a controversy; a demonstration of truth, and a refutation of error. Hence both the demonstration and the refutation should be so arranged as to effect the conviction of the errorist, and the preservation of truth, which is the scope of Polemic Theology.

For this purpose it is especially requisite, that the premises should be *infallible;* whence arises this FOURTH rule:

Since, in Polemic Theology, truth should be so demonstrated, that the results may be certain; therefore we should neither confide in our own, nor in another's authority, because it is a fallible premise, or principle.

For a demonstration ought to rest on premises which are certain; and such premises must be derived from reason, or from Revelation; or there must be on earth, some man who is infallible, whose judgment, incapable of error, can decide even without demonstration on any article of faith

But experience, independent of the testimony of Sacred Scripture, affords sufficient proof, that such a man, who is truth itself, and incapable of deceiving or being deceived, never existed; Hence in religion no confidence should be placed in human authority, whether our own or another's, except it be supported by demonstration: But we should recur to the simple principles of reason or revelation, where we may find solid bases on which we may securely rest our feet. For both reason and revelation acknowledge God as their author.

From this maxim, that truth must be demonstrated, it is particularly necessary to observe this FIFTH rule:

If truth is to be demonstrated to the conviction of another, that method should be observed in communicating it, which will surely produce conviction, unless the opponent labors to be blind.

For, to convince another by a demonstration of truth, there must be some method observed in the demonstration. The method should be this: let indubitable principles be premised, and from these, by just connexion and correct ratiocination, let others be deduced; those principles, therefore, should always be premised, from which the subsequent can be understood and demonstrated.

This method should be employed in treatises on doctrines

of faith, lest, by an unnatural and restricted method, the truth be founded on such premises as the opponent still doubts, which will greatly obstruct conviction.

The doctrines of faith should therefore be taught in such connexion, that one may always rest upon another, and the latter always derive light from the former.

For if those principles which are especially fundamental in religion, are assumed as granted, and others are founded upon them; all conclusions drawn from such principles cannot but be doubtful to an opposer of truth: but when the foundation of the whole edifice is correctly laid, the superstructure will be immoveable.

All the doctrines of faith will inevitably be uncertain to him, who errs respecting the foundation of the Christian religion; unless the truth both of natural and revealed religion, and the peculiar foundation of the religion of a sinner, which is *perfect salvation by Christ alone*, are first demonstrated. These fundamental articles being established, all the other doctrines of faith may be founded on them.

Hence these primary principles, on which the certainty of all the other doctrines depends, should never be treated cursorily, unless all the conclusions derived from them *ought* to be rendered doubtful.

In a demonstration which has for its end the conviction of another, there must be the evidence of demonstration.

Hence arises this SIXTH rule:

In Polemic Theology all obscurity should be avoided that

by the evidence of demonstration, the opponent may be rendered certain of the proposition in debate.

For the reason why the opponent should assent to the truth, is, because he perceives the connexion and force of the demonstration; but while he does not comprehend the demonstration, he cannot be drawn to assent; or if he should assent, unless there is perspicuity in the reasoning, his assent will be *blind assent.*

Wherefore all obscurity in the reasoning should be avoided, and simplicity carefully studied, that nothing may remain doubtful.

Hence, in the first place, all indefinite phraseology should be excluded, and the most simple diction employed: for obscure terms rather deceive than persuade, and are adapted only to disseminate disputes and logomachies, whereby the truth is greatly injured; especially since under these very terms much meaning is frequently concealed.

In the second place, in the communication of truth, the argumentation should be so arranged, that the opponent may perceive the connexion between the predicate and the subject in debate; for on this depends the evidence of a demonstration, and wherever this is wanting there can be no certainty with respect to the subject which was to have been proved.

These are special rules, which must be observed in the demonstration of truth, if we would attain the end proposed: in the same manner, in the refutation of error, all those means which

conduce to the end must be employed, and all those which may obstruct it must be avoided.

But above all, unless we design to wander from the point in debate, the state of the controversy, or the errors to be refuted, should be well understood, in the manner we have already expressed.

Whence this SEVENTH rule:

To refute the errors of any sect, the whole system of that sect must be well understood in its connexion, that the state of the controversy may be correctly defined.

Every sect has prejudices* and hypotheses peculiar to itself, to which it is extremely attached; but among these hypotheses, there are certain primary prejudices which are fundamental to their other sentiments.

Now the whole of any system of error should be examined in connexion, that we may know how one error is allied to another, and how every particular error contributes a share to establish a general hypothesis.

For in this way only will the system of the errorist be well understood; and its foundation being undermined, the whole edifice will inevitably fall.

Therefore they are inconsiderate, who manage controversies by explaining and refuting individual errors, separately considered, having no regard to the whole system and to the mutual relation of one error to another; because the import and scope of most errors can be understood only in connexion one with another.

* Prejudgments, or preconceived opin-

As errors are to be refuted, and errorists convinced of the truth, the entire system of truth should be very well known; whence arises, this EIGHTH rule:

No one can refute the errors of another, and demonstrate to him the truth, unless he has a knowledge of every thing which tends to establish the truth, and thus understands the whole system of truth.

For as it is highly important that the real sentiments of the opponents should be known by us, so it is equally important, before we attempt a refutation, that we should understand the system of truth in its various relations and connexions, in the manner we have already represented.

And *first:* The divine oracles, the fountain of all saving truth, must be studied with diligence and meditation, that instruction and wisdom being derived from them, all cavillings, all false philosophy, all objections, and all sophisms of the rebellious heart, may be easily detected and unfolded.

We must acquire so correct and extensive a knowledge of truths in the sacred oracles, that we may perceive the consistency and connexion of all essential truths; how each flows from its primary principles, and how each accords with the general system.

And *secondly:* Since even those principles are to be refuted in Polemic Theology, which, being avowedly repugnant to revealed principles of religion, can be repelled only by the principles of Philosophy:—therefore a knowledge of this science is highly useful in Polemic Theology.

For true philosophy greatly assists the human mind in its researches after truth, teaches it to form clear and definite ideas, and habituates it to decide with caution. This science assists the mind to apprehend the truth with correctness, and to detect and demolish error with facility. These general advantages and qualifications, should be sought by the theologian in proportion to his obligation to secure himself from error, and to labor for the acquisition of indubitable certainty.

Further, Philosophy teaches some truths which revealed Theology presupposes to have been demonstrated: such are the existence of God; his attributes; especially his justice, which is the foundation of all religion; his providence and universal government; the nature and spontaneity of the soul, subjected however to divine guidance; the immortality of the soul, and others.

The more intensely the theologian applies to acquire certain and indubitable knowledge in this science, the greater will be his ability and skill in refuting errors derived from this source.

It would even conduce, not a little, to a clear knowledge of essential truth, if the systems of eminent theologians, as well as the mystical books, should be examined with attention.

Polemic Theology is not to be solicitous concerning every error; hence we form this NINTH rule:

In the selection of errors, there is need of consummate prudence, lest we refute those which are unimportant; or, falling into the other extreme, spare those which are directly hostile to essential truth; or, lest we esteem those principles erroneous, which are a part of the truth itself.

For errors are of different kinds: some lie, as it were, entombed with the ashes of their authors, and are forgotten; some are more and some less important, while many principles appear erroneous which are really true.

Hence a selection of errors should be made, as well for the sake of the authors, as for the sake of the sentiments. Nor should all the errors, which have ever been published, be accumulated from every quarter; it is sometimes better not to know them, than to recall them from the dead.

Here we might adduce instances which prove that errors have frequently been disseminated, and embraced by multitudes, in consequence of the opposition made to them. Caution should then be used in the refutation of any new-born error, lest we thereby occasion its dissemination. For such is human nature, that whenever the reading of any bad book is prohibited, or its sale interdicted by the chief magistrate, or opposition made, every one desires to read it, whether he can understand it or not, or whether he is first convinced of its truth or not; and thus the ignorant may be seduced. But in my opinion, it would be judicious never to prohibit the reading of such a book, lest common people should be rendered more desirous of obtaining and reading it, which can scarcely, or rather cannot, be prevented; but if learned and pious men would procure another edition, furnished with such notes and explanations, as would utterly overturn the errors of the book, the result would be, that the reader would have before his eyes truth opposed to the error, and by its light would gain instruction.

It is sometimes prudent to spare those prejudices, which are not essentially injurious to the Christian church, lest by refuting them, we neglect, or occasion the advancement of, more important errors.

This however is so to be understood, that if we undertake to refute the whole system of any sect, no principles should be omitted in it, lest we should appear to attack only those which are very easy of refutation, which would be an evidence of unskilfulness, or of a bad cause.

Those errors, which constitute the primary hypotheses of a sect; which affect the very foundation of faith and threaten extensive injury; which well accord with carnal wisdom and exclude men from spiritual life and salvation, ought especially to be attacked. These should be opposed; these should be thoroughly eradicated.

But as on one side moderation must be exercised, so on the other the number of articles in dispute must not be too much diminished; lest, while wishing to avoid Charybdis, we fall on Scylla, and while disposed to extend the bounds of religious toleration, we become charge-ble with an indifference to all religion, or, (pardon the expression,) at least with latitudinarianism.

Furthermore, we should be cautious lest we mistake that for error, which is perhaps a part of truth. This may happen, especially in those articles, which surpass the human understanding; whose sublimity rises above the utmost scope of mental vision, or whose wide extent exceeds the narrow comprehension of human intellect.

That this may be true with respect to the sublime doctrines of the divine decrees and predestination, not to mention others, any one will readily perceive.

Since we should aim to *convince* our opponent, this TENTH rule must be observed:

If we desire not merely to vanquish an errorist, but to convince him, we should treat him in such a manner, that he may perceive we are influenced solely by the love of truth, free from sectarian partialities.

Because, in Polemic Theology, it is our object not only to preserve divine truth in its purity, but also to convince others of it; hence every thing should be avoided which may obstruct their conviction.

Special prudence and caution should then be employed, that the opponent may not indulge any unfavorable suspicions respecting the person who undertakes the controversy; either, that he is tinctured with prejudices, or that he is disposed to reject reason and argumentation, and, assuming the character of a judge, to decide on every subject by his own authority.

Our controversies must so be conducted, that we arrogate nothing to private opinion and private judgment, and yield nothing to sectarian partialities, but decline adducing the authority even of the most eminent divines and of the church itself, lest we should appear desirous of prescribing laws to the understandings and consciences of others.

The reasons of the opponent are to be treated with attention, not with contempt; they are to be allowed their proper influence, and all difficulties are to be examined. For as soon as we speak contemptuously of the arguments which another adduces in support of his sentiments, we seem either to despise his intellectual talents, or, at least, to be tinctured with prejudice, and not to allow his arguments a proper examination

Whence in Polemic Theology a dispute is to be commenced, as though we were not zealously attached to any form of religion, and were very remote from partialities to any sect; for frequently it is highly conducive to the conciliation of an opponent, that, where it is not improper, we should, for a short time, appear to hesitate in pronouncing our decision in favor of either sentiment.

Thus says Minutius Felix, Octavius, Sec. 5: Your understanding should be so well instructed, that you may hold the scale of an impartial judge, nor rashly incline to either side, lest your decision appear to originate in your own perceptions and feelings, rather than to be the result of our mutual disquisitions.[*]

From the preceding sections, arises this ELEVENTH rule:

In Polemic Theology we are to aim at the conviction of the errorist; and this conviction can be effected only by demonstration; hence, if we wish to convince another, we should not rage with violence, but reason with deliberation.

As we are to address another's conscience by a demonstration of truth, that he may perceive the correctness of our proposition, surely no external force should be employed.

To induce another to renounce his former doctrines and to imbibe others, is an effect which cannot be produced by compulsion, but must take place with the utmost liberty of mind. It is a gradual operation. For the understanding cannot be violently forced to believe those doctrines false, which it has hitherto regarded as true, nor those true which it has regarded as false.

Since no man has dominion over another's thoughts, we cannot induce another to adopt our sentiments except by arguments; if another should be forced by menaces and violence to profess our sentiments with his mouth, this would not be faith but mere hypocrisy.

No profession, except voluntary, can be acceptable to God; since in his word he uniformly requires voluntary worship: although therefore another may be compelled by violence, by

sword, by exile and other punishments, to profess our sentiments, yet he cannot be compelled to believe them.

If, as all will readily grant, the conviction and assent of the heart, not the external profession, constitute religion; then no one can be violently compelled to embrace another religion.

Were it granted that the professors of one religion had any right to persecute those who were inclined to another, perpetual war would pervade this whole earth; which is divided into numerous parties and sects. This would not be a contest to refute errors, but to exterminate errorists.

How far the civil magistrate may exercise his power in restraining heresies, and in what cases he may employ external force, we shall have occasion to show hereafter. Chap. 5. on Heresy.

As the system of errorists should be correctly understood, so he who is about to confute another, ought to exhibit the proposition according to the views of the opponent; hence we derive a TWELFTH rule:

No principle is to be ascribed to errorists, which they do not support; therefore we should abstain from deducing any pernicious and alarming consequences, which are not designed to convince their understandings, but to wound their feelings.

For since in this science we should aim principally to acquire the truth, and to convince others of it; hence on one side we should treat the opponent with candor, and, on the other, we should employ no means

[*] See the Cel. S. R. Praffius. Primit. Tab. Dissert. post de præjud. Theol. Sec. 9. p. 136.

which may obstruct his conviction, such as the excitation of his anger, and the perturbation of his feelings.

If we affix false conclusions to another's words, we do not exhibit, in his estimation, a mind ardently attached to the truth, but rather an ardent desire to offend and injure.

We use sincerity and uprightness with our opponent, when we express the meaning of his words according to their true import, without perverting them to an inferior sense, or adducing them in a mutilated and disconnected form.

But we act an ungenerous part, if, without carefully reading the whole of his books, we judge of the whole from a part; or if, insisting upon propriety of diction, we attend to words rather than their proper interpretation.

Some leave the foundation of error untouched, neglect the pursuit of truth, and derive such consequences from the opponent's doctrine as are designed to obscure his reputation;—consequences, which are either inconsistent with his doctrine, or which he strenuously denies to flow from it. Such persons are called 'Consequentists.*

These assume the first consequence as they please; from this they deduce others, and studiously annex to the opponent's words many dangerous and fatal results.

All consequences, however, are not to be rejected, if proper cautions are observed in deducing them. [Note omitted.]

These special cautions are to be observed:

* An appellation of reproach.

First; Consequences are never to be derived from words simply considered, but from their true import when considered in their proper connexion.

For a scrupulosity about one or two phrases is not sufficient to condemn a book; the whole series of reasoning must be taken into consideration. Every thing cannot be said at once in one place; and there are some principles, which, taken separately, may be contradicted, but, when viewed in their proper connexion, are strongly fortified by the combined influence of others.

Heresy relates to the ideas, not to the words; the sense, not the expression, constitutes the crime.

Secondly; The conclusion should flow, not through a winding channel, but directly, from the doctrines of the opponent; and with such clearness, that he will be obliged to reject his principles, or admit the conclusion.

Thirdly; A consequence which flows from the opponent's doctrines, should not however be imputed to him, since perhaps he did not discover or anticipate it.

Here a distinction should be made between those who are acute in judgment, who value themselves for the faculty of perceiving connexions and distinctions, and those who possess less philosophic penetration; between teachers and hearers; between the learned and unlearned. For to the latter consequences should not be hastily imputed, although they may clearly flow from their doctrines.

Fourthly; It is evident we should abstain from deducing

those conclusions which are suited only to injure our opponent, and expose him to ridicule and contempt.

To convince an errorist, we are to avoid every thing which may disturb his feelings and excite his anger; but these are the effects, when we employ such reasonings as render the opponent and his doctrine odious to others.

Such arguments are called *invidious*; hence a THIRTEENTH rule:

In Polemic Theology we must abstain from arguments derived from envy, since the mind is not thus conciliated but confirmed in error.

The argument is derived from envy:

First; When any one, desiring to ruin the reputation and fortune of another, whom he would refute, enviously and maliciously explains his sentiments.

Hence it happens, that some principles are esteemed erroneous, which are really true, and thus innocent men are often greatly injured.

Since this is directly opposed to the rules of Christian love, to Sacred Scripture, and to reason, and does not promote the truth, nor the honor of God, nor the conviction of man, it should be avoided with the utmost care.

Secondly; The argument is derived from envy, when the doctrines of the opponent are compared with the favorite sentiments of those men, who are already stigmatized and disgraced.

This happens, for example, when ancient and obsolete heresies are charged upon modern errorists, or upon the really innocent.

Thus by the Romish Pontiffs and priests, the Protestants are compared to the Simonians, Novatians, Sabellians, Manichæans, Donatists, Arians, Pelagians, Nestorians and others.[e]

Since it may rarely occur, that any modern will adopt the whole system of any ancient sect, it would be foolish to charge him with the whole heretical system, on account of any single sentiment, which he may hold in common with them.

However, if the design is upright and the reason sufficient, such a comparison may be made, both to exhibit the new tenets of any heresy, and to fortify others against it. [Note omitted.]

Here, also, a spirit of persecution should be entirely avoided.

Thirdly; The argument is derived from envy, when the importance of the question in debate is exaggerated, and those, who are not fundamentally erroneous, are proscribed as heretics, and anathemas are fulminated against them.

Fourthly; The same is true, when the opponent's doctrine is defamed by invidious epithets: thus the doctrine of the reformers respecting predestination is called by some *blasphemy*, *Stoic fatality*, *church security*, and other invidious names. When,

---

Bellamine, Vol. 2d Controvers. Book 4. de Ecclesia c. 9; and, not to mention others, the crime of Manichæism is very often charged upon the Reformed Churches.

Fifthly; The arguments of the opponent are concealed, or are not expressed in all their force. Or,

When, in an unimportant controversy, the favorable conclusions, which may be derived from the opponent's principle, are concealed, and the unfavorable conclusions only, with which it is incumbered, are exhibited.

Since the conviction of the errorist is to be sought, and since external force is not to be employed, this FOURTEENTH rule should be observed:

Not the persons of errorists, but their errors only, are to be attacked.

The end of Polemic Theology and humanity itself, oblige us to treat errorists with lenity, while we destroy their errors: wherefore Augustine thus writes (Book 4.) against the Donatists: Love men, while you destroy their errors; contend for truth without severity; pray for those whom you confute and convince.

The examples of Christ and his Apostles are not to be alleged; as when Christ, after much delay, employed severe expostulations with the Pharisees and Sadducees, calling them *a sinful and adulterous generation,* Matt. xiv, 4; *children of the devil,* John viii, 44; and John, calling them *generations of vipers,* Matt. iii, 7; and Paul, calling Elymas, the sorcerer, *a child of the devil,* Acts xiii, 10.

For as the examples of Christ and his apostles are presented to us for imitation, so there are some cases in which we cannot lawfully imitate them; because Christ was free from immoder-

ate zeal, possessed absolute and supreme authority, and was endued with omniscience and infallibility; and the apostles, in their official capacity, were also endued with infallibility.

It was therefore proper for Christ and his apostles to employ such means against their opponents, as no other men can properly employ.

Nor should the conduct of the ancients, who treated heretics with undue severity, be here alleged by way of excuse; their mode of conduct is not our supreme rule, nor should their warmth, when too great, be applauded. [Note omitted.]

Rule FIFTEENTH:

Nor should we employ a satyric style in writing. All raillery, severe reproach, and virulent banter, with which we evidently gall our opponent, are to be carefully shunned.

Since we aim to convince our opponent, his feelings should not be disturbed, nor his anger and moroseness excited; but the satyric mode of writing will never induce our opponent to change his sentiments, but will rather provoke his indignation and excite a spirit of revenge: wherefore, if we desire to convince another, all scoffs, and jests, and sneers, must be avoided.

This satyric style in composition arises from a malignant contempt of another, which disposes us to subject him to derision and contempt; but since this is improper in itself, and extremely exasperates the opponent, it is by no means to be indulged by the theological writer.

Nor can those, who prefer

truth and sound argument to this fallacious method, be easily induced to assent to such a style.

Neither Christ, nor his apostles employed this mode of refutation; for the gravity of the subject in debate, requires that it should be treated with seriousness and reverence.
[Note omitted.]
Nor does it accord with the principles of theology or moral Philosophy, that he should be disturbed and harassed, who deserves either pity or contempt.

Nor are the examples of the Fathers, who sometimes used this style, here to be imitated; since, being seduced by a spirit of persecution, they followed inclination rather than truth.

Although many Empectæ have hitherto existed; and will exist, who, in a scurrilous style, being deficient in argument, expose to derision the venerable mysteries of sacred religion; yet a refutation is not to be conducted, according to their example, by those who, being taught better things, have learned to treat sacred subjects in a sacred way.

But since men, especially young people, are often captivated with this satyric mode of attacking religion; it should be shown, how ridiculous are the arguments these scoffers adduce, and that nothing in the world is so true, so sacred, and so venerable, which may not be made a sport, and exposed to ridicule; it should be shown, that they advance nothing new, but that all the mysteries of religion, and the cross of Christ, have long since appeared foolish and contemptible to the Gentile nations, fascinated with their worldly wisdom. This the

apostle Paul asserts, who was well versed in profane literature, 1 Cor. i, 23.
[Note omitted.]
Rule SIXTEENTH:

Nor should we employ this perverse method of convincing and refuting infidels, which to the extreme injury of the Christian religion, rejects those properties and qualities which constitute its essence.

Verily I understand that mode of converting infidels, in which for their sake, all mysteries and whatever surpasses human intellect, or exceeds natural religion, are laid aside.
[Note omitted.]
Against this, we shall at present make only one remark: that, in this way, the path is beaten, and an occasion is offered, to theological Pyrrhonism or universal scepticism, by which every doctrine of the Christian religion is called in question, nay its truth perverted.
[Note omitted.]

For the Panoplist.

SINNERS, THOUGH BLIND AND DEAF, COMMANDED TO SEE AND HEAR.

Hear, ye deaf; and look, ye blind, that ye may see. Isa. xlii, 18.

PROBABLY some, who may have read my first paper on this passage, will say, "If sinners are blind and deaf, what propriety is there in addressing them, and what benefit can they derive from being addressed?"

To this inquiry I reply, that such feelings, on this point, are not new. A desperately wicked heart produced the same fruit, many centuries ago. It is to be expected, that blind and deaf sinners will feel and talk in this manner. But it is a matter of unspeakable joy, that every body does not feel thus; and that there are some, who are sensible of the wickedness of such thoughts, and who are solicitous for the restoration of the blind to sight. Nor do they hesitate, what means to apply for such a restoration Deaf and blind as sinners are, Christians and Ministers must imitate the example of the prophet, and call on them to see and hear. Nor can enlightened Christians be persuaded, that it will be of no avail The following are some of the reasons, which urge them to the duty, and animate them with hope in performing it

1. This blindness of sinners is of their own seeking. Say not, my fellow immortals, that you inherited this blindness from your parents; nor plead this in excuse. Were such a plea valid, our first parents must bear all the sins of their posterity. Admit that you inherited an evil disposition from your parents; they have not compelled you to exercise it: And you have been warned of its unreasonableness, and exhorted to exercise kind, virtuous, and holy affections. Whatever may be the result of metaphysical speculations on this point, it still remains a truth, that an *unholy temper is cherished* by sinners, and that sinful objects are loved and chosen. Now this love of sinful objects *constitutes* the spiritual blindness, of which all unrenewed men are the subjects. Hence, clearly, so long as sinners love

and choose sinful objec must be allowed, that blindness is of their own ing. You cannot, then, dou propriety of expostulating them upon their exceed wicked choice. How plai is the duty of all, who kno folly and guilt of sinners t monish them Nor can a b olent mind cease from en ors to dissuade them f choice so cruel to thems and so highly displeasing i sight of a holy God. ' their blindness of a ki which they bore no pe agency, the case would be rially changed. But sinn bear an immediate and tial agency in the continua their moral blindness; and case is, therefore, an u one. Instead of being cause of surprise, that (tians should address them it is a matter of still greate prise, that they do not ac them with increased earne and a more unyielding im nity. Because

2. Sinners are incurri mazing guilt, by persist this spiritual blindness. very thing, which const their blindness, is a crime deepest die. It consists love of sin, and in *enmity a, God.* Can there be a g evil than this? This e against God is known to l foundation of every evil, has existed among intel beings. Spiritual blindn this enmity persisted in.

I am aware, that there ar ny persons, who have been sensible of this enm themselves. This, how does not prove that it h existence there. Such persons have, probably, never contemplated the character of God with solemn attention, as it is exhibited in his word; or they have never noticed, carefully and impartially, the exercises of their own hearts. 'If God is a holy being, all love of a *sinful* object is *enmity* against him.

The evil of such a disposition and such a choice, is too great to admit of an adequate description. As spiritual blindness consists in the love of sin, it is easy to see, that all, who are under its influence, are constantly incurring guilt. As days revolve, their guilt in the sight of God accumulates. And can the benevolent mind behold all this and be silent? Can the faithful Minister behold the storm of divine wrath gather blackness over the heads of his hearers, and give them no warning? How cruel, as well as unbecoming his silence. In this view, his duty is both plain and imperious. He will, and he must, give them solemn warning to flee from the wrath to come. And in reply to all their cavils he will utter the prayer of the dying but conquering Redeemer. *Father, forgive them; for they know not what they do.*

3. All, or nearly all, who have yet been brought to their spiritual sight and hearing, have been restored by these means. In all periods of the world, a greater or less number have been cured of these spiritual maladies. Nor do I recollect a single instance of restoration, in which the subject has not been addressed in the language of the prophet. *Hear, ye deaf; and look ye blind, that ye may see.* This is the method, which it hath pleased God to appoint: and he will always *bless* the means of *his* appointment, and *none but these.*

It is indeed true, that in itself considered, it does no good to call upon sinners to see and hear. There is no efficacy in the call, or in the person who gives it. And it is equally true that, in itself considered, it would do no good for Naaman to wash seven times in Jordan; for Moses to smite the waters of the red sea with his rod; or for Christ to make clay to anoint the eyes of the blind man. In themselves considered, there was no efficacy in the waters of Jordan, or in the rod of Moses, or in the clay used by the Savior. But in all these cases the method pursued was the one *appointed*, and the end was secured. It betrays both ignorance and folly to say, the end might as well have been effected in another manner. In all instances, when any end is to be accomplished, in the divine purposes, the means necessary to effect it are placed in a train; and *none* of them can be omitted without a failure in the accomplishment of the end. Hence when sinners are to be renewed in heart, and restored to sight and health they must be addressed, warned, exhorted, invited, and urged.

4. Ministers were appointed and commissioned for this express purpose. The example of Ezekiel is a full illustration of this truth: *Son of man, I have set thee as a watchman unto the house of Israel; therefore, thou shalt hear the word at my mouth and warn them from me.* His vision of dry bones presents us with the whole truth on this

point. The vision is familiar. He was commanded to prophesy, that is to preach, to a valley of dry bones. What a strange command. What a gloomy and hopeless task. How easily might he have pleaded an excuse. But he cheerfully obeyed. With confidence in God, and joy in the means of *his* appointing, he preached to dry bones the solemn truths, which he was commanded to declare. Nor did he labor in vain. The Spirit of the Lord crowned his labors with success. Who can any longer doubt, that the means which God appoints will, invariably, prove successful.

God now commands his Ministers to preach the Gospel to blind, deaf, and dead sinners: *Hear ye the word of the Lord.* Let them obey, and let them be encouraged in the duty. They need not doubt of success. For this they are not answerable. Their great concern should be, to discharge faithfully their duty; never yielding to the obstinacy, or reproach of sinners; never doubting the power and mercy of God, or the immutability of his promise. *Lo, I am with you always to the end of the world.*

A full discussion of this point comes not within the design and limits of this short essay. It is enough for my present purpose, if I can fasten the attention of sinners upon the *fact*, that the preaching of the word is the *appointed* method, for the restoration of fallen man from a state of ruin, to a state of salvation. This appointment was made with a perfect knowledge of the deplorable state of man. When God commands his Ministers to call upon sinners, he knows that they are

deaf and blind. And si has represented, in his that this is an indispe mean, we must forever d of the salvation of souls other way. Then why w: ners persist in the profan il, so common in the mo men? Why will they eternal life, because it is tainable in the precise m which their own perverte son would dictate. Hav forgotten the universal d "A Jewish writer intr Noah, from the ark, expo ing with those who were p ing, because excluded. pleaded that they had us rious means of securing selves, in case the deluge come, though they had de his invitation to betake selves to the ark: but he ces all their pleas at on saying, that they had refu avail themselves of God *pointed* way of salvation: a ery other method must b vailing." Let their ex warn and deter others. sinners prize the precious pel; use all the instituted of instruction; believe, saved. *How shall ye esc ye neglect so great salvatio*

AL

EXAMINATION OF AN OI
STATED BY O. E.

To the Editor of the Pan

Sir,

YOUR correspondent, C seems to be of opinion, that to possess religion implie existence of religion in the He thinks "it implies a c diction to say, that we ch thing which we have natural power now to have, and yet do not have it."* I am not satisfied, that his reasoning is conclusive, or his opinion correct. I believe his argument contradicts the experience of both saints and sinners.

It contradicts the experience of saints. It very obviously implies, that they have, at all times, as much religion as they desire. But was this the case with the man, who cried out, and said with tears; *Lord, I believe; help thou mine unbelief?* Was this the case with the disciples, when they said unto Jesus; *Lord, increase our faith?* Was this the case with Paul, when he said; *O wretched man that I am; who shall deliver me from the body of this death?* And where is the Christian who will presume to indulge a hope, that he loves God as much as he ought, or as much as he desires? If any should say that they are perfect, would it not prove them perverse?

The argument of O. E. appears no less contrary to the experience of sinners. The evidence appears very strong and abundant, that sinners in general, who are rationally convinced, that the Bible is true, are desirous to escape hell—to gain admittance into heaven—to possess that holiness without which no man shall see the Lord. And their desire of holiness is strong in proportion to their sense of danger. If sinners do not desire holiness, why do they manifest such solicitude and make such exertions for conviction and conversion, in times of awakening? If sinners do not desire

to be converted, why do they often feel such envy and indignation, when others are taken and they are left? If they do not desire conversion, why do they desire others to pray, that they may not be left to deceive themselves and fail of the grace of God?

Christians, in general, can remember the time, when they were without faith and without God in the world. And cannot such remember, also, that, while they were in that wretched condition, they desired to be converted, that their sins might be blotted out, and their title to heaven made sure?

If I may be allowed, in this case, to adduce my own experience, I can say, with the utmost confidence, that I do desire to be conformed to the blessed image of Christ; though I am by no means confident that I am a Christian. And I am likewise very confident, that, if I have any conformity to God, I desire more. I have the evidence within myself, that the argument of O. E. must be fallacious.

Though sinners have no holy desires; though every imagination of the thoughts of their hearts is evil, and only evil, continually; though they do not desire holiness for what it is in itself, nor because it is reasonable and fit, nor because they are under obligations to love God; yet no doubt, many of them do desire holiness as sincerely and as ardently as they desire to escape damnation. Though they have no definite and distinct ideas of the nature of holiness, yet, be it what it may, they desire to possess it, to shield their souls from the wrath of an angry God.

The views of O. E. upon the infinitely important distinction between natural and moral inability, are probably not very erroneous. In the present case, however, he seems to have drawn a conclusion that is contrary to facts; and probably not the least injurious of errors. Tell a sinner, that the impenitent have no kind of desire for religion; and he will either believe you or not. In either case, the consequence may prove ruinous. If he believes you, he will be likely to conclude, with great assurance, that he is a Christian; and his false hope may prove his destruction. If he does not believe you, he will be in great danger of disbelieving and disregarding the great evangelical truths, which you may endeavor to urge upon his conscience; and thus die in sin and stupidity.

E. O.

For the Panoplist.

INQUIRY RESPECTING THE WORD ATONEMENT.

Mr. Editor,

I HAVE been led to believe, not only that the Scriptures exhibit one uniform, entire, and consistent scheme of doctrine; but that their several parts are useful to elucidate and explain each other. The Old Testament harmonizes with the New, and when both are well understood, the one will, I trust, throw light upon the other. In examining the subject of the atonement, (and thoroughly to understand this doctrine is worthy of more labor, than is commonly bestowed upon it,) I have remarked, that various terms are used as ex-

pressing, in appearance, cisely the same thing; bu are generally interpreted k positors of Scripture, as i ing very different thing the New Testament, *aton* and *reconciliation* are in ently rendered from the original Greek word, as in chap. v. In the Old Testa the same English words a ed in application to the subject, as in Levit. chap. v xvi. Now as I am, unha not versed in the Hebrew guage, my inquiries are so ed, that I cannot satisfy n upon this point; and as miscellany is open to whose biblical learning m equal to the task, my requ that some one will undertal solve the question; Wheth *atone* and *to reconcile* are same original import, as words are used in defining itical rites and institution whether they may be consi as synonymous with the G word, in the New Testa once translated *atonement* *reconciliation* in most, if all, other instances.

For the Panop

PRAISE AND BLAME.

Mr. Editor,

I AM pleased with seeing portant subjects introduce to your magazine, both o count of the light that is di ed, and the stimulus that is en to inquiry. Among o that of *"praise and blame"* been touched upon,* thou has not undergone that mi

* See Pan. vol. ix, p. 311,

and elaborate discussion, which would have been gratifying to at least *one* of your constant readers. I deem it material, not only to understand in what praise and blame consist, but to be able judiciously and correctly to proportion them among the several actions, to which they apply. The question has been stated; "Are moral agents as worthy of praise for exercising holy affections, as they are of blame for exercising sinful ones? In the very brief solution that was given, in the piece above alluded to, it seems to be taken for granted, as it undoubtedly ought to be, that in holy exercises, such as all true Christians are the subjects of, there is as *real* a desert of praise, as there is of blame in the exercises of the wicked. But a negative answer is given to the question, upon the principle, that when moral agents are holy, they are just what they are under obligations to be; but in sinners there is a direct violation of their obligations.

Perhaps the writer of the ensuing remarks is singular, in his ideas upon this subject; but he is willing and desirous to be brought to the test of Scripture and sound reason, that he may be convinced of all the error, with which he may be chargeable. He frankly declares, that he does not perceive strength and conclusiveness in the reason that has been given for the opinion, that the holiness of creatures is not as praise-worthy, as their sin is blamable. The argument, which has been supposed to prove this proposition, is as follows; "Were it possible that we could be under no previous obligation to practise holiness, and avoid sin, we might deserve as much praise for being holy, as blame for being sinful. But as we are under the strongest obligations to be holy, the question should receive a negative answer." The author of this reasoning seems not to be aware, that to suppose *a moral being under no obligation to practise holiness and avoid sin*, is a perfect solecism; for he does not appear to deny, or to doubt, the possiblity of the existence of such a thing.

Here a gross mistake seems to have been committed. Instead, therefore, of inferring, as he does, that *if we were under no previous obligations to practise holiness and avoid sin, we might deserve as much praise for being holy as blame for being sinful*, I should rather conclude, from our being in such a state of indifference towards good and evil, that *we could not be the subjects of any moral desert whatever*. I know not what ambiguity there may be in the term *obligation;* but if it will apply to all moral beings of whatever grade, then to be free from obligation is to be incapable of either holiness or sin. In an extensive signification of the term, I take it there is no impropriety in saying, that God *is under obligation* to be holy. Would any one hesitate to affirm that He *ought* to do right, rather than to do wrong? But this does not imply, that there is any other being, of superior rank and authority, to whom he is accountable. Should it be said, that the circumstance of being under a superior power belongs to every case, where obligation exists; upon such a supposition it is evident, that obligation can apply only to creatures. But would it be any shock to common sense, or to piety, to say, that God is as much bound, or obligated, to do right as creatures? I think it would not; although it be true, that the obligation depends, in no measure, on his standing related to some higher power. The very nature of right and wrong, I apprehend, implies moral obligation; and hence the conclusion appears to me infallible, that to be *under no obligation to practise holiness, and avoid sin,* would be the same, as to be incapable of moral merit or demerit, of praise or blame. I know of nothing to show, why doing *more than we ought,* or than we are obligated to do, would not be as real a fault, as to do *less.* Every instance of true virtue is the fulfilment of some obligation. The same *general* reason may be given, why we should be employed in almsgiving, according to the means we possess, as that we should abide by our own voluntary contracts, and pay what we call our honest debts. The example, therefore, that has been taken to illustrate and evince the doctrine, that so much praise does not attach to our good exercises, as blame does to our bad ones, is not in point. The question has been put; "Suppose A. owes B. a hundred dollars; in paying that sum A. does right. But does he deserve as much commendation for this act, as he would deserve blame for refusing to pay it? and not only refusing to pay it, but robbing B. of a hundred dollars besides?"

Setting aside the supposed robbery, I would ask, why paying a debt of a hundred dollars is not as commendable, as a refusal to pay it is reprehensible. If we estimate the rectitude, on the one hand, and the wrong, on the other, by the requirements of the divine law, they will be equal; for it is the same command, which determines the one act to be virtuous, and the contrary to be vicious. If we compute by the effects produced, is it not as greatly to a man's advantage to receive a payment of a hundred dollars, as it is to his disadvantage not to receive it? Then again, let an act of robbery be set over against an act of charity, or bounty; and is it not as great a good, for a person to be unexpectedly put in possession of a gratuity of a hundred dollars, as for one to be deprived of the same sum, contrary to his will, provided the one be no poorer after his loss, than the other was before his gain? As to the evils attendant on robberies, aside from the loss of property, they are not to be brought into the account, but are matters of separate consideration. No one will deny, that giving is as really a virtue, enjoined in the law of God, as robbery is a crime forbidden. And why does not a liberal person deserve as much praise from a man, who has been made better by him, to the amount of a hundred dollars, as he does blame from another, who has been made worse by him to the amount of an equal sum? And why, again, is not Gabriel to be as much commended and praised for his unshaken fidelity to God, as Satan is to be blamed for his apostasy and rebellion? There is no evading the position, that holiness deserves praise to as great a degree, as sin deserves blame, only by adopting the principle, that has been assumed, not by one only, but by many, viz. that in order to deserve praise one must go beyond what he is under strict obligations to do. But if this principle be correct, is it enough to say, that the holiness of men is not worthy of *so much* praise, as their sin is of blame? Ought it not rather to be affirmed, that it deserves none at all? For if a man's owing his all to God, does not stand in the way of his receiving *some* praise, when he performs real acts of duty, by what rule shall we determine the exact point, at which this praise ought to stand? or *how much less* his praise should be than the blame of persons of an opposite character. The principle in question, if it does not utterly annihilate praiseworthiness, as connected with upright conduct, certainly goes to diminish it; else it would not be said, that the praise due to men, on account of their holy exercises, is less than the blame incurred by wickedness, because men are under obligations to do right, or to be holy. It follows, therefore, by inevitable and fair consequence, that in proportion as our obligations to holiness are strengthened, our praiseworthiness for the duties we actually and faithfully perform is lessened. If it be true then, that persons may be placed in circumstances to enhance their obligation to love God and do his will, the tendency of those circumstances will be to bereave them of a part of the praise, or reward, of their piety, to which they would have otherwise been

entitled. If, then, religious obligation increases with the increase of divine light, holiness must, in the same proportion, degenerate and sink in worth, or in its desert of praise; so that it will become exceedingly problematical, whether we have not labored under a great mistake in wishing, *that many might run to and fro, and that knowledge might be increased.* In opposition to a theory, leading to such conclusions, I have rather embraced the opinion, that holiness will, in every sense, bear to be weighed against sin; and that they, who keep God's commandments, may be certain of a reward as great, as will be the punishment of those who break them. The beauty of holiness I believe to be as great in one, who is purified by grace, as is the deformity of sin in the reprobate and impenitent.

If, Mr. Editor, I have conceived amiss, upon so weighty a subject, or have laid myself open to consequences, incompatible with the general tenor of Scripture doctrine, you may enlighten and confirm others, while you are kindly rectifying my misapprehensions and mistakes.

FRANK.

For the Panoplist.

GENERAL BIBLE SOCIETY,

THE subject of promoting religious truth has been so often brought to the public view, and its importance is at this time so generally acknowledged, that a further discussion of it would here be comparatively useless. At a period, when the Christian community is daily urged to the diffusion of sacred knowledge by innumerable tracts, sermons, and addresses, it may be more profitable to inquire how this great object may be most effectually accomplished. There is but little advantage in persuading men that the Gospel of Christ is designed to promote the happiness of the world, while they remain ignorant or careless of proper methods to extend its blessings. It may even be injurious to leave this matter on a general conviction of its utility; for correct opinions have such an effect of complacency upon the mind, that the satisfaction, which results from a knowledge of duty, frequently causes us to forget the evil of neglecting it.

We believe that the time is approaching when *the knowledge of the Lord shall fill the earth;* and we believe, with equal reason, that those societies and nations, which now call upon his name, will be employed to proclaim it before the heathen. We rejoice to say, that multitudes, in all Christian countries, have wisely taken heed to this sure word of prophecy. It is to be mentioned with gratitude that Societies have been formed for the propagation of the Gospel; that missionaries have been sent; that the Bible has been translated into various languages, and that converts to the Christian faith have been multiplied. But these things have been effected by limited and partial exertions, and the word of life is still confined to a small portion of the world. While the duty of all Christian nations to unite in this cause of God, is felt and acknowledged, few national efforts have been made. Our own country, so dis-

tinguished through all the periods of its history for religious privileges, has, till lately, seemed to forget, that millions, in other lands, were *perishing for lack of vision;* and what is still more remarkable, that its own poor are still destitute of the Scriptures. Even now it has done but little, in comparison of duty; and there is reason to fear that but little will be done, till new, and more extensive plans of operation shall be devised and pursued.

These considerations have convinced me of the importance of the measure, which has recently been proposed in a number of the Panoplist; that of forming a Bible Society of the United States. It appears to be an object which is peculiarly worthy of general attention, and which the friends of religion should labor steadily to accomplish. It promises great and extensive usefulness, not only as a mean of giving to the heathen a knowledge of the truth; but also of arresting the progress of infidelity among ourselves; of alleviating the various evils which we suffer; of saving us from the destruction of those, who shall be found among the enemies of God and of the Lamb.

But it may be proper to examine more particularly the grounds on which the utility of this measure rests; the extent of the evil it is designed to remove; and the deficiency of other remedies which have been applied. In doing this, it will appear that multitudes at home and abroad, who are dependent upon our charity, are destitute of the Bible; and that those societies, which have been formed among

still incompetent to their
It is hoped that the no-
these facts will be attend-
h profit; and that those,
ave heretofore believed
ough might be done by
and desultory exertions,
ow be led to inquire,
r a time has not arrived,
his nation is called upon
age, as one man, in the
n of sacred truth.
are first led to consider
te of our own country in
to this subject; and if we
o go no further, it is
t that sufficient reason
be found to vindicate the
al of a General Bible So-
Although the question is
sked, where is a family in
ored land that is destitute
Scriptures? it appears
he estimates which have
made even in New Eng-
hat they are wanting to
than a sixth part of the
ion. In certain districts,
larly in New Hampshire,
Island, Vermont, and the
e of Maine, the propor-
still greater. Hundreds
lies live from year to year
this guide to heaven; and
r of the public schools re-
instruction is entirely
ed, because parents are
or unwilling to afford Bi-
their children. Thus the
ld customs of our fathers
wing obsolete. Their
xample is forgotten; their
structions are ridiculed;
e precious relics of that
ok, which they purchased
much labor and suffer-
scattered by the careless
usness of their profane
ants. If we add to this
the western and south-

ern sections of the country, the
evil becomes still more alarming. There are fewer religious
institutions, fewer ministers of
the Gospel, fewer copies of the
Bible than among ourselves. In
some of the territories annexed
to the United States, religious
instruction is a thing unknown;
and very few, certainly not one
third of the inhabitants, are possessed of the Scriptures.

These facts alone give sufficient evidence that the Societies,
which have been formed, are inadequate to the supply even of
our own wants. Not only remote parts of the country, but
also the very districts in which
these institutions are founded,
have been found more or less
destitute of the Bible. Their
exertions, though so far successful as to give encouragement for
more comprehensive schemes of
benevolence, have not been proportionate to the evil, which is
to be removed. The moral state
of society has become more and
more corrupt; and, in many instances, intemperance, neglect
of the Sabbath, profaneness, and
other kindred sins, have marked
whole communities with wretchedness and infamy. Nor can it
be reasonably expected, that these
minor associations will greatly
extend their influence. They
are not constituted for great
efforts, and are most useful in a
narrow sphere. They may be
fitly compared to the grammar
schools established in the different districts of a state or country, which regulate the confined
departments of elementary instruction, but have no direct influence beyond their appropriate
limits. Each district looks to its
own seminary for its quantum of

improvement; but for a common source of useful knowledge, all eyes are upon the "Alma Mater."

If we regard then merely the population of the states, and the territories on this side the Mississippi, the importance of the proposed establishment is apparent. We are not, however, to stop here. The claims of the French Catholics in Louisiana, and the Missouri Territory, have recently been exhibited. Of these there are 50,000, who have not the Bible, and who are represented as exceedingly desirous to obtain the means of religious instruction. Their Priests are disposed to favor any designs for diffusing among them the Scriptures, and nothing but an exertion of Protestant benevolence is wanting to carry them into effect. We have also been directed to the inhabitants of New Spain, whose wants, and applications for relief, will, probably, soon solicit our attention. Here an extensive field is open for the circulation of the Scriptures, and we should never give occasion for reproach, in leaving it to be occupied by more remote, yet more zealous friends to the cause of the Redeemer. Our Bibles should even find their way across the Isthmus, and cause the streams of peace and mercy to flow throughout the southern portion of our continent. Christians of the nineteenth century should convince the descendants of those, who were butchered, for the love of God, by Pizarro, by Cortes, and their cruel followers, that the God we serve is not, in truth, silver and gold. But who is sufficient for these things? what can be expected from those So-

cieties, which are, as yet, to relieve the more imm objects of their charity?

Is there need to seek reasons for the measure has been proposed? I wo fer to the moral history Eastern world. I woulc that land of slavery, whi so long been filled with vi and woe to feed the ava more enlightened natio would rehearse too the choly account of an emp 330,000,000, from who Scriptures have been with the seal of death. I ask if we have already fol the tears, we so lately she the mournful story of Hin perstition and misery? if ing shrieks of the widov male, sinking amid the k fires of the funeral pile never reached our ears? cry of woe, wafted on the breeze, has never echoed shores the horrid name c gernaut? I might recap the accounts which are brought from heathen cou and tell of more than 500,C of souls, that know noth the truth as it is in Jes might profit by the pio searches which have been from time to time, and mention of whole natior tribes of men, as good by as ourselves, who still war the wilderness without from heaven. But these are already known. I wi ask, to what extent has our try obeyed the command blessed Savior, which is e binding upon Christian and individuals, to make the blessings of the Go every creature? We are i ed by facts, we are reproved by conscience, we are reproved by the word of God for having done but little; and, if the considerations, which have been urged, have any weight, it may be affirmed, that but little can be done, in comparison of our duty, till a new, a general, and united effort shall be made. I am aware, that on this subject there is need of prudence and moderation. I know that the day of small things is not to be despised; and that a sanguine, adventurous spirit, which waits not for calculation, and hardly stops at the limits of possibility, will at length find disappointment and defeat. But, is it not a sober truth that the world is to be evangelized; that the Bible is to be translated into every language, and distributed among every people under heaven? Is it not a sober truth that we are to be made instruments in this work; that we must impart of our substance to carry on these great designs of Providence? When we see, moreover, how much yet remains to be done; when we reflect that millions are suffering a famine of the Word, and that all means, hitherto adopted, are incompetent to their relief; does it not seem also to be a sober truth, that a national effort, in forming a Bible Society of the United States, has become, not only expedient, but an imperious duty?

It may be proper to mention more distinctly some of the peculiar advantages of such an Institution.—It will unite the resources and influence of all denominations, and thus be enabled to extend the blessings of the Gospel to every part of our own land, and to every class of its inhabitants. It will make the influence of truth commensurate with that of ignorance and error. It will afford encouragement and aid to the local establishments which are already formed; will be able to found new ones as auxiliaries, and will effectually remove the objections that are made against forming societies in the new settlements, that there is no parent institution, to which information may be communicated, or from which assistance may be obtained. It will save much expense in the publication of the Scriptures. It will prevent the inconveniences of that complicated system of management, which necessarily attends any co-operation of various distinct societies. Being single and unconfined in its movements, it will be able to meet any particular exigencies with a promptness and facility, otherwise impossible. Besides, to use the language of a respected friend, "there is a grandeur attending a National Association, which will win many, and, it may be supposed, induce more to contribute their property to the benevolent purpose, than are now attracted by the minor institutions."*

* I cannot forbear to make known the sentiments which have been expressed on this subject by a distinguished friend of literature and religion, to whose pious example and benevolent exertions, our eastern seminaries and churches are much indebted. "For myself, I earnestly hope the design will meet encouragement. "Their circumscribed influence;" [the different local Societies] "the paucity of members of which they consist, and the comparatively. inadequate funds they possess must form strong arguments against leaving them the whole ground of such labor. There is a grandeur attending a National Association, which will win many, and, it may be supposed, induce more to

The Institution proposed will afford much important assistance to our Missionary Societies. It is by no means desirable that the object of these Societies should be delayed; and this would be the case, if they were occupied in any distinct employments. The concerns of translating and publishing the Scriptures would necessarily lessen the number of their Missionaries, would increase their labor and responsibility, would perplex all their operations. They are the proper agents to ascertain the circumstances of the destitute, and receive the Bible for distribution. In this sense, our Board of Commissioners call themselves a "Foreign Bible Society." But it is obvious, that to procure translators, to establish presses, and direct the business of publication, would far exceed their ability and design.* All this, however, would

contribute their property to the benevolent purpose, than are now attracted by the minor institutions. Yet these, I think, would by no means be neglected. On the contrary, a general attention would be excited, that, in the end, might embrace both the branches and their stock at once."

* Our correspondent is under some misapprehension, as to the design of the American Board of Commissioners for Foreign Missions. It has ever been the design of that Board to superintend translations of the Scriptures, as soon as this can be done with a rational prospect of success. Till that period shall arrive, the Board will patronize such translations as promise to be of the most immediate utility.

We do not think it correct to say, that missionaries and translators should be confined to their distinct employments. The first translators of the Scriptures into any new language, we apprehend, should be missionaries; and should have learned the language by frequent intercourse with the people. Indeed, we do not see how any others beside missionaries can, with hopeful prospects, translate the Scriptures into

be conducted by the pro establishment with compar ly little trouble or emba ment. The work of Mi would thereby be not onl uninterrupted, but would a relieved from many bu which now oppress it, a continually reinforced with means, which are indispe to its success. "The divi labor," says the Christia server,* "has never app applicable to any departm human exertion, more th missionary efforts. The i sibility of reserving a suff portion of a general fund fo special, and comparativel mote purpose; the extensi quiries necessary for proc

languages, which have not been pre written; and a very large part human race speak such languages. ly all the translations of the Scri which have lately engaged the atte mankind, have been made by m ries. It is true, that as translato become more and more employed work of translation, they have nee become less employed as missi but they were fitted by the one e ment for the other. The natural has been pursued in Bengal The lators obtained an indispensable their qualifications while they a missionaries only; they have sin barked deeply in the work of tran they have obtained very respectabl for the work by their own exertio the exertions of their friends; an as an immeasurable field opens them, the British and Foreign Bi ciety comes forward to their ass with the most exalted beneficen catholicism.

But this statement does not wea argument of our correspondent, a advantages of a National Bible So this country. Such an institution be excellently calculated to patron publication of the Scriptures in guages. It would merit the heart port of all the friends of all the oth gious and charitable institutions am

* Review of Prof. Dealtry's Ser propagating Christianity.

persons willing and fit to go upon this most important of all embassies; the cares and embarrassments incident to a multiplicity of foreign transactions;—all point out here a natural line of division for our common labors in the Christian cause."

It would be a pleasing employment to enumerate other advantages of this establishment. But these will doubtless suggest themselves to the minds of all, who have an interest in the leading object of my remarks. I would not, however, neglect to make mention of the noble example which is set before us in the "British and Foreign Bible Society," whose success may remove every doubt of the utility of a similar establishment in this country. The reports of that Society are the most interesting papers brought before the Christian public; and the blessings which have come upon it, from thousands ready to perish, supply the most powerful motives of zeal and activity to the friends of Zion. It is an institution, which may be justly called one of the strongest bulwarks of the Religion we profess; which the Church of Christ may acknowledge as the firmest pillar of her glory, the noblest engine of her power. Millions of grateful hearts, in every quarter of the globe, daily unite in praise to Him, who has given to "the kind strangers in England" a disposition to spread through every nation "the Word that saves men's souls."

With regard to the manner, in which a General Society may be formed, perhaps nothing can be as yet determined. Nor is it necessary that any single plan should be immediately proposed. When the subject shall have been fairly considered, and its importance generally understood, we may believe that a better way of procedure will be discovered by the Providence of God than might now be devised. Indeed, while the views and purposes of different, remote portions of the community are unknown, it is impossible to fix upon any particular method that would commend itself to all. Let us, then, wait direction from Him, "who turneth the hearts of men." Let us, who rejoice in the future glory of the Church, renew our prayers, that "He, who is the Head, even Christ," may employ this people in the great work of *Universal reformation.* Let us quicken our exertions that we may realize the blessings we hope from a National Institution, which may unite us all in promoting the glory of that kingdom, which is boundless and everlasting. Who of us will not joy to contribute to its formation, and to pray for its success? Who of us will not love to contemplate the happiness it may dispense to millions of our degraded, miserable race? Who of us will not delight to follow the streams of salvation it may send forth to "the dark places of the earth," and to behold them mingling with the waters of that "River of God," which has already begun to flow through the nations with mercy, truth, and righteousness upon its peaceful bosom?   .N*.

For the Panoplist.

ON PREJUDICE.

NOTHING is more common, than for men of different and opposite sentiments, to accuse each other of prejudice. "It is prejudice," says the infidel, "which induces such multitudes to believe the Bible to be a revelation from God." "It is the blinding influence of prejudice, produced by education, and an established habit of thinking," exclaims the Socinian, "which leads so many to profess their belief in the doctrine of the proper Deity of Christ, and a trinity of persons in the Godhead." "It is prejudice," says another, whose conduct is thought to be suspicious, and whose religion is called in question, "which causes many good people to give an unfavorable representation of my character, and to withhold from me their charity." This practice of charging others with prejudice is a short method of answering their arguments, and an expedient easily adopted for the purpose of casting odium upon their opinions. It is far easier, than for a man to defend his own positions, and confute those of his opponent; and less arduous, in many cases, than, by an appeal to facts, to vindicate his character from the imputations brought against it.

That a person may be able to determine, whether or not prejudice may justly be attributed to him, it is important that he should examine its nature, its causes, and its effects, and faithfully scrutinize his heart to detect it. Every lover of truth will deplore any wrong bias given to his judgment, and will desire ever to be in such a state of mind as that he may thoroughly investigate, and candidly weigh, all the evidence which he can obtain for settling his opinions and directing his conduct.

Prejudice has its seat in the depravity of the human heart. In this corrupt fountain are found selfishness, pride, envy, hatred, and a multitude of other malignant passions. Whenever the mind is under the controlling influence of either of these passions, it is prejudiced. A man in this state will neither attend to nor admit the force of evidence, which, if duly estimated, would persuade him to desist from the object, which he is now pursuing; because he apprehends the accomplishment of *this object* will greatly promote his own interest and honor. He is determined, that the object *shall not* be relinquished. The most convincing proof, that it *ought* to be abandoned, will then pass by him like the wind, and the understanding will be constrained to bow implicitly to the will.

He has adopted an opinion, for instance, to which he is extremely attached because it is his *own*, or because he thinks it highly honorable to him. His passions are enlisted to defend and maintain it. Consequently, there is no evidence or argument to which he is at all inclined to listen, which does not corroborate his preconceived opinion. The reason of this is, that he is too much interested, or too proud, to acknowledge that he is in an error.

He has found his own interest and reputation concerned, per-

ecommending or de-
the character of a-
le will, then, in the
ed manner repel ev-
entation, which does
rt with his previous
views, however seri-
be in its nature, and
r authority it may be

e disinclines the mind
s fully, and to appre-
', the evidence which
inst any favorite con-
Wherever it operates,
ent is bribed by pas-
s pure mind of an an-
all the objects of its
as they are, and esti-
a accordingly. But a
r the influence of pre-
srepresents the sub-
s attention. He mag-
ry circumstance and
which falls in with his
esires, while every
contrary description
to reduce to the low-
e account. The fear
harged with inconsis-
f being constrained to
hen differing from him
stes and opinions, are
nmendable for their
iscernment, and cor-
than himself, deter-
not to renounce his
h, however erroneous,
alter his conduct, how-
able. The genuine
i of his feelings is, "I
ight so hitherto, and
so still."
e truly candid man,
ad is open to' convic-
ad of justifying him-
ingenuously acknowl-
error, whenever evi-
presented, which, if
a the balance of truth,

preponderates against an article
of his belief, or reproves any
part of his character. Yet he is
not to be accused of prejudice
for refusing to renounce an opinion, or discard a doctrine, upon
the exhibition of proof which
seems to militate against it, unless such proof does in fact outweigh the evidence upon which
he had before grounded his conclusions.

The subject is too extensive
to be fully treated in the present
paper. I would therefore conclude by observing, that an honest, benevolent and pious heart
is the only effectual remedy for
prejudice. With such hearts
let us come to the light of divine
truth, that we may see whether
or not *our deeds are wrought in
God.*   **D.**

For the Panoplist.

ON ADMONITION.

Mr. Editor,

In reading the piece "On the duty of
admonition," in the Panoplist for Nov.
last, page 450, I was very forcibly reminded of a transaction, which took place about
three years ago, and which I then penned
down under the head of "Good effects of
seasonable admonition." As the narrative
is calculated to impress the remarks of the
writer of that piece more deeply on the
mind, and may possibly influence some of
the readers of your excellent work to administer reproof and advice to the vicious
and profane, I shall submit to your disposal
what I then wrote, assuring you it is a
faithful statement of facts.   **P.**

BEING called to transact some
business upon a wharf in one of
our large towns, I was grieved
to hear some workmen, at a little distance, talking with much
anger, and uttering most dreadful oaths and imprecations. Directing my attention to the place,

I noticed a person who appeared to be superintending the business, in which the men were employed, and hoped he would put a stop to their shocking profanity. Being disappointed, I went to him and requested that he would interpose his authority, and check the profane language of his workmen. He made no reply; but suddenly turned to them, *and swore, if they did not desist, they should leave the wharf.* I immediately addressed one of the men, and told him, in as solemn a manner as I could, the awful consequence of such conduct, if unrepented of. He endeavored to justify himself, by alleging that he had been abused by one of his fellow-laborers. I replied, that he could not be justified in using such language, whatever might be the provocation, and returned to my own business.

They ceased their angry and profane talk for a time; but from their mutterings and malicious looks at each other, I foresaw a quarrel would ensue; and soon heard them talking again in a loud and passionate manner. I instantly hastened to the spot, just in season to step between two, who were upon the point of coming to blows. They were uttering the most tremendous oaths. Several persons were standing by, silently witnessing their behavior. I expressed my astonishment, and abhorrence of their conduct; and reminded them of the solemn account they must one day give of their worse than idle words. I entreated them to desist, and seriously reflect on what they were doing.

The youngest of the t
one I had previously add
turned and walked off.
other, a man more th
years of age, attempted
cuse his conduct, by de
he had been abused and
ed by the other. No
said I, can justify or pallia
a proceeding. Would ye
to offer this plea at the
future retribution? This
had the effect to calm h
sions; and he replied in
erate tone, *I do not kno*
it is right. With a fi
unusual to me I rejoine
know it is wrong. We
a better example than th
one of your years. You
to remember, that you m
only give an account o
conduct in the day of jud
but answer for all the per
effects *your example* ma
upon others.

Having delivered this r
I left the man to his own
tions; and had not procee
before the other met me i
and said, *he was heartily*
that he had hurt my feelin
hoped I would forgive
assured him that I felt
will towards him; that
had said and done was de
for his good; and d
him to consider, that th
of that day, and all the sin
life, had been committed
God; that to him he mus
confession of his guilt; a
without sincere repentan
reformation, he would c
feel the weight of God'
nal wrath. *O!* said he, th
still flowing from his
know I have sinned; I am
sinner; I hope I shall nev

foolish and wicked again. If I had not been stopped, perhaps I should have killed that man, or he me; and then what would have become of my poor soul! That, said I, is a solemn consideration Would not God have done justly to have cast you down to the regions of darkness and despair? Yes, replied he, he would, for I am a great sinner. I assured him it gave me much satisfaction to find he was sorry for his conduct; but added, there was reason to fear he would again indulge his evil passions, and profane the name of God. With sighs and tears, he replied, I hope you will never hear of my conducting so again. What you say may proceed from the heart, I added, but your future life alone can satisfy others of your sincerity. He thanked me for my interference, reproof, and advice.

About a year after the above transaction, I had opportunity to see this person again; reminded him of what is here related; and inquired if what was said to him on that occasion had produced any permanent effect. He had a distinct recollection of the circumstances, and assured me, that the reproof he received made a deep and lasting impression upon his mind; that he had never used any profane language since; and that he had frequently admonished others on account of their profanity.

RELIGIOUS INTELLIGENCE.

BIBLE SOCIETY IN THE COUNTY OF MIDDLESEX.

In consequence of a notice previously given in the newspapers, a number of gentlemen from different parts of Middlesex county met at Concord, on the 8th uk. for the purpose of forming a Bible Society in that county. After a full discussion of the subject, it was determined to be expedient to form such a society; but as the notice was thought not to have been sufficiently general, the meeting was adjourned to the 16th inst. then to meet at the same place for the further consideration of the same important business.

The Rev. Dr. Stearns of Lincoln was Moderator of the meeting, and Samuel Hoar, jun. Esq. Clerk.

A Committee was appointed to prepare a constitution, and report it at the adjourned meeting, consisting of the following gentlemen; Gen. John Brooks, the Rev. Mr. Ripley, of Concord, the Rev. Dr. Morse, the Rev. Mr. Stearns, of Bedford, the Hon. Asahel Stearns, Esq. the Rev. Professor M'Kean, and Dr. Grosvenor Tarbell.

The same Committee were directed to send a circular letter on the subject to every clergyman in the county, to be communicated to the people of his charge as he should think proper.

The meeting was opened with prayer by the Rev. Moderator.

On the 16th inst. a respectable number of gentlemen from the most distant, as well as the more central, parts of the county assembled according to adjournment. It was determined, without a dissenting voice, that the persons present would then proceed to form themselves into the contemplated Society.

The Committee previously appointed for that purpose then reported a Constitution, which, after discussion and amendment, was unanimously adopted as follows:

CONSTITUTION.

WHEREAS the general diffusion of the Holy Scriptures is the great mean of promoting the temporal and spiritual interests of man, we the subscribers associate for that end and adopt the following Constitution.

I This Society shall be styled, THE BIBLE SOCIETY IN THE COUNTY OF MIDDLESEX.

II. The sole object of the Society shall be the distribution of the Holy Scriptures

In the first place, a principal regard shall be had to the supply of those in Middlesex county, who are destitute of the Scriptures and unable to purchase them. When this county shall be well supplied, the Society, should any surplus means be left in their hands, will direct their efforts wherever they appear to be most needed.

The common version without note or comment is the only one, which shall be distributed in the English language. Whenever the Society shall assist in the distribution of the Scriptures in other languages, the version above mentioned shall be the guide in the selection of the versions in said languages, which shall, also, be distributed without note or comment.

III. Every person who engages to pay one dollar annually, shall be a member of the Society so long as his or her subscription shall be paid Every person, who shall pay twenty dollars at any one time, shall be a member for life; and two thirds of all the payments made by members for life, shall be appropriated to form a permanent fund, the annual income of which shall be expended in promoting the objects of the Society Any sum of money will be thankfully received, and religiously applied to the purpose of the institution. Whenever donors shall prescribe the direction of their donation to the general fund, or for immediate distribution, their desires shall be complied with.

IV. The officers of the Society shall be a President, as many Vice Presidents as the Society shall see fit to appoint at any general meeting, a Corresponding Secretary, a Recording Secretary, a Treasurer, an Auditor, and a Board of Directors consisting of seven persons; all of whom shall be chosen annually by ballot. The other officers named, shall be at liberty to attend, and act, at all meetings of the Board of Directors. The names of the several officers, except that of the Board of Directors, sufficiently express their several duties.

It shall be the duty of the Board of Directors to superintend the purchase and distribution of Bibles and Testaments; to appoint committees in the several towns, parishes and districts of the county for the purpose of facilitating the distribution of the Scriptures; to draw orders on the Treasurer; and in general to transact all the executive business of the Society. The Board of Directors shall appoint a Secretary of their own body, whose duty it shall be to keep a fair record of their proceedings, which record shall at all times be open to the inspection of the Society.

The Board of Directors, and the Treas-

urer, shall make reports, respectively the Society at every annual meeting

The Officers shall hold their office others are chosen in their stead.

V. The Society shall hold an a meeting on the last Wednesday of A at such place, as shall be appointed a preceding annual meeting. At ea nual meeting, a sermon shall be prea or an address delivered, by some me of the Society previously chosen for purpose at the annual meeting; an ter the religious exercises, a colle shall be made for the benefit of the ety's funds.

VI. Twenty one members shall b cessary to constitute a quorum to tra business, at any annual meeting.

VII. The Society shall aim to ac plish their object as well by furni Bibles at reduced prices to the wel posed, whose means are small, and have a desire to do what they can, giving to the destitute.

VIII. Any alteration of this Con tion, if proposed by the unanimous of the Board of Directors, may be a ed by a major vote at any annual m ing; and any alteration proposed by member of the Society at an annual ing, may be adopted by a major vot subsequent annual meeting.

The Society voted to choose five Presidents at the present meeting, proceeded to the election of officers, the following gentlemen were ch viz.

Gen. JOHN BROOKS, of Medford, *Pr*
The Rev. CHARLES STEARNS, D. Lincoln,
The Rev. EZRA RIPLEY, of Concor
The Rev. DANIEL CHAPLIN, of Gr
The Rev. PAUL LITCHFIELD, of Ca and
The Rev. JEDIDIAH MORSE, D. Charlestown,

Vice President

Mr. LEVI HEDGE, Professor in Ha College, *Corresponding Secre*
SAMUEL HOAR, jun. Esq. of Con *Recording Secretary.*
Dea. JOHN WHITE, of Concord, *Tre*
Dr. —— WYMAN, of Chelm *Auditor.*
Dr. ISAAC HURD, of Concord,
The Rev. SAMUEL STEARNS, of Bed
The Hon. ASAHEL STEARNS, Es Chelmsford,
Dr. GROSVENOR TARBELL, of Linco

* *The Vice Presidents and Dire are intended to be arranged accordi seniority.*

The Rev. Joseph M'Kean, Professor in Harvard College,
The Rev. William Collier, of Charlestown,
Jeremiah Evarts, Esq. of Charlestown,
Directors.

The first annual meeting of the Society will be held at Concord, on the last Wednesday of April, 1815. The Rev. *Charles Stearns,* D. D. was appointed to preach on the occasion; and the Rev. *Samuel Stearns* was appointed his substitute. The business of the meeting was conducted with great harmony, and the members of the Society separated with a strong conviction that their united exertions would be attended with the most desirable effects.

It is expected that the Board of Directors will soon enter upon some plan calculated to draw forth the benevolence of individuals in all parts of the county, and to supply the wants of the destitute.

BRITISH AND FOREIGN BIBLE SOCIETY.

The *Ninth Annual Report* of this illustrious Society has been reprinted in New York by Messrs. Whiting and Watson, in a neat duodecimo form. We are happy to announce it to the religious public, and hope the patronage will be sufficient to insure a republication of all future reports of that Society. We now present our readers with the cash accounts of the Society for the year which ended, on March 31, 1813, expressing the various sums in Dollars and cents, at the rate of $4 44 to a pound sterling. Ed.

RECEIPTS.

Annual subscriptions,	$13,203 52	
Donations and life subscriptions,	18,958 00	
Congregational collections,	5,117 27	42,278 79
Legacies,		5,060 00
Dividends on Stock, (deducting the property tax,)	1,559 77	
Property tax returned,	183 21	
Interest on exchequer bills,	2,609 83	4,352 81
Remittances from Auxiliary Societies,		244,885 30
From the Edinburgh Bible Society, in aid of printing the Icelandic Bible at Copenhagen,		222 22

Carried forward $296,799 12

Brought forward $296,799 12

Insurance on account of the loss by the Elizabeth for Bengal,		444 44
Total Net Receipts, exclusive of sales,		297,243 56
Received by sales, viz.		
For Bibles and Testaments	42,332 44	
For use of stereotype plates of the French Bible	166 67	
For Annual Reports,	57 05	42,556 60
Total Net Receipts, inclusive of sales,		339,800 22
For exchequer bills sold,	59,258 21	
Bills not due, in the Treasurer's hands at the last audit,	5,847 39	
Cash in the Treasurer's hands, at the last audit,	791 43	65,897 03

Grand Total $405,697 25

PAYMENTS.

For Bibles and Testaments in various languages, and binding ditto, viz.

English, Welsh, and Gaelic,	$195,926 76
Irish Testaments,	878 02
German Bibles,	2,792 39
—— Testaments,	3,478 30
Portuguese Testaments,	1,145 39
Italian Testaments,	658 89
French Bibles,	3,876 42
—— Testaments,	175 99
Swedish Bibles and Testaments,	263 22
Dutch Bibles,	1,462 72
—— Testaments,	845 04
Icelandic Bibles,	888 89
Arabic Bibles,	130 05
Esquimaux Gospels,	238 93
Finnish Testaments,	24 44
Hebrew Bibles,	1,144 43
Ancient Versions for India,	1,502 50
Modern Greek Testaments,	1,906 24

To the Corresponding Committee in Bengal, additional grant, voted March 7, 1812, $8,888 89

To the same Committee invested in Bibles, Testaments, and printing paper, including 2000 reams, voted as an

Carried forward $8,888 89 $217,328 63

8,888 89 £217,323 63

additional grant on account of the loss sustained by the fire at Serampore, 27,473 87—36,362 76

For translating, printing and circulating the Holy Scriptures in the Chinese language, by the Rev. Robert Morrison of Canton,   2,222 22

To the Hibernian Bible Society,   2,222 22

To Foreign Bible Societies, viz.

Berlin, in aid of printing Bohemian Bibles   £1,363 33

Abo, for Finnish Bibles,   3,333 35

Stockholm, for distribution of Swedish Scriptures to to the poor,   1,333 33

New Jersey,   444 45

Philadelphia, in aid of English cast stereotype plates for a Bible,   444 45—6,888 89

To the Rev. E. Henderson, for superintending the printing of the Icelandic Bible, at Copenhagen   £444 44

For Bibles and Testaments to be circulated in various parts of the continent of Europe, as directed by the Rev. Mr. Steinkopff, in his late tour, at the request of the Committee,   12,055 56—12,500 00

£277,524 72

The following expenses may be considered as incidental; viz.

To the Rev. J. Paterson for various important services relating to the Swedish and Laponese Scriptures, and for expenses incurred in correspondence in 1811,   973 33

To the same on account of travelling and other charges, in Sweden, Finland, and Russia, in 1812, connected with the formation of the Bible Societies at Abo and St. Petersburgh,   888 89

To the Rev. Mr. Steinkopff,

Carried forward £279,386 94

Brought forward £279,3

as travelling expenses on his tour including losses on exchange at various places,   1,44

Travelling expenses of the Secretaries, attending the meetings of the Auxiliary Societies,   1,5

Salary of Assistant Secretary,   1,1

Gratuity to the Assistant Secretary, for the two last years,   44

Commission to Depositary upon £96,725 22, (being the amount of the Bibles issued, at reduced prices,) at 5 per cent, including warehouse rent, packing paper, cord, and porterage,   4,2

Per centage on collecting annual subscriptions, at 5 per cent,   9

For completing 20,000 annual reports for the eighth year, and 9,500 without the appendix,   5,4

Completing 20,000 summaries for 1812; 39,000 brief views; and 20,000 circulars, containing regulations and extracts from correspondence,   1,6

For paper and printing on account of 20,000 copies of the ninth annual report,   6,6

Shipping charges, export duty, freight, carriage, and packing of donations of Bibles, Testaments, annual reports, and sundry other parcels,   1,5

Insurance on goods shipped, and on the Society's property from risk of fire,   6

Stationary, stamps, &c.   2

Use of Freemasons' Hall for annual meeting; fitting up do; repairs of furniture damaged, and other expenses on that occasion,

Advertising, and inserting an account of the annual meeting, in some of the principal London newspapers,

Use of rooms for the committee, and other purposes of the Society, and for the Society's Library and care thereof,

General Disbursements, including postages from auxiliary

Carried forward £307,5

Brought forward $307,226 00

' societies, &c. messengers, and
other incidental expenses, 1,648 26

Total Net Payments.* $308,874 26
Purchase of Exchequer Bills,
bills in the hands of the Treasurer not yet due, and cash in
the hands of the Treasurer,
in the whole amounting to, 96,822 99

$405,697 25

Besides the above balance of $96,822 99
the Society possessed different kinds of
stock, estimated to be worth $34,084 86;
making, in the whole, a balance on hand
of $130,907 85. The receipts, during
the ninth year, exceeded the expenditures by nearly $31,000.

The Society was, at the time of printing
the report, under engagements, which
would fall due in 1813, to the amount of
about $155,000.

NORFOLK BIBLE SOCIETY.

We are happy to publish the following
address, and abstract of the Constitution
of a Bible Society lately formed at Norfolk, (Vir.)

ADDRESS OF THE MANAGERS.

A Society having been lately established in this place under the title of "THE
NORFOLK BIBLE SOCIETY," the managers
submit its constitution to the public, and
earnestly invite their aid and co-operation
in the advancement of its design.

The object of this Society, (as will be
seen by the 2d article) is simply to distribute Bibles and Testaments *to the
Poor of this Borough and of the neighboring counties,* and also to furnish contributions to the Bible Society of Virginia,
to aid the design of that institution, "the
distribution of Bibles and Testaments *to
the Poor of our country and to the Heath-
en.*"

After this simple statement, it would
seem entirely unnecessary to say any
thing to recommend a plan of such obvious utility to the best interests of mankind. If the Gospel is indeed *the power
of God unto salvation to every one that
believeth,* can it remain a question, whether it is our duty to use our utmost exertions for its diffusion? Can there be any
charity of such plain and certain benevolence, as that which disseminates the

means of life eternal? Or is there one
which can appeal with fairer hopes to the
blessing of our Creator, *who will have all
men to come unto the knowledge of the
truth;* and who has established his Gospel as the medium of faith, and the instrument of grace?

But if it is thus our duty to diffuse the
word of God to all mankind, is it not peculiarly our duty to distribute it to the
Poor? Let us consider their situation in
life, and remember that God who has
given us the means of benevolence, and
we shall feel at once the duty and the
delight of providing for their happiness.
But in what manner can we do this, more
certainly and more effectually, than by
giving them this blessed volume of *glad
tidings,* with all its hopes and consolations, to cheer their fire-sides and their
bosoms? And let us remember that our
Lord and Savior has made it one of the
peculiar distinctions of his religion, and
one of the strongest evidences of his own
divinity, that the "*Poor have the Gospel
preached to them.*"

If any further motive could be wanting
to animate our zeal, we might find it in
the fact, that the present time seems to
be the æra of such exertions. It is but
little more than ten years* since 'the
"British and Foreign Bible Society,"
established in the metropolis of Great
Britain, upon a broad and liberal plan,
first called the attention of the world to
this subject; and similar institutions, in
great numbers, have already been formed, and are daily forming, in that country,
on the continent, and in these United
States. At this very moment, the Bible
Society of Virginia, established in our
own metropolis, stretches forth her hand,
and invites our co-operation in her benevolent design. Never before were there
such zeal and such unanimity, among
Christians of all countries and denominations, to diffuse the blessings of their
common religion. Never before were
their exertions so signally favored by
Heaven. Now then, when our fellow
Christians are every where rising around
us, as by a divine impulse, in the service
of our Creator, is it possible for us to observe the progress of their toils, without
feeling the generous ambition to participate in their exertions and their reward?

It is therefore with the clearest conviction of duty, and the fullest assurance of
success, that we call upon our fellow
Christians, of all churches and denominations to unite with us in this institution.
It is not the work of a sect, or of a party.
It is the cause of Christianity, of mankind, and of Heaven. Let us engage with

* *There is an error of nearly $4 in
this amount; but it is not thought necessary to go over the whole process in order
to detect so small a mistake.*

* *[illegible] years.* ED.

sincerity, with zeal, and with constancy, in the work before us, and the blessing of God will be upon ourselves and upon our labors.

The following is an abstract of the Constitution.

The title of this Society shall be "THE NORFOLK BIBLE SOCIETY."

2. The object of this Society is to distribute Bibles and Testaments *to the Poor of this Borough, and of the neighboring counties;* and also to furnish contributions to the Bible Society of Virginia, to aid the design of that institution, "the distribution of Bibles and Testaments *to the Poor of our country, and to the Heathen.*"

3. The Bibles and Testaments distributed, shall be such as are in common use, without note or comment.

They shall also be stamped in some manner, at the discretion of the managers, to prevent persons from transferring them improperly.

Art. 4th specifies the officers and the time of election.

Art. 5th prescribes the meetings of the managers.

6. In case of the resignation, or death, or disability of any of the managers, the vacancy may be supplied by the remaining managers until the next general election.

7. Persons of every religious creed or denomination may become members of this Society, upon paying Two Dollars subscription money, and binding themselves to pay the same sum annually, so long as they choose to continue members. The payment of Twenty-Five Dollars, however, in advance, shall constitute any person a member for life, without further contribution.

Art 8th prescribes the duties of the managers.

Art. 9th fixes the time and place of the annual meeting.

Art. 10th specifies the mode of calling special meetings.

11. Two-thirds of the members of the Society may make alterations in this Constitution, when it may be expedient; except that the first section of the third article shall be unchangeable.

Art. 12th regulates general meetings of the Society.

The following gentlemen are chosen officers for the present year. As their titles are omitted in their official publication, we are unable to supply them.

JAMES NIMMO, *Pres.*
WRIGHT SOUTHGATE, *Vice Pres.*
WILLIAM MAXWELL, *Cor. Sec.*
WILLIAM T. NIVISON, *Rec. Sec.*
JOHN M'PHAIL, *Treas.*
JOHN D. PAXTON,

RICHARD L. GREEN,
JAMES MITCHELL,
WILLIAM K. MACKINDER,
ROBERT ROBERTSON,
GEORGE W. CAMP,
ARTHUR COOPER, *Managers.*

The following paragraphs are extracted from a communication addressed to the Editor of the Norfolk Herald by a "Member" of the Society.

"But some perhaps may not be fully aware that there is any very pressing necessity for this work of benevolence. Would to Heaven it were indeed the fact, that our labors were entirely superfluous! But any man at all acquainted with the actual state of this Commonwealth, and even of our neighborhood, to look no farther, will see that it is far otherwise.—The truth is, and it is a shameful and mournful fact, that while too many neglect to read the Bibles which they have, many others among us have no Bibles to read. There is indeed a dearth, if not an actual famine, of the word of the Lord. I appeal to the knowledge of our Baptist and Methodist friends, and other Missionaries, who have gone out with admirable zeal into the hedges and highways of our States to bring in stray sheep to the fold of our Great Shepherd.—They have done much, it is true, and they deserve the thanks of all Christians for what they have done. But much is still left for us to do.—We must put the Bible into the hands of every poor man within our reach. The poor must have the Gospel not only preached unto them, but put into their hands. They must not be left to drink life at the muddy stream defiled by ignorant man, but must be led up to the sacred fountain itself, to quench their thirst with water from the rock.

"If the field then is thus open to us, have we not a right to anticipate that our exertions will be highly useful to the community, as well as honorable to ourselves? Sir, they cannot fail to be so. The Society will and must prosper. It will have a tendency, small and feeble as it may be, to excite the attention of Christians, to stimulate their zeal, and unite them more closely in the sacred bands of Christian friendship, presenting a solemn and interesting object worthy of their common counsels and labors.—It may perhaps awake the negligent from their sleep, and draw them home to a closer inspection of that blessed volume which we invite them to diffuse. Nay, Sir, may we not be allowed to hope, that by God's blessing, it may prove, "the savor of life unto life" to some, many, who are now in the shadow of death?—This is not merely speculation; it is experience. These happy effects

and uniformly followed sim-
is in other parts of the world,
arefore, be fairly anticipated

one difficulty indeed, Sir,
all have to encounter at the
nd I confess it wears a formid-
lut we shall conquer it, and
t subservient to new purposes
his difficulty is, that many of
whom the Bible should be
nable to read. No matter,
into their hands. It will
Let the managers take care
a them the duty, nay, the
ity of their knowing its com-
persuade myself that they
instances at least) take pains
t an iron chest into the hands
and tell him that there is gold
the may have, and he will
ey to open it. Put the Bible
d of an illiterate man, and
ily sensible of the inestimable
he treasure it contains;—
rhich we are told upon the
xrity is "more to be desired
m than much fine gold"—and
ll soon find the way to read it.
ill thus furnish a powerful mo-
to learn himself, or at least
children taught. But he is
means will never be wanting
t desire. Benevolence, ani-
al to diffuse the word of God,
to provide them.—Churches
will rise together around us.
d knowledge will go hand in
h our State, diffusing their
very side. The solitary place
br them, and the forest and
n will rejoice and blossom as
ndeed, Mr. Editor, consider
in its true spirit, and it is not
l to say, that the Bible Society
nay be designed in the Provi-
d, to be the seminal principle,
in of mustard seed, of a great
ution, whose future increase
l ample harvest of blessings to
sterity.

, if any one shall smile at my
s in promising such magnifi-
from such simple causes, I
at gentleman to remember,
, as I have a right to count,
istance and blessing of Jeho-
il own work. He has inspir-
will bless it He has already
l it with no doubtful marks of
ion and favor. Will any man
int the means are unequal to
ir, look at the history of the
s the delight, the prerogative
to accomplish great things by
It has already pleased God,

by the foolishness of preaching, to effect
the most sublime revolution that ever
blessed the world, the introduction of
Christianity: and if there is truth in his
word, he will use the same simple instrument to accomplish the still greater miracle of his grace, in the moral regeneration
of mankind.

"The present time too is pointed out by
the finger of God, as the peculiar season
for such exertions. The sure word of
prophecy is upon the eve of its accomplishment, when the Gospel shall be published to all nations, to prepare the way for
the harvest of the Lord—Now then is the
golden moment for Christians to exert
themselves with the certain prospect of
success. The whole moral world is already in motion. The impulse has been
given by a Divine hand, and the finger of
a child may continue its progress.

"Let Christians of all denominations,
then, come forward with one mind and
spirit, to engage in the sacred work to
which they are invited.

"I know we shall have to encounter difficulties, chiefly in the beginning. We
must prepare ourselves to meet the hostility of infidels, the ridicule of scorners,
and what is perhaps still more painful and
discouraging, the calm indifference of professing Christians. None of these things
must move us. We must set our faces
as a flint. Let us march at once. The
Spirit of the Lord calls to us from the
throne, 'Go on, I will be with you.' "

We have published the foregoing extracts, constitution, &c. both on account of
their intrinsic excellence, and because it
is desirable, that our readers should be
informed how leading individuals, in different parts of the country, feel in relation
to the great subject of evangelizing the
world. Let the North and the South animate each other in the great work in
which all are invited to engage, and for
which the labors of all will not be more
than sufficient.

CONNECTICUT BIBLE SOCIETY.

We have been sometime desirous of presenting our readers with an abstract of
the latest reports of several Bible Societies in this country. The press of other
matter has deferred such an abstract till
now. We first take up the fourth annual
report of the Connecticut Bible Society;
a Society which justly ranks high among
similar institutions for the zeal, intelligence, and activity, with which its affairs
have been conducted.   Ed.

The Directing Committee reported to
the Society, at

May last;—That the exertions of the Committee had been attended with as great success as could reasonably be expected; that the objects of the Society's beneficence in the state of Connecticut had been supplied, so far as they had come to the knowledge of the Committee, and the word of salvation had been sent to many of the destitute in other states; that this precious gift had been received with gratitude; and that pleasing accounts had been received, not only of the grateful reception of Bibles, but of the divine blessing, which had accompanied this exalted charity.

The Committee state the truly liberal and enlarged views of the Society, in the following words:

"To supply the poor of this state is considered a primary object. But the benevolence of the society will not end here. It embraces the destitute in the wilderness as well as in the city; in the various and distant parts of our land, and in other lands so far as the funds of the society will admit.

"Since the last meeting of the society there have been distributed 2341 Bibles. Of these 200 have been sent to the Oneida Bible Society for distribution; 200 to the Ohio Bible Society; 200 to the Bible Society in Orange County, state of New-York; 200 to the Vermont Bible Society; 300 to Rhode Island Missionary Society; 50 to the Genesee Missionary Society; and 387 to agents in this state.

"The whole number distributed since the formation of the society is 7644."

This is a larger number, if we mistake not, than any Bible Society in this country has distributed

The Committee proceed to state, that though great relief has been afforded to individuals, yet but little has been done toward supplying the wants of the numerous poor in the new settlements.

The Committee with commendable sympathy and liberality voted 500 dollars toward repairing the loss at Serampore, which was remitted accordingly.

The Report closes with the following paragraphs:

"While your committee desire to be grateful to God that the society have been able to do so much to promote his cause, it would rejoice their hearts could they have the means of doing much more. They have done as much as your funds have enabled them to do. They trust that Christian benevolence will enable the society to extend their views still further. *Whoso hath this world's good, and seeth his brother have need, and shutteth up his bowels of compassion from him, how dwelleth the love of God in him?*

How much more forcibly must this apply when a brother needs the word of eternal life, the guide to heavenly glory? If those who give to supply the bodily wants of their fellow men have the promise that it shall be given to them again, how much more may they expect who give to supply their souls with that spiritual food which is necessary to their eternal welfare?

"Do Christians desire and pray for the extension of the Gospel and the glory of the Church? This is one of the means which God will use to hasten on this glory. And from the liberality of the Christian world to aid in this and similar ways, have we not reason to believe the glory of the church is at hand? Surely the day dawns and the dark shadows of the night are rapidly fleeing away."

The *receipts* during the year previous were, donations and subscriptions, $1,728 00
Interest of money   112 90

     $1,840 90

The payments were, for Bibles, &c.   1,437 63
Loss by a counterfeit bill,   5 00
Toward repairing the Serampore loss,   500 00

     $1,942 63

The balance on hand was $2,960 64, of which $1,890 constituted the permanent fund. Sixty three persons, and associations, had become members for life, by paying $40, or more, at one time.

The following gentlemen are the present officers of the Society:

His Excellency John Cotton Smith, *President.*

The Hon. Jedidiah Huntington, of New London.
The Rev. Samuel Nott, of Franklin,
The Rev. Lyman Beecher, of Litchfield,
The Rev. Samuel Merwin, of New-Haven, *Vice Presidents.*

Henry Hudson, of Hartford, *Secretary.*
Joseph Rogers, of Hartford, *Treasurer.*
His Hon. Chauncey Goodrich, of Hartford,
Samuel Pitkin, Esq. of East-Hartford,
The Rev. Amos Bassett, of Hebron,
Hon. Theodore Dwight, of Hartford,
The Rev. Henry A. Rowland, of Windsor,
The Rev. Calvin Chapin, of Wethersfield,
The Rev. Andrew Yates, of East-Hartford,
Ichabod L. Skinner, Esq. of Hartford,
The Rev. Samuel Goodrich, of Berlin, *Directing Committee.*

Rev. Andrew Yates, *Clerk of the Directing Committee.*

Rev. Abel Flint, *Agent for purchasing and distributing Bibles.*

Ichabod L. Skinner, Esq.

The Rev. Calvin Chapin, and

Hon. Theodore Dwight,

Committee of Accounts.

Agents have been appointed in most of the towns in the State of Connecticut for soliciting and receiving subscriptions and donations.

The Rev. Messrs. Calvin Chapin, Andrew Yates, Samuel Goodrich, and Ichabod L. Skinner, Esq are a Committee to correspond with those Agents, with powers to appoint Agents for the above purposes, as from time to time they may find necessary.

Payments of monies, are to be made to Mr. Joseph Rogers, the Treasurer. Applications for Bibles, are to be made to the Rev. Abel Flint.

PHILADELPHIA BIBLE SOCIETY.

The Managers of this Society state, in their fifth annual report, that the whole number of Bibles and Testaments distributed by this Society, since its institution, is 7,845.

During the year preceding, the managers had committed to various societies and individuals for distribution 359 copies of the Bible in English; 150 in Gaelic; 90 in German; 97 in French; 172 English Testaments; 1 Spanish Bible; 1 Spanish Testament; and 100 Bibles and Testaments, (English, German, and French;) besides having distributed a number of copies of the Scriptures individually.

In reviewing the congregational collections, the managers cannot conceal their regret, that so few churches have manifested their zeal and liberality in contributing to the benevolent work of circulating the words of eternal life among the poor and ignorant. They indulge the hope, that many more will feel it incumbent on them to assist in making the Gospel known among all nations. We extract the account of two donations in the words of the managers; the former of which relates a very interesting anecdote:

"It will be interesting to the society to receive an account of two other contributions to their funds. The one amounts to no more than one dollar and eighty-four cents; but, like the widow's two mites, honored by our Savior's particular notice, it merits special commendation. It is the gift of a little girl; and was accompanied by the following letter from a respectable merchant of this city.

"The donor of this small sum is a dear little female, about six years old. She reads the Scriptures daily, and never omits morning and evening prayers. Some time last fall she read, or heard read, an address of the Society on the importance of distributing the Bible. Her little heart seemed immediately impressed with the duty of saving her cents to buy Bibles for the *Indians.* Ever since that period she has not spent one farthing her parents gave her as her accustomed weekly allowance. Her residence is in the country. During the last week she paid my family a visit, and brought the box with her treasure in her hands My children took her several times to town; and, in order to try her, showed her every thing the shops or fruit-stalls afforded, and asked her repeatedly whether she would not lay out her money for some of the articles which she saw. Her answer was uniformly, that she would like to have many things she saw; but she would not spend the money that was to buy Bibles for the Indians. I requested her to take the money home: she seemed affected, and thought I did not like the trouble of disposing of it." How easily can God touch the heart, and multiply streams of liberality to replenish our funds! When he gives the word, even children shall hasten with their little offerings to his altar; and, by their zeal, chide the sluggishness of age in the discharge of an important duty.

"The other donation comes from the British and Foreign Bible Society. It will be recollected that they voted the sum of two hundred pounds sterling, as soon as they heard of the establishment of this society; and, since that period, they have made handsome donations to a number of the Bible societies existing in the United States. The present donation amounts to one hundred pounds sterling. It was granted in consideration of the heavy expense incurred by this society in procuring a set of stereotype plates for printing the Bible. Your managers, duly appreciating their obligations to this noble and generous society, immediately on receiving the information of this new instance of liberality, passed a resolution, that their thanks should be presented for it; and directed their corresponding secretary to transmit to the British and Foreign Bible Society a copy of this resolution."

How does the self-denial of the little girl, mentioned in the preceding extract, reprove the sluggishness of multitudes of professed Christians!

The managers congratulate the Society, and we congratulate the country, on the safe arrival of the stereotype plates of the Bible. The Society are certainly to be commended for their early efforts to procure these plates. Before this report was drawn, an order had been issued for printing 3750 copies of the Bible.

The whole expense of the plates, including the expense of insurance and conveyance, amounts to $3,594 67, government having very properly remitted the duties on the importation.

The managers will supply Bibles to any amount to other Societies and to individuals; and their copies of the Scriptures are superior to those which are generally in market.

The managers have addressed a circular letter to influential persons, in different parts of the state, urging them to constitute auxiliary Bible Societies. Particular measures have been devised for infusing more life into this Society, and exciting a greater interest in its annual transactions.

The managers pay the following deserved tribute to the memory of the late Dr. Rush:

"While the Managers of this Society offer their gratitude to Almighty God, for preserving their body, during past years, from vacancies produced by death, they are, on this occasion, called to the mournful duty of paying a tribute of respect due to their late venerable associate, Dr. Benjamin Rush of this city. It was with deep regret they heard of his decease. He was not merely an honor to his profession and to his country as a physician, but an ornament to religion as a zealous friend of the Bible. Among the first to give existence and energy to this Society, he drafted its constitution; and ever since its establishment he was one of its Vice-Presidents."

The report concludes with the following animating paragraphs:

"In surveying the labors of the year past with a view to prepare this report, your Managers were led to contemplate some interesting events to which this Society owes its existence.

"The establishment of Missionary and Bible Societies forms a new era in the Christian Church; to which unborn generations will look back with gratitude and praise to the God of all grace. These Societies, nearly cotemporary in their origin, pursue, with growing ardor the same glorious and benevolent object, the universal diffusion of the knowledge of the Son of God among our fallen and benighted race. To Missionary Societies, however, is due the praise of having taken the lead in this ennobling work of Christian charity; and probably to the excitement of public zeal for the cause of our

great Redeemer produced by the may be traced the origin of Bi ties.

"How sublime the conception ed at the formation of the Londo ary Society, that their design wa less than to effect a general mov the Church on earth! Improbab peared the accomplishment of thi purpose, at that time when rel throughout Christendom in a sta guid, and the efforts of infidelity and prevalent, we have lived to alized. A general movement Church of Christ, on earth, has ed the establishment of that Soci

"The man who first conceived of forming a society for di gratuitously the Holy Scriptures, note or comment, among the which the active exertions of C of all denominations have been ously combined in diffusing the pure light of heavenly truth; deemed a benefactor of mankh vast importance of this principle most interestingly displayed; fir establishment and exertions of th and Foreign Bible Society, an quently in the formation and labo merous similar societies in Euro and America; by whose agency of God has been put into the several hundred thousands of who might otherwise have lived without possessing this invalu necessary treasure.

"Nine years have this day el the British and Foreign Bibl was formed; and, during that pe have labored in the great cause tianity, with a zeal and liberal will throw upon the present and century a lustre that will distingu in Christian history. The effort Society are marvellous, and dem every follower of Christ grati praise to him who "worketh," i ple "both to will and to do of pleasure." May the blessed Sp preserve that Society, and, from time, renew and increase its ze erality!

"In imitation of the laudable set by this PARENT Society, n auxiliary societies have been f Great Britain: and in this count tians have shown a disposition to the conduct of their transatlanti ren.

"To the Bible Society of Phi belongs the honor of having in try taken the lead in this noble love; and it enjoys the happines ing been instrumental in giving

tablished on the same prin-
nt States of the American

teresting spectacle does the
rch exhibit in this day of
convulsions! What a sub-
has she assumed' While
it s of this world are con-
mastery, and are, in their
sts, desolating the earth;
are tottering, kingdoms fall-
nity bleeding at every pore;
r head amid the noise and
d, contemplating, with the
her divine Lord, the mis-
kind, she is meditating
eir deliverance. Animated
promises of her God, and
d, with holy exultation, to
glory, she has commenced
rprise, which will, we trust,
n that grand and long wish-
on, by which nations shall
the Prince of Peace, and
illed, which announces the
in these reviving words,
is of this world are become
of our Lord and of his
e shall reign forever and

r of the Society, during the
g, were as follows:
xther Bible Soci-
repaid in stereo-
- - - - $1,254 44
nts of members 652 00
tions and dona-
- - - 312 71
S. stock - 128 46
————
$2,347 61

ts were as follows:
tereotype plates
transportation,
se of them - $1,032 70
r and printing
lates - - 450 00
urchased before
f these plates 390 00
5 per cent for
annual subscrip-
- - - 49 50
ts and transpor-
les - - 94 74
————
$2,016 94

hand, beside about $2,000
$566 29.
the Bible Societies in this
eep these stereotype plates
hout intermission, till they
and will then procure new

The officers appointed at the annual
meeting are as follows:
Rt. Rev. William White, D. D. *Pres.*
Rev. F. H. C. Helmuth, D. D.
Rev. Joseph Pilmore, D. D.
Rev. William Staughton, D. D. } *V. Pres*
Rev. Jacob J. Janeway,
Rev. James Gray, D. D. *Corres. Sec.*
B. B Hopkins, *Recording Secretary.*
Robert Ralston, Esq. *Treasurer.*

Rev. Philip F. Mayer.
Rev. Samuel Helffenstein.
Rev. George C. Potts.
Rev Thomas Sargeant.
Rev Jackson Kemper.
Rev. James C Brownlee
Rev James K. Burch
Rev. John Joyce.
Edward Pennington, Esq.
Godfrey Haga, Esq.
Thomas Haskins, Esq.
George Krebs, Esq.
Laurence Seckel, Esq.
James Moore, Esq.
Peter Vanpelt, Esq.
William Haslett, Esq. *Managers.*

NEW HAMPSHIRE BIBLE SOCIETY.

THE Board of Directors of this Society'
in their second annual report, Sept. 1813
state, that they had purchased nine hundred Bibles, nearly all of which had been
distributed, that the Society had been incorporated by the Legislature, with ample provision for holding personal estate;
that the Directors see more and more reason to prosecute their design with renewed ardor; that the demand for Bibles in
that state is greater than was expected;
that the Bible is received with gratitude;
that it is much wanted in the District of
Maine, and that the Directors have heard
of the formation of seven Bible Societies,
during the past year, in the United States.

The Directors extend their views, with
a truly enlarged and liberal zeal to the
destitute in Asia, in every part of our own
continent, and in every part of the world.
They argue with conclusive effect, that
exertions to send the Bible abroad will increase the exertions to distribute it at
home. We present our readers with the
close of the report, in the following paragraphs:

"It would seem that little if any doubt
can remain, as to the application of the
following prophetic passage: 'And I saw
another angel fly in the midst of heaven,
having the everlasting Gospel to preach
unto them that dwell on the earth, and
to every nation, and kindred, and tongue,
and people, saying with a loud voice,
Fear God, and give glory to him; for the
hour of his judgment is come: and worship him that made heaven, and earth,
and sea, and the fountains of waters.

And there followed another angel, saying, Babylon is fallen, is fallen, that great city, because she made all nations drink of the wine of the wrath of her fornication.* Does not the present period furnish an accomplishment of these predictions? Do we not manifestly behold this flying angel with the everlasting Gospel, in the Missionary exertions of the present day? What movements have there been in the Church, the symbolical heaven; and how many, with zeal and great speed, have gone forth as Gospel heralds! How greatly do these exertions increase! How many zealous Missionaries are still going to preach the Gospel to every nation, and kindred, and tongue, and people!—Has not the hour of God's judgment come? When was there a more signal period, than the last twenty years, of war and carnage, of calamity and distress to nations? Is not Babylon falling? Is not the papal power almost annihilated?

"There is another prediction equally interesting: 'And it shall come to pass in the last days, that the mountain of the Lord's house shall be established in the top of the mountains, and shall be exalted above the hills; and all nations shall flow unto it. For out of Zion shall go forth the law, and the word of the Lord from Jerusalem '†—The same is predicted by another prophet.‡ In the last days, when all nations come to the knowledge and worship of the true God; out of Zion shall go forth the law; and the word of the Lord from Jerusalem: in this way, is that glorious event to take place. But by Zion and Jerusalem, we are undoubtedly to understand the Church and people of God By these the sacred Scriptures are to be extensively distributed, in order to the conversion of the whole world. Do we not enjoy the unspeakable privilege of witnessing, at least in a pleasing degree, the accomplishment of this prediction? When was the like ever before attempted?

"These are the two grand means by which the nations are to be brought to the obedience of faith, and *the kingdoms of this world become the kingdoms of our Lord, and his Christ.* They are means of like importance, and should be pursued in connexion. Neither Bibles alone, nor preachers alone, will produce the desired effect. These means have mutual influence. One helps the other. Let them be vigorously prosecuted, and all nations will soon flow unto the house of the Lord. Swords will be beat into ploughshares, and spears into pruning hooks, and the nations shall learn war no more.

* *Rev. xiv, 6—8.*   † *Isaiah i , 2, 3.*
‡ *Micah iv, 2.*

"Dear Brethren, our work is b... It is a glorious, a most blessed w... will succeed; it will prosper. Lord's time, the world will be co... This time is near. THE COMING LORD DRAWETH NIGH. *Be ye therefore, and let not your hands b... for your work shall be rewarded.*

At the annual meeting of th... Hampshire Bible Society, at Pl... September 22, 1813, the following were elected for the ensuing yea...

Hon. John Langdon, Portsmouth
Rev. Seth Payson, D. D. Rindge,
Ebenezer Adams, Esq. Hanover,
Rev. Nathan Parker, Portsmouth
Rev. John H. Church, Pelham, S...
Jonathan Wilkins, Esq. Concord,
Daniel Emerson, Esq. Holles,
Rev. John Smith, Salem,
Major John Mills, Dunbarton,
Rev. Reed Paige, Hancock,
Rev. Abraham Burnham, Pembr...
Dea. Abiel Rolfe, Concord,

Voted, That the thanks of the be presented to the Printers wl... given notice of this annual meeting papers.

Voted, That the Secretary g... thanks of the Society to Mr. Ja... kins of Newburyport, for his ge... in presenting a seal for stampin... with the name of the Society.

The next annual meeting of th... ty is to be holden at Hanover, Wednesday following the third '... in September, 1814.

JOHN H. CHURCH, *Secr...*

Receipts during the precedi... viz.

Annual payments of members, $
Donations from individuals,
Contributions from towns,
———— from Cent Societies,
For Bibles and Reports sold,
Interest of money,

Expenditures.
For Bibles, $
Printing reports, &c.

Balance in the Treasury, $378
We are informed, that the contr... to the Society have considerably ed since the annual meeting, and Directors have very generously ...

$500 to the Bible Society in Philadelphia, to aid in printing a French New Testament for distribution in Louisiana.

The Directors had also resolved, previous to the last annual meeting, to advance $500 to assist the distribution of the Scriptures in Asia, as soon as the funds of the Society shall admit of such an appropriation.

BOSTON ASYLUM FOR BOYS.

An institution for the relief, and protection of indigent boys has lately been formed in Boston, and incorporated with the designation placed at the head of this article. The design of the founders is highly benevolent; and such an institution has long been wanted in the capital of Massachusetts. A large number of gentlemen, in the course of a few weeks, added their names to the list of annual subscribers; and the public are much indebted to the active exertions of those persons, who took the lead in procuring subscribers.

The following gentlemen have been chosen officers:

BENJAMIN GREENE, Esq. *Pres.*
JONATHAN AMORY, jun. Esq. *V. Pres.*
CHARLES P. PHELPS, Esq. *Treas.*
CHARLES W. GREENE, Esq. *Sec.*
The Rev. CHARLES LOWELL,
Mr. EDWARD TUCKERMAN, jun.
Mr. EDWARD CRUFT,
Mr. WILLIAM BROWN, jun.
Mr. ISAAC WINSLOW,
Mr. GIDEON SNOW,
Mr. JOSEPH AUSTIN,
Mr. NATHAN WEBB, and
Mr. SAMUEL H. WALLEY, *Managers.*

DONATIONS TO SUPPORT MISSIONS AND TRANSLATIONS.

March 1, 1814. From E. and E. of Pulteney, (N. Y.) $6 40
2. From the Foreign Mission Society in the Eastern District of New Haven County, by the Rev. Matthew Noyes, Treasurer,   50 00
From the Foreign Mission Society of New Haven and the Vicinity, by Mr. Timothy Dwight, jun. the Treasurer, viz.
for missions $165 75
for the translations,   19 00——184 75
From the Female Auxiliary Foreign Mission Society of

Carried forward $241 15

Brought forward $241 15
Stratford, (Con.) by the same hands,   45 00
From the Rev. Mark Mead, of Middlebury, (Con.) by the same hands,   3 00
4. From the following individuals and societies by Mr. Henry Hudson, viz.
From the Female Foreign Mission Society in Franklin, (Con.) $27 00
From the Female Foreign Mission Society of South Preston, (Con.)   21 00
From a friend to foreign missions by the Rev. Mr. Bartlett,   9 00
From a friend of missions,   5 00
From the Durham Cent Society, Greene county, (N. Y.) for the translations,   41 50
From a friend of missions in Greene county, (N. Y.) for the translations,   10 00
From a poor widow in Greene county, (N. Y.) for missions,   3 00
From Dea. Benj. Chapman, Durham, (N. Y.)   3 00
From a friend to foreign missions. towards a permanent fund,   100 00
From a friend to foreign missions, of Hampden county, (Mass.) for do.   2 00
From H. H. to make even money,   ,50—222 00
9. From the Hon. Matthew Cobb, Esq. of Portland, by Mr. Levi Cutter,   50 00
From a lady in Gorham, by the Rev. Mr. Hilliard,   3 00
12. From a few individuals in Arkport, (N. Y.) toward the translations, remitted by Mr. C. Hurlburt,   15 20
15. From a friend of missions, in a letter to the Treasurer by mail,*   20 00

Carried forward $599 35

* *The following sentences are extracted from this letter.*
"*Sir,*
It has long since been my wish to do something for the cause of missions. The period has at length arrived, when it is in my power I enclose twenty dollars,

Brought forward $599 35

19. From Mr. Travis Tucker, of Norfolk, (Vir.) by William Maxwell, Esq. (of which $20 are to be applied to the translations,)   30 00

From the Treasurer of the Board, towards a permanent fund,   100 00

24 From the *Essay to do Good Society*, in Kingston, (Mass.) by Maj. George Russell, (half to missions and half to translations,)   6 37

From a person, who had found a five dollar bill, but could not find the owner,   5 00

From the Rev. Mr. Rand. of Gorham, by Mr. Henry Homes,   5 00

From ladies in Portsmouth, (N. H.) by Mrs. A. Tappan,   58 00

$803 72

FOREIGN MISSION SOCIETY OF GLASTENBURY, (CON.)

To the Editor of the Panoplist.

Sir,

In compliance with your request, I transmit you the names of the officers of the Foreign Mission Society in Glastenbury, (Con.) The Society has been instituted but little more than a year, and consists at present of but a few individuals. A small sum only was received the first year: but expectations are entertained that a considerable number of members will be added to the Society the present year, and of course something more be contributed to the funds of the Board, in aid of the great object of its institution.

Rev. WILLIAM LOCKWOOD, *Pres.*
Rev. PRINCE HAWES, *Vice Pres.*
Mr. JOSEPH WRIGHT, *Sec.*
Mr. OLIVER HALL, *Treas.*

LATE MISSIONARY INTELLIGENCE.

Extract of a Letter from Josiah Roberts, Esq. dated London, 21st December, 1813, to Robert Ralston, Esq. of Philadelphia.

"From the present aspect of affairs in Europe sanguine hopes are formed, that the period is approaching, when peace on an enlarged scale, will once more be given to a bleeding world. Let us not cease to

which you will please to appropriate to Foreign Missions. I could wish it were more; but it is, as God hath given me ability. I am young; yet I have seen enough to convince me, that God is about to do great things for his Church."

look up to Him whose prerog[ative] prepare the minds of men for th[e] ble blessing, and then to vend them:—some consolation while the midst of these distressing drawn from the increasing noti which the Holy Scriptures are in the Armies and Navies; amongst prisoners of war, a home, as abroad; instances of effects of which are by no me and in some cases very re Surely no step is so well calc preserve our respective nations hateful consequences, in a mor ligious view, which flow from warfare.

"Recent accounts from B very cheering. A divine blessi sionary efforts is more and more and in some instances Hindoo east have been brought to the edgment and obedience of the t ply by the perusal of the wor without ever having communie the missionaries personally. T incorruptible seed springing up, is giving testimony to his wor the Cape of Good Hope, also, pl counts are received, and also of Otaheite, the first scene of mis born by the London Society; a till the present time, there has encouragement; but the laborer quarter now express a hope that Pomarre has felt the power grace, and is become a Christian after having long manifested a and regard for them. May thei be disappointed."

REVIVAL OF RELIGION, IN SPR (N. J.)

Copy of a letter from the Rev Rains, Pastor of the Presbyte gregation in Springfield, (his friend in Philadelphia.

"Springfield, Feb. 2

My dear friend,

I know your heart will rejoice the prosperity of Zion. God h ed in glory amongst us. He has p this whole congregation, as with rushing wind This is the seven which has taken place where I h though two of them were previo ministry; but this exceeds what fore witnessed. Though there v hopeful prospects last spring, an January after a season of stup great work did not appear until t day of this month. It exceeds o revivals in its *rapidity*, in through all parts of the congreg few days; in its power, producing the sorest anguish of soul, carrying some nearly to despair, and in some instances issuing in conversion in a few days; and in its being so general among the youth, and almost entirely confined to that class. The first evening which I appointed to converse with persons under religious impressions, 29 attended; (all youths but two.) At the next appointment, 30 were present, and only two of them were over 25 years of age. Last week, on Monday evening, one of my elders who attended with me, and took account, said there were 70, exclusive of 7 who had professed religion. And last Monday evening he said there were 100, beside 20 others not reckoned under deep impressions. These were only what could assemble in the midst of the town in the evening. The night was very dark, and the travelling quite muddy; so that many could not attend; and especially from the extreme parts of the parish. In the afternoon of Tuesday last, I appointed to commune with persons under religious impressions, in the most distant corner of the parish; and 32 attended, nearly all youths; and but one had obtained a hope.

"In this general shock, it is difficult to ascertain the number of persons under awakenings. Some say there are not less than 200; but I should say about 150. The work is rapidly progressing and new cases occur every day. Within a few days past it has begun to pass from the children to the parents, and, I hope, many who have sinned away the days of youth will yet find mercy. I have just been informed, that one of my neighbors of about 70, and another of 50 years of age, have lately experienced the love of God shed abroad in their hearts, and are now rejoicing in the hope of glory. One of our elders has 7 children under 25 years of age, who are subjects of this work, and six of them, together with a daughter-in law, have obtained a hope of pardoning mercy. I have conversed with 45, who have obtained a hope that their sins are pardoned through the blood of Jesus. Such a time was never before known in Springfield. We had a revival in 1803, and only 60 were added to the Church in one year. In 1808 we experienced another time of refreshing, and only 54 were received into the Church in the same period. But though we cannot tell what will be the issue of this work, the number will probably be greater. My labors at present are unusually arduous. I feel as though the apostolic direction, *Preach the word; be instant in season and out of season*, is now to me particularly applicable. During 24 days past, I have been attending the devotions of religious assemblies every evening except two; and though the season has been muddy, and the nights dark, these assemblies have been full. I bless the Lord that my health has not yet failed, though it has been shaken; and I am not without fears. Yet, in the present state of things I dare not relax for one day."

OBITUARY.

DIED, at Stockbridge, on the 26th of April 18.3, Dr. HORATIO JONES, A. M an eminent physician in that town, aged 43.

At his interment, a sermon was preached by the Rev. Dr. Hyde of Lee, from Job xix, 21. *Have pity upon me, have pity upon me, O ye my friends, for the hand of God hath touched me.*

The following extract from the Sermon is no more than a proper tribute to the memory of the deceased, and will evince the high estimation, in which he stood among his acquaintance.

"On the present solemn occasion, we see a number of this people, and many of them the professed friends of the Divine Redeemer, in deep affliction. The hand of God hath touched them, in a tender place. Sore is their bereavement; for they have been called to part with a much valued friend.

"If ever there were mourners, who might with propriety and with a deep sense of their loss, *call* for the pity and sympathy of their friends, it may surely be done, by the near relatives and connexions of *Dr. Jones*, whose death we now lament. He was apparently every thing to them, in their respective relations, that can be comprised in the endearing names of husband, father, brother and friend. Tender in his feelings, obliging in his disposition, familiar in his deportment, and easy of access, it was always pleasant for them to *meet* him. He was a man of rare endowments and attainments. With him have departed much excellency and worth. And what adds peculiar poignancy to the grief of his friends is, that he is cut down, by the ruthless hand of death, in the midst of life, activity and usefulness. Indescribably great is the breach, which is made upon them. The world has nothing in it to repair their loss. Under this mighty hand of God, they may suitably adopt the words of afflicted Job, *Have pity* upon us, have pity upon us, O ye our friends, for the hand of God hath touched us.

"If ever there were mourners, who might reasonably expect to have the pity, and share in the sympathy of friends, the mourners, on this occasion, may reasonably expect it. The death of Dr. Jones is no common event. His removal from this world, in the midst of his usefulness, is an unspeakable loss to the community. Rarely has this town, or even this county experienced a greater shock, in the death of a citizen. The mourners are not confined to his particular relatives; they are as numerous as his acquaintance; and his acquaintance was extensive.

"He was a man of science, a man of much general information, and of acknowledged medical skill. He acquired knowledge, on all subjects, with uncommon facility; and by his diligence and perseverance, he had risen to *eminence* in his profession. Extensively acquainted with that wonderful machine, that curious specimen of God's workmanship, the human body, and profoundly versed in the healing art, he was *able in counsel; and his counsel was much sought,* in difficult cases.

"As a *practitioner*, he was highly approved and esteemed, being ever prompt to obey the calls of his numerous patients, and making a sacrifice of his own ease, comfort, and interest, that he might if possible, afford them relief. How many in this, and the adjacent towns, to whom he has administered, in their distresses, by night and by day, must be impelled to sympathize with his bereaved family, and lament and mourn, now he is dead! The speaker sensibly feels his obligation to testify his grief, in this public manner, and to lament the death of this important friend, having so recently experienced his kind attention and friendly aid, in a time of sickness and distress in his own family. The physicians, in this part of the county, must feel and acknowledge the claims of his weeping friends on them, for their pity and sympathy.

"In this strain of lamentation, I forbear longer to speak, and desire to acknowledge, that it is the hand of *God*, which hath touched us all. Dr. Jones was not too valuable and important to die. Though calculated to do much good, he was but an instrument in God's hand. Like the rest of us, he was a worm of the dust, and was ready to acknowledge it. God made him what he was, and God's holy name be praised, that we have had such a blessing in him.

"Unspeakable and wonderful were the mercies of God manifested in his death. He left the world like a Christian, with calmness, with resignation to the will, and with enrapturing views mediation, all sufficiency and glory sus Christ, employing much of his fervent prayer, committing his de ily to the mercy and keeping of G calling upon his Christian friends severe in the ways of the Lord.

peared to die in the triumphs of fail did these feelings and views commen the closing scene of his life. To i his particular friends he made a f closure of them, nearly three mont vious to his sickness. While his l held in suspense, he was heard that he desired to live only that h glorify God, by openly professing l Jesus Christ, and walking in h mandments and ordinances. In h my friends, you have seen, we some of the happy fruits of the work, which God has been carry among you by his Holy Spirit.

"The mourners if they hav taught rightly to appreciate divin cies, have much to comfort them, called to commit to the silent man the dead a friend so highly val would have been their duty to h signed him into the hands of God, they had not been favored with su dence of his union to Christ; but such evidence has been afforded, it be grieving the Holy Spirit to say i hearts, that it was not *enough*—th must have had *more*—that their must have *survived*. This would ting an higher estimate on natur spiritual life; and of course would dervaluing the work of the Holy God can take care of the sorrowful and the daughter, bereaved of the fathers; for He still liveth and in r boundless in mercy. He can supp afflicted brethren and sisters, and numerous relatives. To him le look, and in him let them trust. God, in his infinite mercy, give th pity, the counsel and the fervent p of their Christian friends."

To the foregoing extract is su a more particular account of the ance and conversation of Dr. J. closing scene of life.

He died, of the prevailing epiden on the eighth day of his illness. It God to continue to him, during h ness, the full possession of his reas mind was calm and tranquil, and resigned to the will of heaven. asked, by his wife, in the early stag disorder, if he were desirous of reco he replied, "I think I should rejoice cover, if it is God's will; but, if n not think I wish it. He certainly what is best.". He expressed, as

and fears, respecting the
ul, appearing sensible of the
he was in of being deceived,
nceivable misery into which
tion would plunge him. He
ay, "It is a great thing to be
ie! I have had but little time
! It is a great thing to die!"
xring, for some hours, ex-
distress, he said to his wife,
at of my recovery is small insure, if I do not soon get re-
ntinue but a short time; but
ous. God has a right to dis-
und all others, as he sees fit,
ing to leave it with him."
his sisters, who resided in
d who had been a professor
iny years, he said, "You have
est part of any of our family,
began to love and serve God,
Though you have been un-
other respects, you have had
tion given you Religion af-
atest enjoyment we can have
."
nly daughter and child who
n years old, he said, "Your
ou, and has always loved you
I thank you for all your
affection to me. I am now
e you. You too must die.
shat I have often taught you.
o God, and seek an interest
w while you are young. Be
affectionate to your Mamma,
you can for her comfort."
he drew the face of his wife
related many particulars re-
conversion, which he had not
one; adding, "Though the
had to try myself has been
a consoling hope of an inter-
avior. We must part; but I
paration will be but short."
dressed himself to all, who
t, and said, "I am soon to
orld; but my mind is calm and
a degree, that astonishes my-
so anxiety about myself nor
."
before he died, being the Sab-
ted with his wife, in publicly
rayers of God's people for
r having a note, for that pur-
and read to him, he thought
f *Jesus* was not mentioned,
it might be altered; but on
note again, he found it was
and was satisfied. He was
to say, "Let Jesus and dying
my theme." He observed,
d strength to talk, and could
and unbelievers, with whom I
quainted; it appears to me I
on them. O that my death

might be the means of awakening my intimate friends in this street."

As the sun went down on the Sabbath,
he said, "The last Sabbath's sun is set to
me." A friend observed to him, "I trust
you are about to enter on an eternal Sabbath of rest in heaven." He replied, "I
hope, I trust, I believe, I shall soon enter
upon it."

A female friend coming in, he took her
by the hand, and said, "I am very glad to
see you once more. I have long been sensible of the friendship, which has subsist-
ed between you and my wife, and I trust
it is of that nature, which will be lasting;
and as I believe you have taken an interest with her, for my eternal welfare, I
have desired to thank you for it. If I ever
experienced a change of heart it was last
winter, and instantaneously." Turning
to those around him, he said, "Don't weep
for me. Don't regret that I must die
now; but praise God, that he did not call
me six months ago."

A little before death closed his eyes, he
made a most fervent prayer, and committed his departing soul to Jesus. He
turned himself on his back, extended his
arms each side of the bed, raised his
eyes toward heaven, and said, "Jesus, I
expand my arms to receive thee. Happy!
Happy beyond expression! Ye spirits, in
yonder sky, receive my soul, and take it
to Jesus!"

Thus his spirit took its flight, and is now,
we humbly hope, united with saints and
angels, in ascribing glory and honor and
power to Him, who sitteth on the throne,
and to the Lamb, forever.

POETRY.

For the Panoplist.

PSALM CXXVI.

WHEN the Lord brought us back from
    that barbarous land,
And gave us our city again to our hand,
Like those who awake from a dream of
    the night,
We scarcely believ'd the uncertain delight.

Our lips with sweet laughter delightfully
    rung,
And songs of strange rapture flow'd wild
    from the tongue;
The Heathen look'd on with a wondering
    eye,—
'The Lord hath done great things for Is-
    rael,' they cry.

Yes! the Lord hath done great things for
    Israel, we know,
And therefore these songs of our gratitude
    flow—

Ah! turn, Lord, the rest of our captives
   again!
As the streams of the south swelling over
   the plain.

The harvest is some, and no foe to annoy!
We sow'd it in grief; but we reap it in joy:
The sower with tears gave his seed to the
   land;—
See! smiling he comes with the sheaves in
   his hand.   V.

For the Panoplist.

MALTA.

(Written by a young lady.)

The following thoughts on the island of
Malta, were occasioned by reading the excellent letter concerning Dr. Naudi, inserted in the Panoplist of January 1814.

FAR eastward, where the sea with
   thund'ring tides
Sicilian shores from Afric's sand divides,
Not far from Etna's flame sublime and
   dread,
A little island rears its rocky head.
Its broken cliffs allure the fresh'ning gales,
And flow'rs and fruitage clothe its cheer-
   ful vales,*
Mild breathes the air, as if to wake de-
   light,
And orange groves to soft repose invite.
Phenician lords first gave the natives law,
Till Greece with mightier sway awak'd
   their awe,
Though scarce the shallow soil and scant
   domain
Could tempt the av'rice of the haughty
   train.
Then Carthaginian darts in wrath were
   hurl'd
Till Rome's proud sceptre nodded o'er the
   world,
And, rising from her throne, she bound
   with care
This little gem to grace her flowing hair.
But soon her iron arm was bent and broke,
And this sad island bore a changeful yoke,
Fierce on her temples falls the Gothic
   scourge,
And Norman lords their proud dominion
   urge,
Till o'er her head a host are seen to
   wield
The knightly sword, and shake the trophied
   shield:†

  * *Malta has a most delightful climate.*
  † *This island was given to the knights
of Malta in the year 1529.*

And later times with wond'ring
   hold
High-crested valor guard her ten
While trumpets changing so
   thund'ring shocks
Of warlike engines, rend the vau
While round the walls the Turkis
   gleams,
And flows the Turkish blood in
   streams;
Till sunk with shame the faint
   band
Fly few and feeble to their nati
   Once o'er the raging floods a
   hoar
The tempest's wing a lonely ve
The mountain waves, in awful f
And op'ning gulphs the secret d
   close;
The lightning's pointed spear
   were driven,
And thunders rent the darken'
   heaven;
Loud shriek'd the wild winds
   trackless path,
And lash'd the surge to most u
   wrath,
Till with resistless force the fu
The sinking vessel on the quick-
   Sad, weary, faint, the unprote
Trust their last fortunes to the
   main,
Raise their weak hands above t
   foam,
And think, despairing, of thei
   home.
The natives, watching from the
   soil,
View'd the spent suff'rers at th
   toil,
Held the light torch above the sur
Lent the kind hand to aid the
   shore,
Gave a glad shelter from the stor
And with warm welcome cheer'
   ing mind †
      (To be continued.)

*We very much regret, that
obliged to divide this poem We
that the whole would come within
its, till after the preceding matt
type, and was so arranged, tha
siderable alteration could be m
out great difficulty.*

  * *The memorable siege of Ma
in 1566; and 20,000 Turks were
fore its walls; some say 30,00
knights were very splendid in t
tary equipments*
      † *Acts* xxviii.

TH£

PANOPLIST,

AND

;IONARY MAGAZINE.

APRIL, 1814.   Vol. X.

BIOGRAPHY.

)F JOHN KNOX,
FROM THE WORK
. THOMAS M'CRIE.

to an obliging corres-
ollowing article. The
formers, whose names
in perpetual and grate-
e, were Luther, Calvin
ch more is known of the
 the mass of readers,
r. The writer of the
i here abridged, has con-
ligation on the Christian
ing a durable monument
f this illustrious cham-
l.   ED.

he great Reformer
)r the principal in-
l by Providence in
reformation of that
n the errors of po-
rn at Haddington,
to other accounts
  village of East
05.
lucated at the uni-
. Andrews, at that
t celebrated univer-
nd; in which, how-
Hebrew nor Greek
ight. These lan-
cquired at a later
life. His principal
 the philosophy of
:holastic theology,
n and civil law. In
y be imbibed from
 professor of phi-
heology, sentiments

in regard to the power of the
Pope of Rome very different
from what were generally embraced by the papists, and also
opinions respecting civil government very favorable to liberty. George Buchanan, an eminent Latin scholar and historian,
was his fellow student and
friend, and adopted the same
sentiments in respect to religion and government.

After receiving the degree of
Master of Arts, he taught philosophy in the university, and was
distinguished for his acuteness.
When about 25 years of age he
took orders as a priest in the
Church of Rome, for as yet he
was a papist, although more enlightened than most of his brethren. But in the course of a few
years, by examining the writings
of Jerome and Augustine, fathers of the Christian Church, he
was led to study the Scriptures,
as the only pure fountain of
truth, and was made acquainted
with doctrines very different
from such as were taught in the
Romish Church.

At this period the state of religion in Scotland was most deplorable. The clergy possessed one half of the wealth of the
nation. Bishops and Abbots, instead of being humble men, devoted to their spiritual duties,

19

were distinguished by luxury and splendor, and held the principal civil offices being privy-councillors, and lords of session or judges, and lords of parliament. Not a bishop was known to preach; and the only preachers were ignorant mendicant monks. The lives of the clergy were most immoral and scandalous; for the bishops, being forbidden to marry, openly kept their harlots, and the monasteries which had become numerous, were the abodes of debauchery.

So gross was the ignorance, which prevailed, that many of the priests were unacquainted with the Scriptures, and did not even understand the Latin language, in which religious service was performed. The people were prohibited from reading the Bible in their own tongue. The intercession of the virgin Mary was more frequently solicited than that of Jesus Christ, *the only Mediator between God and man;* and more prayers were addressed to dead saints, than to the living Jehovah. The sacrifice of the mass in which, it was thought, that bread was changed into the real body of Christ, was represented as procuring forgiveness; confession to a priest was substituted for confession to God; and penances, pilgrimages, and other superstitions, were depended on as the certain means of salvation. The sermons of the monks were ridiculous stories, and the churches were almost deserted. If any one dared to speak against the clergy, or expressed any doubts as to the holiness of all this mummery, he was branded as a heretic, and imprisoned. or burned at the stake for the good

of his soul. Patrick Hamilton, a youth of illustrious family, for exposing the corruptions of popery was, in the year 1528, committed to the flames at St. Andrews. From this period until 1540, many excellent men suffered a similar death, while others fled to England and the continent. But notwithstanding the flames of persecution, the friends of the reformed religion increased.

Such was the condition of Scotland, when in the year 1542 Knox avowed his belief of the protestant doctrine. Cardinal Beatoun hired assassins to waylay and murder him, but through the care of providence, he escaped their hands, being protected by one of the Scottish lords.

After having been employed in the instruction of youth several years, during which time he was frequently obliged to flee from place to place, he at length in 1547 took refuge in the castle of St. Andrews. This had been the abode of the cardinal; but few protestants, indignant at his cruelties, had conspired against him, and put him to death, an seized the castle. Although Knox was not privy to the conspiracy, yet he approved of it for he was of opinion that tyrants, stained with blood, who could not be brought to justice in the ordinary way, might be put to death by private individuals.

In the castle John Rough was chaplain, to whom Knox was requested to become colleague, but he would not listen to the invitation In order to overcome his reluctance, Rough one day preached a sermon on the elec.

ministers, at the conclu-
ſ which he addressed
who was present, in these
"Brother, in the name of
d of his son Jesus Christ,
he name of all, that call
my mouth, I charge you
ju refuse not this holy
n." Knox returned home,
nained in the deepest dis-
mind, until he was con-
l to accept the invitation,
was given him, and te
: a public preacher of the
ispel. His distress is to
buted to his view of the
duties and awful respon-
of the minister of Christ,
ll be required to give an
: of his stewardship, as
to his sense of the dan-
d trials, which he would
led to meet, in conse-
of his exposing the cor-
s of the Romish Church.
ermination resulted from
ction, that it was the will
he should stand forth in
: of the truth; and, relying
ie protection of God, he
s fears to the winds.
s first sermon, in the parish, he boldly attacked
ile system of error, de-
the Romish Church
the synagogue of Satan,
: Pope to be the Anti-
the man of sin. So suc-
were his labors, that
if the inhabitants of the
a addition to those in the
made a profession of the
ant faith, and he adminis-
i them the sacrament of
-d's supper.
ane .547, a French fleet
ind forces sent to assist
vernoi of St. Andrews,
d the cystle, and obliged
irged to capitulate. The

terms of the capitulation, at the
solicitation of the Pope and of
the Scottish clergy, were violated; for those, who were taken,
instead of being set at liberty on
their arrival in France, were detained as prisoners of war. The
principal gentlemen were
thrown into different dungeons,
and Knox with others was confined on board the galleys, bound
with chains, and treated with
great severity Great efforts
were made, but in vain, to induce him to conform to the
popish worship. One day a
painted image of the virgin was
presented to a Scottish prisoner,
supposed to be Knox himself, to
kiss; but he refused, declaring
that such idols were accursed.
As the officers insisted upon his
compliance, and put the image
to his face, he took hold of it,
and watching an opportunity
threw it into the river, saying,
*Lat our Ladie now save hirself;
sche is lycht anoughe, lat hir
leirne to swyme.* It is not stated,
whether or not this object of
worship went to the bottom;
but the *Ladie,* after this incivili-
ty, was not again obtruded upon
the prisoners.

During his confinement, Knox
wrote two or three small tracts
to confirm his religious friends
in Scotland in their attachment
to the truth. When dangerous-
ly sick with a fever, he expressed his confident persuasion,
that he should recover, and again
open his mouth to the glory of
God in the church of St. Andrews. At length, after being
confined 19 months, he obtained
his liberty in Feb. 1549.

He repaired to England, and
as his ▓▓▓▓▓ was well known,
the ▓▓▓▓▓▓▓, being anxious

—

for a reformation of religion, sent him as a preacher to Berwick, where he remained two years. Here he labored with the utmost zeal to demolish the idolatry of the popish church and to propagate the protestant doctrine, and his exertions were attended with a blessing, especially among the soldiers of the garrison. In the beginning of 1551, he was removed to Newcastle, a sphere of greater usefulness; and in the same year was appointed one of king Edward's chaplains in ordinary. Being consulted in regard to some alterations in the book of common prayer, he caused the notion of the corporeal presence of Christ in the sacrament to be excluded, and guarded against the adoration of the elements. While he resided at Berwick, he became acquainted with Miss Marjory Bowes, a young lady of an honorble family, whom he afterwards married.

At this period he usually preached every day in the week, and was indefatigable in his studies. The adherents of popery persecuted him in various ways; but he triumphed over their malice.

His constitution having been much enfeebled by his confinement in the French galleys, in the year 1553 he suffered several violent attacks of the gravel. In a letter to Miss Bowes, he says, "your messenger found me in bed, after a sore trouble, and most dolorous night; and so dolor may complain to dolor when we two meet. But the infinite goodness of God, who never despiseth the petitions of a sore troubled heart, shall, at his good pleasure, put an end to these

pains, that we presently and in place thereof shall us with glory and immo forever." When archl Cranmer offered him the living of *All-Hallows* in L he refused it because he not in conscience conform English church, which he ed contrary to the institut Christ. He particularly o ed to the law which oblige isters to allow the unwor participate of the sacra Kneeling at the Lord's he also considered as an tion of men. By the spec quest of king Edward V was also offered a bish which he refused, declar the same time, that the e pal office was not of divin thority. He could not that the king, any more the Pope, was the head o Church; he acknowledged to be true bishops, but st preached personally with substitute; and he could no sent to the introduction of monies, not authorized by ture. Among other thin also objected to the secul tles and dignities of the bi and to the total want of ec astical discipline

In preaching before the he was most faithful and gent in reproving some o great officers of state, obse at one time in allusion t prime minister and lord treasurer, who were prese am greatly afraid, that A phel be counsellor, that bear the purse, and that S be scribe, comptroller, treasurer."

After the death of Ed which occurred July 6,

ccession of the bigot-
atholic Mary, he retir-
north; but in the follow-
h he returned and re-
s labors, the queen hav-
icly promised not to
be conscientious prot-
But the Roman Catho-
on was soon restored,
rotestant worship pro-
y law, so that before
of the year many min-
re committed to pris-
g in imminent danger,
as induced by the in-
: his friends, although
ctance, for he thought
· could die in a more
arrel," to flee to Diep-
nce, where he landed
8, 1554. At this place
a strict scrutiny into
sterial conduct, while
ith the opportunity of
; the Gospel, and
ch to deplore and con-
was much dissatisfied
nself. He lamented,
d not been more faith-
eeding the lambs and
Christ; that selfish mo-
sometimes hindered
visiting the ignorant
ssed; that in his pub-
es he had not been suf-
aithful and fervent; and
etimes he had been
too attentive to his
when he should have
upied in the discharge
cial duties. Although
sters have been equal-
t; yet he had reason to
Lord! be merciful to
offence; and deal not
according to my great
but according to the
of thy mercies."
n transmitted to Eng-
xposition of the sixth

psalm, and a large letter, for the
purpose of warning his protestant friends against a sinful compliance with the idolatrous worship of the popish religion. In
the eloquent conclusion of the
letter, he says, "Let it be known
to your posterity, that ye were
Christians and no idolaters; that
ye learned Christ in time of rest,
and boldly professed him in times
of trouble. The precepts, think
ye, are sharp and hard to be observed; and yet again I affirm,
that compared with the plagues,
that shall assuredly fall upon obstinate idolaters, they shall be
found easy and light. For avoiding of idolatry, ye may perchance be compelled to leave
your native country and realm;
but obeyers of idolatry without
end shall be compelled to burn
in hell. For avoiding idolatry,
your substance shall be spoiled;
but for obeying idolatry heavenly riches shall be lost. For
avoiding of idolatry ye may fall
into the hands of earthly tyrants; but obeyers, maintainers,
and consenters to idolatry shall
not escape the hands of the living God. For avoiding of idolatry, your children shall be deprived of fathers, friends, riches,
and of rest; but by obeying idolatry they shall be left without
God, without the knowledge of
his word, and without hope of
his kingdom. Consider, dear
brethren, that how much more
dolorous and fearful it is to be
tormented in hell than to suffer
trouble on earth; to be deprived
of heavenly joy, than to be rob-
bed of transitory riches; to fall
into the hands of the living God,
than to obey man's vain and uncertain displeasure; to leave our
children destitute of God, than

to leave them unprovided before the world;—so much more fearful it is to obey idolatry, or by dissembling to consent to the same, than by avoiding and flying from the abomination, to suffer what inconvenience may follow thereupon"

In February 1554, he left Dieppe, and travelling through France came to Switzerland, in which country he visited with much satisfaction most of the protestant churches. At Geneva he formed an intimate friendship with CALVIN and in that city he resolved to reside during the continuance of his exile. Although about the age of 50, he now applied himself to study with the ardor of youth, and among other acquisitions made some proficiency in the Hebrew language. It was supposed, that in this year eight hundred learned English protestants fled to the continent. Many of them established themselves at *Frankfort on the Maine*, and having requested Knox to become their minister, he, with the advice of Calvin, repaired to that place in November, and entered upon the duties of his office. In March 1555, he was however induced to retire from Frankfort in consequence of the bigotted attachment of a part of the congregation to the forms of the English church; and he returned immediately to Geneva.

In August 1555, superior to the fear of danger, he took a journey to Great Britain. Landing on the borders of Scotland, he immediately went to Berwick, and found his wife and her mother still firm in their attach-

ment to the pure Gos
Christ. He soon went s
to Edinburgh, and in th
and in different parts
kingdom preached inces
and for some time bei
came to the knowledge
clergy. They were alarm
the progress of the truth
his preaching; but they ca
vain upon the queen reg
apprehend and punish
Having summoned him
a convention of the cler
obeyed the summons; bi
enemies not being confi
the regent's support, and
of his great talents, did n
pear against him, but unde
tence of informality cas
summons.

Being invited to take c
of the English congregat
Geneva, he was induced
ten to the request, and ir
1556 left Scotland with hi
ly. The clergy then imme
ly renewed the summons
him, and as he could not a
they sentenced his body
flames, and his soul to he
burned him in effigy.

His visit to Scotland v
vast importance. He di
ed his brethren from atte
the Catholic worship, anc
encouraging in any mann
"damnable idolatry," and
advice they held frequent
meetings, which greatly
moted the protestant doc
His withdrawment fron
kingdom was the means o
serving his life, and of en
him at a future time to
again upon his labors witl
plete success.

(*To be continued.*)

ELIGIOUS COMMUNICATIONS.

For the Panoplist.

Y FAITH, NOT BY
2 Cor. v, 7.

e features of the
tracter, in a person
l, is both pleasing
ve. In him these
marked, prominent,
, in their symmetry,
model, as nearly re-
e *divine pattern*, as
itnessed in a mere
writings we learn
n of his feelings;
w with admiration
vith which he ap-
standard of excel-

ion with the words,
at the head of this
hibits the strength
; and declares the
m to be so interest-
ious, as that all the
time, in comparison
their importance.
persons in their at-
object which is fu-
hich, to the eye of
oth unseen and un-
ld become so en-
ed, may, to a care-
tupid sinner, appear
l enthusiastic. But
one be informed,
who indulge the
animated the apos-
ded by motives dif-
any, and from all,
the efforts of men in
their worldly con-
ry *walk* by faith, *not*
In the case of St.
is companions, this

principle of action was lively and
powerful. All, in whom it is
found, move in a higher sphere,
aim at a nobler end, and share
in a brighter inheritance, than
the wisdom, the riches, and the
parade of this world, can proffer,
or bestow. Reader, permit me
to tax your time and thoughts,
with a few remarks, explanatory
of the apostle's language.

To walk is often used, in
Scripture, *to behave*, i. e. as descriptive of moral and religious
conduct. *To walk by faith*, is
to rely upon Christ for salvation,
and to live in the firm belief,
that the promises of his word
will be accomplished. It implies a reliance upon Christ, as
freely given us in the Gospel
and the receiving of his *grace*,
"to make progress in holiness
and towards eternal glory." In
the Gospel, Jesus Christ is revealed as the only Savior of sinners Here his character is exhibited, and all the duties he requires of his followers are explicitly stated. He, who receives
this testimony concerning Christ
as *true*, believes in him. And
if he likewise receives with joy
and gratitude, the requirements
of Christ as reasonable; if he
places confidence in the doctrines of Christ, imbibes their
spirit, and is habitually influenced by them, he may be said to
walk by faith.

Faith respects objects unseen.
Hence the apostle defines it to be
*the substance of things hoped for,
and the evidence of things not seen.*
The rewards, which the Gospel
proposes, are proper objects of

faith, because, in their greatest richness and beauty, they are future; and all the influence, which the anticipation of these rewards produces on the minds of men, is properly denominated the *fruit* of faith. He, therefore, who learns from the Gospel suitably to estimate these rewards, and the means by which they are secured; and, at the same time, with sincerity and perseverance uses these means, may be said *to walk by faith.*

This language is peculiarly significant. In the use of it, St. Paul seems to challenge an investigation of his motives, and to invite the strictest scrutiny in regard to his life. 'You seem to stand amazed at our conduct, and to wonder that we should make such sacrifices, and persevere in such efforts, without a nobler object in view. But you mistake our motives; you discern not our aim. *We walk by faith.* For our Master, Leader, and King, we take the once crucified Redeemer, whose *kingdom is not of this world.* He teaches to deny all selfish affections, to abstain from every sinful deed, and to serve God habitually, *being fervent in spirit;* and he points to the commencement of our existence beyond the grave, as the period when all our toils shall cease, and our fidelity shall be rewarded. We believe him, and act accordingly. And in all the difficulties, in which obedience to his commadments involves us, we are supported and animated by his promises which cannot fail. What he has *promised* we believe to be as sure, as if it were already in our possession. And in the anticipation we rejoice, and encounter with

patience every evil which meets us in the path of duty. Thus we *walk by faith.*'

Walking by faith, implies a *deadness to the world*, a heart devoted to God, and delighting supremely in his service. In a word, all *walk by faith*, who make religion the great business of life, and who refuse to be diverted from the path of duty, by the frowns or the flatteries of the world. Such are called to the performance of many duties, for which there is no temporal compensation. But, with the eye of faith they look forward to the *recompense of reward reserved for the just;* and this reward, though future, operates as an excitement to action equally strong, as if it were present.

In the Gospel, there are, likewise, some truths presented for their reception, which human reason cannot fathom. But they receive them without hesitation, and experience from them an abiding influence to faithfulness in duty. What is *known* to be communicated from God, they implicitly believe; and experience no uneasiness because they cannot explain it, or tell the reasons why it should be so. This is a distinguishing trait in the character of those who *walk by faith.* They deem it in no respect inconsistent, to believe what they cannot comprehend, and to adore a holy God, in view of the mysteries of his nature, and the mysteries of his word. This implicit confidence in their perfect guide, gives them peculiar advantages; and, borne on the wings of faith, they rise to a purer region for their happiness, while a sinning and thoughtless world views them as enthusi-

ities their servitude, and
them with reproach. I
, *all revealed truth* is re-
and maintained by them
humility and gratitude.
wish not to make a selec-
They know their incom-
y. They dare not reject.
ove the *whole.* They ad-
he plainness, excellence,
blimity of the Scriptures;
ile they pray to be spirit-
nlightened, they realize,
revelation from an in-
Being to finite minds,
necessarily contain things
their comprehension.
ese same incomprehensi-
ths proceed from the same
source with those, which
sy and plain, and furnish
nal evidence, that what
an comprehend is from
Thus, even that portion
Scriptures, which is hid-
om the researches of hu-
ason sheds a lustre on the
nd the humble believer
in every part, proofs of
livine original, and dis-
new sources of richness
auty.

let us not lose sight of the
it, which was more imme-
in the apostle's mind,
he used the words under
eration. *We walk by faith;*
all the happiness we now
from our obedience to the
is by no means to be com-
with what we shall enjoy
:er. Our present conso-
is *great;* but the joy we
ate is unspeakably *greater.*
ject of our hopes, which
all soon attain, is an intui-
sion of the glory of God,
rnal felicity in his imme-
X.

diate presence. Hence, while in
this life, *we groan being burdened;* feel as if absent from *home;*
and hold ourselves in readiness
to depart and go to be forever
with the Lord, when it shall
please him to command us.

With this idea in view, we
can be at no loss, what meaning
to attach to the phrase, *walk by
sight.* The apostle meant by it,
that he had not attained the grand
object of his desires. He did not
possess that enjoyment of God,
that view of the divine glory,
which filled his hopes, and which
he knew was the reward of faith.
For this reason, he considered
not himself as perfect, or that he
had already attained. On the
contrary, so *wide* was the prospect before him, and so enrapturing the view, that he felt disposed to forget his present and
past attainments, while, with all
the ardor of hope and the devotion of faith, he pressed forward
towards *the mark, for the prize of
the high calling of God in Christ
Jesus.* Reader, may these features
in the Christian character be
thine. Contemplate them, and
be encouraged. Review them,
and be admonished.   ALPHA.

A SHORT SERMON.

To the Editor of the Panoplist.

Sir,
I have been led to suppose, that an occasional solemn address to sinners, in your
very useful magazine, might add to its
value. It has an extensive circulation;
is read by persons of all descriptions,
and ought, therefore, to contain a word
in season for all. If you think, that this
short sermon will be useful to any, into
whose hands the Panoplist may fall, you
will, I presume, give it a place. Should

this appear in your pages, you may ex.
pect to receive something further of the
same kind.

MATT. vi, 13.

*Enter ye in at the strait gate,
for wide is the gate and broad is
the way, that leadeth to destruction; and many there be which go
in thereat.*

In this, as in many other passages of Scripture, human life is
with great propriety compared
to a journey. This world is not
our home. We have here no
continuing city. We are strangers and sojourners on earth, as
all our fathers were. We are on
a journey to another country.
We are daily advancing toward
that land, whence no traveller
returns. We are all, my friends,
hastening to our eternal home—
to the place of our everlasting
abode. We are all walking,
either in that way, *which leadeth
to destruction,* or in that, *which
leadeth unto life.*

The way to destruction is
broad; and the gate through
which it is entered, is *wide.*
Every passion, every appetite,
every corrupt desire of the human heart, opens this gate.
Whichever way you turn your
eyes, you may see an entrance
for sin; and behold a thousand
temptations—a thousand allurements to vice. In order to find
this gate, no searching, no inquiry, no diligence is necessary.
The thoughtless, the inconsiderate, the stupid, cannot miss it.
Nor is there the least obstacle to
oppose an entrance. The irres-
olute and slothful will not be
compelled to labor in order to
procure admission.

But it is no less easy to continue in the *way,* than to enter
the *gate* of iniquity. It is a *broad
way.* It is confined to no definite course. It comprehends an
extensive—an unbounded range.
Within its limits are all the
crooked paths of wickedness;
and in most of these paths you
may find leaders and companions. The proud infidel is there:
*He, that believeth not, shall be
damned* * The base hypocrite is
there: *Except your righteousness shall exceed the righteousness of the Scribes and Pharisees,
ye shall in no case enter into the
kingdom of heaven.†* The bold
blasphemer is there: *The Lord
will not hold him guiltless, that
taketh his name in vain.‡* The
giddy, the thoughtless, the irres-
olute are there: *Strive to enter
in at the strait gate; for many, I
say unto you, will seek to enter
in, and shall not be able.‖* There
too are the impure, the fraudulent, and the intemperate: *Neither
fornicators, nor adulterers, nor
thieves, nor extortioners, nor
drunkards shall inherit the kingdom of heaven.§* There, in a
word, are all impenitent sinners,
—from the unprincipled youth
to the hoary-headed transgres-
sor;—from those, who simply
live without God in the world, to
those, who drink in iniquity, like
water;—from the man, who allows himself in one sinful indulgence, or the habitual neglect of
one known duty, to him, who rejoices in iniquity, and glories in
his shame. *Those eighteen, upon
whom the tower in Siloam fell,
and slew them, think ye, that the*

* Mark xvi, 16.   † Matt. v, 20.
‡ Ex. xx, 7.   ‖ Luke xiii, 24.
§ 1 Cor. vi, 9 and 10.

above all men, that
·usalem? I tell you,
:cept ye repent, ye
·ise perish. Verily,*
· unto you, except a
again, he cannot see
of God.† Thus wide
·nd broad is the way,
to destruction; and
·s the multitude of
enter this gate and
way.
·end, art thou one of
·e—art thou in this
and consider! The
·rely important, all
or, as we have seen,
·ay; and, as we are
adeth down to hell.
·epend on the word
·f truth, it will end
·;—not annihilation
being—not a state
·us existence;—but
·l ruin, endless mis-
ng destruction from
·f the Lord and the
·power; perpetual
·to ·uter darkness,
·eeping and gnash-
where their worm
·l where the fire is
·§

O impenitent sin-
·er thou art—con-
·ings. Remember,
·e in sin, that ye are
·ay of death—on the
·leth to destruction.
·nd tremble at your
·cts. Remember,
the wrath to come.
·not your ruinous
·ingle day. Be per-
·· short in your mad
·ent and be convert-
·, for why will ye

·d 5.   † John iii, 3.
·Mark ix, 44. 2 Thes i, 9.

die. Enter the strait gate, and walk in the narrow way. Flee unto Jesus. He is the door of the sheep; he is the gate of salvation; he is the way—the *true way*—the *only way* of life.

ON THE CHIEF END OF THE DIVINE ADMINISTRATION.

For the Panoplist.

Mr. Editor,

As an attentive reader of your valuable periodical publication, I look to it for instruction upon subjects of the highest importance, as to doctrine and practice. I do not conceive, however, that the opinions, offered to the public through this channel, claim *implicit* assent and approbation from any one. How highly soever I esteem such a production, I do not understand that it pretends to infallibility; or that a thought, which is suggested to the public through this medium, may not be admitted with diffidence, doubt, and hesitation; and even examined as liable to be inaccurate. The advantage of having a theological repository, like yours, is not, I take it, that we may be dictated to by any human authority whatever; but that we may have access to important sentiments, with the reasons on which they are founded, that our understandings may be enlightened, and our stock of knowledge increased. New thoughts stimulate to new inquiries; and in this way improvement may be gained, even where we are not so happy as to be presented with truth unmixed with error. If these remarks, Mr. Editor, are in harmony with your views, and no incompatibility with the plan of your publication should stand in the way, I presume you will not object to admitting, from a correspondent, who, until now, has contented himself with reading the productions of others without offering any thing of his own, a brief examination of some thoughts on a paper entitled, *the chief end of the divine administration*, published in the Panoplist for Sept. last, p. 311.

The writer of that essay has made an attempt to conciliate two opposite theories, upon a point distinguishedly important in theology. He aims at nothing less than showing, that to say, *God administers his government for the good of creatures*, is tantamount to saying, that *he does it for his own glory;* and that they, who adopt these different modes of expression, do, in substance and effect, declare the same thing. Whether they do so indeed, I desire liberty to inquire.

There is an indistinctness, and indefiniteness, with an unfortunate inattention to the consequences of his reasoning, in the positions of that writer, which constitutes, as I think, a real defect in his treatise.

1. He seems not to be sufficiently clear and distinguishing, where he speaks of the connexion there is between the glory of God and the happiness of creatures. Because one cannot be supposed to exist without the other, he concludes they may be viewed as one complex object, or as parts of one object equally necessary to constitute one great whole. It is granted, indeed, that so far as the perfections of God are actually displayed in the

happiness that creatures enjoy, there is a certain and necessary co-existence of the glory of God with the happiness of the creature; but this no more supposes, that they must be parts of the same object, than that cause and effect are always and necessarily so blended, as to make but one idea. Cause and effect are relative terms, and to set either of them aside, is to break up the relation; and this involves a complete destruction of the whole. But because the existence of the one is necessary to the existence of the other, do we say, that they are not different things, but the same? The grace of God, as a divine influence, vouchsafed under the Gospel, is the cause, and the believer's faith is the effect. They are reciprocally necessary to each other. But does this imply, that they so belong to each other, as to make but one subject?

2. The proposition, that "the chief end of the divine administration is the good of the universe," is indefinite. What is meant by the universe? If it means God and his creation, then the universe had no existence, until after that act of the divine administration was put forth, which gave birth to creatures. And can that part of the universal divine administration which was antecedent to the creation, be supposed to have been prompted by a regard to the welfare of creatures, as comprehended in the universe, whose good is sought? If so, creation was produced for the good of creatures, which is to suppose, that a man's well being may be the motive of his creation; and, consequently, that a non-exist-

ng may be the occasion or
its being brought into ex-
s; which has strong ap-
ces of an absurdity
l it be said, that creation
had an existence in the
and counsel of God, this
it be denied; but the order
ngs is not changed; and,
ore, it is improper to place
rst in the divine counsel,
stands last in the order of
, as actually brought about
vidence. Means and ends
he same relations in the
l mind of God, as when
re exhibited to the view
a. In our conception of
, the end has always a pri-
o the means. The end is
hosen, and then means de-
for attaining it. Things
us represented in those
of Scripture, which relate
present subject; as when
postle speaks of God, as
; *created all things by Jesus*
t to the intent that now
ie principalities and powers
venly places might be known
church the manifold wis-
f God; according to the
l purpose, which he pur-
in Christ Jesus our Lord.
n the reasoning, against
we object, there is an ev-
inattention to consequen-
The writer thus explains:
be glory of God we can
lean nothing but that illus-
display of his attributes,
he is making in the view
ated intelligences." The
of creatures comes into
ory, as one of its essential
icuts, because God dis-
his attributes in those
, by which creatures are
happy. The argument,
as it has force, results in

this conclusion; viz. that whatever is of use in displaying the
divine perfections, is a part of
that display, and, therefore, belongs to the sum total, which is
expressed by the phrase, *the glo-*
ry of God. If the premises be
good, it ought to have been foreseen, that they will prove more
than has been assumed; and that
the glory of God is to be identified, not only with the happiness
of creatures, but with their misery also; for it is as certain, that
God glorifies himself in the misery of the wicked, as that he
does so in the happiness of the
righteous. What God inflicts
upon Pharaoh is to *make his*
power known, and that *his name*
may be declared throughout all
the earth, as really as the same
effect is produced by his mercies to Moses and Israel. And
therefore we are unto God *a*
sweet savor of Christ in them that
are saved, and in them that per-
ish.

Again. Another unhappy consequence should have been foreseen, when it was affirmed, that
to attribute to God an ultimate
respect to the happiness of creatures, *in itself considered, is lit-*
tle more than a paraphrase of the
proposition, that the glory of God
is his chief end, because *it is his*
nature to promote this happiness,
and in the production of such im-
mense good consists that illustri-
ous display of himself, which he
styles his glory. This reasoning being admitted as sound, and
the most complete selfishness
becomes perfectly synonymous
with the most genuine benevolence, and the purest piety; for
if God seeks his own glory, ultimately, when he has an ultimate
regard to the creature's happi-

ness, *in itself considered*, then creatures, who have an ultimate view to their own happiness, *in itself considered*, and make this the supreme object of their desire, do really, and in effect, by this exercise of entire selfishness, (for I know not how selfishness can be otherwise defined,) seek the glory of God, just as he himself does, and as they are required to do; because *in the production of such immense good* the glory of God consists. Should it be replied, that this objection is nullified by an explanatory remark, which accompanies the reasoning to which we except, viz. "By the good of creatures, as here used, we must understand that kind of enjoyment which the Bible sanctions —that pure and holy delight which the righteous will for ever enjoy;" how can this, we inquire, be any more than a begging of the question: since, if the Bible authorizes the sentiment of God's *ultimately* seeking his own glory by having an *ultimate* aim at the happiness of creatures, *it sanctions that kind of enjoyment*, which the selfish man derives from a scheme of Providence, that gives himself such pre-eminence in the system. According to the doctrine, upon which I am, remarking, selfishness is no mark of a want of holiness. My objection then remains in force. I see not why Dr. Fuller has not well expressed himself, when he observes: "Though the happiness of creatures be not admitted to be the final end of God's moral government, yet it is freely allowed to occupy an important place in the system." Gospel its own

Witness, Part I. chap. beginning.

The answer we me the question; What is end of the divine admi viz. *that it is the good verse;—that as it respe is his glory;—as it re tures, it is their happ* me either unintelligib satisfactory. No dou chief end, with respe who are ultimately ma is their happiness; an spect to those, who miserable, it is thei But there is a still fu to which these, *respec* made subservient, viz. of God, which is as dis the others, as God distinct from creatur true, that God's chief respect to any creatu use to which that cr put; but how this pr trates, or exemplifies, trine, that the glory of the happiness of cre inseparable and undis ble, I see not. I kn view of God, as he dis self, will necessarily righteous happy fore is it not equally cer others will be made miserable under a lik ery? And in what se be said, that *of him, an him, and to him are* if there be any thing and final, as creature garded?

The glory of God, i me be suffered briefly is his character. Mo lence is the principal constitutes it, though glory also in his natur

Nothing that is done in
, earth, or hell, does in
l to or diminish from his
al perfection. But the
of his nature shines
h the medium of his
· This beauty, consisting
al worth, may be seen and
plated in various sab-
but it is God's glory in
aints are represented as
ry of Christ; and it is be-
hey are in his image; his
ness is put upon them;
irit dwells in them; they
ade the righteousness of
n him; and according to
mple they walk. *But we,
ten face, beholding as in a
he glory of the Lord, are
d into the same image,* &c.
: the command, that we do
ngs to the glory of God,
, that our conduct should
exhibition of true right-
ess, even the righteous-
f God, or Christ dwelling
by faith. This is a genu-
ever-failing source of hap-
s to the believing soul;
shows in what sense our
happiness is united with
lory of God; not that they
e expressed in the same
though they have a neces-
relation to each other, even
ood conscience is a foun-
f comfort to all the faithful
rist Jesus. *For this is our
ing, the testimony of our
ience, that in simplicity and
sincerity; not with fleshly
m, but by the grace of God,
ave had our conversation in
vorld.* F. J.

For the Panoplist.

OUTRAGES ON THE SABBATH.

A GROWING profanation of the
Sabbath is an evil which is observable in many parts of our
country. The frequency and
audacity, with which this day
of hallowed rest is violated,
have weakened in the minds of
men those sentiments of reverence, with which it ought always
to be regarded, and are doing
much towards breaking down the
distinction, which still remains
to the Sabbath. A careless and
irreligious habit of thinking with
respect to this venerable institution of God, is widely diffused;
and it threatens extensive desolation to our moral interests.
This growing evil cannot be contemplated by the friends of piety,
law, and order, without fearful
apprehensions for the safety, and
prosperity of their country. The
following statement of *facts* will
exhibit a melancholy specimen
of the progressive evil under
consideration.

On a great road in the western
part of this commonwealth, public decorum and morality have
for some time past been outraged,
by the running of a stage on the
Sabbath. This, to be sure, is an
event, which, in the present re-
laxed state of morals, is not very
uncommon; but, that a combination should be formed, for the
purpose of defeating the execution of the laws, and indemnify-
ing the proprietors of the offending stage, for all fines and costs
which may be recovered against

them. is an enormity of a character which we hope has no parallel in our country. This stage runs on one of the great roads between Boston and Albany, and the combination alluded to has been formed by a number of individuals, in the western part of Massachusetts, who have associated themselves for the specific purpose of shielding the proprietors of the stage from any pecuniary penalties. Some of the persons, who belong to this combination, are men of wealth and influence. They are men too, who own no part in the stage. A respectable magistrate, who lives on the route, has instituted prosecutions for the repeated offences I have mentioned. The combination have obliged themselves, *by writing,* to defray all the expense, which has already accured to the owners of the stage, on account of any prosecutions now instituted against them; and verbal engagements have been entered into, to secure a perfect indemnity against all future prosecutions. The reasons, which induced the prosecutions, were cogent and pressing. The profanation of the Sabbath, which they were designed to suppress, were *unnecessary* and *flagrant.* They were *unnecessary* because there was no contract existing between the owners of the stage, and the government, which required them to carry the mail on the Sabbath.*

They were *unnecessary,* there was sufficient time plete the route, withou ling on the Lord's day, a Monday following, the s by all day in Albany. were *flagrant,* because t was to run, every Sabb distance of seventy mi would necessarily requ whole range of post-offic route to be opened, and taverns into a state of bu confusion for the acco tion of the passengers. were *flagrant,* because rangement was voluntar part of the owners, wa trifling with the feeling religious public, and w sisted in, after a suitabl and request had been p stop running on the Sabb

But the continuance of complained of, is the r this unblest combination magistrate, before com the prosecutions, had a c tion with the driver on ject, who gave him to stand, that the stage sh run on Sunday except i of extreme necessity; conformity to this dec for one Sabbath after, he drive. And here in all p ity would have termina evil, had not the member combination stimulated t etition of the offence, t conversations with the and promises of pecun demnity. Thus, by this nation, prosecutions for lation of the Sabbath are

* We hope our correspondent does not intend to admit the necessity of carrying the mail regularly every Sabbath, on any route. That cases may occur, which will justify government in sending expresses on the Sabbath, will not be denied; but we have always viewed it as a national evil of great magnitude, and one which calls for national repentance and reformation, that the mails are carried, and the post-

offices kept open, on that holy da part of our country. This evil, c by the national authority, and without any considerable oppositi more influence in breaking down t than any other single cause wha

defeated of their object; divine authority, and human laws, are fearlessly trampled in the dust, by the passing of the stage on each successive day, which God has destined to holy repose.

These facts are not communicated, for the purpose of prompting the inquisitive to discover the guilty individuals, who have formed the combination above described, that they may be brought forward into the light. Those unhappy persons I leave to their own consciences, and their God, and cannot but desire, that a serious and deliberate survey of their conduct, with its baleful influences on society, may induce them to tread back their erring steps. The only object proposed to be attained by communicating these facts to the public, is, to cause the religious community to come forward and put an effectual arrest upon this sin of violating the Sabbath, which is now displaying itself in open day, and bringing down upon us the judgments of offended Heaven.

May I not speak in the name of multitudes, and say, We call upon the *ministers* of the living God, to proclaim the public guilt, and danger, and point out the shame, bondage, and woe, which the enemies of society, the violators of the venerable institutions of religion, are preparing for us. We call upon them to fix the attention of the public upon the necessity of combined efforts for repressing ' the sin, which is endangering our remaining virtue and happiness. They are watchmen, appointed to descry approaching danger, and sound the alarm, and if, through indolence or the fear of man, they shrink from their duty,

the blood of those who perish will be required at their hands.

We call upon public *magistrates*, who are also the ministers of God, and guardians of the morals and order of society, to put the laws for the preservation of the Sabbath into vigorous execution. It is their business to attend on this very thing, and *"see that the commonwealth receive no detriment"* We call on them to display their veneration for the laws, by a persevering and determined suppression of those outrages, which are rapidly dissolving the moral elements, that bind society together. We call *on all the servants of God*, whether in public or private life, and on all the friends of order, to unite their efforts for the support of the civil magistrate, in the execution of the laws. Every thing may be done by combined exertion. The splendid results which have already attended the efforts of combinations for the suppression of vice, in different parts of our country, afford a joyful presage of their ultimate success, and ought to excite those, who have not yet arrayed themselves, to prosecute similar measures with ardor and alacrity. If we put forth our strength, every consideration, which can awaken confidence, and brighten our prospect of success, presses upon our view. We have the omnipotent God on our side; we have the consciences of the guilty on our side; and vice is easily hurried into dismay, and driven into darkness, when it is met by virtue in a firm and erect attitude. Virtue has always the advantages attributed to her by the greatest of poets:

——"Abash'd the devil stood,
And felt how awful goodness is, and saw
Virtue in her shape how lovely;"—

Let all the friends to society publicly range themselves on the side of virtue, and lend their combined exertions, to maintain the barriers of religion and order. The moral spectacle, which the transgressions of our country exhibit, cannot fail to impel the de-

vout Christian to weep places, and offer up hi intercessions to the o Being, who disposes th of nations, and the co individuals, that He wo from us the fearful toke anger, with which we ar and spare his heritage : struction.

March 12, 1814.

MISCELLANEOUS.

CHRIST THE GREAT PHYSICIAN.

To the Editor of the Panoplist.

Sir,

SHOULD the following remarks contain any thing, which, in your opinion, may be profitable to your readers, you may give them place in your periodical publication.

The same sin, which king Asa was charged with, is chargeable upon the people of God in general, at the present day.

It is said of Asa that he had a great disease in his feet; *yet, in his disease, he sought not to the Lord, but to the physicians.**

Many, who profess religion at the present day, apply in the first place, when they are sick, to physicians, and seem to place all their dependence on them. The physician, as regardless of God, perhaps, as his patient, will promptly say, that he can shortly remove the disease. But in defiance of all his supposed power, the patient grows worse, and begins to doubt whether he shall ever recover. The physician affirms that he can cure the disease. Again the sick man is de-

* 2 Chron. xvi, 12.

ceived, not remembering issues of life and deat God's hands, and not in sician's. He still grov and the doctor begins t Other physicians are They say that the case i ate. Then the patient his hope from an arm o destroyed; and begins to on Jesus Christ, the gre cian, by whom alone dis be cured. Thus Jesu who is always able, is on to, when the sick are co that they can have no h man. They make an arn their trust, until they fi possible for man to help

Many, who are calle tians, are not only guil sin of not seeking to t but to physicians; they e it of no consequence whe physician be a Christian an atheist, or a sceptic does this argue? Is it nc that their help is from not from God? that the need the blessing of G case? that the skill of th cian is adequate to ren disease? Is it not placi dependence on man than

this a daring affront to the
r and Preserver of life?
physicians, who are desti-
f religious principles, do
hey do without feeling any
dence on God. They
not have any thing men-
to their patients about
or eternity; but would de-
them with false hopes, and
troy the soul, lest its anxie-
uld in some way injure
dy.

unlike this conduct is
the Christian physician.
ls his dependence on God.

about to prescribe, he
tly desires God to direct
feeling his responsibility.
daily prayers, he remem-
e cases of his patients, in
l to both soul and body;
eads for Christ's sake, that
ould heal their diseases,
ve their souls from eter-
th. He daily exhorts them
to God for help, and, if
s that they draw near unto
sits down and converses
them about their soul's
interest, and prays with
r them.

, my Christian friends, on
efforts do you think you
the most reason to expect
sing? On his, who fears
and feels his dependence
countability; or on his,
egards not God? In the
ures of truth, it is thus
n: *The prayer of faith shall
he sick, and the Lord shall
im up; and if he have com-
ains, they shall be forgiven*

e will say, that they want
ayers of the Christian; but
like to have the skill of
ne who possesses skill,
er he be infidel or Chris-

tian. There is no incompatibility between piety and skill. If
the Christian's prayers are good
and acceptable, are they not as
likely to be answered when he
asks for direction, as when he
asks for a blessing on what is
used?

I do not mean, that Christians
ought never to employ a physician, who is not a man of faith
and prayer. But I contend that
they, who profess to believe,
that God alone *healeth all their
diseases, and all manner of sickness,* and to believe also that God
is a God hearing prayer, act inconsistently when they employ
the ungodly in preference to the
pious. The religious physician
has as great an opportunity of
doing good to the sick, as a faithful minister. He daily visits the
sick, and converses with them
about their immortal interests.
And if pious admonition and
counsel are ever likely to do
good, it is at such a time. They,
who employ irreligious physicians, lose all the good, which
may be derived from the counsel and prayers of those of an
opposite description.

My Christian friends is it not
God, who woundeth and bindeth
up? If God maketh sick, he
hath some important object in
view. It cannot be that a merciful God afflicteth, simply for
the sake of giving pain. He
useth sickness as a rod of correction, with which he cor-
recteth for sin. Therefore we
ought to look to God through
Christ for relief, with a penitent
heart. *Come, and let us return
unto the Lord; for he hath torn,
and he will heal us; he hath smitten and will bind us up.*

OBSERVER.

For the Panoplist.

ON THE INEFFICACY OF ADVICE AND REPROOF.

THERE are few things, which would be attended with a happier influence on society, than a general reverence, on the part of the young, for the advice of wise and experienced men. Such a disposition would remedy, to a great extent. the want of experience; and would give the young, when they most need it, a portion of that wisdom, which is seldom acquired, till those follies have been committed the bad effects of which it is impossible to prevent. In a retrospect of past life, many dangerous situations are discovered.—many wrong courses are perceived, which are wholly invisible to those who behold life in prospect only. Would the inexperienced suffer themselves to be guided by the counsel of those, who know the difficulties, and the temptations with which this world is crowded. how many alluring avenues to pain, to mortification, and disgrace, might they shun! How many abortive schemes for their advancement in worldly prosperity might they avoid! How many vicious propensities might be nipped in the bud, which are now too often cherished till they become ungovernable! Were we, indeed, to form to ourselves a picture of happy society, it would be that which is governed not by physical force, but by moral suasion: that in which the vicious are not terrified into obedience by the rigor of the laws, but won over to virtue by the influence of the judicious and experienced part of the community. But this is a state

of things, which can be plated only in imaginatic vice and reproof, althou have been bestowed wi eral hand, have been ac ed without producing, considerable extent, thei effects. Seldom are th tionate warnings, repro intreaties, even of par ministers, attended w permanent success whi sired. But if precept tioned by the most v and endearing of all 1 so frequently prove ab is no wonder that advic by persons in a less f situation, is seldom e that it is rarely listened patience, and still mer remembered or obeyed.

By some, the inefficac vice and reproof is at principally to the fault persons advised and re by others, to that of the sellor himself. It will object of the ensuing to inquire how far each opposite opinions may rect; and to ascertain, if to what extent the evil 1 mits of a remedy.

It must be acknowledg all, whose province it is late the conduct of othe to struggle with many tant difficulties. As far vice is of a moral or r nature, opposition to it expected, in consequenc hostility to moral truth, characteristic of the heart. But to be made ject of advice, of whatev is in itself disagreeabl contains an indirect ch ignorance and liability t However aware a pers

be of his own ignorance and inexperience, he always wishes to
maintain the contrary character
among his fellow men. It is
extremely painful to find, that
the deficiencies, which we had
fondly hoped to conceal, have not
escaped the notice of others. Of
all deficiencies, however, (unless
it be that of cowardice,) perhaps
there is no one, the charge or intimation of which is so galling
and humiliating to most men, as
that of ignorance of one's self and
the world; yet this is generally
implied, in regard to any one
to whom advice is addressed.

But if we are mortified, by
finding that we have been unable to conceal our own deficiencies, we are no less apt to be disgusted, by that superiority,
which is virtually assumed by
the counsellor. The superiority of others, especially if their
ages and stations in life differ
not materially from our own, is
always painful, however suggested; but when suggested by
the subject of this superiority
himself, even with the best intentions, it can scarcely fail to be
repulsive and disgusting. For
these reasons, advice is so far
from being received with gratitude, that it is very often considered by him to whom it is given,
as a species of attack upon his
character which he is bound, at
all events, to repel; and usually
leads to a scrutiny into the character of the adviser himself. In
these circumstances, vanity and
self-esteem will generally be
sharp-sighted enough to discover such defects in the character
of the adviser, as that his advice
may be triumphantly returned
upon himself.

If all attempts of this kind

prove unsuccessful, advice may
be repelled by ascribing it to
mercenary or sinister motives.
Many who cannot overcome,
by argument, the force of precepts delivered from the pulpit,
or question the superiority of
the preacher's character, will
excuse their neglect, and quiet
their consciences, by alleging
that this is the preacher's business,—the trade by which he
gains his subsistence. Not un-
frequently, those who attempt to
offer friendly advice are charged
with intermeddling in that, with
which they have no concern; and
are desired, for the future, to
keep their advice to themselves,
till it is asked for.

I have hitherto gone on the
supposition, that the person to
whom advice is addressed is
fully sensible of his need of
guidance, and of the competen-
cy of his superiors in age and
experience, to direct him. But
even this, perhaps, cannot be
said of most persons; and, least
of all, concerning those who
stand the most in need of advice;
I mean that class of young persons who are just entering on
the stage of action. There are
few individuals of this class, who
do not prove by their conduct,
that they feel better qualified to
direct themselves, than their
parents are to direct them. The
language of Dr. Young on this
subject is not more forcible, than
it is just, and agreeable to daily
observation.

——————"When young indeed,
In full content we sometimes nobly rest,
Unanxious for ourselves and only wish,
As duteous sons, our fathers were more
                            wise.
At thirty, man suspects himself a fool;
Knows it at forty, and reforms his plan.

The reason is obvious. It is natural for every one to raise his estimate of his own character as high, as his opportunities of bringing his knowledge and talents into a competition with those of others, will allow him. On this account, it is often remarked concerning those of every age, whose talents have seldom been forced into a comparison with those of others, that vanity is their prevailing characteristic. If this remark is correct, it is not to be wondered at, that those who have never had years or experience enough to convince them of their ignorance, should think themselves knowing; or that they, who think themselves better fitted to give than to receive counsel, should neglect it, when offered by others.

The preceding observations are applicable, with additional force, to *reproof.* Advice supposes only peculiar liability to error: reproof supposes actual criminality. If it is mortifying to find, that our defects have not escaped the notice of others, much more so must it be to discover that we have not succeeded in concealing our faults. Besides, those, whose moral character is actually stained, must be expected to possess less sensibility to moral obligation, more attachment to vice, and less respect, of course, for the precepts of the wise and virtuous, than those who are not necessarily in fault, but merely in peculiar danger of becoming so.

But whilst those, who assume the province of guiding the conduct of others, justly complain of the opposition which they

experience from vanity, sufficiency, and moral de tion, it becomes them to whether their want of s is not chargeable, in some ure, to their *own* misco Let them candidly ask of selves, whether their advi their example are not o variance? Whether they sometimes feel elated b superiority over those they undertake to counse when they feel this supe whether they do not of discover it? Whether they often obtrude their advi seasons in which they know that it will be of no se Whether they are always ciently careful of the repu or of the feelings of those they advise? Finally, whethe are sufficiently careful to appear, that their conduct tated by disinterested mo Unless they can satisfy selves, that they are fau none of these respects, the not ascribe their failure o cess wholly to the pride, nacy, and self-sufficiency which they have to conter

To point out, with any c erable precision, the m and degree in which an e important and justly lamer the usual inefficacy of sa advice, admits of a re would, were I competent task, lead me beyond the r able limits of a single ess may be remarked, howev general, that as far as th depends on those, who a objects of advice, it is su ble of no direct remedy. as far as the fault is char to the counsellor himself,

ground to hope that it
removed; for the pre-
1 is, that they who are
to guide others, will
·es be guided by reason,
1atever source it may

ose, who undertake
counsel to others, are
the performance of this
y have no reason to ex-
least success. The de-
ns of Scripture against
leaders of the blind, are
able to those who make
·es *blind guides*, by giv-
:e in an improper man-
·rom improper motives,
·se who fail through ig-
If, on the other hand,
ithfully perform their
ey have much encour-
both from experience
divine promises, to be-
t their exertions will be
in a good degree with

I become them, there-
they intend that their
shall have the least
·o be peculiarly careful
ntradict their precepts
conduct. How can a
ect that motives sho..ld
more influence on oth-
they have on himself; or
he be believed to be se-
urging that upon others
he has no regard, in
1g his own conduct? So
producing its intended
lvice, offered by such a
will be retorted upon
and indeed will
ively detrimental, by
the influence of
·hose precepts and ex-
;ree. Where, as in the
instance, there is a pro-
o depreciate the merits

of a particular class of persons,
what is in reality the fault of a
few will be charged to the
whole. Again, the counsellor
should carefully avoid, on the
one hand, assuming any undue
superiority over those whom he
undertakes to direct, and, on the
other, divesting himself of authority to such a degree as to
render his precepts contemptible. To preserve this medium
will be one of his most difficult
tasks. Many of those, whose
business it is to guide the conduct of others, insensibly acquire
an authoritative and dictatorial
mode of delivering their precepts. This habit is fatal to success; for nothing is so repulsive;
nothing so soon provokes opposition. The counsellor should
endeavor, as far as possible, to
disguise a remedy so unpalatable; to administer it indirectly;
and at those seasons in which
his own experience will teach
him that the mind is best fitted
to receive it. He will, also, if
the person of whom he has the
guidance be young and inexperienced, make his instructions as
particular as possible; he will
derive them from passing
events; and will avoid general
and abstract precepts, which
neither strike the young mind
with force, nor are capable of
being applied by it to particular
circumstances of life. He
should be careful to convince
those, whom he advises, that
their benefit is his ultimate object; and that his esteem for
them will be confirmed by obedience, but forfeited by neglect
of his instructions. He should
be no less careful to avoid giving
advice, and especially reproof,
to any individual, in the pres-

ence of others, whose esteem the person concerned is anxious to retain. He who reproves in public, unless compelled by necessity, acts the part of an informer; and will be so far from making a useful example of the person reproved, (which appears to be the only object of reproof given in this manner,) that he will inflame the hatred and opposition of all present; for no one can know how soon his own character will be attacked in the same manner. In fine, the man who would hope for success in the arduous work of guiding the conduct of his fellow men, must exercise discretion, not only with regard to the nature, the time, and the mode, of delivering advice, but with regard to the persons themselves, to whom it is addressed. Some are too hopelessly abandoned to warrant the least expectation, that advice will be successful in reclaiming them; or to render it proper that any one should expose himself to derision by attempting it. The precept of Solomon, *Reprove not a scorner lest he hate thee*, was doubtless intended for characters of this description; persons who have lost all sense of shame, who have become callous to the dictates of reason and conscience, and over whom moral suasion has lost its influence. Such characters, however, before they are resigned to the more powerful arm of public justice, ought to be reminded of the critical and awful situation to which they have reduced themselves. *He that being often reproved,' hardeneth his neck, shall be suddenly destroyed, and that without remedy.*   Q.

ON SENDING FOR PHYSICI[ANS]
THE SABBATH.

For the P[

Mr. Editor,
I BELIEVE it to be a pret[ty com]mon fact, that country [physi]cians have more freque[nt calls] in their profession on the [Sabbath] Day, than on any othe[r day of] the week. This fact be[ing ad]mitted, it is natural to [inquire] into the cause. Is the a[ir or the] diseases most active up[on the] day which the Lord hath [blessed] and in the hours which [he calls] his own? Is it then that [men] are most exposed to si[ckness] so that fevers, colics, &c[. make] this season as the favora[ble time] of beginning, or repeatin[g their] attacks?

I am inclined to thin[k that] neither of these surp[ositions] will be deemed a ratio[nal ac]count of the fact. Perha[ps] what I am about to off[er may] be rejected as equally un[satisfy]ing; but with your leave, [I] shall venture to give my [opin]ion, with some of the rea[sons] which it is founded. As [men] will not allow us to atten[d to] secular concerns more t[han six] days in the week, (which, [by the] way, some think a grea[t hard]ship,) men of business a[nd en]terprise are generally d[isposed] to make the most of eve[ry day] till the appointed day of [rest ar]rives. Hence they cann[ot well] afford to be sick on wee[k days] as this would be an inter[ruption] to their business;— nor c[an they] spare time, unless the [case is] very urgent, to go or s[end for] the physician, if he li[ves at] any considerable distance[. Ac]cordingly, when one of [their] persons feels indispose[d]

ard to keep about
he week, intending, if
ot get better, to spend
th in the use of medi-
:move his complaint,
ply at that time, if ne-
or medical aid.

myself known more
person act on this
and I presume, Sir,
' readers will easily
similar instances,
ve fallen under their
rvation.

any persons are often
from public worship,
ss, who are very rare-
ed, by the same cause,
:ager and active pur-
1eir secular interests!
ural consequences of
omical scheme are ob-
the first place, by neg-
) take diseases in their
state, many, who adopt
eme, really become
k, and *must* send for a
1, on the Sabbath.
oo, who would wait a
;er, if they were equal-
osed on Thursday, or
nd it very convenient
1e Sabbath for this pur-
t nothing of this kind
rfere with an early re-
: to business after the
is over. If these ob-
1s are well founded,
'rd a satisfactory answer
quiry, suggested at the
g of this paper.
:esult, I acknowledge,
t give rise to any very
train of reflections.
1ld be glad to believe
ry body anticipates the
1 of God's holy day, not
1son of sloth and carnal
1ce, or of paying that at-
to bodily health which

might and ought to have been
paid before, but as a season of
holy rest and religious improvement We must, however, when
speaking of the conduct of men,
take it as it is, not as it should
be. I have only to add, that
possibly even some professors
of religion may be able to recognize their own conduct in
this rough and hasty sketch. If
so, let me earnestly exhort them
to consider well, whether they
can answer it to their consciences and their God. Let no one
misunderstand me, as if I meant
to insinuate, that it is improper to send for physicians and
take medicine on the Sabbath.
Ali I mean to insist on is, that
there is no reason why physicians should be more employed on that, than on any other
day, and that every calculation
to gain time by setting apart
that holy day for medical applications is sinful. Whoever does
it, is chargeable with neglecting
the health of his soul as well as
of setting a pernicious example
before his family, and depriving
his physician of the benefit of
public worship.   MIKROS.

ON THE GOOD USES, WHICH
MIGHT BE MADE OF THE MON-
EY NOW EXPENDED IN WAR.

For the Panoplist.

IN a paper published in the
Panoplist for Nov. 1813, (part
2,) p. 444, I offered to the public some calculations on the ex-
pences of war. From these calculations it appeared, that the
Christian world expended in the
year preceding Sept. 9, 1813,
the enormous sum of $2,360,
000,000, the annual interest of

which, at 6 per cent, would be *one hundred and thirty five millions and six hundred thousand dollars.*

On reflection, I have no reason to suppose this result larger than the truth. If some items of the account are too large, though I do not admit that they are, others are certainly too small. The money raised by Great Britain, for instance, as I put the sum down from memory, was stated to be £103,000,000 sterling, whereas it was in fact £113,000,000.

I computed, also, that the loss of life and of productive labor, in consequence of war, during the same year, involved a loss of property equal to $975,000,000, at least. The interest on this sum would be *fifty-eight millions ana five hundred thousand dollars.*

At the close of that paper I proposed to "pursue this subject, by specifying some of the good purposes to which this money might be applied."

Let us imagine, then, that all the armed men in the Christian world, on the 10th of Sept. 1813, and all their attendants, and all their employers, had been suddenly changed in their moral character, and become so thoroughly transformed, as to *do justly, and to love mercy, and to walk humbly with their God.* It is very clear, that hostilities would have immediately ceased; all the armies would have returned to their respective countries; and by the first of January 1814, those, who had been engaged only in war and violence, would be ready to enter upon the useful and profitable labors of life.

Let us imagine further people of all Christian were willing to make pecuniary sacrifices, *for year*, with a view to pro temporal and eternal goo fellow creatures, as the the year preceding, in on offensive and defens and we shall find, that *nent fund* would be raise at 6 per cent interest produce $194,100,000,

I do not say, that it be wise to raise such but only that such sacri have been specified, it. It would certainly however, for Christian n exert themselves on scale, and in their nati pacities, for the promul the Gospel and the civ of mankind.

But to return: If war cease, never to be ren nations called Christi mankind were universa vinced of the fact, the the present systems of t after the single year abo tioned, might be almost devoted to the extingu of the war-debts, whi press upon many natio enormous weight. To t purpose might be applie ever could be derived fr sale of the brass, the i steel, &c. &c. which is various kinds of arms, bu might be converted to purposes. The material tifications, which would molished, might be sol converted into dwelling arsenals might be rent commercial ware-house of war might be convert ships of trade; and eve

reparation might answer
valuable end, and contri-
o the wealth and comfort
public. The least valua-
uld be used for fuel, and
the words of Scripture
be fulfilled by *burning*
ariot with fire. It is rea-
le, that those walls, which
een erected by the toils of
r twenty successive gene-
s, which have been mois-
with the sweat and ce-
d with the blood of un-
millions, should be made
viate the national burdens.
would be an immense
of productive labor to ev-
tion; so that, in these vari-
ays, every national debt
be discharged in a few

ile this process was going
e internal condition of ev-
tation would be receiving
and unexampled improve-
. Schools would be every
supported; the children
poor would every where
ucated; churches would ev-
here be erected; the Sabbath
l every where shine with
ious effulgence, and, as of-
is it returned, would be a
f joy and salvation to assem-
myriads. The writer of
reflections has been assur-
a gentleman, who travel-
l over England about the
1792, and again about
ears afterwards, that the
ess of internal improve-
in that kingdom within
ty years is amazing, and
exceeds the increase of
xternal commerce. This
nent may be depended on,
e gentleman travelled, in
rst instance, to use his own
ssion, 'with a young, in-

quiring eye,' and, in the second,
he went over the same ground
with a particular view to make
a comparison. If this is the
fact, notwithstanding the pressure of external war, how much
more rapid and extensive would
be the progress in a time of profound peace, and when all the
vast resources of the kingdom
should be gradually withdrawn
from their destination, as the
public debt melted like snow under an April sun.

As the liberated resources of
every nation would abundantly
suffice for every domestic improvement, and would meliorate
the condition of the people, in
relation to temporal things and
spiritual privileges, let us suppose the income from the permanent fund, raised by the
saving of *one year's war ex-*
penses, to be devoted solely to
the promulgation of the Gospel
among the heathen nations, and
nations partly heathen. And
surely it is not unreasonable,
that men should make such a
sacrifice for such an object. It
is now more than eighteen hundred years since the hymn of the
angels was heard in Bethlehem,
Glory to God in the highest, and
on earth peace, good will to-
wards men. The full import of
this hymn will hereafter be understood by mankind. As to the
past, men have always devoted
the best of their resources, their
wealth, their talents, to the arts
of war. Every year since any
nation has become nominally
Christian, has seen the prime of
every thing devoted either to actual war, to a preparation for it,
or to repair the breaches which
war had made. It is time that
men had found out, that war

is not the way to happiness; let them pursue a different plan; let them become faithful subjects of the Prince of peace, and use all their efforts to extend his dominion.

After these preliminary observations, I proceed to state some of the purposes, to which the sum of $194,100,000 might be applied, in carrying on the great work of evangelizing and civilizing mankind. The great end should be the promulgation of the Gospel. This should hold the first place, not only in fact, but in appearance. Civilization would be a necessary attendant. The notion of civilizing first, in order to Christianize afterwards, is chimerical. Is not the Gospel beyond all comparison the greatest mean of civilization to be found in the universe? But I have not time now to refute at length an opinion, into which some well meaning persons have fallen. I proceed therefore to state,

1. That a part of this sum might be expended in distributing copies of the Holy Scriptures, in various translations now existing, among vast multitudes of the human race, who may be called partly heathens. They have heard of the Gospel, but know little or nothing about it. Of this description are many of the Laplanders, the Finlanders, the inhabitants of many Russian provinces, many natives of Asia who are more or less acquainted with the Dutch and Portuguese languages, and many natives of New Spain, and South America, who have learned the Spanish language This class of people must embrace many millions; and I have no doubt,

that five millions of copies of the Scriptures might be distributed among them to advantage. Here need be no delay for want of translations. Stereotype plates, kept in constant use, would soon furnish the requisite number of copies. The expense of Bibles, in different languages, would be different; as, in some of the Asiatic languages, much more paper is requisite than in European languages. But, though the paper would cost more, labor costs less. On the whole, I think it a liberal allowance, in all these calculations, to suppose, that copies of the Scriptures, well bound, will cost the average expense of the English, Welsh and French Bibles to the British and Foreign Bible Society; which is *one dollar and thirty cents each*, in the cheapest form distributed by that Society. The English Bible costs the Society just a dollar; it could be furnished from stereotype plates in this country, and bound as well as the English copies, at eighty cents or less. It is furnished, I understand, by the Philadelphia Bible Society, bound in sheep, for fifty cents a copy. I think it may be taken for granted, therefore, that 5,000,000 copies of the Scriptures might be furnished for distribution among nations partly heathen, at an expense of $6,500,000.

But the great work is to supply those, who are altogether heathens, totally involved in moral darkness, and utterly ignorant of the Savior of men. It is desirable, that the Bible should be translated into every language of the world; and, therefore, *Colleges for translations* should be es-

in all the principal na-
ribes, of the heathen
pecuniary means were
College for translations,
scale should be insti-
China. Cochin-China,
Thibet, Siam, Pegu, at
Wales's Island for the
population of Asia, at
Calcutta, Benares, Ma-
mbo, Bombay, in Per-
ia, Turkey, Georgia,
k Islands, Palestine,
Abyssinia, Madagascar,
Holland. Smaller es-
nts of the same kind
made in various other
e world; in Greenland,
or, in Lower Canada,
estern parts of the Uni-
, in many regions be-
Mississippi, and on the
t coast, in South Amer-
mg the western coasts
at the Cape of Good
eastern Africa, in the
the Pacific ocean, at
tka, Japan, and in the in-
Asia. Of these smaller
probably two or three
would be necessary; say
red and fifty.
be objected, that the
ents of the heathen
would not permit such
ments to be made in
ritories. This may be
art; but in the great ma-
instances there is rea-
lieve that no opposition
made. China would be
ely to be permanently
, than any other country;
t is far from certain, that
d influence of the courts
t Britain, Russia, and
would fail to procure a
ulation of the Scriptures,
the governments of the
world exert themselves

as much to open a way for the
unmolested propagation of the
truth, as they have done for ambitious or commercial purposes;
let these exertions be accompanied by the prayers of all the
pious; and who can say, that any
proper attempt will be unsuccessful? But if China should refuse the precious gift at first,
some suitable place might be
chosen in the vicinity of that empire, where all the Chinese books
could be procured and natives engaged to assist. After the Scriptures should be well translated
into Chinese, they could be published and distributed as opportunity should be presented. Mr.
Morrison seems well calculated
to superintend such a College.

At Calcutta, the establishment
of the Baptist missionaries would
only need to be enlarged in order to form such a College. After the addition of new buildings,
new laborers in the work of
translation, and an increase of
the library, it would be an establishment precisely of the kind
here intended. Indeed, the College of Fort William in Bengal,
as formed by Marquis Welles-
ley, came very near being a college of this description. It
doubtless embraced many other
objects; but a principal regard
was had to a preparation for giving the Scriptures to Asia, in
her most widely diffused languages; and, for this purpose, a
hundred learned natives were collected from every part of India,
from Persia and from China. The
expense of this College was complained of by the East India Company, and was probably considerable. The salary of Dr. Carey,
as professor of Shanscrit, is
about $6,000 a year; that of the

other professors was probably the same.[*] Colleges on a large scale, with extensive buildings, great libraries, and a large number of professors, tutors, and students, strike the eye as expensive establishments; and they do in fact cost something. Yet compared with arsenals, and army hospitals, they cost very little. If funds were ample, and exertions were made worthy of the cause, each of the larger of the colleges above mentioned should contain a competent number of learned missionaries, and of learned natives; at least a hundred of both classes, on an average. In some countries, there is nothing that can be called learning; yet, even in these, natives should be trained up to learning, and should be present, as a translation progresses, to ascertain whether it conveys the meaning of the original. The expense of supporting these hundred persons might amount to $100,000; the proper buildings to begin with $50,000; the library well furnished with the most important books in biblical literature $25,000; the casting of extensive founts of type attached to each college $25,000; the support of a few printers merely to commence the work $10,000; and a small supply of paper $15,000: the whole amounting to $225,000; —or $5,175,000 for the 23 large colleges.

Let each of the smaller establishments cost one third as much as the larger, or $75,000; the ex-

pense of the whole 25(...) $18,750,000. These (...) would be establishment (...) a part of the instructors (...) forth occasionally into t(...) boring districts. and (...) missionaries. But bes(...) another class of mi(...) would be needed, who w(...) etrate. in every practic(...) into heathen countries. (...) ering, that there are (...) 650,000,000 heathens (...) hometans in the world, (...) not be a large allowance (...) one missionary to 25,0(...) or 26,000 missionaries (...) tion to those occupied i(...) leges and their viciniti(...) expense of supporting (...) $600 each, would be 1(...)

Permit me here to re(...) the sake of illustration, (...) appears by the foregoi(...) ment, *two hundred an(...) three new colleges* could (...) tuted, with new buildin(...) libraries, more than 10 (...) fessors, and about 3,000 (...) in the whole, and with (...) type and a stock of pape(...) ing to each; and that 26(...) sionaries could also be e(...) at four or five thousand (...) stations, at an expense a(...) to that incurred in a sir(...) by the United States in (...) ent war. The above (...) ments would contain nea(...) active, diligent, faithful (...) greater part of whom we(...) families; the whole m(...) Christian population of n(...) a hundred thousand so(...) tered as lights in the da(...) of the earth. But to pr(...)

Beside the foregoing, (...) useful class of men migl(...) ployed in diffusing ligh(...) struction; I mean nativ(...)

---

[*] It is proper to state here, that the salary of Dr. Carey is put into common stock, with the earnings of his brethren, and they all draw out for their expenses according to the same rule. What remains is devoted to the great work of the mission.

olmasters, who could in-
the Scriptures exten-
the children and the
the population, as has
nd easily practicable in
Thus $5,000,000 would
e Scriptures into 25,000
and neighborhoods, and
stated reader of them
and to small circles as-
for the purpose. There
lations enough already
d in Asiatic languages
h copies of the Bible to
ders. It is to be under-
at all missionaries, not
e fully employed, would
he children wherever
ould be formed.

of the great scheme of
zing the world, numer-
ies could be formed, and
moderate distances from
er, on the skirts of every
ed and heathen country.
of these should contain
nen, one faithful Gos-
ister, one or two good
asters, and a handicrafts-
every useful trade. All
e industrious; all should
fear of God in their
nd exhibit proofs of up-
and benevolence in
duct. In the commence-
these colonies, the outfit
ssionaries, and the trans-
of all their goods, the
g millions would be ex-
as the extent of the col-
ld be regulated accord-
he money should hold
this way, the surplus
n of some parts of Eu-
ld be drawn off, and the
s would improve their
ondition, as well as com-
the knowledge of sal-
the ignorant.

As a part of this scheme, instead of a thousand ships of war,
Great Britain would have need of
a thousand ships for the transportation of Christian missionaries and colonists; but the difference in the expense, is well
worthy of notice. One seventy
four gunship costs not less than
20 large, elegant, commodious
vessels for the conveyance of persons and merchandize; and the
expense of keeping them, respectively, in active employment,
is in about the same proportion.

Possibly I may hereafter furnish a paper, on the small expenses which men, which even
Christians, seem willing to incur
for the noblest of all purposes,
compared with those which they
incur, sometimes willingly, for
the support of war.   A. B.

HAPPY REFORMATION.

To the Editor of the Panoplist.

Sir,
If you think the following account will promote the cause of religion, please to insert it in your useful publication.

In a town about 20 miles north
of Montpelier, (Ver.) there lived
a very poor man, who was in the
constant habit of laboring on the
Sabbath. Last spring he had a
Bible given him by the Bible Society in this state. Upon reading
it, he felt condemned for laboring
on the Sabbath; and, on examining the Scriptures, he became
fully convinced of his sin in this
particular, and of his sinful state;
and in a few months was brought
into the liberty of the Gospel.

Soon after, a neighbor came to
see him on the Sabbath; but he

had no relish for the company of his visitor, on that day. He was at a loss how to communicate his feelings; at length he took his neighbor to the barn, and said; See how the Lord has blessed me this year. I never before had so good crops of grain and hay; and I have done no work on the Sabbath to obtain them. I have been better prospered with six days, work than I used to be with seven.

Montpelier, Nov. 1813.

VOLUNTARY ENGAGEMENT TO SUPPRESS INTEMPERANCE.

THE following paper has been circulated for signatures, in a country town, with a view to combine the exertions of the well-disposed. The subscribers, after pledging themselves in this manner, are to meet and agree upon such a course of proceeding, as may be thought expedient.

WHEREAS the use of ardent spirits in our beloved country, has

become so general, and in instances so excessive, as minish the property, corr morals, destroy the happin endanger the eternal wel of thousands, and may ju viewed as one of those sins, on account of which as a nation enduring the ments of heaven; which orations have greatly alarm considerate and benevole excited them to ende check the growing evils fore, we the subscribers, i ants of the town of —, do with, and unite in, such b lent attempts, by engaging ert our utmost endeavors, within the sphere of our ence may walk at such a d from that awful precipice which so many thousand fallen and been dashed in as, by divine aid, may sect own safety and that of all with whom we are conne on whom we have any inf

REVIEWS.

LIX *The Juvenile Spelling Book, being an Easy Introduction to the English Language, containing easy and familiar lessons in spelling, with appropriate reading lessons, calculated to advance the learners by easy gradations, and to teach the orthography of Johnson, and the pronunciation of Walker. By* A PICKET, *Author of the 'Juvenile Expositor, &c.* Newburyport; E. Little and Co.

THOUSANDS of years since, it was foretold by the voice of prophecy that HOLINESS TO THE LORD

should be written on the the horses, when God sho to fight agains· those, w fought against mount Zion the piety of his people wi forth conspicuously; the ture of their houses, thei ments, and even the trapp their horses, will indica consecration of all work sessions to God To n their zeal for their Red to enforce the doctrines ties of his Gospel; to prove selves his faithful servan be the dearest objects o hearts. Do not the Mis

the Bible Societies, the
cieties, and other be-
institutions, which have
sen, like new stars
leavens, to guide the
the Savior, argue that
lay of glory is dawn-
us. To these considera-
y we not add others
onclusive, though less
in their aspect. Many
t professedly religious,
Holiness to the Lord
upon them. Though
. or science is the ap-
object of the author,
ggests some religious
ers to some religious
octrine, and imbues his
a a religious spirit. Of
iption is the Univer-
raphy, the Gazetteer of
rn Continent, and the
r of the Bible. In de-
countries, which have
subjects of prophecy,
facts suggested very
g reflections of a relig-
ncy. The same may
ncerning some of our
ies for schools. Among
ol books of a similar
on, the Juvenile Spel-
k holds a respectable
is a spelling book, it
aguished merit. The
y easy gradations from
nost simple to what is
the analogical arrange-
he words, according to
l of the vowels, present-
oung learner with the
of the English lan-
their proper order, and
g perspicuity, and sim-
e important character-
his work. But the fea-
important in our view,
oral instruction of its

lessons. It breathes a religious spirit, such as ought to be found in every book, put into the hands of children. While the child is learning to read such a book, he may be insensibly learning to be good; while the instructor is teaching orthography and pronunciation, he may be rearing a little immortal for celestial glory; while the parent sends his child to school, he may place him in a seminary of spiritual life. We select the following passage, as a specimen of the work, and the spirit of the lessons.

"The good and dutiful son is one, who honors his parents, by paying them the utmost deference and respect; by a becoming reverence for them, a filial affection for their persons, a tender regard for their safety and preservation, a constant and cheerful attention to their advice, and a ready and implicit obedience to their commands. As he becomes every day more sensible of his obligations, he grows every day more solicitous to repay them. He employs his youth to support their age, his abundance to relieve their wants, and his knowledge and strength to support their infirmities. He is more careful of his character and reputation in the world, because their's depends upon it. Ever anxious for their welfare, and attentive to their happiness, he endeavors by every method in his power, to prolong their days, that his own may *be long in the land.* He rests assured, that God will not only bless obedient children; but reward them with the possession of heaven, where it will be well with them forever, and where we shall all join, son and father, daughter and mother, wife and husband, servant and master, all the relations and connexions of this life, to honor our great Parent, the Protector, the Lord, and the Master of us all"!

This little book is recommended by several presidents of our colleges, and by a number of instructors and clergymen of eminence; and well deserves the patronage of the public.

intemperance upon civil society. It emancipates its subjects invariably from the fear of the Lord, influencing either the conscience or the heart. It is also a contagious sin; it is a moral pestilence, before which the bloom of Eden would fade, and sicken, and die; it impairs the physical strength of a nation; it breaks the spirits, damps the courage, annihilates the enterprise, dissipates the wealth, and debases the morals of a people. It undermines every civil and religious institution. It prepares men to become slaves, delivers them, at length, to the tyrant whom God has prepared to rule them with a rod of iron, for the punishment of their sins.

"4. We learn, from the subject, the importance of the Christian Sabbath. It preserves in the world the knowledge of God, and the influence of his moral government. It upholds his worship, and, by unceasing repetition, keeps alive in the minds of men the precepts and the sanctions of his law. It forms the consciences of men, and preserves them. It multiplies men of moral principles; the only men who can be trusted in the hour of temptation. It makes freemen, who are capable of being free, and lays the only foundation for permanent civil liberty. It promotes health by the intermission of labor, which, if unremitted, would prematurely exhaust the human constitution. It promotes wealth, by the new vigor which it weekly gives to man, to resume his labor; and by keeping back those crimes, which debilitate the body and dissipate the substance. But especially, is the Sabbath the power of God and the wisdom of God to salvation. Where there is no Sabbath, there is no ministry of reconciliation; no knowledge of salvation; no worship of God; no fear of the Lord; and no influences of the Spirit to convince of sin, to convert the soul, and prepare men for heaven. The extinction of the Sabbath would be the return of idolatry with all its darkness, impurity, and blood. It would be to put out the Sun of Righteousness, and leave benighted men to grope their way to hell through the region of the shadow of death!

"5. It appears from our subject, that those immoralities which trespass upon the rights of Jehovah, are as proper subjects of legislative prohibition and punishment, as those crimes which invade directly the rights of men; for they terminate, in the second step, in the same thing. The profane man may not of course be a thief, but his profanity tends to emancipate others from the fear of God, who tempted, will not fail to steal and may not be himself dishonest; neglects, he contaminates his often his neighbors, till the pernicious influence, become dishonest; Sabbath-breaker may not be respects, an immoral man, but setting the influence of his example down the Sabbath, he overthrows his influence extends, the government of God; and lets loose war upon each other, as they are by circumstances and by their ity. Is it proper, then, to man who sets fire to his neighbor's And shall he escape who and by his influence prompts Should the sword of justice villain brandishes the dagger the fire-brand, and smite work of ruin is accomplished

"6. It follows from what I that it is both the duty and legislators to countenance religion, and its institutions desperately wicked, and must ed somehow. Civil rulers are God, appointed for this very bound to exercise their best to provide for public safety. the Lord is the most salutary influence that can be addressed man mind. This influence the Gospel and its institutions gislators desire the temporal men, if they seek national power and greatness only, romize Christian institutions there is so much impotence such power in the Providence carry headlong the best con scheme, that all government ked and contemptible, from of God is exiled.—They men need to supply the their wisdom, by taking ho dom of God; and hide their taking hold on his strength."

Many consideration curred to us, while re paragraphs and the parts of the sermon; been so liberal in our that we must leave reflections of the read

RELIGIOUS INTELLIGENCE.

AMERICAN MISSIONARIES.

istian public have been for some
ous to hear from the missiona-
Asia. The impediments, which
at war has thrown in the way of
idence with that quarter of the
e often embarrassing.

be recollected, that our last intel-
om Messrs. Nott and Hall left
board ship, about the last of Nov.
hey had taken passage from Cal-
Ceylon, or Bombay, (being un-
t which place they should at-
fix themselves,) and wrote back
ot boat after leaving the banks of
es. The last that we have heard
Newell is, that he left the Isle of
r Bombay on the 24th of Febru-
. It was not to be expected that
arrive there before the date of
ing letter; but with a prosperous
se would meet his brethren soon

ve strong hopes, that the appre-
expressed by Messrs. Nott and
not been realized; and that they
mitted to remain quietly at Bom-
he new charter of the East India
reached that place; which it
did in Nov. or Dec. last. After
il of this act of parliament, it is
l that no peaceable, prudent mis-
will be molested by the local gov-
.

lowing letter has the London post
Oct. 7; it having been probably
to some person who forwarded it.
ssionaries had been sent to Eng-
sey thought it possible they might
hould probably have heard from
ore this time.

. Nott and Hall very properly
ief sketch of what they had writ-
vious letters, and as their summa-
ciously expressed, and may re-
minds of readers, we publish
le letter to the Corresponding
r of the Am. Board of Commis-
s for For. Missions.

"*Bombay, March* 17, 1813.
r. and dear Sir,

pathize with you and our distant
general, in the grief you must
e unexpected war in which our
involved. We daily unite our
nth yours to the "Giver of Peace

and Lover of Concord," that you may
speedily be delivered from the evils which
it must have introduced, and that those
which you fear may be averted from you.
We had hoped, with the friends of Jesus
we believe both in England and America,
that these kindred nations would have
lived in love and unity, and been joined
in diffusing their religion far and wide.
We hope so still. The prayers, offered
up by Christ's real friends for this, will
not, we trust, remain long unanswered. That there are such prayers, indeed, does not fail to induce in us the continual expectation of hearing the good
news of peace. But you will be more
anxious, dear Sir, we doubt not, to learn
our situation, than to hear our views of
yours.

"We are happy to inform you, that
through the goodness of God, we are at
length arrived upon the ground, which
we have chosen as the seat of our missionary labors; though, as you will presently
see, not with the most flattering prospects.
We arrived on the 12th ult. eleven weeks
after leaving Bengal. Five weeks of this
time we spent on the Coromandel coast,
at the French settlement of Pondicherry,
from whence we wrote you our last letter.*
Though we shall have room for but little
in this letter, we shall, as the events of
the war may have prevented your receiving some or all of our letters, notice such
of the principal occurrences, as will give
you a general view of the past, and prepare you to understand our present situation

"Soon after our arrival in Bengal,
which was early in August, we were ordered to return to America in the ship
which brought us. With expectations,
which we finally gave up, we obtained
leave to go to the Isle of France. Though
our arrangements were made, at a very
early period, to go to that place, we were
detained by causes not under our control,
till we were led by further inquiries to entertain hopes of succeeding in this place,
of which we had previously despaired
After this, we first thought of coming by
the way of Ceylon; but finally obtained
passports departing † After all this was

* *This letter has not been received.*
† *This is probably the technical phrase
for a general passport to leave the
country*

intemperance upon civil society. It emancipates its subjects invariably from the fear of the Lord, influencing either the conscience or the heart. It is also a contagious sin; it is a moral pestilence, before which the bloom of Eden would fade, and sicken, and die; it impairs the physical strength of a nation; it breaks the spirits, damps the courage, annihilates the enterprise, dissipates the wealth, and debases the morals of a people. It undermines every civil and religious institution. It prepares men to become slaves, delivers them, at length, to the tyrant whom God has prepared to rule them with a rod of iron, for the punishment of their sins.

"4. We learn, from the subject, the importance of the Christian Sabbath. It preserves in the world the knowledge of God, and the influence of his moral government. It upholds his worship, and, by unceasing repetition, keeps alive in the minds of men the precepts and the sanctions of his law. It forms the consciences of men, and preserves them. It multiplies men of moral principles; the only men who can be trusted in the hour of temptation. It makes freemen, who are capable of being free, and lays the only foundation for permanent civil liberty. It promotes health by the intermission of labor, which, if unremitted, would prematurely exhaust the human constitution. It promotes wealth, by the new vigor which it weekly gives to man, to resume his labor; and by keeping back those crimes, which debilitate the body and dissipate the substance. But especially, is the Sabbath the power of God and the wisdom of God to salvation. Where there is no Sabbath, there is no ministry of reconciliation; no knowledge of salvation; no worship of God; no fear of the Lord; and no influences of the Spirit to convince of sin, to convert the soul, and prepare men for heaven. The extinction of the Sabbath would be the return of idolatry with all its darkness, impurity, and blood. It would be to put out the Sun of Righteousness, and leave benighted men to grope their way to hell through the region of the shadow of death!

"5. It appears from our subject, that those immoralities which trespass upon the rights of Jehovah, are as proper subjects of legislative prohibition and punishment, as those crimes which invade directly the rights of men; for they terminate, in the second step, in the same thing. The profane man may not of course be a thief, but his profanity tends to emancipate others

from the fear of God, who, if the tempted, will not fail to steal. The ard may not be himself dishonest, neglects, he contaminates his childre often his neighbors, till they, by hi nicious influence, become dishonest Sabbath-breaker may not be, in oth spects, an immoral man, but by co ting the influence of his example to down the Sabbath, he overturns, a his influence extends, the whole government of God; and lets men lo war upon each other, as they are te by circumstances and by their own d ity. Is it proper, then, to punish man who sets fire to his neighbor's l And shall he escape who laid the and by his influence prompted to the Shall the sword of justice sleep wh villain brandishes the dagger, and the fire-brand, and smite only wh work of ruin is accomplished?

"6. It follows from what has bee that it is both the duty and the po legislators to countenance the Ch religion, and its institutions. Me desperately wicked, and must be re ed somehow. Civil rulers are mini God, appointed for this very thing bound to exercise their best dis to provide for public safety. The the Lord is the most salutary rest influence that can be addressed to t man mind. This influence is embo the Gospel and its institutions. If tl gislators desire the temporal well men, if they seek national wealt power and greatness only, they wi tronize Christian institutions—B there is so much impotence in ma such power in the Providence of (carry headlong the best concerted l scheme, that all governments appe ked and contemptible, from which t of God is exiled.—They who rul men need to supply the deficien their wisdom, by taking hold on th dom of God; and hide their weakn taking hold on his strength." pp. 1

Many considerations hav curred to us, while reading paragraphs and the succee parts of the sermon; but we been so liberal in our quota that we must leave them t reflections of the reader.

RELIGIOUS INTELLIGENCE.

AMERICAN MISSIONARIES.

The Christian public have been for some time anxious to hear from the missionaries in Asia. The impediments, which the present war has thrown in the way of correspondence with that quarter of the world, are often embarrassing.

It will be recollected, that our last intelligence from Messrs. Nott and Hall left them on board ship, about the last of Nov. 1812. They had taken passage from Calcutta to Ceylon, or Bombay, (being undecided at which place they should attempt to fix themselves,) and wrote back by the pilot boat after leaving the banks of the Ganges. The last that we have heard from Mr. Newell is, that he left the Isle of France for Bombay on the 24th of February, 1813. It was not to be expected that he would arrive there before the date of the following letter; but with a prosperous passage, he would meet his brethren soon after.

We have strong hopes, that the apprehensions expressed by Messrs. Nott and Hall have not been realized; and that they were permitted to remain quietly at Bombay till the new charter of the East India Company reached that place; which it probably did in Nov. or Dec. last. After the arrival of this act of parliament, it is presumed that no peaceable, prudent missionaries will be molested by the local governments.

The following letter has the London post mark of Oct. 7; it having been probably enclosed to some person who forwarded it. If the missionaries had been sent to England, as they thought it possible they might be, we should probably have heard from them before this time.

Messrs. Nott and Hall very properly gave a brief sketch of what they had written in previous letters; and as their summary is judiciously expressed, and may refresh the minds of readers, we publish their whole letter to the Corresponding Secretary of the Am. Board of Commissioners for For. Missions.

"*Bombay, March 17, 1813.*
"Rev. and dear Sir,

We sympathize with you and our distant friends in general, in the grief you must feel at the unexpected war in which our country is involved. We daily unite our prayers with yours to the "Giver of Peace and Lover of Concord," that you may speedily be delivered from the evils which it must have introduced, and that those which you fear may be averted from you. We had hoped, with the friends of Jesus we believe both in England and America, that these kindred nations would have lived in love and unity, and been joined in diffusing their religion far and wide. We hope so still. The prayers, offered up by Christ's real friends for this, will not, we trust, remain long unanswered. That there are such prayers, indeed, does not fail to induce in us the continual expectation of hearing the good news of peace. But you will be more anxious, dear Sir, we doubt not, to learn our situation, than to hear our views of yours.

"We are happy to inform you, that through the goodness of God, we are at length arrived upon the ground, which we have chosen as the seat of our missionary labors; though, as you will presently see, not with the most flattering prospects. We arrived on the 12th ult. eleven weeks after leaving Bengal. Five weeks of this time we spent on the Coromandel coast, at the French settlement of Pondicherry, from whence we wrote you our last letter.* Though we shall have room for but little in this letter, we shall, as the events of the war may have prevented your receiving some or all of our letters, notice such of the principal occurrences, as will give you a general view of the past, and prepare you to understand our present situation.

"Soon after our arrival in Bengal, which was early in August, we were ordered to return to America in the ship which brought us. With expectations, which we finally gave up, we obtained leave to go to the Isle of France. Though our arrangements were made, at a very early period, to go to that place, we were detained by causes not under our control, till we were led by further inquiries to entertain hopes of succeeding in this place, of which we had previously despaired. After this, we first thought of coming by the way of Ceylon; but finally obtained passports departing † After all this was

---

* This letter has not been received.

† This is probably the technical phrase for a general passport to leave the country.

done, our passage paid, and part of our
baggage on board, we were on a sudden
informed, that provision was to be made
for our passage to England on the fleet
then to sail in five days. As both we and
our captain had taken the regular steps
for departure, we embarked according to
our previous arrangements, and arrived at
this place as was mentioned above.

"This field, which we chose, we think,
after deliberate and prayerful examination, is so eligible, being connected in its
language with a country immense and
populous, and, as a commercial place, with
many countries immense and populous,
that we presume, should we succeed in
staying, our choice will not fail to meet
your highest wishes. Our objections to
Birmah were, the unsettled state of the
country—its particular jealousy of Europeans—the dangers and difficulties with
which the Baptist mission there has been
struggling,—and the fear that an attempt
by us would be followed, not only by its own
defeat, but likewise by the defeat of that
mission. In a word, *this* is the field we
esteem the most desirable;—but there is
some reason to fear, that we shall not be
suffered to remain.

"The Governor, (Sir Evan Nepean,
Vice president of the British and Foreign
Bible Society,) bears the character of a
religious man; and is, we have much
reason to believe, himself inclined to
favor us. The only difficulty arises from
the strong recommendation of the supreme government that we should be sent
away. This strong recommendation results from their own original desire, and
from their displeasure at the manner of our
leaving Bengal; with the regularity of
which we believe they were not thoroughly acquainted. We have stated our desires and explained our conduct to the
Governor, and are informed by him, that
he has nothing further to say to us at
present. Our hopes of staying are so
strong, that we have already commenced
learning the Mahratta language.

"As the general government have been
offended, you must not be surprised, if,
when we write again, our letter should be
dated in England; or if you should hear
from our own lips the story of our trials
and disappointments. God forbid that we
should be so severely afflicted in this way,
and give us rather our sufferings in our
work than by taking us from it. Pray
for us, that we may never faint in our
minds, and may be prepared, if that be
the will of God, to enter upon a new
course of wanderings and to be baffled by
new disappointments.

"We repeat a wish contained in our
former letters, that the communications
made to us by the way of Bengal may, for

the present, be committed to t
Dr. Carey.

"As to our funds, you may we
them low. We hope some effecto
of replenishing them has alr
adopted. Should we remain in
an economy, which you would
will not more than make our sal
port us. Besides, we shall soon
of many native books, which c
tained only at a very high rate
must immediately be at conside
pense for native instructors.
these things that the truth may
and must leave the measure o
mittances to your power and
ment; assuring you that at p
have no plans of spending, and
never shall have, but such as w
ling to submit to you, and that w
all in our power for our own
which can be done without inju
plans of usefulness. We are t
that, because we may not soon ha
opportunity of writing, and an
arrangement on these points wi
important to our progress in
We beg leave to mention, (if th
not already been adopted,) as pr
best way of remitting, that yo
should be lodged in some merca
in London, and they be directed
immediate advice. This indeed
ly safe way in our present uncer
will at any time furnish us with
the least loss. Dear Sir, if we
we shall greatly need your pr
the prayers of the Christian pub

"The three islands of Bor
sette, and Caranja, contain at
hundred thousand natives, mo
rattas; and the adjacent Mahr
tories, many millions; while to
and the north there stretch une
regions, which present a pitiful
tive spectacle to Christian be
You will perceive, from the
of the field, that we shall
be strengthened by two breth
need they delay to learn the
our attempt. Should we fail,
for reasons which will not affect
instead of coming to Calcutta, t
come to Madras, Ceylon, th
France, Batavia, or even to t
Good Hope, and then direct
place. We do hope, that be o
as it may, this field will not be
—a field than which we believe
sesses more claims or more facil
for immediate and final usefu
case our brethren must be long d
come to Calcutta, we wish they
thither. They may succeed as m
peans have done—as we hope t
we will forward to Calcutta som

able them to be more discreet
re.

Prudential Committee, and the
ommissioners, we tender our
pect and our Christian affec-
their prayers and yours beg a
emembrance. We are, Rev.
a the Gospel,

SAMUEL NOTT,
GORDON HALL "
uel Worcester, D D.

If our letters have been receiv-
ll know in full the history of
rethren. Brother Newell is at
France, and we hope will join
en J. and R. will pursue a sep-
n, having changed their senti-
aptism, and been baptised at

EONT BIBLE SOCIETY.

Report of this Society was
annual meeting, Oct 21, 1813
etors state. that they had ap-
nts in different parts, to ena-
carry into effect the designs
ety; that they had procured
and 200 Testaments, the
t of which had been distribut-
) Bibles had been received as
from the Bible Society of
.; and that the want of the
eh greater than had been ap-
The Directors state the fol-
, and ground suitable reasoning

r poor woman, in a message
the Directors, begging for a
ed that her son was fifteen
and that she had never had
er house, since her marriage.
hers came, or sent, to the
n, informing that they neither
, nor the means of procuring
e was one family, also, whose
furniture was burnt about six
fore, which had no book, nor
le page of a book of any kind.
deeply to be lamented, that
ir cases are to be found, in this
ntry, it is with much pleasure,
rectors observe, that the Bi-
ave been distributed, have been
fully received, and, there is
elieve, have already, in some
ances, been instrumental of

whole, the Board have the
o state, that the success of this
ty, to procure and distribute
hitherto exceeded expectation,
to whom the word of the
cious, have been made exceed-

ing glad by the gift of this inestimable
treasure, and that others, who have been
indifferent towards it, or treated it with
contempt, have been induced to read it,
with serious attention, and to realize their
own concern in its interesting and solemn
truths. Far, therefore, from despising
the day of small things, we have great
reason to take encouragement from these
promising beginnings, to persevere in, and
increase our endeavors to extend the
knowledge of salvation by grace, by
the distribution of the Bible. The unparalleled exertions, and the wonderful
success of similar Societies both in Europe
and America, while they call aloud for the
liveliest expressions of gratitude to Him,
by whose inspiration the Scriptures were
given, which are able to make us wise unto salvation, through faith in Christ Jesus,
should also excite, in us, a fervent zeal, to
co-operate with our brethren, in diffusing
the knowledge of the truth, and ushering
in the glorious day, when the Bible shall
be read in every tongue, and its saving
truths made known to every inhabitant
of the globe."

The report closes with the most weighty considerations, which can be addressed
to men:

"There is reason to believe, that the
happy influence of Bible Societies will not
be confined to those, to whom their charity extends. Many others, beholding
what exertions are made to give the Bible
to the destitute, and perceiving the blessed effects of these exertions, in the saving conversion of sinners, who were ready
to perish, and the consolation drawn by
the humble believer from this well of salvation, will be excited to inquire into its
importance to themselves. More Bibles
will be purchased; they will be more read;
the knowledge of divine truth, drawn from
this uncorrupted fountain, will increase;
and there is reason to hope, that it will,
by many, be received with faith and love,
and thus become the power of God to
their salvation. These Societies, it is apprehended, are calculated to do great good,
as they have a happy tendency to break
down the wall of separation, which prejudice and party spirit have too long placed
between many, of differe t religious denominations, who really love our Lord
Jesus Christ in sincerity. As the Bible
is the standard, to which professing Christians, of all denominations appeal, because
the great truths of religion are here made
known, not in words, which man's wisdom teacheth, but which the Holy Spirit
teacheth, all the real disciples of Jesus can
cheerfully harmonize in exertions for
causing every one to be supplied with
this precious source of divine instruction.
And having an object, of such vast impor--

tance, to concentrate their exertions, and harmonize their views, and coming together, with the spirit of the Gospel, their prejudices against each other gradually subside, 'they feel themselves drawn together, by the cords of Christian affection, and learn how good, and how pleasant it is, for brethren to dwell together in unity. Nor is this all. Those, who become engaged in the good work, of putting the Bible into the hands, and recommending it to the attention of others, can hardly fail to be excited to give more attention to it themselves, and to receive proportionable benefit. The more the Scriptures are studied, with a disposition to receive instruction, in the things of God, the more light and comfort will be drawn from them. This, again, will tend to enliven zeal for causing the instructions of the Bible to be received by others. For, certainly, the more the love of God, and the love of Christ, are perceived and felt, the more fervent must be our desires, and the more active our exertions, that others, also, may taste and see that the Lord is good.

"Were it only in relation to the happiness of the present world, the universal distribution of the Bible, and influence of our holy Religion, would be vastly important. Let all become possessed of the amiable temper, and be governed by the benevolent precepts, of the blessed Gospel, animosity, and hatred, and discord, and bloodshed, would be banished from our now distracted and miserable world. Men would love as brethren. Righteousness would every where prevail; and the work of righteousness would be peace, and the effect of righteousness, quietness and assurance forever. In relation to the eternal happiness of guilty men, however, the importance of the instructions of the Bible, rises immeasurably high. Here it is, that life and immortality are brought to light. Here, only, a way of salvation is made known. The situation of those, who are destitute of the Bible, as described by an Apostle is, That they are aliens from the commonwealth of Israel, strangers from the covenant of promise, *having no hope,* and without God in the world. What benevolent heart, then, but must bleed, in view of the vast multitudes, the hundreds of millions of our fallen race, who are, at this moment, in this most affecting and awful situation! Who but must ardently desire, that they may be delivered from this deplorable state, and obtain salvation with eternal glory! Would you, dear brethren, be instrumental in promoting this benevolent and glorious object? Lend your aid, then, in sending them the Bible, in which are contained the words of eternal life. Send them

this treasure, and by the blessing of God, they may receive instruction, and become wise unto salvation. Then, a single Bible, which many very lightly esteem, will be worth more, to these now benighted souls, than all the wealth of the Indies—Yea, and the blessing of some poor soul, now ready to perish, may come on you.

"If any thing more is wanting, to arouse us to the most vigorous and active exertions, let us go to the cross of our bleeding, dying Savior. There let us remember, that God so loved the world, that he gave his only begotten Son, to sufferings and to death, that whosoever believeth in him, might not perish, but have everlasting life. Let us remember, that our Lord Jesus Christ, though he was rich, for our sakes became poor, that we through his poverty might be rich. Let our hearts here be warmed with love, and gratitude, for what has been done for our own salvation, and melted into tenderness and compassion for others, for whose salvation the blood of Jesus flowed. Let us behold this wonderful display of the love of our Redeemer, and remember that the voice of inspiration has declared, If any man have not the spirit of Christ he is none of his.

"In behalf of the Directors,
CHARLES MARSH, *President.*"
The Society had received $765 27, and had expended $353; leaving a balance of $412 27.
The following gentlemen were chosen officers;
"At the annual meeting of the Vermont Bible Society, at Montpelier, Oct. 21, 1813, the following officers were elected, viz;
Hon. Charles Marsh, Esq. *Pres.*
Hon. William C. Harrington, and Rev Aaron Leland, *Vice-Pres.*
Rev. Heman Ball,
John Noyes, Esq.
Rev. Leonard Worcester,
Rev Chester Wright,
Doct. William G. Hooker,
Doct. Joseph Winslow, and
Hon Chauncey Langdon, *Direc.*
William Page, Esq *Sec.*
Gen. Abner Forbes, *Treas.*

It is in contemplation to form an Auxiliary Bible Society, in each county in Vermont. We believe some of these Societies are already formed.

NEW YORK BIBLE SOCIETY.

THE fourth annual report of this Society, which was made at the annual meeting in Dec. last, contains a particular account of the doings of the Society during the year

ng. Since the last report 1355
ad been distributed in the city of
ork, on board of vessels, and by
magers, and 954 in the country;
2,309 in the whole.*

Trustees mention with pleasure the
on of *An Auxiliary Bible Society*
g men of different religious denomi-
in the city of New York. They
lso in terms of high commendation
xertions of Messrs. Schermerhorn
lls, in the course of their missiona-
through the western states.

Trustees close their report with
owing paragraph:

n and brethren! Can you behold
ritual need of your fellow-creatures,
nt up your bowels of compassion
them?" The pressure of the times
d heavy, and the claims on your
ience are already numerous and in-
g. But can there be an object
eserving of your Christian charity,
hat of dispensing the bread and
er of life to perishing sinners? Has
Providence blessed you abundantly
basket and your store? Remember
whom *much* is given, from him
ill be required: "Freely ye have
d, freely give." Have you but
spare? "The Lord accepteth ac-
to what a man hath." He who
ich honorable mention in his Gos-
the widow's *two mites*, and who
ared that "a cup of cold water
n his name, shall not lose its re-
will surely not withhold his bles-
om those who become "fellow-
s with *Him*," in contributing to sup-
r sinners with the rich treasures
word, which is able to save the
rough faith that is in Christ Jesus."
then be excited to renewed ex-
in this glorious work, in order to
sh the exhausted funds of the So-
nd to enable it to effect the impor-
signs in contemplation. We are
g under the desolating scourge of
rine, then, and let us present upon
ar a portion of our substance as
e-offering to the *Prince of peace*"
an tell, but for *his own name's*
is righteous anger may be turn-
y from us, and that he may again
pon us, and upon our land, and
with the return of peace upon all
ders, and cause us to "sing of mer-
ell as of judgment." Let us not
y in well doing: for "in due sea-
shall reap, if we faint not." "

receipts of the Society, during the
ug year were,

ice the institution of the *Society*
Bibles have been distributed.
L. X.

In subscriptions and dona-
tions, $770·09
Donation from the British
and Foreign Bible Society, 364·44
For Bibles sold at cost to the
Female Bible Society of
Geneva, 50·00
_____
$1,184·44

Expenditures.
Paid for Bibles, $1,384·45
Paid William Burk, his ex-
penses in travelling through
the country to distribute
Bibles, 120·00
Whiting and Watson's bill
(particulars not stated,) 100·97
Commissions on monies
collected, 29·78
Other contingent expenses, 54·06
_____
$1,689·26

Balance remaining in the
Treasury, $266·92

Though this balance was inadequate to
the immediate engagements of the Society, yet the Trustees express a confidence,
that their funds will be replenished, and
that the Society will be enabled to print
the French Bible for distribution in
Louisiana.

The following gentlemen were chosen
officers of the Society.

Officers and other Managers for the
present year.
Rev. Dr. Philip Milledoler, *Pres.*
—— Mr. John Williams,
—— Dr. Alexander Mc Leod,
Col. Henry Rutgers, and
Peter Wilson, LL. D *Vice-Pres.*
Mr. John E. Caldwell, *Sec.*
— Samuel Whiting *Clerk.*
— Leonard Bleecker, *Reg.*
— Cornelius Heyer, *Treas.*

Other Managers.
Rev. Dr. John M. Mason,
— — John B. Romeyn,
— Mr. Christian Bork,
— — Joseph Crawford,
— — Archibald Maclay,
— — Thomas Hamilton,
— — James M. Matthews,
— — Gardiner Spring,
Dr. J. R. B. Rodgers,
Mr. Divie Bethune,
— Elisha Colt,
— Richard Duryee,
— John Kane,
— Isaac Lakin,
— Zachariah Lewis
— Archibald
— John

Mr. John P. Mumford,
— John Stoutenburgh,
— George Sukeley,
— John Withington,

MASSACHUSETTS SOCIETY FOR PROMOTING CHRISTIAN KNOWLEDGE.

The Sermon delivered before this Society, in September last by the late lamented Rev. Dr. Prentiss, has been published with a very interesting appendix. The Sermon is from 2 Thes. iii. 13. *But ye, brethren, be not weary in well-doing.* The appendix contains a particular account of the labors of the missionaries employed by the Society in Rhode Island and New Hampshire. We intend to take further notice of this appendix hereafter.

The following account of the funds of the Society we print at large:

STATE OF THE TREASURY.

May 20, 1813. Amount of ORIGINAL FUND	2,773	12
June 5. A legacy from Mrs. Whitwell of Boston	33	
Payments by six Members on admission	60	
Interest received	19	69
	$2,885	81

DISTRIBUTING FUND.

May 20, 1812. Balance in the Treasury	701	85
Annuity paid by Members	135	
Annual subscription of		
Miss Eliza. Bromfield	20	
Mrs. Eliza Rogers	10	
William Lambert Esq.	10	
DONATIONS from		
Mr. Henry Homes of Boston	10	
an anonymous Lady by Rev. Mr. Greenough	1	
Elijah Stearns Esq. of Bedford	2	
a Female Friend by Rev. Samuel Stearns	0	
a Female Friend to missions by Rev. M. Stone	2	
a Female Missionary Society in Newburyport	30	
a Female Friend by Rev. Mr. Greenough	5	
Rev. Timothy Davis	2	
an anonymous Friend by Rev. Mr Greenough	8	
an anonymous Friend by do.	10	
Sons of Rev. Dr. Morse	3	
Mrs. Sarah Holmes	10	
Mrs. Susan Cook	2	
Mr. Samuel Sparhawk	2	
Collected by Mr. Josiah Salisbury	30	

by Rev. Mr. Eastman on his mission	13	15
by Rev. Mr. Turner do.	3	
by Rev. James Johnson do.	10	13
CENT CONTRIBUTIONS communicated by		
Rev. Mr. Greenough	10	92
from Ladies in Boxford by Rev. Mr. Eaton		
From Ladies in South Parish of Andover, communicated by Rev. Dr. Pearson, collected by		
Mrs. Rebecca Abbot	12	36
Mrs. Hannah Poor	25	25
Mrs. Rachel Furbush	12	25
Mrs. Phebe Abbot	8	54
	58	
from Ladies in Rev. Mr. Huntington's Society, Boston	21	
from a Female cent Society in Newburyport	27	
From Ladies in Charlestown, (for 1812*) communicated by Rev. Dr. Morse, collected by		
Miss Deborah Tufts and Miss Martha Edes	47	41
from Ladies, collected by Miss Mary Cooke	5	20
In Cambridge First Parish, collected by		
Mrs Kezia Walton	26	62
Mrs. Nancy Moore	6	75
	33	37
In Second Parish by Mrs. Eliza Livermore	10	60
from sundry Ladies by Rev. Micah Stone	2	56
from Ladies in Harvard, collected by Miss B. Wilder	9	37
in Royalton, by Miss Lucy Lee	8	50
in Welfleet, by Mrs. Catharine Davis	1	55
in First Parish in Dedham, communicated by Rev. Mr. Bates	35	50
Collection after a Sermon by Rev. Dr. Dana in the Old South meeting house, Boston	68	92
Interest on Securities	100	83
Balance of Loan to Trustees of Phillips Academy, paid	200	
	$1,670	95

EXPENDITURES IN SAME PERIOD.

Paid Rev. Asa Lyman for missionary service	189	57

* *The amount collected in this town, by the same persons in the year 1813, and paid to the Treasurer by Dr. Morse, was* $113 20.

phraim Abbot   do.   200
aniel Waldo   do.   200
imothy Hilliard   do.   100
ohn Turner   do.   150
ames Johnson   do.   50
Elphalet Pearson for
and expenses of a mis-
of inquiry in New
pshire, by request of
ciety   25
illiam Hilliard for books
d printing   578 75
l Expenses   3 50
in the Treasury, May
is   263 31

$1670 93

NATION AND INSTALLATION.

D, at Burlington, (Mass.) on the
st. the Rev. SAMUEL SEWALL.
by the Rev. Dr. Ware from
i, 21.
ED, on the second ult. the Rev.
MASON, over the church and So-
Barkhamstead, (Conn.) Sermon
ev. Dr. Perkins, from 1 Tim.

IONS TO SUPPORT FOR-
MISSIONS AND TRANS-
ONS.

25, 1814. From Mr.
el Austin, of Charles-
y the Rev. Dr. Morse $10 00
a friend, for the trans-
2 60
1. From the Foreign Mis-
iety of Boston and the
, it being the balance then
ag in the Treasury.   90 23
om Mr. John Burknap,
ham, (Ver.) by the Rev.
t Fowler of Windsor.   1 00
rom Mrs. Martha Jen-
(a widow,) of Milford,
by Mr. Timothy Dwight
50 00
the Foreign Mission Soci-

Carried forward $153 23

Brought forward $153 23
ety of Litchfield County, by Uriel
Holmes, Esq. the Treasurer, deposited at the Hartford Bank.   793 67
From persons convened at a
prayer-meeting for missionaries, in
Charlestown, (Mass.)   10 77
From individuals in Dunstable
(Mass.) paid to the Rev. Dr.
Morse, by Deacon Zebedee Ken-
dal   53 25
18. From Mr. Joseph Thayer of
Barre, by Mr. S. T. Armstrong   5 00
20. From a subscriber to the
Panoplist, Norfolk, (Vir.) who
declined having his name published; by William Maxwell Esq. for
the translations.   10 00
From two females, friends to
foreign missions, in the north parish of Andover.   4 00
22. From the "Aiding Foreign
Mission Society of Plympton and
the Vicinity," by the Rev. Elijah Dexter.   17 00
23. A New Year Offering from
ladies in Beverly, by the Rev.
Joseph Emerson   53 07
26. From individuals in New
Ipswich, a contribution after a sermon, by the Rev. Richard Hall.   74 68

$1,175 27

The Treasurer of the Board has lately
remitted more than $1,000 to Asia, on
account of the translations, and is about
to make another remittance soon for the
same object.

The religious public are requested to
bear in mind, that millions of the natives
of Asia are at this moment earnestly
stretching out their hands to receive the
Bible; and that money can' be immediately expended, as soon as it reaches Calcutta, in furnishing copies of the Scriptures, in the languages of that vast continent.

FOREIGN MISSION SOCIETIES.

AT the Annual Meeting of the Foreign
Mission Society for the County of Litch-
field, (Con.) held at Litchfield on the 9th
of Feb. last, the following gentlemen
were chosen officers:
His Excellency JOHN COTTON SMITH,
Esq. *Pres.*
Rev. LYMAN BEECHER, } *V. Pres.*
Rev. JONATHAN MILLER, }
JAMES MORRIS, Esq. *Sec.*
URIEL HOLMES, Esq. *Treas.*
AARON SMITH, Esq. *Aud.*

because he hath anointed me to preach th- Gospel to the poor &c.

The amount of the donations from this Society appears above in the list of donations.

The Rev. Joseph Harvey was appointed preacher for the next annual meeting, and the Rev. Lyman Beecher his substitute.

The Foreign Mission Society of Middletown, and the vicinity was instituted in August 1812. The officers of the Society are,

The Rev. DAN HUNTINGTON, *Pres.*
Rev. SAMUEL GOODRICH, *V. Pres.*
THOMAS HUBBARD, Esq. *Sec.*
Mr. SAMUEL GILL, *Treas.*

Besides these officers there is a committee of ten members.

LITERARY AND MISCELLANEOUS INTELLIGENCE.

NEW WORKS.

A SERMON, delivered in Boston before the Massachusetts Society for promoting Christian Knowledge, Sept. 15, 1813. By Thomas Prentiss, D. D. Pastor of the Congregational Church in Medfield. Andover; Flagg and Gould. 1813.

A Sermon delivered at the ordination of the Rev. Thomas Brattle Gannett to the pastoral care of the church in Cambridgeport, Jan. 19, 1814. By Abiel Holmes, D. D. Pastor of the First Church in Cambridge. Cambridge; Hilliard and Metcalf. 1814.

A Sermon delivered at the installation of the Rev. Preserved Smith, over the church and society in Rowe, Dec. 2, 1812. By Jonathan Grout, A. M. Pastor of the church in Hawley. Greenfield; Denio and Phelps. 1814.

A Sermon on prayer; preached at Dorchester, Dec. 12, 1813 By John Codman, A. M. Pastor of the second church in Dorchester. Boston; S. T. Armstrong, 1814.

INTERESTING OCCURRENCE.

LIEUT. ASA KENDALL of Ashby, (Mass.) having reached the 80th year of his age, and having a desire to see all his descendants together at his house on his birth day, the 28th ult. gave them an invitation to attend; at which time his sons, sons-in-law, daughters, daughters-in-law, with their offspring to the number of 102, convened, (8 of his descendants being absent.) The Rev. Cornelius Waters, the minister of the place, read the 73rd psalm, 3rd part, which was sung; after which he made a pertinent address to the aged sire and his descendants, and then addressed the throne of grace in a prayer adapted to the occasion. The company next partook of a generous repast. They were then

spread abroad, on a pleasant plat of ground according to the seniority of their families; when the father of the numerous and respectable company took his place in front, addressed them in a solemn and appropriate manner, and pronounced his benediction upon them. On returning to the house they sung another psalm, after which the Rev. Mr. Waters made another affectionate address and prayer. The whole was conducted with order and decorum, and was highly gratifying to a number of spectators.

PLEASING FACT.

THE keeper of the prison in Boston gives notice, that there is not a person confined within the prison walls for debt;—a circumstance which has never before happened since his connexion with the prison.

AWFUL CALAMITY.

Extract of a letter from Smyrna.

"WE have received intelligence of a dreadful calamity having overtaken the largest caravan of the season, on its route from Mecca to Aleppo. The caravan consisted of 2000 souls; merchants and travellers from the Red Sea and Persian Gulph; pilgrims returning from performing their devotions at Mecca, and a numerous train of attendants, the whole escorted by 400 military. The march was in 3 columns. On the 15th of August last they entered the great Arabian Desert, in which they journeyed seven days, and were already approaching its edge; but, alas! they were not permitted to return in safety.

"On the morning of the 23rd just as they had struck their tents and commenced their march, a wind arose from the northeast, and blew with tremendous

ey increased the rapidity of
to escape the threatening
he fatal Kamsir had set in.
dense clouds were observed,
nity obscured the horizon,
face of the desert. They
se columns and obscured the
L. Both men and beasts,
struck by a sense of common danger, uttered loud cries. The next moment they
fell beneath its pestiferous influence lifeless corpses. Of 20 to so composing the
caravan, not more than 20 escaped this
calamity. They owed their safety to the
swiftness of their dromedaries."

OBITUARY.

THE REV. SAMUEL NILES OF
(MASS.) WHO DEPARTED
JAN. 16, 1814, IN THE 70TH
IS AGE.

minister of Christ, a son of
Samuel Niles, of Braintree,
at the College in Princeton,
the early part of life, he discovered particular sobriety; but was, on
unusually thoughtless and triwhile a member of College,
he a subject of those religious
which issued in his hopeful
to divine truth. He was
to the pastoral office in Abington; where he continued to discharge the duties of his office, until pre-
paralytic shock, which took
more than two years before
'rom that shock he so far recover
he was able to ride, and several
ended public worship, but he
nearer in the midst of that
embly, which he had so often,
h deep solemnity, addressed
entous concerns of eternity.
recollected all his acquaintance
visited him during his last
iced to see them, evidently
id took a deep interest in their
, especially on religious subjects unable to articulate more
ords himself. When his parents
in the ministry inquired of
ng the state of his mind, during illness, he gave them to
hat he was happily resigned
ensations of divine Providence
joyed the consolations of that
ich he had so many years
others. Being asked a short
his death, whether he should
ame religious sentiments he
ould he return to active life
wered with peculiar emphasis
rmative. Though frequently
th great bodily pain, he was
patient, meek, and humble,
that he was treated with unkindness by his heavenly Father.
g sentences, with reference

to his own situation, he often repeated.
"All is done, all done—All is right, all
right." This was evidently the language
of his heart. With such a submissive,
quiet spirit, he close his sufferings on
earth. The passage of Scripture, which
was chosen as the foundation of the sermon preached at his funeral, and which
was thought to be peculiarly pertinent on
that occasion, was the words of the Apostle Paul to Timothy, (2 Epistle, iv, 7, and
8;) *I have fought a good fight, I have
finished my course, I have kept the faith;
henceforth there is laid up for me a crown
of righteousness, which the Lord the
righteous Judge shall give me at that
day; and not to me only, but unto all
them also that love his appearing.*

The object of the discourse was to
exhibit the trials, duties, and rewards of a
faithful minister of Christ. From such
trials our deceased friend was not exempted: for he preached those doctrines,
which are calculated to awaken the resentment of the human heart, and set in
motion the tongue of slander. "But
none of these things moved him, neither
counted he his life dear unto himself, so
that he might finish his course with joy,
and the ministry which he had received
of the Lord Jesus to testify the Gospel
of the grace of God." The various trials
incident to the Christian ministry he endured with exemplary meekness and fortitude. He *ran with patience the race
set before him, looking unto Jesus the
Author and Finisher of his faith.* That
he, as well as the rest of his brethren,
was a subject of much indwelling corruption, he was deeply sensible of, and often
lamented. Though he was a burning and
a shining light in the golden candlestick in
which he was placed, and eminently useful as a minister of Christ, yet he often bewailed his own barrenness and unfruitfulness. He had an affecting sense of the
evil nature of sin, and ardently strove to
gain a conquest over it in his own heart,
and to rescue others from its awful dominion. He was always ready to instruct
the ignorant; to comfort the disconsolate,
and to preach the Gospel to those who de-

sired it. His services, on the Lord's day, did not constitute the whole of his ministerial labors. He preached abundantly on other occasions, especially during revivals of religion in his own, and neighboring societies. He *was instant in season, and out of season; he reproved, rebuked, exhorted with all long suffering and doctrine.*

Among the doctrines, which he preached, the following held a conspicuous place. God from eternity adopted and unalterably fixed a plan of government, which, in its operations, will afford the brightest display of his own character, and bring into existence the highest possible good of the intelligent system. *All scripture is given by inspiration of God.* Jesus Christ, in his highest character, is the JEHOVAH of the Bible; co-equal and co-eternal with the Father.* The whole human race, in their fallen state, are totally depraved, and must have eternally perished without an atonement. The atonement made by Jesus Christ, though sufficient for the salvation of the whole world, does not render the situation of a single individual safe, until he becomes interested in it by that repentance and faith which the Gospel requires. To these conditions of salvation sinners are utterly opposed, and will never comply with them unless made willing by the irresistible influences of the Holy Spirit. All true religion consists in a principle of disinterested benevolence, and its corresponding fruits. A definite number of the human family were given to Jesus Christ in the covenant of redemption, and, before the foundation of the world, predestinated to everlasting glory. Not one of this number will eventually be lost.— But all, who are not included in this number, will infallibly abuse the means of instruction they enjoy, and finally be doomed to a state of endless punishment; to whom all the means of moral instruction they enjoyed in a state of probation will be a savor of death unto death.

These doctrines, in their various connexions and consequences, he well understood, and illustrated and defended with irresistible force of argument. His manner of preaching was peculiarly plain, luminous, solemn and impressive. By the friends of truth he was loved and admired.

* *In a charge, he gave at the ordination of a minister in the County of Plymouth, we meet with these words: "The following dilemma is unavoidable You must admit the real and proper Deity of Jesus Christ; or that the first Christian martyr died in an act of gross idolatry. If the former be admitted, you cannot fail to preach it If the latter, keep nothing back"*

And no person could hear him w ference. His object was to se consciences and hearts of his hea to make them feel in some me they will, when standing before t nal of their final Judge. Nor di ways fail of success. The profoun and deep solemnity frequently di by his audience evinced, that im were made, which could not eas faced His labors were manifest panied with the influences of t Spirit, and unquestionably instru the salvation of many souls. He unspeakable pleasure to witness five remarkable revivals of religio the people of his charge; the go of which are yet visible.

With respect to his prayers, with strict propriety be said, th uncommonly full of thoughts, p comprehensive, fervent, solemn, pressive, and often produced a effect on those, who had opper unite with him before the throne cy. At such seasons, he somet peared to be raised above all scenes, and permitted to look w vail.

Among other things, he was bly wise in council. Hence his a assistance were often sought in th ment of ecclesiastical difficulties. occasions, it is well known to his acquaintances, he was preeminent

To the preceding observati specting the character of Mr. N following may with propriety be s As a man he was peculiarly in and agreeable. In conversation pleasant without levity, facetiou malignity, and serious without He was thoroughly acquainted principles of human nature, and discern the motives by which characters in society are governe friend, he was distinguished fo dence and fidelity. His heart w net, in which the secrets of othe be locked as safely, as in th Though not affluent, yet his hou mansion of hospitality. No ma enjoyed his friends, nor more sought to make them comfort happy. Although, owing to circumstances, he was not a ma most extensive reading, yet he very superior powers of min few better understood *the art of t* or profited more by it. His id clear in his own mind, and were expressed with uncommon pe A fair specimen of his talents seen in a work which he had nea pleted for the press, when arre the paralytic shock before m

rk has since been published. It
d, "Remarks on a sermon preach-
the Association of Ministers, in
l congregational society in Mid-
gh, September 26, 1816, by
sed, D. D. Pastor of the first
and congregation in Bridgewater."
remarks the talents of the author
physical discussion, are strikingly
l. It is believed, that no candid
after examining them, will hesi-
knowledge, that he was thorough-
rount with the abstruser parts of
. Since such was the character
leceased friend, it is obvious that
has sustained a great loss on his
, and that the church of Christ is
l of one of its ornaments. But the
dispensation, which has deprived
such a blessing, has, it is hoped,
his personal benefit. Since he
a good fight, finished his course,
the faith, he has undoubtedly
receive a crown of righteousness,
he Lord, the righteous Judge will
all his faithful ministers at the last
y, and not to them only but unto
also, that love his appearing. A
an heaven has said, they that be
all shine as the brightness of the
ment, and they that turn many to
teness as the stars for ever and
What our Lord said to the angel
ter of the church of Smyrna, he
each of his true ministers. Fear
those things, which thou shalt suf-
thou faithful unto death, and I
e thee a crown of life. A similar
reserved for all his sincere follow-
o all such in presence of the as-
l universe he will ere long say,
ye blessed of my Father, inherit
rdom prepared for you from the
ion of the world. There all sin
bring will be done away. There

they will live and reign with Christ forever and ever; and make an endless progres-
sion in knowledge, holiness and happiness.
What powerful motives present themselves to the view of Christ's ministers and
to all others, to be faithful in his service!
*Blessed are the dead, who die in the
Lord; for they rest from their labors and
their works do follow them.*

DIED, at Paris, Col, CHARLES LOUIS
PREVOST DE BOISSY, an officer of Bonaparte's legion of honor, shot as a spy.

At Woburn (Mass.) on the 23rd ult.
of an apoplexy, the Rev. THOMAS WA-
TERMAN, pastor of the Baptist church in
that town, aged 39.

At Princeton, (N. J.) Mrs. CHRISTIA-
NA GREEN, wife of the Rev. Dr. Green,
President of Princeton College.

At Belchertown, (Mass) the Rev.
JUSTUS FORWARD, Senior Pastor of the
Congregational church in that place, aged
83.

At Lexington, (Vir.) the Rev. DAN-
IEL BLAIN, Professor of languages in
Washington College, aged 42.

In Maryland, the Hon. WM. M'CRE-
RY, Esq. formerly member of Congress
from that state.

At New Haven, (Con.) JESSE ATWA-
TER, Esq. postmaster, aged 45.

At Concord, (Mass.) the Hon.
Ephraim WOOD, Esq formerly a Judge
of the Court of Common Pleas, aged 81.

At Providence, AMOS THOOP, Esq.
President of the Exchange Bank.

At Taunton, Mrs. ELIZABETH HOP-
KINS, widow of the late Rev. Dr. Hopkins of Newport, aged 75.

At St. Johns, (N. B.) the Rev. MA-
THER BYLES, D. D. late rector of that
city, aged 80. He was son of the celebrated
Dr. Byles, who was for many years pastor of Hollis Street Church in Boston.

POETRY.

For the Panoplist.

PSALM CXXXVII.

rivers of Babylon there we re-
fin'd,
e thought of our home and our
country behind;
nquish'd and low by our enemies'
spears:—
ught upon Zion—and melted in
tears.

We had hung up our harps on the sad
willow trees,
And they wildly and mournfully sigh'd to
the breeze;
When the foes of our city in scorn pass'd
along,
And tauntingly bade us to raise them a
song.

'Come, one of your national ditties,' they
cry;
Our sighs and our tears were our only
reply—

Oh! how shall we sing them the song they
demand,
Now captive, forlorn, in a barbarous land.

No! if I forget, my dear Zion, thy fate,
If my heart cease to sigh for thee early and
late,
This harp, my delight, be for ever
unstrung,
And the sweet song of pleasure grow
strange to my tongue!

Remember these children of Edom, O
Lord!
Remember and give them their dreadful
reward;—
How they cried in the day of Jerusalem's
sighs,
'Destroy her, destroy her, she never shall
rise.'

O! daughter of Babylon destin'd to woe!
How soon in a deluge thy sorrows shall
flow!
The blood of thy infants shall moisten the
stones,
And the shouts of our victory rise with thy
groans.   V.

For the Panoplist.

MALTA.

(Written by a young lady.)

Concluded from p. 144.

As round the blaze their sea-beat forms
they drew,
Forth from the flame a deadly viper flew,
Swift to a guardless hand his venom'd dart
Shot that quick poison which corrodes the
heart
Exclaim'd th' astonish'd natives as they
saw—
"This wicked man hath broken heav'n's
great law,
And though he 'scap'd the doom the waves
prepare,
Yet righteous vengeance will not longer
spare."
With fixed gaze they anxiously await
The fearful purpose of avenging fate;—
But when they saw the wound with ven-
om fraught
No change—no horror, in their guest had
wrought,
"A God'—a God'"— their mingled voice
proclaims,—
"A God, whose power the viper's venom
tames!"
Ah simple train, ye knew not that ye
saw
A friend of *Him*, who vanquish'd nature's
law,

Who, on his glorious a
say,—
"No deadly thing shall b
way;
On scorpions they shall t
pain;
And serpents dart their
vain "
Ye knew not that ye saw
Who through a host of e
ran,
Whom no reproach, no
threaten'd doom,
Nor present woes, nor vis
Nor height, nor depth,
nor sword,
Could sever from the love
To you was given with
impart
Those gentle deeds, that
ger's heart;
And though more spaci
chance, display
A richer soil, a titled train
Yet, lonely Isle, thy praise
That shall remain to Time
And in thy soil, made so
An unseen Hand has so
grain;
Though weak its stalk, its
first,
Yet by the dews of hea
nurs'd,
And deep the growing
spread,
And high the cherish'd t
head,
Till in its boughs the fowls
rest,
And wounded nations in i
And thou, so skilful in t
Who fain would'st pour a
heart,
Whose holy zeal the noble
Impell'd thee journeying
wave,
Still prop the broken form
cere,
Still pour the sounds of m
Still let the sacred rule
guard,
And stand expectant of thy

March 1, 1814.

TO CORRESPON

THE *Comparisons* of R. N
ficiently accurate and str
our inserting them.
A Series of Essays on th
be commenced, in our ne
We have received sever
tions, both in poetry and p
we have not had sufficient
an ultimate opinion.

THE
PANOPLIST,
AND
[M]ISSIONARY MAGAZINE.

| 5. | MAY, 1814. | VOL. X. |

BIOGRAPHY.

[LIFE] OF JOHN KNOX, [ABRIDG]ED FROM THE WORK [OF] REV. THOMAS M'CRIE.

(Concluded from p. 156.)

two years he resided at [Geneva,] happy in the friendship [of Calvin,] and of the other minis[ters. B]ut nothing could extin[guish his] regard to Scotland, ar d [he was desirou]re of promoting there [the estab]lishment of the reform[ation. B]eing requested by some [of the n]obility to return to Ed[inburgh,] he bade adieu to his [congreg]ation and repaired to Di[eppe. A]t this place, discourag[ing lette]rs from Scotland reach[ed him,] together with a [intelligen]ce of occasion such [danger o]f discord and bloodshed [as he ex]pected, induced him to [relinquis]h his journey. By his [letters, h]owever, he still advanc[ed the] reformation. In one of [them, sp]eaking of the doctrine [of pred]estination, he says, "If [we take] any thing, which God [hath p]redestinate and appoint, [and grant]ed he wisdom and free [regimen] [or government;] or if [nothing] was ever done, or yet [ever sh]all be done in heaven or [earth] which he might not [have im]peded (if so had been [his good] pleasure,) then is he

not omnipotent; which three properties, to wit, wisdom, free regimen, and power denied to be in God, I pray you what rests in his Godhead? The wisdom of our God we acknowledge to be such, that it compelleth the very malice of Satan, and the horrible iniquity of such as be drowned in sin, to serve to his glory and to the profit of his elect."

Knox returned to Geneva in the end of 1557, and in the following year was engaged in making a new translation of the Bible into English, which is called *the Geneva Bible*. He also wrote several treatises, of which the one, that made the greatest noise, was *The first Blast of the trumpet against the monstrous Regiment of Women*, in which he assailed the practice of entrusting the reins of government in nations to females. The first sentence is—"To promote a woman to bear rule, superiority, dominion or empire, above any realm, nation, or city, is repugnant to nature, contumely to God, a thing most contrarious to his revealed will and approved ordinance; and finally it is the subversion of all equity and justice." It was undoubtedly the cruelty of queen Mary of England towards the protestants

X.

which incited him to blow this blast. It was his intention to sound his trumpet thrice; but on the accession of queen Elizabeth, who favored the protestant cause, he was induced to abandon his design, although his opinion remained unaltered.

His letters to Scotland had the effect of encouraging the protestant lords, and they soon renewed their invitation to him. Bidding adieu for the last time to Geneva he went to Dieppe, and thence sailed to Leith, where he landed in May 1559. In the preceding year an aged priest was committed to the flames on a charge of heresy;—an event, which awakened the general indignation of the people, and strengthened the protestant interest. On his arrival he found, that the queen regent was determined to suppress the reformed religion, all the preachers of which she summoned to trial at Stirling on the 10th of May. In reference to this order he says in a letter, "Satan rageth even to the uttermost, and I am come, I praise my God, even in the brunt of the battle. For my fellow preachers have a day appointed to answer before the queen regent, when I intend (if God impede not) also to be present; by life, by death, or else by both, to glorify his godly name, who thus mercifully hath heard my long cries. Assist me with your prayers, that now I shrink not, when the battle approacheth." As a large number of the protestants were preparing to assemble at Stirling, the queen by a profligate promise to put a stop to the trial induced them to return to their homes. But on the day of trial the accused were

outlawed for not a When the news of thi ry came to Perth, wl had just preached against the idolatry of and image worship, t in their indignation, standing his efforts t them, destroyed all ments of the church a ished the monasterie grey and black friars Carthusian monks.

The evident disposi queen to maintain with the Catholic religion ir protestant lords to e close bond of union, determined, where th ity extended, to abolis ish superstition. St. was thought the fittes beginning the reform cordingly Knox went June, and proposing to the cathedral the arch sembled an armed for clared, that if he appe pulpit he would give the soldiers to fire The noblemen on c advised him to de preaching, as their r small, and the queen v hand with an army, re port the bishop. But in the heroic spirit of tian, that he was dete preach. "As for th danger, that may cor let no man be solicit he, "for my life is in t of Him, whose glory I desire the hand nor no man to defend m next day and for the cessive days he pre numerous assembly v slightest opposition o tion. Such was his

that the inhabitants agreed to set up the reformed worship, and the church was stripped of images and pictures, and the monasteries pulled down. In a few weeks the houses of the monks were destroyed in other parts of the kingdom, even at Stirling and Edinburgh. Knox entirely approved of the destruction of the monasteries, for he observed, that "the best way to keep the *rooks* from returning was to pull down their *nests*."

At the end of June, he went to Edinburgh, and was chosen the protestant minister in that city. But he soon was sent on a tour of preaching through the kingdom, and in less than two months travelled over the greater part of Scotland, and was the means of opening the eyes of the nation to the abominations of popery. He was also at this period much employed in some negociations with the English court, to persuade to an effectual support of the protestant cause in Scotland against the queen regent, and the French soldiers sent from France to her aid. His exertions at this time were incredible; and although the papists publicly offered a reward to the person who should seize or kill him, he was not deterred from the discharge of any duty. The protestants, thinking it necessary to effect a revolution in the government, met at Edinburgh in a large assembly consisting of nobles, barons, and representatives of boroughs, and it being proposed to depose the queen regent, the opinion of Knox respecting the lawfulness of that measure being required, he gave his opinion, that it was lawful

and necessary. She was accordingly deprived of her authority. He was of opinion, that that there was a mutual compact, implied if not explicit, between rulers and their subjects, and that if the former became tyrants and oppressors, the latter have a right to depose them from office, and to elect others in their stead.

An English army entering Scotland in April 1560, the French troops retired to Leith, and a treaty was made with France, by which it was provided, that the troops should be removed from the kingdom, and that a free parliament should be called. This treaty was fatal to popery in Scotland, which was supported by force only, and the reformed worship was every where set up.

In 1560 Knox had a principal hand in organizing the national church of Scotland. At the first *General Assembly*, Dec. 20th, he was one of the six ministers present. About this time he was called to a heavy affliction by the death of his wife, and the care of his two young children was devolved upon him.

In Mary, queen of Scots, who had been educated in France, and who came to Scotland and assumed the reigns of government August 19, 1561, the protestants found a most determined and artful enemy. As she immediately set up the Roman Catholic worship in the chapel of Holyrood house, Knox took occasion to observe the next Sunday in a sermon against idolatry, that "one mass was more fearful to him, than if ten thousand armed enemies were landed in any part of the realm.

on purpose to suppress the holy religion." The queen was very much incensed, and had several interviews with him, in which he conducted himself with great skill and firmness. "Think you," said the queen, "that subjects, having the power, may resist their princes?" "If princes exceed their bounds, madam," replied he, "no doubt they may be resisted even by power. For no greater honor or greater obedience is to be given to kings and princes, than God has commanded to be given to father and mother. But the father may be struck with a phrenzy, in which he would slay his children. Now, madam, if the children arise, join together, apprehend the father, take the sword from him, bind his hands, and keep him in prison till the phrenzy be over, think you, madam, that the children do any wrong?" At an interview, occasioned by his predicting in the pulpit, that great evils would be the consequence, if she should marry a papist, the queen was dissolved in tears, but he remained firm to his purpose. As an apology he protested, "that he took no delight in the distress of any creature; that it was with great difficulty that he could see his own boys weep, when he corrected them for their faults; far less could he rejoice in her majesty's tears;" an apology, which so enraged the proud queen, that she ordered him immediately from her presence. In an adjoining room he addressed himself to the court ladies, "O fair ladies, how pleasing were this life of yours, if it should ever abide, and then

in the end, that we might pass to heaven with all this gay gear!"

Mary soon afterwards caused him to be brought to trial on the charge of treason; but he was honorably acquitted. "That night," says Knox, "there was neither dancing nor fiddling in the court, for madam was disappointed of her purpose, which was to have had John Knox in her will, by vote of her nobility."

In the church of Edinburgh he preached twice every Sabbath, and thrice on other days of the week, besides attending to much ecclesiastical business. In 1563 John Craig was established as his colleague. In March 1564 he married, for his second wife, Margaret Stewart, daughter of lord Ochiltree.

In 1566 he was induced to take a journey to England, partly from regard to his personal safety, and partly from affection to his two sons, who were at one of the English seminaries. While he was absent, the king, queen Mary's husband, was murdered, Feb. 9, 1567, and she soon afterwards married Bothwell, generally supposed to be the chief agent in the murder; a circumstance, which, in connexion with others, left no doubt on the mind of Knox, that Mary was accessary to the crime. She was obliged to resign the government, and the Reformer, on the 29th of July, preached the sermon at the coronation of King James VI. While Mary was held in confinement he publicly maintained, that as she was charged with murder and adultery, she ought to be brought to trial, and if guilty to be punished with death. At the close

', the parliament rati-
acts, which had been
1560 in favor of the
religion; and Knox
lcity of seeing the su-
ernment in the hands
at, the earl of Mur-
telligent and pious
in whose wisdom and
he had the greatest

regent being soon as-
the country was in-
gain in dissensions
ed upon the spirits of
in Oct. 1570 he had a
apoplexy, which for
impaired his speech.
his life was in immi-
from the hostility of
who wished to restore
One evening a mus-
was fired in at his win-
friends were under
city of watching his
ing the night, and
gth persuaded him to
St. Andrews. Here he
to preach, although
walk to the pulpit
distance. But when
y his subject he was
eloquence. One of
s represents, that he
d to lean on the pul-
irst entry; "but ere he
with his sermon he was
and vigorous, that he
thing the pulpit in blads,
s,] and fly out of it."
lat 1572, he returned
rgh in feeble health,
is to leave the world.
preached, his voice
be heard by half the
on. On receiving
of the general massa-
protestants in France,
nveyed to the pulpit,
urged the vengeance of

heaven against the cruel mur-
derer, the king of France; and
desired his ambassador to tell
his master that sentence was
pronounced against him in Scotland, and that divine vengeance
should pursue him unless he repented. The ambassador, having in vain required the regent
to silence Knox, left the kingdom.

In November, James Lawson
was installed as his colleague,
on which occasion he preached and preached for the first
time. As he returned to his
house, his hearers thronged the
streets to take the last sight of
their beloved pastor.

It was his ordinary practice to
read every day some chapters
of the Old and New Testament;
to which he added some of the
psalms of David, the whole of
which he perused regularly
once a month. Nov. 10th he
was obliged by sickness to desist
from his course of reading;
but he directed the 17th chapter
of John, the 53d of Isaiah, and
a chapter of the epistle to the
Ephesians to be every day read
to him. He exhorted his servants, when he dismissed them,
to walk in the fear of God. Nov.
15th he sat at table for the last
time. A friend dining with him,
he ordered a hogshead of wine to
be pierced, and with hilarity requested him to send for some of
it, as long as it lasted, for he
himself should not tarry until it
was all drunk. Nov. 17th he
had a most affecting interview
with the session of his church,
and addressed them in the following words: "The day now
approaches and is before the
door, for which I have frequently and vehemently thirsted, when

I shall be released from my great labors and innumerable sorrows, and shall be with Christ. And now God is my witness, whom I have served in spirit, in the Gospel of his Son, that I have taught nothing but the true and solid doctrine of the Gospel of the Son of God, and have had it for my only object to instruct the ignorant, to confirm the faithful, to comfort the weak, the fearful, and the distressed by the promises of grace, and to fight against the proud and rebellious by the divine threatenings." Nov. 20th he said to Lord Ruthven, who professed his readiness to serve him, "I care not for all the pleasure and friendship of the world."

Nov. 21st, he desired his coffin to be made, and often said, "Come Lord Jesus, sweet Jesus, into thy hands I commend my spirit. Be merciful, Lord, to thy church, which thou hast redeemed. Give peace to this afflicted commonwealth."

Nov. 23d, he frequently uttered pious ejaculations, and exhorted and prayed. Nov. 24th was the last day of his life. In the afternoon he desired his wife to read the 15th chap. of 1 Corinthians, and said, "O what sweet and salutary consolation the Lord hath afforded me from that chapter?" Being tempted to think that he merited heaven on account of his faithfulness in the ministry, "blessed be God," said he, "who has enabled me to beat down and quench this fiery dart by suggesting to me such passages as these: *What hast thou, that thou hast not received? By the grace of God I am what I am: Not I, but the grace of God in me.*" About 11 o'clock in the evening he gave a deep sigh and said, *Now it is come,* and soon expired without a struggle.

He died in the 67th year of his age, exhausted by his extraordinary labors of body and anxieties of mind. Few men were ever exposed to more dangers, or underwent such hardships.

Nov. 26th he was interred in the church yard of St. Giles's, Edinburgh. A great concourse of people attended his funeral. When his body was laid in the grave, the Regent, Morton, pronounced his eulogium in these words: "There lies He, who never feared the face of man."

He was of a small stature and of a weakly habit of body. According to the custom of the times he wore his beard long, reaching to his middle.

His principal work is the History of the reformation in Scotland. His defence of *Predestination* is written with perspicuity and acuteness.

RELIGIOUS COMMUNICATIONS.

For the Panoplist.

ON THE SABBATH. NO. I.

Introductory Paper.

IN nothing were the Fathers of New-England more highly or more honorably distinguished, than in their sacred regard for the Sabbath. Too wise to indulge the visionary notion, that religion, or sound morality, can long exist without it, and too pious not to rejoice in its week-

heir first care, when
to this country, was
such regulations, as
are at once its bless-
ti perpetuity. They
a corner stone of that
ce of morals and re-
ich has in these latter
a ad much defaced,
ved so many rude
in the hands of their
sons—an edifice, the
of which are still so
it. Justly regarding
it as, in a sense, the
of their infant settle-
ly raised around it a
part of wise laws, and
some of the best and
tial of their number
and guardians.
they rest here. Sound
sincere piety were
conspicuous, in the
ployed by our ances-
petuate a reverence
tal institutions, than
t legal protection of
tutions. Fully sensi-
strength of early hab-
the potent and abiding
of first impressions
nds of children, they
temselves with zeal
verance to the govern-
nstruction of the ris-
tion. This they made
their daily business.
bbath was more par-
levoted to these im-
jects. Each tender
ent, almost as soon as
te shoot. Children
bt, both by precept
le, to remember the
ly, and in anticipation
oach, to prepare them-
sonably to enter upon
riate duties. Instead
dulged in their child-

ish sports at home, or allowed
to range the fields and walk the
streets, as if but too common in
our day, they were kept close
from morning to night; and were
not in general allowed to go a-
broad, or engage in any vain re-
creation, either on the evening
preceding, or on that succeeding
God's holy day."

Nor was the weekly rest,
which they were taught to observe, permitted to be wasted
by them in sloth; nor yet was it
devoted to what, in strictness of
speech, are termed mere mental
improvements. The grand object of parents, in that golden
age of New-England, was to instil correct moral and religious
principles into the tender minds
of their children, and to mend
their hearts. In the prosecution of this object, they persevered from Sabbath to Sabbath,
and from year to year. To this
end the young members of almost every family were required to commit to memory select
portions of Scripture, and appropriate psalms and hymns, as
well as the catechisms of Dr.
Watts, and of the Assembly of
divines. In the mean time, great
care was taken to inspire the
rising generation with such a
love for public worship, and other religious exercises, that the
Sabbath might not be considered as a burden, but as a *delight,
the holy of the Lord, honorable.*
It was reasonable to indulge the
hope, that a course of religious instruction so early begun, so judiciously pursued, and so powerfully enforced, by the general example of heads of families, would,
by the divine blessing, produce
the happiest effects. This hope,
if not realized in all its extent,

was so far answered, in the conduct of those concerning whom it had been indulged, as to gladden the hearts of the pious pilgrims, as they descended to the grave, imploring a thousand benedictions upon their posterity.

It is certain, from the most faithful and candid records of those times, that for many years after the first settlers were dead, things remained, as nearly as could be expected, in the state in which they left them.

When at length, innovations began to be made, their progress was too slow and insidious, at first, to excite any considerable alarm. If parents of the third and fourth generations, were not quite so exact in sanctifying the Sabbath, as their fathers had been, they certainly reverenced it as an institution of God, the gross profanation of which would inevitably jeopardize the best interests of society. If they yielded to their children some few indulgences, which they had not received themselves in childhood, their family regulations were still such, as would be esteemed extremely rigid, by most of the present generation. But though the decline was slow, it was steady, and at length became rapid. The laws against Sabbath-breaking were less and less faithfully executed. Occasional travelling upon business and pleasure came in time to be winked at, by informing officers and magistrates. Each succeeding generation took greater liberties than the preceding had done, and, with some few exceptions hereafter to be mentioned, the evil has been increasing to this very day. I will not say, that the corner stone is remov-

ed from its place; tho
certain, that it retains
of its ancient beauty:
its enclosure is who
away; because the law
protection still retain tl
in our statute-books.
ly the general ineffic
these laws must be o
every one. We migl
suppose them buried u
ery turnpike road, so
men of this generatio
their gains and their j
with almost as little inte
as if no divine or hun
requiring the sanctif
the Sabbath, were no
ence. To a most alar
tent has light and vain
tion usurped the place
prayer, and the pious in
of children. Voyage
news-papers and nov
gained quiet possessio
shelf, which was once
by sermons, Bibles
chisms. Many a clos
verted into a count
The frugal meals of
tors, which were usual
ed on Saturday, have gi
to luxurious dinners,
with much labor upo
which the Lord hath r
in the hours which he
own.

Instead of regularly
public worship, as serv
once permitted and
ed to do, they may now
employed in their ordin
or driving their mast
cles of pleasure. Mar
of high rank, and very
influence, take the lea
hesitation in violating
and setting the magistr
fiance. So fashionab
become, especially in

ge towns, to make ex-
s for pleasure on the
l, that, if I am not misin-
, all the environs are
:d with persons of every
l of all ranks; a motley
de of statesmen, law-
merchants, tradesmen,
l, sailors, pedlars, and
:ants, some on foot, some
-se-back, and the rest
;es, coaches, phaetons,
air icles, chaises and ev-
ier vehicle which fancy
vented. I wish I could
it these and other fashion-
blations of the Lord's day,
where prevalent but in
but our principal towns.
mentable fact, however, is,
e Sabbath is greatly pro-
n our small, as well as
blaces; in the country as
the city. This leaven of
r has been fermenting and
ing, till almost the whole
I leavened. While throngs
ple are pursuing their
is and pleasures upon the
roads, multitudes are
ring about their fields, ex-
g the state of their farms,
ewing their cattle and
and others are sailing,
, and taking their pleas-
the water.

ie mean time, pretences
xcuses for engaging in
l labor, especially in time
ting in hay and harvest,
ltiplied to a most alarm-
gree; and actual violations
law in this particular have
e very frequent. Nay,
:es are not wanting, in
fines imposed and col-
by a regular civil process,
een returned to the delin-
, by a formal vote in pub-
m meeting.

. X.

These practices would give
great pain to every pious and reflecting mind, even if they were
confined to what is generally
considered as the loose and unprincipled part of the community. But how much severer pain
does it inflict to perceive, that
the poison has spread wide even
among those, who have sworn
to execute the laws, and that the
church of God itself is infected!
Painful as is the admission of
this statement, it is in vain to
think any longer of denying or
concealing the fact, that informing officers, justices of the
peace, judges of courts, and
members of our state and national legislatures, are frequently
guilty of profaning the Sabbath,
in all, or nearly all the ways that
have been specified. Equally
notorious is it, that the names of
many professors of religion
might be enrolled to swell the
melancholy list. Some even go
so far, as to maintain, with singular confidence, that the Sabbath, under the Christian dispensation, is a mere human institution; and that the laws, which
require its observance, infringe
the liberty of conscience.
Among those, who consider this
notion as unscriptural, and distinctly foresee the ruinous consequences which must result
from its becoming general in
any community, a considerable
number would readily tolerate
practices, which are directly subversive of the sacred institution
now under consideration. I am
afraid, that but few, of the most
strict and conscientious among
us, are fully aware of the broad
extent of the fourth command.
I am afraid, that some very worthy and pious people do things

26

on the Sabbath, which they ought not to do, and omit things which it is their duty to perform.

A minute investigation of the causes, of this wide and sinful departure from the principles and practice of our ancestors, would not comport with the designed brevity of this introductory paper. Some of these causes, however, I shall just mention.

In the first place, it is well known to every person, acquainted with the early history of this country; that after the first settlers had established themselves, and begun to turn the wilderness into a fruitful field, they were followed by adventurers from the mother country, who were very different from themselves, in all their views and habits. These adventurers, by mixing with the earlier emigrants, gradually gained an influence, with many of the young especially, by which their high regard for divine institutions was materially weakened. Considering what human nature is, this single cause, continuing to operate from one generation to another, would have produced very alarming innovations.

But secondly; our sad degeneracy is probably owing still more to the demoralizing influence of the several wars, in which this country has borne a conspicuous part. Hardly any thing so deranges the settled order of things, as war, even in its mildest forms. The passing of expresses, the firing of alarm guns, the march of armies, the transportation of provisions, clothing, and all the munitions of war, upon the Sabbath, as much as on any other day, must

unavoidably divert the
of multitudes from th
priate duties of holy t
weaken the sense of o
to perform these duties
same time, many are
take advantage of thes
and, under pretence o
service, or without a
tence at all, to pursue t
private interest. The
ble effects of our revo
war, in this particular,
distinctly remembered
the aged now living.
myself heard numbers
speak of it with the de
gret.

Thirdly; the unexan
crease of wealth and li
New England, since the
the war just mentioned,
a demoralizing influen
the people, and has, in
contributed largely to
profanations of the Lo
The natural consequen
sudden influx of wealt
men forget the God tl
them, and trample upor
thority.

But whether the c
which I have merely
passing, be, or be not,
and principal causes
gradual and mournful
tion of our sabbatical inst
is not very material. It
more important, to poin
extent and perpetuity o
vine precept, on which
founded; to awaken pub
tion to a subject, which
the highest temporal a
nal interest of the pres
of future generations; to
whether or not an
measure can be devised
serve what is left, and
what has been lost; and,

se one grand and united
in this sacred cause; the
of the church, the cause
country, and the cause of
ity. Z. X. Y.

E PRACTICAL TENDENCY OF ERROR.

For the Panoplist.

Editor,
g that you inserted my commu-
t, *On the Causes of Error*, I
is liberty to send for your dis-
i few remarks on *the practical
cy of error.* A. D.

he Apostles travel from
y to country, endure fa-
nd hunger, brave the rage
s and Gentiles, of civiliz-
tions and barbarians, to
doctrines, that have little
connexion with practice?
in it: the doctrines they
, if embraced sincerely,
een and still are produc-
f holy living; while the
ry doctrines have always
contrary effect. However
tionable the opinion may
a many, at the present day,
vertheless true, that erro-
doctrines will lead to sin-
conduct. *Do men gather
of thorns or figs of this-
A good tree cannot bring
vil fruit, neither can a cor-
ree bring forth good fruit;
orrupt tree bringeth forth
uit.* Our Savior knew the
of men, and the connex-
ween doctrines and works,
ould judge unerringly of
ects of error on the lives
n. The decision, which
e, is abundantly confirm-
observation. A careful
of men, their sentiments
spduct, will convince us,

that, in morals, *grapes do not
grow on thorns.*

If one believes, that God is so
far above the human family, that
he feels no concern in what takes
place among them, does not hear
their prayers, overrules no events,
nor requires any account of
their actions; the natural consequence of these opinions
will be, that this man will not
have God in all his thoughts;
he will not pray to him, nor fear
to offend him by profaneness or
injustice. Such a man has no
principle to guide his conduct
but worldly policy; no restraint
on his passions but what self-interest imposes. What security
have others against his injustice
or rapacity? The sad effects of
such libertine principles are
clearly shewn, by the confused
and wretched state of the world
at the present time.

If one does not believe, that
Christ was God, with the Father
in the beginning, he will not
*honor Christ as he honors the
Father;* he will not pay him that
adoration, love and obedience,
which the Gospel requires.
While he considers the Savior
as a mere man, he will treat his
commandments as the commandments of men; he will entertain
low thoughts of the Son of God;
he will be negligent and remiss
in duty towards Him.

If one does not believe, that
the human heart is totally depraved, he will not earnestly beseech God to give him a new
heart. He will not advance in
holiness and virtue; for he does
not see, that he lacks these
things.

If one believes, that he is indebted to Christ for nothing but

the pardon of his sins, he will not feel that heart-felt love and gratitude, which fills the soul, that ascribes to the merits of the Redeemer's sacrifice, *righteousness, sanctification, and redemption.* Can he consistently with his principles ask the Father, for Christ's sake, and in Christ's name, for spiritual gifts and graces? And if he does not ask them in the name of Christ, has he any reason to expect a favorable answer to his prayers?

If one believes, that there is no bestowment of special grace, will he seek any? Will he not rather *strive to enter in at the strait gate,* relying on his own strength, and with low and unworthy motives?

If one does not believe the words of Christ, that *without me ye can do nothing;* or the saying of the Apostle, that it is not the Christian that lives, but Christ that lives in him, will he live near to God? Will he sincerely and unreservedly give himself up to the direction and will of his Savior? Will he not rather trust too much to himself, and go on in his own strength when he ought to rely on the grace of God for ability to run his Christian race? Is not this the reason why we see so many, who deny with strong asseveration the divine sovereignty, and as strongly assert man's ability to perform good works, come far short of the Christian standard, and live so as to bring dishonor upon the cause of Christ? They object against the doctrines of free grace and man's moral inability, because, they say, these are discouraging doctrines, and enough to paralyze all moral exertion. But this objection is so

far from being true, that it exact reverse of the truth; leads men away from Go great fountain of living w and brings them to *broke terns, that can hold no* He, that lives nearest to will best obey his will; a will live nearest to God, puts all his trust and confi in Him?

If one believes that the bath is not holy time,—h not keep the day holy. H spend in worldly busines amusements that sacred p of his temporal existence, God has appointed fo religious improvement and duties He will lose the sing attached to the obec of the command. His chi allowed to spend the day in ness, will contract habits of and become noxious memb society.

From the preceding ob tions, we learn the fallacy c maxim, so often repeated present day, "That if a thinks himself right, he *is* r As if sincerity in any o₁ made that opinion true. A¹ ing to this maxim,—the pheming Jew, the deludet hometan, the idolatrous he the superstitious papist, scoffing infidel, the deba epicure, and the cannibal s who eats the mangled lim his enemy, offered to his i₁ nary God, are all right; doubt not, that some of all classes are honest and si₁ Merciful Savior, may I crucify thee afresh by ack edging so monstrous a n May I never repay, by s₁ vile act of ingratitude, th nite condescension and which led thee, to pass through unparalleled sufferings to redeem sinners.

We see how necessary it is for those, who are well instructed in the distinguishing doctrines of the Gospel, to teach them with fortitude and diligence, disregarding the opposition and reproaches of the patrons of error. No wonder they are opposed to the truth, for its brilliant light discovers their shame and depravity. They, whose deeds are right, have nothing to fear from the dissemination of truth. *Ye know by their fruits those who walk in darkness; they hate the light and will not come to it, lest their evil deeds should be reproved.*

For the Panoplist.

A MORSEL FROM THE PROPHECIES.

Bishop Horsley, in a treatise on the 18th chapter of Isaiah, published in 1799, interprets the three last verses of the preceding chapter as relating to the fall of Antichrist. The verses contain the following prophecy.

Verse 12. *Woe to the multitude of many people, which make a noise like the noise of the seas, and to the rushing of nations, that make a rushing like the rushing of mighty waters.*

13. *The nations shall rush like the rushing of many waters; but God shall rebuke them, and they shall flee far off, and shall be chased as the chaff of the mountains before the wind, and like a rolling thing before the whirlwind.*

14. *And behold at even-tide trouble; and before the morning he is*

not. *This is the portion of them that spoil us, and the lot of them that rob us.*

The bishop also observes, that the French nation ever since the late revolution, "has been a conspicuous and principal branch at least of the western Antichrist." There appears indeed the utmost reason for this opinion. The propriety of interpreting the prophecy above quoted, as relating to the overthrow of Antichrist, appears from its being immediately followed by the prophecy of the restoration of the Jews, in the 18th chapter. For what should so naturally precede the conversion of the Jews, and the general prevalence of the kingdom of Christ, as the signal vengeance of God on the enemies of his kingdom?

According to this interpretation, there can be little room to doubt, that the prophecy in these three verses has been fulfilling in Europe ever since the middle of the year 1812. The Antichristian power is represented as surviving the first overthrow; but only to experience new troubles and a speedy dissolution.

H. S.

A LETTER FROM A YOUNG LADY, GIVING AN ACCOUNT OF HER FATHER'S DEATH.

My dear Aunt,

ALTHOUGH my brother has written by this opportunity to my grandfather, informing him of the particulars of my father's sickness and death, yet, as I know whatever relates to these melancholy scenes will be highly interesting to you, I cannot refrain from dwelling more particularly upon some parts of them than he has done.

It must be a source of joy and consolation to us all, my dear aunt, to reflect upon the last days of my dear and most excellent father. His character as a Christian shone at this awfully trying season, most transcendently bright. Although at times racked with agonizing pain, yet he was patient and resigned, constantly affirming that his sufferings were less than he deserved, and dwelling with the most lively gratitude on the numerous blessings with which he was still surrounded. But if temporal mercies awakened his gratitude, much more did those of a spiritual nature. Oh! I trust I shall never forget how continually, and with what ardent affection and thankfulness, he spoke of the blessed Redeemer. Never was faith more firm, more entire than his. He rejected with abhorrence all reliance upon any merits of his own; again and again declaring to those, who spoke to him of the excellence of his character, that he was a poor unworthy sinner, and had no hope, no consolation, but what he derived from the atonement, righteousness, and intercession of his Almighty Savior. He was a firm believer in the great truths of our holy religion, and lamented exceedingly, the great and dangerous errors, which have crept imperceptibly into the Christian church. The supreme Deity of our glorious Redeemer was a doctrine dear to his heart, and which he constantly endeavored to inculcate. The doctrines of the depravity of the human heart, and the absolute

necessity of regeneration [
influence of the Holy Spiri
truths, which made an ess
part of his system. Those
trines, although branded wi
name of enthusiasm, and
nounced by an unthinking
titude to be unfriendly to t
terests of morality, he l
valued.

Whenever his strength
permit, the Bible was his
panion and comfort; and
he became too feeble to
that, and the latter part of
dridge's Rise and Progre
Religion in the Soul of M
would frequently beg my n
to read to him. Precious t
(he would frequently ex
oh! what comfort, what co
tion is there! The two last
ters of Doddridge's, the
tian rejoicing at the prosp
death, and the Christian l
ing God by his dying condi
listened to with peculiar
ure. The advice given l
last chapter, he endeavor
far as his exhausted str
would permit, to imitate
we have to regret, that
many of the last days of hi
he was rendered incapal
conversing. Thus have
tempted to give you a
(but oh! how faint,) of the
bed of my dear lamented p
O that you had been he
have witnessed his humilit
trition, resignation, and ho
umph. I hope and pray
these solemn, mournful, a
pleasing scenes, may ma
impression upon all our t
which time shall never b
to efface. May we die the
of the righteous, and ou
days be like his. We hav
deed, abundant cause to

for ourselves; for we have lost a most affectionate parent and friend, and my mother, a tender and excellent husband: but we mourn not as those without hope; for we feel a strong, a perfect assurance, of his having entered upon a glorious immortality, where he will be forever with that Savior, whom, while he was with us, he loved, honored and obeyed; and be released from that imperfection, that sin, which he has so often, and so feelingly lamented.

I regret that I am obliged to close my letter, for when I enter upon this subject, I am unwilling to relinquish it. May God, of his infinite mercy in Christ Jesus; unite us all at last to the society of angels, and the spirits of just men made perfect, where friends shall no more be separated, and where we shall spend an eternity together, in celebrating the praises of him, *who hath washed us with his blood, and made us kings and priests unto God.*

July 20, 1813.

AN ADDRESS TO CARELESS SINNERS.

For the Panoplist.

My dear friends,

As you have entered upon an existence that must run parallel with eternity, and are blessed with powers and faculties capable of everlasting improvement in glory and excellence, it must fill every benevolent heart with pain to behold you living without hope and without God in the world; to behold you indifferent to your own best interests, and pursuing a course of conduct, which, unless timely repentance intervene, must inevitably sink your souls in endless woe. Standing, as you do, upon the margin of the invisible world, it is astonishing beyond expression, that you should bound your views by the short term of mortal life, and as though earth were your final residence, your everlasting home. Your attachment to things seen and temporal, while you neglect those which are unseen and eternal, is a convincing, though lamentable proof, that *the heart is deceitful above all things and desperately wicked.* You are by nature children of wrath, enemies to the great and glorious Jehovah, and obnoxious to the penalty of that holy law, which thunders in the ears of transgressors, *The soul that sinneth, it shall die.* But from the cross, pardon peace, and salvation, smile on a dying world, and invite the acceptance of all, *without money and without price.* The gate of heaven, barred by the lapse of man, is now opened by the hand of the Savior, for the admission of all, who will cordially submit to the terms of the Gospel. The garden of the Lord, blooming in eternal spring, and filled with delights unknown in our earthly Eden, is now opened for the reception of perishing souls just on the verge of death and hell. Can you neglect this great salvation? Can you coldly turn from the cross, and, slighting all the joys of heaven, press your way to the regions of woe. O my friends, I beseech you, act not so mad a part. Awaken from your guilty slumbers before you lift up your eyes in the torments of the bottomless abyss. You stand on a tremendous precipice, down which you are liable to be precipitated into the gulf beneath. Should you *die in your sins;* should you perish, after all the invitations, and warnings, which you have received in this world, how awful must be your doom, how aggravated your condemnation! God declares, that all the finally impenitent shall have their portion in the *lake which burneth with fire and brimstone,* where there is *weeping, and wailing and gnashing of teeth* In that dark and bottomless pit, the sunshine of hope never disperses the rayless gloom; the life-giving sound of a Savior's voice is never heard; but all is interminable and ceaseless misery, remorse and despair. Will you make this your dreary abode? Why, O why, will you die? Why will you murder your everliving souls for the worthless, short-lived pleasures of this delusive world? Why will you continue to tread the broad and beaten road, when another step may plunge you in everlasting ruin? Will you not take alarm, and hide yourselves from the gathering tempest, in the pavilion of God? Delay not. *Your life is a vapor that appeareth but for a little time, and then vanisheth away.* Your moments are inconceivably precious, and while you are busy here and there about the veriest trifles, they speed their flight never to return. Boast not of to-morrow; for ere to-morrow shall arrive, the hand of death may blast your expectations, frustrate your schemes, and send your trembling spirit to its Maker. You are ever on the brink of the grave, on the threshold of eternity. Death waits his commis-

sion to sever the brittle thread of life, and seal your retributive state unalterably.

It is a serious thing to die. The moment, which dissolves the union between the soul and the body is big with everlasting realities, which the language of mortals cannot explain, nor the heart of man fully conceive: Then the fascinating charms of the world, and the deceitful pleasures of sin, which now engross your supreme attention, and for which you hazard the welfare of your immortal souls, will all vanish like a dream; leaving you to the pangs of unutterable disappointment. Were you possessed of all the honors, riches, and joys, which grow on earthly soil, they could not extract the sting of death, nor ward off his fatal shafts. Say; my dear friends, how can you meet that eventful period; how salute the universal conqueror? Shall you not want a religion, which can pour heavenly light upon the dark and gloomy vale, and point you to mansions of bliss on high? Shall you not need a Savior, whose presence can allay the swellings of Jordan, and whose hand can bear your departing spirit to the celestial Canaan beyond?

Let me intreat you, then, to make a good use of present opportunities, by laying up a treasure in heaven. Rest not, till you are the subjects of that change of heart which is indispensably necessary to a preparation for heavenly bliss. Repent of your numerous and aggravated sins, and seek vigorously, and unremittingly, for an interest in the atonement of Christ. Seek after

mes, without which you see God, nor relish the sake of redeemed spirits...
your... dying world, and... ...things above. Thus passed for the inheritance saints in light, and will be strengthened... vision of God... you possess peace... amidst all the... of life, and if the adversity shall cover... resignation shall... smile in your com... and your hearts shall in gratitude and joy... reach the end of... in the wilder... the vital lamp glim... shades of death, you... dently, repose on the... Savior, and... look forward to the... Christian pilgrims... their voices in com... the praises of their... ...ductor. To that up... your departing spirit... and, blessed with... youth and vigor, shall... to the uncreated... light, making con... ...gression in felicity... ...ence.

... my dear friends, re... force of all these... ... Be assured they... ...offspring of a wild... but solemn truths... the signet of heaven... and therefore war... deep and constant at... may they sink deep... hearts, and have an... ...pression, and a salute... upon your actions... Spirit seal... in... your minds, lead... the path of wisdom, and...

X.

by his divine teachings and ti... ...tional prepare you for... rest, which remaineth for the peo... ple of God! CLAUDE

DEATH OF LIEUT. FINLEY.

The following account of the religious feelings expressed by Lieut. Finley, on his death-bed, was drawn up by the Rev. Dr. M'Leod, of New York, at the request of Mr. Elisha Coit, of that city, and is now published with the consent of the writer.
This young gentleman entered Harvard College, and continued a member of that institution a considerable part of the regular term of four years. After leaving college, he entered the army and was profane and careless of religion till his last illness. His exact age, and the circumstances of his life, are not known to the writer.

New York, 2d March, 1814.

Mr. Coit,

AGREEABLY to your request, I send you a statement of the conversation which I had at two different times with Lieut. Finley, at the first of which you were yourself present. It may be gratifying to his surviving relatives to know how his mind was exercised before he left this world.

When I first called on him, he was involved in doubts and fears respecting his eternal welfare. Although he did not expect sudden death, but still cherished a hope of partial restoration to health, he seemed to be persuaded, that his disorder did not admit the hope of a full re-establishment of his bodily constitution, and that it must in the end prove mortal. Under these circumstances, the awfully important question, *Wherewith shall I come before the Lord?* deeply affected his troubled spirit.

Without attempting to administer any palliatives, my first object was to ascertain the extent and the nature of his convictions. Upon inquiry, it appeared, that in his earlier years he had been instructed in evangelical principles; that while a student at college he became a Socinian; that afterwards, by a natural and easy process, he became an Infidel, and brought forth the fruits of infidelity in a life of vanity and profaneness; and that he now felt, in the prospect of death, that such systems were deceitful, vicious, and comfortless. He expressed a deep sense of sinfulness, and earnestly requested me to point out to him some source of comfort.

Apprehensive that some particular transgressions, obviously criminal even in the estimation of an unsanctified conscience, might be the cause of his uneasiness, I asked him whether some certain acts of his life had not occasioned the sorrow for sin, which he expressed, and from which he desired relief.

"Oh no," was his reply, "my actions have indeed been bad; but it is the sinfulness of my nature that grieves me—my whole life has been wicked—I am a sinner in every thing—I have no righteousness—no good in me."

I approved of this sentiment, and having confirmed it, by repeating some texts of Scripture, I inquired, whether the general inoffensiveness of his life, and his regret for his natural failings, might not now suffice to set his mind at rest, seeing God is merciful? He looked sternly at me: I caught his eye; there was some disappointment in his countenance; and when he said, "I can depend upon nothing

but the merits of Je[sus] it was in a manner cated some suspici had met with an un guide. I then sugge sibility, that he mig some doubts respecti of the Scriptures, th Jesus Christ, and the the atonement. He

His principles w correct. *He believe bied.* He repeated, w ing earnestness, the I should point out t source of comfort.

Aware of the da founded hopes and de I urged him to reflec form me what comf tional being convin own guilt, he most d

"O," said he with sis, "that I may kno sins are pardoned, a soul shall be saved." knowledge, my frien which I have not mys ing you, and which c have it not in my pow to you. This remark sired effect. It startle quickened his attenti I added, it is in the necessary for you to your sins may be par it is soon enough, wl has become a matter reflect upon the benel der it an occasion o quickly asked, "How I obtain the pardon of

This question, I re answer unhesitatingly it perfectly, because self hath clearly rev his holy word. I pr explain to him the covenant of grac nature of faith in Jes

...read from the Scrip-
...persuade him, that he,
...since, had a perfect
...the offer, the invita-
...the commandment of
...admit his soul for sal-
Jesus Christ, with as-
...ance that he should,
...as he had when he...
...upon his bed that it...
...part his body, or when
...upon the solid earth,
...certainly bear him
...
...me with profound
...I then put the ques-
...you willing to accept
life, as the free gift of
...Christ, and to con-
...to him with confi-
...he will save you? If
...your objections. He
...I continued, He is
...to the uttermost,
...reason together, al-
...sins be as scarlet,
...be white as snow;
...cometh shall not be
He has pledged his
word of God, who can-
...he will receive you;
...authority, I, as his...
...invite you, even
...up yourself to him
...assurance, that he will
Can you refuse? He
...replied, "I have no
...I will trust in the
...esus Christ."
...versation then turned
...character of man as a
...and accountable crea-
...doctrine of a future
...divine perfections—
...of sin and holiness—
...and mediation of our
Redeemer—and ef-
...by the Holy Spir-
...these points, he glad-

...ly received information and appeared to entertain correct ideas.
At his request, I prayed with
him, and promised soon to repeat my visit. This was on
Monday, ...th of Feb. and on
Thursday the 17th, I again called upon him...
On my second visit, I found
him ... The little
noise occasioned by my entering his apartment, awaked him.
He instantly recognized me, and
stretching out his hand to me,
said, with some ...,
dear doctor, I have found Jesus,
and in ... have peace. ... Taking his hand, I replied, Being
justified by faith we have peace
with God ... our Lord Jesus
Christ—...world you ...
have trembled, ...
shall ... ... said
he, pressing my hand, with
him, this bed is comfortable.
Fearful lest in his present
state of bodily debility, his mind
might have been under some
undue excitement, and this ex-
clamation be caused by a delusio-
ry hope, I took my chair, watched his features, changed the subject of thought, and inquired
for the state of his health, since
I last saw him. He was perfectly composed and collected.
I then gradually directed the
conversation to the Providence
of God—the duty of resignation
to his will—and of tracing out
his footsteps in the several incidents of life. He spoke with
ease, joined in the conversation
with freedom, observing, that
he had been brought not only to
acknowledge the justice of God
in his own afflictions, but able to
rejoice in the wisdom and mercy which directed the time and
the circumstances of his ...

"God," said he, "hath laid his hand upon me, and brought me to this place, that I might meet you, and by your help find my Redeemer, whom I had been denying. I know now, that God has called me to trust in his Son; I trust in him for my salvation, and I am comforted."

I again changed the subject of conversation, watchful to discover to what objects of thought his affections inclined. Having inquired about his age, natural constitution, connexions, and his hopes of recovery; he replied with candor and sensibility. He did not anticipate a speedy death. He was willing to die; but he wished, if it were the will of God, for an opportunity of glorifying his Redeemer by a public profession of that religion, which he had before disclaimed. He added, "The night after your first visit, while I was meditating upon the character of Jesus Christ, and admiring its suitableness to my own case, I experienced an indescribable sense of his goodness, and since that time I am happy. At times, indeed, I am transported with gratitude; but my sense of joy is not always the same. I now feel very little emotion, and almost forget how grateful I ought to be. How comes it, that my frame of mind does not continue the same?"

In the course of this conversation, all my fears that he would give way to delusion were dispelled. I found him so humble, discreet, and correct in his views and feelings, that I threw off all suspicion, and indulged him in expressing his emotions in his own way.

He told me he had never been

baptised, and expressed to participate both of the ment and of the Lord's He was anxious to go the several parts of Chris ty, as soon as possible; an ed me, when I thought h pared to make a profess administer these sacram him, asking whether it not be done in his chamb

I expressed my appi of the principle of shew Christian obedience by ing these ordinances with speed, assured him that i made no difference, and chamber was just as sa the most costly edifice; b blind observance of any useless and dangerous, of being desirable.

I then explained to doctrine of the sacramen New Testament—shewin they belonged, not so personal religion, as to C societies organized acce order—that they were for the Church, and only dividuals as connected visible Church—that the not so much in the wan the neglect, of these po stitutions—that while by ill health his not parti of these ordinances criminal, and of course rious to him—that even forts of the Gospel were ited to ecclesiastical ri dispensing the sacram of the due order, and anxiety to receive them, more of superstition tha liness—and that all th ments of superstitious were to be avoided as e dangerous to the soul.

He appeared to be

and eagerly expressed a hope, that he should meet me in heaven, and thank me for the good he derived from my instruction on earth.

After prayer, I retired; but not without receiving an invitation to pay him an another visit, as soon as convenient.

I saw him no more. On Sabbath morning, he breathed his last. Your's respectfully,

ALEX. M'c LEOD.

ON THE CHIEF END OF THE DIVINE ADMINISTRATION.

For the Panoplist.

Mr. Editor,

I HAVE been deeply interested with two papers, that have recently appeared in the Panoplist, *on the chief end of the divine administration;* the first in your number for Sept. last, p. 211, and the other in your number for April, p. 155.

With the latter, signed F. J. I was pleased for several reasons. In the first place, I was gratified, that you had acquired such a correspondent; earnestly hoping, that so able a hand would not soon be withdrawn from the public service. I was particularly pleased with his introductory remarks, and still more with the spirit of the whole. As it is rather uncommon, so it is peculiarly pleasing, to discover the Christian temper shining through a controversial discussion. It is doubtless, in a great measure, owing to the gall, with which controversies are so often embittered, that so many Christians are disgusted at the very name and thought of controversy. Hence has arisen the maxim, *Never dispute concerning re-*

ligion; a maxim as unreasonable as it is unscriptural.[*] God forbid that Christians should give occasion any more to use this proverb.

I should have been still more pleased with F. J. if I had considered him as perfectly correct. I will mention a few things, with regard to which my views do not exactly accord with his.

It does not appear to me, that the writer of the first piece, (whom, to avoid circumlocution, I shall denominate K.) "has made an attempt to conciliate two *opposite* theories." There is, indeed, a kind of circumstantial inconsistency between these theories. No man can, at the same time, suppose that God administers his government *exclusively* for his own glory and *exclusively* for the good of creatures. But there is no such repugnance between these theories, as F. J. seems to intimate,—no such repugnance, as there is between selfishness and benevolence, light and darkness, good and evil. If either of these theories were the very reverse of what it is, then the repugnance would be manifest. That is; to say that God administers his government for his own glory, would be repugnant to saying that he does it for the *evil* of creatures; or to say that he does it for his own *dishonor* would be repugnant to saying that he does it for the good of creatures.

The two theories, which K. has attempted to unite, so far from being opposite, appear as harmonious, as any two theories can, which relate to the same subject. Nay, if we only omit

[*] Acts iv, 29; and xv, 2, 7; and xvii, 17 and xix, 8. Jude 9.

the circumstance of *exclusive-ness*, are they not harmonious parts of the same scheme? and parts, which God has actually joined together? Is it not a fact that God does promote both, at the same time, by the same means, and in the same way? Is it not true, that he never promotes either, without equally promoting the other? And is it not manifest, that God might determine to accomplish, what he actually does accomplish, and that he might make it the chief end of all his operations, to promote, to the utmost, his own glory and the good of creatures?

I cannot, therefore, perceive, that the theory of K. is inconsistent with itself; or that it is an attempt to reconcile incongruities.

The difficulty in the mind of F. J. seems to arise from the apprehension, that the theory of K. implicitly denies the infinitely important distinction between selfishness and benevolence. It is not strange, therefore, that he manifests so much zeal and acuteness in attempting to disprove it. "Another unhappy consequence," he observes, "should have been foreseen, when it was affirmed, that *to attribute to God an ultimate respect to the happiness of creatures, in itself considered, is little more than a paraphrase of the proposition that the glory of God is his chief end, because it is his nature to promote this happiness, and in the production of such immense good, consists that illustrious display of himself, which he styles his glory* This reasoning being admitted as sound, the most complete selfishness becomes perfectly synonymous

with benevolence, and th est piety; for if God see own glory, ultimately, w has an ultimate regard creature's happiness, in considered, then creature have an ultimate view t own happiness, in itself ed, and make this the su object of their desire, do and in effect, by this exer entire selfishness, (for I not how selfishness can b erwise defined,) seek the of God just as he himself and as they are required because in the product such immense good the g God consists."

The above passage, t doubtless very plain t writer, may appear to so certainly it does to me, acute than perspicuous. sentences are unhappily lo complicated. I think, ho it has a meaning, which, several attentive perusals, discovered. It appears ply one or two mistakes, w shall endeavor to point ou order to this, it may be to premise a few observ upon selfishness and be lence.

Selfishness is an undue to self—a regard to self a Benevolence is the opposi is a disregard to self as As far as a man is selfis regards his own interest, ly because it is his. As fa man is benevolent, he regard to any interest mere cause it is his. The hear is entirely selfish, regar supremely, and regards s premely because it is self. benevolent heart cannot self supremely, except (as case with God only) self is entitled to supreme regard. The selfish heart is disposed to prostrate every interest that comes in its way, except its own interest. The benevolent heart never can invade the rights of another. Selfishness is implicitly, or explicitly, enmity against God. Benevolence loves God supremely. Selfishness rises and rages against every thing, that is calculated to obstruct its gratification. Benevolence surrenders its own gratification, whenever the surrender will promote a more important good. Selfishness is the consummation of partiality; preferring an inconsiderable, and perhaps a merely imaginary, good to one that is real and infinite. Benevolence is perfectly impartial; always preferring a greater good to a less. He, who is selfish, regards every object according as he supposes it will affect his interest; and *merely* because he supposes it will affect his interest. He who is benevolent, regards every object according as it appears to be really important, and *merely* because it appears to be really important. Selfishness sets up a separate interest. Benevolence coalesces with the interest of the whole.

To these remarks, I suppose that F. J. and every other well informed friend to the truth, can most heartily subscribe.

F. J. appears to have made a mistake in supposing, that benevolence cannot induce God, or any other being, to have "an ultimate regard to the creatures' happiness, in itself considered." To have an ultimate regard to any object, is the same as to make that object an ultimate end.[*] Now it appears to me, that benevolence not only allows, but requires, both God and creatures to make the happiness of every being their ultimate end, so far as they can promote that happiness, consistently with higher obligations. For happiness is a real good in itself considered, and ought to be valued and sought for its own sake. Benevolence does not require a man to disregard the good of his own soul, nor that of another's. Comparatively indeed, it may require him to *hate his father and mother, and wife and children, and brethren and sisters, yea and his own life also.*[†] But, positively, it both permits and requires a man to seek his own welfare; not because it is his own, but because it is a real good. For the same reason, he should regard and seek the welfare of other creatures, and the glory of God, according to their importance, and his ability to promote them. And he should regard and seek the welfare of himself and other creatures, to the utmost possible extent, so far as it can be done without invading the rights of any.[‡] But here, to prevent mistake, it may be observed, that as the glory of

---

[*] An ultimate end is sought for its own sake; a subordinate end, for the sake of something else.

[†] Luke xiv. 26. See also Matt. x, 37—39.

[‡] It is generally the duty of a man to do more for the promotion of his own welfare, than for that of another; not because it is his own, but because he can much better realize its importance, and also because it is particularly committed to his care. For the same reason, it may be a duty for a man to do more for his particular connexions and friends, than for others; and more for his own country than for any other.

God is infinitely more important than the good of creatures, so all are bound supremely to regard and seek the divine glory.

Benevolence in God is of the same nature as benevolence in creatures. And it is not possible, that the infinitely benevolent God should positively disregard the welfare of any creature. Comparatively he may disregard the welfare of millions, and consign them to eternal woe. But as far as can be, consistently with the highest good of the universe, he must be disposed to promote the welfare of every individual to the utmost. And when he promotes the happiness of his creatures, he regards that happiness as a real good in itself considered, and makes it an ultimate end, in all that he does for its promotion.

But I would by no means intimate, that the happiness of creatures is not, in any sense, a subordinate end. Mr. Edwards very justly remarks, "that a thing sought may have the nature of an ultimate, and also of a subordinate end." The happiness of creatures will undoubtedly subserve the glory of God; and, in relation to that, it may be considered as a subordinate end. I am further of opinion, that the happiness of creatures is much more important, considered as a subordinate end, than considered as an ultimate end.

But while the happiness of creatures is made to promote the glory of God, the same glory of God is made to promote their happiness in a still higher degree. There is reason to believe, that the *holiness* of creatures will promote the glory of

God and be promoted by the same manner. And the doubt, the glory of God an good of the created univ will mutually promote eacl er, to a higher and highe gree in infinite progressior

F. J. appears incorrect suppose, that if creatures an ultimate view to their happiness, in itself conside they must "make this th preme object of their de: I think it must be manifest the above remarks, that we desire our own happiness, i sense, as an ultimate end still higher sense as a sub nate end; and supremely and seek the glory of G the same time.

In the sentences above qu F. J. clearly implies, that creature to seek his own h ness, as a separate intere selfishness. This is doul correct. But he seems fa to imply, that this selfishne allowed by the theory of K. this he appears by no n correct. As I understand theory of K. it allows the ture to desire and seek hi happiness as an ultimate er connexion with the glor God; and as a subordinate in subserviency to that glo not as a separate interest not with supreme regard.

I will take the liberty to a few remarks upon one pa: more in the strictures of

"No doubt," he obse "God's chief end, with re to those who are ultim made happy, is their happi and with respect to those are made miserable, it is misery. But there is a sti

hich these respec-
le subservient, viz.
God, which is as
the others, as God
istinct from crea-
writer would here
od has, in all re-
me regard for the
wicked, as for the
the righteous, he
rrect. God pro-
ppiness of the one
happiness is a real
ecause it will be
vient to a further
flicts misery upon
ot because it is a
not,) nor because
but wholly on ac-
good, to which it
subservient. Ac-
d is represented as
and deep regard
ion of his people.
presented as being
having any such
the ruin of repro-
he delights in
ament is his strange
ive, saith the Lord,
asure in the death
ieth.
am not prepared
prove, or wholly to
production of F. J.
am of opinion, that
the latter upon this
he most correct. I
least doubt, that the
ltimate end, which
lew in all his works
providence, and
good of the uni-
ighest possible in-
fare of himself and
onsidered as one
lite whole. There

appears to be no absurdity, nor the least shadow of difficulty, in supposing, that God had a real regard for the welfare of his creatures while they and their welfare, were non-entities. Had any benevolent person the power of creating beings completely happy, I am confident he would find a motive for exerting that power, in the happiness he would thus impart.

A benevolent being necessarily regards the interest of others, as his own. In reality, their interest is his. He cannot, knowingly, neglect the interest of any. The infinitely benevolent God cannot have any interest distinct from the welfare of creatures; as his real friends can have no interest distinct from his. The bond of perfectness, unites all holy beings in the most endearing union. Their hearts are one; their interests are one: And to promote this general interest must be the great aim and end and exertion of all.

This is a point, which I conceive has been set in the clear light of demonstration by the illustrious Edwards, in his dissertation concerning the *end for which God made the world.*[*] That performance, though probably in some respects not perfectly correct, I do not hesitate to rank among the greatest and most valuable productions of the greatest man, who has yet adorned the American church.

MEDIUS.

[*] See Edwards' Works, vol vi.

MISCELLANEOUS.

For the Panoplist.

ON CHURCH DISCIPLINE.

Mr. Editor,

A constant reader of your interesting publication submits to your disposal the enclosed thoughts on church discipline. The subject is important; but little attended to, and still less understood, especially by Christians in general. The enclosed was intended as a solution of most of those little questions, which usually arise in the *real practice* of discipline. How far the writer has succeeded, yourself and the public will judge.   X. W.

CHURCH discipline is a very solemn and important part of church duty. On a proper exercise of it seems to depend, not barely the well being, but almost the very existence of the church. It may be defined to consist in reproving and admonishing offending members, and in using all other orderly instituted means, to recover them to the path of duty.

I pretend not here to enter upon a full discussion of this important and much disputed subject; but shall content myself with suggesting and answering two or three questions, which very naturally arise on a consideration of it. If what is here offered throws no new light on the subject, but only excites a spirit of inquiry in abler minds, and quickens churches to be more faithful in this part of their duty, the writer will think himself amply compensated.

It is pretty generally understood, in this part of our country, that the power of disciplining its members is vested in every church. Our first question may then be,—*Who are the subjects of church discip*

In answer to this, it is that none can be properly to the discipline of a p church, but those who ar bers of it. Professors of may reprove the immoral the world; and indeed the to do so; but never m treat those who are out church, as subject to th pline of that sacred body. also may notice and repr orderly professors, who belong to the same chur themselves; but never offender be considered ject to a process of discip any church, but that to w really belongs.

The visible church is c ed of visible saints, or i words, of such as are visi ly. When, therefore, a has ceased to be visibly h has become visibly wicl has dishonored his pro and is a proper subject discipline of his brethren. may be thought that this *visibly wicked*, is not suffi explicit, to note the prop jects of a whole process o pline. My brother may l bly wicked in my eye; opinion his conduct may l sinful, while this is the of no one else. Or he r visibly wicked to me o another account, which cause no one else has any edge of his offence. T may not misapprehen phrase, *visibly wicked*, l state two circumstances, ought always to apply to

ers; at least if their offences are to be made known to the church.

1. Their supposed offences are to be unquestionably real ones, in the opinion of the complainant. Their conduct must be so clearly sinful, as that its criminality can rationally be supposed capable of being shewn, both to them, and to the world. Notwithstanding the world is so full of opinions, the judgment of mankind respecting the morality of actions, is, especially in Christian countries, pretty generally uniform. At least, there are very many actions so palpably wicked, as to be condemned without dispute. Of this character should be the conduct of offenders, especially if their offences are to be made known to the church. Indeed, a man's own opinion of right and wrong must guide him in the first step of discipline, which is only private reproof. If *I think* my brother has done wrong, I must reprove him. But I may not bring his offence to the church, unless its criminality is so unquestionable, in my opinion, as that it may rationally be supposed capable of being shewn, both to him, and to the generality of mankind.

2 An offending professor is not a proper subject of discipline before the church, unless his offences are capable of proof. If his offences cannot be proved against him by at least two credible witnesses, the church, as a body, is not to believe him guilty, and cannot proceed to discipline him in a regular manner. If a member offends privately, the brother who knows of his offence, may labor with the offender in a private way; but no one, in such a case, can be a proper subject

of discipline before the church. It appears, then, on the whole, that professors of religion, who, a*re visibly wicked; who* are guilty of some undoubted offence, which can be proved against them, are proper subjects, and the only proper subjects, of a full process of church discipline.

Question second: *What are the proper steps to be taken, in a process of church discipline?*

These are summarily stated by our Savior, in the 18th chapter of Matthew. If thy brother has trespassed against thee, the first step, according to his directions, is, to *go and tell him his fault between thee and him alone. If he shall hear thee, thou hast gained thy brother. But if he will not hear thee*, then proceed to take the second step in church discipline; which is, to *take with thee one or two more, that in the mouth of two or three witnesses every word may be established. And if he shall neglect to hear them*, then proceed to the third step, which is to *tell it unto the church. But if he neglect to hear the church*, the fourth step only remains to be taken, which is, to cast him out, and cause him to become to your sacred fraternity *as an heathen man and a publican.* These directions are so explicit, as to need but little comment. Two simple questions, which may arise respecting them, will be answered. 1. Does Christ refer to *personal offences* only, when he says, *If thy brother shall trespass against thee;* or does he refer to sin in general? Personal offences are such as are aimed against the life, property, or reputation of some individual person or persons. Such are slander, theft, dishonesty in dealings,

&c.—and it has been the opinion of some, that Christ, in the passage under consideration, refers exclusively to such offences. But there is no necessity for this opinion; since the words under consideration are evidently, and very naturally, susceptible of greater latitude. The word here translated *trespass*, is usually and literally rendered *sin*. If it had been so rendered in this place, the passage would then have been, *If thy brother shall sin against thee.* The church is one body—the body of Christ. (1 Cor. xii, 27.) If, therefore, a particular member sins, he sins against and offends the whole body, and every particular member of it. If my brother is guilty of the sin of profaneness, or drunkenness, he sins against, and offends me, although he commits nothing against me personally. We see, then, that there is nothing in the words themselves, which should lead us to suppose that they referred exclusively to personal offences. They may very naturally be taken in a greater extent, as referring generally to the sins of professors. I now add farther; that the words under consideration not only may—they *must* relate to other offences, than those of a personal nature. It is evident that Christ must, somewhere, have given an universal rule respecting discipline—one which will apply to all cases. But we find no such rule in Scripture, except in this passage. This, then, must be an universal rule;—the directions here given must refer and apply to *all supposable offences*, and cannot refer to personal offences only. If Christ in this passage refers exclusively to

personal offences, he has then given no rule respecting the discipline of such members, as are chargeable with intemperance, idolatry, profaneness, &c. and the church cannot be justified in admonishing, or in excommunicating such offending members. But an error so palpably gross, will find no advocates. It seems certain, that in the passage I have considered, Christ refers not only to personal offences, but to all the manifest, undoubted sins of his covenant people. 2. In the passage, *Go and tell him his fault between thee and him alone*, does the command of Christ extend to any brother, who has a competent knowledge of the nature and circumstances of the offence; or is it limited to the particular brother, who may have been personally offended. I am of the decided opinion, that the command of Christ, in this case, is not to be limited; that any brother may rightfully undertake this business, and labor with the offender, who has a competent knowledge of the nature and circumstances of the offence. Indeed this is a clear inference from what has been said. If, as we have seen, in his directions respecting offences, Christ does not refer exclusively to such as are *personal*, then his command in the present case, cannot be limited to such as have been *personally* offended. The same brother is to go and tell the offender his fault who has been trespassed against, or sinned against, by the offender; and this, as we have seen, is every brother in the church. Any one of the brethren then has been sinned against by the offender, and any one, who has a compe-

ledge of the nature
stances of the offence,
ally go to the offender
m of it. But farther:—
ther may go and labor
offender, except he
een personally offend-
o offences can be dis-
y the church, except
s of a personal nature.
r cannot be disciplin-
temperance, or profane-
... any other crime,
ot personal in its na-
t, by such a crime he
end any of his breth-
ually, and of course
s brethren have a right
and labor with him.
ch must retain the in-
person, the profane
d many other persons
characters; since, on
ple I am opposing,
s provided no way in
y can be dealt with,
t reclaimed, cast out.
surdity so glaring will
ally disclaimed; and
ust be disclaimed the
rom which it has flow-
er: If no brother, ex-
an one as has been
offended, can proper-
ith an offender, then,
ll offences, which are
al, but very many *per-
ices,* will be shut out
otice and discipline of
h. Suppose a pious
have been personally
—suppose that she has
dered by some other
brother, in the church.
she do? and what can
a do? On the ground
sing none of the breth-
eal with the offender;
of the brethren have
ually offended. And

the injured and offended sister cannot deal with the offender; as she will not be permitted to tell her grievances to the church and support them there; since *it is a shame to a woman to speak in the church.* (1 Cor. xiv, 35.) Again: Suppose a church member to give personal offence to a neighbor, who is out of the church. Suppose him, (for the case is certainly possible) to defraud, to belie, to slander such a neighbor. Now what can be done? No brother in the church can deal with this offender; since none of the brethren have been personally offended. And certainly he cannot be disciplined by the abused neighbor, who is out of the church. In both these cases, offences strictly personal, and perhaps highly aggravated, must be overlooked by the church; since it is impossible, on the principle I oppose, that they should be noticed in a regular way. Such are some of the absurd and evil consequences of the principle that no brother has a right to deal with an offender, unless the offender has offended him personally. We shall therefore be justified in discarding this principle; and in supposing, in opposition to it, that any brother, who has any competent knowledge of the nature and circumstances of an offence, may rightfully go to the offender and deal with him.

Question third: What is the proper satisfaction to be made by an offender, after a process of discipline has been commenced?

In answer to this, let it be observed, that he must always be humble and penitent for his faults, and must make a proper confession of them. This is to believed will be admitted by all. The only question then is—what confession is proper for an offender? Must it be public or private? This must depend wholly on the nature and circumstances of the offence. The confession must be as public, as is the offence. A private confession cannot make satisfaction for a public offence; and a public confession is not needed, and probably ought not to be made, in order to satisfy for a private offence. After the first or even the second step has been taken with an offender, in a process of discipline, if his offences are still in a degree private, a confession as private, as are his offences, will satisfy for them. But after a complaint has been entered against him to the church, his offences have become in a lawful way public, and a public confession alone can make satisfaction. Some have distinguished between offences publicly committed, and those, which, having been privately committed, afterwards became public; and they have supposed a public confession in the former case necessary, and not in the latter. But it is evident, that all public offences, whether publicly committed, or made public after commission can be satisfied only by a public confession. This alone can wipe away the stain, and reinstate the offender in the affections of his brethren, and in the esteem of all good men. If I offend privately, and my offence becomes public not by my means, the sin of needlessly publishing it, must lie on some other. But still, as the offence has unhappily become public, I can make satisfaction only by a public confession. I can in no other way satisfy myself; satisfy the church; and satisfy the world around. We have now seen what is the proper satisfaction to be made by an offender, after a process of discipline has been commenced against him. If his offences are private, a private confession only is necessary. But if they are public, as they always are, after they have gone to the church, then nothing but a public confession can satisfy for them.

These observations will be closed with a few remarks.

1. We see from what has been said, that no brother can excuse himself for not reproving and laboring with an offender, by the consideration that the offender has not personally injured him. This is too often made an excuse by professing Christians. "To be sure, such a brother or sister has done very wrong; but he has not injured me—and why should I meddle with what is none of my business?" But from what has been said, we see, that this excuse is utterly inadmissible. The offending brother or sister does sin against the whole church—the body of Christ—and against every particular member of it. *Every* brother is offended—and *any* brother if he has a competent knowledge of the nature and circumstances of the offence, is called upon to reprove the offender.

2. It is a remark very important to be noticed, that a process of discipline ought to be kept as private, as the nature of the case will admit. It is to be commenced in private, and it is, if possible, to be closed in private. The reproving brother may not mention it any oftener than

requires; and if it come
church, no church mem-
a right to mention it be-
the world. The law of love
as this—the honor of re-
requires it—and the com-
of Christ does, at least im-
require the same.
church discipline, it seems,
every stage of it, a labor of
The offender is a wander-
in the fold of Christ—from
path of duty—and from the
heaven. In this dread-
ation, one of his brethren
him. His heart is touched,
kindly offers to take his
brother by the hand, and
him back. Is not this an
ace of friendship and broth-
love? How ought the offen-
y thank this kind brother,
this brother, to follow
back, and to be grateful for

It is of the utmost impor-
to churches, faithfully to
ain the discipline of Christ.
hey have this power in their
s, they are justly accounta-
or all the impunities, which
offered to remain in the vis
church. Certainly then, as
ches regard themselves—as
regard the honor of relig-
they regard the conver-
of sinners and the good of
and as they regard the
mands of their ascended
they will carefully main-
the discipline which he has
ituted.

LETTER FROM THE LATE MRS.
NEWELL.

following letter was forwarded some-
he ago for publication; but was deferred on account of the more urgent
claims of other communications.

Haverhill, Dec. 13, 1811.

"I HAVE long been wishing for a
favorable opportunity to return
my thanks to my dear Miss
W——d for her affectionate letter received last June. A multiplicity of avocations, which
could not possibly be dispensed
with, have deprived me of this
pleasure before. Though my
friends have been neglected, yet
they have not been forgotten.
Oh no! dear to my heart are the
friends of Immanuel, particularly those with whom I have walked to the house of God in company, and with whom I have tak-
en sweet counsel about the
things which immediately concern the Redeemer's kingdom,
Zion, the city of our God. These
dear Christian friends will retain
a lasting and affectionate remembrance in my heart, even though
unfrequented forests and stormy
oceans should separate me from
them, during my short pilgrimage below. There is a world,
my sister, beyond this mortal
state, where souls, cemented in
one common union, will dwell
together and never more be separated. Adieus and farewells
will be unknown in that land of
pure delight, where Jesus sits
on the throne, and where his followers will forever reign. Does
not your heart often burn within
you, when, in humble anticipation of future blessedness you
engage in the delightful service
of your Redeemer?

"The toils of this short life
will soon be over. Yes, my
friend, we shall soon bid an eternal farewell to this passing

world, and, if interested in the covenant of redemption, we shall find that rest which remaineth for the people of God. I thank you sincerely for the affectionate interest you have professed to take in my future prospects in life. I feel encouraged to hope, that not only your good wishes, but fervent prayers will attend my contemplated undertaking. I know, that the earnest supplications of the faithful will avail with God. Plead, then, my friend, on my behalf: The path of duty is the only way to happiness. I love to tread the path which my Father, my Guide, and my Director points out for me to walk in, though it leads to unnumbered trials and is replete with privations, and hardships. Who, my dear Miss W——, that has felt the love of Jesus, the worth of souls and the value of the Gospel, would refuse to lend her little aid in propagating the religion of the cross, among the forlorn and perishing heathen, when presented with a favorable opportunity? However great the discouragements attending a missionary life, yet Jesus has promised to be with those who enter upon it with right dispositions of heart, even to the end of the world. When will the day dawn, and the day star arise in heathen lands? Oh when will the standard of the cross be erected, and all nations hear of the glad tidings of salvation? When will the millennial state commence, and the lands which have long lain in darkness, be irradiated by the blessed Gospel? When will the populous regions of Asia and Africa, where "Moloch, horrid king, besmeared with blood of human sacrifice and parents'

tears," now reigns tri[umphant] unite with this our [c]country, in one general praise to God? Though [error] and error now prevail, fai[th] over these lofty mount[ains] beholds, with unutterab[le] port, the dawning of th[e] righteousness, the re[ign of] peace and love.

"The clock strikes t[wo, I] must leave you, my fri[end;] tired nature requires res[t.] much of me, my sister, [write] often for me. Write [im]mediately upon receiv[ing my] hasty letter, if it dese[rves] answer.

Affectionately your[s,]
HA[RRIET]

ON RELIGIOUS CHAR[ITIES.]

For the [——]

IN a paper published in [the] op[l]ist for April, I offer[ed] calculations, respecting [the] uses which might be [made of] the money now expe[nded in] war, and proposed to of[fer some] remarks on the comp[arative] small sums which C[hristians] seem willing to give to charities

Before I proceed to [the ac]complishment of this [I] must premise, that C[hristians] sometimes expose the[ir] causes to ridicule, by [ex]travagant exultation at a [rel]atively trifling subscri[ption to a] charitable object. [They raise] their expectation so [high that] they tempt every in[fidel and] scoffer, who stands b[y to say,] "*These people [must not]* *religion at [a] [cheap rate, see]* *how they [are]* *thousand [——]*

gious charity. They
f a most extraordinary
taken place. If there
e but infidels, in this
and wealthy city, who
ny considerable sum of
uch exultation would
o strange But when
ssing Christians of this
might pay a million of
d never feel the sacri-
seems rather curious,
should assume so
dit for giving a thous-
t of that sum. If a the-
be erected, a *hundred
dollars* can be raised
he least difficulty. If
d actresses are wanted
ported from London,
se can easily be borne,
egular dramatic exhibi-
go on, at an expense
t *two hundred thousand*
uring one winter, for
xtra dress, coach-hire,
In a popular war, this
l raise five millions in
lay to carry it on; in the
st Satan, which these
s profess to wage with
vigor, they think they
y if they can raise for
scheme of warfare, a
andth part of that sum.
n their sincerity. If I
a Christian, give me
st Moravian, who acts
; to his professions;
ile he says he is the
f God, actually dispos-
his earnings and *all* his
is he thinks will most
to the spread of re-

I can well imagine,
the language of an in-
infidel; and let me ask
If there is not ton
for it is not a
t.

fact that many Christians, both
in the city and the country, act
according to a shamefully low
standard, so far as religious
charities are concerned. In one
of our largest cities, for instance,
the merchants pay a million annually in duties to government;
the inhabitants expend two millions in erecting new private
buildings: they add a million to
their banking capital; they add
half a million to the furniture of
their houses; they lend some
millions to government; they
have some millions lying by unemployed; and how much do
they give to Christ? Not a tenth
part of a tithe of what they might
give—of what they ought to
give. Before Christians should
give largely of their property to
religious charities, there are two
questions to be settled. Is the
cause worthy of pecuniary sacrifices? Will the *giving of money*
really promote the cause?

As to the first question, it
would be an insult to a Christian community, were I to attempt to answer it. As to the
second, let the inquirer look
around upon the ignorance, the
vice, the irreligion, which prevail in the world. These evils
may be removed by instruction,
admonition, and example, accompanied by the divine blessing. Instructors, who will exhibit a good example, may be
found and employed, if pecuniary means are not wanting: and
the experience of the church
has shewn, that the divine blessing usually accompanies faithful attempts to do good. It is
plain, then, that very great pecuniary sacrifices should be
made without delay by Christians, for the general diffusion

of religious .... Let us
compare the expense actually
incurred for this object with
those which are incurred for
...... purposes are concerned. In
...... the writer would not by any
means ...... party feeling ...... he is
bound to premise, that he does
neither wish ...... to him at the
justice or injustice of any particular war, as far as relates to
one party engaged in it rather
than the other. All men admit,
that no war can be justifiable on
both sides. Every war must,
therefore, be owing to the wickedness of man; and the whole
expense, on both sides, must be
charged to that cause. To all
reflecting Christians, then, it
must appear a melancholy, a
bitter, a lamentable thing, even
in regard to any war which they
may deem just and inevitable,
that so enormous a tribute
should be paid to human depravity; that millions after millions
should be raised by professed Christians, to hire men to
engage in the unhappy em-
ployment of killing their fellow men; that the Sabbath
should be broken down, vice
and immorality become awfully prevalent, and thousands after
thousands of immortal beings,
be driven away in their wickedness; while it is so difficult to
support the fainting cause of virtue in the world, and to bear any
extraordinary expense incurred
by the endeavor to make mankind, wiser, better, and happier. I now proceed to shew, that
the greatest charitable expenses
are very small compared with
the expenses of war.

The British and Foreign Bible Society is one of the noblest
charities, in the pro...
which Christians have ...
ed. It has received a ...
tensive patronage—s ...
sive, that Christians ...
generally been astoni ...
magnitude:—a patro ...
which it is perfectl ...
and which could be use ...
ployed if increased tw ...
This Society expende ...
the year which ende ...
1813, about *three hu...*
nine thousand dollar...
...... large; but it is ...
...... hundredth ...
war expenses of the ...
pire, exclusive of the ...
penses of the British ...
for the last year. In w ...
it would not pay the se ...
see, as they accrue, ...
...... for a single ...
days. It would not ...
arms and ammunition ...
by ...... advanced ...
the battles of Leipsic ...
scarcely furnish lint t ...
the mangled limbs of th ...
ed da ...... those battles ...
scarcely grease the ...
the waggon, and still ...
it would scarcely feed ...
geons of the army or ...
water, while actually ...
in amputating limbs an ...
ning fractured skulls; ...
scarcely repair the dam ...
to a ship of the line, ...
fought battle; it would ...
give a morsel of brown ...
each of the widows and ...
children, whom a sin ...
paign has reduced to-t ...
tion. Some few gener ...
may give more to the ...
ciety, than they pay to ...
expenses of war; but ...
proportion, even of t ...

subscribers, do not give a hundredth part so much, as falls to their share of these expenses.

To cross the Atlantic and return to our own country:—From the best computation, which I am able to make from the documents before me, I suppose the missionary Societies in the United States expended 25,000 dollars the last year, and the Bible Societies will spend the current year about 20,000 dollars. Supposing our war expenses to be $45,000,000, which is generally considered as a pretty low estimate, it appears that the people of the United States, which is a professedly Christian Country, and in which many thousands of real Christians are to be found expend *one thousand* dollars in war for a *single dollar* laid out in supporting missionaries and distributing of Bibles. In other words, the money expended for these purposes would support our war expenses only *nine hours and thirty seven minutes.* It would scarcely load the guns, in all our forts and vessels, for a general salute on account of one of our victories; it would scarcely afford pine coffins for our young men who have died in our army hospitals.

Some individuals among us, (I record it for the honor of the Christian name,) make pecuniary sacrifices for the cause of their Redeemer with as much zeal, as those, whom the world calls patriots, ever made sacrifices to support a popular war. The number is small but increasing; and it will continue to increase. The time is coming, when the opinions of mankind are to be changed on these subjects; when the real interests of

men will be perceived and promoted; and when those things, which have been hitherto *highly esteemed among men,* will be found to be an *abomination in the sight of God.* A. B.

PRAISE AND BLAME.

For the Panoplist.

Mr. Editor,

A WRITER in your number for March, p. 114, has advanced some sentiments on *Praise and Blame,* which are, I believe, very erroneous. He thinks, "that holiness deserves praise to as great a degree, as sin deserves blame; and, "that holiness will, in every sense, bear to be weighed against sin."

It is not my design to enter into an examination concerning the gross mistake which he supposes I committed some time ago in writing on this subject; nor to endeavor to show, particularly, the fallacy of the arguments which he has used. If there can be found some short and easy method to prove clearly, that the question, Are men deserving of as much praise for their holy actions, as blame for their sinful ones, should receive a negative answer, my present object will be accomplished. I would now ask those, who hold that as much praise and consequently, reward, are due to a holy creature, as censure and punishment to one that is sinful, whether they believe, that the wicked deserve on account of their iniquities, to be forever fixed in a state of sin and misery? If they allow this, I would inquire, whether accor-

ding to their principles, angels and whether the Deity
and our first parents before their interposing to prevent
fall, did not, for their holiness apostacy, has not faileth
deserve to be forever continued ing them their due irrec...
in a state of sanctity and bliss.

POETRY.

To the Editor of the Period

Sir,

You will oblige a reader, if, consistently with the object
work, you can insert the enclosed. If otherwise, will y
sign it to the flames.

BUCHANAN.

Several years since, it was reported, and believed, that the Rev. Dr.
intended visiting the Holy Land. The following lines were written in co
of that belief.

Whence comes yon bark that ploughs the wat'ry plain
A lonely wanderer on the trackless main?
There sails a hallow'd ship from Britain's isle,
By angels led, and cheer'd by heav'n's own smile;
And there Buchanan quits his native strand,
And points his course to Palestine's land.
'Late came the sacred sage from India's shores,
Climes of the morn, where worshipp'd Ganges pours.'
What object there engag'd his constant care,
Ask'd every toil, and call'd his ceaseless prayer?
To burst the chain, that bound the Hindoo's mind,
The soul to wake in Pagan sleep confin'd;
Realms lost in night to warm with genial day,
And light to heav'n with truth's immortal ray.

To Juggernaut, (where frantic myriads raise,
Screams of wild joy, and yells of senseless praise,)
He trod the path of death, and woe, and gloom;
The porch of hell, a nation's boundless tomb:
There maddening crowds the bloody demon hail,
And howl their transports to the sobbing gale;
Orissa's fields are there th' unmeasur'd grave;
The mangled corpse there chokes the rustling wave,
O'er the wide champaign gorg'd hyenas roam,
And sin and death, exulting, find a home.
"There thou hast seen the Inquisition's fire;
The victim fetter'd for the lustral pyre;
Heard the shrill shriek, the groan of pale despair,
The yell of anguish on the wearied air.

There 'twas a sin to doubt, a crime t' inquire,
And saints arose from Persecution's fire:
There martyr'd virtue fed th' assassin's steel,
Glutted the axe,—or gasp'd upon the wheel.
Yet, follower of thy GOD, lament no more;
The shriek, the groan, have startled Albion's shore:
Fierce on the fiends, see! sternest ruin frowns;
Echoing the crash, the eastern shore resounds.
Hark! 'tis the shout of joy that myriads raise;
And through the expanse is heard all India's praise.

Thence to sad Judah's sons was bent thy way;
Reft from their kindred tribes of orient day;
The lorn remains of proud Assyrian power,
From joy exil'd on India's distant shore;
Unknown, unknowing, outcasts from mankind,
They wait their country's morn, to woe resign'd.

But now the theme again awakes thy lyre;
For them thy bosom burns with hallow'd fire;
Now, through the Central Wave to Israel's land
Points thy bright track from Britain's rocky strand.
The same pure passion now exalts thy mind;
The recreant soul with virtue's bond, to bind;
To bid the outcast leap at Jesus' name,
To glow with love, and feel an angel's flame,
To bid that darken'd race their throne resume,
And joy inspire the breast, and truth illume.
Low art thou fall'n, once beauty of the morn!
No more the smiles of peace thy land adorn,
No more a Hebrew monarch fills thy throne;
Nor trembling realms thy proud dominion own:
But, stretch'd in dust, thy sacred glory lies;
Stern on thy ruin'd temple frown the skies;
Around thy walls the Crescent sheds its gloom;
And mosques arise o'er blest Messiah's tomb.
Where Jordan once refresh'd thy verdant vales,
And drank the fragrance of thy spicy gales;
Through dreary wastes he rolls his sullen wave,
While nought disturbs the stillness of the grave;
O'er thy bleak deserts wide destruction reigns,
And fearful horror shadows all thy plains.

O sacred Salem! daughter of the skies!
Unseen, forgot, thy ancient glory dies.
O lov'd of heav'n! o'er fairest regions fair!
The pride of Asia! plung'd in deep despair.
I mourn thy fall, I weep thy splendors gone;
Yet still I hail thee beauty of the dawn.

On distant shores, thy sons thy misery mourn;
Fall'n from the skies, from peerless greatness torn;
They weep for joys long past, to come no more;
And breathe their sighs where western oceans roar;

Or in thy mould'ring walls to hoped'gs giv'n,
They sink beneath the angry frown of heav'n;
There, crouching 'mid the waning Crescent's gloom,
They mourn around their sek-nown Savior's tomb;
Still look for Bethlehem's star, where morning broke,
Herald of joy, precedes unchanging day.

  But lo! Buchanan on thy strand appears,
To cheer thy furrow'd brow, and wipe thy tears;
To spread the sacred word thy tribes among,
To bid the song of heaven employ thy tongue,
The rescued wanderer to his Father's care,
And call the prodigal, repenting, home.

  Though scorn assail,—though rancor blast thy name,
Though sin and sorrow tell the world thy shame,
Yet hush thy murmurs; soon the desert smiles;
Thy glory shines, and breaks on distant isles.
He that announc'd Messiah's birth, again
Points to thy clust'ring tribes their native plain;
Again the sun of peace thy land illumes;
No more a waste, thy field with Eden blooms;
And lo! the Warrior-Angel o'er them flies,
The cloud descends where hostile myriads rise;
The fiery pillar points their destin'd way;
And soon o'er Zion bursts millennial day.
Go then, thou saint, 'gainst every foe contend;
Pursue thy path; complete thy destin'd end;
Hear from yon countless throng the burst of praise;
For thee the strain of grateful joy they raise.
"Thou, thou hast freed the captive wretch from pain,
Cheer'd the desponding heart to peace again,
The Hindoo brought where holy pleasures rise,
And led the trembling Pagan to the skies."

  With thine compared, how poor the Warrior's fame,
Though climes applaud, and ages shout his name;
His praise is mingled with the echoing groan;
And devastation claims the chief her own;
In fields of gore his rising glories bloom;
Beneath his trophies yawns th' insatiate tomb.
But thou hast felt a purer, holier flame;
And the poor heathen leaps to hear thy name;
For thou hast raised to heav'n the darkling mind,
While o'er thy path celestial glory shin'd.

  Compar'd with thine, how poor the Poet's praise,
Who bids th' applauding world his glory raise;
Though genius lights him with immortal ray,
Though fairy forms around his fancy play,
Though he o'ertakes the sun-beam in its flight,
And the moon traces borne on silver light;
For him though beauty springs with fairer bloom,
And fresher, sweeter, breathes the gales perfume,

Yet the bright scenes are all illusion there:
No lasting radiance makes the rainbow fair.
  How poor the joys that Learning's sons inspire,
Though multitudes her valued stores admire:
With thine compar'd what need can Science claim,
The sun that lights the sage's deathless name.
Though by her eye we view the comet roll,
And count the stars that circle either pole;
Though Nature's book its countless stores unfolds;
And heav'n's own work th' unfetter'd mind beholds:
Yet, here no virtue shines, nor GOD appears;
In mis'ry's helpless hour no angel cheers;
Nor saints invite, nor seraphs bid them rise,
On faith's strong wing, to bliss beyond the skies.
  Go, then, thou saint! haste, haste to Syria's wilds;
On thy blest work th' Eternal Spirit smiles.
  With faith, with transport, run thy blest career;
Bid the lorn Jews Immanuel's Gospel hear,
Proclaim the sacred word their tribes around,
And make each each plain JEHOVAH'S name resound.

                         Y.

RELIGIOUS INTELLIGENCE.

AMERICAN MISSIONARIES.

e following letter from Mr Nott to his
ents contains some particulars, not
utioned in the letter to Dr. Worces-
, published in our last number.

Bombay, March 5, 1813.

MY VERY DEAR PARENTS,

m sometimes led to fear that the
nts of the war may have prevented
r receiving the several letters which I
Mrs Nott have written since we left
erica, and may still be in suspense con-
ning us You may be assured you
e not been forgotten, and I hope you
e received our letters as a witness that
have not

n the whol , the past year has been
ry prosperous one with us, though
have been once visited with sickness,
have not been without some other
ls; but of all these things I hope you
e been before this fully informed Af-
we left Bengal we landed first at Pon-
cerry, a pleasant French settlement on
Coromandel coast, where in a pleas-
and studious retirement we spent five
eks, the ship being accidentally detain-
Our voyage from that place to this
s about a month: the weather gener-
y pleasant—but Mrs Nott was as usual
ick. We arrived here on the 11th

of February, and landed on the 12th.
Three or four of the first days we spent
at Dr Taylor's, who was formerly a Missionary from the London Society, for
whose hospitality and active friendship we
have reason to be very grateful. We are
now living in our own hired house, in the
enjoyment of many domestic comforts,
and in the possession of perfect health
We have much hope that this place is to
terminate our wanderings and to be the
scene of our future labors We have also
fears. The governor of this Presidency,
we believe inclined to favor us, but the
Bengal government, besides endeavoring
to send us away from them, have strongly
recommended a similar step to the gov
ernment here What will be the event
is very uncertain; all we can say is, that
we may be sent to England We trust,
however, that the Lord has something
for us to do here. We have found
friends among the English inhabitants
here, who interest themselves in our stay,
and some who seem to do it from good
motives. We are deeply encouraged by
one instance of *deep serious concern* The
person whose mind is affected is a young
Lieutenant in the Artillery, who has been
in the country about six months. His education was not religious, and his character, till within these four months, trifling
He was awakened by reading Cowper's

Poems, and who comes to receive *relig-ious instruction* of us, and to *encourage our hearts* by exhibiting that this place to which we have come, is one that God designs to visit.

Though our state is uncertain, we are content to ongthe Mahratta language—"we walk by faith, not by sight." A very talkative black gentleman, is to sit by us, and *beat it into us,* three or four hours every day.

As yet we do nothing as preachers—but shall hope to if we stay * * * * *

* * We do long to hear from you and from our parents of the other family. We think of you and daily pray for you, and hope that God recompenses our absence to you, by crowning you with loving kindness and tender mercies, and cheering your hearts in your way with the hope of glory.

We experience no evils from being in an *enemy's* land, as perhaps you may fear. However we most earnestly desire that there may be a *firm* and *lasting* peace between the parent country and our own.

At this season of the year the climate is delightful. Indeed the evenings and mornings are quite cool—it will soon, however, be very hot. But we are told that this is the most healthy place in India.

We send our united love to all the family—and wish you to remember us with respect and affection to our other parents, and all their house. Forget not our neighbors and intimate friends, for whom we wish the enjoyment of all *spiritual* and *temporal* blessings.

I am, my dear and hon. Parents,
   with continual affection,
     Your dutiful son,
       SAMUEL NOTT, JUN.

NEW ENGLAND TRACT SOCIETY

A short time since a Society with the above designation was formed, and has began its operations on an extensive scale. In consequence of the beneficence of a few individuals, the Executive Committee have been able to print 300,000 tracts, comprising a variety of fifty different kinds, the first cost of which, exclusive of contingent expenses, will be about 3,000 dollars. The nature and design of the Society will be manifest from the following Constitution and Address.

CONSTITUTION.

During the last twenty years many millions of Religious Tracts have been distributed by Christians, in Europe and America, and during the last twelve

years the religious public in [land] have taken an active pa[rt in the] labor of love. The experience [which] affords abundant encourageme[nt to con]tinue and extend efforts of th[is descrip]tion. For the purpose of dir[ecting and] combining all the energy an[d zeal] which can be brought into op[eration in] this cause, a number of indi[viduals in] different parts of New Engl[and have] agreed to form themselves into [a Society,] and have adopted the followi[ng consti]tution.

Art. 1. The Society shall [be called] THE NEW ENGLAND TRACT S[OCIETY.]

Art. 2. The object of this S[ociety is to] promote the interests of vital [religion] and good morals, by the dist[ribution of] such Tracts, as shall be calcul[ated to re]ceive the approbation of seri[ous Chris]tians of all denominations.

Art. 3. Any person, who [shall pay] twenty dollars, or more, into t[he treas]ury of the Society, at any one [time, shall] be a member for life; and a[ny person] who shall engage to pay two [dollars, or] more, annually, shall be a m[ember so] long as his subscription shall be [paid.]

Art. 4. Every member shall [be entitled] to receive three fourths of the [amount of] his subscription, in Tracts, at c[ost; and] any person, who shall engage [to pay a] less sum, annually, than is a[bove fixed to] constitute him a member, sha[ll be enti]tled to receive Tracts in the [same pro]portion, and at the same rate.

Art. 5. There shall be an an[nual meet]ing of the society in Boston, o[n the] day preceding the General E[lection, at] 6 o'clock, P. M. when a Presid[ent, a Vice] President, a Corresponding S[ecretary, a] Recording Secretary, a Tre[asurer, an] Assistant Treasurer, an Audit[or, and an] Executive Committee, shall be [chosen] by ballot.

Art. 6. It shall be the duty [of the Ex]ecutive Committee to super[intend the] publication and distribution of [Tracts, to] procure a place of deposit in [Boston, to] appoint corresponding commit[tees, to ap]point a general agent, who sh[all conduct] the sales, and to make repo[rt of their] doings at each annual meeting.

Art. 7. Any religious or ch[aritable So]ciety, or any association of p[ersons, for] the reformation of morals o[r the sup]pression of vice, shall be enti[tled to re]ceive Tracts at cost.

Art. 8. No tax shall be laid [upon the] members.

Art. 9. At any annual mee[ting such] amendments of the constituti[on may be] made, as shall be recommen[ded by the] Executive Committee, and a[pproved by] two thirds of the members pr[esent.]

IE FRIENDS OF RELIGION IN NEW
ENGLAND.

the extensive distribution of cheap
, must have an important influen ce
he community, cannot be doubted
fluence will be good or bad accord -
the nature of the Tracts distribut-
he splendid talents of Voltaire,
ever employed against Christianity
s much effect, as when they were
d to the writings of small Tracts, of
its tendency, for gratuitous disper-
ing common people. A respect-
iter, who had ample means of in-
on, affirms, that the industry and
of a few infidels, directed to this
was a prime instrument of produc-
se terrible convulsions, which have
aken the civilized world. The
Christians, taught by the zeal and
ise of Infidels, resolved "to foil the
at his own weapons." A society
med, whose design was to print
s Tracts, in so great quantities,
so cheap a rate, that good men of
eans might be able to give them
nd that all the hawkers and little
et shops in the kingdom, might be
l, from the ordinary love of gain,
neir circulation. The success of
ertaking surpassed the most san-
expectations of its friends. From
report of this ociety, it appears
Tracts have circulated "from the
f the Baltic to the Cape of Good
hrough the whole of Europe and
nd were pressing upon the
nts of China, and that within
rt period since the Institution
need its operations, no less than
EN MILLIONS *of Tracts have been
ted by its agency.*"

n the same period, similar socie-
e been established in various coun-
Europe, particularly in Denmark
dcn. By one parish of the latter
, 600,000 Tracts have been dis-
: and 500,000 m another place, by
evolence of a single wealthy in-

ferent parts of our own country,
ve engaged in the same good work
inconsiderable zeal and success.
the amount of good already acted in the United States, by
of religious Tracts, can never be
ed, till it is revealed in the light of
. But much remains to be done,
ety has hitherto been established,
n of operations sufficiently exten-
d permanent, to answer all the
rposes for which such an institu-
ceded. To create a society that
asess means, adequate to these

.. X.

purposes, is the design of the plan herewith presented to the public.

It is to be distinctly understood that
this society is not designed to interfere
with the province of religious Magazines.
Much of the matter which renders these
periodical works especially valuable to
their readers, is not adapted to the design of Tracts. These must be simple,
serious, practical. They must be intelligible to the "way-faring man," and the
tenant of the cottage. Learned criticism, discussions in polemic theology, and
even articles of religious intelligence, unless comprised in a few sentences, can
no place in these little pamphlets,
which are designed for promiscuous and,
to a great extent, gratuitous dispersion
among those, who otherwise would
scarcely read any thing. Instead of diminishing, they will doubtless increase the
demand for religious Magazines.

It is to be understood also, that this Society is not intended to supersede, or to
interfere with any of those Tract or
Moral Societies which are already established. On the contrary, its primary object is to aid such societies wherever they
are formed, to multiply their numbers, to
encourage and increase their efforts, till
their salutary influence shall be felt in every village of New England.

Too long have good men stood still in
criminal supineness, or silent despondence, while a flood of licentiousness has
been sweeping away the institutions of
Christianity, and the land marks of our
fathers. It is time that they, who have
slumbered amidst these growing impie-
ties, or have wept over them in secret
places, should unite in a *common effort* to
"strengthen the things that remain, and
that are ready to die."

The period is portentous. While war,
with its dire calamities, rages over Christendom, while the worst passions of men
are let loose from restraint, while the
world is overturned and the earth rent in
pieces; it becomes the friends of Zion to
adore the righteous Providence that is
smiting the nations. But it becomes them
not to sit down in sloth. God has made
every man responsible for the use or
abuse of his personal influence. Whether
that influence is great or small, he is sacredly bound to employ it in doing good. The
field for action is extensive: the motives
to action are various and momentous. In
this Christian land, the Sabbath is dread-
fully profaned, and in some places, is in
danger of being utterly forgotten. Multitudes throng the road of death. These
immortal creatures can not be brought to
consideration, till they are first brought to
read They cannot read without books:
and a great proportion of them will ne r

er have books, unless they are furnished by the hand of charity. Here then is an urgent call for the exercise of Christian benevolence, on a large scale. The New England Tract Society is established for the purpose of publishing a great variety of the best Tracts that can be procured, by selection or original composition, and in such quantities as to supply all the demands of individuals or societies, in different parts of the country. The deep interest which this subject has already excited, the promptitude and liberality with which many have entered into the plan, and contributed the means for its execution, is regarded as an auspicious omen that it will be attended with the blessing of Heaven, and the cordial co-operation of the friends of religion.

MIDDLESEX BIBLE SOCIETY.

THE Board of Directors of this Society have appointed local committees in all the towns in the county of Middlesex, and formed a general plan for soliciting subscriptions, ascertaining the want of Bibles, and distributing them. This plan is communicated to the local committees, by a circular letter, which closes with the following Address.

CHRISTIAN BRETHREN AND FRIENDS, IT is no new subject to which we ask your attention. The utility, and the urgent necessity of Bible Societies are now universally acknowledged by those who have examined the subject, and who look with a favorable eye on whatever promotes the happiness of mankind.

Since the institution of the British and Foreign Bible Society, about ten years ago, nearly two hundred Bible institutions have risen in Great Britain and Ireland, a great number on the continent of Europe, and nearly forty in the United States. The experience of every one of these institutions has added to the proof of their utility, and of the duty of supporting them, of enlarging their exertions, and of increasing their number. Though the exertions of Bible Societies already existing have evinced commendable zeal and activity, yet the wants of the destitute are by no means supplied. So great and so widely extended are these wants, indeed, that if Bible Societies were multiplied twenty fold, there would be occasion for their benevolent labors for many years to come.

Unless we are greatly mistaken, a large number of Bibles is wanted to supply the destitute in this County; as there are not only the poor, strictly so called, who will put in their claims; but many apprentices

and hired laborers of both sexes, benefited by receiving the Scriptures at reduced prices, or gratis when the destitute in this county perfectly supplied, there are many tute places in the neighboring and in the new settlements, which in pressing need of our beneficence

Permit us to state, that we party feelings, of any description ever, will be suffered to divide or our efforts in the cause. We are bers in the sight of God; we have partakers of his unmerited bounty heard the offers of his great merc Let us unite in the good work of ing the word of truth to our fell ners, and thus enable them to have access to the fountain of spiritual edge.

Brethren, let us not procra Let us be active and diligent now days are rapidly passing away. W but a short time to obtain good communicate it, here on earth. low creatures, also, are dying arou many of them without this preciou which contains the words of eterna and which we have it in our po bestow. Soon will the present gen descend to the tomb, and be no more within the reach of human b lence. A thousand consideration to immediate and persevering exer

The committees, and all who ta active part in procuring subscri will consider, that the time conse these labors will be employed for t blest purposes, and will, as we fondly produce the most desirable result.

Suffer us, brethren, to ask a liber scription. The sum to constitute bership was fixed at one dollar, view to embrace all who are in eas ble circumstances; but we hope to whom God has given an abun will not think of limiting themselve small a sum. It is the right and th of every man to judge for himself, gard to his charitable offerings, a as in regard to religious doctrines. every charitable offering should be ly voluntary, but cheerful. While truths are admitted, and even none of us can be ignorant, that in munity like the one which is here a ed, there are many persons abun able to make liberal offerings to the many persons who ought to make and, unless we are mistaken, man sons who will make them.

The motives to Christian bene are numerous and weighty; but the we trust, too well known to need t peated here. Our Savior inculcated, ample and by precept, and enforced

rful sanctions, that genuine
evenly charity, which prompts
t action. He will gloriously
who feel the force of his pre-
mitate his example.
timents of respect, we are,
pars in the bonds of Christian
    JEDIDIAH MORSE,
    LEVI HEDGE,
    JEREMIAH EVARTS.

RELIGION IN KINGSTON, N. H.

ted in a letter to the Editor of
the Panoplist.]

ir,
ee with your wishes, I trans-
rief account of the revival of
Kingston, N. H. the past sea-
was neither general nor at-
any peculiar circumstances, I
d whether it should be noticed
bly useful magazine. In one
r not, perhaps, be uninterest-
firms the truth, that God often
pious exertions and faithful
is ministers, after the instru-
id aside,—the laborers called

nguished literary and theologi-
ments of the late Rev. Dr.
his minister of Kingston, are
known. His sermons were
zeal, and his manner of deliv-
rate. His prayers were devo-
thors unweari., his life exem-
is death tranquil. During his
high was of about 35 years con-
ur additions were made to the
this settlement, it consisted of
umbers; at his death of 17. One
er only remained; and he was
rarely to attend public wor-
state of that people, when the
was truly lamentable. To use
guage, it appeared, that "God
to write Loammi upon them,
wholy memorial of departed

ne year after Dr. Thayer's
h was the last of March 1812,
Divine truth, which he had
his strength to sow, which he
was watered with his tears, and
d to the blessing of God by
gan to spring up. A num-
a manifested an unusual seri-
'able worship was more gener-
d. The countenances of the
are unusually solemn, their at-
ted, and numbers were drown-
A divine energy appeared to
nstructions given in the sanctu-

ary, and in the family. No irregularities
were manifested in any of the religious
meetings. A profound solemnity uniformly pervaded them. It was the still small
voice of Elijah's God, which pierced with
the arrows of conviction, or consoled with
the promises of the Gospel. In private
conversation, those under serious impressions generally expressed a deep sense of
the depravity,—the pollutions of their
hearts;—a conviction of the awful demerit
of sin, particularly that opposition of heart
to God, and his government, which they
discovered in themselves. The convictions
of sin were so pungent, as to be almost
overwhelming. A view of their guilt rather
than their *danger*, rendered those who
were under conviction comfortless by day,
and almost sleepless by night.

Many among those, who became hopefully pious, stated, that their attention had
been gradually excited to view the importance of eternal truths, from their studying
the Scriptures in a social manner. Where
hopes were obtained, distress of mind was
succeeded by a tranquil frame, which
sometimes excited fears, lest they were returning to a state of stupidity. This composure was usually attended with a degree of hope in the merits of Christ, and
an expressed delight in the character, government, word, worship and ordinances of
God, with earnest desires to be wholly devoted to his service. When inquiring of
one, whose distress had subsided, what
was the state of her mind, she answered to
this effect. "I cannot better describe my
feelings, than by using the language of
Jacob: *Truly God is in this place; and I
knew it not.* My mind has been exploring distant regions to discern the being
and perfections of God; but this morning
I seem to behold him in every thing. His
perfections are conspicuous in *all* his
works. They are pre-eminently displayed in the glorious work of redemption.
What appears most lovely in the character and government of Jehovah, is that
HOLINESS which shines with such lustre in
them. I seem to have lost that opposition
of heart to God which I once possessed."

The awakening continued from March
to August, 1813. Twenty-four were added
to the church, more than one third of
whom were male members. Some of
these were persons who had previously
entertained hopes. Some, who then obtained hopes, have not yet professed religion. The fruits of this awakening, as
far as my observation and information extend, are a prayerful temper of mind, and
a humble, circumspect, and exemplary
conduct. That the Lord would graciously
visit all our towns with a *rain of righteousness;*—that He would bless all you

exertions to disseminate religious knowledge, and advance the Redeemer's cause, are the ardent desire of your affectionate friend and humble servant,

HERVEY WILBUR.

MORAL SOCIETIES.

THE formation of small societies, in towns, parishes, and districts, for the suppression of vice and the promotion of good morals, is one of the happiest omens, which are now to be discovered among us.

A letter from a clergyman in Vermont to the editor of the Panoplist states, that a society had been formed in the town where he resides, for the suppression of profaneness, intemperance, sabbath-breaking, and other prominent immoralities. He adds, "Moral Societies are forming generally, I believe, through this state."

REVIVALS OF RELIGION.

THE following particulars respecting late revivals of religion in Vermont, are taken from a letter dated April 6, 1814, and written by a student in Middlebury College to a clergyman in Massachusetts.

The revival at Bridport began about a year ago, and continued in a progressive, silent, but solemn state, through the summer. Towards the latter part of autumn, it began to be more powerful in its operations, and became more extensive. There was hardly a family but shared in its blessed efficacy to subdue the stubborn and heal the wounded. During the winter, it became still more general. It was confined to no age, character, nor sect. The young and the old, the moralist, the universalist, and the infidel, have been made the monuments of God's victorious grace. Eighty have already united with the church, and about thirty more are ready to come forward, and join the same heavenly band. Notwithstanding the revival has already been spreading and increasing more than twelve months, there is this circumstance attending it, which exists in but few revivals of equal duration and extent, that it still appears to be rising towards its zenith. The Lord is still carrying on his own glorious work in a truly marvellous manner. The minister of the place is a faithful, rousing preacher, and his labors have been abundantly successful in awakening the careless and directing the inquiring.

Of the revival at Pawlet I have not heard particulars; and can only observe, that it has been pretty generally spread through the society. The work has been powerful in its progress, and glorious in its effects I have not heard the precise number of persons, who are supposed to have shared in its saving grace, but believe, that not far from a hundred have tasted and seen that the Lord is gracious since last fall.

The awakening at Hebron commenced but a few weeks ago, and is now spreading under the most favorable circumstances. A large number, have already, we have reason to hope, become the subjects of renewing grace.

At Weybridge the attention has but just begun. A small number have obtained a hope.

DONATIONS TO SUPPORT FOREIGN MISSIONS AND TRANSLATIONS OF THE SCRIPTURE

April 29, 1814. From the Merrimac Branch of the Foreign Missionary Society, by Mr. Richard Bartlet, the Treasurer,	$200
From a person in Andover, (north parish,) who last year sent the same sum, for the translations,)	3
April 30. From persons in Kingsborough, (N. Y.) viz. from Dea. Samuel Giles, (half to missions and half to translations,)	$20 00
The Rev. John Truair, of Vermont,	5 00
A friend to foreign missions, (half to translations,)	6 00
From a friend to missions,	5 00
From John Manrow,	1 00
From Rebecca Wells,	1 00
From Eunice Wells,	1 00
From a friend to foreign Missions,	1 00
From Jennison Giles,	,50
From Nine friends of foreign missions, in sums less than a dollar each,	2 44—43
May 2. By cash collected at a prayer-meeting for missionaries, in Charlestown,	
3. From the following persons by Gen. Huntington of New London, viz.	
Col Samuel Green,	2 50
Nathan Belcher, Preston,	6 00
Azariah Stanton, Stonington,	2 00
From the Foreign Mission Society of New London,	11 00
From the Female Foreign Mission Society, at Plain-	

Carried forward $21 50

ught forward $21 50 $253 36
a.) by Mrs. Han-
son, Treasurer, 12 00—33 50
Miss Lucretia Whit-
the translations, 2 00
cash of Mr. Anson
ps, of Hartford,
alf to missions and
analations, 100 00
Mrs. Sarah Norris,
y, for the transla-

5 00
om Christophilos,* 5 00
om the Plympton
of the Heathen's
ociety, (a society of
) by Mrs. Mary

22 06
a friend to the mis-
ause, 10 00
r cash from the La-
at Society in Nor-
the Rev. Mr. Swan,
by Mr. T. Dwight,

40 00
Mr. Samuel T.
ng, as the clear
Memoirs of Mrs.

100 00
rom the Female
ciety in Plymouth,
Abigail Judson, 20 00
———
$590 92

EVANGELICAL SOCIETY.

gladly give publicity to the fol-
ommunication

To the Editor of the Panoplist.

-ting the following, in your ex-
and excellent publication, you
lige a number of your friends,
robably, the friends of the Gos-
uatry in general.

ED with the duty we owe to the
nd to our liberal donors, especial-
ve some further account of the
e, and progress of the *Evangel-*
ety, formed principally within the
of Pawlet and Rutland Associa-
Vermont.
ber of Ministers, of Pawlet Asso-
et in Pawlet, March 6, 1804, and
emselves by constitutional regula-
hich they then adopted, for the
purpose of aiding pious and needy
en of promising talents, in acquir-
ation for the work of the Gospel.

ort extract of a letter from
hilos will appear in our next.

ministry. The Society soon became re-
spectably numerous.
The officers of the Society are, a President, Vice President, Secretary, Clerk,
and Treasurer, who are chosen annually.
The funds of the Society are at the disposal of a Board of Trustees, consisting of
nine members, chosen annually.
The Trustees are directed, by the Constitution, to aid pious, and needy young
men of promising talents, whose professed
object is to engage in the work of the Gospel ministry, by lending them money,
without interest, for a necessary term of
time.
In the year 1806, the following donations were received by the hand of the
Rev. William Jackson, from our liberal
Patrons, whose names and liberalities are
as follows:

At Salem, (Mass.)

William Gray,	$100
John Norris,	50
Nathaniel West,	40
John Derby,	20
Elias H. Derby,	20
Henry Gray,	20
Benjamin Pickman,	15
John Jenks,	10
Jerethmiel Pierce,	10
Aaron Wait,	10
Mrs. Ward,	5
Daniel Jenks,	5
Daniel Lang,	5
Walter P. Bartlet,	5
A female friend,	4
Female friends,	3
Rev. Samuel Worcester,	2
Dea. —— Adams,	4

At Newport.

Hon. George Champlin,	20
William Patten, D. D.	52
Ruth Wright,	10
A friend,	10
Mr. —— Main,	5
Jabez Denison,	3
Rev Caleb J Tenny,	2
Mr. —— Clery,	4

At Boston.

Hon. William Phillips,	50
William R. Gray,	50
Dea. S. Salisbury,	30
A Friend,	30
Henry Holmes,	50
A friend,	15
John Derby,	20
Hon. James Sullivan,	20
Joseph Eckley, D. D.	10
Rev. Charles Lowell,	9
A friend,	10
A friend,	10
Perkins Nichols,	10
A friend,	10
A friend,	5
Dr. Jonathan Jov.	10
Richard Derby,	5

Daniel D Rogers,	10
Joseph W. Jenkins,	10
Jonathan Harris,	10
A friend,	10
J. W. Walley,	10
A friend,	5
Joseph Bumstead,	6
Charles Walley,	10
William Wells, jun.	5
Thomas Dawes,	10
William Thurston, Esq.	10
David Tilden,	5
John West,	5
William Pelham,	3
A friend,	10
A friend,	5
Rev. John Elliot, D D.	5
John Alkin,	5

In Books.

David West,	10	75
Thomas & Andrews,	30	
White, Burdit, & Co.	15	
Oliver C. Greenleaf,	5	
Manning & Loring,	11	07
Etheridge & Bliss,	12	63
E. Cotton,	5	
A friend,	3	

At Providence.

Nicholas Brown,	20
Jabez Bowen,	10
Thomas P. Ives,	10

[At Charlestown, (Mass.)

Editors of the Panoplist, (in books,)	100
Jedidiah Morse, D. D. (in books,)	50
Richard Devens, Esq.	10
Joseph Hurd,	10
A friend,	5
Oliver Keating,	10
David Woodward,	10
John Austin,	5
Artemas Ward,	10
Skinner & Hurd,	10
A friend,	15
John Pratt,	5

At Danvers.

Joseph Torrey,	5
Enoch Poor,	5
Samuel Walker,	4
Jacob Pool,	6
Robert Shelaber,	10
Ebenezer Shelaber,	5

At Beverly

Col Israel Thorndike,	50
Thomas Davis,	5
John Dike & J. Ellingwood,	5
Betsey Eaton,	3
A friend,	4
Mrs. Packard,	3
A female friend,	1
A friend,	5
Rev. Joseph Emerson,	2
Elizabeth Lovett,	3
An unknown friend.	10

At Newburyport.

Moses Brown,	20
Nicholas Pike, Esq.	6
A friend,	6
Charles Whipple,	5
Dr Charles Coffin,	10
Dea. Thomas Thompson,	5
William Bartlet,	20
John Pettingel,	10
Elias Hunt,	5
John O'Brien,	5
Benjamin Wyath,	3
A friend,	5
Richard Pike,	10
Jonathan Marsh,	6
Leonard Smith,	10
John Pearson,	10
John Rollins,	2
Joseph O'Brien,	3
Robert Foster,	3
Nathaniel Smith,	5
A Friend,	3
Jeremiah Nelson,	5
Joseph Noyes,	2
A friend,	1

At Rowley.

Rev. David Fuller,	5
Friends at Exeter,	5

Since we received the above donations the funds of the Society, by entrance money, which is one dollar for each member, or ten dollars for life, and by annual payments, which are one dollar per annum, for each member, and by small donations from Churches and individuals amount to $2,282 80.

Much more aid has been solicited by young men of promising talents, patronized by the Society, than our scanty funds would enable us to afford. We have, however, assisted in educating twenty three young gentlemen, of whom we entertain raised expectations of eminent service to the churches. Nine are already settled in the work of the Gospel ministry, and are called faithful. Five are now promising candidates for the ministry, and others are pursuing their collegiate or theological education.

Since ministers of the Gospel are generally embarrassed, and their usefulness impeded, by the want of pecuniary support, especially in new settlements, how desirable it is, that indigent young men rich in talents, who labor to devote themselves to the arduous work of the Gospel ministry, should receive such aid in obtaining their education as will leave them free from a load of debt, when settled in their work.

By order of the Society,

NATHANIEL HALL, Sec.

P. S. The Evangelical Society contemplates a union with Middlebury College

le Society, which was lately form-
e promotion of the same benevo-
gn.
lle, N. York, March 14, 1814.

f ENGLAND TRACT SOCIETY

>osite of the New England Tract
bas been opened in the chamber
. S. T. Armstrong's Bookstore,
Cornhill. This deposite contains
a moral and religious subjects of
rent kinds, amounting in the
300,000 Those of 24 pages 12
be sold to members and Auxilia-
. Societies at $2 33 1-3 per hun-
o others, not members, at
-3 per hundred. Smaller Tracts
ild in the same proportion.
ollowing are the titles of the
ow published, viz,
tion, Address, &c
k of the Holy Spirit
nperance
ns on Hebrews xii, 11.
; Voice
gue between a Traveller and
M
py Negro
ord's Day
ryman's Daughter
pherd of Salisbury Plain
or the best
'hird Commandment
Spectator of a Funeral
rer of Truth
gress of Sin
sulutions
he Porter
ialogues between a Minister and
his parishioners
ber the Sabbath Day to keep it

Companion, or a help to Self-
nation

The repentance and happy death of the
Earl of Rochester
Copy of a Letter from the celebrated Dr'
Isaac Watts to Madam Sewall on the
death of her children
The Christian indeed
The importance of Sobriety illustrated by
the evils of Intemperance
Sin, no trifle
Parental duties
The instruction of the Rising Generation
in the principles of the Christian Relig-
ion recommended
A Serious Address to children and youth,
relating to the great and necessary du-
ty of prayer
Advices to Children, relating to prayer
The Westminster Assembly's Shorter
Catechism
To a Child
Hymns for Infant Minds
Sermons to Children. To which are add-
ed, Short Hymns suited to the subjects
A Present to Children at School
Divine and Moral Songs for Children
To Children
Early piety recommended, the history
of Miss Dinah Doudney, of Portsea,
(Eng.)
Filial Duties
An Affectionate Address to young Chris-
tians
A persuasive to Public Worship
The importance of Speaking Truth
Moderation in Food
An Address to Youth
No life pleasing to God but that which is
useful to mankind
Subjects for Consideration
To the afflicted
To the Aged
A Sketch of the life of the late Rev
John Cowper
The Swearer reproved, or his oath ex-
plained
Family Worship

OBITUARY.

England, the Rev. Mr Hor-
of the denomination of Metho-
) anxious were many of his ad-
) possess some memorial of the
, that his effects, books, &c were
1e most extravagant prices. A
worth six pounds sold for 200
in old arm chair, not worth five
for sixty guineas, and a hymn
irth half a crown, for twenty-six

brook, (Con) the Rev. SAMUEL
ged 60.
th Hero, (Ver) on the 29th of
Col. ELIJAH SAWYER, aged

94, formerly of Lancaster, Mass. He
was an officer in the provincial armies,
in the reigns of George II, and George
III, and in the American army during
the revolution.
At Rutland, (Ver) Mr. JOSEPH
CHILDS, aged 27, murdered.
At Medfield, on the 28th of Feb. last,
the Rev. THOMAS PRENTISS, D. D minister of the Congregational church and society in that town, aged 66
At Wiscasset, on the 1st of March last,
the Hon. SILAS LEE, Attorney of the U,
S for the District of Maine. He was
graduated at Harvard College in 1784, a

Representative in Congress in 1801, and
since that time till his decease he has held
the office above-mentioned. For several
of the last years of his life, he held the
office of Judge of Probate for the county
of Lincoln. His age was 53.

At Essex, (Vt.) Mrs. SARAH MORGAN,
wife of the Rev. ASAPH MORGAN, aged
52.

At Concord, (Mass.) on the 24th of
Feb. last, Mrs. LYDIA BALL, aged 99.

At Boston, MOSES BASCOM, Esq. Representative of the town of Gill in the General court, aged 53.

At Brookfield, the Hon. PLINY MER-
RICK, Esq.

At Stonington, (Con.) Mrs. CONTENT
LANGWORTHY, aged 105.

At Boardman, (Ohio) Maj. RICHARD
ELLIOT, formerly of Kent, (Con.) The
circumstances of his death are thus stated
in the newspapers.

On returning at evening from the town
of Poland, he observed two lights coming
towards him in the shape of a half-moon;
and when the lights met him, they seemed to enclose him in a circle round his
breast, when he heard a voice distinctly
say, *Are you prepared to die?* to which he
answered, *If it is God's will, I think I
am.* The lights then passed him a short
distance, but turning back followed him
until he arrived against the burying
ground, where they made a stand, and
he could observe them on looking back
for half a mile. On reaching home, he
stated the above circumstances to his
family, and afterwards to several of his
particular friends, adding his full belief
that he was soon to die, and making his
preparations accordingly with manifest
resignation to the will of Providence.
On the third day after seeing the lights,
he was seized with the prevailing epi-
demic, and died the next day.

At Easton, (Md.) JAMES EARLE, Esq.
Cashier of the Farmers' Branch Bank.

At Waterford, (N. Y.) a Mrs. ELDRED,
killed her husband while he was (as it
is supposed) in a fit of insanity.

At New York, Mrs. BRIDGET RAG-
LAND, a native of Ireland, she had been
thrown into the fire by her husband, and
was burnt so as to occasion her death.
Verdict, *murder.*

At Millbury, (Mass.) on the 26th of
Feb. last, Col. JONATHAN HOLMAN, aged
87, an active officer in the revolutionary
war.

At Boston, on the 13th of March last,
Mr. JOHN P. CLARK, late cashier of the
State Bank, aged 34.

Near Bladensburg, (Md.) Lieut. HALL,
of the U. S army, *murdered* in a duel by a
brother officer.

At Parma, (Italy,) JEAN B.
BONONI, the most celebrated pai
Italy, aged 73.

In France, Gen. Count WA
colonel of the Imperial horse
aged 52.

At Lancaster, (Ohio,) Mr. JOH
LAP, aged 100.

At Leicester, (Mass.) JARED B
Esq. a member of the H. R. o
from Lee.

At Guilford, (Con.) Gen. Ar
COLLINS, for many years a mer
the H R. of that state.

In the district of Columbia, E
H. BRYAN, murdered in a due
Lieutenant of U. S. army. Bry
tols missed fire twice.

At Enfield, (Con.) Rev. GEOR
WELL.

At Philadelphia, on the 2d h
Hon. NICHOLAS GILMAN, Esq. a
of U. S from New Hampshire.

At Ipswich, (Mass.) Mrs.
WHEELER, aged 100.

In Spain, the Marquis of SOME
late Governor of Cuba.

At St. Johns, (N. B) in the 76t
of his age, the Hon. WILLIAM H
member of the Executive Coune
the formation of that province in 1

Near Paris, killed in the b
March 30th, RAPATEL, the aid of t
Gen Moreau.

TO CORRESPONDENTS.

THE paper of H. S. on *The P
of the Vials* and the *Remarks o
xiii,* we decline to insert; princip
cause brief interpretations of pr
when they relate to difficult p
often perplex the minds of read
sometimes diminish their revere
the prophetical writings. This
does not apply, in our apprehen
the *Morsel from the Prophecies,*
we have admitted.

We are again under the neces
reminding our correspondents,
obituary notices can be inserted,
the persons who communicate th
known to us, or we have authentic
mation of their accuracy from som
er quarter.

We received, sometime since,
per containing *Objections to
Female Missionaries,* and anothe
ten by a person who had seen the
in manuscript containing *Answ
these Objections* We have not d
whether the discussion of this
will be useful.

Our poetical correspondents a
quested to exercise patience

THE

PANOPLIST;

AND

ISSIONARY MAGAZINE.

JUNE, 1814. VOL. X.

RELIGIOUS COMMUNICATIONS.

For the Panop ist.

SABBATH. NO. II.

itution of the Sabbath.

Sabbath was originally
by divine authority, is
eve, questioned by any,
ss to regard the Scrip-
revelation from heav-
cannot, therefore, be
to spend a moment in
clear a point. Happy
e, if the same just coin-
f opinion existed re-
every material ques-
ected with this impor-
ct. That this however
r from being the case,
fficiently obvious, in the
of these numbers.

g granted by all parties,
abbath was originally a
itution, the first ques-
presents itself, in the
h I propose to pursue,
*hat time, and on what
was the Sabbath insti-*

uestion, as it appears to
nequivocally answered,
ond chapter of Genesis,
inning. *Thus the heav-
he earth were finished,
e host of them. And on
th day, God ended his
ich he had made, and he
.*

rested on the seventh day from all
his work which he had made. And
God blessed the seventh day, and
sanctified it, because that in it he
had rested from all his work,
which God created and made.
Here is nothing ambiguous,
either in the words themselves,
or in their connexion with the
preceding narrative. The plain
and obvious account is, that as
soon as God had finished the
great work of creation, he not
only rested from it himself, but
appointed the very next, or seventh, day to be observed by our
first parents, as a day of holy rest,
in commemoration of the grand
event. Whatever reasons any
persons may think they see for
ascribing a much later date to
this sacred institution, they will
not surely say, that any of these
reasons were first suggested to
their minds by the perusal of the
passage before us. Even *they*
must concede as much as this,
that the passage *seems*, at first
view, to favor the construction
which I have given it. But it
has been contended, that this
cannot be the true construction,
because neither the observance,
nor the existence, of a Sabbath, is
once mentioned by the sacred historian, from the second chapter of
Genesis, to the sixteenth of Exodus, including a period of about

31

2500 years. Many very pious men, it is added, certainly lived within that long period, who would have solemnly observed the sacred weekly rest, if it had been appointed, which observance must have been somewhere recorded by Moses.

This argument has some degree of plausibility, I admit, but nothing more. It is true, we are no where expressly told, that holy men before the flood, or that the post-diluvian patriarchs observed a weekly Sabbath. That they did, however, seems highly probable, independently of other considerations, from the division of time into weeks, which obviously took place, long before the giving of the law to Israel. Such a division is pretty clearly hinted at, more than once, in the eighth chapter of Genesis. After sending out the dove the first time, Noah waited seven days, and then sent her forth a second time, and, at the end of just seven days more, he sent her forth a third time. This regard to the number seven might, I grant, possibly have been accidental; or Noah might have had reasons for it, of which we know nothing;—but when we view the subject, in connexion with the passage above quoted from the second chapter, it seems altogether more probable, that every seventh day was kept by the patriarch and his family as a Sabbath; and this accounts for the division of time, by him and his posterity, into weeks.

The same division is again incidentally mentioned, by the sacred writer, in the twenty-ninth chapter Genesis. *Fulfil her week*, said Laban to Jacob, *and we will give thee this also,* (i. e. Rachel;) *for the service which thou shalt* * *with me yet seven other y And Jacob did so, and ful her week.* That the week referred to consisted of s days, must, I think, be obv to every one, who will take trouble of comparing this sage with others, in both T ments, where the same wor curs. And this furnishes sumptive proof, of no incons able weight, that one day o seven, in each week, was kr and kept as a Sabbath. But posing that no allusion what to this sacred institution we be found in the history of patriarchs, it would not on extremely illogical to infer, they had no knowledge c since, in a history so very cise, millions of events r necessarily be passed ove silence; but the argument this additional misfortune, tl it proves any thing it prove much. It equally proves, the Sabbath was entirely known and unobserved, from days of Joshua to the reig David, no mention being r of it, in the history of that pe If mere silence be taken proof, in the former case, it r in the latter also. If, on other hand, the highest de of probability forbids the i ence, that the pious Judg Israel paid no attention to G holy day, notwithstanding t observance of it is not men ed, on what principle can inferred, that the Sabbath not appointed till 2500 y after the creation, and that mentioned by Moses, in the ond chapter of Genesis, nc having commenced in para but in the wilderness?

ally fatal to this favorite
ent of Dr. Paley and oth-
the same side of the ques-
s the silence of the inspir-
lume, respecting the ob-
ce of the rite of circum-

from a little after the
of Moses to the days of
iah; that important seal of
venant not being so much
e mentioned, or even al-
to, in the history of that
, including more than 800

Will it be maintained,
be believed, that all the
kings, together with the
Jewish nation, for eight
ies paid no regard to a
command of God, requir-
ery male to be circumcis-
) be consistent with them-
all those must adopt this
ible supposition, who in-
t mankind were left with-
Sabbath, for more than
-five centuries, merely be-
the observance of the Sab-
not particularly mention-
the sacred history of that
.

n the whole, then, it is
ully submitted to the can-
der, whether the objection,
I have been considering,
iot be given up; first, be-
the institution seems to be
ntly alluded to in the in-
records of patriarchal
and, secondly, because,
'ere not thus alluded to,
'nce of those records could
ssibly prove any thing a-
the existence of the insti-

proceed:—That the Sab-
as instituted in Paradise,
it in the wilderness, I

, from the words of the in-
penman, already recited.

Having told us what was done on
the first and each succeeding
day of the creation to the sixth
and last, he proceeds in the same
tense, and without giving the
least intimation that what follows
is spoken by way of anticipation,
to record the important fact, that
on the seventh day God rested
from all his work, blessing and
sanctifying the day, on account
of his having thus rested. Now,
if the divine example, in resting
on the seventh day, was of any
significancy to men; if it was
designed for their imitation; then
it became their duty to rest one
seventh part of the time,—and to
observe every seventh day as a
Sabbath. And if God's resting
was a reason why they should
rest, then his resting on the first
seventh day, was a reason why
that day should be their first
Sabbath.

Again; *God blessed the seventh
day and sanctified it.* That is,
he separated it from common
secular employments and consecrated it for a day of religious
worship. This solemn consecration most evidently took
place, on the very day when
God rested from all his work,
and not twenty-five hundred
years afterwards, as some have
labored to prove. If the Sabbath was instituted to commemorate the stupendous work of
creation, what can be more absurd than the supposition, that
this commemoration was deferred, till the world was more than
two thousand five hundred years
old! The miraculous deliverance
of Israel from Egypt, was commemorated in the annual feast of
the passover, *from the time* that
the Lord brought them out.
The independence of these Uni-

ted States has been annually celebrated, ever since they were declared independent. In like manner, are all those eras and events celebrated among mankind, which are thought worthy of being kept in remembrance by stated festivals, or other demonstrations of rejoicing. The commemoration in each case, commences at, or near, the time of the event, which it is designed to perpetuate. How extremely improbable, that the appointment of a day, to commemorate the creation of the world, should form a solitary exception! But if it does not form an exception, then the Sabbath was ordained and sanctified from the beginning, which was the thing to be proved.

I flatter myself, that on this ground I might safely rest the argument. But a few brief remarks, on the supposed *anticipation* of the passage in the second chapter of Genesis, may serve still further to expose the weakness of the opposite side of the question. If the Sabbath was not instituted, till after Israel's emancipation from Egyptian bondage, what occasion had Moses to say any thing about it, when writing the history of what took place between two and three thousand years before? Could the placing of events, (which were, on the scheme here opposed, so remote from each other,) side by side in the history, serve any other purpose, than to mislead and perplex the reader? It will not, surely, be pretended, that the mention of God's blessing and sanctifying the seventh day could not have been deferred and inserted in its proper place. With what color of prob-

ability can it be mair then, that in directing what to write, the Spirit c dictated an arrangement, instance, so contrary to t ular order of the sacred tive, and so much better c ted to mislead, than to gu biblical student into all tr

I shall only add, that same grounds, on which contended, that the Sabl first spoken of by anticipa might be argued, that the tion of the world is spol in the same manner. If t spired writer teaches us, : ample, that the sun and th were created on the fourt he is equally explicit in ing to us, that on the s day God rested from all hi and blessed the seventh d sanctified it. There therefore, no difference phraseology, we must su that if the latter event is of by way of anticipation, the former. In other we we suppose Moses to sp the second chapter of G not of what actually took on the seventh day of the but of what was done aft lapse of thousands of year we must suppose him in t chapter, to speak of the s moon, not as being creat the fourth day, but at son ture and distant period. same must be supposed of is said to have been do each of the six days, em by God in the work of cr and so we shall be consti out of regard to consister consider the sacred histor representing the heaver the earth as brought into ence *by way of anticipatio*

ıe Sabbath was not giv-
ıel in the wilderness, as
ıtitution, and, of course,
ıs instituted in paradise,

lly, from the address of
ı his brethren on the
in the sixteenth chapter
ıs, connected with what
:ely precedes that ad-
The Lord had given the
ıanna for bread; a quan-
hich, sufficient for one
nsumption, they were
to gather every morn-
ıs they did, till the sixth
ıd *it came to pass, that
xth day they gathered
much bread, two omers
ıan: and all the rulers
:ongregation came and
ea. And he said unto
ıs is that which the Lord
, To-morrow is the rest
y Sabbath unto the Lord:
which ye will bake to
seeth that ye will seeth,
which remaineth over
ır you, to be kept until
ıng.*
ıst thing worthy of re-
this passage is, that
ıny order, or direction,
s appears, the people
twice as much manna
xth day, as on either of
:eding. How shall we
'or this, but by suppos-
the Sabbath had been
ly instituted, and that
some idea, at least, of
·e and design of the in-
Why, on any other
.on, should they gather
of two days in one; and
ıey did, should they wait
sixth day before they
is double provision for
·es and their families.
ıey had any knowledge

of the Sabbath, at that time, it is
certain, that it was not then first
ordained; and, of course, that
when Moses told them, in the
next verse, *To-morrow is the
rest of the holy Sabbath unto the
Lord*, he spoke of it, as an institution already existing, and not
as then for the first time made
known to mankind.

This supposition is not a little
strengthened, by the language,
in which the Jewish lawgiver
addressed the congregation on
the subject. This is that which
the Lord hath said, *To-morrow
is*, (not to-morrow shall be,) *the
rest of the holy Sabbath, &c.*
This is not the manner, in which
a lawgiver would speak, in appointing any new festival, or
other commemorative observance; but it is precisely as men
naturally speak of existing institutions. In strict propriety we
say, that to-morrow *is* the Sabbath, although the day is yet future, because it is an old institution; but if there never had been
a Sabbath and to-morrow were
to be consecrated on the first
day of holy weekly rest the lawgiver would not say it *is*, but it
shall be, the Sabbath.

Thirdly, Christ tells us that
the Sabbath was made for man.
The obvious meaning of this is,
that it was appointed for the use
and benefit of the whole human
family; and, if so, it must have
been from the beginning. The
Sabbath was made for man; for
man in every age and under every dispensation. Concerning
the proof which this text furnishes, of the perpetuity of the
Sabbath, I shall have occasion to
speak more particularly, in my
next number. I would only infer from it here, that if the Sab-

bath was made for the benefit of all men, it is unreasonable to suppose, that its institution was deferred till the time of Moses, or indeed, that it was deferred a single week. after the creation of our first parents.

Fourthly, the testimony of a great many profane writers might be adduced. which could scarcely fail to lead the mind to the very same conclusion, at which I have aimed. in all my preceding observations. I shall not, however. detain the reader long with quotations, deeming it unnecessary.

Josephus, the Jewish historian, affirms. "that there is no city, either of Greeks or barbarians, or any other nation. where the religion of the Sabbath is not known."

Philo says, "that the Sabbath is not a festival peculiar to any one people, or country; but is common to all the world: and that it may be named the general and public feast, or the feast of the nativity of the world."

The learned Grotius, after quoting several very ancient authors, and among the rest Homer and Hesiod, says, "that the memory of the creation's being performed within seven days, was preserved, not only among the Greeks and Italians, but among the Celts and Indians, all of whom divided their time into weeks." The same is affirmed by other authors, of the Assyrians, Egyptians, Arabians. Romans, Gauls, Britons and Germans.

How is this remarkable agreement in the practice of nations so remote from each other, and between many of whom little or no intercourse ever existed,

to be accounted for? Wi said, that they were indeb the Jews for it? By who me ask, was it borrowed that despised people? Wo Egyptians permit themsel be instructed, by a nation civil and religious insti they abhorred? Would the rians? Would the Ar Would those proud and r masters of the world, the C and the Romans? No. more rational solution problem is, that the divi time into weeks, togethe some knowledge of the Sa was handed down from the ly of Noah, through all i merous branches, and tl process of time, spread ov greatest part of the world, same manner as tradition counts of the general d have found their way amo nations. This solution us directly back, far beyo age of Moses, and fur strong collateral evidence the Sabbath was known ante-diluvians, and of quence, that, according plain account of the sacred rian, it was instituted in dise.　　　　　Z. X

For the Pan

A PERSUASIVE TO RELI RETIREMENT.

OF the general duty, wl would inculcate upon the tr, Christ Jesus was an er example. Though engag the most important worl was ever undertaken on he found time for devout tude. He sent the mul

t he might be alone
. It was his frequent
Sometimes he contin-
ght in prayer. He re-
secret communion with
relief from fatigue,
parative for his labors'
ings.
at notice the reasons
re often been urged, to
e neglect of retirement.
ll content myself with
remarks. First: It is
ase, that no business
can afford a just ex-
neglecting the duties of
votion. Our eternal
are infinitely important,
be attended to, though
pense of our worldly in-
But, secondly, we
re care, that every du-
s proper share of atten-
igence in the concerns
rld will give time for
priate duties of relig-
member these duties,
lay out your secular
and undertake no more
can accomplish con-
with a life of piety.
gaging in any business
rtance, seriously in-
ether it will allow you
me for daily meditation
er. If we exercise
wisdom in the arrange-
ur business, and dili-
the execution of it, no
r duty needs to be neg-
Life is long enough
rformance of the whole
ich God has given us

beg your attention,
reader, to a few con-
s, which show the im-
of religious retirement.
Religious retirement
see the hurtful impres-

sions, which are made upon the
mind by our intercourse with the
world. We are apt to receive
impressions from what we see
and hear By conversing constantly with sensible objects, we
are liable to be too much under
their influence The things of
the world obtain a dangerous as-
cendency over us They occupy our thoughts, strengthen our
earthly passions, and weaken
every sentiment of piety. *Religious retirement* is fitted to
cure these disorders. By withdrawing our attention from sensible objects, it weakens their
influence. It gives us opportunity to consider the vanity of
earthly things, and to correct the
false estimate, which we before
made of them. In seasons of in-
consideration and busy care we
are prone to set far too high a
value upon the riches and honors of the world. But this error is likely to be corrected in
retirement. In the silent, solemn hour of secret meditation
and prayer, what trifles do
earthly riches and honors appear,
compared with the riches of
Christ, and the honor which
cometh from God!

Intercourse with the world
tends to make us familiar with
the sight of immoral and sinful
practice, and so to wear away all
affecting sense of its evil. The
continual exhibition of impiety
and profaneness gradually diminishes the horror, which they
once excited in our minds. We
are in danger of conforming to
the maxims of the world; of
sliding insensibly into a compliance with prevailing fashions;
and of imbibing the immoral
sentiments, which govern others. We are often carried away

with the multitude. Their number, noise, and influence overpower us. To our closets we must retire, in order to rise above these impressions, and escape these dangers. In devout retirement we behold the ungodly world pursuing shadows, and going swiftly down to destruction.

We learn, that conformity to the principles and fashions of the world, is the certain way to perish with the world. Thus we are awakened from our dream, and secured from fatal evils.

Secondly. *Religious retirement affords the best opportunity for becoming acquainted with God and divine things.* Intercourse with the busy world, instead of giving any right views of divine things, tends to keep us in ignorance of them, or to instil erroneous opinions into our minds. How can we hope to obtain divine light by having much to do with the world, which lieth in darkness? But retirement withdraws the mind from earthly objects, and puts it in a suitable frame for contemplating the perfections and ways of God. Our best views of these subjects are commonly obtained in retirement. In secret meditation and prayer, we can fix our eye most steadily on heavenly objects, being most free from every thing, which beclouds the sight, or turns it away to other objects. Religious retirement night and morning is the best means of promoting spiritual knowledge. Whereas, without this, every other means will be exceedingly ineffectual. Even the instructions of God's house will contribute little to our progress

in knowledge, unless [...] structions are reviewed [...] gested in private. The [...] chamber, the secret gro[...] lonely mountain, has be[...] the most profitable schoo[...] attainment of heavenly [...]

Thirdly. *Retirement [...] able, in a high degree, t[...] joyment of communion w[...]* Public prayer and famil[...] have their peculiar adv[...] and ought to be conscie[...] performed at their pro[...] sons. But in neither [...] have we the perfect liber[...] may be enjoyed in secre[...] secluded from the world [...] best discover our wants, [...] unreservedly make them [...] to God. We can most a[...] ly examine our hearts [...] lives, and thus prepare [...] for the most penitent co[...] The clearer views of Go[...] are obtained in retiren[...] cite more ardent love, a[...] unwavering hope. Ne[...] haps, can believers say, w[...] earnest feeling, as in ret[...] *As the hart panteth [...] water-brook, so panteth [...] after thee, my God. [...] my rock, my fortress, an[...] liverer, my God, my str[...] whom I will trust.*

Fourthly. *Retirement [...] peculiar assistance in t[...] fication of sin.* Amid [...] ness and pleasures of th[...] even Christians are apt [...] sensible of their moral [...] tions. While a thousan[...] invite and forcibly en[...] attention, we have little[...] nity, and often less i[...] to look into our own [...] search out the decei[...] ings of sin there. [...] not only prevents [...]

ng the corrupt affections of
earts, but affords much to
sh and increase them. By
il customs, it furnishes the
with many pleas to justify
it keeps out of view the
f God, the perfect standard
ness. Against all these
retirement is a powerful
eb. In pious solitude we
leisure to look within our-
s, and discover the corrup-
f our hearts. And as the
ts, which excite those cor-
us, are withdrawn, we are
peculiar advantages to
progress in sanctification
an expose the excuses, by
indwelling sin justified it-
We can perceive the fals-
the maxims, by which the
has so often misguided
We find that the advantag-
ich a deceived heart ex-
d to obtain from sin, have not
obtained; or, if obtained that
re worse than nothing, be-
e price of our innocence.
m make penitent co des-
before God, set a guard
t future snares, and apply
precious blood which
eth from all sin.

hly. *Retirement directly
ates to the growth of*
While the corruptions
heart thrive most amid
rrying business and tempt-
asures of the world; grace
hes most in retirement.
grace is modest and hum-
It seeks not the public
It operates with the great-
edom, which no one else,
oth. When surrounded
rthly objects, we find
ndrance to the exercise
The objects of re-
e out of sight, and our
are occupied with

X.

things. And are we not sometimes guilty of checking the impulse of grace in our hearts,
lest, by yielding to its influence,
we should incur the reproaches
of the world? In retirement it is
not so. When conversing in pious solitude with God, we fear
not man. The world with its allurements and terrors, is far out
of sight. Divine and eternal objects are present to our view.
We have opportunity undisturb-
edly to contemplate the errors
and vanities of the world, the
value of the soul, the beauty and
glory of God, the excellence of
Christ, approaching death, judgment, and eternity. With these
great objects in view, love, repentance, faith, and every grace
is excited. Beholding as in a
glass the glory of the Lord, we
are changed into the same image
from glory to glory

Sixthly. Retirement not only
excites and strengthens the holy
affections of believers at the present time, but by inspiring them
with firmer resolution and constancy, *prepares them for future
scenes.* Few Christians pass much
time in the company and business of the world, without finding
their pious resolution weakened. Their minds must be constantly raised and invigorated,
furnished for duty and armed
against temptations, by secret
reflection and prayer. Besides
the direct, natural influence
which secret devotion has upon
them, it secures that divine assistance, without which their
own strength is weakness.

Religious solitude prepares
Christians for the day of adversity. In retirement, they learn
what the world is, and what expectations they have a right to

indulge of enjoyment here. They see that all is vanity and vexation of spirit. They accustom themselves to anticipate the day of adversity. Their thoughts become familiar with all the common trials of life. Thus they are prepared for affliction, so that they are not surprised and thrown into confusion when the time of trouble comes. Their previous reflections and prayers with reference to affliction have given firmness and strength to endure. It is in a great measure by devout meditation and secret converse with God that they are prepared for the solemnities of the final judgment.

Finally. *Devout retirement affords the purest pleasure.* They, who know not the pleasures of secret religion, are justly objects of compassion These pleasures as much exceed the pleasures of the world, as divine and heavenly things exceed those which are earthly, or as eternity exceeds a moment. What an unspeakable pleasure is it to devout souls in retirement, to be freed for a while from the noise and wickedness of the world; to look at temptation as distant; to see themselves out of man's reach, and to be able to indulge within themselves, this holy, triumphant thought; *let the world say and do what it will; let it flatter or frown; ere in my pious retirement I am safe; here I am happy, for God is with me.* What pleasure do Christians derive in retirement, from the undisturbed exercise of holy affection; from unwavering confidence in God and submission to his will; from the contemplation of divine truth; and from the

humble hope of perseve goodness, and of enjoying er the friendship of th changeable God! How sa tial, how purifying, how an ing, these pleasures are, n can fully describe.

The foregoing remark gest the reason, why imp sinners dread the hour of meditation, and restrain before God. It is not b secret prayer would intru on the proper business o and occupy time, which be better employed. The retirement, because it bri view objects which are di ing to the impenitent Should they give themsel secret to the sober conside of eternal things, they discover the unlawfulne their favorite pursuits; would behold the wrath o and the approaching end their pleasures. Their cor ces would be awakened, enjoyment interrupted, a tressing fears excited. T the great reason why the v shun religious retiremen find no pleasure in sacr ties. Moral impurity is p at the sight of infinite ho It is wounding to the l worldly pleasures, to se those pleasures must ha end; and what can be mor tressing to guilt, than to s face of a righteous, Alm Judge!

In this subject, candid r you have a criterion of c ter. *The followers of poseess his Spirit. Th* communion with God, *he had such enjoyment,* enjoyment to *them.* W can retire from earthly,

iverse humbly with God,
ouls are satisfied as with
and fatness. There is no
lty of enjoying the bles-
of heaven without a
o delight supremely in
nion with God. The
sposition, which renders
ssatisfied with the wor-
d service of God in this
uld render them much
ssatisfied with the wor-
d service of God in heav-
heaven there is nothing
igion. The holy service
not day or night. How
y, who are tired and dis-
with the little religion
mong the saints on earth,
fied with the perfect un-
pied religion of the heav-
ate. From the praises
s of the celestial world
ould turn away with dis-
aying, *Oh what a weari-
When will it be ended!*
wer of Christ, receive
monition, which is here
stered to you. Is it not
omission, or careless per-
ce of secret duties, that
ist in a great measure as-
our low attainments in re-
What knowledge of God
vine things might you
ttained,—what mortifica-
sin,—what spiritual mind-
—what usefulness,—
minence in grace,—what
ation for the presence of
heaven, had you, with
diligence, employed
portunities afforded you
gious retirement! Peni-
review past neglects; and
future guard against ev-
ing, which would inter-
mmunion with God. Re-
live as Jesus lived.
member your weakness

and inconstancy, and repair continually to God in whom is
everlasting strength.

A SHORT SERMON. No. II.

MARK X, 20.

*All these have I observed from
my youth.*

"ALL these have I observed from
my youth"—my childhood—my
infancy. Self-deceived young
man! Little had he attended to
the subject, when he thus declared, that he had kept the commandments. Little did he know
of the spirituality and extent of
the divine law. Little had he
examined his heart, or considered in what true obedience consists. He probably had not
openly violated the letter of
those moral precepts, to which
his declaration related, by actually committing murder or adultery; by fraudulent dealing or
false accusation. In the view of
his fellow men, therefore, who
looked on the outward appearance alone, and in his own superficial view, he had kept these
commandments. But all this
might be done under the influence of the most sordid and selfish motives—upon principles of
mere worldly wisdom—with a
supreme regard to public opinion, or human authority, or private emolument. All this might
be done without the obedience
of the heart—without submission to the will of God—without
religious principle—without
exercising one holy affection, or
performing one act truly virtuous and good in the sight of
Heaven.

e person, who made

the declaration in our text. was destitute of true religion and in a state of self deception, the sequel of his history abudantly proves; and that many, who make a similar profession. are in the same condition, we have too much reason to fear. How often do we hear the thoughtless and inconsiderate justifying themselves in precisely the same manner, as he did! How many, who have not God in all their thoughts;—who follow the inclinations of their corrupt hearts, who walk according to the course of this world, are nevertheless insensible of their danger! How many even justify themselves in this state of carelessness and impenitency, adopting the very language of our text; "all these have we observed from our childhood." "We have never committed murder; we have defrauded no man; we have nothing to repent of, and nothing to answer for!" Ah! thoughtless sinners, you know not your own hearts The god of this world hath blinded your minds. Your understandings are darkened, through the ignorance that is in you, because of the hardness of your hearts. You have never considered, how exceedingly broad are the divine commands. You have never entered your secret chambers and examined yourselves before God, with a spiritual understanding of his law. *Be not deceived.* Remember who hath said, that *there is no man that sinneth not.* Forget not the declaration of our Lord himself to a mixed multitude, and through them to us all; *Except ye repent, ye shalt all likewise perish.* Pause and consider. Examine your

conduct. Try your princ Scrutinize your motives. S into the secret recesses of souls. Humble yourselv fore God. *Repent and b verted.*

Young men, these ad tions and exhortations with peculiar force to yo all, who are in the morn life. The person who, u the language of our text, ' appears by a comparison Evangelists, a young m young man of some disti possessing property, pow influence—a young man, external deportment was. lar, who united in his many amiable qualities, Jesus loved. Yet he lack one thing needful; he we from Christ sorrowful, a awfully short of that ki to which he supposed he nearly approached.

Young men! Young w Read the interesting na in our context. Medit the character, which it c: and apply the warning, w furnishes. It is indeed who have not sincerely i solutely devoted themse. the Lord, a most soler important warning—sole eternity, and important soul is precious!—What, ask, (and be intreated yourselves,) what are hopes? Where is your i Whence do you derive support? Are you trust self-rightousness, becau: have externally observed of the divine command you building your hopes o en on your supposed inn because you have been ke the commission of what nominated great sins? Are you content with your state, because no one has accused you, and because no one can justly accuse you, of immoral conduct? Are you satisfied—are you pleased with yourselves, because your amiable social qualities have rendered you pleasing to your friends—because the personal charms, natural to youth, have procured for you the flatteries of a deceitful world? All these natural qualities—these social accomplishments—this imaginary innocence, this freedom from scandalous crimes, this partial, external obedience to the divine commands, this flattering approbation of man;—all these things may you possess, and yet lack one thing, without which you can never enter the kingdom of heaven. All these things are indeed amiable and desirable; and it were to be wished, for the good of society, that all our youth possessed even these—that none were profane, impure, intemperate, scoffers, liars, slanderers; disturbing the harmony of society; destroying the peace of families; wounding the hearts of the pious, and spreading mischief and misery through the whole circle, in which they move.—But although you, my young friends, should be able to say, that you are free from these gross and scandalous iniquities; yet let me intreat you not hence to conclude, that you are safe—that you are holy in the sight of a heart-searching God—that you are fit for the kingdom of heaven. If you have no religion, except what consists in a negative morality, or a cold, partial, selfish obedience—if you have never been humbled for sin, and led

to embrace the Savior by faith—if the love of God has not been shed abroad in your hearts—if you have no established principle of holiness, leading you habitually to do that, which is good, as well as to abstain from that, which is evil—if you are not striving to walk in all the ordinances and statutes of the Lord blameless—if you are not ready to renounce every pleasure, every vanity, every earthly distinction, every temporal interest, which duty requires—if, in a word, you are not prepared to forsake all and follow Christ; you are yet no nearer the kingdom of heaven, than was the young man, who uttered the self-deluding language of our text. He could say all, perhaps more, than you can say; and still his heart was not right with God—still he loved the world supremely—still he went away from Christ sorrowful. He had in him many things amiable; but when brought to the test of obedience—when weighed in the balance of the Gospel, he was found wanting. He would not give up his idol for the sake of Christ. He loved Mammon more than God. He was unwilling to forsake all, take up his cross, and follow the King of glory. So would it be with you. *Would be*, did I say? *So it is* with every one, who lives in a habitual neglect of known duty—with every one, who refuses to devote himself without reserve to the service of God—with every one, who does not renounce every practice, and give up every object and pursuit, inconsistent with supreme love to God, and a sincere, unreserved, self-dedication to him.

Once more; young men, young women. I invite you, I entreat you, I beseech you in Christ's stead; be ye reconciled to God. Trust not to a refuge of lies. Rely not on a defective morality—an imaginary innocence—a selfish righteousness. Say not, *I am rich and increased with goods, and have need of nothing:* whilst *thou art wretched, and miserable, and poor, and blind, and naked.* Be persuaded to examine yourselves. Repent of your sins. Devote yourselves to the Lord. Take up your cross and follow the Savior of sinners. By the preciou of your immortal souls—b agonies of a crucified Rede —by the mercy and just God—by the love and terr the Lord—by the uncertain life, and the certainty of de by the solemnities of that ment-seat, before whiel must all appear, and that er state of retribution, on we must shortly enter—by thing interesting to ration accountable beings, I e you to attend immediately things, which belong to everlasting peace!

MISCELLANEOUS.

ORIGINAL LETTER OF PRESIDENT EDWARDS.

The following letter from the great President Edwards to his friend Dea. Lyman of Goshen, (Con.) has never been published.

"*Northampton, Aug.* 31, 1741.
"Dear Friend,

In my prodigious fulness of business and great infirmity of body, I have time to write but very briefly concerning those things you mention.

"Concerning the great stir that is in the land, and those extraordinary circumstances and events that it is attended with, such as persons crying out, and being set into great agonies with a sense of sin and wrath, and having their strength taken away, and their minds extraordinarily transported with light, love, and comfort;—I have been abundantly amongst such things, and have had great opportunity to observe them here and elsewhere, in their beginning, progress, and consequences: and ho there may be some mixtu natural affection, and some of temptation, and some il dences and irregularitie there always have been, a ways will be, in this imp state; yet, as to the work ir eral, and the main of wha be observed in these extr nary things, they have a clear and incontestable evi of a true divine work. I be not the work of God, I all my religion to learn again, and know not what make of the Bible.

"As to any absolute pro made to natural men, the i is exceeding plain. God i no promises of any future nal good to fallen man, i other covenant but the cov of grace; but how can the; any interest in the prom the covenant of grace, tha no interest in the Media that covenant, and never have performed the condition of that covenant, which is faith in the Mediator? The Scripture is ignorant of any other way of coming to a title to any promises of God, but only laying hold of the promises by faith, which surely men that have not faith don't do.

"As to the ministers that go about the country to preach, I believe most of the clamor that is made against them must needs be from some other principle than a regard to the interest of religion; because I observe now there is vastly a greater outcry against ministers riding about to preach the Gospel, than used to be heretofore, when ministers rode about on the business of a physician, though that be so much more alien from their proper work, and though they were gone from their own people five time as much. But I observe that now-a-days no irregularities are so much cried out against as exceeding in religion. As to ministers that ride about the country, I can't say how the case is circumstanced with all of them; but I believe they are exceedingly misrepresented. Mr. Pomroy and Mr. Wheelock have been* ——— as much as most; and by particular opportunity I have had to know how it has been with them, they scarcely ever are absent from their people on the Sabbath, and are very careful not to leave them destitute, and are not wont to go abroad but only where they are invited, and not to go into other ministers pulpits without their consent, and rarely without being desired by them;

and, at the same time, are more abundant in labors among their own people than ever.

"I rejoice to hear of the flourishing of the work of God in your parts. I hope God will cause it to prevail against all opposition. Let us look to God to plead his own cause, and to get to himself the victory Seek to him to direct you, and give you wisdom, and humility, and zeal. I desire your prayers for me. I am your sincere and entire friend,

JONATHAN EDWARDS."

"P. S. The Rev. Mr Williams of Hatfield died this morning.†"

CUMINGS ON THE CHERUBIM.

To the Editor of the Panoplist.

SIR,

I HAVE just finished the perusal of a little work entitled, *Contemplations on the Cherubim,* by Abraham Cumings, A M. printed by John Eliot, Jun. Boston, 1812. I have neither leisure nor ability to give you a proper review of this publication; but I take the liberty to recommend it, as a work of curiosity, genius, and candor, to studious theologians, for whose use it must have been designed; the subject being too much out of the way of ordinary inquiry, and the manner of discussing it being much too literary, for common readers. It is deficient, especially at the beginning, as to a distinct statement of the author's design. He gets you to the conclusion before he makes

* A word is here lost in the M. S

† Mr. Allen in his very valuable Biog. and Hist. Dict. p. 611, states that Mr. Williams died in 17.. This P. S. corrects the error.

you well understand the premises: There are some things perhaps fanciful, and too much in agreement with the extravagancies of the Hutchinsonian philosophy. But, for the most part, the book seems to me replete with sound sense and accurate criticism. It is a work uncommonly learned for this country. It exhibits a mind, that has been long exploring and gathering rich treasures of knowledge from high antiquity, and a watchfulness over the genuine Gospel doctrine, the doctrine of the Trinity, which is certainly the basis of the whole Christian scheme. It contains refutation strong of the absurd, misshapen theory, lately obtruded upon the public in a work entitled Bible News; and with a good deal of success, in my opinion, opposes the unfounded pretences of Dr. Priestley, and his disciples, that the doctrine of the Trinity, has its rise, not in a just interpretation of the sacred writings, but in the schools of the Platonic philosophy. As a

lover of literature, and ardent lover of the trut not but give my thanks Cumings for this work Whatever may become expositions of the diffic ject of the Cherubim, I but commend him, for gence, and accuracy; and ly wish, that his work m with deserved attention 1 religious public.

With your leave, Mr. I will also call the atter your readers to anothe work, lately published in sor, Vermont. The at the Rev. Stephen Fa Claremont, N. H. It co a series of letters to th Noah Worcester, in refu his Bible News. It is plete refutation. The at is conducted with ingen precision. It does hono Farley, especially con that he is a young man, ar enjoyment of but in health. I wish this wor have an extensive circul

CA

REVIEW.

LXI. *Proceedings of the Second Church and Parish in Dorchester; exhibited in a collection of papers. Published agreeably to a vote of the church.* Boston; S. T. Armstrong. 1812. pp. 124. 8vo.
The Memorial of the Proprietors of the New South Meeting House in Dorchester, to the Ministers of the Boston Association. Together with their

Report on the same. Watson and Bangs. 18 48. 8vo.

THE controversy betwe Rev. Mr. Codman and a his parishioners has ex very considerable intere one end of this countr other. This interest alor ever, would not have ind to admit the subject in pages. But the ostensible and real causes of this controversy are of general and permanent importance, and *ought* to excite a correspondent degree of interest. In most parish disputes we find too many indications of unfairness, imprudence, anger, detraction, and hatred of the truth. All the bad passions of man's depraved nature, are, indeed, occasionally brought into exercise. While these passions assume only their usual forms, there seems no good reason why their effects should be commemorated. It rather appears desirable that these effects should be buried in oblivion, as soon as possible. But when a parish controversy originates in opposition to the Gospel, and enlists on its side a powerful party,—a party in the constant habit of proclaiming its own strength, and wisdom and learning, and liberality,—a party always vigilant to extend its influence, and active to bear down those who stand in its way,—a party, which, under the guise of charity and candor, is aiming to establish a strong and lasting domination,—it appears highly proper, that the true nature of the controversy should be explained, the principal facts stated, and the Christian public enabled to judge of professions by the conduct which accompanies them. Such, in our apprehension, has been the controversy between Mr. Codman and some of his people; and such is the party from which his opposers have derived all their consequence, if not all their means of annoyance. We are too well acquainted with this party not to know, that many of its members will be extremely angry with the above description, and with every thing,

indeed, which tends to expose their views; and that they will attempt to conceal their anger by protesting that they hold us in the most perfect contempt. We have not inserted a single clause in this description without full deliberation, an unwavering persuasion of its truth and justice, and a conviction that we are able to prove the propriety of its application.

Though the party in question is no other than the liberal party in Boston and the vicinity, yet we are desirous to have it understood, that all the individuals of that party are not chargeable with lending their influence to drive Mr Codman from his people. Though the influence of the party, as a body, was certainly against him, there were individuals of the party who uniformly declared his opposers in the wrong; and though they might have thought it expedient that he should ask a dismission, they were not backward to acknowledge, that he was persecuted for his religious opinions.[*]

* The following anecdote may be related without impropriety.

A minister, who would undoubtedly be ranked with the liberal party, met Mr. Codman during the progress of his parish troubles, and addressed him substantially as follows: "I am sorry, my dear Sir, for the opposition which you experience. It is an unreasonable opposition. But I can tell you for your comfort, that you have the prayers of many pious Christians in distant parts of the country. You have my prayers that you may be supported, and I shall continue to offer them. You cannot invite me to preach in your pulpit, consistently with your own opinions. I am not offended at this; though I should be glad to preach to your people once, with a particular view to tell them *how improperly they behave*. I commend you for acting according to the dictates of your own conscience; though I differ from you in religious doctrine. My own principles, however, do not prevent my desiring you to preach in my pulpit; and I shall

As in most other party questions, it is probable that a comparatively small number took a lively interest in consulting; the great mass lent their good wishes, and the influence of their opinions, against what they were taught to consider as bigotry and intolerance; and a few dissented from the opinions of the party. The latter could not for their lives see, that a love of candor and liberality made it their duty to condemn a brother for exercising a right, which all ministers of the Gospel claim for themselves; viz. *The right of regulating their ministerial conduct by their own sense of duty.*

We now proceed to state the particulars of the case; in doing which we shall make free use of the publications before us, and admit many additional facts derived from authentic sources.

On the 9th of Sept. 1808, the second church of Christ in Dorchester unanimously elected Mr. Codman, then a licensed candidate for the ministry, to be their pastor. A few days after, the parish concurred in the election, with only four dissenting voices. The pastor elect was immediately informed of the result, and requested time for prayer and consideration. As the church had heard him preach on two Sabbaths only, and at one lecture, and had enjoyed but little opportunity of becoming acquainted with his religious

opinions, Mr. Codman determined to make a co nication to them on the s He therefore wrote them and affectionate letter, w express design 'to ente some explanations, whic highly interesting to hi them,' and "to prevent difficulties." He procee state, 'lest there should doubt on the subject, th felt it his duty to declare shaken faith in those doc that are sometimes call doctrines of the reformatic doctrines of the cross, the liar doctrines of the C These doctrines he inten preach, and it gave him ure to say, that his faith same with that of our ve forefathers; 'particularly that of the former pastors church in Dorchester, W Maverick, Mather, Burr He subjoined the followi agraph on the subject trines:

"As *Arian* and *Socinian* error late years crept into some of our C I think it my duty to declare Church of Christ, of whom I n the pastoral charge, that I bel *Father, Son, and Holy Ghost to l living and true God;* and that i in general, is conformable to the bly's catechism, and to the con faith drawn up by the elders and gers of the Congregational Chu the year 1680, and recommende Churches by the General Court c chusetts." p. 12.

Before concluding his Mr. Codman requests, other things, that Dr. V Psalms and Hymns may l in public worship; from it seems, they had been ed to make room for I knap's. On this subject serves,

be much obliged to you, if, whenever your own pulpit shall be supplied, you will come and preach to my people. I call the opposition to you a persecution, *and a persecution for religious opinions.*'

Some others of the liberal party are known to have entertained the same sentiments, as are here expressed. We shall rejoice to find, that the number of these persons is greater than we had supposed.

collection now used contains
ellent hymns, particularly those
Steele's, Dr. Doddridge's, &c.
But on many accounts it appears
eedingly defective. Unwarrant-
ties are taken in altering Dr.
nguage.
xologies of Dr. Watts, the as-
if praise to the glorious Trinity,
ally left out, and the preface
xpressions in my humble opin-
ntory to the glory due to the
Father, Son, and Holy Ghost."

whole communication of
odman evinces perfect
as, an earnest desire not
misunderstood, a deep
f responsibility to God,
implicit determination
ccept the call, unless he
lo it with a prospect of
harmony and usefulness.
ild not be misapprehend-
er in regard to his relig-
inions, or his intentions
ing the communication,
by a person totally igno-
the present state of relig-
this vicinity, and of the
nts of Christianity. As
attempt in the *Memorial*,
, it appear, that Mr. Cod-
ommunication was inex-
we shall take notice of
another place.
communication was ac-
and the requests con-
in it complied with, by
rch and parish; of which
dman was notified, in an
nate letter from a com-
chosen for the purpose.
etter, which was unani-
approved at a parish
g, begins with stating,
communication 'was re-
with pleasure and gener-
faction; that the writers
e the principles of their
ers, especially of the pi-
l worthy pastors of the

church in Dorchester, and are
happy to find Mr. C. agreeing
with them in sentiment.'

The invitation was now accepted by Mr. Codman, and, in
his letter of acceptance, he
thought it proper, as the committee had alluded to 'the promotion of peace and friendship
among his people,' to explain
his views as follows:

"The promotion of THAT PEACE, which
is founded on *true Christian principle*,
and not on *carnal security*, and of *that
unanimity*, which is the *effect of the general reception of evangelical truth*, and
not of indifference to religious opinions,
will be the subject of my prayers and the
object of my life.

"It will be my earnest endeavor, *as far
as consistent with the faithful discharge
of ministerial duty*, to promote peace and
friendship among the people of my charge;
—to do all in my power to continue and
confirm it among our sister churches and
their Pastors, and to promote the best interests of the university, of which I shall
be an overseer." pp. 16, 17.

Before the council proceeded
to the ordination, which took
place Dec. 7, 1808, the pastor
elect communicated his confession of faith, which was orthodox
and full on the following points;
viz. *the Trinity, the decrees of
God, election, the temptation and
fall, original and actual sin, the
character of Christ, as uniting
the divine and human natures
and having made an atonement,
the character of the Holy Spirit,
as the Renewer and Sanctifier of
men, regeneration, sanctification,
justification by faith, adoption,
repentance, good works, perseverance, the final and unalterable
states of the righteous and the
wicked*, and on several other important articles of doctrine and
practice.

Although no objections to this
creed were stated at the time,

Mr. Codman had not labored many months among his people before it was found, that the preaching of those *doctrines*, which he had all along professed and inculcated, gave serious offence to a part of his hearers, who soon began to form and organize a regular opposition. That this opposition originated, in fact, from a dislike of the *great truths* which Mr. Codman preached, and the correspondent strictness of moral deportment which he urged, we have the fullest persuasion; and we think no candid man, having an intimate acquaintance with the parties and the controversy, can entertain a doubt on the subject. Had Mr. C. delivered smooth harangues on the native benevolence and dignity of man; complimented his people, occasionally, on their candor, catholicism, and liberality; inveighed earnestly, and with a very significant air and tone, against creeds, intolerance, bigotry, and enthusiasm, and countenanced such *innocent amusements*, as playing at cards, and midnight revelling, it is altogether possible that he would have remained unmolested by those who took a lead in the controversy with him, and that the question of *ministerial exchanges* would have been suffered by them to sleep in silence. It would not do, however, to bring any accusation against Mr. Codman, on the score of his religious opinions, as it is a fundamental principle with the liberal party, that no man is to be called on to declare, explain, or defend such opinions; and as his opposers claimed to belong to this party, a claim which they amply supported in the course of their op-

position. When any nu persons are leagued toge party purposes, they wil be in want of ostensible r however different these from the real ones. A known, that Mr. Codm conscientious scruples in to introducing into his any man, who disbeliev tain fundamental doctrine Gospel, no great sagac necessary to determine, parish difficulty could b easily and successfully r the subject of exchang on any other. This sul forded a fine opportunit claim on the duty of charity, peace, and c Hence it happened, tha Mr. Codman's opposer carrying on their opposit uncommon violence, and ing in unprovoked and bi tility, they professed to l ing only for peace.

The first intimation, Mr. Codman received f disaffected members of t ish, that he was desired l to enlarge his circle changes, was communic two of their number, to w gave, in substance, this That in regard to excha ministerial labor he sho deavor to act conscien that he should conform wishes of his people, on t ject and every other, s his own sense of duty wo mit; and that he could no himself to exchange v man, or body of men, wl This is the same answer he had given to an indiv the parish, who applied his settlement, to know tentions in regard to e

answer he steadfastly ad:
i every part of the con-
.
s than a year after Mr.
's ordination, forty of
ishioners communicat-
iim a written address,
that a dissatisfaction ex-
the parish, the principal
which was, that Mr. C.
make exchanges gener-
h those ministers, who
the public lectures in
on Thursdays, and with
discriminately.' "This,"
d, "we did expect, and
think we have a just
expect, from your own
tions previous to your be-
ed as our minister." The
was enclosed in a re-
letter from a committee,
clared that 'if any one
e of the enclosed should
ght expressed in a harsh
:orous manner, or if any
it could be so construed
ave the least semblance
rative language, the same
error of judgment and
esign.'
is letter and address Mr.
i returned an immediate
—took a respectful no-
its various topics;—re-
the determination which
formed on the subject of
ges;—protested that he
ver, from any observa-
eviously to his being set-
their minister, given the
ers any claim to expect
course of exchanges as
equested;—and assured
but 'in his exchanges, as
part of ministerial duty,
d be his endeavor, as it
aad been, to conciliate the
is and to promote the
and happiness, but e'

pecially the spiritual welfare of
the people committed to his
charge' *Pro.* p. 24.

In April, 1810, some of the
disaffected members of the parish made a legal application to
have the following articles, in
substance, inserted in the warrant for a parish meeting; viz.
'To know if it is the desire of the
parish that Mr. Codman should
exchange with the ministers who
compose the Boston association,
&c. To know if the Society will
exchange the psalm-books now
in use, and use Dr. Belknap's
in their stead:—To know if the
Society are willing the meeting-
house shall be opened for private lectures.'

At the parish meeting, the
motion to desire Mr. Codman to
exchange with the ministers of
the Boston association was nega-
tived 52 to 34; the article respecting psalm-books was dismissed from the warrant; and
the meeting-house was declared
to be in future under the control
of Mr. Codman, in respect to
lectures, as usual.

One would have thought, that
the disaffected members of the
parish, with all their professions
of candor and their ardent desires of peace, would have now
rested a while from their opposition. They *professed* no dislike
of Mr. Codman's preaching; they
professed no dislike of the preaching of those ministers with whom
Mr. C. had exchanged; they admitted, (or at least they did not
deny, and they subsequently admitted,) the *right* of Mr. Codman to regulate his own exchanges; they had requested indiscriminate exchanges, on the
plea that the peace of the parish

would be promoted by such a measure; but the parish, in a legal meeting, had refused to support them in the request. Instead of remaining quiet, however, they entered upon a course of more determined hostility. The leading members of the dis-affected party resorted to such low and vulgar methods of personal insult and provocation, as are not worthy to be particularly mentioned. In August, they publicly offered 38 pews for sale, by advertisement in the Centinel, when in fact the pews were not for sale, and several of the owners of them knew nothing of the advertisement till they saw it in print. This advertisement, inserted in a paper which has a more extensive circulation than any other in New England, appeared, on the face of it, to be intended to prejudice the public at large against Mr. Codman. For this purpose it was doubtless intended, and for another purpose equally worthy; viz. to be used as proof that the parish was in a broken, divided, unhappy state.

In September, the disaffected party applied for another parish meeting, and specified the advertisement above-mentioned, as one of the reasons of their application. This is a fair example of the manner in which the controversy was conducted by them. One outrage was made the pretext of another, and that of a third, and so on to the end. Indeed, if a recipe is wanted for the best method of driving away a faithful minister, who has given no just cause of complaint, it may be comprised in the following brief directions: Begin the quarrel with great boldness and

great violence; set afloat
titude of stories, no matt[er]
false, or absurd, or how
disproved. If they shoul[d]
fact disproved, be careful
peat them, and keep the[m]
ing briskly, and make [some]
some addition to them. A[s]
the fact, that the very ex[istence]
of such a state of things [proves]
that the minister's useful[ness is]
gone. Profess a strong
for the peace of the paris[h]
at the same time, inflam[e]
passions of anger, malic[e]
envy, by every species o[f false]
hood, and every vulgar a[rt]
which ingenuity can
Seek occasion to convers[e with]
your minister on the par[ish dif-]
ficulties; and a moderate
of cunning will enable yo[u to ac]
cuse him openly and pub[licly of]
falsehood. By this time
number of persons, sc[attered]
through the vicinity, will
to say, "The man *must ha[ve been]*
imprudent; he must have
some occasion, or these
could not exist. His use[fulness]
is gone; and the sooner he
his people the better."
us return to the narrative.

The parish meeting
mentioned was held on
of Oct. 1810. The oppos[ers of]
Mr. Codman had by thi[s time]
gained such strength as t[o pass]
the following vote; viz.
the Rev. Mr. Codman
quested to exchange wi[th the]
ministers who compose th[e Bos-]
ton association of which
member."[*]   A commi[ttee]

thirteen was appointed to present this vote to Mr. Codman, and to receive an answer. At an adjourned meeting, an answer was reported in the following words: "That he [Mr. C] cannot pledge himself to exchange with any man, or any body of men, whatever." The parish then proceeded to vote, 40 to 35, that '*the connexion between themselves and Mr. Codman become extinct.*' They also voted, "that a committee be chosen to write to the ministers in the several towns, with whom the Rev. Mr. Codman has been in the habit of exchanging, requesting them *not to preach in his pulpit any more,* until the difficulties, which now seriously threaten the parish with destruction, are removed.".

The committee wrote a circular, in accordance with the preceding vote, and addressed it to the Rev. Mr. Greenough and the Rev. Mr. Homer, of Newton, the Rev. Dr. Morse, of Charlestown, the Rev. Dr. Griffin and the Rev. Mr. Huntington, of Boston, the Rev. Mr. Strong, of Randolph, the Rev. Mr. Bates, of Dedham, and the Rev. Mr. Gile, of Milton. For this curious document the read-

put laborers out of employment, and to see others who were indebted to them, unless they would vote against Mr. Codman. It has been stated by members of that party, that at their meetings for consultation and preparation, the more wealthy treated the rest very generously with spirituous liquors. On the days of the parish meetings, all the voters of the opposition were rallied.

Mr. Codman's friends, on the contrary, were apparently overawed, and astonished, by the violence with which the opposition was conducted. Being friends of peace, and entirely unused to such a state of parish war, they shrunk from the conflict.

er is referred to the *Proceedings,* pp. 29. 30. This measure was not less inconsistent with the preceding measures, than unprecedented in its character. Dr. Morse and Mr. Huntington were members of the Boston association, and the parish had endeavored to *compel* Mr. Codman to exchange with ministers of that association, "*indiscriminately;*" yet these two gentlemen are now requested *not to exchange* with Mr. Codman. The disaffected party had professed no dissatisfaction with the labors of any of the gentlemen above-named, but had requested Mr. Codman *to enlarge* the circle of his exchanges. As he declined pledging himself to do this, they were determined that he should not *exchange at all,* nor even admit *into his pulpit* some of his highly respected brethren in the ministry, against whom they could state no objection. Further; professing the strongest desire of promoting peace and harmony in the churches, they wrote a letter to eight pastors of neighboring churches, which could hardly be construed any otherwise, than as a direct insult to Mr. Codman and those to whom it was written.

Before the transmission of this letter, Mr. Codman had agreed upon an exchange with one of the gentlemen to whom the letter was addressed. It was not thought that the arrangement should be altered, in consequence of the receipt of such a letter. When the Sabbath arrived, and the gentleman was about entering the door of Mr. Codman's church, he was nearly surrounded by these lovers of peace and concord, and rudely and boisterously assailed by several passionate voices at once. In the afternoon, he was again attacked in a similar manner, though with increased violence. He was surrounded by persons, who conducted in the style of an angry mob, and demanded 'why he came thither?' to which he replied, that 'he came to preach the Gospel.' He was charged with impudence, and not suffered to proceed till he had repeatedly demanded a passage.

Dr. Morse and Mr. Bates' wrote long and affectionate, though plain, and faithful, letters to the committee, which one would think, must have excited some feelings of shame and compunction; but which were never communicated to the parish, though written with the express design of being thus communicated. Mr. Bates's letter was, in fact, addressed "to the second parish in Dorchester." *Pro.* pp. 36—42. We regret that our limits will not permit us to make extracts from these interesting letters.

During the progress of the outrageous proceedings, which we have been detailing, Mr. Codman's friends felt it to be their duty to give him a public and formal proof of their attachment. Accordingly, *seventy three* male members of his parish signed and presented an affectionate address, from which we select the following passage:

"Nearly all your parishioners appear satisfied with your performances, and acknowledge you have conformed to the doctrines and principles held out to us in your communication, previous to your ordination; and the foundation of the difficulties professedly is, your declining to exchange ministerial labors with the association of ministers to which you be-

long. And you know by the applications and individual reque ny of the subscribers, that we very happy to see all gratified i spect, as far as circumstances an ence of theological sentiments v mit. But, the right being ves by the custom of ages, to decide to exchanges, and as many may exist which are unknow understood by us, and are not c control, but depend in a great the opinion and convenience ministers and their people, such tions cannot be demanded as without an invasion of the rig ers, which we hope our brethr majority will take into their se sideration, and will see that the able request, as it is termed, subsequent proceedings has gro to a most positive demand; s have all the same interest to pre reconciliation is very desirable that we shall not, on either sid erned by our feelings, but by ment,—not by our prejudices, reason, and that we may not l ced by the calumny, threats, man, but by a regard for justi the love of God and our neighb 31.

This address was su by another, signed by c *dred and eighty one* fema bers of the parish Th and temper of this pa appear from the perusal following sentences:

"We, beloved Sir, when you tled as our pastor, echoed the v that proceeded from our hus thers, brothers and friends; an we could not become public ad your settlement, the eye of a disclosed the happiness of the h power of sympathy has never l ed us, the virtue of sincerity not withheld . With affection thy and Christian sincerity, you to bear up against the host that beset you, and like a good Christ, having on the whole a gospel, we hope you will fgh and come off conqueror and conqueror, in this important so

"You have this consolation hearts gratefully bear witne truth,—that your preaching ha m vain, but, that by a blessing your faithful and affectionate.

ten of the word, many of us have been advised, comforted, animated, and strengthened." p. 32.

Of these addresses Mr. C. took suitable notice in an anniversary sermon preached soon after, and of which an extract is given at p. 32.

About this time, another advertisement appeared, in the Centinel and the Chronicle, offering 69 pews for sale, and containing a gross insult on Mr. Codman. It was prepared and inserted by the leaders of the disaffected party; and for no other imaginable purpose, than to give some public expression of their spleen and resentment.*

During the progress of the controversy, Mr. Codman's opposers gradually withdrew from public worship, till scarcely any of them attended; yet his congregation gradually increased, as many persons, who did not belong to the parish, chose to attend on his ministrations. In Jan. 1811, a number of the inhabitants of Dorchester and Roxbury petitioned the legislature for permission to join Mr Codman's parish. The petition was referred to the next General Court by consent, and never after brought up, as it was supposed that a general law, passed at the same session, rendered any legislative interference in this particular case unnecessary. We mention this to shew, that Mr. C. had encouragements mingled with his trials.

In April 1811, another address was presented to Mr. C. by his friends, in which they declared, 'that they saw nothing to justify the origin or continuance of the existing evils,' and gave assurance of their 'determination to support him as their pastor, so long as he should continue to sustain his present character as a minister of the Gospel, and give no other occasion of complaint than that which was alleged against him ' This address was signed by fifty-four.

At a parish meeting, June 24, 1811, a committee was appointed to act under the following instructions: 1. To request a separation between Mr. C. and his people. 2. In case Mr. C. should decline such a separation, to propose a mutual ecclesiastical council. 3. In case Mr. C. should not accede to either of the above propositions, to call an *ex parte* council, prepare articles of charge, &c. &c. In these proceedings, the parish distinctly recognized Mr. C. as their pastor, though they had declared, eight months before, that *the connexion was extinct*. Soon after a council had been determined on by the parish, Mr. Codman's friends met, and appointed a committee to assist him in his defence, should it be necessary. A discussion arose between the parish committee and Mr. C., as to the mode of communication, which, it was finally agreed, should be in writing. The committee then requested an answer to the first proposition. Mr. C., in reply, goes ... the manner ... and of ... declaration

---

* It is understood that the Editors of the Centinel knew nothing of the advertisement till after it was ... Otherwise he would not have suffered it to appear.

of his religious sentiments, which he then made, on purpose to avoid *"future difficulties."* He laments, that an opposition should have been excited by some of his parishioners, 'who openly profess a system entirely opposite to the one, upon which he was settled.' He freely yields to his opposers perfect liberty of conscience, while he claims it for himself. He asserts his fidelity in the performance of his pastoral duties, professes a strong attachment to his people, desires the parish to reconsider their proceedings, and requests, if the application for his dismission should be persistin, that the committee would state the *reasons* for a separation, with *all the specific articles of complaint* against him. This reply appears to have given great offence to the committee, as an *evasion* of their request. They refused to state their reasons and their charges, on the ground that it was impossible for Mr. C. to be unacquainted with them. Through ignorance of the meaning of the word *ostensible*, they stumbled upon it, in such a manner as to give, unintentionally, a just description of the whole controversy. "I must therefore repeat, Rev. Sir," says the chairman of the committee, "that you cannot be at a loss to know what the ostensible ground of complaint is with the parish." *Pro.* p. 51.

Mr. C. returned for answer, 'that if the committee were ready to say, that they had no other reasons for wishing a separation, than those which formed *"the ostensible ground of complaint,"* by which he understood the objections that had been

made respecting his ex his answer would be quivocal as they coul but. if they had other he wished to see them larly stated.' This le also construed as an eva the committee requeste swer to the second pro i. e. the calling of a mu clesiastical council. M gues at some length, i to show the reasonable his request, utterly d any design to evade the ositions, expresses his ness to unite in a (though he sees no nece it.) and concludes by insi being furnished with *specific articles in writin* condition *absolutely ina* ble.

The committee ne sad complaints of the *conduc'*," which Mr. pursued, decline stating ticles of charge. and thi a statement will be in sea he shall have answered proposition, or agreed them in calling a counci decide, however, 'that usefulness as a minister Gospel in that society is, opinion, at an end.'

As no reasons were t the Committee to prove cessity of a separation, the *ostensible* one abo tioned, Mr. C. gave a answer to the first pro As to a council, he re proceed till his reque furnished with the spec cles of complaint should plied with.

The committee, aft cavilling and complai length consent to exhib articles of complaint which at the present time they may have a knowledge of;' but they cautiously add, "that it is their intention to offer to the council every article of complaint, which has transpired, not within their knowledge, or which may transpire before the result of the council.' Mr. C. replied, as he very obviously might, that he did not wish the committee to exhibit 'articles of complaint *of which they had no knowledge, or which had not yet transpired!*' He remonstrated against being tried in reference to such charges; but expressed his willingness to unite with the disaffected members of his society in choosing a mutual council, upon their exhibiting, in writing, "all the articles of complaint which *had* transpired, and of which the committee *had* a knowledge.'

This letter appears to have given great offence to the committee. They spiritedly declare, that they "will not agree to a proposition, that may deprive them of bringing forward and laying before the council, all such articles of charge, or causes of complaint, as, in their opinion, may be thought expedient." They threaten to break off the communication, 'unless a speedy and satisfactory decision can be had on the point in dispute,' and to proceed to the third head of instructions in the parish vote; i. e. to call an *ex parte* council. They complain of the month's delay, which had been occasioned by the correspondence.

Mr. C. adhered to his determination; but the committee again refused to accede to it, appointed a time and place, at which to choose a mutual council, and invited Mr. C. to attend. This he utterly declined, till the articles of complaint should be furnished; and went into a considerable argument to show, what is indeed very evident, the reasonableness of his request. He urged, that even the parish vote described the council as being chosen 'to hear and determine all matters of controversy *existing* between him and the society;' which precluded the idea of being tried on articles of complaint, which had not then transpired.

The committee met, at the time and place appointed, to call a mutual council; but, as Mr. C. did not join them, they proceeded no further. Nearly a month elapsed before any other step was taken. The committee then came forward with all the articles of complaint, which they could muster, reserving the right of stating any additional articles, provided any new causes of complaint should transpire; in which case they would seasonably furnish Mr. Codman with a copy.

The correspondence between Mr. C. and the committee, after the parish had determined on a council and before the specific articles of complaint were exhibited, is extended through nineteen letters, some of them of considerable length. The committee are often querulous and disposed to make great difficulties out of little things Mr. C. is patient, self-possessed, and steadfast in his resolutions. Many topics are started, which we have not deemed it necessary to notice; but it appeared to us that the reader could hardly be

In possession of the case without a brief sketch of this correspondence.

The articles of complaint, or the reasons why the parish wished the pastoral connexion between Mr. C. and his people dissolved, are these:

"1st. Because the great disappointment, that a respectable number of your Church, and a majority of your society, have experienced at your not exchanging ministerial labors, with the Rev. Clergy composing the Boston Association generally, more especially those that were present and performed at the dedication of the meeting-house, and at the organization of the Church; and those that were particularly concerned and assisted in your ordination; which the parish had every reason to expect, from your intimations, both antecedent and subsequent to your settlement.

"2d. Because, though we would not deny to a minister all discretion in the choice of those with whom he changes pulpits; yet you have, in our opinion, gone in this respect, to such an improper and unwarrantable extreme, as in effect to make us a separate religious society; cutting us off from that intercourse with the greater part of those Christian societies (and of our own denomination) with which we have been on terms of friendship and communion.

"3d. Because we conceive, that the lectures and religious meetings which you appoint, or encourage, are so frequent, and held at such times and places, as that they tend rather to disorder and the interruption of domestic union, comfort, and duties, than to the promotion of the social virtues and genuine religion.

"4th. Because of your unfeeling and unnatural conduct, in attempting to prevent the neighbors and friends of Mr. Thomas Crehore, from attending the funeral of his son, by urging several of them personally to attend your lecture; and requesting them to call on your friends to do likewise; also, threatening to forsake them, in case of refusal.

"5th. Because you personally, or by your instigation, circulated cards in Rev. Mr. Harris's parish, respecting the catechism, cautioning them to beware of innovation; undoubtedly meaning for them to guard against their Rev. Pastor; who had previously introduced Dr. Watts's Catechism, agreeably to the printed directions of the School Committee of which you are a member.

"6th. Because of your overbearing conduct in neglect of the wishes of a majority of the parish in admitting into a number of ministers, whom the ... a legal meeting, had request... preach therein, until their ... rebuilded; also, your endeavor... vent the customary tolling the funeral, as an interference with ... ture.

"7th. Because of your hard observations, towards some of you and brethren in the ministry believe, sustain unimpeachable both as men and Christians.

"8th. Finally, because we ... while your ministerial relation... continue, there will be no pro... restoration of that harmony, ... brotherly love, which have been... ply interrupted, and which we wish may soon return." pp. 6...

About the same time, ... grieved members of the ... preferred articles of ch... gainst Mr. C., to be laid... church-meeting, which ... previously requested to b... These articles are, in a... (for we cannot spare ... print them at large,) as ...

1, "We are aggrieved ... we *fully* believe, that y... *designedly* practised upo... *arts of deception.*" Un... head two instances are s...

2. 'Because Mr. C.'s r... to exchange ministerial... &c. &c. is inconsistent ... charitable spirit of the ... and tends to interrupt, if ... stroy, the fellowship ... church with the neig... churches.'

3. 'Because Mr. C. ... changed with some m... who had been requested... preach in his pulpit.'

4. 'Because Mr. C. h... lated an express rule of... by refusing an aggrieved... an opportunity to tell hi... ances in private.'

The church formally ... these complaints, and ... them to a committee,

, to which they relat-
a committee Mr. C.
a long letter, taking
arge and vindicating
n every just cause of
His statements in
e, as afterwards ap-
re the council, were
accurate; his mode
ig the various topics
e and dignified; and
ig perfectly conclu-
defence occupies
ges; and ought to be
ively by any person,
, to understand the
ly. The aggrieved
fused to produce any
a support of their
i the pretence that
was prejudiced in
r. Codman and had
do with the subject;
church is, according
bridge platform, the
tribunal for the trial
es, unless the parties
rch agree upon some
iod of terminating
ities. The commit-
church enter into a
ation of the various
so far as they have
nity of judging, and
bjection to a mutual
ough they see no
such a measure.
me, Mr. C. entered
angement, which a-
a voluntary relin-
of a great part of his
ugh the whole had
equal to his necessa-
s.
these preparations
ade, the calling of a
ncil came very near
ited, as the parish
could not prevail on
to give up the

chance of preferring any new
charges, which might be discovered before the sitting of the
council. This obstacle was at
length removed; and it was a-
greed that the council should
decide, as to the propriety of
admitting new articles of charge.
There seems to have been little
occasion for so much pertinacity
on this point; for the parish
gave Mr. C. notice, before the
sitting of the council, that the
third article of charge would be
abandoned. Indeed, the legal
advisers of the parish committee, as we have learned from
authentic sources, would have
much preferred, that the subject
of exchanges should be the only
ground of complaint. The third
article, it will be recollected,
had reference to the frequency
of religious meetings, which
Mr. C. had encouraged in the
parish. Had this article remained among the charges, he
would have confessed to the
Council, what he admitted in
his defence to the church, that
he had established a weekly
lecture, on Tuesday afternoons;
and that he had encouraged
prayer-meetings, in different
parts of the parish.

A mutual council was at length
agreed upon, to consist of twelve
ministers and a delegate from
each of their churches; six of
the churches to be selected by
Mr. C. and six by the parish
committee. The ministers and
delegates from the churches selected by Mr. Codman, were the
following: viz.

From the church in Medfield,
The Rev. Thomas Prentiss, D. D.
    Artemas Woodward, Delegate.
Hatfield, Rev. Joseph Lyman, D. D.
    Isaac Maltby, Del.

Newton, Rev. William Greenough,
    Dea. Joseph Adams, Del.
Worcester, Rev. Samuel Austin, D. D.
    Moses N. Child, Del.
Charlestown, Rev. Jedidiah Morse, D. D.
    Jeremiah Evarts, Del.
Salem, Rev. Samuel Worcester, D. D.
    John Punchard, Del.

The ministers and delegates
from the churches selected by
the parish committee, were the
following: viz.

From the church in Bridgewater,
The Rev. John Reed, D. D.
    Simeon Keith, Delegate.
Watertown, Rev. Richard R. Elliot,
    Dea. Moses Coolidge, Del.
Dedham, Rev. Thomas Thacher,
    Dea. John Richards, Del.
Worcester, Rev. Aaron Bancroft, D. D.
    Joseph Allen, Del.
Weston, Rev. Samuel Kendall, D. D.
    Nathan Hagar, Del.
Lancaster, Rev. Nathaniel Thayer,
    Ebenezer Torrey, Del.

The council met on Wednesday, Oct. 30, 1811, and was occupied in the public hearing of the parties, by themselves, their agents, and advocates, till Saturday. The Hon. Samuel Dexter, Esq. and Benjamin Parsons, Esq. managed the cause of the parish; the Rev. Mr. Bates, of Dedham, appeared as the advocate of Mr. Codman; and Daniel Davis, Esq. the Solicitor General, as representing Mr. Codman's friends. The discussion of all the various topics was ample, and was closed by Mr. Dexter on Saturday, in an elaborate speech of three hours. Were that speech in print, we should think it peculiarly worthy of examination.

The council met again on the Monday following, and continued their deliberations till Thursday, when their decision, technically called their *result*, was published. In regard to the account,

which we propose to gi
private discussions. in t
cil, it is proper to say
have not inserted it wi
ing great pains to hav
rect.

It ought here to b
that Mr. Codman utter
ed offering any testi
show with what temper
position had been carr
any further than was in
the reading of the writ
uments in chronologic
He wished to criminate
but simply to defend
Supposing the case to b
in his favor, and hoping
council would pronounc
so, he was unwilling to
testimony, which, thoug
illustrative of the true i
the controversy, would
increase the irritation of
posers. He earnestly w
do them good, and to d
all the duties of a faithf
to them.

At the formation of t
cil, the Rev. Dr. Pren
appointed Moderator,
Rev. Mr. Thayer, and t
Dr. Worcester, Scribes.

In the course of the
proceedings, the 7th
charges made by the par
abandoned; the one be
jected to as too indefi
other as being no charge

Upon the remaining
the council expressed t
cision as follows:

"Voted, 1. That the charg
tional deception, as stated in th
cification of the aggrieved bret
not been supported.
2. That the charge of *inte
ception*, as stated in the secon
tion of the same article, *has* n
ported.

t the charge *of having violated
as rule of Christ, in refusing an
d brother an opportunity to tell
ances*, as stated in the fourth ar-
he aggrieved brethren, *has not
ported;* although it appears, that
Mr. Codman and brother Field
stood each other in the attempt
be first step.
t the charge *of unfeeling and
d conduct*, as stated in the
article of the parish, *is not sup-
as it appears*, that the interfer-
he Rev. Mr. Codman, in the ten-
quies of a funeral, was made un-
liar circumstances; and that his
nt explanations ought to be con-
is satisfactory.
at *the circulation of a card by
. Mr. Codman, in the town of
ter*, alluded to in the fifth article
harges of the parish, was an in-
and improper act,† *although it is
ed, that there was an evil or un-
design in the transaction.*
at as the parties who brought for-
icles third of the aggrieved breth-
sixth of the parish, deemed them
tant, the council consider them
lly withdrawn.

*reference is, in the original min-
he third article, as the preced-
cle had been withdrawn.*
*an explanation of the circum-
attending the circulation of the
the reader is referred to Rev.
dman's Defence, pages 76, 77, of
oceedings* The card is in the
g words: "A NECESSARY CAT-
Innovations are dangerous. "I
cerely declare," said that great
dman. Dr Watts, in his preface
atechisms for Children*, "that it
om my design or my wish to ex-
le Assembly's Catechism out of
s families; for if that should
done, I have much reason to
our age, there would scarce
better in the room of it." Watts's
vol. 8, p. 214 Jer vi, 16, "Thus
he Lord, Stand ye in the ways,
and ask for the old paths, where
od way, and walk therein, and ye
id rest for your souls" "* These
Mr. C. had caused to be printed
l pieces of paste-board about the
visiting cards. To three females,
s of his church, Mr C had given
of these cards for distribution.
these females belonged to fam-
heads of which were members of
. Mr. Harris's society. The mo-
Mr. C. heard, that the card gave
he ceased distributing it. His
ect was, as he declares p. 77, to

On the preceding votes it will
be sufficient to remark, that the
1st and 2nd passed 20 to 3, and 19
to 4, the Moderator not voting in
any case unless his vote might
either make or prevent a decision. The 3rd passed, we think,
unanimously; and the 4th, 22 to
1. The dissenting member afterwards explained, so that it
appeared, that he did not mean
to vote in the negative.

On the 5th vote, the council
were much more equally divided than on any of the preceding,
though the exact number, who
voted on each side, cannot be
stated. It is certain, however,
that some, who voted in the affirmative, were convinced on reflection, that the vote was too
strongly expressed.

Mr. C. was a member of the
school committee of the town of
Dorchester, and acted as such
in using his influence to prevent
the exclusion of the Assembly's
Catechism from the schools.
His conduct, in this business,
had no peculiar relation to his
own parish.

The 6th vote passed, we think,
unanimously.

The following motion was
then submitted to the council:

"That in the opinion of this council,
the aggrieved brethren and the majority
of this parish, have just cause of complaint against the Rev Mr. Codman for
having neglected to exchange ministerial
labors with the ministers of the Boston
Association, generally, as presented in
the second article of the aggrieved brethren, and in the first* article of the committee of the parish"

*make known the opinion of Dr. Watt
in regard to the Assembly's Catechism,
especially in that town, where an attempt
was made to exclude the Assembly's Catechism by the introduction of Dr
Watts's.*

* The second article of the parish was
considered as included in the pre

This question gave rise to a long debate, which commenced on Tuesday afternoon and lasted, except during the necessary intermissions, till Wednesday evening. The discussion occupied about 13 or 15 hours. All the clerical members of the council, and four of the laymen, offered their opinions and their reasons, at considerable length; and some of them repeatedly. On putting the question, the council was found to be equally divided, the ministers and delegates from the churches selected by the parish committee voting in the affirmative, and the other part of the council in the negative. So the motion did not prevail. The above-cited proceedings, with a suitable introduction, and a closing exhortation to peace and moderation, were published on Thursday, as the result of the council.

The question respecting exchanges was considered by all parties as the only important question. It was repeatedly stated by the agents of Mr. Codman's opposers, during the public hearing, that if he would agree to exchange with the ministers of the Boston association generally, all other difficulties could be settled in five minutes. The council directed their principal attention, therefore, to the discussion and decision of this point. As this is a new subject to many, it will not be deemed uninteresting or improper to give an abstract of the arguments on each side, so far as they can now be ascertained. In doing this, it will be most convenient to represent the arguments as offered by the speakers on each side without any

further discriminations; in fact some topics were upon by one member, and by another.

It was urged in favor above-cited motion,

'That Mr. C. had for a time declined exchange the greater part of the m of the Boston Associati in such circumstances, neglect to exchange wit is tantamount to a refusal a refusal is a denial o ministerial character.

condemnation of a lar respectable body of m heard, a body of men ministerial and moral ch no person will be bold to call in question; a men entitled to particu gard from the stations they occupy, and the rep which they sustain. course of conduct as Mr pursued, must be consid having a tendency to inj character of these gentle impeach their fidelity, stigmatize them as h Though Mr. C. is adm have been sincere and co tious in his practice point, yet he may have b roneous and uncharita forming his opinions, and termining to act in acc with them. In the view who advocate this moti was so; and though his not of such a character a stroy his usefulness in places, it will render it i er for him to continue present pastoral relation, he should feel convince error, and enter upon liberal course of conduct

'It is not to be suppos

any minister, who should exchange with Mr. Codman, would enter upon controverted points, or preach in such a manner as to bring him or his opinions into discredit with his people. No man would be so indiscreet, or so unkind or uncharitable, as to do this.

'The interchange of ministerial labors tends to promote harmony, peace, and charity. It unites neighboring societies in bonds of affection. It causes the ministers, who exchange with each other, to feel a lively interest in each other's happiness and success in the ministry A refusal to commence an intercourse of this nature, unless supported by good reasons, is a violation of that charity, which ought to subsist between ministers of the same Gospel. If a minister is unworthy to be admitted into the pulpit of another minister, he is unworthy to preach. But while he continues worthy to preach,—while he is received and acknowledged by his brethren, and by the churches, as a faithful Christian bishop, it is highly improper to deny him that character, either directly, or implicitly.

'If a difference in regard to particular doctrines is allowed to interpose a separating wall between brethren, it is impossible to tell where the evil will stop. Scarcely any two ministers think alike on all passages of Scripture. Must all withhold communion with each other, because, in regard to some point or other, a difference of opinion exists? In almost every association of ministers, there is a considerable diversity of opinion. But this diversity is perfectly

compatible with mutual respect and affection.

'It is admitted, that the right of controlling his own exchanges belongs to Mr. Codman. The pulpit is to be under his direction, and his ministerial intercourse must be conducted according to his discretion. But he must exercise a wise and charitable discretion. He must not forget, that the people have rights as well as he;—rights which they will claim, and which ought to be regarded. If his sense of duty is such, that he cannot indulge his people in their wishes, in relation to this subject, he may be a very useful minister in some other place, where the same combination of circumstances does not exist.'

In opposition to the motion it was urged,

'That Mr. C has done nothing to bind himself, in relation to exchanges, any further than he is bound by the mere act of entering into the pastoral relation. He has made no contract with his people on the subject. He has made no promise to exchange. On the contrary, he declared before his settlement, what he has frequently and formally repeated since, that he could not pledge himself to exchange with any man, or body of men, whatever. This declaration he has never invalidated, or contradicted, by word or action. Nor has there been the least evidence, that he has pledged himself *not* to exchange with any man, or body of men, whatever. His duty, whenever and wherever he shall discover it, he has expressed himself ready and desirous to perform. What that duty will be, in certain future and imaginable circumstances, he has not ventured to foretel. All the facts in this case, which have any bearing on the subject, are few and plain. Mr. Codman has been settled about three years in Dorchester. During that time he has exchanged ministerial labors with a considerable number of neighboring ministers. For about two years, a part of his people have expressed a great desire that he should exchange with certain others. With this desire he has not complied. He has declared, however, that in his exchanges, as well as in all parts of his ministerial conduct, he shall be guided by a sense of duty, and shall comply with the wishes of his people so far as his duty will permit. He stands, therefore, in the same situation as every other minister, so far as his own engagements are concerned; and the question before this council is, whether they are called upon to interfere, and to establish a *compulsory system of exchanges.*

'As Mr. C. has entered into no express agreement on this subject, and as his declarations have been always guarded against furnishing an appearance, or a pretence, of such an agreement, it is further to be observed, that his letter on receiving an invitation to settle, and his repeated declarations since, have uniformly implied, that he would not consider himself as bound to any prescribed course of exchanges He wished to remain free to act according to his own opinions of duty, in this matter, and not to preclude himself, by any unnecesary engagement, from forming his

opinions with deliberat on the surest foundation

'Nor can it be said, entering the Boston As Mr. C. virtually engage change with the m There never has been a lar course of exchange body; much less *any co course.* A certain ge in this Association ha exchanged with the oth bers; and many of the r exchange with each ot seldom, if at all.*

'It may be proper he scribe an exchange. I an act necessary to com It is merely a supply of pit, occasionally suital proper all things conside in order to be either t proper, it should be voluntary on both sid should never bear the of constraint or com Though an exchange i mission of ministerial cl a refusal to exchange imply a denial of mi character. Such a refi be made for many reason have no relation to such

* Mr. Emerson in his hist first church in Boston, and w h ing the origin of this very a soci "Perhaps there is not a ph world, where the independene ual churches is more perfectl then in this metropolis and its Again, he says, "The indepe congregational churches in E been maintained from the begi perhaps their freedom will b served by keeping clear of *ente liances* It is very remarkal attempt should have been ma a member of this very associati into *entangling alliances* with members, and that such a should have received the warm from the most vehement declab vor of the independence of ch ministers.

ıere neglect to ex-
:h is all that has been
nst Mr. C. is not in
t degree disrespect-
clergyman, either in
ıis public or his pri-
.er. So far is this
the case, that mem-
ıe same association
ted to exchange with
'or twenty years, and
aintained an entire
each other. If an
proposed and declin-
on declining is un-
ation to assign a rea-
ıimply to be consid-
ː acts with sufficient
his own opinion, and
ıons may be perfect-
le with respect and
· all parties concern-
ıl members of the
ıociation, during a
of the last century,
publicly, and system-
ːclined exchanging
ːher; yet no one sup-
by so doing they
charge, or an im-
of ministerial char-
st each other. The
rs. Channing and
declined exchang-
ːodman; yet it is by
ecessary to suppose,
ıid so for improper
ːnt reasons, or that
l to acknowledge his
ːharacter.
e been any usage of
ːs in this country,
ırizes or requires a
course of exchanges?
ı the first settlement
ntry, to the present
ıolitary instance of
ːeding can be found.
compulsory course of
ı England? None.

far as we can find; nor was there
ever. In Scotland? None. In
the Presbyterian churches in
this country? None. Among the
consociated churches of Connecticut? None.

'In England we find instances,
numerous and decisive, to show
that clergymen of the established church decline exchanging,
or inviting each other into their
pulpits, whenever their sense of
duty requires such a measure.
This is done without the slightest apprehension of the possibility of an ecclesiastical censure,
so far as can be ascertained by
attending to the instances which
come to our knowledge. Yet
the clergymen of that church
are obliged to give their assent
to the same creed and the same
plan of church government, before they can be inducted into
office. The late amiable and
highly revered Mr. Newton systematically declined introducing
into his pulpit certain clergymen
of the same establishment with
himself, though he was always
ready to interchange the offices
of hospitality and social intercourse with them. No man, who
knows his character, can suppose him peculiarly deficient in
kindness and charity.

'There being no usage in this
country which requires Mr. C.
to exchange with all neighboring clergymen, and there being
nothing in the nature of the case
which requires it, we infer, That
*where there is no law there is no
transgression.* If Mr. C. is to
be censured, it must be for some
offence that he has committed.
If this vote passes, and Mr. C.
refuses to succumb to it, and to
▇▇▇▇▇▇▇ has been all along
▇▇▇▇▇ ▇e is to receive ▇

scribe the course of duty to
their ministers

'7. It is not desirable, on any
account whatever, that there
should be an extensive, binding,
burdensome system of ministerial exchanges A pastor has
the charge of his *own* people.
For *their* souls he must watch,
as one who is to give an account
to the Lord Jesus Christ, at the
day of his appearing. Some
ministers think it useful to exchange frequently; others very
seldom. One of the distinguished ministers of the Presbyterian
churches in this country has declared, that for a considerable
number of years he had exchanged but twice Those, who
are acquainted with this gentleman, know that he is not deficient in love and respect for his
brethren. His own view of
ministerial duty, and his peculiar attachment to his own people,
led him to pursue the course
which has been mentioned;
while he was perfectly willing
that others should pursue a different course, according to their
own judgment.

'8. A minister may have many good reasons for declining to
exchange with a neighboring
minister, which reasons he would
not be justified in assigning to
the public. To say that he shall
exchange, or assign his reasons,
would be reducing him to a situation in which he could not, as
the case might be, obey the
plainest commands of the New
Testament. He might, for instance, have the fullest evidence,
that a neighboring minister is a
rank infidel. This is not an imaginary case. It has actually occurred. Yet he might not be
able to bring the evidence be-

fore the public. To take a more
common case. He might have
the fullest conviction, that a
neighboring minister preaches
doctrines ruinous to the souls
of men;—doctrines which have
nothing of Christianity in them;
—doctrines which are utterly
subversive of the Gospel Yet
the case might be such, as that
no advantage would accrue from
his making a public declaration
of this conviction. It might be his
duty to remain in silence, and
to preach the truth to his own
people. He might have a perfect conviction, that the levity,
or the anti-ministerial character,
or the immoral character, of a
neighboring minister ought to
exclude him from every pulpit.
Yet it might be improper for
him to bring forward any public
accusations.

'But it is said, that every minister is to be supposed a faithful evangelical minister, till he
is regularly deposed. In some
places this argument would have
weight. It might not be applicable to exchanges; but it would
be entitled to very respectful
consideration. In the case of
Mr. Codman, the use of such
an argument certainly borders
on the ridiculous. Supposing,
for the sake of example, that
Mr. C. had the most undoubted
evidence, that any one of the
members of the Boston Association was a decided enemy of
the Gospel. How is he to procure this minister's deposition?
Is it not perfectly notorious,
that many ministers of that association would look with ineffable scorn upon an attempt, by
a person not a member of their
own church, to bring them to
trial for error in doctrine or

Is it not altogether
iat their own church-
lismiss with indigna-
ge against their min-
eferred by Mr. Cod-
iot the principal proof
i is the most liberal
: world, that the min-
hurches are perfectly
it of all mankind, and
o no human tribunal?
l it be proved, that a
' opinion, on some of
mportant doctrines of
l, is not fundamental,
ald be of very per-
idency that different
iuld be preached from
ulpit. Such a course
inish the regard for
: would bring the Bi-
intempt.
id, that no judicious
controvert Mr. Cod-
ines from his pulpit.
served, that the grand
r of *indiscriminate* ex-
lleged by Mr. Cod-
sers, is, that they want
at can be said *on all*
v this will be accom-
' hearing men, who
hemselves bound to
no side, can hardly be
.
id, that charity, lib-
l catholicism, require
nce with the wishes
ih. Let us not be de-
nere sounds. There
ers of this council,
ieard all the changes
rung on the delight-
charity and candor,
ie of thirty five years.
similar words can be
ry pleasant tune; but
is nothing more than
he words charity and

candor prove just as much in favor of the religious character of
those who use them most, as
the words liberty and equality prove in favor of the political
character of those who use them
most.

'But how does it appear, that
Mr. C.'s conduct has been either uncharitable, illiberal, or un-
catholic?

'What is charity? In the supremely beautiful delineation of
this greatest of Christian virtues,
in 1 Cor. xiii, we are told, that
charity *rejoiceth in the truth*.
This grand characteristic of
charity is peculiarly exemplified by a faithful minister. He is
set for a witness and defender
of the *truth*. He is to preach
the *truth*. By preaching the
truth he is to be the instrument
of producing that mighty transformation of the human character,
which must take place be-
fore any man can see the kingdom of heaven But charity
does not judge without evidence;
she does not decide against the
highest evidence, the express
declarations of the word of God;
she does not trust to mere professions. Charity laments over
the sins and errors of men; but
she does not declare them not to
be sins and errors.

'What is liberality? Not every
thing which assumes that title.
The truly liberal man never enlists under the banners of a party. Though he may think and
believe with many others, he
still thinks and believes for himself. He will put the most favorable construction on the
words and actions of others.
He will
fender

not persecute and punish a man, for happening to be, in his estimation, less liberal than himself.

'Catholicism is principally distinguished from bigotry, by a willing admission of what is good though found in an unexpected quarter, and mixed with much infirmity. It will prompt its possessor to unite with all men, so far as may be practicable, in the promotion of every good work; and where difference of opinion is inevitable, it will differ in good temper and with good will; and with as little noise and controversy as possible.

'In what manner does the clergyman, who neglects to exchange with the ministers of the Boston Association, prove himself to be defective in charity, liberality, or catholicism? He proceeds, from Sabbath to Sabbath, and preaches himself, or supplies his pulpit in some other way, according to his own sense of duty. How can it be proved, that this springs from narrow views? from an uncharitable temper, or a bigoted mind? No such thing has been proved in this case. How can it be proved, in any given case, that the minister has judged incorrectly? He may have reasons, which, in the view, of every man, would completely justify him. How is this council to be assured, that Mr. C. has not such reasons? But they ought to be assured before they proceed to censure him.

'We are not to forget, that Mr. C. has been a successful minister in this place. God has prospered him. His church manifest a strong attachment to him; an attachment highly honorable to him and to themselves. He has made great sacrifices of time, of property, and of quiet, for the Gospel. During this long trial his character has appeared to great advantage. There probably is not a clergyman present, against whom a more formidable list of imprudences could not be arrayed and supported, than has been sustained against Mr. Codman.*

'It seems to be a curious fact that the warmest declaimers in favor of charity, and the right of *private judgment*, are unwilling to have Mr. C. decide for himself, as to the duties *which the Lord Jesus Christ has imposed upon him*, as a minister of the Gospel;—that the champions of liberality are clear and strong in the opinion, that Mr. C. should be *compelled* to be as liberal as themselves, in regard to exchanges, under the penalty of ejection from his parish;—and that a course of rigid conformity to the views of a party, a regular, authoritative, compulsory course of exchanges; (a course which has never been attempted, so far as we can ascertain, by any rigid church es-

* While on this part of the subject, the delegate of the church in Medfield, the pastor of which was Moderator, expressed the sentiment of the text in nearly the following words:

"For my part, Mr. Moderator, I know not where the minister is to be found, whose character would appear to greater advantage, than Mr. Codman's has appeared, during the whole of the public investigation. I am not willing to admit, that any man has a higher respect for his minister than I have for mine; or a more entire confidence in his character. Yet I think it highly probable, that a zealous, persevering opposition to my minister, would enable his opposers to produce more instances of what some persons would call imprudence than have been produced against Mr. Codman."

iment on earth;)—that such
se should be attempted in
on, which proclaims itself
the most liberal, enlight-
and catholic in the world.
is indeed a curious and
rful fact.

s to be remembered, how-
that it is possible for men
warm and violent in the
of moderation; reproachful
just under the banners of
lity; malignant and cruel in
earts, while the sounds of
y and catholicism are issu-
rom their lips. These
are to be remembered,
r the sake of applying
in this case, any further
be on our guard against
sions, which are unsup-
l by reason or Scripture.

this council has no proof
it, that Mr. C. has done
in regard to his exchang-
has no authority to censure
r conduct, which may have
ltogether proper and com-
ible, or to say, that the par-

ish has just cause of complaint
against him.'

It appeared unhappy, that the
council should have been equally
divided on the only important
question that came before it.
We say the only important question; for though some of the
charges of the parish appear formidable on paper, it was evident
that no great reliance was placed
on them by the complainants.
And Mr. Dexter declared, in
their name, as has been already
stated, that if the question of exchanges could be terminated, all
the other charges of the parish
could be settled in five minutes.
Though the council was not so
happy as to decide the controversy, the discussions were carried on, in general, with good
temper, and apparent good will;
and when the council was dissolved, the members separated
with many expressions of tenderness and respect.

(To be continued.)

RELIGIOUS INTELLIGENCE.

MEETING OF THE MASSACHUSETTS MISSIONARY SOCIETY.

iety held its fifteenth annual meet-
Boston, on the 24th and 25th days
y last. The meeting was opened
ging an appropriate psalm, after
the Rev. Dr. Spring, in the ab-
of the President, offered a prayer.
Society then attended to the fol-

REPORT OF THE TRUSTEES.

ren,

HE season has again returned, at
is made the duty of the Trustee,
t to you their doings, and such in-
as may be interesting and useful,
l to the great object for which we
ia id

N.

At the last anniversary, such information was communicated, as had then been
received from Messrs. Schermerhorn and
Mills, who, under the patronage, partly of
this Society and partly of other Societies,
were engaged in a missionary tour in the
western and southern parts of our country. But they had not then returned; no
was the Board then in possession of a full
account of their mission. As general intelligence for the use of missionary soci-
ties was a great object of that mission, an
as the two missionaries were remarkabl
industrious in collecting intelligence; it
thought right to report a brief summary
what, since their return, they have largel
communicated, as the result of their obse-
vations and inquiries. The summary is as
follows.

In the state of PENNSYLVANIA, west
the Alleginy mountains, there are about

200,000 inhabitants; 101 Presbyterian*
churches, and 57 ministers; two Methodist circuits, in which are employed 12 itinerant preachers; very few, if any Baptists;
a few Halcyons; and a society of Germans,
who have all things in common, are remarkable for industry, sobriety and order,
and have a preacher, zealous in directing
their attention to divine things. In this
district, there are two small colleges,
whose pious instructors make it a very particular object to prepare young men for
the ministry; but the means of general education are scanty. The Synod of Pittsburg, composed of Presbyteries partly
within this district and partly within the
adjoining state of Ohio, acts as a Missionary Society; and expends annually,
about one thousand dollars for missionary
objects, a considerable part of which sum
has been applied for the benefit of the Wy-
andot Indians. The churches within the
limits of this Synod, are represented as
having been remarkably blessed with effusions of the Holy Spirit, and as being in a
very prosperous state; but many thousands
around them are unsupplied with the stated means of religion, and are famishing for
the word of life.

In the state of OHIO, containing a population of more than 330,000, there are 78
Presbyterian or Congregational churches,
and 49 ministers; between 20 and 30 Methodist preachers, employed in different circuits; 10 or 12 Baptist societies; several
societies of Friends or Quakers; considerable numbers of a sect called New Lights;
a few Halcyons, a few Swedenburghers,
and too many Universalists and Deists.
The district of this state called New Connecticut, the inhabitants of which are in
great part from the states of Connecticut
and Massachusetts, has received very particular attention from the Connecticut Missionary Society, has been recently favored
with special divine influences, and, on the
whole, presents a comparatively pleasing
and hopeful aspect. In some other parts
of the state some attention is paid to religious institutions, and a few flourishing
churches are established; but in the state
at large the means of religion are but scantily supplied and lightly esteemed, and the
apparent consequences are such as might
reasonably be expected. The Sabbath is
awfully disregarded, gross ignorance of divine things is general, and great laxity of
morals prevails.—At Marietta, Messrs.
Schermerhorn and Mills succeeded in ob-

taining the establishment of a Bi[...]
ety, which received the suppor[...]
pious of different denominations[...]
which three ministers were appo[...]
ride through the state to preac[...]
subject, shewing the importance o[...]
institution, and soliciting subscripti[...]
donations.

In the state of VIRGINIA con[...]
population of almost a million, t[...]
only about 70 churches, Presby[...]
Congregational, and about 40 mini[...]
what is called Old Virginia, or th[...]
the state from the sea board ba[...]
Blue Ridge, the Episcopal churc[...]
formerly held a complete ascenda[...]
was well endowed, is now in a do[...]
condition. To about one hundred[...]
pal societies, which have still so[...]
ence, the number of clergymen is[...]
ed at less than thirty. The socie[...]
for a considerable time been d[...]
and the houses decaying; and th[...]
at large, comprising nearly three f[...]
the whole population of the stat[...]
traversed by itinerant Methodists[...]
tists, yet exhibits, in a religious re[...]
extensive and dreary waste.—Th[...]
between the Blue Ridge and the [...]
mountains presents a different [...]
With scarcely a seventh part of th[...]
population of the state, it cont[...]
about one half of the total numbe[...]
Presbyterian or Congregational [...]
and ministers; and these churches[...]
to be in a more flourishing condit[...]
any elsewhere to be found in the S[...]
States.—In the remaining distric[...]
prising the counties west of the A[...]
there are but twelve Presbyterian[...]
es and three ministers; but the [...]
ists and Baptists are considerabl[...]
ous.—In this ancient and great sta[...]
is a most melancholy famine of the[...]
the Lord.

KENTUCKY, with a population [...]
than four hundred thousand, has [...]
byterian churches, and 40 minis[...]
Methodist circuits, in which about[...]
itinerant preachers are employ[...]
Baptist societies of different dese[...]
and 148 preachers; two Episcop: l[...]
es; several societies of New Light[...]
siderable number of Roman Cath[...]
eties; some Shakers, Dunkers, a[...]
versalists; and many Infidels. Of[...]
tists one entire Association, comp[...]
churches, is Arian or Socinian. [...]
n an Catholics have a Bish p, a[...]
a Nunnery, several Chap. ls in [...]
counties, and are said to be in[...]
The Infidels, though less open [...]
than formerly, are nevertheless a[...]
1812 no less than three infidel pul[...]
issued from the press in Lexingto[...]
of one of which, elegantly bound,[...]

---

* *Under this name are included, not on-
ly the Presbyterians connected with the
General Assembly, but also those of the
Associate Reformed and of the Associate
Synod, Covenanters, and Congregation-
alists.*

:ach member of the Legislature.
ae there are very few schools,
1 said, in great part, to a preva-
it influence, unfriendly to learn-
ma:s of the people, extremely
are either entirely regardless of
r lamentably blown about by ev-
af doctrine. The Sabbath re-
f little religious regard; and in-
e, profanity, gambling and lewd-
revalent vices.
see, with more than 260,000 in-
has 79 Presbyterian churches,
nisters; 19 itinerant Methodist
employed in several circuits;
t churches, and 74 preache. s, a
.ights, and some of various other
ious. The Presbyterian inter-
asing. In East Tennessee, the
ges, one at Knoxville and the
reen County, are great blessings.
er, (of which the Rev. Charles
D. is President,) there were
dents preparing for the ministry,
missionaries were there. In this
s, there has recently been estab-
ociety, Missionary, Tract, and
only Missionary Society, ex-
: Synod of Pittsburg, west of the
In relation to this Society, the
alent Coffin, in a letter to Mr.
iorn, says, "For our Society
more members than means, and
nd than our missionaries can oe-
would anticipate great good were
chusetts Missionary Society to
attention to this state. I was
sisted to organize" that Society;
rejo'ce in its increase, and have
ope they will try to aid us to the
their power."—In West Ten-
o Rev "Mr. Blackburn is of
at many churches might be or,
f there were a proper person
in the business; and regrets that
s so much occupied with his
t he has no leisure to devote to
It might greatly promote reme missionary body would em-
nan in their service, permitting
ie same time, to supply his own
—In this state at large, the pre-
s are the same as in the state of
nor is the general state of soci-
ifferent.

MISSISSIPPI TERRITORY, con-
int 58.000 inhabitants, there are
rian churches, 4 ministers; 9
Methodist preachers; 27 Bap-
ies, and 13 preachers. "The
ciety in this Territory is deplor-
l scarcely see a man ride with-
tol, or walk without a dagger
om It is believed that more
lood is shed in this Territory
.isions, in one year, than in all

the Middle and Eastern States, in ten
years." At Natchez, in this Territory,
Messrs. Schermerhorn and Mills procured a Bible Society to be established under
favorable auspices.

The INDIANA TERRITORY, with about
25,000 inhabitants, has one Presbyterian church and minister; five itinerant
Methodist preachers; 20 Baptist churches, and 14 preachers; six New Light
preachers, and a few Shakers.

In the ILLINOIS TERRITORY, containing about 13,000 inhabitants, there are five
or six Methodist preachers in several
circuits, and about six hundred members
of the Methodist connexion, and five
Baptist churches containing about 120
members.

In the whole great extent of country,
thus surveyed, there are not two thirds
as many ministers, Presbyterian or Congregational, as there are in Massachusetts Proper; but those ministers are generally of respectable attainments in knowledge, of strictly evangelical sentiments,
and of good reputation for piety, and
regular devotedness to their work. In
most of those parts, the Methodists and
Baptists are the prevailing denominations.
The sentiments of the Methodists, and
their general character are much the
same there as in other parts of our country. The Baptists in the western States
and Territories are in their sentiments
extremely various. The better informed
are said to be Calvinistic; but a very considerable proportion are either Antino-
mian or Arminian, and not a few are
Arian or Socinian. Some of them have a
religious regard to the Sabbath; but by
the greater part the sacredness of that
holy day is openly denied. Their preachers are not only unlearned, but they hold
learning in disesteem and contempt.
While they decry human knowledge,
they pretend to divine inspiration. They
pay great attention to dreams and visions,
mysterious impulses and impressions;
and of these the relations and experiences, upon which members are admitted
to their communion, in no small part
consist. The New Lights, of whom mention has been made, are a sect which
sprung up in Kentucky in 1803. Believing that the extraordinary work then
prevailing was the commencement of the
millennium, and that all mystery and obscurity in religion was then to be done
away; they gave license to their heated
imaginations, and proceeded to explain
the Scriptures, according to what they
called reason; and it is a remarkable fact,
that a wild fanaticism in those western regions conducted its votaries to the denial
of the same doctrines, and to the adoption
of nearly the same opinions, as the vaunt-

ed criticism and liberality of other parts of Christendom have done. This sect, which for a while was numerous, is now decreasing. The Halcyons of the West are a sort of mystics, who set out with the avowed design of abolishing all distinction of religious denominations, and uniting all professed Christians in one communion, and under one name. They renounce all creeds, confessions, and catechisms; and profess to receive the Holy Scriptures, as a divine help, handed down from heaven, to aid their reason in forming just ideas of the divine character and of divine things. But say they, "We receive not the Holy Scriptures as the foundation of our faith in religion; for we conceive that other foundation can never be laid, equal to that foundation stone, which was laid before Joshua, (of which the Scriptures clearly speak,) whereon where seven eyes, which we conceive to be the seven communicable attributes of God."[*] They hold that "the office of Christ on earth was to explain the eternal laws of religion to man;" they practise baptism indifferently by sprinkling or immersion; and decline matrimony, under pretence of choosing spiritual mates. This sect is also on the decrease.

On the whole, throughout the States and territories reviewed, there is a deplorable want of the preached Gospel and of the stated and regular administration of divine ordinances; a deplorable want, indeed, of all the means of good religious instruction; (for but a small part of the people possess the Bible:) and therefore a loud and affecting call for the benevolent aid of Missionary and Bible Societies. The General Assembly of the Presbyterian Church has sent a few missionaries, from time to time, into these destitute regions, and the attention of the Philadelphia, New York, and Connecticut Bible Societies has been turned towards them; but unless much greater exertions shall be made, than have yet been made, by the pious and the liberal, it will be long before any adequate supply, either of ministers or of Bibles, will be furnished to them.

But regions of still deeper and more deplorable darkness and corruption are now to come under review; regions but lately annexed to the United States.

In the district of country, west of the Mississippi, called the Missouri Territory, containing a scattered population of about 21,000, there are 445 members of Methodist Societies, among whom six itinerant preachers are employed; and 130 members of Baptist churches, with no settled preachers. It is estimated that about two fifths of the inhabitants are Americans, and the rest French; and

* *II Epist No 44 and 45, Lex. 1803.*

both the one and the other are in a state of extreme ignorance, and the greater part as visibly without God in the world as heathens. A Mr. Stephen Hampstead of St. Louis, the principal place in this Territory, who was formerly of Connecticut, in a letter to our missionaries, say, "I believe the formation of a Bible and Tract Society, would be very useful be I have distributed a few tracts that brought with me; and they were received with thankfulness, and I trust have done good. If any of the Societies in New England will send on some Bibles and Tracts to my charge, I will distribute them among the poor and needy, who are famishing for the word of life. In my interviews with the heads of families and officers of government, they have expressed a strong desire to have a minister of education, piety, morals, and talents settled at St. Louis, and that they would contribute liberally and continually to his support."

The state of Louisiana has a population of about 77,000 free people, and about 35,000 slaves. Of the free people it is estimated that about one fifth are Americans. "The settlements east of lakes Mauripas and Bouchatrain to Pearl river are few and scattering, but chiefly American. The settlements on the Mississippi are very flourishing from Point Coupee to some distance below New Orleans; and on both sides of the river they present almost a continued village. The inhabitants of the upper part of the settlements are from Canada; of the middle, Germans; and of the lower part, French and Spanish from Europe. All speak the same language, and are similar in habits, manners and religion. In the settlements on the Gulph, west of the Mississippi, the people are Spanish, French, and American. On Red River they are principally French, and in the Washita American. The state of society in this country is very deplorable. The people are entirely ignorant of divine things, and have been taught only to attend mass and count their beads. They are without schools, and of the French inhabitants not one in ten can read. Their whole business seems to be to make the most they can of their plantations, and to get gain. They are not intemperate in drinking, but continence is with them no virtue. The Sabbath to them is a high holiday, and on it is committed perhaps more actual sin, than during the whole week beside. Dancing, gambling, parties of pleasure, theatrical amusements, dining parties, &c. are the common business of the day, after mass in the morning. In the whole state there is not one Protestant church, unless it be a small one of Baptists, about to be organized at Appelousas. The Methodists have

Red River and Washita,
igly unpopular. The re-
s entirely Roman Catho-
of this order, however,
s; perhaps fifteen. The
· or five priests reside in
bishop de Bury I believe
iety; and I know that he
aded state of their church
mourns over the deprav-
ess of the place in which
· Bishop and Father An-
establishment of the Lou-
siety, which I trust will
id lasting blessing to the

" says Mr. Mills, "is con-
i of character and of ex-
ion; he came from Balti-
en in New Orleans but a
e gave it as his opinion,
iot at this time twelve Bi-
ty of New Orleans. He
ty as being the most des-
place he had ever been
had been in France, and
of ascertaining the mor-
in the cities of that king-

. Bible Society was estab-
rleans by the exertions of
, while they were there.
was then in session, and
luence, not in the city on-
te at large, became mem-
siderable attention was ex-
ect, and many people be-
i inquire for the Bible.
Bible Society was formed,
s, "I was at the store of
this morning, and during
e, five or six French peo-
m inquiring for Bibles in
Some of them belonged
I some to the country."
wards he writes. ' Mr.
med me this evening that
ple called on him for Bi-
ench Catholics. This is
derful day for New Or-
rkhouse told me that if he
they would all be disposed

Mr. Dow has received,
, twenty or thirty Eng-
n the British and Foreign
'hese were all distributed.
· stay of about three
Orleans, our missionaries
n as they had oppo'tunity.
iuth Mr. Mills says; "In
congregation was numer-
c; perhaps 200 attended.
erhorn preached. It was
ho had lived in the city a

considerable time, they never saw so full
a meeting before. After sermon, a collection of 84 dollars was made for the missionaries."—Mr. Schermerhorn had an invitation, a pretty pressing one, it would
seem, to remain at New Orleans, and settle in the ministry there. In relation to
this he says, "I regretted it could not be
so; for I believe the Lord has much people in that city; that it is an ample field
for usefulness, and the most important situation in the western country."

"In West Florida," says Mr. Mills,
"the people are extremely ignorant. The
attention of some of them has been lately
called to religious subjects. Numbers of
them lose no time in soliciting for a Bible,
whenever a prospect, that they may be
supplied is presented, which is very rare.
There are some families in this part of our
country, who never saw a Bible, nor heard
of Jesus Christ; and some there are,
hopefully pious, who cannot obtain a Bible or even a Testament. The people to
whom I now refer speak the English language."

The view now given of these extensive,
dark, and famishing regions of our country, can hardly fail deeply to affect the
hearts of the friends of the Redeemer, and
of those for whom he died; and if it have
the effect to wake up the members of this
Society and others to more earnest prayer
and exertion for the imparting of the blessings of the Gospel to such as are perishing
for want of them, the design of presenting
it will be answered.—From this distant
excursion we return to things nearer
home. (*To be continued.*)

LETTER FROM MR. WILBERFORCE.

THE following paragraphs are extracted
from a letter lately received by the Rev.
Dr. Morse from the Hon. William Wilberforce, Esq. a gentleman whose excellent character and admirable exertions
for the promotion of human happiness,
are familiarly known in this country. Dr.
Morse, in the letter to which the following is an answer, had lamented the existing war between Great Britain and the
United States, particularly as it impedes
the efforts of Christians in both countries
for the diffusion of Christianity.

"*N. London,** *March* 17, 1814.
"My dear Sir,
I VERY lately received from your son
your obliging and, to me, I can truly say,
most interesting letter, dated, I think, in
Nov. last. I put it yesterday into Mr
Henry Thornton's hands, and therefore
I am not able to name its date. In the

* *North London, we presume*

very few lines with which your son accompanied it, he was so kind as to offer to take charge of any answer which I might transmit to him for you; but till this moment, when I was casting my eye on it in order to learn his address that I might direct a note I had written to invite him to Kensington Gore, (my residence,) I did not observe that he said a letter must be sent to him, early in this week in order to be forwarded. I am sorry to say, that this is Thursday. Still, I *may be* in time; and I am so very unwilling to lose this opportunity of exchanging, *from the heart,* your *peaceful* salutation, that I instantly lay aside some very pressing business, in which I was engaged, for the purpose of scribbling a brief and hasty reply to your most welcome epistle.

"The wise man, or rather the Wisdom of Revelation, has compared "good news from a far country" to the gratification of the most importunate of our bodily wants and appetites; and surely this news is justly more grateful, when it conveys the the accents of peace and love from a country, once a land, literally as well as figuratively, of brethren, but since rendered not only strange but hostile; and when those accents are strictly in unison with the feelings of the person to whom they are addressed, and, as notes in unison are wont to do, call forth responsive tones of kindred harmony. Indeed, my dear Sir, I have scarcely been able to confine myself to metaphorical language, while I have been writing the above sentence. We do not lament the death of a wife, or a child in couplets, but in broken and rude sentences; and I have with difficulty restrained my pen from more simple expressions of unaffected grief on account of this sad war, in which our two countries are engaged."

"It is balm to my wounded feelings to indulge, as I justly may, the reflection, that these feelings of mine are by no means peculiar to myself, but that they are those of almost all good men among us; and surely this consideration may both lead us to hope, that the war will not be of much longer duration, and also that, when peace shall once more be restored, it will be peace indeed, and the two countries will not be likely again to suffer themselves to be drawn into a rupture. But I must turn to other topics, and hasten to a conclusion of my hurried scrawl; for by keeping it beyond to-day, I may lose altogether the opportunity of conveying it to you.

"It rejoices my heart to find, that the friends of religion, on your side of the Atlantic, are interested for the benighted millions of our Indian empire. I will take the liberty of sending you a copy publication of two of my speeches together,) on that subject. The tian Observer's kind partiality my efforts on that occasion so that, were reputation my object, have abstained from printing my But they contained some passa tracted from the ponderous vo East India Documents laid on the the House of Commons, during gress of the measure,) which me decisive on the controverted the moral character of the Hind therefore, as the only way of pro the diffusion of these, I consent publication. On consideration I you four copies, as you may be able to circulate them among ligious friends and connexions parts of America."

"Farewell, my dear Sir. I r think, that amid war and tu sources of peace and happines only true sources,) are multiplyin number and exuberance of their streams, in both our countries. T yet still growing success of the ciety, (the British and Foreign I mean,)—the increased yet still ing prevalence of the missionary the advanced and the continually ing progress of education amon and even the aged, as well as am dren, with various other particula I could specify — above all, creased and increasing number and truly enlightened and ferve ters of our Church Establishmen as the success and growing chari rious classes of Dissenters;— quite warm my heart, and fill hope, as well as, I trust, with It is with difficulty, that I fore to conclude with begging you to re me and my wife, and dear childre prayers, and assuring you, that I real esteem and regard, my dear
    Yours very sincerely,
        W. WILBERF

DONATIONS FOR THE SU OF FOREIGN MISSION TRANSLATIONS.

May 23, 1814. From the For sionary Society in Salem and the by Mr. John Jenks, the Treasu
  Contribution at the annual meeting, $76 5
  Donations to the Society by a friend, by the hand of the Rev. Mr. Walker,   50 0

      Carried forward $126

Irought forward 126 33
u by a member 5 00
t of annual sub-
aid in, 140 00—271 33
m Mrs. Mary Beattie,
roman, communicated
eath-bed, by the Rev.
, 8 00
ie Female Cent Society
ster, by the Rev. Dr.
25 86
Mrs. Mary Green, by
Paul Litchfield, of Car-
1 00
re children in S. Read-
e tra slations, 41
dividuals in Hopkinton,
r. Nathaniel Howe, 10 42
m a pious young woman,
ated on her death-bed,
temas Woodward, 1 00
males in Sandwich, half
and half to translations,
v. Jonathan Burr, 5 12
Ira. Eunice Kingsbury,
gham, by Mr. N. Willis, 80
female friend, by the
a Cleaveland, for the
a, 1 00
two young ladies in
85 each, for the trans-
the Rev. Dr. Emmons, 10 00
on the following sources,
. W. Gallaudet; viz.
of missions in
parish, Stam-
.) by the Rev.
faher, 8 50
d to missions in
ry, 3 00
l to missions by
. B. Gleason,
5 00
muel Whiting, of
1 00
ladies in Windsor
rong, 5 57—23 07
i sincere friend to the
y the Rev Eli Smith, 10 00
m the Auxiliary For-
on Society of Franklin
y Jerom Ripley, Esq.
irer, 200 00
r. Solomon Goodell, of
Ver) by the Rev. Dr.
o the permanent fund,
ed to the diffusion of a
of the Holy Scriptures
t, 198 00
he Rev. Elipha-
1, of Woodstock,
the Rev. Dr. Ly-
rds the perma-
40 00

Brought forward $40 00 $766 01
From Dea. Edward Walk-
er, of Wardsborough,
(Ver.) for do. 2 00
From Mrs. Prudence
Clark, of do. for do. 1 00
From a friend of missions
of do. for do. 50—13 50
31. From the Female Cent So-
ciety in Winchendon, remitted
by Mrs Sara: Pilsbury, the
Treasurer, by the hand of Samuel
Prentiss, Esq. (half for missions
and half for translations,) 43 44
From Miss Lucy Hale of Win-
chendon, by the same hand, 1 00
June 2. From the Rev. Jona-
than Cogswell and another sub-
scriber to the Foreign Mission So-
ciety in Saco, 6 00
From the Cent Society in Hard-
wick, remitted by Mrs. Sarah
Holt, 5 84
From the Female Cent
Society in . Montpelier,
(Ver.) by the Rev. Chester
Wright, 50 00
From an individual in
Randolph, (Ver.) by the
same hand, 1 00—51 00
3. From the Female Heathen's
Friend Society in New Bedford,
half to missions and half to trans-
lations, 30 45
From a branch of the same So-
ciety in Fair Haven, 16 00
From the Female Cent
Society in Harford, (Penn.)
by Mr. Henry Hudson, 12 12
From the Middlesex Aux-
iliary Foreign Mission So-
ciety, 20 00
From a friend of Foreign
Missions, 20 00—52 12
From Mrs. Orange Osgood, by
the Rev. Jonathan Osgood, of
Gardner, Mass. towards the translations, 5 00
4. From a Society in Cummington, toward the translations, 82 00
6. From Mr. Amasa Frissell, of
Peru, Mass. by John Leland, jun.
Esq. 5 00
7. From the Female Religious
Society in Braintree, by the Rev.
R. S. Storrs. 18 90
From individuals in Braintree,
by the Rev. R. S. Storrs, 10 00
18 From the Foreign Mission
Society of Bath and the Vicinity by
Mr. Jonathan Hyde, the Treasurer, 94 00
22. From a female friend of
missions, by Mr. N. Lord, 1 00

Brought forward $1241 96
From Miss E. M of Goshen,
Mass. by Mr. Horatio Bardwell,   5 00
  24. From Mr Isaac Porter, of
Westfield, Mass. by the Rev.
Isaac Knapp,   3 00
  27. From a female friend of
missions, by Mrs. Hardy,   5 00
From the Foreign Mission Soci-
ety of North Yarmouth and the
Vicinity, by the Hon. Ammi R.
Mitchell, Esq. the Treasurer,   60 00
From the Aiding Foreign Mis-
sion Society in Plympton, by the
Rev. Elijah Dexter, the Treas-
urer,   18 97
From the Plympton Branch of
the Heathen's Friend Society, by
Mrs. Mary Dexter, the Treas-
urer,   9 50
     $1,340 73

N. B. The following letter was omitted
last month.

      "F——. *April,* 1814.
  "Dear Sir,
  I TRANSMIT you the trifling sum of five
dollars, in support of the Gospel of Christ,
among the poor heathen of India. I would
leave it at the discretion of the Society,
whether to devote it to the purpose of
translating the Holy Scriptures, or of
supporting faithful missionaries in the
ends of the earth.

  "This is the first donation I have ever
made for the promotion of the religion of
Jesus, our dear Redeemer; but, with his
blessing, I shall strive to bestow as much
every quarter; confident that in the times
of revolution and peril, this is the only
fund, where the stock of the Christian can
be safely lodged.
          CHRISTOPHILOS.
  The Treasurer of the Board of Commissioners for Foreign Missions."

MEMOIRS OF MRS. NEWELL.

TO THE PUBLIC.

As there have been some mistaken reports, respecting the profits arising from
the sale of Mrs. Newell's Memoirs, it
may not be improper to make the following statement of facts.

For the labor of preparing the Memoirs for the press, the Compiler received,
as the avails of the first edition, nearly *fifty
dollars,* beside what was sufficient to pay
several small sums to several persons,
who had assisted him as transcribers.

Early in May, the Compiler committed the work and whatever interest he

had in it, in trust, to the Rev.
and Jeremiah Evarts, Esq. for
tage of the Foreign Mission 1
ion; leaving it entirely to thei
whether he ought to receiv
in addition or not. They dec
certain additional sum ought 1
which would increase his comp
one hundred dollars in the w
Compiler has no pecuniary in
work, and never expects any
it, except what is stated above

OBITUARY.

DIED, in France, of his wounds
ESTIAN, a prisoner to the allie
  In England, Maj. Gen Sir J
LAS, the defender of Acre in P
  Also, Capt. JOHN STOCKMAN
manded the Thunderer, 74, i
of Trafalgar
  In the state of New York, I
LEN, of U. S. army, shot by
whom he was attempting to e
his duty.
  At Portsmouth, N. H. the 1
THAN WARNER, aged 88, and
Mrs. *Sherburne,* relict of B
burne, Esq. aged 95.
  At Burlington, Mass. Mrs
JONES, relict of the Rev. *The*
formerly minister of th't place
  At Boston, on the 13th ult.
ROBERT TREAT PAINE, Esq
He was one of the signers of
ation of Independence, had be
of the Supreme Judicial Court
chusetts, and sustained many
portant offices.
  At Courtlandt, (N Y)
PIERRE VAN COURTLANDT,
He had been a member of Co
Lieut Governor of the state of
  In London, the Rev WILLIA
a member of the Royal Acad
celebrated painter.

TO CORRESPONDE

WE have on our files man
which are necessarily deferre
gret this necessity, particular
to several obituary notices, and
of the Benevolent Society in Yu

The remaining part of the *Re*
Trustees of the Massachuseta
ry Society will appear next mo
are compelled to divide this vah
ment much against our inclina
pecuniary accounts of the S
also be found in our next numbe

T̲H̲E̲

PANOPLIST,

AND

SSIONARY MAGAZINE.

JULY, 1814.   VOL. X.

REVIEW.

·*view of the Dorches-*
Controversy.

ded from p. 281.)

·se of this review, the
been brought to the
of the first council.
every reflecting per-
t, in the progress and
at council. and in the
continuance of the
roversy, that mutual
re most inadequate
Whenever the par-
ish controversy differ
f real importance, the
is very great, that
d ministers, who dif-
ch other in the same
d who will be dispos-
ort the parties with
respectively agree.
cases, such a differ-
npatible with fairness
, and ought to bring
h on those, who ad-
her side of the ques-
other cases, prejudice
iews may overpower
f reason, and clamor-
and their victim. In
classes of supposable
nds of justice will be
strated by relying on
ouncil, chosen equally
arties: for whether

the parties are moderate or violent, candid or prejudiced, honest or dishonest, they will naturally and almost inevitably select
such ministers, as are known to
agree with them, respectively,
in opinion. How is such a council to come to any decision? If
there should unexpectedly be a
decision by a single vote, how is
such a decision to command the
respect and cheerful submission
of the party against whom it is
made? What would be thought
of a political arrangement, which
should refer all important legal
questions to a court composed
of members, half of whom should
be selected by one party and half
by the'other; especially if the dispute hinged on some great question, such as the constitutionality
of a law, on which there was a
diversity of opinion, and men of
intelligence had taken opposite
sides? What would be thought
of making arbitration the *only*
method of deciding questions of
property, liberty, and life? Arbitrations are sometimes useful;
but it is a notorious fact, that
they are sometimes the sources
of monstrous injustice, either
from ignorance, a silly attempt
to please both parties, or a timid
yielding to popular clamor.
Though the regular courts of

justice are not absolutely free from exposure to these evils, they are much less exposed to them, than any tribunals could be, which were selected by the parties, with a particular view to each controversy. We hesitate not to say, that the political condition of this country would be intolerable, if questions affecting character, property, and life, were to be decided only by arbitrations, in the preparation for which the creditor and debtor, the person injured in his reputation and the slanderer, the public and the criminal, should have an equal influence.

The same reasoning applies, in a considerable degree at least, to ecclesiastical disputes. If differences of opinion will arise, concerning which the interests of the church require a decision to be made by others beside the parties, it is certainly wise to have some tribunal agreed upon, *previous to the origin of the differences*, in order to avoid endless bickering in the attempt to constitute a tribunal, after the *roots of bitterness* have struck deep, and extensive parties have been formed. But if, on the other hand, there is no such thing as ecclesiastical authority sanctioned by the Scriptures; or if each church is perfectly competent to settle within itself all questions and disputes which can exist; or if no church has a right to settle any question, or give any opinion, but every professor of religion must be left by his brethren to do *what seemeth good in his own eyes*;—on any of these suppositions, mutual councils are much worse than useless. They aggravate parish contests, while, on either of

these suppositions, they ought to possess no remedial authority.

So far as the charges against Mr. Codman's moral and ministerial character were concerned, the decisions of the first council were highly beneficial; as these charges have not since made any impression upon a single person, so far as we have been able to ascertain.

Had the motion prevailed, which censured Mr. Codman in regard to exchanges, it was the avowed intention of the advocates of that motion, to introduce another motion to the following purport: That the council advise to a dissolution of the connexion between Mr. C. and his people, unless he will engage to exchange ministerial labors with the members of the Boston Associationg enerally. No person, however, undertook to show the consistency of this motion with the admission, that Mr. C.'s first refusal to pledge himself to exchange with any man or any body of men whatever was a correct reservation of his rights.

After the decision of the first council, there was a good opportunity for Mr. C.'s opposers to lay aside their hostility. They still professed no dislike to his preaching; they still professed to think favorably of his talents and ministerial character. The charges of a moral nature, which, as was evidently the case, they had thrown into the scale, as makeweights merely, they professed themselves willing to take out with their own hands, if Mr. C. would pledge himself to exchange with their favorites. The council was unable to decide the question of exchanges Mr. C. was not censured on this ac-

Why did not these lovers
e sit down quietly, and
eir minister in p ssses-
those rights, which all
n ministers have enjoy-
time immemorial? The
loubtedly was, that the
l of exchanges was a
ndle, as it was forcibly
by a member of the
in the course of the de-
f'be opposers of Mr. C.,
ir friends out of the par-
ited to drive from this
i faithful minister, who
oxious to them. It was
or granted, that he had
p his mind on the subject
anges, and that, sooner
eld to any compulsory
ts, he would leave his
Shall we be called un-
le in saying, with the
r of the council, that the
n of exchanges was mere-
dle? Let the reader call
l, that charges of *inten-*
leception were solemnly
gainst Mr. C , and persist-
o the last. Yet those,
ide these charges in one
offered in the next to
w them, if the question
anges could be settled.
incharitable to suppose,
en who who would use
makeweights as these,
ise such a handle as the
n of exchanges?
now proceed with the

it the time of the first
, twelve inhabitants of
ister and Roxbury appli-
oin Mr. C.'s parish, un-
act of the legislature,
had recently passed.
oplication was refused a
; by Mr. C's opposers,
are now able to carry any

vote which they felt disposed to
carry. The decision of the first
council was made, as we have
stated, on the 7th of November,
1811. On the 28th of the same
month, a parish meeting was
held, for the purpose of calling
another council. Accordingly, a
committee was chosen for that
purpose. The parish instructed
this committee to unite with
Mr. C. in choosing a mutual
council. In case he should refuse to unite with them, the
committee was instructed to
call an *ex parte* council. Two
questions were to be submitted.
1. Whether Mr. C. had not giv-
en just cause of complaint in regard to exchanges? 2. Whether a dissolution of the connexion between Mr. C. and his people should not take place, on
account of the divided and unhappy state of the parish? The
makeweights were not again
thrown into the scale.

Previously to this arrangement, Mr. C. had exchanged,
for the first time, with a certain
member of the Boston Association. Many persons, both among
the friends and the enemies of
Mr. C. put a misconstruction
upon this act. They considered
it as a dereliction of the principles, for which he had all along
contended. Some among his
friends deeply lamented it.
His opposers were greatly enraged by it. They seriously
feared, that they should lose
their only plausible pretext of
opposition. So anxious were
they, on this account, that they
held a meeting for consultation
the very evening of the day, on
which the exchange took place;
and, in eleven days afterwards,
they warned and held a parish.

meeting for the purpose of calling a second council as above stated. Instead of rejoicing at the prospect of an alteration in in Mr. C.'s plan of exchanges, as they had professed themselves ready to do, they sneeringly charged him with giving up his conscience rather than give up his parish. They did all in their power to hasten the sitting of the council, lest Mr. C. should, in the mean time, yield the very point, which he had from the first maintained, and to make him yield which they had professedly begun and continued the dispute. They made it the principal charge against him, that he had *neglected to do the very thing*, which they were now much afraid he would do, and thus deprive them of their great resource. We mention these facts for the purpose of shewing the nature and temper of the opposition to Mr. Codman, and of correcting some misapprehensions among his friends. We know not that his friends in the parish ever had any misapprehensions on the subject; but many of his friends, out of the parish, certainly had. These misapprehensions are sufficiently corrected by the following note, at p. 115, of the *Proceedings.*

"As much conversation has taken place, and many mistakes and misrepresentations have been made in consequence of this exchange; the Rev. Mr. Codman thinks it a duty he owes himself and the public to state, that the exchange was made *consistently* with the principles which have uniformly governed him in his ministerial exchanges."

The church seeing the parish determined on a further prosecution of the controversy, took measures to afford all the support in their They appointed a com who made a report, th material part of which w

"When, in compliance with mous wishes of the church, o was ordained to the work of th among us, we esteemed it a b We anticipated from him a faithful labors and affectionate to promote our good. We che sincerely pledged ourselves t those kind offices which are du Christian church to a belove And we hoped and prayed so blessings upon us and our childr

"We solemnly give thanks to day, that the anticipations, b the time of the Rev. Mr. Codm nation have been in some go realized; and the mutual prom expressed in some good degree

"As our pastor had, before ment, stated most fairly and the doctrines which he intended and the manner in which he in discharge his ministerial duty, what to expect from him in this concern. And, after three y elapsed, we are not able to per he has deviated from the cours duct, which he then so explicitly ed to himself. On the contrary ourselves constrained to declar the services of the pulpit, he h ously and zealously inculcated truths which he then professed, followed them by pressing on science and the heart the duties tianity.

"We have always regarded hi now regard him, as a faithful l the vineyard of his Lord, as a who needeth not to be ashame dividing the word of truth; as a tious minister of the New T who watches for souls, as one give an account, and who strive bors, and prays for the salvat people. In his private interco the members of his church an we recognize the disinterested ing, beneficent spirit of th We rejoice in saying, that we b to be remarkably actuated by t that in his visits to houses of aff is a minister of consolation; that who are enquiring what they s be saved, he is an affectionate counsellor; and that in private as well as in the pulpit, on othe

well as on the Sabbath, he is
his people.
 also to state, with devout
od, that we have reason to
.or's labors have been man-
ed with a Divine blessing.
as have been made to our
r his ministry; the attention
as been directed to religion,
of the Spirit have appeared,
e. in the increase of vital and
r."* pp. 116, 117.

nmittee express it as
led opinion, that "*there
ause for a separation
e Rev. Mr. Codman
ish*, and that it is the
is church to do all in
r to prevent such a
." This step was ta-
12, 1811. The church
, reasons, in support
inion, either of which
y sufficient to justify
he course which they
The fifth reason is
ords:

re that the complaint against
with respect to exchanges,
many only *ostensible*, and
on to his *religious doctrines
al cause of complaint and
n;* which, we have reason
ald not cease, nor become
ble, should Mr. Codman
as his friends would sacrifice
nciples and feelings, and be-
subservient to those, whose
ons of *liberality* do not pre-
from the greatest *intoler-*
9.

rch accepted the re-
ppointed a committee
lowing purposes; viz.
mpt an accommoda-

*time of the Rev. Mr. Cod-
tion, in Dec. 1808, the sec-
in Dorchester consisted of
Since which 52 have been
ofession, and 14 have been
other churches; 5 have died,
esent number, (April 1812,)
49 are males, and 100 ...*

tion between the parties in the
parish. 2. If an accommodation
should be impracticable, to unite
with Mr. C. in choosing a part
of the council. 3. To make
such representations to the council, as truth and justice might
require.

In order to an accommodation,
the friends of Mr. C. made the
following propositions to the
committee of the parish; viz.

1. "That the friends of Mr. Codman
purchase all the pews of his opposers in
the South Meeting House, who are willing
to sell (and will leave the society) at the
cost, viz. what they were appraised at, and
what was given for choice; notwithstanding the pews sold for $10,400 more than
the cost of the house and land, and other
expenses."
2. "It is proposed, that three referees
be chosen by those in the parish who are
disaffected to the Rev. Mr. Codman, and
three more by his friends; and that said
six referees choose the seventh; and that
said referees decide which party shall retain the present meeting-house, and
which shall be considered the second parish; those, who hold the present house, to
purchase all the pews of those, who wish
to sell and leave the society, at such
price, and to pay in such time, as the referees shall determine." pp. 122, 123.

Neither of these propositions
were accepted. The church
then prepared for the worst.
A worthy and pious member
gave a deed of seven acres of
land, as a site for another meeting house, should they be compelled to leave their present one.
In that event, the church were
determined to adhere to Mr. C.,
so long as he should maintain a
good character, and consent to
stay with them. Though he
could expect but a very small
salary, not one quarter enough
for his support, he might possess the affections of a grateful
people, and enjoy the satisfaction
of having preserved a church

from wandering as sheep without a shepherd.

We now leave the printed documents, and rely principally, for facts, upon a written account of the subsequent proceedings, kept by a very candid and respectable man, a member of the church and a most useful friend of Mr. C., during the whole course of his troubles

Many letters were interchanged between the parties, in reference to the time of convening the council, and to the letters missive. At length the council met, May 12, 1812. The Rev. Dr. Lathrop of West Springfield, was mutually agreed upon as the moderator and umpire; it being supposed a very probable event, that the remaining part of the council would be equally divided. Dr. Lathrop was requested to attend without a delegate. The plan adopted to unite in the other members was, that each party should name two churches among those, which had been represented in the former council, and two churches which had not been thus represented. The ministers and delegates from the churches selected by Mr. C. and his friends were as follows; viz.

From the church in Medfield,
The Rev. Thomas Prentus, D. D.
   Artemas Woodward, Delegate.
Newburyport, Rev. Daniel Dana,
       William Coombs, Del.
Bedford, Rev. Samuel Stearns,
   Dea. Moses Fitch, Del.
Salem, Rev. Samuel Worcester, D. D
   John Punchard, Del.

The ministers and delegates from the churches selected by Mr. C.'s opposers, were as follows, viz.

From one of the churches in Salem,
The Rev. Thomas Barnard, D. D.
   Ichabod Tucker, Delegate.
Bridgewater, Rev. John Reed, D. D.
     Dea. Noah Edson, Del.
Duxbury, Rev. John Allyne,
   George Partridge, Del.
Lancaster, Rev. Nathaniel Thayer,
   Ebenezer Torrey, Del.

The council opened on Tuesday and began the public hearing, which was continued till late on Wednesday. The result was published on Thursday morning

The parish committee appeared to rely principally on the divided state of the parish, though the question of exchanges was brought distinctly into view. The committee of the church represented, that the best way of settling the whole controversy was, to agree that those who disliked Mr. C. should join the parish of Mr. Harris, to which most of them had formerly belonged; and that others, now belonging to Mr. Harris's parish, should be permitted to join Mr. Codman's. This proposal appeared the more reasonable, as the parishes were not divided by local limits, and the whole town had till lately constituted Mr. Harris's parish.

The church laid before the council a paper, signed by 305 attendants on Mr Codman's ministry, purporting, that the subscribers were satisfied with his pastoral services, and continued desirous of enjoying them in future. Forty seven others were stated to be regular attendants on his ministry, and decidedly friendly to him; though they did not sign the paper, either through absence, or some other cause. Of 150 church members all but 7 or 8 were anxious to re-

C. as their minister; and
lerable number of per-
shed to join the parish,
ild not legally do so at
c.

ave already mentioned
erator of the council; the
were the same as at the
ouncil. The principal
acted upon was expres-
he following motion.

opinion of this council, under
reumstances it is expedient, that
terial and pastoral relation be-
e Rev. Mr Codman and the
'ish in Dorchester be dissolved."

question of exchanges
we are informed, made
at basis of this motion;
as not discussed to any
rable extent. On taking
estion, the ministers and
es from churches select-
he parish committee all
1 the affirmative; the min-
and delegates from the
es selected by Mr. C. and
irch. all in the negative.
ev. Dr. Lathrop was then
upon for his vote, and he
l the question in the neg-

He found it desirable,
r, to explain his vote;
he did by the following
aph, appended to the re-

he question before the council,
it were expedient, that the Rev.
dma should be dismissed from
oral and ministerial relation to
nd parish in Dorchester, I gave
in the negative, on a full belief
g persuasion, that from this time
he would open a more free and
ntercourse with his ministerial
, and thus remove the only ob-
Beged against him, and the on-
urged for his dismission. If his
onduct should be the same as in
st, in this respect, I should be
isappointed and grieved; and if I
ind myself thus disappointed, I

should certainly have no hesitancy in giving my vote for his dismission, if called in
Providence to give my voice on the question."

On the subject of exchanges,
the council unanimously agreed
in the following judicious observations:

"While they view it an important privilege of the Christian minister to regulate
his exchanges with his brethren according
to the unbiased dictates of his own mind
and conscience, they are sensible that this
right ought to be exercised with prudence
and tenderness. If he treat with wanton
disregard either the wishes of his people,
or the sensibilities of his ministerial brethren, he is undoubtedly culpable. Errors
of this kind, however, are of different degrees, and are not all to be treated with
the same severity."

After offering such exhortations to peace and union as were
thought suitable, the council
closed their result with the following words:

"In this result and exhortation the
council are unanimously agreed; presum-
ing that your pastor will be disposed to
pursue a liberal plan of exchanging with
his brethren in the ministry, and that in
all other respects he will diligently unite
his efforts with yours to promote the cause
of Christian truth, holiness and love; praying, at the same time, that you may be
each other's crown and joy both here and
hereafter."

We entirely approve every
thing, which is said in the result,
taking the words, "liberal plan
of exchanging," in their proper
sense, and not allowing of any
strained interpretation which favors a party.

In reference to the explanation, which the moderator appended to his vote, we have a
few words to say; after premising, that we highly venerate the
Rev. Dr Lathrop, as an able and
pious divine, and an amiable and
upright man, whose life exhib-

its a bright example of the Christian virtues.

From several remarks made by that gentleman, while at Boston and Dorchester for the purpose of attending the council, it appeared to be taken for granted by him, that there was some regular method of deposing any minister, who should embrace dangerous heresy and continue to propagate it. But this is not the case. Suppose a minister, (and such a one we now have in our mind,) to teach doctrines which Dr. Lathrop would pronounce to be fundamentally heretical; suppose him to live in the constant habit of reviling Trinitarians as bigots and Pagans, and of expressing his hatred and contempt for those, who uphold the religion of our forefathers, in a style of such insolence and vulgarity, as decency forbids us to describe. How is such a man to be deposed? The very attempt to bring him to trial would cover the person who made it with odium and reproach. Nor would this be all. The attempt would be perfectly impotent. He would acknowledge no tribunal but his own church; perh. ps not even that. If consistent with his principles, he would not acknowledge any ecclesiastical authority whatever. But if he admitted the authority of his own church, it would be of no avail; for his church would undoubtedly support him. Must he be treated, then, during his whole life, as a minister of that Gospel, which he is constantly laboring to pervert and destroy?

Again: The Rev. Dr. Lathrop seemed to have received the opinion, that Mr. Codman condemned a large part of t[h]... ton Association in the m... that he pronounced the ... etics in an imprudent and ... tifiable manner. But n... thing appeared in evid... either council; and we a... suaded that no such thing be proved. Mr Codm... perfectly free to exchang... nearly all the individuals ... Boston Association, so fa... declarations, in referenc... dividuals, were taken in ... sideration.

Further: Dr. Lathrop ... ed to take it for granted, ... ministers of the Boston A... tion were agreed in mos... doctrines, which are usu... led the doctrines of grac... ticularly in the doctrines ... tification by faith, regen... the saving operations ... Holy Spirit, and the ato... We are informed, that ... some reason, from what h... and saw on the spot, to t... for granted. But such an... ment does not exist i... There is a great variety ... ious doctrine professe... taught by the different m... of the Boston Associatio... decided Calvinism to the ... grade of Socinianism, ... some grades lower. ... many opinions, which w... radically erroneous, and ... Dr Lathrop, we presume ... deem so too, the follow... held by one or another ... Association, viz. That ... was a mere man;—That ... doctrine as that of the ato... is taught in the Scriptures ... the idea of an atonement ... fectly ridiculous;—Th... common opinion of con... is fanatical;—I'll at reaso...

elation;—That the re-
nature is of higher
than book-religion;—
ntance of sin is all that
I for the enjoyment of
here or hereafter;—
are justified by their
'hat those, who do not
his world, will become
repent, and be happy,
re world;— That there
general judgment;—
soul sleeps with the
death to the resurrec-
it Christ made but two
le additions to the re-
ankind; viz the *fact* of
ection of the body, and
ution of the Chris-
.ry;—That the soul of
terial;—and many oth-
tural notions.
scription is not given
nsideration. With re-
ery one of these opin-
ive either heard it de-
m the pulpit, in un-
erms, by some mem
: Boston Association,
en assured by compe-
sses, that it was so de-
that it was clearly and
maintained in conver-
but two of these opin-
been delivered from
; and most probably
also.
ould Dr. Lathrop ad-
ithful minister, who
doctrines of justifica-
th, the atonement, re-
i, and the operations
y Spirit, as at the foun-
all religion, to ex-
th a man, clothed in
of a minister, who
se doctrines the butt
ual ridicule, and the
unmeasured and most
if not impious, re-

proach? Would Dr. Lathrop
compel a faithful minister, under
the penalty of ejection from his
parish, to exchange with such a
man? We are persuaded he
would not.

But how is the faithful minister to know, that a man, clothed
in the garb of a minister, is
guilty of such conduct, he being
in regular ministerial standing?
He is to know, we answer, by
the evidence of his own ears,
and by the unanimous testimony
of multitudes, who have the evidence of their own ears. Is it
to be taken for granted, that a
minister cannot furnish evidence
against himself till he has been
tried? especially in a case where
no trial will be permitted or, if
permitted, where a trial would
be a mere mockery?

It is to be remembered here,
that it is not necessary for a candidate to be examined as to his
religious doctrines, either for
license to preach, or for ordination He need only profess to
believe the Bible to be the word
of God; and this profession may
be made in the most general
terms conceivable.

That we may not be misun-
derstood, we again say, that the
Boston Association contains
members, who differ widely from
each other in doctrine; and that
they range from decided and
consistent Calvinism down to
the lowest Socinianism, if not
down to the station of Geddes;
whom we should place about
half-way between Socinus and
Voltaire.*

* Whatever proof Mr. C. might have
had, with respect to the erroneous opinions of any member of the Boston Association, it would have been highly improper for him to disclose it, as such member
was not on trial before the council

We again proceed with the history, in the detail of which we must be brief.

In about two months after the decision of the council, the parish committee addressed a letter to Mr. C. stating, that the council had sanctioned their complaints, and requiring a categorical answer, whether or not he intended to exchange with twelve ministers, (naming them,) of the Boston Association indiscriminately. To this application Mr. C. returned for answer, that he should endeavor to comply with the true spirit and meaning of the result of the last council; that the right of regulating his exchanges was admitted to be in him; that the council could not have intended, that he should bind himself by any pledge, as to exchanging with individuals; that he should endeavor to preach at home as much as possible; and that, when he did exchange, he should consult the feelings and wishes of his people in general.

Things remained in this state more than two months longer. In the mean time, Mr. C. had exchanged with two, out of the twelve, ministers named by the parish committee in their late application. On the 30th of September, a number of individuals, professedly in the name of a majority of the parish, addressed a long letter to Mr. C. complaining of the infrequency of his exchanges. "Are one or two stars," say they, "though of the first magnitude, to content us for the light which might be derived from all the planets of our system, revolving in regular suc-

cession?"* The burde[r] letter, however, was an to persuade Mr. C. tha[t] ish could never be unite[d] and that he would con own ease and usefulnes[s] ing a dismission. In re C. refers the writers to preceding letter, and sta 'he had already opened free and liberal intercou his ministerial brethr should continue to do s[o] as time and circumstanc[e] admit' What rule M[r] prescribed to himself, perplexing business. w[e] profess to know. He u declared, that he had no the principles of his but that he considered cision of the moderato second council, as en very respectful attent pecially in doubtful case new exchange, though perfect conformity to th ples for which Mr. C. inally and uniformly co he viewed as "a more liberal intercourse." I ly was so in public es

The parish difficulti now rapidly approaching On the 27th of October, disaffected members of ish wrote another long Mr. C. stating 'that noth separation would resto quillity to the chu ch ar ty,' and intimating, in t expressive terms, that now too late to think of

*To all, who are so happy that Boston and a few neighbo contain the greatest and most n.en in the world, the above se appear eminently beautiful.

ciliation by means of exchanges. Mr. C. replied, that he had made up his mind *not to ask a dismission.* His letter breathed a spirit of benevolence, in regard to his opposers, and a strong desire to promote their spiritual interests. It was dated Nov. 12th.

On the 24th of that month, a parish meeting was held for the purpose of dismissing Mr Codman. The plan now was, to dismiss him by a vote, and to keep him by force from the pulpit If he resorted to the law for the recovery of his pulpit, or his salary, he would be branded as litigious. Besides, it might take two or three years to decide the question; the whole controversy would be brought before a court and jury; the pulpit would be supplied, in the mean time, by the opposers, according to their wishes; the friends of Mr. C. would have no convenient place of worship, and would hesitate as to leaving the meeting house immediately and erecting a new one; the expenses of a tedious law-suit would be enormous; and the opposers of Mr. C. construed a late decision of the supreme court in such a manner, as to encourage them with the belief, that the ultimate decision of this case would be in their favor. They had tried two councils; and now said they would have no more to do with councils. The present plan was a promising one; but most unfortunately for its projectors, *it did not succeed;* though they were not deficient in boldness and zeal.

At the parish meeting Mr. C. was dismissed by a vote, which was carried 55 to 45, and which was founded on twelve allegations, expressed in most intemperate language. The vote declared that Mr. C. had forfeited his office; that his pastoral relation should become extinct after Thursday of the same week; and that the parish would not allow him to preach any more in their meeting house The reasons, on which the vote was founded, were merely the old charges new vamped. They were drawn out to a great length. The following is a faithful abstract:

'1. Mr. C. has violated his agreement with the parish.

'2. He has frequently been guilty of immoral conduct by practising deceit and falsehood.

'3. He has, in some respects, neglected, and wilfully refused to perform the duties of a Christian minister.

'4. He has not sustained an irreproachable character for moral and Christian virtues.

'5. He has treated with "wanton disregard the wishes of his people, and the sensibilities of his ministerial brethren."*

'6. He has not endeavored to comfort, but has attempted to wound the feelings of, the afflicted.

'7. He has circulated a card† in favor of the Westminster catechism, and otherwise ungenerously attempted to wound the feelings of the Rev. Mr. Harris.

'8. He has violated an express rule of Christ, by refusing an aggrieved brother an opportunity to tell his grievances.

'9. He has treated, in a most disrespectful, indecent, and contemptuous manner, the university in Cambridge, its governors, &c.

'10. He has repeatedly declared, and solemnly called God to witness, that he could not conscientiously exchange with Dr. —— and others, &c. &c. notwithstanding which he has exchanged with Dr. ——, still professing not to have changed his own principles.

'11. He has not complied with the result of the last council.

"12. Lastly, because by having committed the aforesaid and numerous other imprudences, immoralities, slanders, deceptions, and falsehoods, he has rendered himself so obnoxious to a large majority

---

* See above p. 295, in the result of the second council

† For an account of this card see p. 271 *of our last number.*

of this parish, that his dismission has become essentially and indispensably necessary to the restoration of peace, and harmony, and brotherly love within the parish."

We need not inform our readers, that the preceding charges were groundless and therefore highly slanderous and libellous; nor remind them how easy a thing it is, to prate about charity, candor, peace, harmony, and brotherly love.

What now remained was to keep Mr. Codman from his pulpit in future. It was known to his opposers, that he had engaged to exchange on the next Sabbath, with one of the twelve members of the Boston Association, whom they had named to him, and with all of whom they had endeavored to compel him to exchange. They sent a deputation to this gentleman, requesting him not to preach for Mr. C., as there would be difficulty if he did. He accordingly called on Mr. Codman and excused himself. The opposers now looked round for a man to preach under their auspices, on the following Sabbath; and, in a neighboring town, they discovered one, (not a settled minister,) just suited to their purpose.* For several reasons we shall relate the succeeding transactions with considerable particularity.

On Saturday evening Mr. C. was informed, who was expected by his opposers to supply the pulpit for them, and to keep him

* We have hesitated whether it is our duty, or not, to mention this person's name. He certainly has no claims upon us, or us on the public, for indulgence. But we had rather err on the side of lenity and forbearance, than on that of severity.

from it. He immediate quested three of his frie wait on the person, with lowing note. The urge the occasion will accou the decided terms, in whi expressed.

"Dear Sir,

I have this moment heard which I hope is not true, that yo gaged to preach in my pulpit to

"I think it my duty to inform I shall consider such a measure part as very unkind, and an infr of my rights; and shall feel myse bound to maintain them again any other man whatever.

"You must be sensible, that I dismiss d from my people, eith mutual, or an *ex parte* council, vote of the parish, on the ground prudences, immoralities, slander tion and falsehoods."

"By preaching in my pulpit, t without my consent, you will their proceedings, and place me t disagreeable necessity of interm complaint against you

"I am, dear Sir,
respectfully yours,
John Col
Dorchester, Nov. 28, 1812.
Rev Mr. ——

Mr Codman's friends cred this note, and urge the person, to whom it dressed, the impropri preaching in Mr C.'s without his consent, and ry to the wishes of the and many of the congre The person replied, that great respect for the church in Dorchester; t was sorry he had not the mation sooner; but that h fulfil his engagements wi C.'s opposers, and had no that Mr. C. would be di by the supreme court, charges which the pari exhibited against him.

On Sabbath mornin addressed the following

the chairman of the committee who had waited upon him.

Nov. 29, 1812.

"Dear Sir,

The very friendly manner in which the Committee called on me last evening, and the Christian temper which they manifested, in stating the feelings of the second church in Dorchester relative to my preaching there this day, have induced me to write to the parish committee, giving them notice, that I shall not preach for them, unless they shall make it appear, that I can do it without violating the duty of a Christian, or debasing the sacred office of a Gospel teacher. Whether they will make a y further communication to me, I know not.

"As to Mr Codman's note, it savors so much of the temper with which he has for a long time treated me, without the least provocation, that I shall treat it with the contempt which it deserves.

"I am, Sir, very respectfully,
    your obedient and humble servant,"

——— ———

To this note a mild and proper answer was immediately returned, and the friends of Mr. C. hoped that no violent measures would be adopted on that day. It is proper to state here, that Mr. C. utterly disavows having given this man any cause of personal offence. What arguments the parish committee used in order to change his resolution 'not to preach for them,' we are not so fortunate as to know. It seems, however, that their arguments were effectual.

Mr. Codman and his friends, hearing that he was to be excluded from his pulpit, went to meeting rather earlier than usual on Sabbath morning. What must have been their surprise at entering the house of worship, to find eight sturdy men posted on the pulpit stairs, four on each side of the pulpit, in such a manner, as to obstruct the passage entirely. Mr. C was determined to do all in his power to maintain his rights. He advanced, therefore, in his way to the pulpit, till he crowded hard against the bodies of the rioters; and, finding in them no disposition to yield, he turned into the seat under the pulpit, and soon after began public worship. In the mean time, he had expressly demanded admission into the pulpit; and one of his friends, senior deacon of the church, and a magistrate of the county, made a suitable declaration, and ordered the rioters to desist from their unlawful purposes. All this had no effect; and the agitation of the assembly was now considerable. When Mr. C. began public worship, all became quiet, and the exercises were unusually solemn and affecting. In the midst of the first prayer, the redoubtable preacher for the parish committee made his appearance; and his guard of honor opened and gave him entrance into the pulpit. There he staid during the remainder of the services; and, strange as it may seem, he made no further disturbance till Mr. C. had pronounced the blessing; unless it be, that he discovered sundry symptoms of uneasiness, and appeared anxious, as the audience shrewdly imagined, to find some gap, or break, into which he might thrust the commencement of *his* services. But no such gap, or break, was he able to find, and he made no noise or other disturbance.

When Mr. C. had dismissed the assembly, he stepped forward into the middle of the house, addressed the said preacher by name, expressed surprise at such an intrusion, and forbade his preaching in that place. The magistrate, to whom we have alluded, confirmed the statement of Mr. C., and declared such an intrusion to be a violation of all law, order, and propriety. Several others urged the same thing

The preacher replied, in substance, that he did not wish to do any thing contrary to the peace of the parish. (not he, good peaceable soul, not he.) but he must proceed The magistrate then made proclamation, that all the friends of law, order, and decency, would be expected to retire. They retired accordingly, and the preacher was left to address a comparatively empty house. He went through with his exercises, had a very short intermission, and was nearly through his second sermon, when Mr. C. and his friends assembled for worship in the afternoon. It seems that the redoubtable preacher was quite a legal character, as he could tell, at the first blush, how the supreme court would decide Mr. C.'s controversy; and, being such a legal character, he well knew that possession was a great point in the law. He therefore wisely determined to keep possession of the pulpit during his short intermission. The refreshment, which was afforded him, he took without leaving the house. After the completion of his services, he and his hearers retired, and Mr. C. ascended the pulpit, and preached as usual. The preacher of the parish committee had 48 hearers on the lower floor of the house, at his afternoon service; Mr. C had 220. The proportion in the gallery was probably not very different. Mr. C.

preached A. M. from words: *Casting all your upon him; for he careth f* P. M from—*Father them; for they know no they do.* Though his a had no allusion, not the sli to the parish troubles, the thought to apply admirab

Though the preacher parish committee was a man, and though Mr. C.'s sers were all, all liberal m it does not follow that a liberal men were willing with them to such a pitch travagance. This was v from being the case. proceedings, on this S were condemned by me parties; and by none mo ingly than by distinguish sons in the liberal party. of these persons advised to mediate prosecution of the ding preacher for a trespa all saw, that these riotou ceedings had removed plausible covering of the and characters of Mr. C. cipal opposers in the When these opposers can Boston, on Monday m they found the current so and overwhelming agains that they offered terms o promise, on that very day were ultimately accepte which secured the house to Mr. C. and his and to himself the perfec of exchanging ministerial according to his own s duty and propriety.

It may be thought, th exhibition of himself, m the preacher of the paris! mittee, is unworthy of the tion bestowed upon it review; but we think it f teaches several useful lessons. The attentive reader will be struck with the fact, that on Sabbath morning, when the preacher was about to exclude a neighboring minister from that minister's own pulpit, by a most unwarranted and disorderly intrusion of himself; and while he was expressing his *contempt* for a regular, faithful minister of the Gospel, who had never done him any injury; and while he was supporting a violent party, in all their slanderous and libellous proceedings;—he should yet talk about "friendly manner," and "Christian temper," and "the duty of a Christian," and "the sacred office of a Gospel teacher." This fact teaches a useful lesson, and one which must not be forgotten by the people of New England. It shows how little confidence is to be placed in mere words; in the miserable, thread-bare, singsong of charity and candor.

The foundations of the compromise, between the two parties in the parish, were as follows:

1. That Mr. C. and his friends should purchase the pews of all members of the parish, who would sign a declaration that they were disaffected towards him, on the 1st of Dec. 1812; the price to be the sum given for choice added to the original cost:

2. That each one of these disaffected persons should give a bond to Mr. C. in the sum of $1,000; conditioned that the person bound should not vote in any parish meeting, nor take any part in parish concerns, nor in any way molest or impede Mr. C. in the discharge of his parochial duties, while he should continue the minister of the parish.

3. That Mr C. should give a bond of $1.000, to each disaffected person. conditioned that Mr. C should cause all parish taxes to be refunded, which might be assessed on such person, during his ministry

4. That Mr. C. and his friends would not oppose, but, on the contrary, would favor and support, any petition, which his opposers should prefer to the legislature, to be set off as a separate parish.

5. That the second parish in Dorchester should cause to be paid over to Mr. C.'s opposers a proportion of the ministerial fund, &c &c. according to a rule agreed upon.

6. That a parish meeting should be held, as soon as convenient, at which the opposers of Mr. C. should resign all the parish offices which they held.

Upon these bases the parties set themselves about making an accommodation, which, we are happy to say, was completed at last, though after much trouble and many new impediments. We have no inclination to dwell on these topics; but a scene of overreaching and injustice could here be disclosed, which would astonish those, who are most versed in parish contests. After the affairs of the parish were again committed to the friends of Mr. C., they arrived at the most satisfactory conclusion, that there never was a fair majority of legal voters opposed to Mr. Codman. The number of alterations made in the tax list, for the purpose of admitting and excluding voters, and for other party purposes, would appear incredible, were not the principal facts proved by written official documents.

In fulfilling the terms of compromise, Mr. C. and his friends purchased pews of his opposers to the value of about $10,000, only $3,000 of which now remain on Mr. Codman's hands; and it is a pleasant circumstance, as indicating the growth of the congregation, that every pew owned by Mr. Codman is rented on such terms, as to produce the interest of the purchase money. Beside the expense of the pews, the parish, which is very far from being wealthy, has been unjustly burdened with some great expenses attending the two councils. Many unreasonable charges were allowed and paid from the parish treasury, by Mr. C.'s opposers, after they had entered into the terms of compromise above stated, and after the time had elapsed when they were to resign their parish offices; and the treasury was thus drained of the money which had been raised for the payment of the minister's salary and other necessary expenses. However, the separation is at length accomplished, and we believe no subject of dispute now exists.

In the summer of 1813, those who had been the opposers of Mr. C. erected a meeting house; and, when it was nearly completed, they applied to the Boston Association to dedicate it. On this occasion, the Memorial, the title of which we have placed at the commencement of this article, was presented to the Boston Association. A few words upon this paper will be sufficient.

The object of the memorial-

ists was to make out a cl for themselves, so th might boldly ask for the nance of the Associatio this purpose they pre elaborate memorial, writ more than ordinary care i ity, which occupies 28 pages. They attempt t lish the following poin That the memorialists h contending for the pe harmony of their chur society, and of churches cieties generally; that the were disaffected towards had reason to expect fron different course of cono regard to exchanges, fro which he pursued; that ! letter to the church and before his settlement, fi being explicit and par was general and indefini if this letter had been e explicit in regard to doct would have been no inc of Mr. C 's intentions ar changes; that Mr. C. i condemned for conceali designs as to exchanges, making illiberal and grot insinuations against his bi in the ministry, rather t be praised for his fran that a refusal to exchang a minister is virtually a co nation of him without tri the dismission of Mr. C. b violent proceedings of N 18:2, was legal and prop founded on a decision of preme court;[*] that Mr C.

[*] In the passage which the m ists quote from the opi ion of tl delivered by the late chief justice two causes only of the dismis-ion ister by a parish are mentioned; moral conduct," and "a wilful a neglect of public preaching, or of turing the ordinances, or of pe

his, by refusing to ap-
laws for redress; and
memorialists made
ifices in point of inter-
ling, by consenting to
om the second church
, We do not say, that
xpressed these points
ls of the memorialists;
l have taken up too
n; but we have endeav-
re the substance faith-
e memorialists admit,
r things have been said
y individuals, *on both
h*, in their cooler mo-
ey will condemn, and
deliberate judgment
can approve." The
l not consider this as
admission, after what
red.
morial was presented
ssociation, read, and
; and it was finally re-
iat while the Associa-
ve of the great object
the memorialists pro-
tend, they do not con-
aselves called upon to
nent, in their official
on the proceedings of
ty in this affair; yet as
no probable method

of composing these differences
without a separation, and as the
separation appears to have been
the result of a mutual arrangement, *Voted*, that we comply
with the request of the memorialists.'

The Association, therefore, as
a body, attended at the dedication
of the meeting house, and performed the religious services according to the request of the memorialists, Oct. 6, 1813. We are
informed, that the new society has
received more encouragement
and support from clergymen of
a certain description, so far as
ministerial services are concerned, than any other new society
in this vicinity has received
within the memory of man.

Mr. Codman, who had some-
time before taken a dismission
from the Boston Association,
complained to individuals of that
body, that their proceedings on
the memorial did in fact implicitly condemn him and justify his
opposers; for the memorial was
expressly designed to justify the
memorialists on all the principal
points, in order to make it proper for them to ask the countenance of the Association; and
they adhered to all their charges
of gross immorality against Mr.
Codman. The Association say,
they will not pass judgment in
the case; yet they comply with
the request of the memorialists.

Let us state a different case.
Suppose some disaffected members of the Rev. Mr. Channing's,
or the Rev. Mr. Lowell's, society
in Boston, should prefer charges
of gross immorality against their
minister, and should persevere
in these charges for years: suppose these charges should be declared groundless by a compe-

ial duties." There is no
tence that either of these
d in the case of Mr. Codman.
the dismission of ministers,
uncil, the Convention of the
al clergy thus express them-
s. "We do not find, on the
enquiry, a single instance of
ational church from the first
l the country to the present
has deposed or dismissed its
r, or pastor, without the advice of neighboring churches;
a dismission has been effectual consent of the elder and
, even in this case, it appears
s been before adduced, that
on is irregular, and contrary
ution of these churches.

tent tribunal: suppose the disaffected persons should finally separate and erect a new house of worship: suppose they should request the Boston Association to dedicate their house, premising, however, that they could not expect this favor, unless they could justify themselves in the course they had taken: and suppose they should insist upon all their old unsupported charges of immorality. Would it be thought liberal and correct for the Association to say, we give no opinion in this controversy; but we will comply with the request? Would it not be more liberal and correct to say; We cannot *receive* charges against a minister, as we have no authority to try them: we are bound to consider these charges as slanderous till they are proved to be just, especially as one competent tribunal has declared the most of them to be unsupported: take back your memorial, and ask simply for the dedication of your house, without attempting to criminate a man, whom we are bound to consider as innocent; and it may probably be our duty to dedicate any house, erected for the worship of God, by persons formed into a regular religious society?

We have no hesitation in saying, that we think Mr. C. had just grounds of complaint against the Association His feelings were stated to that body, and a vote was passed, which, after a suitable preamble, recites the proceedings of the Association, and adds the following paragraph:

"This Association also desire their Scribe to state, that they have never considered themselves a tribunal instituted to

examine and decide upon charges a ministers or churches. In conf with this sentiment, it was their and purpose, in their proceedings this occasion, to avoid the express any opinion whatever on the subj the late differences in Dorchester their language on this point appe them so unequivocal, as to need planation. If, however, there ar sons, who, notwithstanding this carr ceive either from the language of th or from any circumstance attend that it sanctions charges, which the moral character of any indi the Association are ready to declar this effect was in no degree inten foreseen; and they regret that such struction should be given to a pros which was designed to encourage tend the institutions of religion."

In the appendix to the m rial, p. 42, 43, there is a de tion, which seems calcula make an impression unfave to Mr. Codman, where th cumstances are not known is but justice to state, wh know to be the fact, the deposition varies in two important particulars fro testimony of the depone the first council. So st was the difference of th dence, as given at the two cils, that a large number c sons who were present at and several of whom took the testimony at the first c in writing, were greatly ast ed at the confidence of th nesses.

Our readers will be ha hear, that Mr Codman left perfectly free on the s of exchanges The fol declaration, first prepare committee, has been unan ly approved by the parish it has been newly organi

"As it is the important privile Christian minute to regulate be ges with his brethren according unbiassed dictates of his own r

=; we think it expedient, that the
=ould agree, that Mr. C. should
=fined in his exchanges, the ad-
=ny council or member thereof
=anding, as the advice, which was
= upon the expectation, that the
=d were to continue active mem-
=e parish, which is not now the
=l that the exercise of this privi-
=not again be made the subject
=int before an ecclesiastical coun-
= parish."

need only say, in conclu-
=at Mr. C.'s character has
='ered by the long trials,
=a which he has passed;
=parish is now very flour-
=as more persons attend
=istry than has been the
=t any previous time; and
=, and many of his friends
='y part of the United
=think there is abundant
=o bless God, that the con-
=y has been brought to so
=le a termination.

*The Christian's Confi-
=: A Sermon preached at
=ham, at the funeral of the
=Rufus Anderson, A. M.
=15. 1814. By SAMUEL
=CESTER Boston; S. T.
=trong. pp. 24.*

thor of this sermon has
=ed several occasional dis-
=, within a few years
=All, which have come to
=ds, (and we believe we
=id all that have been pub-
=abound in good sense,
=ousness, and in a happy
=ation of doctrinal and
=l instruction. They are
=ly the production of a
=a mind, which is deeply
=bitually impressed with
=onsibility of the ministe-
=:e, and solemnly intent
=e discharge of its duties.

The only reason that we have not
noticed these discourses, in their
order, is, that we are able to devote but a moderate portion of
our work to reviews. Perhaps
this reason is not sufficient; but
it is all we have to offer.

The sermon before us is from
these words of Paul: *Nevertheless, I am not ashamed; for I
know whom I have believed, and
am persuaded that he is able to
keep that which I have committed
unto him against that day.* 2
Tim. i, 12

The preacher divides his subject in the following manner:

"Let us, I. Attend to some particulars,
which were comprised in Paul's knowledge
of Christ, and on the ground of which he
felt secure;

"II. Consider what he had committed
in trust to Christ; and then,

"III. Contemplate, more directly, the
reason which he had not to be ashamed."
p. 4.

The knowledge of Christ,
which the apostle had, is described, and set in a forcible light, by
apt quotations from his writings,
under each of the following
topics; viz.

"His knowledge of Jesus Christ, we may
assure ourselves, was correct, ample,
deep, and experimental. He knew
Christ to be a person in the highest sense
divine;—he knew him to be the propitia-
tion for the sins of the world;—he knew
him to have been raised from the dead, and
exalted upon the throne of the universe;—
he knew him to have power to restore to
the divine favor all true believers in him—
he knew him to b the resurrection and
the life—and he knew him to be the final
Judge of all." pp. 4, 5.

The other divisions are judiciously filled up, and succeeded
by two reflections: "1 Our subject opens to us a glorious view
of the riches of divine grace
presented in the Gospel" "2.
Of what infinite importance is a

true knowledge of Christ." We omit further remarks, for the purpose of inserting the latter part of the sermon, which we do as a just and honorable tribute to the memory of a worthy and faithful minister. The delineation of Mr Anderson's character is thought, by those who were particularly acquainted with him, to be very faithful and accurate. Unless we are mistaken, our readers will pronounce the following extract to contain several passages of genuine pathos, and solemn exhortation. The closing paragraph must have made a deep impression on the hearers, and ought not to be slightly regarded by any reader.

"I need not tell you, my brethren, how happily these sentiments have been exemplified in the instance of him, whose mortal part now lies in the shrouds of death before us. Of him you expect me to say something; and it is right that something should be said, for the "memory of the just is blessed," and ought to be embalmed in the hearts of the survivors.

"This beloved servant of Christ was born at Londonderry, (N. H.) on the 5th of March, 1765. Blessed with pious parents and a religious education, his mind was early imbued with the truths of the Gospel; and by means of those truths, under the power of divine grace, he appears to have been early brought to a saving knowledge of Christ. Having devoted himself to God, his thoughts and his heart were gradually turned to the Gospel ministry, until he became settled in the persuasion, that duty required him to consecrate himself to this sacred work. Under this impression, and with this object steadily in view, he commenced and prosecuted a regular course of study; during which, as he has been often heard to say, his great concern was to qualify himself for the holy vocation which his heart had chosen. He was graduated at Dartmouth college in 1791. After spending about three years, partly in direct application to theological studies, and partly as a licentiate preacher, on the 22d Oct. 1794, he was ordained the pastor of the second church in North Yarmouth, where he continued about ten years. His labors

there were abundant; and in some degree successful, his trials, various but salutary in their influence and in their results. Many predicts his ministry there, as we are to believe, will be his joy and at the appearing of the Lord separation from that people good mutual understanding circumstances, which appear no imputation of particular blame one side or on the other. On however, it was tenderly painful necessity of it was deeply regretted dear flock at North Yarmouth, special charge, he ever continued witness, to bear on his heart, affectionate regard and concern without personal knowledge, them his memory has been cherished great tenderness and respect.

"Of the beloved flock in this place installed the pastor, on the 1805. Concerning his ministry need not be particular. "For know, brethren, what manner in he had unto you;"—and fully known his doctrine, purpose, faith, long suffering, tience;—how gentle he has been you, even as a nurse cherisheth them;—how affectionately desirous of you, even to a willingness to parted unto you not the Gospel only, but also his own soul, be were dear unto him;—how justly, and unblamably he behaved self towards them that believe, wards all men—warning every teaching every man, in all These distinguishing traits of character should not be applied my deceased friend and brother the present solemn responsibility not confident of a ready testimony consciences, that the application ingly just.

"Mr. Anderson was possessed natural talents, improved by diligent study, especially in the study of Writings. His mind was active cient; and, in regard to objects him important, would easily kindle ardor. His passions, naturally strong, restrained and sanctified grace, diffused around him a benign, a warming and cheering In his various relations, as a father, a friend, a brother, a citizen of his country, and a Zion, the benevolence of his h manifest, in constant endeavor desires unequivocally expressed, vidual happiness, and for public conversation was distinguished fo plicity and godly sincerity, and

th grace seasoned with salt; and
s rarely to be found of whom it
said with more evident apposite-
ᵈhold an Israelite indeed, in
re is no guile."
minister of the Gospel, he was
aany who corrupt the word of
r as many who deem it prudent
ᵈ, or but indistinctly, or ambigu-
declare their views of divine
t "renouncing the hidden things
esty, not walking in craftiness,
ling the word of God deceitfully;
nanifestation of the truth," he
anxious only to "commend him-
very man's conscience in the
3od." A firm and enlightened
n the doctrines, distinctively de-
d the doctrines of grace, of these
he was never ashamed; but to
testimony to them, to shew their
l importance, and to press them
the consciences and hearts of
s the great business of his life.
l preacher of Jesus Christ, and
ified: of Jesus Christ, as truly
truly man; and of him crucified,
ropitiation for the sins of the
nd the only name given under
mong men, whereby we can be
his thoughts, his sentiments, and
er, were his own; his thoughts
mous, his sentiments were rich,
er was plain and unaffected, but
affectionate, and impressive.

. ; - - - - - *"Much impressed*
as conscious of his awful charge,
ious mainly that the flock he fed
eel it too; - - - - - - - - -
he violated law spoke out
ers, and by him, in strains as
t
le use, the Gospel whispered
s."

as eminently a man of prayer;
rayers were distinguished for the
eathed into them of unaffected
lively faith. In them, as in all
id, his devotedness to Christ and
was manifest. Zion,—the pur-
he Redeemer's blood—Zion, the
God's everlasting love—was ever
seart. He took pleasure in her
e favored her dust. His heart
t whatever concerned her pros-
was forward to lend his aid to
ures for her enlargement which
h and brighten the present age;
ailed with holy gladness the evinces of her King, to put an end
s of her mourning, and to "ex-
se to her like a river, and the
the Gentiles like a flowing

"As he lived, so he died. His last days
were serene. Knowing whom he believed, he was persuaded, that he was able to
keep what he had committed to him. "I
have the assurance," he repeatedly said,
"I have the assurance of faith: though not
constantly the assurance of hope." In the
truth of the doctrines which he had
preached, he maintained an unwavering
and lively confidence; and his greatest
grief appeared to be that any should
preach another Gospel. His tender concern for his dear people, his ardent love
to Zion, his sacred devotedness to Christ,
were conspicuous to the last.

"Such was the servant of Christ, who
statedly, for years, dispensed the word of
life, from the sacred place in which I
stand. But the eyes that have seen him
here, will see him here no more. At a
much earlier day, than our affections and
wishes would have marked for the event,
his divine Master, whose will 'is always
good, has called him to rest from his labors. To him we believe it is gain; to us
only who survive it is loss. Upon his dear
family, upon this church and people, upon
our ministerial circle, and upon our Zion,
the breach is great.—Might an expression
of personal feeling be indulged, I would
say, I am distressed for thee, my brother
Anderson; very pleasant hast thou been
unto me!—But the sorrows of others claim
condolence: the sorrows particularly of
the afflicted widow, and fatherless children, and of this bereaved flock.

"Upon you, dear Madam, the stroke is
heavy. But the anguish of it is relieved,
we trust, by the consideration that it is
from the hand of your heavenly Father;
and we pray that his consolations may not
be small with you. Thankful should you
be in this day of your mourning, that you
have not to sorrow as others who have no
hope. The lover and friend indeed, who
is now put far from you, will not return
to you;—but you must go to him. Follow
him then with your affections and desires
to that better world. Let the precious
Gospel which he preached, and which
was all his salvation and all his desire,
dwell richly in you; look steadily forward
to the end of your faith; and the time will
not be long, ere your spirit shall join his,
in the presence of God, where there is
fulness of joy, and at his right hand, where
there are pleasures forever more.

"Dear Youth, Sons of the deceased, he
who has been your friend, your guardian,
your guide, your example, who gave you
to God, who has instructed you in the way
of peace, who has sought your welfare
with many prayers and tears;—your worthy and beloved father—is now no more
with you. He has left you at a critical age,
and in an evil world. But his death may

of you to God, his instructions, his examples, his prayers and tears will not, we trust, be in vain. They constitute a precious legacy; a legacy more valuable, than thousands of gold and silver; a legacy in the possession of which you may be truly rich and happy. "Know then the God of your father, and serve him with a perfect heart and with a willing mind;" and he will be your God; will supply all your need; will guide you with his counsel, and afterward receive you to glory.

"Brethren and Friends of this Church and religious Society, the present is a solemn day to you. He who has watched for your souls with most affectionate care, is gone to render up his account to his Judge and your Judge; and you are left as sheep not having a shepherd. We grieve for your loss; we feel a deep solicitude on account of your destitute state: we are devoutly desirous that this solemn dispensation may be sanctified to you. We pray God the breach made upon you may not be irreparable. Has not your beloved and lamented pastor left a testimony in all your consciences, that he is pure from your blood;—that he has not shunned to declare unto you all the council of God;—that he has taught you the way of life in truth and with all fidelity. And as he is now gone to render up his account, does it not behove you individually and seriously to reflect, how the account must stand as it regards you. Happy, if you have received the truths of the Gospel, dispensed by him into good and honest hearts, and are built up and established in the most holy faith. Mournful the fact, if in regard to any of you, he has labored in vain, and spent his strength for nought, and been only a savor of death unto death!—His great concern in his last days was, lest, "after his departure grievous wolves should enter in among you, not sparing the flock." "Therefore, we beseech you, watch, and remember, that by the space of eight years, he ceased not to warn every one night and day with tears." And could he now speak to you from his bright abode, what could he more, than repeat in effect the instructions, exhortations, and entreaties, which while here he so affectionately delivered to you. Brethren, it is not a small thing, if a prophet has been among you. O may his message abide in your minds and in your hearts; may even his death be as life from the dead to many of you. May the dews of heavenly grace yet cause the good seed, here sown by him, to spring up into a rich and glorious harvest, and may the breach here made by his removal, be soon repaired by the great Shepherd and Bishop of souls.

"My fathers and brethren in the ministry, our beloved brother and fellow laborer in the ministry is gone. Let us deposit his sacred remains, to be kept by Him to whom his all has been committed; affectionately drop a tear upon his grave; embalm his memory in our bosoms; and return to our labors with quickened diligence, fidelity and zeal. Soon will our Lord call also for us. What we do for him, and for the souls committed to our care, we must do quickly; we are dying—our people are dying. Let us seize the moment, and, in view of the judgment seat, declare to them all the counsel of God, warning every man, and teaching every man with all wisdom and fidelity. God grant we may so preach, and so live, and so die, as to save ourselves and our dear people.

"My hearers of this numerous assembly, the hope and the end of the true believer have been set before you: the hope is full of glory, the end is peace. But, alas! how different the hope, and the end of them that believe not! They live without God in the world; in continual transgression of his law, abuse of his grace, and refusal of his Son the only Savior. Die they must; but when they die—ah! what will become of them! Their souls and their bodies they have neglected to commit to the Savior's hands. Their sins are not forgiven; their persons are not sanctified; they have no title to heaven—no preparation for that holy place—no treasure laid up there. In the dark valley of death, no light from heaven cheers them; no convoy of angels atte ds them; no friendly hand is extended to guide or support them. Hopeless and forlorn, the distracted soul is torn away from its earthly tenement, and hurried by demons down into the abyss of eternal darkness and woe; and the body is consigned to the dust—to rise indeed, when the trump of God shall break the slumbers of the grave—but to rise to shame and everlasting contempt. At the final day, when the heavens are passing away with a great noise, and the earth is dissolving before the splendors of his throne, they must stand at the bar of their Judge:—whose mercy they have refused, whose blood they have spurned, whose terrors they have defied—and hear the dreadful sentence, "Depart from me, ye cursed, into everlasting fire, prepared for the devil and his angels."—O be warned my hearers, every one of you, and flee from the wrath which is to come. Flee for refuge to the hope set before you. Repent and believe in the Lord Jesus Christ; and live the life, that you may die the death of the righteous, and your last end be like his. Amen."

MISCELLANEOUS.

lECTION OF AN ERROR.

To the Editor of the Panoplist.

pleased with your review
low's Columbiad, as con-
; many just strictures on
lse sentiment and false
f that work. In this coun-
ere every man is suppos-
e at liberty to think what
ases, and utter what he
it is not strange that men
be found willing to write
or nonsense, so long as
ley write may be publish-
sold, without any respon-
at the tribunal of criti-
Perhaps it is a natural con-
ce of our habits as a people,
all know, or at least pro-
know, a little of every
Not a few, therefore, sup-
at they know a little more
hers, concerning some fa-
subject; and that they are
alled to communicate that
dge to the public. If our
reputation were to be es-
d by the *number*, and not by
ity of the books we pro-
ve should have no reason to
ious for the result. Our
authorship does not extend
h voluminous works as
f Erasmus or Lord Hale.
an American folio would
ost as great a curiosity, as
erican ship of the line.
r shelves are loaded with
lets, concerning many of
we hesitate whether to
hem to the binder, or con-
em to the rubbish of the

ly, Mr. Editor, we need a
table literary censorship
over the press. Nothing short
of this can save us from being
inundated with trash, from the
vanity, the cupidity, or the wan-
tonness of writers and booksellers. If this subject were duly
considered, wise men certainly
would not complain of well written reviews, in our periodical
publications. Many of your
readers, I am sure, wish to have
this department of the Panoplist
made an object of increasing attention; and to see it regularly
filled with the labors of sound and
enlightened criticism.

But the principal object of
this communication is to recal
your attention to a passage in the
review of the Columbiad, on the
86th page of your number for
Feb. last. After some general
remarks on Mr. Barlow's version
of the psalms omitted by Dr.
Watts, the reviewer says:

"His edition of the psalms was at one
time quite popular, and contains some
happy efforts of poetry. His 137th, which
it is strange that Dr. Watts should have
omitted, as it is justly pronounced by Chateaubriand to be the "finest of all canticles
on the love of country," begins as follows

"Along the banks were Babel's current
flows
Our captive bands in deep despondence
stray'd,
While Zion's fall in sad remembrance
rose,
Her friends, her children mingled with
the dead.

"The tuneless harp, that once with joy we
strung,
When praise employ'd and mirth inspir'd the lay,
In mournful silence on the willows hung,
And growing grief prolong'd the tedious day."

These stanzas are worthy of particular
praise. It is a sorrowful reflection, that

talents which might have been a credit to any good cause, and any country, should have been utterly perverted and abused; and that a man, born and educated under favorable circumstances, where the true God is known, the Bible is understood, and pure worship offered, should have a-postatized from the religion which he once preached, and plunged into the gulf of Atheism."

It has always seemed strange to me that this 137th psalm, which is indeed one of the most melting strains of poetry that can be found in any language, should have been overlooked by the ethereal spirit of Watts. The version of it in Barlow's collection doubtless possesses all the merit which the reviewer ascribes to it; but none of that merit belongs to Barlow. The writer of that beautiful psalm was Dr. Lemuel Hopkins, late of Hartford, Con. and the original manuscript is now in the possession of his family. This mistake, though really of small importance, it seems but a piece of literary justice to correct.

N. S. O.

YALE COLLEGE BENEVOLENT SOCIETY.

THIS Society was formed in July, 1813. The annual meeting is on the day before Commencement, when an oration and a poem will be delivered. The Society consists, at present, principally of students; though a few generous subscribers from abroad have joined it, or sent their donations. It has already afforded assistance to a number of worthy young men, and promises great usefulness. It receives donations in books, particularly in those classical books which every student must possess; and in this manner is enabled to lessen the expenses of education to indigent students very considerably. These books can be lent in such a manner, as that one complete set will accommodate several persons, at the same time. We shall gladly take some future occasion to urge this subject upon the opulent, particularly upon the *Alumni of the College.* The designs of the Society will be clearly seen by the following

CONSTITUTION.

Art. I. The Society shall be styled THE YALE COLLEGE BENEVOLENT SOCIETY; and its object shall be to assist indigent young men, of good talents, and unblemished moral character, in obtaining an education at this College.

Art. II. Any person may become a member of the Society, by paying the sum of two dollars; and may continue a member by paying one dollar annually. And any person may become a member for life, by paying, at any one time, thirty dollars; or, within the space of four years, forty dollars.

Art. III. The officers of the Society shall be a President, Vice President, and Committee, from the Senior Class; and a Secretary from the Junior Class: all of whom shall be appointed by ballot at each annual meeting.

Art. IV. The Committee shall, with the consent of the President of the College, and the Professors of Mathematics, Languages, and Chemistry, appropriate all monies belonging to the Society.

Art. V. One half of the money annually contributed shall be appropriated to form a permanent fund; the interest of which, and that only, shall be annually expended. This fund shall be placed in the hands of the President and Fellows of Yale College, who shall keep and manage the same, in such a manner as they, or their Treasurer, may think most advantageous to the Society.

Art. VI. All persons making donations to the Society shall have the privilege of adding their money to the permanent

'placing it exclusively in
.ls of the President and
ors or of appropriating
sively to the education of
.aen intended for the min-

7II Such person or per-
may subscribe one hun-
llars annually, shall have
rilege of designating the
who shall receive his or
nation: provided the per-
designated shall possess
ifications required by the
ition.

VIII. No person shall
assistance from the So-
inless he produce suffi-
stimony of a good moral
:r and respectable talents;
he shall have been a
: of College at least one

: VIOLATION OF THE
.TH BY PERSONS OF
AND INFLUENCE.

been high'y pleased with an
n the Christian Observer for
ier last, on the violation of the
; and have determined to pre-
· readers with the whole of it.
:uity, the independence, the
, exhibited by the Editor of that
t publication in admitting a
hich reprehends, in decided but
terms, the conduct of the Prince
the acting chief magistrate of
:h Empire, and the source of
honor, are worthy of admiration.
I be a shame to us, if, in this re-
country, and in New England,
.e Sabbath is much more gener-
rved than in Great Britain, we
ie afraid to mention the delin-
of our rulers on the same sub-
imitation of the Christian Ob-
e take this opportunity to state,
jes of the highest courts in New
have b·en known to travel on
ath, without a iy plea of neces-
.tever; and that instances of
relling have multiplied of late.
:atly evident, that a judge should
X.

not travel on the Sabbath, unless in a
case of extreme necessity, and he should
then take special care to apologize for
his conduct, and to state the necessity
with such particularity and concern, as
to counteract the pernicious tendency
of his example.   ED.

To the Editor of the Christian Observer.

I BELIEVE that not only all serious Christians, but all good citizens, are agreed as to the importance of maintaining, in the
minds of the great body of the
people, a respect for the institution of the Christian Sabbath.
The Christian, indeed, values it
chiefly on account of the spiritual benefits with which its due
observance is fraught. But even
its civil and political advantages
are by no means of trivial moment; and they ought to secure,
on the part of our magistracy,
and of all the friends of good order, the tribute at least of their
external respect to so beneficial
an appointment.   The temporal
sanctions by which our forefathers have protected the sacredness of the Sabbath from secular
occupation, is sufficient evidence
of their sentiments on this point.
The law of the land requires that
its repose should not be unnecessarily disturbed; and were it only for the sake of the general
principle of cherishing a reverence for the laws in the minds of
the community at large, I should
have hoped that our senators,
our judges, and our governors,
would themselves have scrupu-
lously abstained from any open
infraction of them.

These reflections, Sir, were
suggested to me last Sunday, at
a large county town where I had
rested during a journey, by the
circumstance that on that day the
Prince Regent and his suite

passed through the town in one direction, and a judge of the circuit in another, both travelling rapidly, and communicating of course abundant activity to all the inns and stable-yards where they had occasion to stop. But this was not the only evil. The public curiosity was naturally awake to see the Prince Regent. The consequence was, that instead of the crowded church, or the quiet family party, all was bustle, and confusion, and clamor. The streets through which he had to pass were filled with spectators, and the grave aspect of the Sabbath was changed for the levity and frivolity of a fair or a race course. Surely the advisers of his Royal Highness are to blame, when they induce him thus to weaken the obligations of religion, and of the laws by which religion is fenced, by journeys on the Sunday, for which, in his case at least, no plea even of expediency, much less of necessity, can be advanced. The judge, however, I think still more to blame, as he must have acted from his own mere motion, and without the intervention of any adviser; and as his experience on the circuits must have taught him, in innumerable instances, how much of the crime which it falls to his lot to punish, had originated in those violations of the sanctity of the Sabbath which his example has tended to encourage.

Should this paper meet the eye of the judge to whom I allude, or of any other judges, I trust it will not be without its use in inducing them to avoid similar occasions of offence.

C.

THE OPINION OF THE LEGISLATURE OF MASSACHUSETTS IN REGARD TO THE SABBATH.

We cannot follow up the preceding communication better than by publishing the recent, solemn, recorded opinion of the Legislature of Massachusetts, in relation to the momentous subject of the Christian Sabbath. Let this paper be well pondered; let the great truths which it states be separately considered; and let the public awake to the paramount importance of making a vigorous and united effort to restore to New England the ancient sanctity of the Sabbath. Ed.

THE committee appointed by both houses to consider what further provision is necessary to enforce a due observance of the Lord's Day, and to whom were committed several petitions from the people on this subject, with leave to report by bill or otherwise, have attended to the duty assigned them, and respectfully offer the following

REPORT—

We find a law passed March 8th, 1792, and another passed March 11th, 1797, the provisions of which extend not only to all the evils mentioned in the petitions, but to all such as are in any other way known to us to exist, in regard to the outward observance of the Sabbath. The provisions of these two laws we think are sufficient to accomplish the end proposed, if they were faithfully and discreetly executed. The preamble to the first law is solemn, clear and impressive. It states the design and use of the Lord's Day in a manner well calculated to excite in the minds of the people, and of the officers named

aws, a just sense of their
ibility and duty, and to
e them to corresponding
. The specifications and
:d penalties, which fol-
ear not to us to require
ther additions from the
ure, until it shall ap-
m a fair experiment in
g the laws, that the
: not removed.

hile we thus report, that
er legal provisions are
l from this honorable
e are still impressed
leep sense of the extent
ortance of the evil com-
of, both by the clergy
people, and are earnest-
ous to give all the aid in
er to the execution of
, by our renewed sanc-
l the full expression of
iments and feelings.

elieve, that an enlight-
iform and pious observ-
the Lord's Day, in at.
public and private in-
and worship ourselves,
fraining from all actions
ctices which may dis-
worship and instruc-
thers, is a duty solemnly
upon the conscience of
ndividual. We believe
tliout the appointment.
tinuance of the Lord's
blic instruction and wor-
uld soon languish, and
entirely cease: that pri-
rship and the best virtues
l life would share the
te: that the Scriptures,
ng the records, the prin-
he duties, and the hopes
ligion, would soon pass
: recollection of multi-
our citizens who now
hem, and never become
o the great body of the
eneration: that the pow-

erful and happy influence which
they now exert upon public sentiment and morals would be
seen no longer: that the safety
of the state, the moral and religious improvement of the people, the personal security and
happiness of all, are intimately;
if not inseparably connected
with the uniform and conscientious observance of the Lord's
Day, and its various institutions
and services; and that we are all
bound to make every just and
proper effort to secure the execution of the laws, which have
been already made upon this
important and interesting subject. However wisely and
skilfully laws may be framed,
they must greatly depend upon
the public sentiment and virtue,
and especially in all measures of
a moral and religious character,
for their final and complete success. We trust the public sentiment and virtue in this Commonwealth are sufficiently elevated and powerful to secure the
execution of just laws for the
observance of the Sabbath, when
once the public mind shall be
properly and simultaneously directed to this object, and to the
reasons which enforce it.

We therefore recommend the
following measure to be adopted by the Legislature:

That this Report be printed,
and a copy sent to each minister
of every denomination in the
Commonwealth.

That each minister be re-
quested to read in his pulpit, on
the Sabbath, the existing laws,
for the due observance of the
Lord's Day, and to address the
people on the subject; pointing
out as fully and explicitly as the
occasion and the circumstances
of his people may require, na-

cording to his own judgment, the importance and value of the Sabbath, and the reasons which bind us to observe it, and to obey the laws of the Commonwealth:

That the people be especially and distinctly called upon to elect such moral and religious men to fill the office named for the particular execution of the laws in regard to the Sabbath, as shall give the public a rational confidence, that all proper means will be adopted to meet the just expectations of the Legislature, and of all the lovers of righteousness, peace and order:

That the people be distinctly reminded of the necessity of supporting such public officers in the faithful discharge of their duty, by uniting and preserving the common sentiment in their favor, and not permitting it, by neglect or irritation, to turn against them to injure their reputation, business or happiness:

And that the officers themselves, who are, or may be thus appointed, should be discreet, judicious and benevolent, while they are yet honest and firm in the execution of their trust, according to the oath of office prescribed in the statute. All which is respectfully submitted by order of the committee.

D. A. WHITE, *Chairman.*

In Senate, June 14*th,* 1814.

Read and accepted, sent down for concurrence

JOHN PHILLIPS, *President.*

In the House of Representatives, June 14*th,* 1814. Read and concurred,

TIMOTHY BIGELOW, *Speaker—*

RELIGIOUS INTELLIGENCE.

EXTRACTS FROM MINUTES OF THE PROCEEDINGS OF THE GENERAL ASSOCIATION OF MASSACHUSETTS PROPER.

AT a meeting of the General Association of Massachusetts Proper, holden by previous public notice, in Dorchester instead of Boston, June 28, 1814.

Present the following delegates from the associations specified, viz.

Berkshire Association.
Rev. Joseph L. Mills, and
Rev. Thomas Punderson.

Mountain Association.
Rev. Caleb Knight.

Franklin Association.
Rev. Preserved Smith.

Hampshire central Association.
Rev. Evan Johns, and
Rev. Experience Porter.

Hampden Association.
Rev. Timothy M. Cooley, and
Rev. John Keep.

Brookfield Association.
Rev. Thomas Snell, and
Rev. Samuel Ware.

Worcester South Association.
Rev. Samuel Austin, D. D.

Westminster Association.
Rev. Joseph Estabrook.

Haverhill Association.
Rev. Isaac Tompkins, and
Rev. Joshua Dodge.

Essex Middle Association.
Rev. William Balch, and
Rev. James W. Tucker.

Association of Salem and Vicinity.
Rev. Samuel Thurston, and
Rev. Samuel Dana.

Union Association.
Rev. Jedidiah Morse, D. D. and
Rev. Samuel Gile.

Delegates from the General Assembly of Presbyterian Church.
Rev. Aaron W. Leland, and
Rev. John Johnson.

Delegates from the General Association of Connecticut.
Rev. Royal Tyler, and
Rev. David L. Perry.

Delegates from the General Association in New Hampshire.
Rev. Josiah Carpenter, and
Rev. William F. Rowland.

Delegates from the General Convention in Vermont.
Rev. Sylvester Sage, and
Rev. John Fitch.

Rev. Enoch Hale, Secretary, and Rev. John Codman, minister of the parish.

The Rev. Jedidiah Morse, D. D. was chosen Moderator, and the Rev. John Keep was chosen Scribe. The Rev. Thomas Punderson was chosen assistant Scribe. The meeting was then opened with prayer by the Moderator.

Rev. Messrs. Cooley, Hale, and
vere chosen a committee of ar-
nts.

Brethren, who were delegates
a body to the associations in our
n, in the General Assembly of
byterian church, in Connecticut
r Hampshire, reported.

, That the association attend a
ssture on each evening during the

, To set apart a season for prayer,
rsday morning, commencing at
k.

prayer by the Moderator, ad-
to meet to-morrow morning at
in the meeting-house.

day morning, June 29, met ac-
to adjournment and joined in
rith the Moderator.

, That the Rev. James Murdock,
delegate from this body to the
Association in New Hampshire,
' other delegates who may be
be invited to sit as honorary
.

That the associational sermon
red at 2 o'clock, in the afternoon.
mmittee of arrangements made
ort in part, which was accepted.
That future reports of delegates
om this body be made in writing.

That Rev. Messrs. Dana, Tuck-
'orter, be a committee to audit
nts of the association, to report
of the funds, and such measures
e thought expedient respecting

That the association attend to
tives of the state of religion, im-
/ after public worship, and that
Messrs. Murdock, Leland, and
a committee to take minutes,
epare a report.

To hear and to take order upon
ures proposed, in an ancient Doc-
epared, "To serve the great in-
f religion, which is lamentably
in the country," by the Minis-
Massachusetts, convened at Bos-
e years 1704, 5 and 6. It was
at a committee be appointed to
a Manual of discipline for the
al churches in Massachusetts, in
with this association; whereupon,

To refer this subject to a com-
three, and that the Rev. Samuel
D. the Rev. Jedidiah Morse,
d the Rev. Enoch Hale, compose
mittee.

llowing Brethren were chosen
to the ecclesiastical bodies with
association is connected; viz.
muel Shepard, and Rev. Samuel
delegates to the General Assem-
e Presbyterian Church in the
ates, to be holden in Philadel-
he 3d Thursday in May, 1816.

Rev. Evan Johns, and Rev. Timothy
M. Cooley, were appointed substitutes.

Rev. John Codman, and Rev. James
W. Tucker, substitutes to the Rev. Theophilus Packard, and the Rev. Nathan
Perkins, delegates to the General Association of Connecticut, to be holden in Dan-
bury, on the third Tuesday in June next.

Rev. Joseph Estabrook, and Rev. Experience Porter, substitutes to the Rev.
Joseph Blodget, and the Rev. Joseph
Field, delegates to the General Association of New Hampshire, to meet in Hanover, on the 3d Tuesday of Sept. next.

Rev. John Keep, and the Rev. Richard S. Storrs of Braintree, delegates to the
General Convention of Vermont, to meet
in Woodstock, at the house of the Rev.
Mr. Chapin, on the 2nd Tuesday in Sept.
next, at 2 o'clock, P. M.

The Committee on the document, &c.
bearing date 1704, 5, and 6, reported.

Voted, That the consideration of this
report, be deferred till tomorrow morning.

Adjourned to meet in this place, immediately after the public exercises, in
the afternoon.

The associational Lecture was preached
by the Rev. Thomas Snell, from Prov.
xiv, 12. *There is a way, which seemeth
right unto a man; but the end thereof are
the ways of death.*

At 4 o'clock, P. M. met according to
adjournment. The Rev. Moderator stated, that it was necessary for him to be
absent till to-morrow morning. He was
therefore excused, and the Rev. Samuel
Austin, D. D. was chosen to preside as
Moderator in his absence.

The association agreeable to assignment
proceeded to attend to the narratives of
the state of Religion.

Adjourned, after prayer by the Moderator till to-morrow morning, 8 o'clock.

Thursday morning, June 30. Met according to adjournment. The meeting
was opened with prayer by the Moderator.

The Committee appointed to audit the
accounts of the association, made their report, which was accepted.

Voted, That the Rev. Ebenezer Porter,
Bartlet Professor in the Theological Institution at Andover, be invited to sit with
the association, as an honorary member.

The business assigned by previous vote
to this hour was discussed, and the following vote passed, *nemine contradicente.*

"Whereas an ancient document has
been presented to this association, containing an answer to the question, "What
further steps are to be taken, that Councils may have their due constitution, and
efficacy, in supporting, preserving, and
well ordering the interest of the churches
in the country?" and "Assented to by the

delegates of the associations, who accordingly to former agreement at Boston, Sept. 15, 1705," and "further approved and confirmed, by a General Convention of the Ministers at Boston, 30, 3d month, 1706:"

Voted, That a committee of seven be chosen by ballot to inquire into the history of the above mentioned document; and particularly to ascertain, whether the resolves it contains were carried into execution at the time, and to what extent; and to report at the next annual meeting of this association, on the expediency of a recommendation by this body of the plan of discipline there proposed, either entire, or with alterations and amendments, to the consideration of the associations and churches in our connexion.

Rev. Jedidiah Morse, D. D. Rev. Samuel Austin, D. D. Rev. Leonard Woods, D. D. Rev. Samuel Worcester, D. D. Rev. Enoch Hale, Rev. Joseph Lyman, D. D. and the Rev. Timothy M. Cooley were chosen a committee for the purpose above specified.

The Committee appointed to consider the liberal proposal of Mr. John S. Schermerhorn, reported as follows:

"That it is expedient for the associations, in connexion with this body, to form themselves into Societies, for the purpose mentioned by Mr. Schermerhorn, and that being formed, they act as auxiliaries to the religious charitable society in the county of Worcester, one avowed object of which is, the assisting of pious indigent young men, in obtaining a public education, in reference to the ministry; and that the Secretary be a committee to receive the books offered by Mr. Schermerhorn, and to distribute them in equal proportions to those associations which shall be thus organized; and also, to transmit information to him of their organization, on or before the first day of May next.

It is recommended likewise to pass a vote, directing the Secretary to express, suitably, their thanks to Mr. Schermerhorn, for the generosity he has manifested toward this body. The report was accepted.

Voted, That a committee be chosen to take into consideration the subject of petitioning the Congress of the United States, to put a stop to the transportation and opening of the mail on the Lord's day; and if they shall think it expedient to concur with the late measures of the General Assembly of the Presbyterian church, and the General Association of Connecticut in regard to this object, that they send printed petitions, prepared at discretion by themselves, and in such numbers as they shall think necessary, to the several associations represented in this body, and to others as they shall think proper, for the purpose of procuring subscribers to such

petitions, to as great an extent as is practicable, and transmit them, on fore the first day in December such members of Congress, their opinion, he disposed to p their design, to be laid by them this great Council of the nation Samuel Austin, D. D. the Rev. Murdock, and the Rev. Thom were chosen a committee for the purpose.

The Committee appointed to tak ntes from the narratives of the religion, reported, which, after corr was accepted as follows:

The Committee, appointed to p a narrative on the state of religion the communications made to thi beg leave to offer the following Rep

From a general survey of the our churches, it will appear, th friends of Zion have cause for inc joy and confidence.

While our political affairs have l a state of peculiar embarrassment the angry and ferocious passions ha excited by the din of war, and whi titudes have been suffering in the poral interests and happiness, the l of the Gospel have not failed to forth as the messengers of salvation guilty world, and to put forth thei gies, in dependence on sovereign for the enlargement and prosp that kingdom, which shall def flourish beyond the narrow bou time. Though in some instances tention of Christians has been too engrossed with political and things, yet the churches under ou have generally manifested more so licitude for those things into whi angels desire to look.

Several of our churches have, dur year, enjoyed a precious season of r ing from the presence of the Lord. of the revivals mentioned in the l nual report have continued down t a part or the whole of the presen A pleasing work of grace has begu ing the past year, in Long Meade vey, and Gloucester, and is still go ward. In several towns there app be an increasing attention to th and ordinances of God: and g throughout our limits, external ort decency, and with few exceptions, adherence to the faith once deliv the saints, give evidence that the still in the midst of our churches.

The attention of Christians: h much called to the state of public and noble and combined efforts a ing, with the most flattering prosp the suppression of the helping an temperance, Sabbath breaking, an ty. The Theological Institution dover continues to prosper, and th

st, and other religious chari-
, are still pursuing their re-
ts with that pious ardor,
n so astonishingly displayed
ars past, both in Europe and
some parts of our limits
on has been given to cate-
uation; and an increasing
er is visible in many of our

le, it is believed, that not
a lamentable degree of for
piritual deadness is apparent
s, and in others the friends
godliness see much to grieve
have great occasion to re-
ovenant faithfulness of God,
he prosperity of our churches.
e things are presented with
mits, it is with peculiar satis-
n speak also of the fruits of
er sections of the American

limits of the General As-
Presbyterian church, sev-
have been visited the past
e extraordinary effusions of
irit. Especially ought we to
rark, and the towns adjacent
f New Jersey, that highly
which has repeatedly been
refreshings from the Spirit
In general the state of re-
pears from communications
body, is gradually rising.
General Association of Con-
have also joyful evidence
rd hath not forsaken them,
st High hath not forgotten
Spirit is poured out in
es within their limits; and it
e have been larger accessions
m of Zion the last year, than
eding since the year 1800.
public morals is also improv-
friends of the Redeemer are
re and more united in re-
, and in promoting the wel-

e limits of the General As-
New Hampshire, although
ous fanatical errors prevail,
ices are destitute of the stat-
ations of the Gospel, yet the
of previous revivals remain,
able zeal and faithfulness
aracterize the exertions of
ho are contending earnestly
. The exertions made the
y the Massachusetts Society
ng Christian Knowledge, to
he things which remain, and
ready to die, in the counties
aro and Strafford, by their
, and the dispersion of relig-
od tracts, have been crowned

with pleasing success, and encourage a
hope of the speedy resettlement of the
Gospel, in several towns, which have long
been destitute. The attention to the instruction of youth and children, and the
efforts for the suppression of open violations of the Sabbath, and other public vices,
afford the animating hope, that their labors, through the divine blessing, will be
followed with salutary effects.

From the General Convention of Vermont no information has been received of
any extraordinary reformation of recent date, except in the towns of Pawlet
and Bridport. While we lament that a
great portion of that state is destitute of
the stated administration of the bread of
life, and that vice and error so extensively
prevail, we see also some tokens for
good, particularly in the formation of Bible
and Moral Societies, and much to induce
Christians to intreat the Lord of the harvest, to send forth laborers into this part
of his vineyard.

From a general view of the state of religion throughout the world, it appears,
that the cause of Zion is advancing; and
notwithstanding the opposition from the
powers of darkness, the church is gradually rising from her depression and laying
aside her sackcloth. The period foretold
when "many should run to and fro and
knowledge be increased," is come. In
view of the animating prospects before
us, we anticipate the time as not far distant, when it shall be said to Zion. "Arise,
shine; for thy light is come, and the glory
of the Lord is risen upon thee."

By order of the Committee,
JAMES MURDOCK, *Chairman.*
John Keep, *Scribe.*

Voted, That the Rev Jedidiah Morse,
D. D. and Jeremiah Evarts, Esq be a
Committee to publish in the Panoplist, at
their discretion, the minutes of this association.

A statement having been made to this
association, from good authority, of the
energetic measures, lately pursued by the
peace officers and tythingmen in Belchertown, to prevent the profanation of the
Lord's day,

Voted Unanimously, That this association are deeply and gratefully affected by
this information, and hold in respect and
honor the officers aforesaid; and that they
anticipate the best results from these noble efforts to maintain the authority of the
laws, and the sanctity of the Sabbath

Voted, That the Secretary be requested
to transmit a copy of this vote to the se-
lectmen of Belchertown, to be communicated by them to the officers aforesaid.

Voted Unanimously, That this association hear with great satisfaction, that zeal

gun efforts are making in different districts of the commonwealth, and particularly in the towns lying on the roads between Boston and Hanover, in N. H. for the suppression of the multiplied violations of the Sabbath, which have been witnessed with so much grief by the friends of piety and order.

Voted, That the Rev. Mr. Codman be requested to express the thanks of the Association to his Society, for the very kind and respectful treatment they have received during their present session; and their satisfaction that they conformed to the wishes of the association in not ordering upon the table at the public dinner any spirituous liquors.

Voted, That the next annual meeting of the association be holden in Royalston, at the house of the Rev. Joseph Lee, on the last Tuesday in June, 1815, 5 o'clock P. M. and that the Union Association be requested to appoint the preacher.

Adjourned till to-morrow morning 6 o'clock.

Friday morning, June 30. Met according to adjournment. Prayer by the Moderator. The minutes were read and corrected.

Voted, That the publishing Committee cause to be printed 150 copies of Minutes of this Association, and that they forward such numbers to the bodies in this connexion, as they shall deem proper.

After uniting in singing an hymn, and in prayer with the Rev. Mr. Johnson, the meeting was dissolved.

JEDIDIAH MORSE, *Moderator.*
John Keep, *Scribe.*

THE following Document, copied from the *Original* M. S. by the Rev. Professor JENKS, who now has it in his possession, was lately put into his hands, by Madam H. CROCKER, of Boston, grand-daughter of Rev. Dr. COTTON MATHER, and is now published, so far as is known, for the *first time.* The Christian public are left to make their own comments on this invaluable *relic* of our venerable and pious forefathers.

"*Boston,* 1d. 4m. 1704.

To serve the great intentions of religion, which is lamentably decaying in the country; it is proposed,

1. That the Pastors of the churches, do personally discourse with the young people in their flocks, and with all possi-

his prudence and coundeavor to win their en the covenant of grace; glorious articles of it.

2. That unto this pur pastors do take up that but engaging practice of their personal visits, the families, that belo their congregations.

3. That the Pastors way of proceeding, their people, as far as publicly and solemnly to nize the covenant of G come into such a degree church-state, as they made willing to take th tion in; but not to leave they shall be qualified for, suaded to, communion church is all special ord

4. That for such as mitted to the governm Christ in any of his ch no Pastors of any other es, any way go to shelt under their wing, from cipline of those from wh have not been fairly mended.

5. That they who have tually recognized their tion to the discipline o in his church, yet shoul upon their obstinate re such a subjection, or thei into other scandals, be treated with proper tious: About the meth manner of managing w monitions, the Pastors w several churches, will unto the exercise of th discretion.

6. It is desired, and h if the Lord please, that General Convention of t isters, there may be giv

f the Pastors present, an
t of their progress and
a in that holy undertak-
hich has been proposed:
o the Lord may have the
if his grace, and the con-
>f religion in the country
e the better known and
among us.

.s a subserviency to these
ind great intentions, it is
ed; That tne Associations
Ministers in the several
>f the country may be
bened, and that the sever-
>ciations may by letters
ore free communications
ie another.

d and unanimously con-
unto.

esent,

uel Willard, *Moderator.*
iezer Pemberton,
amin Colman,
  Hancock,
nas Blowe,—?
>n Mather,
dal Rawson,
:miah Walter,
nas Barnard,
:s Allen,
iel Torrey,
:s Fiske,
>h Green,
  Fox,
land Cotton,
.han Pierpont,
than Sparhawk,
>h Belcher,
  Clark,
amin Wadsworth,
>h Gerrish,
r Thatcher,
is Sherman,
han Russel,
nas Bridge,
  Danforth.

:st. What further steps
be taken, that Councils
X.

may have their due constitution
and efficacy, in supporting,
preserving, and well-ordering,
the interest of the churches in
the country?"

It was proposed,

I. That the ministers of the
country form themselves into
Associations, that may meet at
proper times to consider such
things, as may properly lay before them, relating to their own
faithfulness toward each other,
and the common interests of
the churches:—And that each
of these Associations have a
Moderator for a certain time,
who shall continue till another
be chosen, who may call them
together upon emergencies.

In these Associations,

It is expected, that questions,
and cases, of importance, either
provided by themselves, or by
others presented unto them,
should be upon due deliberation
answered.

That advice be taken by the
Associated Pastors, from time to
time, ere they proceed to any
actions in their particular
churches, which may be likely
to produce any embroilments.

That the Associated Pastors
do carefully, and lovingly treat
each other with that watchfulness, which may be of universal
advantage. And that if any Minister be accused to the Association, whereto he belongs, of
scandal or heresy, the matter
shall be thus examined; and if
the Associated Ministers find
just occasion for it, they shall
direct the calling of the council,
by whom such an offender is to
be proceeded against.

That the Candidates of the
Ministry, undergo a due trial,
by some one or other of the As-

sociations, concerning their qualifications for the evangelical ministry: And that no particular Pastor, or congregation, employ any one in occasional preaching, who has not been recommended by a testimonial under the hands of some Association.

That they should together be consulted by bereaved Churches to recommend to them such persons, as may be fit to be employed among them for present supply, from whom they may in due time proceed to choose a Pastor.

That hereunto may be referred the direction of proceedings in any of their particular churches, about the convening of the councils, that shall be thought necessary for the welfare of the churches.

That the several Associations in the country maintain a due correspondence with one another; that so the state of religion may be better known, and served in all the churches:—And particularly it is thought necessary to the well being of these churches, that all the Associations in the country meet together, by their respective delegates once in a year, to concert matters of common concern to all the churches.

And, finally, that ministers, disposed thus to associate, endeavor in the most efficacious manner they can, to prevail with such ministers, as unreasonably neglect such meetings with their brethren in proper Associations; that they would not expose themselves to the inconveniencies, that such neglects cannot but be attended withal.

II It is proposed,

That these Associated Pastors, with a proper number of delegates from their several churches, be formed into a standing or stated council; which shall consult, advise, and determine all affairs, that shall be proper matter for consideration of an Ecclesiastical Council, within their respective limits. Except always when the cases are such, as the Associated Pastors may judge more convenient, to fall under the cognizance of some other council.

III. That to this end these Associated Pastors, with their respective churches, shall consociate and combine, according to what has been by the synods of these churches recommended; that they act as consociated churches, in all holy watchfulness, and helpfulness towards each other: And that each church choose and depute one or more, to attend their Pastors, as members of the council, in their stated sessions, or occasionally, as emergencies shall call for.

IV. That these messengers from the several consociate churches, shall be chosen once a year, at the least.

V. It is propounded, as that which from our beginnings has been recommended, that the churches thus consociated for these purposes, have a stated time to meet in their council; and once in a year seems little enough, that they may enquire into the condition of the churches, and advise such things as may be for the common advantage of our holy religion. But the more particular time is best left to the determination of each respective Association.

VI. That the Association shall direct when there is occasion for this council to convene on any emergency; and shall direct whether the whole, or only a certain number of, these consociated pastors and churches shall convene on such occasions.

VII. It appears agreeable to the present condition of our churches, and from our beginings acknowledged; that no acts in the councils are to be received as concluded, and decisive; for which there has not been the concurrence of the major part of the Pastors therein concerned.

VIII. The determinations of the councils, thus provided for the necessities of the churches, are to be looked on as final and decisive; except aggrieved churches or persons have weighty reasons to the contrary: in which cases there should be provision for a farther hearing.

And it seems proper, that the council convened on this occasion should consist of such Pastors and churches, as may be more for number than the former: And that they should be such as shall be directed to, and convened for this purpose, by the ministers of any Association near to that, whereto these of the former council belonged: Unto which the aggrieved should accordingly apply themselves; and in this way expect a final issue.

IX. If a particular church will not be reclaimed by council from such gross disorders, as plainly hurt the common interests of Christianity, and are not mere tolerable differences in opinion, but are plain sins

against the command, and kingdom of our Lord Jesus Christ; the council is to declare that church no longer fit for communion with the churches of the faithful; and the churches represented in the council are to approve, confirm, and ratify the sentence, and withdraw from the communion of the church, that would not be healed:—Nevertheless, if any members of the disorderly church do not justify their disorders, but suitably testify against them; these are still to be received to the wonted communion of the churches:—And if after all due waiting the church be not recovered; they may (upon fit advice) be actually taken in as members of some other church in the vicinity.

These proposals are assented to by the delegates of the Associations met according to former agreement, at *Boston*, Sept. 13, 1705, to be commended unto the several Associations and Ministers, in the several parts of the country, to be duly considered, that so what shall be judged for the service of our great Lord, and of his Holy Churches, may be further proceeded in.

Samuel Willard, *Mod.* ⎫
Cotton Mather,   ⎬ *Boston.*
Ebenezer Pemberton,   ⎭
Samuel Torry,   ⎱ *Weymouth.*
John Danforth,   ⎰
Samuel Cheever,   ⎱ *Salem.*
Joseph Gerrish,   ⎰
Grindal Rawson, *Sherburne.*
Samuel Danforth for Bristol *Association.*

Further approved and confirmed, and a resolution to pursue,

with the Divine assistance, in all suitable methods, the intention of the said proposals:—By a General Convention of the Ministers at *Boston;* 30d. 3m. 1706.

Attested by

SAMUEL WILLARD, *Mod.*"

THE following Document, from the pen of a distinguished Divine of New-England and one of the Committee, who prepared the preceding Resolutions, was written about the year 1700, and is published in this connexion, as indicating the state of religion and discipline in the New England churches, at that period, with more correctness and precision, than any thing that has fallen under our notice. The churches being in the situation here represented, the movements which followed, from 1704 to 1706, as exhibited in the preceding document, were natural and to be expected from good men, who were disposed and determined, at all hazards, to do their duty. Like causes will always produce like effects.

"*More particular prognostications upon the future state of* NEW ENGLAND.

But, Oh my dear *New England,* give one of thy friends leave to utter the *fears* of thy best friends concerning thee; and consider what fearful cause there may be for thee to expect sad *things to come?* If every wise man be a prophet, there are yet some in thee that can prophesy. Predictions may be formed out of these

Reasonable Expectations.

I. Where schools are not vigorously and honorably encouraged, whole *Colonies* will sink apace into a degenerate and contemptible condition, and at last become horribly *barbarous.* And the first instance of their *barbarity* will be, that they will be undone for want of *men,* but

will not see and own what it was that *undid* them.

II. Where faithful ministers are *cheated* and *grieved* by the *sacrilege* of people that rebel against the express word of Christ, *Let him that is taught in the Word, communicate unto him that teacheth in all good things;* the righteous judgments of God will impoverish that people; the Gospel will be made lamentably unsuccessful unto the souls of such a people; the ministers will be either fetched away to Heaven, or have their ministry made woefully insipid by their incumbrances on earth.

III. Where the ministers of churches in a vicinity despise or neglect *Formed Associations* for mutual assistance in their evangelical services; *Wo to him that is alone.* 'Tis a sign that either some of the *Pastors* want love to one another; or that others may be conscious to some *fault* which may dispose them to avoid inspection; but fatal to the *churches* will be the tendency of either.

IV. Where *churches* have some hundreds of souls under their *discipline,* but the single pastors are not strengthened with *consistories of Elders,* or an agreeable number of wise and good and grave men, chosen to join with the *pastor* as their *president* in that part of his work, which concerns the *well-ruling* of the *flock,* there *discipline* will by degrees be utterly lost; the *grossest offenders* will by degrees and through parties be scarce to be dealt withal.

V. Where *pastors* do not quicken orderly *private meetings* of both elder and younger Chris-

r exercises of religion
neighborhood, the power
'ion will observably decay
those Christians: the *seed*
n *public*, will not so
rosper for want of being
I in private. And when
tor shall fall sick, there
. be so much as one com-
f Christians in all his
at can come together to
: his life.

Where *churches* profes-
great *Reformation* shall
o represent in their con-
n unto the *world* the ho-
f the Lord Jesus Christ
is *heavenly kingdom*, they
come loathsome to that
rd; their *glory* is gone
ir *defence* goes with it;
adful wrath of Heaven
onish the *world* with the
t will do unto them.

Where *churches* are loath
unto *councils* regularly
omplaints enquiring into
ministrations an account
'tis much to be suspect-
they are chargeable with
inistrations; and if the
f regular *councils* come
be trod under foot by
ticular *churches*, all scri-
n will be afraid of join-
such *unaccountable socie-*

Where a mighty body
le in a country are set
nning down the ancient
ate in that country, and
ent for the hedge about
munion at the Lord's ta-
broken down; and for
ho are not admitted unto
munion, to stand on equal
in all *votes* with them
, the *churches* there, are

not far from a tremendous convulsion, and they had need use a
marvellous *temper* of resolution
with circumspection to keep it
off.

IX. Where *churches* are bent
on backsliding, and carried away
with a strong spirit of *apostasy*,
whatever minister shall set himself to withstand their *evil bents*,
will pull upon himself an inexpressible contempt and hatred,
be his merits never so *great;* a
thousand arts will be used for to
make him *little;* he had need be
a man of *great faith* and *great
prayer;* but GOD will at length
honor such a man with great
recompenses.

X. Where a fountain shall become *corrupt*, there the *streams*
will no longer *make glad* the
city of GOD.

XI. The *Gospel* of our Lord
Jesus Christ we have with much
expense lately sent into several
of our *Southern plantations.* If
it be rejected, there are terrible
things to come upon them;
'twere better to have lived in
Sodom than in one of these *plantations.*

XII. GOD prepare our dear
brethren in *Connecticut* for certain *changes* that are impending
over them.

Finally, there was a town called *Amyclæ*, which was ruined
by *silence.* The rulers, because
there had been some false alarms,
forbade all people, under pain of
death, to speak of any *enemies*
approaching them. So when
the *enemies* came, indeed no one
durst speak of it, and the town
was lost. *Corruptions* will grow
upon the land, and they will gain
by *silence.* It will be so invidious

to do it; no man will dare to speak of the *corruptions*, and the fate of *Amycla* will come upon the land.

Reader, I called these things *prophecy;* but I wish I be not all this while writing *history.*

Now if any discerning persons apprehend any *dangers* to impend over *New England* from any of the *symptoms* mentioned, it is to be hoped they will employ their best thoughts how to anticipate those *dangers;* and whereas 'tis the sense of all men, who discern any thing, that it is in vain to hope for any good until a *spirit of grace* be poured out from Heaven to dispose men to it; I beg them to consider whether the only way to obtain that *spirit of grace,* be not humbly to *ask* it by *prayer* with *fasting* before the GOD of Heaven.

It was therefore an article in an advice agreed upon by some of the principal ministers in this province, and with the mention of that advice (which doubtless all but the *sleeping* will follow) I'll conclude: "Solemn days of *prayer* with *fasting* celebrated in our *churches* to implore the grace of GOD for the rising generation, would probably be of blessed consequence for the turning of our young people unto the GOD of our fathers. The more there is this way ascribed unto *grace,* the more the grace of GOD is like to be communicated; and there is in this way a natural and plentiful tendency to awaken our unconverted youth unto a sense of their everlasting interests, which were it generally accomplished a remarkable reformation were therein effected."

THE following *Remarks* close a *quisition concerning Eccle[si] Councils,"* by the venerable I[n-] CREASE MATHER, published 171[9]

"I COME now to that which the main thing inducing m this disquisition. I woul[d] by what I have written be understood, as if I were [af-] fected to the *consociatio[n]* *churches,* in order to the [pres-] ervation of the faith and or the Gospel professed by [us.] I know no man that has sp[end-] ed in this cause more t[han I] have done. For as to the [con-] sociation of churches, agr[eeing] among themselves, that no churches shall be owne[d by] them, or pastor ordained [or de-] posed, or the like matte[r of] common concernment [done] without the approbation of n[eigh-] boring pastors and chu[rches,] I have more than once de[clared] publicly my judgment con[cern-] ing it, as that which is no[t only] lawful, but *absolutely nece[ssary]* for the establishment of [the] churches. The light of n[atural] reason, as well as Scrip[ture] teaches churches in co[mmon] with other societies, to ass[ociate] and combine for their co[mmon] safety. This was pra[ctised] among the churches, in [the] primitive times of Christi[anity,] and it is so in most of t[he re-] formed churches in Euro[pe to] this day. Some who ar[e not] Christians, have seen a ne[cessi-] ty of consociating, to upho[ld the] false religion professed by [them.] To say nothing of many [mod-] ern instances, a late lea[rned] writer informs us, that [some] ages since there happe[ned a] great contention among [the]

* *Vindiga de Synod[is.]*

synagogues then in
:arried on by three Rab-
iote among them, who
that account cast out of
iagogues, but others ad-
them; what had been
oved insignificant, until
ie to a consociation, the
iereof was, that the be-
of the schism were made
le of giving them any
trouble. Now if the
of this world shall be
in their generation, as
ir and consent for the
ig superstition; why
not the churches of
iaving the countenance
ord in their doing of it)
: consent maintain the
order of the Gospel?
tion would sometimes
:he deficiency of the
i in New England in
icular; and he did with
emnity recommend the
ation of it to Mr. Mitch-
famous pastor of the
n Cambridge) when he
i the Right-hand of Fel-
at his ordination. And
before he went to be
he spirits of just men
rfect, he drew up, "Pro-
concerning the conso-
and communion of
i, tendered to the elders
hren of the churches,
consideration and ac-
according to God."
propositions falling into
i, I published them to
d above forty years ago.
it of a church govern-
i been objected to us,
we have one gathered
e Word of God, by those
servants of his, who
:hurches in New Eng-
What else is our Plat-

form of Church Discipline? Our
only want is an agreement to
practise what has been our profession: which neglect will in
time endanger the overturning
our church government, and our
churches too, and it may be introduce another church government not gathered out of the
Word of God. In the Synod
which met at Boston, in the year
1662, although there was not an
universal concurrence in the answer to the first question concerning the subjects of baptism;
in answer to the second question about the consociation of
churches, there was a *marvellous unanimity;* not one elder,
nor so much as two brethren in
all that reverend Assembly dissenting, which I am the better
able to testify, in that I was of
that Synod; which very few
men now living were. Not one
other that I know of. Such an
unanimity, seems to be of God,
and the consideration of it should
be of weight with the churches.
The pastors in this Province, did
at a general convention of them
at Boston, May 30, 1700, pass
the following vote; To prevent
the great mischief to the evangelical interests that may arise
from the unadvised proceedings
of people to gather churches in
the neighborhood, it is provided,
that the result of the Synod, in
1662, relating to the *Consociation of churches* may be republished, with an address to the
churches, intimating our desires
(and so far as we are concerned
our purposes) to see that advice
carefully attended, and the irregular proceedings of any people hereafter, contrary to that
advice, not encouraged. This
was the vote which passed at the

mentioned convention. When also he that writes these lines, was desired to address , the churches accordingly. What has hitherto retarded, I need not mention. I am now taking. my leave of the world, and of these churches; having been in a public capacity, serving Christ and them (after a poor weak manner) for more than five above a jubilee of years. I have been often thinking with myself, what I should leave with the Lord's people in this land as my last legacy. I have considered, that the churches have now greater cause than formerly to be concerned by ecclesiastical and scriptural methods to preserve the faith and order of the Gospel, which has been delivered to them. A due attendance to what is from the Scripture declared in the Synod mentioned, with respect to the communion and consociation of churches, will, by the blessing of our Lord Jesus Christ, be a good means to prevent degeneracy, and to establish them in that holy faith and order of the Gospel, which has been professed and practised among them; and by which the religious people in New England have been distinguished from other people. I have therefore caused those Synod conclusions, to be republished herewith, and recommend the consideration of them, and an agreement to practise according to what is there determined, with a steadfast adherence to the Platform of Discipline, as my dying farewell to the churches in New England. *So will New England remain New England.*"

The "Synod's pro concerning the *Consoc churches,*" here referred contained in a late editi Cambridge Platform, Mr. Armstrong, and oth sellers in Boston.

MASSACHUSETTS MISSIONARY

*(Report of the Trustees
from p. 285.)*

At the annual and semiannu of the Board for the year no the following missionary ap were made: viz. The Rev. An gill, for six months, on the no western frontiers of, our co Rev Jotham Sewall, for the v in the counties of Somerset beck, Maine, the Rev. John four months, in Garland and ity, county of Hancock; the Warren, for three months, in the vicinity; Mr. Joshua Dea six months, and afterwards weeks, Mr. Philip Colbey, fir months, and afterwards for ei Mr. Robert Crowell, for thre and Mr. Benjamin C. Meigs, weeks: these last four to occu tions or fields of labor, in the Maine, as our Committee of Missionary Society should judg visable All these, exceptin Pettengill and Meigs, who we ed by particular circumstance their appointments, and hav their missions to the satisfac Board.

Mr. Colbey's labors were Waterville, Farmington, Vas Fairfax, and Readfield in the Kennebeck, Paris, in the cou ford; and Norridgwalk and the county of Somerset. Bea ing on the Sabbath, he preach days as often as he had oppo as in some of the places he fou venient for the people to at meetings on secular days, he of his time in visiting from hou which he thought he found to ful as more frequent preaching he says, "being most of the u ary, located in particular plac ties were more like those of a parish, than of a travelling n "In all the places where I ha is, "I have found people not only courteous to... the missionary places, meetings have been solemn, and affecting." "Very... essed gratitude to the Missionary for their goodness to them... sionaries amongst them." ... under date of Lord'sday, Nov... "After meeting (at Vassalville to the upper part of... preached an evening lecture. Lord appears to be specially... For several weeks past, the e been very attentive to ser... and it is thought that about this little neighborhood have ght to the knowledge of the... house was crowded, and ev... ned listening as for eternity." ngregational society in Paris, of about thirty families, he as very much interested for... Surrounded with Sectarians, Universalists, and others, the med like a good man struggling ity. Their candor, sincerity, ve solemnly pleased me much peared to be many inquiring g them. They are worthy the Missionary Societies, and de prayers of the friends of Zion." gewock he says, "While in this versed with some young per... deep convictions, and, from ld discover, have strong hope, is about to pour out his... and revive his work, which have been pretty much suspend general reformation for about years. Christians seem much prayer and sinners appear sol tentive." In some other places some encouraging appearances ng the National Fast and one which he kept at Norridgewock, ell's labors were chiefly at Wa d Wayne, in the county of k. At Waterville he noticed rable appearances, and in his der date of Monday, Oct. 4, It was signified to me, through for procuring preaching, that here wished for preaching, and for several Sabbaths it I would cannot but hope that the day distant, when the people of this little village will no longer be to God and his ordinances, as o has preached Gospel." For reasons, and especially on ac n urgent request to return to a re he had been preaching, as a Mr Crowell spent out eight the missionary work, but his ars to have been off-and-... employed.

X.

Mr Dean was stationed at Hampden on the Penobscot. "Although," he says, "I have preached regularly in that town, I have also preached frequently in other places, particularly in Frankfort, and in Plantation No 2. Besides preaching 158 sermons, I have attended, as opportunity presented, to such other duties as are common to missionaries. The people, among whom I have labored, appeared solemn and attentive, and uniformly manifested a strong disposition to hear the preaching of the word, and, though I have not the pleasure to state any special success, that attended my labors, I trust my efforts have not been without effect. The people feel grateful that they have been provided with preaching, and wish to return the Missionary Society their acknowledgments for the favors conferred on them." Desirous of enjoying the stated ordinances of the Gospel, the people of the congregational order in Hampden and Plantation No 2 have expressed a desire to have Mr Dean regularly ordained over them as his united charge, and for this purpose, they have made subscriptions to a considerable annual amount. But not finding themselves able at present to provide a full support for a settled minister, they have made application to the Board for assistance from the funds of this Society.

In aid of the support of the Rev Mr Williams of Brewer, Maine, who was settled under the patronage of this Society, and with expectation of continued assistance from it for some time, the Board have appropriated for the current year one hundred dollars; and from information received they have the satisfaction to believe, that the money appropriated to this object, is very usefully applied.

Fifty dollars were also appropriated for the purpose of supporting in part Mr. Ezekiel Rich in missionary service in the state of Rhode Island.

The plan of more stationary missions, and especially of assisting parishes and societies, desirous of a permanent ministration of the Gospel, but not yet quite able to support it, appears to meet with very general favor, and to promise great and lasting benefit to many. Besides the application from Brewer, which has been complied with, and that from Hampden which is under partial consideration, the wishes of some other societies in our Eastern District, for similar aid, have been communicated to the Board, and will deserve attention. Calls indeed, of this kind seem likely to multiply faster than our funds, unless some special exertion be made to augment them, will admit of their being satisfactorily answered, and it is still the opinion of the Board,

Brought forward $1,536 56
tions in the second parish
of Weymouth by Mr S
Torrey,   1 00
   Eliza do do do.   1 25
   From do. do. do. ,25———2 50
From the Rev. Mr
Strong's society in Ran-
dolph,   50 00
  From a Cent Society
do.   10 00———60 00
From the Rev Dr Austin's
Society in Worcester, 86 52
From the Rev D. Parish's
Society in Byfield,   41 62
From the Rev. Mr Thomp-
son's Society in Rehoboth, 14 61
From the Rev Mr Thom-
as's Society in Abington, 25 13
  From a Cent Society,do. 19 00———44 13
From the Rev Mr
Tucker's Society in Roxbury 21 75
From the Rev. Mr. Judson's
Society in Uxbridge, 38 13
From the Rev Mr Howe's
Society in Hopkinton, 18 00
  From a Cent Society do 4 68———22 68
From the Rev Mr Backer's
Society in Middleborough, 49 13
From the Rev. Mr. Waters's
Society in Ashby,   25 12
From a Cent Society in Dan-
vers, by Mrs Walker, 17 60
—— —— in Fitchburg, by
the Rev W. Bailey, 6 25
From three children, by do. ,18
From the Cent Society in
Wrentham, by the Rev Mr
Fiske,   6 30
—— —— in Milford, by Dea
N. Chapin,   1 75
—— —— in Medway, by the
Rev Luther Wright, 4 00
From an unknown person,
enclosed to Mr. Asaph Leland, 1 00
From a friend, by the Rev.
John Cleaveland, for the pur-
chase of Bibles, 3 00
Collection at the Old South
Church, after the annual ser-
mon,   178 65
  9. From the First Congre-
gational Society in Paris, Maine,
by Mr Philip Colher, 6 56
June 7. From the Rev, R S
Storrs's Society in Braintree, 23 60
  16 From a friend by the
Rev Dr Spring, 4 00
  17 From the Rev Free-
grace Reynolds's Society in
Wilmington, 10 62
From a friend of
missions of the Rev Mr
Reynolds, 2 00———12 62

Carried forward $2,240 2

Brought forward $2,244
From a Cent Society in
Northborough, by Mr. A. Rice, 1
  From 96 members the annu-
al payment for one year, $192
From 11 do. for 2 years, 35
From 1 do. for 3 years, 6
From 1 do for 5 years, 10
From 1 do. for 7 years, 14
From 1 do for 8 years, 16
From 1 do for 9 years, 18
From 1 do for 11 years, 22———300

$2,591

DONATIONS FOR THE SUPPORT OF MISSIONS AND TRANSLATIONS.

July 2. 1815 From the following per-
sons in Danville, Ver by the Rev. J
Fitch; viz.
Amos Clement, $1
Joseph Hall,   1
Ebenezer Cheney, 1
Oliver Morse,   1
Miss Rhoda Brainerd, 1
Rev John Fitch,   2
Jacob Morrill,   5———$10
From Dea Eliph Goddard of
Athol, by the Rev Josiah Esta-
brook,   —
  4 From an unknown person
by mail,*   50
  6 From Mr Jesse Heskel, of
Rochester, toward the transla-
tions,
From a female friend to mis-
sions in Rochester,
  7 From an unknown person by
mail,†

Carried forward $9

* A fifty dollar bill was enclosed i
following letter. "District of Maine.
donor of the enclosed bill sometime
presented a smaller one to the Ame
Board of Commissioners for Foreign
sions, with an implicit engagement,
he would add thereto as the Lord
prosper him." And the may be com
ed as a grateful acknowledgement
being thus prospered, as well as a tok
his reliance on the promise, *He that w
eth shall be watered also himself*"

† A five dollar bill was enclosed i
following letter. "County of Hamp,
June 30, 1814.

"Sir,

I am a man in low circumstances, an
my bread by the sweat of my brow
have named the name of Christ, and
(though not without many doubt
trust) that my sins are washed aw

Brought forward $95 60
m a friend of missions
'. Dwight, jun $2 00
Mrs. Abigail Clark
xilge, Con.   3 00
the Female Chari-
iety in Great Bar-
              23 35—33 35
rm the Female Cent
in Arkport, Steuben
N Y. for the transla-
                       13 00
Mr Samuel T. Arm-
¿ear profits of Memoirs
Newell,   200 00
om an unknown person
                       10 00
om the Rev. John Turn-
Biddeford, Maine, and
subscriber to the Saco
leford Foreign Mission
                        6 00
om females in the first
t Canterbury, (Con) by
mas L. Paine,   68 00
om Mr Solomon Good-
manea, Ver towards the
on of the Scriptures in
                      100 00

Carried forward $525 35

l of Christ. I have for some time
I felt for the poor destitute heath-
um a member of a branch of the
missionary society. But I have
al the Memoirs of Mrs Harriet
with much pleasure, and I trust
feel myself called upon to extend
ing hand to the miserable millions,
ow nothing of the blessed Jesus.
this offering is small; yet I trust,
who noticed the widow's two
d overlooks not a cup of cold wa-
i given in his name, will grant his
upon it, so that it shall accomplish
which it is given. Please to use
 used five dollars for the further-
he missionary cause, and accept
es of a yearly offering, as the cir-
xes of an unworthy subject of di-
earance will admit.
                      A MECHANIC "
ter, in the hand writing of a fe-
d with the Salem post-mark, con-
re above donation. The following
ract.
ear Sir.
t I could not well spare my sem-
ination for the support of Foreign
at present; and I had concluded
old it accordingly. But the argu-
Christophilos, in the last number
panoplist, occasioned me to change
rmination, and forward you the
bill."

Brought forward $525 35
21. From the Rev. Heman
Humphrey of Fairfield, Con.
                        5 00
From Mrs Sophia Humphrey,
wife of the Rev. H. H.
                        5 00
From the Sheffield Female
Charitable society, by Mrs. Margaret Bradford, the Treasurer,†   36 65
22. From a female, enclosed
in a letter with the Jaffrey post-
mark,   5 00
27. From a society of Young
Ladies in Wrentham, remitted
by Miss Olivia Hawes, the Secretary, by the Rev. Elisha Fisk,   50 00
                     ————
                      $627 00

DONATION TO THE MIDDLESEX BIBLE
SOCIETY

THE following letter, enclosing three dol-
dollars and a quarter, was lately received from some unknown person by the
Rev. Dr. Morse. The resolution of the
writer is recommended to the serious
consideration of every reader of the
Panoplist.   ED.

"Sir,
HERE is enclosed a small sum, which I
wish you to transmit to the Trustees of
the Bible Society in the county of Middlesex. I will explain to you the manner in
which this sum was collected, and what
induced me, in the first instance, to lay
so small a sum aside for charitable use.
About a year since, I was reading Paley,
where he treats of being charitable upon
a plan. The thought struck me in this
manner, that though I was poor, I was
able occasionally to give a little something,
and I thought this little in a lump would
do more good than the same sum divided. I have every Sabbath for one year
past laid aside one sixteenth of a dollar I
had never concluded in what charitable
manner to bestow it, until I heard of the
formation of this society; and thinking that
this small sum, laid out in the manner
contemplated by the society, might be

† The Secretary of this Society in a letter accompanying the donation says
"With gratitude to the Board for having
engaged in the great work of evangelizing
the heathen, and accepting and appropriating our mite to the object intended, this
year's collection is cheerfully committed to
their disposal."
Many donations are accompanied by letters, which abound in affection toward the
great object for which the donations are
given, and in respect for the Board as the
instrument of dispensing this charity.

the happy means of enlightening some one, who is ignorant, I freely give it. Should this purpose be answered I shall be highly gratified.

A WELL WISHER TO MORAL AND
RELIGIOUS INSTITUTIONS."

Rev Dr Morse.
June, 1814.

BOSTON FEMALE SOCIETY FOR MISSIONARY PURPOSES.

This Society has existed nearly fourteen years: It was instituted in Oct 1800; and is believed to be the first of its kind in the United States. Its object is to aid Missionary undertakings. Its members are, (principally professors,) of the Congregational and Baptist denominations. Each member pays two dollars annually and the subscriptions and donations of each are devoted to societies of objects patronized by her own denomination. These funds have been applied to the purchase of books, the support of domestic missions, the translation of the Scriptures, to Foreign Missions, and the purchase of Bibles for distribution, as the openings of Providence have suggested the path of duty. The Society meets on the first Monday afternoon of every month, the two denominations meeting harmoniously together.

In March 1812, this Society in an address to the female friends of Zion, (published in the Massachusetts Baptist Missionary Magazine,) requested correspondence by letter from similar Societies in our country; and also proposed to them to set apart the same time for special prayer for the out-pouring of the Holy Spirit, and a blessing on Missionary exertions. The result has been pleasing. They have received information from about 40 Societies, which have cordially engaged to unite in concert with them. These are in the States of Vermont, New Hampshire, Rhode Island, Massachusetts, Connecticut, New York, Pennsylvania, and Ohio.

May not a hope be indulged, that He, who inclines his children to pray, will return answers of peace in his own time. Should other Societies be disposed to unite in concert and correspondence with this, letters directed to Mrs Mary Webb secretary of the Society, to the care of Messrs Lincoln & Edmands, No 53, Cornhill, would undoubtedly be received with pleasure, and duly attended to.

BOSTON SOCIETY FOR THE RELIGIOUS AND MORAL IMPROVEMENT OF SEAMEN

The Committee of this Society lately made their second annual report. It ap-

pears that the Society has tracts among the seamen of ships. The following paragraph tracted from a sensible letter the chaplain of U. S. frigate the Committee.

"If you could but prevent t sion of some sins, your Societ amply rewarded for its benev tions. But I believe that you means of doing more;—of sav wretch from sinking beneath t of everlasting misery.

"I pray God to bless, as I will reward, your exertions men, who deserve the atte pious and benevolent."

EXCELLENT REGULATI

The Government of U. S. military order "directing the censed from service of any ed officer, who shall send or challenge to fight a duel, or ing that any other officer accepted, or is about to send challenge to fight a duel, sha diately arrest and bring to fender."

SOCIETY FOR PROPAGATING T

This Society, at its late annu chose the following officers fo ing year, viz
His Honor WILLIAM PHILLIP

The Rev. JOHN LATHROP, D

The Rev. ABIEL HOLMES, D
The Rev. WILLIAM E. CHA

Dea SAMUEL H. WALLEY,
Mr. JOSIAH SALISBURY, T.
SAMUEL SALISBURY, Esq
ALDEN BRADFORD, Esq.
The Rev. JEDIDIAH MORSE,
The Rev. ELIPHALET PORT.
Mr. JAMES WHITE,

Select C

ORDINATIONS

ORDAINED, at Dedham, on March last, the Rev. TITUS the office of deacon in the Church, by the Rt Rev. world. Mr. Strong is to off James's Church in Greenfield

At Peru, (N Y) on the last the Rev. DAVID PLUM pastor, pearl of the church in Sermon by the Rev. James T

brough, (Ver) the Rev. Era-
Newton. Sermon by the Rev.
Jonaf m 2 Thess. ii, 3, 4.
an, on the 20th of April, the Rev.
its, over the church and soc. e-
hird parish of that town. Ser-
e Rev. Mr. Ripley of Concord.
nd, (Con.) on the 5th of May,
Augustus Bollesto the pastoral
e Baptist church in that place.
y the Rev. Dr. Baldwin of

dbury, Con. on the 25th of May
Rev. Josea Treat, as an evan-
a view of laboring as a mission-
e western parts of the United

imer, (N Y.) on the 16th of
t, the Rev. Joas B Whirtel-
the Presbyterian church in that
ermon by the Rev Dr Backus,
of Hamilton College
ville, (Penn.) on the 16th of
, the Rev. Oliver Hill, over
and societies in that town and
nl. Sermon by the Rev. Eben-
sbury from Ez. iii, 10, 11.
vham, (Ver.) on the 30th ult.
David O Morton, over the
ional church and society in that
ermon by the Rev Dr Davis.

At Jerico, (Ver.) on the 6th i m the
Rev. Joseph Lanule, over the congre-
gational church and society in that town.
Sermon by the Rev. Thomas A. Merrill.

INSTALLATIONS.

Installed, at Woodbury, (Con.) on the
25th of May last, the Rev. Henry P
Strong, to the pastoral care of the church
and society in that town. Sermon by the
Rev. William L. Strong of Somers.
At Rowe, (Mass.) on the 31st. of Dec.
last. the Rev. Preserved Smith. Ser-
mon by the Rev. Jonathan Grout, of
Hawley.
At Boston, on the 30th ult: the Rev
James A Winchell, as pastor of the
First Baptist Church in that town Ser-
mon by the Rev Dr. Baldwin from Acts
xx, 24

CONSECRATION.

On Friday, the 29th of April, St. Mary's
Chapel in Newton was consecrated as an
Episcopal church, by the Rt. Rev. Dr.
Griswold, bishop of the eastern diocese.

OBITUARY.

APHICAL SKETCH OF THE REV.
T DICKINSON, LATE PASTOR OF
URCH OF CHRIST IN HOLLISTON,

rrect maxim, that *example* is
reserve and efficacious, then *pre-
*rtial sketches of the lives of men,
or piety, activity, and usefulness,
divine blessing, be not only in-
but beneficial, to the living.
rter of the humble and devout
is an interesting and instructive
, particularly that of the dili-
, and faithful minister of Christ.
rily to delineate *such a charac-
*obiect of this communication.
e Rev Timothy Dickinson was
ious and respectable parents at
, Mass. June 2 , 1761. He was
of eight chil ne ; four of whom
, and four daughters; and who
o be settled in the family state.
bject of this me noir, in the ear-
of childhood, manifested a tem-
rkably mild, pleasant and pacific.
utiful, obedient, and submissive
rents. So amiable and pacific
tural disposition, and so inoffen-

sive and engaging were his manners, that
he was universally beloved, not only by
his nearest relatives and youthful associates, but by all who knew him. While a
child he manifested a great fondness for
books. Although his constitution was
naturally slender, and his health feeble
and interrupted, he devoted a large portion of his leisure hours to study.
He lived with his parents, and labored
upon a farm until he was sixteen years
of age. At that period, he took a very
lively interest in the revolutionary struggle of his country. His youthful mind
was so engaged in the cause of liberty and
independence, that he would not be dissuaded by his friends from entering into
the active service of his country. He accordingly joined the army, as a private
soldier in the militia, in which capacity he
served for about 15 months. It is said.
that while in the army his conduct was
so dutiful and obedient to his officers, and
so engaging to his fellow soldiers, that he
obtained special tokens of favor and esteem from both.
Immediately after he left the army, he
was fitted for College; principally at
Northampton, under the tuition of the

Rev. President Dwight, who was then a young man, instructing a private school at that place. It is believed on good authority, that Mr. Dickinson was induced, principally, to seek a liberal education, in consequence of his witnessing so much depravity and wickedness in the army; by which his sensibility was often and severely wounded. This depravity and licentiousness, which he found to be more or less acted out by mankind generally, he felt determined to combat; and, that he might be enabled to do it the more effectually, he sought the aid of a public education.

At the age of about 18, Mr. Dickinson became a member of Dartmouth College. Although at this period, he was "a child of nature only," his disposition was so amiable, his temper so mild and pacific, and his manners so engaging, that he soon secured the friendship and esteem of the officers and students of the College.

In the first year of his collegiate course, it pleased a sovereign God to visit the College and its vicinity with a special and remarkable revival of religion. This promising youth, and most of his class, were hopeful subjects of this glorious work. At this season of divine manifestation and power, "young Dickinson was made for the first time to notice the deep depravity of his own heart, and to renounce all dependence upon his own strength. Then was he taught in the school of Jesus the equity of the divine law, the ability and willingness of the Redeemer to save, and the greatness of his salvation. At this period, he hopefully arrived at the knowledge of the truth as it is in Jesus, and imbibed a love for those doctrines of grace, which he so manfully espoused, and faithfully preached through life, and which were the ground of his support in the hour of death." Having made a public profession of the religion of the Gospel, he was enabled, amidst the various temptations to which youth are exposed, to adorn his sacred profession by an humble and circumspect walk before God.

While at College, Mr. Dickinson was diligent and persevering in the prosecution of his studies, appeared to advantage at recitations and all the literary exhibitions of his class, and acquired the reputation of a correct, classical scholar. A friend to the officers of the College, and a steady supporter of its laws, he was always one of the first to suggest the cautions of prudence, and to restrain the impetuosity of the more eccentric and ardent part of his class, in any enterprise hazardous to morals or good order.

One of the most prominent traits in his character, at College, was that of a peacemaker. He not only cautiously kept himself from unhappy contentions and injurious disputes, but when any of his classmates were contending, he was ready to interpose his efforts, as a reconciler of the parties.

In fine, such was the sincerity of heart—the simplicity of his manners, and the uniform consistency of his character, that he was universally esteemed, both by the officers and particularly by his classmates, who graduated in the year 1785.

For the substance of this account of Mr. Dickinson's collegiate character, the compiler acknowledges his obligation to three very respectable clergymen, who were his classmates; and one in the class immediately preceding.

After Mr. Dickinson took his degree, he was immediately appointed to Moore's charity school, which is an academy connected with the College. Being employed one year in the instruction of this school, he felt it his duty to place himself in a situation, in which he might pursue his favorite theological studies in a more systematic and uninterrupted manner. To this end, he studied divinity under the instruction of the Rev. Mr. Tappan, late Professor of Divinity in the College, then a minister in ——— (Mass.) He was next licensed as a candidate for the Gospel ministry, preached at Exeter and Hampton, New Hampshire, and in several parishes in the northern part of Massachusetts, where he is now remembered with great affection by many serious and religious persons.

After having preached a suitable time at Holliston, (Mass.) he received an invitation, from the church and people of that place, to settle with them in the ministry. Having seriously and prayerfully deliberated on the subject, he gave an affirmative answer to this call, and was solemnly set apart to the work of the ministry, Feb. 18, 1789, and settled in great harmony with his former instructor and patron, the excellent Dr. Tappan, preaching on the occasion.

On the 26th of November following, he was married to Miss Margaret, the eldest daughter of his predecessor in the ministry.* By this lady* he had seven children, one son and three daughters, five of whom are now living. May a judicious and faithful instruction, and the pious example be duly appreciated by them, that each child of Mr. D. (a daughter,)

* At the request of Mrs. ——— family, some words of commendation, which the writer had used, are omitted.

n, Feb. 2, 1806, aged 15 years
very amiable, dutiful, and promis-
and from the patient and sub-
ness in which she endured a
ease, and in which she left the
rom of her hopeful circumstan-
s reason to trust that she fell
so. They have also buried
a.

contemplate the character of
on as he stood at the head of
y, it shines with peculiar lus-
so kind, tender, and provi-
d—an affectionate and indul-

His house was eminently
oth his example and precepts
inced, that he adopted the
pious Joshua of old, *As for
house we will serve the Lord*
may be said of him with as
iety as of almost any man,
efore his house with a perfect
greatly excelled in family gov-
d instruction. He united
h energy, and innocent indul-
proper restraint. His instruc-
ample were so uniform, judi-
nsistent, and so expressive of
benevolence, that all, under
cure, felt conscious that his
re wisely and affectionately
he promotion of their present
d usefulness, and to the attain-
for future and eternal good. His
e a passion for hospitality,
ted peace. He always receiv-
ven in the ministry, and his
iends, with great cordiality
as of only entertaining and
t peculiarly instructive. So
impressive was his sense of
nce of time, that it was his
favor, that his social inter-
his friends might be mutually
improving. To communicate
with modesty, and receive it
le and pleasure, were prom-
his character. His favorite
conversation were the great
duties of the Gospel, relig-
nee, cases of conscience, and
ry thing pertaining to the
God. At the same time, he
means indifferent to literary
seful subjects. Possessing a
ngitative turn of mind, and
the most benevolent feelings
kind, he was ever desirous to
own fund of useful information,
contribute to the improve-
ers. He possessed a peculiar
rest the attention, and to un-
inds of children and youth
of instruction was too young,
or too obscure to escape his

benevolent exertions, when opportunities
presented for doing good.

But the character of Mr. Dickinson
shines with a peculiar brightness when
viewed in connexion with the discharge of
the immediate and appropriate duties of a
Gospel minister.

As a preacher, he was plain, faithful,
and affectionate. He ever spake "*as a
dying man to dying men.*" As he firmly
believed in the truth and importance of
those doctrines, which are usually denominated *the doctrines of grace,* he felt it
his duty often, plainly, and affectionately
to state and illustrate them. The native
and total depravity of sinners; the necessity of regeneration by the special operations of the Holy Spirit; the doctrine of
personal election; the necessity of disinterested and holy affections towards God
and men, in order to become interested
in the atonement of the Savior; the Deity
of Christ, and the doctrine of a Trinity
of persons in the Godhead, together with
those doctrines, which naturally grow
out of the preceding sentiments, are
truths which he firmly believed, and
which he considered as of the greatest
importance. No considerations of popu-
larity or self-interest could deter him from
a plain and frequent exhibition of those
divine truths, which are so offensive to the
carnal mind. Believing that *all Scripture
is given by inspiration of God, and is
profitable for doctrine, for reproof, for
correction, and for instruction in righteousness,* he ever felt it his indispensable
duty to contend earnestly for the faith
which was once delivered to the saints.

The writer of this paper can in no way
do better justice to the character of
Mr. Dickinson, than by subjoining the
following extract from the Rev. Dr. Em-
mons's sermon delivered at his funeral,
from these words of the apostle Paul in
his second epistle to Timothy. *For I am
now ready to be offered, and the time of
my departure is at hand. I have fought
a good fight, I have finished my course, I
have kept the faith. Henceforth there is
laid up for me a crown of righteousness,
which the Lord the righteous Judge shall
give me at that day, and not to me only
but unto all them that love his appearing.*

"Mr. Dickinson was naturally endowed
with that placid countenance, that mild
disposition, and those social and mental
excellencies, which attracted the love
and esteem of all his friends, connexions,
and acquaintances. But these are not
worthy to be compared with those moral
excellencies, which diffused a radiance
around his religious and ministerial character. He was very apparently a man of
God, who exhibited the reality and beauty

43

Rev. President Dwight, who was then a young man, instructing a private school at that place. It is believed on good authority, that Mr. Dickinson was induced, principally, to seek a liberal education, in consequence of his witnessing so much depravity and wickedness in the army; by which his sensibility was often and severely wounded. This depravity and licentiousness, which he found to be more or less acted out by mankind generally, he felt determined to combat; and, that he might be enabled to do it the more effectually, he sought the aid of a public education.

At the age of about 18, Mr. Dickinson became a member of Dartmouth College. Although at this period he was "a child of nature only," his disposition was so amiable, his temper so mild and pacific, and his manners so engaging, that he soon secured the friendship and esteem of the officers and students of the College.

In the first year of his collegiate course, it pleased a sovereign God to visit the College and its vicinity with a special and remarkable revival of religion. This promising youth, and most of his class, were hopeful subjects of this glorious work. At this season of divine manifestation and power, "young Dickinson was made for the first time to notice the deep depravity of his own heart, and to renounce all dependence upon his own strength. Then was he taught in the school of Jesus the equity of the divine law, the ability and willingness of the Redeemer to save, and the greatness of his salvation. At this period, he hopefully arrived at the knowledge of the truth as it is in Jesus, and imbibed a love for those doctrines of grace, which he so manfully espoused, and faithfully preached through life, and which were the ground of his support in the hour of death." Having made a public profession of the religion of the Gospel, he was enabled, amidst the various temptations to which youth are exposed, to adorn his sacred profession by an humble and circumspect walk before God.

While at College, Mr. Dickinson was diligent and persevering in the prosecution of his studies, appeared to advantage at recitations and all the literary exhibitions of his class, and acquired the reputation of a correct, classical scholar. A friend to the officers of the College, and a steady supporter of its laws, he was always one of the first to suggest the cautions of prudence, and to restrain the impetuosity of the more eccentric and ardent part of his class, in any enterprise hazardous to morals or good order.

One of the most prominent traits in his character, at College, was that of a peace-maker. He not only cautiously kept himself from unhappy contentions and ruinous disputes, but when any of his mates were contending, he was ever to interpose his efforts, as a mediator, to reconcile the parties.

In fine, such was the sincerity of his heart—the simplicity of his manners, and the uniform consistency of his character, that he was universally loved and esteemed, both by the officers and particularly by his classmates. He graduated in the year 1785.

For the substance of this account of Mr. Dickinson's collegiate character, the compiler acknowledges his obligation to three very respectable clergymen, who were his classmates; and to ___ in the class immediately preceding.

After Mr. Dickinson took his degree, he was immediately appointed preceptor of Moore's charity school, which is an academy connected with the College. Being employed one year in the instruction of this school, he felt it his duty to place himself in a situation, in which he could pursue his favorite theological studies in a more systematic and uninterrupted manner. To this end, he studied under the instruction of the Rev. ___ pan, late Professor of Divinity at ___ College, then a minister in N___ (Mass.) He was next licensed as a candidate for the Gospel ministry, preached at Exeter and Hopkinton, New Hampshire, and in several parishes in the northern part of Massachusetts, where he is now remembered with great affection by many serious and religious persons.

After having preached a suitable time at Holliston, (Mass.) he received an invitation, from the church and people of that place, to settle with them in the ministry. Having seriously and fully deliberated on the subject, he gave an affirmative answer to this invitation, and was solemnly set apart to the work of the ministry, Feb. 18, 1789. He settled in great harmony and peace. His former instructor and patron, the excellent Dr. Tappan, preached on the occasion.

On the 26th of November following, he was married to Miss Margaret ___, the eldest daughter of his venerable predecessor in the ministry, a lady[*] he had seven children, four sons and three daughters, five of whom are now living. May a gracious God ___ faithful instructions, and promises ___ be duly appreciated by them. The first child of Mr. D. (a daughter,) died ___

tion, Feb. 2, 1806, aged 15 years a very amiable, dutiful, and p.omo-d; and from the patient and submanner in which she ended a disease, and in which she left the d from o.her hopeful circumstan-ive reason to trust that she fell Jesus. They have also buried son.

we contemplate the character of .inson as he stood at the head of mily, it shines with peculiar lus-was o kind, tender, and provis-and—an affectionate and indul-nt. His house was eminently

Both his example and precepts . evinced, that he adopted the i of pious Joshua of old, *As for ty house we will serve the Lord.* it may be said of him with as opriety as of almost any man, *d before his house with a perfect* le greatly excelled in family gov-and instruction. He united with energy, and innocent indul-h proper restraint His instrue-example were so uniform, judi-l consistent, and so expressive of and benevolence, that all, under nal care, felt conscious that his were wisely and affectionately to the promotion of their present and usefulness, and to the attain-ieir future and eternal good. His saves a mansion of hospitality,), and peace He always receiv-ethren in the ministry, and his s friends, with great cordiality. y was not only entertaining and but peculiarly instructive. So nd impressive was his sense of rtance of time, that it was his endeavor, that his social inter-h his friends might be mutually l improving. To communicate on with modesty, and receive it tude and pleasure, were promi-s in his character. His favorite of conversation were the great and duties of the Gospel, relig-ligence, cases of conscience, and every thing *pertaining to the of God.* At the same time, he > means indifferent to literary r useful subjects. Possessing a inquisitive turn of mind, and by the most benevolent feelings mankind, he was ever desirous to its own fund of useful information, y to contribute to the improve-others. He possessed a peculiar interest the attention, and to im-e minds of children and youth. et of instruction was too young, de, or too obscure to escape his

. **X.**

benevolent exertions, when opportunities presented for doing good.

But the character of Mr. Dickinson shines with a peculiar brightness when viewed in connexion with the discharge of the immediate and appropriate duties of a Gospel minister.

As a preacher, he was plain, faithful, and affectionate He ever spake *"as a dying man to dying men"* As he firmly believed in the truth and importance of those doctrines, which are usually denom-inated *the doctrines of grace,* he felt it his duty often, plainly, and affectionately to state and illustrate them. The native and total depravity of sinners, the necessi-ty of regeneration by the special opera-tions of the Holy Spirit; the doctrine of personal election; the necessity of disin-terested and holy affections towards God and men, in order to become interested in the atonement of the Savior; the Deity of Christ, and the doctrine of a Trinity of persons in the Godhead, together with those doctrines, which naturally grow out of the preceding sentiments, are truths which he firmly believed, and which he considered as of the greatest importance. No considerations of popu-larity or self-interest could deter him from a plain and frequent exhibition of those divine truths, which are so offensive to the carnal mind. Believing that *all Scripture is given by inspiration of God, and is profitable for doctrine, for reproof, for correction, and for instruction in right-eousness,* he ever felt it his indispensable duty to *contend earnestly for the faith which was once delivered to the saints.*

The writer of this paper can in no way do better justice to the character of Mr. Dickinson, than by subjoining the following extract from the Rev. Dr. Em-mons's sermon delivered at his funeral, from these words of the apostle Paul in his second epistle to Timothy. *For I am now ready to be offered, and the time of my departure is at hand. I have fought a good fight, I have finished my course, I have kept the faith. Henceforth there is laid up for me a crown of righteousness, which the Lord the righteous Judge shall give me at that day, and not to me only but unto all them that love his appearing*

"Mr. Dickinson was naturally endowed with that placid countenance, that mild disposition, and those social and mental excellencies, which attracted the love and esteem of all his friends, connexions, and acquaintances. But these are not worthy to be compared with those moral excellencies, which diffused a radiance around his religious and ministerial char-acter He was very apparently a man of God, who exhibited the reality and beauty

4 3

of religion in his private conversation, as well as in his more public and official conduct. He carried religion with him wherever he went, and made it manifest to all around him, that he was habitually under the influence of the love and fear of God. He gave convincing evidence, that he loved those doctrines of the Gospel which he taught to others, and taught them in love to their souls. The whole tenor of his preaching plainly indicated, that he sought to please God rather than men, for he did not *shun* to exhibit the most essential, the most humbling, and the most heart-searching truths, in terms too plain for any to misunderstand. He had a clear, strong, and pleasant voice, which enabled him to speak with peculiar propriety and energy. And as he aimed to draw the attention of his hearers to his subject, rather than to himself, so he seldom failed of deeply impressing their hearts and consciences. He loved to converse upon religious subjects, and greatly excelled in private discourses with his people, whether they were in prosperity or adversity, whether they were in health or sickness, whether they were concerned or unconcerned about the state of their souls, and whether they were under the hidings of God's face, or enjoyed the light of his countenance. He assiduously performed the most self-denying duties of his office. He took heed to his ministry, and left no proper methods unemployed, to promote the spiritual benefit of his people. He preached the word in season, and out of season, and he privately reproved, rebuked, and exhorted, with peculiar tenderness, plainness, and fidelity. He endeavoured to guard his whole flock against those wolves in sheep's clothing, who lie in wait to deceive and to destroy. *He fought the good fight of faith,* and zealously contended for the doctrines, which he supposed to be according to godliness, and continued through life, to exhibit all the common marks of a pious Christian and of a faithful minister.

"But this is not enough to say of Mr. Dickinson, for in some Christian and ministerial virtues, he shone with a peculiar lustre. His meekness resembled the meekness of Moses. His patience resembled the patience of Job. His fortitude and zeal resembled the fortitude and zeal of Paul. When he was convinced he was right, whilst he was calm, he overcame evil with good. He colored himself against oppression with fortitude, and with a zealous regard to knowledge, he promoted the cause of Christ, at home and abroad. He was among the most zealous ministers and Christians to spread the Gospel and to extend the kingdom of Christ through the world. By his noble example in these

things, Mr. Dickinson, though dead, still speaketh to his brethren in the ministry, and calls upon them, to *go and do likewise.*

"His death was correspondent to his life, for when he had finished his ministerial course, and the time of his departure drew nigh, he found good reason to hope and rejoice in the nearest views of eternity. His lingering disorder, which did not directly affect his intellectual powers, gave him ample opportunity of reflecting upon the past, and of anticipating the future. Though he was frequently afflicted with extreme bodily pain and distress, during a long season of debility and languishment, yet he manifested the same calmness and serenity, the same meekness and patience, and the same submission and fortitude, that he had uniformly exhibited in the time of health and activity. When he had nearly given up all expectation of living, he freely conversed about death and eternity, in a realizing view of those solemn scenes, with apparent peace and full assurance of hope. He seemed to have nothing to fear from the sting of death, or the terror of the grave, nor to prevent his saying, with the departing Apostle, *I am now ready to be offered, and the time of my departure is at hand. I have fought a good fight, I have finished my course, I have kept the faith: henceforth there is laid up for me a crown of righteousness which the Lord the righteous Judge shall give me at that day.* He certainly gave us sufficient evidence to trust that he has fallen asleep in Christ, and will be amply rewarded with a crown of righteousness, when the Lord shall come to be glorified in his ... and admired in all that believe.

"The death of such a pious and faithful minister, in the midst of his days and of his usefulness, is a loud call upon the cause and interest of Christ. It is a day of deep declension, in city and country, and the love of many is waxing cold. Intemperance, errors, and delusions, are coming in like a flood upon us. We need the Nobles, and Jebs, and Deacons, and ... others, to stand in the gap and by the fervent prayers and zealous endeavors, to strengthen the things which

...et are ready to die. This immortality gives us just cause to *Look for the god'y in the coming of the day of God, hastening the coming of the day...*

...who left this world of distress al, July 6, 1814, to enter the reward of a faithful servant. He was the 82nd year of his age. The testimony of all, who knew him, was that he was an able, reverend, and affectionate minister of Jesus Christ. Although he had no general revival of religion in his own and persevering labors, a hopeful instrument of the conversion of a goodly number, and of comforting and edifying the people of God he preached. The writer is in indulging the consoling hope, that ere long, the seed which he has sowed, will be springing up, that *they that do sleep, shall be in the end rest from their labors, and their works follow them.*

At... ...rn, (Mass.) March ... Mrs. Maria Dewey, aged 45, wife of the Hon. David Dewey, Esq. ... Mrs. D. was to a large circle of acquaintance, the writer among that number, and worth remembered only on the monument ... and not, indeed, be seen by her friends,—but was never more to be interesting and useful... Death took from one of the most delightful in the family, and possessed in many advantages, mental and religious. These she ... to good purpose, and the improvement of her powers of mind continued in life. Her natural was well cultivated, her judgment discriminating,—her person amiable, mild, and ... manners were refined, and to a ... degree of communicativeness. In the several relations, as a wife, a mother, a sister, a friend and neighbor, she was in the duties of... ...with no small portion an import... in society. To her amiable and ... the gospel of Christ, she was endeared,—to them her death was a ... They became sensible of the extensive sphere she filled, and the strong hold she had on the affection of their hearts. ...had been, for several years a member of the church, and sustained a...

...ther was the Hon. David Noble, ... of the Court of Common ... ...of Berkshire.

...character unfavorable in the view of her Christian friends. But, though her conduct was good, she was too well acquainted with her own heart to be satisfied with herself. She felt her sinfulness, and her desert of punishment. But to her, Jesus Christ, upon whom she appeared to place her reliance and hope, had *brought life and immortality to light.* She believed the important, humbling truths of the Bible, and trusted that, through the grace of God, she should be admitted to the mansions of light and glory. Actuated by the operative faith of the Gospel, she wished others to enjoy its rich blessings, and, as a member of the Female Charitable and Religious Society of the town, she sought as well as in other ways, to do good to her fellow-sinners. Her prayers... bosom... interest to the East—the conveyance of the knowledge of the Gospel was a very interesting to her heart.

This winter and spring of 1813 was noted with the prevalence of that disorder, which has so rapidly hurried thousands into eternity. Though her disease was not, properly, she probably fell a victim to that disorder. For a considerable time before her sickness, even while health prevailed, she was impressed with the belief that she had not long to live. This quickened, and animated her in the performance of duty. It was evident to her Christian friends, for months before her sickness, that she was fast advancing in the Christian course. There was something in her that gray and somber, which seemed to say, I am not at leisure, but I shall soon reach it—and much more first be done. At length disease violently seized her, and, in less than three days, she reached, (as we confidently trust,) her heavenly home. Mrs. D.'s sickness usually was most desirous to make preparation for death till a dying hour. Racked with severe and untiring pain, and partially bereft of her reason at times, she had no opportunity for preparation. To this she had already attended, and, though surrounded with everything which could render it desirable, was ready to depart, when her heavenly father called. Sensible of her approaching dissolution, she said to her aged mother, at the commencement of her sickness, "Be submissive, be resigned." And whenever she expressed her feelings they indicated a mind, humble, resigned, with dependence upon the mercies of God through the Redeemer. Several hours before her death, she perfectly possessed her peace of mind—the great struggle of nature and disease was past—and reason at once completely resumed their place. This minutes period she employed ... husband and children a final ... bidding adieu to them such consolation...

consolation and instruction, suitable to
their situation and years. To one she gave
a Bible, as the most precious legacy which
could be bestowed.

When this most interesting and affecting scene was closed, she seemed to have
accomplished all that she wished—composed herself to rest—and lay in compar ative
ease and quiet, till all the power of life was
spent.

In the death of Mrs D. her friend had
much to lament, but more to give them
joy. Her place was vacant, but she had
gone to fill a glorious one. The reader
has much to warn and instruct him. Her
death strikingly exhibited the calmness and
meekness, which the religion of Jesus, the
religion of the heart, can impart to the
dying hour. It was mournful, and it was
most satisfying,—it was not the most triumphant, but it was most consoling. It
did not exhibit the armor of passions, but
the assurance of faith; not the shout of victory, but the meekness and firmness of
heavenly certainty. May her friends—
may all, so live, that their *last end may be
like that of the righteous*. At the funeral,
a sermon was preached by the Rev Dr.
Fitch, President of Williams College,
from Psalm cxvi, 15. *Precious in the
sight of the Lord, is the death of his
saints.*

Died at Troyes in France, M Gay, shot
by order of Bonaparte, for wearing a badge
of the Bourbon dynasty. This was probably the last murder perpetrated by the
tyrant under the formality of a military
execution.

In England, the venerable Dr. Burney,
author of the History of Music, aged 88.

In the Isle of Sky, Scotland, Mrs
Mary Jones, aged 127. She lived to see
the sixth generation, and retained the use
of her faculties to her last day.

At Wheeling, (Vir) Noah Linsley,
Esq aged 41, counsellor at law He was
graduated at Yale College in 1791, a tutor
at Williams College in 1795, and at Yale
College in 1794 He was a native of Bran-
ford, Con He left a legacy of $3000 to
Yale College, and a sum to establish a
school in Wheeling.

At Springfield, the Hon. Moses Bliss,
Esq. lately one of the justices of the court
of common pleas.

At Walpole, (N. H.) Capt. Stephen
Parker, aged 76 He served three cam-
paigns in the Old French war, and through
nearly the whole of the revolutionary contest.

At Higham, Abner Lowell, Esq
of Dorchester, attorney at law, aged 33.

At Windham, Maine, James Lovell,
Esq naval officer of the port of Boston
and Charlestown, aged 76 He was a

member of Congress under the old confed-
eration.

At Burnham, Eng. Thomas Thornton, Esq author of *The Present State
of Turkey.*

At Paris, M. Mercier, author of
Tableau de Paris, Member of the Insti-
tute.

At Herkimer, (N Y) Gen Michael
Myers, an officer in the revolution
war.

At Globe, (Vir.) the Rev. Henry H
Fernan

At the city of Washington, during
last winter, the Hon. John Dawson, E
for many years a representative in C
gress from Virginia, aged 52.

At the same place, in April last, Sa
ml A. Otis, Esq. Secretary of the Sen
since the organization of the governm
under the Constitution, aged 73

At Wiscasset, Me while on the circe
the Hon. Samuel Sewall, Esq. L.L.
chief justice of the Supreme Judi
Court of Massachusetts, aged 56.

At Rochester, (N. Y.) the Rev. Jo
nathan Moore, aged 75.

At Plattsburg, (N. Y.) Mr. Isaac Co
aged 103.

At Waltham, (Vir) Mr. Jeremi
Griffith, age 20. He walked up a le
of rocks, and ventured near a precipi
when the rock on which he stood fell w
him 115 feet. He was delirious till
death.

At Detroit, Rev T. Wilson, for
years chaplain of Congress

In England, Alexander Crump
Esq F R S an eminent professor of
chemical science

Also, the Rev S Palmer, at the
of whose books the pulpit Bible of the c
ebrated *John Bunyan* was purchased
S Whitbread, Esq M P. at the price
20 guineas.

In Jamaica, Capt Hassard Sto
roll, late commander of the British f
ate Statira, murdered in a duel by the
Lieut of the Argo

At Farmington, (N. Y) Mr. Tho
Hine, aged 60, in consequence of be
stung by bees He survived the calar
but about an hour

At Newburyport, William Coo
Esq a man of uncommon worth, and
truly Christian character, aged 78

At Pompey, (N. Y) Mrs Eliza Sa
wood, aged 101. She retained her m
tal faculties to the last

In England, Robert Digby, Esq.
died on the Red, Senior Admiral of
British Navy excepting the Duke of C
rence

In Germany, Prince Ernest of Me
lenburgh Strelitz, brother of the Qu
of England, aged 60

w, Ireland, MARTHA EAKIN,

, Cambridge, (Mass) JOSEPH
q. Attorney at law, aged 31
ngton, (Mass) on the 8th ult
WALKER, aged 52 He was
ury professor of the Christian
d had been repeatedly honored
nfidence of his fellow-citizens.
ained the offices of representa-
egislature, a magistrate of the
Middlesex, a military officer and
of Pres of U. S

a Yarmouth, the Rev THOMAS
, M pastor of the Baptist
hat place, aged 53
land, Admiral ALEXANDER
ord Bridport,) aged 87
ford, (Con) Mr THOMAS
aged 100 He attended divine
w days before his death, and
rational faculties till his last ill-
had professed religion in the
f life
nd, the Rev TIMOTHY PRIEST-
er of the late celebrated Dr
aged 80
Orleans, Mr BERTEL GYEMA,
Being indisposed in the middle
t, he sent for Dr FARETAS,
minutes after feeling the pulse
d, fell down, and they both ex-
e same instant.
urn, RICHARD G LEE, Esq.
n the Branch Bank at Norfolk

BIBLE MISSIONARY SOCIETY.

l report of this Society was mis-
on papers, or we should have
en notice of it
nal meeting was held at North-
Aug 19, 1813 The report is
and animating
penditures of the Society for
ing year were as follows:
missionaries, $717 41
books,   589 54
nt expenses,   51 67
                       ─────────
                       $1,358 62

ok presented by the

ples.
er bound volumes
ieer at tics, sermons.
pamphlets
cipts of the Society were as

tions in towns and
                        $651 37
he Female Association
unty, for the purchase
                         360 48

Carried forward $1,611 85

Brought forward $1,611 85
From the Female Charitable
Society in Whitestown, (N. Y.)   123 81
From a friend of missions,   50 00
From Mr Joseph Warner, of
Amherst, in notes payable in
1816, and 1817,   127 84
From the Rev David H Wil-
liston of Tunbridge, (Ver.)   10 00
Contributed in new settle-
ments,   123 70
Contributions at the annual
meeting,   55 00
Avails of Panoplist and Maga-
zine,   19 79
From other sources,   5 26
                               ─────────
                               $1,527 25

The property of the Society, as appears
by the report of the auditors, amounted
to about $3,000, though a part of this sum
was due for missionary services   Nearly
all the funds were in a productive state.

NEW ENGLAND TRACT SOCIETY.

AT the first annual meeting of this Society in Boston, May 23, 1814, the following
gentlemen were chosen officers viz.

WILLIAM BARTLET, Esq. of Newbury-
port, *President*
The Rev JEDIDIAH MORSE, D D. of
Charlestown, *Vice President*
The Rev Dr MORSE,
The Rev LEONARD WOODS, D D. of An-
dover,
The Rev JOHN H CHURCH, of Pelham,
(N H)
The Rev JOSEPH EMERSON, of Beverly,
and
SAMUEL FARRAR, Esq of Andover, *Ex-
ecutive Committee.*
The Rev JOHN CODMAN, of Dorchester,
Corresponding Secretary
The Rev JOSHUA HUNTINGTON, of Bos-
ton, *Recording Secretary.*
HENRY GRAY, Esq of Boston, *Treas-
urer.*
Mr SAMUEL T. ARMSTRONG, of Boston,
Assistant Treasurer

The Depository of the Society is at Mr
Armstrong's bookstore, No 50, Cornhill,
Boston

NEW WORKS.

THE Place of the Church, on the grand
chart of Scripture Prophecy, or the Battle

* *As Mr Gray has declined accepting
the office of Treasurer, all communications relating to that office will be since
to Mr Armstrong*

of Armageddon. In four Discourses, the three last of which were delivered on the annual Fast, April 7, 1814. By Thomas Andros, Pastor of the Church of Christ in Berkley. Boston. S. T. Armstrong. 1814. pp. 48. 8vo.

The Covenant of God's mercy made known to Abraham, ratified with him, and the consequent duties obligatory upon his spiritual seed; illustrated in two Discourses. By Clark Brown, A. M. Minister of the Congregational Church and Society in Swansey, N. H. Keene, John Prentiss. 1814. pp. 60. 12mo.

Human Life not always desirable. A Sermon, delivered at Richmond, N. H. Nov. 19, 1813, at the Funeral of Mr. Solomon Atherton, aged 73. By Clark Brown, A. M. Keene, John Prentiss. 1814. pp. 22. 8vo.

Heirs of Grace. A Sermon, delivered at Charlestown, Sept. 26, 1813, occasioned by the death of Mrs. Abigail Collier, consort of the Rev. William Collier, Pastor of the Baptist church in said town. By Thomas Baldwin, D. D. With an Appendix, containing extracts from Mr. Collier's Diary, Letters, &c. Boston. Manning and Loring. 1813. pp. 92. 8vo.

A Song to Zion. A Sermon, delivered on the occasion of a meeting of a Singing School for exhibition, at Cummington, Mass. March, 1811. By Jonathan Grout, A. M. Pastor of the Church in Hawley. Northampton, William Butler. 1812. pp. 14. 8vo.

Two Sermons delivered at Morris-Town New-Jersey; to which is annexed an Address to the Presbyterian Congregation in that place. By Rev. Samuel Fisher, A. M. Pastor of the First Presbyterian Church in Morris-Town. Morris-Town, Henry P. Russell. 1814. pp. 64. 8vo.

An address on Sacred Music, delivered at a public meeting of the Rockingham Sacred Music Society in Hampton, Oct. 6, 1813. By Daniel Dana, A. M. Pastor of a Church in Newburyport. Exeter, Charles Norris, & Co. 1813. pp. 24. 8vo.

A Sermon, delivered before the Society for propagating the Gospel among the Indians and others in North America, at their anniversary, Nov. 4, 1813. By Joshua Bates, A. M. Pastor of the first Church in Dedham. Boston, Cummings & Hilliard. 1813. pp. 44. 8vo.

A Sermon, preached January 12, 1814, at the Old South Church, Boston, before the Society for Foreign Missions of Boston and the Vicinity. By William Greenough, Pastor of the second Congregational Church in Newton. Boston; Nathaniel Willis. pp. 29. 8vo.

Correct view of that part of the United States, which lies West of the Alleghany Mountains, with regard to Religion and

Morals. By John F. Schermerhorn, and Samuel J. Mills. Hartford; Peter B. Gleason, & Co. 1814. pp. 52.

An Oration, delivered at Tolland, Connecticut, before the Washington Benevolent Society, February 22, 1814; in commemoration of Washington's Birth-day. By John Hall. Hartford; Hale & Homer. 1814. pp. 25. 8vo.

Guatonwenta wontewrienstakwa, engraved *yawennontakon:* A Spelling Book in the language of the seven Iroquois nations. By Eleazer Williams. Plattsburgh, (N. Y.) F. C. Powell. 1813. pp. 24. 12mo.

A Dissertation on the subject of procuring the education of pious youths for the Christian ministry, addressed to the religious Public. Boston, S. T. Armstrong. 1814. pp. 40. 8vo.

A Sermon, delivered at the Ordination of the Rev. Ephraim Abbot to the pastoral care of the Congregational Church and Society in Greenland, Oct. 27, 1813. By the Rev. Eliphalet Pearson LL. D. Andover, Flagg & Gould. 1813. pp. 40. 8vo.

An Appeal to the Public, on the controversy respecting the revolution in Harvard College, and the events which have followed it, occasioned by the use which has been made of certain complaints and accusations of Miss Hannah Adams against the Author. By Jedidiah Morse, D. D. Charlestown, 1814.

A Narrative of the controversy between the Rev. Jedidiah Morse, D. D. and the Author. By Hannah Adams. Boston, 1814.

Remarks on the Controversy between Doctor Morse and Miss Adams, together with some notice of the Review of Dr. Morse's Appeal. Second Edition, with Additions. Boston, S. T. Armstrong, 1814.

Sermons by the late Rev. J. S. Buckminster. With a Memoir of his life and Character. Boston, 1814.

A Sermon delivered before the General Association of Massachusetts Proper, at their annual meeting in Dorchester, June 29, 1814. By Thomas Snell, pastor to the church in North Brookfield. Boston S. T. Armstrong. pp. 22.

A Sermon delivered in the North Meeting house in Salem, before the Bible Society of Salem and Vicinity, at their annual meeting, April 20, 1814. By Thomas Barnard, D. D. To which is added, the third report of the Society. Salem, T. C. Cushing. pp. 28.

A Discourse delivered at Portland, May 5, 1814, before the Bible Society of Maine, at their annual meeting. By Edward Payson, pastor of the second church in Portland. Published by request. Portland; Arthur Shirley. pp. 24.

A Charge pronounced before the

Republicans of Charlestown,
4 th 1814. By Joseph Emer-
Shurtleff town; S. Etheredge, jun
on preached before the Ancient
nable Artillery Company, Ju
ne 6, 1814, being the 177th an-
of their election of officers. By
rey, one of the ministers on the
oston T Wells pp. 26.

urse delivered in Newburyport,
4, in commemoration of Amer-
eminence, and of the Deliver-
rope. By Daniel Dana, A. M.
church in Newburyport Wm.
pp. 20

on preached before the Massa-
Missionary Society, at their an-
ng in Boston, May 26, 1814.
hompson, A M pastor of the
Rehoboth. Boston, S T.
; pp 29

POETRY

For the Panoplist.

MAN IS BORN TO DIE

rn with youth and flush'd with

t begin our life's career,
n poverty or wealth,
ree from pain and free from

the scenes of careless joy,
sing each intrusive sigh,
e thought our hope alloy,
m is frail and born to die.

journey on through life,
see tells a mournful tale,
is full of woe and strife,
hes low in sorrow's vale.

ful homes, our transient towers,
e the lightning through the sky,
g, whisper in our ears,
, like them, are born to die

of him, who once was great,
who once charm'd ev'ry eye,
s of our life claim late,—
they liv'd—like them we die

that dress upon our race
decree doom, that we must die,
s to God's abounding grace,
's offered from on high.

n the Savior's love,
in the grave our ashes lie,
shall mount to realms above,
; to sin, no more to die.

OLNEY.

mpshire, 1814

*... on the tyranny and fall of the In-
quisition, occasioned by reading accounts of its abolition in Spain and
Goa, in the Panoplist for Oct. 1813
p 533.*

BY A YOUNG LADY.

IN distant ages, number'd now and gone,
When Superstition sat on Reason's throne,
When o'er the world her veil of darkness
    hung,
Forth from the deep abyss a monster
    sprung,
Earth trembled as his foot her verdure
    prest,
And hollow groans seem'd murm'ring in
    her breast
  At first a weak and with'ring wand he
    bore,
The mask of Sanctity his features wore,
Though dark resolve, and deeds of
    fiendlike spite
Lurk'd in his heart, scarce hidden from
    the light.
A holy zeal he prais'd with vile intent,
And to the holy church obsequious bent,
Bow'd like her slave,—then as her cham-
    pion rose,
Though leagu'd in secret with her deadly
    foes.
Swoln with success, his brow was seen to
    low'r,
And his rude hand to grasp the rod of
    pow'r,
While with her thunders arm'd, her
    pomp array'd,
O'er her own head he shook his reeking
    blade.
  Deep draughts of blood in secret cells
    he drains,
His ear finds music in the clank of chains,
Loath to the rack the tortur'd form he
    leads,
Devouring flames with guiltless victims
    feed,
With bolts and bars his wretched prey
    confines,
And holds in vassalage immortal minds.
  His lofty dome rose frowning on the
    shore,
Black as his sins, and mystic as his lore.
When midnight wrapt the world in dark-
    est shade,
The first accursed stone was hewn and
    laid,
Hell from beneath behold the proud de-
    sign,
And lent him treasures from her burning
    mine.
Deep in the cavern'd vaults with malice
    fraught,
Dire Cruelty and Superstition wrought;

Mistaken zeal the pond'rous arches rear'd,
Paus'd o'er her work, and, as she saw it,
  tear'd;
And close-veil'd Mystery with finger slow
Plac'd on the massy gates the seal of woe
  High on the dome her audit Terror
    kept,
While in the hidden cells pale Misery
  wept,
And prison'd Virtue scarce with constant
  care
Could keep her lamp from quenching in
  despair.
The voice of Cruelty, the groan of pain,
And shriek of anguish fill'd the drear do-
  main:
Meek Innocence expir'd, in pangs severe,
And Death receiv'd his nightly banquet
  here.
  Long this dark power the humbled na-
    tions sway'd,
Crown'd heads and sceptred hands their
  homage paid;
Hard on the neck the yoke of bondage
  prest,
The belt of iron bound the throbbing breast,
The burden'd spirit sunk to rise no more,
And Nature shudder'd at the load she bore.
  Once as the monster with infernal sport
Held the dark revels of his blood-stain'd
  court,
A heavenly ray with quick effulgence
  stream'd
Through those drear cells where light
  had never beam'd.
He heard the bursting bars, the captives
  free,
The breaking chains, the shouts of liberty,
Saw through his grate a form of heavenly
  birth,
With seraph steps imprint the grateful
  earth;
In frantic rage his blood-shot eyes he
  roll'd
Internal pangs his changing features told;
His champions fled—his guards forsook
  their place,
His horrid temple totter'd to its base;
Its cleaving arch receiv'd the sweeping
  blast;
Its mould'ring columns fell in ruin vast.
Down sunk the fiend with rage and mal-
  ice fir'd,
And in his fabric's pond'rous crush ex-
  pir'd.
Hoarse moving thunders roar'd a migh-
  ty knell;
The glad earth shouted, as the prison fell;
The pow'rs infernal join'd in one fell
  moan,
And Satan trembled on his burning throne.
  On came the conqu'ring One:—no arm-
    ed host,
Or martial trump, her silent footsteps
  boast,

No scourge she rais'd—no flaming
  she wore,
And not on raven's wings her fl—
  bore;
But as the day-star lifts a gentle f—
To gild the dim and troubled ski—
  eanie.
Her eye was rais'd, her knee was
  pray'r,
Her arm sustain'd a wreath divine
A cross of crimson sparkled at her
In robes of flowing light her limb
  drest.
  Oh blest Religion! raise thy gent—
Lift thy mild voice, erect thy—
  throne,
Still turn the heart from vice and
  eread,
Still in soft chains thy willing—
  lead,
Hush the wild passions, snatch the—
  of strife
And pave the entrance of the Pr—
  Life.
  He to one fold his ransom'd flo—
    draw,
The gather'd isles shall listen to hi—
The warring nations fear th'aveng—
Old Ethiopia stretch her arms to G—
Peace with white wing the trouble
  invest,
The savage lion with the lambkin—
The blinded eye the light of hea—
  ceive,
The harden'd heart be touch'd, the—
  believe
The skies shall sparkle, man to joy
The new-rob'd earth the harp of g—
  take,
Seas shout to seas—to mountains,
  ans sing,
And Nature welcome her victoriou—

March 20, 1814.

TO CORRESPONDENTS

No III. *On the Sabbath*, did n—
us in season for this number

The line, *On the Excellency of—*
like most of the poetry which is o—
us, were written too hastily

D. *On the Misapplication of—*
tire, has just come to hand. Th—
a useful paper at some future time

We have on hand a large nu—
communications. Delays must o—
be experienced, in regard to som—
papers, which will ultimately be pu—

тнв

PANOPLIST,

AND

SSIONARY MAGAZINE.

AUGUST, 1814.　　VOL. X.

ELIGIOUS COMMUNICATIONS.

For the Panoplist.

SABBATH.　NO III.

tuity and Change of the Sabbath.

ly results from the di-
ntment of the Sabbath
:, that it must be obli-
on the whole human
ie end of time; unless
iade to appear, either,
the law respecting it
d by its own limita-
secondly, that it has
ally repealed by God
These two being the
in which any of his
s can either be set
ose the smallest de-
heir original binding
Vhen men impiously
o make void the law
raditions, they do it at
. No human authori-
er interfere with the
nts of Jehovah. It
infinitely less daring
l, for the meanest sub-
: greatest earthly po-
declare the fundamen-
f his empi e null and
or man, who is a worm,
) against his Maker,
pt to set aside *his* sa-
utions. The ceremo-
: the Jews, commonly
t.

called the law of Moses, was in
its nature limited and temporary.
No other nation was ever bound
by it, and even to the Jews themselves it was only a shadow of
good things to come. When the
Messiah, who was prefigured in
its costly rites and ceremonies,
came, it had begun to wax old
and soon after vanished away.

Not so the law of the holy rest
ordained in Paradise. It is a law
of universal and perpetual obligation, for, first, it never can expire by its own limitations. The
reason is, it contains no limitations　The terms, in which it is
promulgated, are general and
indefinite. *And God blessed the
seventh day and sanctified it; because that in it he had rested
from all his work, which God
created and made.* Now if this
solemn consecration of one seventh part of time imposed an obligation upon our first parents
to keep that part of time holy, it
obviously imposes the same obligation upon all their posterity;
no intimation whatever being
given, that the observance of the
sacred institution was intended
to be confined to a part of mankind, in the first ages, or to any
limited period of time. The
law, then, still remains in full
force, and will so remain,

44

through all succeeding generations, unless God has seen fit, or
shall hereafter see fit, to repeal
it. This I will venture to observe, secondly, he has not done.
Let those, who think he has,
point out the repealing act. It
will be easy for them to show
that the Jews, immediately after
the resurrection of Christ, were
released from their obligations
to keep the seventh day of the
week. But this does not touch
the question. They may prove,
too, that the Jewish Sabbath was
never binding upon Gentile converts to Christianity. But neither is this at all to their purpose.
It is incumbent on them to point
us to the chapter and verse,
where the institution of the holy
rest of one seventh part of time,
which was originally enjoined, is
explicitly annulled.

It has been said, as I am well
aware, that the repealing act is
recorded in two places: Rom.
xiv, 5, 6, and Col. ii, 16, 17. Let
these passages be examined, not
as detached independent texts,
but as connected parts of the
epistles, in which they occur.
One man, saith the inspired writer to the Romans, *esteemeth one
day above another; another esteemeth every day alike. Let
every man be fully persuaded in
his own mind. He that regardeth the day, regardeth it unto the
Lord; and he that regardeth not
the day, to the Lord he doth not
regard it.* Now, what is the
apostle's meaning here? That
the Sabbath was abolished, when
he wrote, in so far at least, that
it became a matter of indifference what day of the week, or
whether any day, was kept holy?
Surely those, who put this construction upon the passage,

greatly err, not knowing the
Scriptures.

Every attentive reader of the
New Testament must have observed, that the Jewish and
Christian dispensations were for
some time blended together; the
former being gradually abolished,
and the latter as gradually taking
its place. Hence arose some unhappy disputes and divisions,
between the advocates of the
two dispensations Many of the
Jewish converts thought themselves and others bound to observe the ritual law, in the same
manner as before they embraced
Christianity. Most of the Gentile converts, on the other hand,
maintained, that as the ritual law
was abolished, no further regard
to its various distinctions of
meats, days, &c. was admissible.
To put an end to these disputes,
and induce the disputants to exercise mutual forbearance, and
charity, the apostle addressed
them thus: *Him that is weak in
the faith receive ye, but not to
doubtful disputations. For one
believeth that he may eat all
things. Another, who is weak,
eateth herbs. Let not him that
eateth despise him that eateth
not; and let not him which eateth
not judge him that eateth; for
God has received him. Who art
thou that judgest another man's
servant? To his own master he
standeth or falleth; yea, he shall
be holden up, for God is able to
make him stand. One man esteemeth one day above another;
another esteemeth every day
alike. Let every man be fully
persuaded in his own mind. He
that regardeth the day, regardeth it unto the Lord. And he
that regardeth not the day, to
the Lord he doth not regard it*

He that eateth, eateth to the Lord, for he giveth God thanks; And he that eateth not, to the Lord he eateth not, and giveth God thanks. It is plain from every word of this quotation, that it refers exclusively to the controversies which had unhappily arisen, about the observance of the ceremonial law. But the Sabbath, considered simply as a season of rest and religious worship, was not a part of that law. It was appointed and sanctified, more than 2,500 years before the law was given. Some things required of the Jews, in keeping it, might perhaps be ceremonial; but the institution itself could no more be abrogated, than any other moral precept, as a part of the Jewish ritual. Indeed, it is very doubtful, to say the least, whether the passage under consideration contains the slightest reference to the seventh day Sabbath. There were many other days in every year, the religious observance of which was strictly enjoined in the law of Moses. All, therefore, that can fairly be gathered from the apostle's words, is, that the Christians of that time might, or might not, regard those feast days, just as they thought fit, provided they acted conscientiously. If one convert thought it his duty to regard any particular day according to the ritual, he might do so; while another, who considered the whole Mosaic dispensation as abolished, was not to be blamed for declining to unite with his brother in such an observance. On this point, every one must be fully persuaded in his own mind, and act accordingly. If, then, God

has abrogated the Sabbath, we must look elsewhere for the repealing act; for surely it is not found here.

Let us then turn to Col. ii, 16, 17, and see if we can find it there. The words of the apostle are, *Let no man, therefore, judge you in meat, or in drink, or in respect of an holy day, or of the new moon, or of the Sabbath days; which are a shadow of things to come: but the body is of Christ.* Here, say those who maintain that the Sabbath is abolished, here we have the repealing act, in terms as explicit, as human language can furnish. The Colossians, and of course all other Christians, are excused, as well from observing the Sabbath days, as the new moons and other Jewish festivals.

To this construction of the words just quoted, which strikes at the foundation of the Christian Sabbath, not less than three distinct answers can be given.

In the first place, the construction takes for granted the essential thing which ought to be proved, viz. that the apostle is speaking here of the weekly Sabbaths. I say this ought to be *proved;* because, as is well known, the ceremonial law required the Jews to keep several *other* Sabbaths every year. Thus, for example, they were commanded to keep the first day of the seventh month, and also the tenth day of the same, as a Sabbath, throughout their generations. See Lev. xxiii. *And the Lord spake unto Moses, saying, Speak unto the children of Israel, saying, In the seventh month, in the first day of the month, shall ye have a Sabbath, a memorial of blowing of trum-*

pets, an holy convocation. Ye shall do no servile work therein. Also, on the tenth day of this seventh month, there shall be a day of atonement. Ye shall do no manner of work; it shall be a statute forever, throughout your generations, in all your dwellings. It shall be unto you a Sabbath of rest, and ye shall afflict your souls. Now, when it is considered, that all the other things mentioned by the apostle in the passage before us, such as meats, drinks, and festivals, belonged to the ceremonial law, why might not the Sabbath days, which he speaks of in the very same verse, be the ceremonial Sabbaths of the Jews just mentioned, and not their regular weekly Sabbaths? The contrary, I am sure, cannot be proved; and, until it is proved, the text cannot in the least affect the perpetuity of the sacred rest, which was from the beginning. This is my first answer. But

Secondly; allowing, what cannot be proved, that the apostle refers to the ordinary Jewish Sabbath, and excuses every body, under the Christian dispensation, from observing this day, what does it amount to? To nothing more than this, that the observance of the seventh day of the week was no longer obligatory. A Sabbath must still be kept, though the day might be changed, and was intended to be changed, in commemoration of our Lord's resurrection. If, on the one hand, such of the Jews as acted conscientiously were not to be judged, or condemned, for adhering for a time to a dispensation, which was vanishing away, neither on the other, were those Christians,

whether Jewish or Gentile converts, to be condemned, for forsaking at once the Jewish, and adopting the Christian dispensation. This is my second answer.

The third I shall give, in the words of an able foreign writer. "It is evident from the context," says he, "that the apostle was speaking of the ordinances of the ceremonial law, for the neglect of which no Christian was to be condemned. *Blotting out the hand writing of ordinances that was against us, which was contrary to us, and took it out of the way, nailing it to his cross: Let no man therefore judge you in meat or in drink, or in respect of an holy day, or of the new moon, or of the Sabbath days.*

"In this passage the apostle is clearly speaking of burdensome ordinances: of something that was *against* them, and *contrary* to the spirituality of the Gospel. But can any pious person conceive, that the spending of one day in seven in spiritual services, in the delightful employment of social worship and other religious exercises, could be ranked by the holy apostle amongst the things which were against Christianity and contrary to it? Was that institution, which the people of God had been commanded to call a *delight, holy of the Lord, and honorable,* now to be esteemed of so carnal a nature, as to be ranked amongst the things which *Christ took out of the way, nailing it to his cross?* Were those holy persons, who had been accustomed to adopt the language of the Psalmist, *I was glad when they said unto me, let us go up to the house of the Lord,* now taught to esteem

ent in such services, as
f that *yoke, which neither*
atles nor their fathers
le to bear? We must de-
l just ideas of the effects
he preaching of the Gos-
s intended to produce,
we can adopt such an in-
ation of the apostle's

train of reasoning might
ued much further; but it
o me quite unnecessary
ge. The above extract
hink, hardly fail to strike
ler's mind with the force
onstration. And now, in
all that has been said,
stion respecting the per-
of the Sabbath stands
It is a divine and not a hu-
stitution; and therefore
le of being abrogated by
man authority. It was
d and sanctified in Para-
It never can expire by
limitations; because it
e. Its abolition is not
d, in either of the passa-
uch we have examined.
ot declared any where in
le; for no one will pre-
at any other passage can
uced more directly to the
e. Of course, the sacred
ion has never been abro-
y divine authority. If it
as been thus abrogated,
will b ; for the canon
ature is full. The insti-
nust therefore be bind-
the end of the world.
might close. On this
I might confidently rest
ation. But a number of
listinct and independent
ons present themselves
liaries to the preceding;
would be ungrateful to
them from the service.

1. The institution of the Sabbath, in paradise, before the fall,
furnishes a strong argument for
its perpetuity. We should have
been apt to think, perhaps, that
while our first parents retained
their primitive holiness, it could
answer no valuable purpose to
enjoin upon them the religious
observance of any particular day,
in as much as they loved God
with all their heart, and were
disposed to spend every day
in his service. They could not
need the Sabbath, as a season of
rest from toils, such as they
were afterwards doomed to experience; for their labor, if labor
it might be called, was most easy and invigorating. They had
only to dress the garden and
keep it. No more toil, as the
great Epic Poet expresses it,

———————————Than sufficed
To recommend cool zephyrs, and made
  ease
More easy, wholesome thirst and appe-
  tite
More grateful———————————.

God was, however, pleased to
enjoin upon them a stated weekly intermission of their gentle
and delightful care, that they
might have nothing to divert
their attention from the far more
animating employment of united
praise and adoration. For the
same reason, that it was the
duty and the privilege of the
first human pair to keep the
Sabbath, before their apostasy,
would it have been the duty and
the privilege of all their posterity to keep it, if sin had never
entered the world. But how
much more do we, fallen creatures, need such a season of
rest from the laborious employments to which we are doomed?

How much more do we, who have lost the image of God, and are prone continually to forget our obligations and dependence, need the leisure and the solemn stillness of the Sabbath to recall us from our wanderings, and assist us in our preparations for heaven? Had man in his primitive state been totally depraved, and had he since been made perfectly holy as Adam was before the fall; had the Sabbath, moreover, been given him, while wandering and loving to wander; it might have been plausibly argued, after the happy renovation, that such an institution was no longer necessary. But what can be more irrational, than to adopt the reverse of the argument and say, that a religious institution, which God saw necessary for man in innocency, has ceased to be necessary for him since the fall? And yet, this is the absurd conclusion to which all the arguments against the perpetuity of the Sabbath unavoidably lead.

2. That the Sabbath is not a ceremonial but a moral institution, of universal and perpetual obligation, is put beyond all reasonable doubt by its being incorporated into the decalogue. Strange it is, that the morality of the fourth command should ever be questioned, when the duties which it enjoins are moral duties, when it was written at the same time, and by the same divine hand, as the other commands; and when it is placed between the two tables of the moral law, as if to teach us, that piety to God, and the conscientious discharge of the duties, which we owe to one another, depend essentially upon the observance of the Sabbath. Even those, who most strenuously deny the perpetuity of the weekly rest, do not hesitate to admit, in general terms, that the moral law is now in full force, and will continue to bind the consciences of all, who are made acquainted with it, to the end of the world. Well, then, what is the moral law? Does it comprise the whole of what was written on the two tables of stone, and laid up with the ark? or only a part? If it comprises all the ten commandments, then all are still obligatory. If it comprises only a part, then the law, as originally given to Moses, is defective. And if any one of the ten constituent articles may be rejected without authority, why may not another, or even the whole? If we may consider the fourth as having waxed old and vanished away, why not the first, the second, and so on to the last? They all rest on the same ground and must stand or fall together.

But not to insist any longer, upon what is instamped on the very face of the law, let us turn to our Lord's Sermon on the mount; and see, if he has not there settled the question for ever. *Think not,* said he, *that I am come to destroy the law or the prophets: I am not come to destroy, but to fulfil. For, verily I say unto you, till heaven and earth pass, one jot, or one tittle, shall in no wise pass from the law, till all be fulfilled.* Let those who would set aside one whole section of the law well consider the curse, which immediately follows. *Whosoever, therefore, shall*

one of these least com-
:nts, and shall teach men
l be called the least in the
* of heaven "That is,"
: judicious Scott, "either
disciple at all; or one of
it inconsistent and mean
rhole company." Mat. v,
19. That Christ was
g here, not of the cere-
but of the moral law, is
ident; because he pro-
immediately to expound
l'th, and 8th commands of
alogue. If he had intend-
)rogate one tenth part of
, would he have said,
came not to destroy it?
he, without giving the
imation of the repeal, or
l repeal, of one im-
section, have declared,
*jót, or one tittle, should
vise pass from the law?*
he was not in the habit
g such loose and ambig-
positions of Scripture.
te plainly and positively
instance, with respect to
ure and obligations of
. He doubtless intend-
his words should be tak-
eir most obvious mean-
l, if so, we have his au-
for considering the com-
relative to the Sabbath,
/ and as strongly binding
hen present and all suc-
generations, as any part
moral law. *The Lord
oken, and who shall dis-*
.
ie perpetuity of the Sab-
plainly implied if not di-
sserted by Christ, Mark
28. *And he said unto
'he Sabbath was made for
id not man for the Sab-
'hereafore the Son of man is
·o of the Sabbath.* If the
was a gracious institution,

originally designed for the benefit of man, why should it not be
for his benefit to have it continued under the Christian dispensation? Could the great Lord of
the Sabbath intend to deprive
his followers of one of the most
important means, which the
saints had ever enjoyed, of preserving true religion in the
world, and of promoting personal holiness? No, surely. The
wise and gracious economy of
God towards his people was,
from the beginning, gradually
to increase, not diminish their
privileges. It is universally admitted, that these privileges are
more and greater under the
Gospel, than they ever were, at
any period, before the establishment of the Christian
Church. But take away the
Sabbath, and it may confidently
be affirmed, that they would be
less. For experience has abundantly proved, that even the
forms of religion 'cannot long·
be maintained, where the Sabbath is discarded. I shall only
add, under this head, that as
Christ was Lord of the Sabbath,
had he intended it should cease,
he could have repealed the law.
He did not repeal it; therefore
it still remains in force.

4. It is a common argument,
and I think a forcible one, in fa-
for of the perpetuity of the Sabbath, that, in speaking of the
final destruction of Jerusalem,
our Lord directed his disciples
to pray, that their flight from
that devoted city might not be
in the winter, nor on the *Sabbath
day.* The argument concisely
stated is this. Christ was speaking of an event, which was not
to take place till about forty
years. If the Sabbath was ever
abolished, the abolition took

place near the time of the setting up of the new dispensation, or soon after Christ's resurrection. But if the Sabbath were to be abolished then, why did he speak of it as an institution, which would exist, and be binding, so many years afterwards? Why did he direct his disciples to pray, that their flight might not be on the *Sabbath day,* when, according to the supposition, they would no longer be under obligations to regard one day as holy, more than another?

5. The perpetuity of the Sabbath is manifestly capable of being proved from the words of the Apostle Paul, Rom. iii, 31. *Do we then make void the law through faith? God forbid, yea we establish the law.* Now what is it to establish a law? To maintain it, doubtless, without retrenchment or diminution? Could it be truly said, that the moral law was *established* through faith, or by the plan of salvation which the Gospel reveals, if an essential part of the law, to wit, the fourth command, were really abrogated?

6. It is evident, I think, from what the Apostle says, Heb. iv, that the Sabbath is a typical institution. Having spoken of the seventh day Sabbath, and referred to the change from that to the first day, of which I shall have occasion to take notice more particularly in another place, he observes, verse 9, *There remaineth therefore a rest to the people of God.* The rest of the holy Sabbath is an earnest to God's people of that eternal rest, which is reserved for them in heaven. In other words, the sabbatical rest, appointed by God in Paradise, is

the *types* and the rest, or sabbatism, which remains in the world of glory, is the *antitype.* Now it is the nature of a type to continue until its use is superseded by the antitype. Thus the typical institutions of the ceremonial law continued in force till Christ came, to whose person and mediatorial work they referred, and in whom they were accomplished. The earthly Sabbath, then, being a type of the heavenly, it must continue till all the people of God shall have entered into their eternal rest, when there will be no more occasion for it. In other words, it must continue to the end of the world.

I might proceed to show, as a further confirmation of the designed perpetuity of the Sabbath, that it has been religiously kept by the most eminent saints, in every age, from the resurrection of Christ, to the present time. I might, also, avail myself of the aid of several strong arguments, drawn from the application of ancient prophecies to Gospel times. But really I cannot think it necessary. If God instituted the Sabbath, and has never abrogated it; then it must be perpetual. If not one jot, or one tittle, can ever pass from the law, then must the Sabbath be perpetual. If the Sabbath existed when Jerusalem was destroyed; if the law is not made void but established through faith; and if the Sabbath is typical of the heavenly rest, then must it be perpetual. In a word, if all, or if only one, of the above arguments be conclusive, then is the perpetuity of the Sabbath unanswerably established.

not do justice to myself
, a momentary digression
inform the reader, who
gin to look with impa-
or the end of this num-
it I have been insensibly
o a length of discussion,
I had not contemplated;
ass, which I hope will be
ed, when the importance
ubject is duly consider-
, a pledge is given, on
t, not to detain him many
s longer.

ifficient number of the
bvious and conclusive
that the Sabbath has
anged from the *seventh*
first day of the week,
e stated in two or three
paragraphs. The ques-
perpetuity being decid-
e affirmative, we natur-
quire what was the prac-
he Apostles and primi-
irissians. It cannot be
ed, that those holy men,
lly, who were inspired
e the New Testament,
either neglect the Sab-
change the day, without
authority. Which day
d *they* keep as holy time?
st certainly. It was on
ning of the first day of
k, being the very day of
s resurrection, that he ap-
in the midst of his disci-
ho were evidently assem-
social worship, and said
em, *Peace be unto you.*
next *first day of the*
they assembled again,
heir Lord repeated his
d his blessing; John xx.

days after the resurrec-
being the *first day of the*
iey were all with one ac-
one *place*, when their

X.

ascended Savior put a peculiar
honor upon the day by the miraculous effusion of the Holy
Ghost upon the Apostles, and by
the conversion of thousands, under the preaching of one of their
number; Acts, ii. It was on
the *first day of the week*, that
the disciples came together
to break bread, and hear Paul
preach, at Troas; Acts xx, 7. The
church at Corinth was directed
to make contributions, on the
first day of the week, for the relief
of their indigent brethren; and a
similar order had before been
given by the Apostle, to the
churches of Galatia; 1 Cor. xvi.
1, 2. It was unquestionably *the
first day of the week*, which in
process of time, received the
honorable and appropriate title
of the *Lord's day*. *I was*, saith
the beloved disciple, *in the spirit on the Lord's day;* Rev. i,
10.

These facts are, I conceive,
sufficient to establish the point,
that the Apostles discontinued
their religious observance of
the seventh day of the week,
immediately after the resurrection of Christ; and thencefor-
ward kept the first day. This
being admitted, their example
would be decisive in regard to
the propriety and authority of
the change, even if the Scriptures had furnished us with no
special reasons for it. Surely
the Apostles would never have
ventured upon such a change
without authority; and the supposition, that they acted *by* authority, settles the question.
But the *reason* of the change is
not less obvious from Scripture,
than that it actually took place.
The Sabbath was instituted to
commemorate the completion

45

of the stupendous work of creation. God's resting from all his work was a sufficient reason why all mankind should perpetuate the remembrance of the grand event, by resting every seventh day. But the redemption of man was a far more stupendous work, than the creation of the world. How rational and proper then, that the day on which this greater work was completed, viz. the day of Christ's resurrection, should be observed as a day of rest and holy rejoicing, throughout all succeeding generations! How obvious the propriety of honoring the divine Redeemer, by keeping that day holy, on which he *rested from all his work, as God did from his!*

But to proceed; the reality and divine authority of the change under consideration, is, I think, completely established thus. Christ declares himself to be *Lord of the Sabbath day;* John says, *I was in the spirit on the Lord's day.* The argument founded on a comparison of these two passages, is simply as follows. If Christ was Lord of the Sabbath, and if the Lord's day mentioned by John was the first day of the week, as most undoubtedly it was, then the first day of the week is the Christian Sabbath.

Again; the prophetical language of the Psalmist leads to the same conclusion; Psalm cxviii, 24. Having spoken of the rejection of Christ by the Jews, and his subsequent exaltation to be head of the corner, the Psalmist adds, *This is the day which the Lord hath made, we will rejoice and be glad in it.* The day here referred to was

evidently the very day when Christ was made head of the corner; and that was the day when he triumphed over death and the grave. Of course, that is the day, on which Christians should rejoice and be glad; or, in other words, it is the Christian Sabbath. Z. X. Y.

THOUGHTS ON THE LATE MEASURES OF THE LEGISLATURE OF MASSACHUSETTS IN RELATION TO THE SABBATH.

In the last number of the Panoplist, p. 314, appeared the late report of a committee of the Massachusetts legislature, in relation to the Sabbath; which report was sanctioned by both branches of the honorable body to which it was made, and is therefore presented to the public as the solemn deliberate opinion of the highest civil authorities in the commonwealth, on this momentous concern. It is my design, in writing this paper, to offer some reflections, which have occurred to my mind, in regard to this legislative proceeding.

I would premise, that the highest civil authorities of a country are never so well employed, as when directing their power and influence to the promotion of sound morality. By doing this they prevent crimes; (which is a thousand times better than to punish them;) and they thus secure the public happiness from interruption. It is to be lamented exceedingly, that our state legislatures should not, during the last twenty years, have spent more time and care than they have done, in de-

g our ancient and inval-
institutions, either by en-
new laws, or providing
ally for the execution of
y laws already in exist-
Instead of watching the
d progress of innovations
our moral habits, and
ng vicious practices in
early stages. our rulers
een engrossed either with
olitical questions, or with
plications of individuals
ors of a private nature.
e is this, that some aged
st respectable members
community, men every
alified to judge in such
from their acquaintance
ublic business, and their
ppreciation of the great
ts of the present genera-
d of posterity;—such men
id, that our legislatures
scarcely any of their
ad talents to the legiti-
purposes of government.
ations for banks, and oth-
porations, have been
to take up almost the
attention of the legisla-
ssion after session, while
ng could not be obtained,
single hour, on any sub-
ating to the preservation
l morals. Yet it will be
thing in the estimation
erity, whether or not the
l men were able, in
ar 1814, to obtain by
of corporations 7 per
or their capital, which
not otherwise have yield-
n more than five or six.
will be a great thing with
ty to have the primitive
of morals restored to the
of New England,* rather

than to have the Sabbath virtually abolished, and the community hardened in such vices as
gambling, profane swearing, and
intemperate drinking. It is to
be hoped, that our legislatures
will at length be convinced of
the vast responsibility which
rests upon them, as the moral
guardians of the community, and
that they will act accordingly. I
was pleased to see the observance of the Sabbath taken up by
the legislature of Massachusetts. Happy will it be, if this
honorable body shall keep a vigilant eye upon the laws made
for the protection of that sacred
day, so long as legislative interference shall promise to be useful.

Let us now turn our attention
to the report already mentioned.

The legislature begin by
stating, that the laws of 1792 and
1797, enacted to enforce a due
observance of the Lord's day,
'extend to all evils known to exist, in regard to the outward observance of the Sabbath.' The
provisions of these laws are
deemed sufficient, if they can
be carried into effect. The
preamble of the first law is declared to be "solemn, clear, and
impressive." As our readers
generally have not the means of
turning to this preamble, we
quote it for their deliberate consideration.

"Whereas the observance of the Lord's
day is highly promotive of the welfare of
a community, by affording necessary seasons for relaxation from labor and the
cares of business, for moral reflections and
conversation on the duties of life, and the
frequent errors of human conduct; for

---

reason why the writer confines
rvations to New England, is,

that he has little personal knowledge
other parts of the United States

public and private worship of the Maker, Governor and Judge of the world; and for those acts of charity which support and adorn a Christian society; and whereas some thoughtless irreligious persons, inattentive to the duties and benefits of the Lord's day, profane the same by unnecessarily pursuing their worldly business and recreations on that day, to their own great damage, as members of a Christian society, to the great disturbance of well disposed persons, and to the great damage of the community, by producing dissipation of manners and immoralities of life."—

Let the reader here observe, that the legislature declare the 'observance of the Lord's day to *be highly promotive of the welfare of a community,'* and stigmatize the violators of the Sabbath as "thoughtless irreligious persons, inattentive to the duties and benefits of the Lord's day;" and that they declare the profanation of this day to issue in "the great damage of the community, by producing dissipation of manners and immoralities of life."

The pernicious tendency of the allowed profanation of the Sabbath is no new doctrine. It has been held by all enlightened statesmen, in every Christian country. It has been held by every wise legislator in New England, from the first settlement of the country to the present day. It has been expressed in a long series of statutes. It was solemnly declared in the preamble just quoted, which received the sanction of the legislature in 1792. It was solemnly re-affirmed by the legislature in 1797, when additional penalties were imposed, as a defence of the preceding statute. And now, in 1814, the legislature pronounce an eulogium on the same preamble. They do more, as we shall presently see.

In the mean time, it is well worthy of particular attention, that a subject which has attracted the care and vigilance of so many succeeding legislatures, must be presumed, without further examination, to be an important subject. It is no party question, nor a thing of merely temporary interest. It is a question equally important at all periods of the world, and in all states of society. It radically affects the very constitution of a well ordered community. But to proceed with the Report.

The legislature next say, that the penalties of the existing laws appear adequate, at least until "it shall appear from a fair experiment in executing the laws, that the evils are not removed." While they declare, "that no further legal provisions are required," they proceed to observe, that they "are still impressed with a deep sense of the importance of the evil complained of, both by the clergy and the people." It has been too common to sneer at any attempts to enforce the observance of the Lord's day, as visionary, impracticable, unnecessary, and the offspring of a heated imagination. The danger apprehended from the present state of things has been ridiculed as a chimera. But what is the real voice of the community on this subject? The clergy and the people, (the most respectable part of the people too,) petition the legislature to suppress some great evil. Do the legislature say, that there is no evil, or only a small one? Far enough from this. They declare themselves to be *impressed with a deep sense of the importance of the evil.* Nor are they content-

imply bewailing the ex-
of the evil. They 'are
to give all the aid in their
) the execution of the
their renewed sanction.'
t be said hereafter, that
s of the community is
ie execution of the laws
ct the Sabbath. The
the wise, sober, reflect-
scientious part of the
ity, is in favor, most de-
) favor, of a faithful ex-
of these laws. And who
st it? None but shallow
i, and shallow politi-
one but the rash, the
ss, the dissolute; those,
nothing for the public
hing for posterity; who
rant whence the public
s must proceed, and re-
r the temporary gratifi-
their lawless passions.
ue friend of his country
re strength and anima-
i the fact, that the legis-
pledged to give all the
power to the execution
rs in question. He will
ieculiar need of combi-
ictive exertions, under
it sanction of the legis-
He will boldly assume
and manner of a person
iws he is seeking the
i of the community.
gislature next proceed
in a dignified manner,
dition to their approba-
e preamble above quo-
full opinion of the im-
of the Sabbath. "We
say they, "that an en-
l, uniform and pious ob-
of the Lord's day, in at-
public and private in-
and worship ourselves,
efraining from all ac-
practices which may
ie worship and instruc-

tion of others, is *a duty solemnly binding upon the conscience
of every individual.* We believe
that without the appointment,
and continuance of the Lord's
day, public instruction and worship would soon languish, and
perhaps entirely cease:"—Here I
must stop to ask the reader, if he
has been accustomed to regard
the subject in this light. If he
has, I would ask whether he has
made every practicable effort to
prevent so awful a calamity, as is
here contemplated? The legislature plainly view the subject in
its just light. Every person,
therefore, who contributes, by
his influence or example, to
break down the Sabbath, contributes in the same degree to
destroy all public worship, and
to introduce the reign of Atheism and of violence and blood.

"We believe," add the Legislature, "that private worship and
the best virtues of social life
would share the same fate."
How imperious then the necessity and the duty of using every
possible mean to avert so tremendous an evil. Well may the
legislature interpose. Well may
all good men rally to protect,
and preserve for their children,
all that is desirable in social life.
Well may the country be alarmed when the Sabbath is in danger.

The legislature next declare
their belief, "that the Scriptures,
containing the records, the principles, the duties, and the hopes
of our religion, would," were it
not for the Sabbath, "soon pass
from the recollection of multitudes of our citizens who now
regard them, and never become
known to the great body of the
rising generation: that the powerful and happy influence, which

they now exert upon public sentiment and morals, would be seen no longer:"—The writer of these remarks was peculiarly happy to find the preceding opinion so clearly stated by the legislature of Massachusetts, as it is an opinion, which he has uniformly held and inculcated, and one which, unless he is mistaken, has been expressly maintained in the Panoplist. This opinion can be established by reasoning from the most solid principles, and by appealing to the unerring decisions of experience. Into what a gulf of wretchedness would the violators of the Sabbath plunge their country? Their example tends to banish religion from the world, to introduce heathenism, to transform a moral community into a gang of cheats, robbers, debauchees, and assassins. Is this language too strong? Look at the sentence, which follows the above quotations from the opinion of the legislature, and you will see it there asserted, "that *the safety of the state*, the moral and religious improvement of the people, the personal security and happiness of all, are intimately, *if not inseparably*, connected with *the uniform and conscientious* observance of the Lord's day, and its various institutions and services;"—I break in upon the chain of inferences here, to assert the obvious propriety of legislating, in reference to the Sabbath. It has been said, that as religion is a concern between man and his Maker, civil rulers have nothing to do with its commands or observances; and that all laws for the punishment of Sabbath-breaking and profane swearing are improper exertions of au-

thority. But are not rulers bound to regard and provide for "the safety of the state," and "the personal security and happiness of the people?" And, in doing this, are they not bound to consult their own observation and their own consciences, the records of past ages and the opinions of the wise and good in every age? or must they rely upon the bold assumption of Sabbath-breakers and swearers, as a safe directory?

As to the fact, that where the Sabbath is disregarded the Scriptures are unknown and forgotten, and the public morals shockingly corrupted, let any person look at a community, in which a large portion of the people violate the Sabbath, and he will be convinced. Look at the city of London, where more than three quarters of the people pay no religious attention to the Sabbath, and you will find more than half the families, in some of the most populous districts, utterly destitute of the Scriptures. You will find an immense majority of the inhabitants, not excluding the higher ranks from a share, totally ignorant of religion in theory, and vast multitudes grossly immoral in practice. Read Colquhoun's Police of London, and you will be astonished at the number, atrocity, and variety of crimes perpetrated in that vast metropolis, and at the almost incredible multitude of criminals, who live in the habitual perpetration of crimes known by them to be punishable by death. Though the greater number escape the sentence of the law by their cunning and their secrecy, yet the number of those, who are annually convicted of capital crimes

ier executed or trans-
to Botany Bay, is aston-
great. On examining
criminals you will find
abitually Sabbath-break-
ost to a man, and most
y ignorant of the Scrip-
id of the first principles
stianity. Look at New-
, where the Sabbath is
led by nearly, if not
ie whole population, and
ll find a corresponding
of ignorance and crimin-
Walk into the suburbs of
st licentious city, and see
dy avenues filled with
tables, at which several
ls sit down, on every
t Sabbath, to perpetrate
kinds of wickedness at
Search these men, and
find daggers under their
Do you wonder that
:s, piracies, and mur- -
e often committed? or
guilty escape punish-

>se parts of this country,
he Sabbath was formerly
ced by nearly all the
and where the violation
acred rest was not toler-
a single instance, the
of crimes perpetrated
:ceedingly small. With
wing neglect of the Sab-
: number of crimes has
radually increasing. It
ionable whether a single
been executed in this
, within the last fifty
n the administration of
:tice, or whether a sin-
ant of our state prisons
)und, who had not, in ei-
:, been habitually guilty
:cting the Sabbath pre-
to his committing the
rhich brought upon him

the vengeance of the laws.
There is the most abundant
reason, then, for the interference
of the legislature to enforce a
uniform observance of the Sabbath. But let me return from
this digression.

The legislature infer, "that
we are all bound to make every
just and proper effort to *secure
the execution of the laws,* which
have been already made upon
this important and interesting
subject." This is undoubtedly
a pressing duty. Let it be seen
and felt, and urged, by ministers of the sanctuary and magistrates, by parents and teachers
of youth, by all in short, who regard the good of their country,
the welfare of posterity, or the
increase and flourishing state of
the Christian church. Let actions succeed to arguments; and
let not the true friends of human happiness think of resting
in their exertions, till the Sabbath shall be as generally observed as it was fifty years ago;
—till all travelling on that day,
every species of amusement,
the carrying of the mails and the
keeping open of post-offices, with
the exception of cases of necessity, shall be utterly prevented.
No well informed man, if worthy to be called either a Christian or a patriot, would wish to
stop short of this mark. Is it
doubted whether individuals are
bound, in their private capacity,
to exert themselves for the execution of the laws? Let the person who doubts consider, that the
legislature of Massachusetts
have made a direct and powerful
appeal to the people for their
aid in executing the laws. This
subject is introduced by the following just observations. "How-

ever wisely and skilfully laws may be framed, they must greatly depend upon the public sentiment and virtue, and especially in all measures of a moral and religious character, for their final and complete success. We trust the public sentiment and virtue in this commonwealth *are sufficiently elevated and powerful* to secure the execution of just laws for the observance of the Sabbath, when once the public mind shall be *properly and simultaneously directed to this object, and to the reasons which enforce it.*"

Let it never be said hereafter, that it is improper or unnecessary for individuals to combine their efforts and their influence to support the laws; at least, let not this be said, till it shall be first proved, that the legislature of this commonwealth are altogether mistaken in their view of the subject. This honorable body not only calls upon the people for their exertions in favor of the laws, but points out some prominent measures to be adopted in furtherance of so great a design. These measures are,

1. The transmission of a copy of these legislative proceedings to every minister of the Gospel in the commonwealth.

2. The reading of the laws for the due observance of the Lord's day, by every minister, in his pulpit, on the Sabbath.

3. That each minister, by particular request of the legislature, should point out to his people, as fully and explicitly as the circumstances of his people may require, the importance and value of the Sabbath, and the reasons which bind us to observe it, and to obey the laws of the commonwealth.

4. That the people be called upon to elect moral and religious men to the office named for the particular execution of the laws in regard to the Sabbath.

5. That the people be reminded of the necessity of supporting such public officers in the faithful discharge of their duty.

6. That the officers themselves should be discreet, judicious, and benevolent, while they are honest and firm in the execution of their trust, according to the oath of office prescribed in the statute.

I have abridged this part of the report for the sake of presenting the different points to the mind of the reader at once. As a reason of the *fourth* recommendation above cited, the legislature express a desire, 'that the public may have a rational confidence that all proper means will be adopted to meet *the just expectations* of the legislature, and of all the *lovers of righteousness, peace and order.*' As a reason of the *fifth* recommendation, the legislature represent the people as obligated to protect the public officers, "by preserving the common sentiment in their favor, and not permitting it, by neglect or irritation, to turn against them, to injure their reputation, business or happiness."

On the preceding measures, and the reasoning of the legislature, I beg leave to offer the following brief remarks, in addition to what has been already said.

First: The legislature represent themselves as entertaining *just expectations* that the laws

:ting the Sabbath will be
ted.

ondly: They represent all
)ers of righteousness, peace
·der as entertaining the
just expectations; conse-
y all persons, who oppose
ecution of these laws, are,
opinion of the legislature
:assachusetts, *haters of*
ousness, peace, and order.
·dly: The legislature with
est propriety assume a transac-
ental character, in the con
which they discover for
otection of faithful public
s. This is the most no-
ad dignified trait, in the
valuable report which I
een considering. If the
ature would frequently ap-
before the public in this
cent character, they would
end themselves to the
and consciences of the
·, and would take strong
f the affections of all good
as. Such a course would
ery powerfully to perpet-
ur republican institutions,
store them to their for-
urity.

rthly: The legislature re-
the oath of office as a sol-
ledge for the faithful per-
ice of arduous duties, and
an unmeaning formulary.
· earnestly is it to be de-
that oaths of office should
arded as they really are,
y are intended to be un-
od, and as they will be in-
ted at the great day by the
of the world.

s one of the most awful
of human depravity, that
of office have been evad-
:plained away, or shame-
iolated, in every commu-
any considerable duration,

„ X.

within the whole extent of history. The downward progress is
slow at first, but afterwards astonishingly rapid. A striking
instance of this is to be seen, in
the conduct of church-wardens
in Great Britain. So entirely is
their oath of office disregarded, an
oath imposed to preserve the purity of the Established Church,
that the Christian Observer, a
work conducted by members of
that church plainly intimates,
that the periodical visitations
present to the eye one immense
mass of official perjury. But we
need not leave our own country
for examples Let any one look at
the duties imposed by our laws
upon justices of the peace, grand
jurors, select men, constables,
and tything men; and then see in
what manner these duties are
neglected, although every one
of these officers is under oath
to perform *all the duties of his*
office. After such a prospect,
there is no need of going to foreign countries for proofs of public degeneracy.

It might be curious to form
an oath of office to suit the practice of many of our public officers. If I am not mistaken, it
would run somewhat as follows:
"I solemnly swear that I will
faithfully and truly discharge the
duties of a —, as prescribed by
the laws of this commonwealth;
provided said laws are, in my opin-
ion, just and salutary, and have
not become obsolete in consequence
of the improvements of modern
times; and provided it shall ap-
pear to me expedient, that said
laws shall be executed; and pro-
vided I can discharge the said du-
ties, imposed upon said
perfect ease, c
tion to myself.

smallest risk of incurring any personal inconvenience or unpopularity." Would not such an oath be a gross affront to God;—an impudent trifling on a most solemn subject? What must be the guilt, then, of taking a very different oath, and *acting* as though it were expressed in the manner above stated? What would be thought of an oath for the President of the United States in the following words: "I do solemnly swear that I will faithfully execute the office of President of the United States, and will, to the best of my ability, preserve, protect, and defend the constitution of the United States; *so far as I can execute said office consistently with a supreme regard to my own ease, emolument and popularity.*" If such an oath would appear shocking, even to be read, how great must be the criminality of a country, in which many thousand guardians of the public peace and welfare systematically act, in violation of their oaths, on the principles expressed in the preceding salvo, which I have placed at the close of the real oath of the Chief Magistrate of the United States?

Lastly: Now is the time for making a noble, vigorous, persevering effort, in every part of our country, to secure the execution of all the laws enacted for the promotion and preservation of the public morals. A large part, and much the best part, of the community is awake upon the subject. A conviction that something must be done is becoming quite prevalent. Let this conviction be enforced and extended in every quarter; let the hands of faithful public officers be strengthened; let their number be increased; let the influence of all the "lovers of righteousness, peace and order," be concentrated, and powerfully directed to one good object after another; and with the blessing of God, we shall soon see a glorious reformation begun, which will terminate in a more glorious consummation, than we should at present dare to anticipate.　　　A. B.

ORIGINAL LETTER FROM THE REV. PRESIDENT FINLEY TO THE REV. DR. BELLAMY.

Nassau Hall, Princeton,
Nov. 10, 1763.

My very precious
　　Brother and Friend,

DID you not sometimes think I had forgotten, or neglected, or become cold and indifferent about you? It was all false. I have had your letter on my desk ever since I received it, that it might be before me. I saw it every week; sometimes every day; and never saw it without thinking of you and of answering it. It will seem mysterious that I could not, in so long a time, scrape a few minutes I could have done so; (though if you were here you would say I had double work for every minute;) but I could not yet redeem so many hours, as to get through your good book on the Gospel, which you desired me to read critically, and give you my opinion. I still put off writing to you, until I could gratify myself as well as you by this thing; and this was what prevented me. I at last resolved I must write, and tell you the case as it is. I have not yet in all the

s of time I could steal, got
hrough the pieces; but I
onestly tell you, that what
e read I read with a full
wing relish, and took the
less of the whole so far
anted, that I recommend-
to Mr. D—, a young Epis-
ian minister of Philadel-
a fine orator, who seems
ve got a new heart, and who
much taken with your Dia-
s, and Mr. Edwards on
ious Affections. The sum
: matter is, I like your
so well that I am not at
until I get through it. If I
ny thing from which I dis-
you shall know it with the
less of a friend, as soon
an get leisure But when
k of apologies for delay-
answers, I could write a
, and yet could hardly
you sensible of all my af-

to the questions about
you desire my opinion, I
be very brief.
Are not the best doings
unconverted entirely des-
of virtue, yea sinful?"
wer. Yes, formally sin-
it not materially.
How can God consistent
he holiness of his nature,
c sinful actions?"
wer. He cannot require
at all; nor, (in answer
: third) does he any
require, that persons
I do actions sinful, or in a
manner.
If God and Christ do not
, to unholy, unconverted
rors, what right have minto do it?"
wer. None at all. But
ne thing to exhort to un-
ndeavors, and another to

exhort unholy persons to endeavor holy actions. To exhort
to unholy endeavors as such, is
absurd; but to exhort sinners to
seek, knock, strive, &c. as God
has commanded, is to exhort
them to holy, not unholy, endeavors. 'Tis one thing to say,
the prayers of the unconverted
are sin; and another to say, it is
a sin for such to pray. Their
ploughing is sin; but it cannot
be their sin to plough An endeavor to pray is an endeavor to
do a holy action; and that endeavor must be as much a duty, as to plough, which is a civil action. God, who does not
require unholy actions, yet requires unholy persons to endeavor good actions: therefore
such an endeavor is materially
holy, and agreeable to the divine perfections to require.

I know not whether I make
my meaning intelligible; but I
cannot take time to better what
I have written, nor enlarge. I
really think Sandeman's scheme
is pernicious, and his talk on
this head a mere twirl of ambiguous words. He seems an
instrument of Satan to divide
the Church, and confuse Christians in their religious course.

I forgot to send you our College Theses; but will now send
you both years' together. I received and distributed your
good sermons according to direction.

The Lord has been very gracious to this College the past
year. A goodly number, I think,
have been hopefully turned to
God—and all carried on smooth-
ly, and unobserved, save to such
as were on the spot. I cannot
be descriptive, but in general I
assure God is here

furnishing ministers for his Church.

Shall I never see you till we meet in heaven? I expect to see you there; but if you knew what a heavy, leaden, laggard, and dull soul I have, you would wonder at my hopes, as I sometimes do myself. Help me with your prayers, which I greatly need and desire.

I do not remember to have written so long a letter in this sort for years. You will see the indications of hurry through it. Assure my old friend, Mrs. Bellamy, that I have not forgotten her. Give her my affectionate regards, and believe me to be, emphatically,

Yours, &c.
SAMUEL FINLEY.
Rev. Mr. Bellamy.

A SHORT SERMON. NO. III.

JOHN V, 40.
Ye will not come to me, that ye might have life.

My fellow sinners, behold here the only difficulty in the way of your salvation. *Ye will not!* An all-sufficient Savior has been provided. An infinite ransom has been found. An unlimited atonement has been made. A door of everlasting mercy has been set open. God has expressly declared, that he is not willing that any should perish, but that all should come to repentance. Christ has invited every weary and heavy-laden sinner to come unto him; and given us an assurance, that he will in no wise cast off any who come. The Spirit and the Bride say, come; and the continual language of the Gospel is, *Whosoever will, let him take the water of life freely.* Yes; and these calls and promises are all *yea and amen in Christ Jesus*—founded on eternal truth, and supported by almighty power. Where, then, can you find the cause of the impenitent sinner's destruction, but in his own choice? To this cause the Scriptures uniformly ascribe it; and beyond this cause they suffer us not to look. *O Israel,* saith the Lord, *thou hast destroyed thyself. Ye will not,* saith the Savior in our text, *ye will not come to me, that ye might have life.* Again he saith, *This is the condemnation that light is come into the world, and men loved darkness rather than light, because their deeds were evil.*

But the cold-hearted speculator, the vain disputer of this world, will object to this truth, and attempt to exculpate the impenitent sinner. He will ask, how man's free agency and accountability can be reconciled with his dependence on divine grace—with the immutability of the divine government—with the certainty of divine foreknowledge—with the eternal purposes of the divine will? To such presumptuous inquiries—to such objections, raised by human vanity, and supported by human ignorance, we have no answer to make. We leave Infinite Wisdom to comprehend infinite subjects. We believe, (because revelation concurs with reason in establishing the belief,) that the Lord reigneth; —that he doeth his pleasure in

d on earth;—that his
s sure and standeth
er;—and yet we be-
cause revelation con-
a consciousness in es-
; the belief,) that men
gents and accountable
. Thus far the Scrip-
ceed; thus far we pro-
l thus far to proceed
tisfactory to every hum-

But to those, who
be wise above what is
ve can only say; *Secret
ong unto God; but the
hich are revealed, un-
our children.*

', however, be further
ay of objection to our
that many are willing
emely anxious to be
no nevertheless have no
l can obtain no hope of
. Our answer to this
is, that a man's hope or
ot always a criterion of
tual state. The hum-
stian may all his life
*his salvation with fear
nbling*, while *God is
in him both to will and
his own good pleasure;*
noughtless sinner, trust-
, refuge of lies, or the
ded hypocrite, seeking
obation and praise of
ty be supported by a
pe, which shall finally
f and perish.

may be said still fur-
it has been said,) that
illing to be saved;—that
a desire to be saved.—
aved from what? from
a corrupt heart and a
life? A strange desire
impenitent sinner! Can a
a sincere desire to be
l from sin without re-

pentance for sin? What kind of
desire is that, which is consistent with an opposite desire?
What kind of desire is that,
which leaves a man opposed to
the object desired, and in love
with that, which he desires to
forsake? No, my friends, an
impenitent sinner never yet sincerely and ardently desired to
be saved from sin. He may
wish to be happy. He may
wish to be saved from misery.
He may wish to go to heaven.
But a desire of holiness cannot
dwell with a love of iniquity.
Where such a desire really exists, it will excite anxiety; it will
lead to repentance; it will produce watchfulness and prayer;
it will cause *a striving* to enter
into the spiritual kingdom of
heaven; it will bring forth fruit
unto holiness. Set it down
therefore, as an established
truth, that if you sin, you sin
freely;—if you perish, you perish voluntarily. Be assured, if
you walk in darkness, it is not
because light hath not come into the world, but because you
love darkness rather than light.
If you have not life, it is not because life is not offered you; but
because you choose death; because you *will not* repair to
Christ.

O Jerusalem, Jerusalem, said
our blessed Savior, while he
wept over that devoted city, *how
often would I have gathered thy
children together, even as a hen
gathereth her chickens under her
wings, and ye would not!* The
compassion of the Redeemer is
still the same; and the obstinacy
of impenitent sinners in reject-
ing him is still the cause of
their destruction. Say not, then

that necessity is laid upon you, and you must perish Say rather, in the language of the returning prodigal; *I will arise and go to my Father. I will repent and return unto the Lord.* O, may every sinner, into whose hand this address may fall, or to whom it may be read, feel himself stripped of his vain pleas, bow the knee to Jesus, and become *willing* to be saved! This, O sinful children of men, is all, that is necessary for your salvation. God is willing to save you. The Father hath invited you to return. Christ hath opened a way for your return. The Holy Spirit is ready to lead you in that way. Whether Jew or Gentile, bond or free, you may find access to the Father of mercies, through Christ by the Spirit—yea access even to the mercy-seat, to obtain pardon for all your past sins, and grace to help in every future time of need. You want nothing but a willing mind—an ardent desire to be saved—a hatred of sin and a love of holiness—a disposition to approach Immanuel and thus be reconciled to this *God with us.* All, who have this disposition, will be saved. *For every one that asketh receiveth; and he, that seeketh, findeth; and to him, that knocketh, it shall be opened.* Wherefore, turn ye, turn ye; for why will ye die. *Let the wicked forsake his way, and the unrighteous man his thoughts; and let him return unto the Lord, for he will have mercy upon him, and unto our God, for he will abundantly pardon.* Amen.

ON THE CHARACTER OF C

For the Pan

ANTITRINITARIANS conf disregard all the argume proof of the Divinity of from his divine dignity, and attributes, on the that he possesses all the the mere pleasure of the But this plea is certain founded and fallacious.

That Christ possesses the mere pleasure of the is strenuously urged wit pect to his character Judge. Repeated testi of Scripture, that Christ dained and appointed the are adduced as decisiv dence, that he will exec office as the mere deputy hovah. But if it can be that he executes the offi his own account, for the tenance of his own right be manifest, that his be dained and appointed Jud not imply that he will act character, as the mere of another.

In the second Psalm, a clear testimony that judge the world as the of his own wrongs. Af telling the establishm Christ's kingdom, notwi ing the opposition of J Gentiles, the prophet solemn admonition. *now, therefore, O ye ki instructed, ye judges of t Serve the Lord with j rejoice with trembling. Son, lest he be angry; perish from the way, wrath is kindled but a li*

Luke xix, 12—27, the
ctions of the last judg-
are illustrated by the par-
f the talents. The noble-
who went into a far coun-
receive a kingdom and
, is evidently Christ; the
rvants are those, who pro-
acknowledge his charac-
Messiah and Lord; the
as, who opposed, intend
wish people, and all the
enemies of Christ's king-
According to this para-
hrist will judge the world
ly on his own account.
passage, *He that falleth
a stone shall be broken;
whomsoever it shall fall,
grind him to powder*, con-
terrible idea of the ven-
e of Christ on his oppos-
The builders rejected the
one of the corner, but it
take its place, notwith-
ng their opposition, and
hemselves, standing in its
rould be crushed by it.
Matthew xxiv, from verse
o the end, Christ, having
ied his disciples that his
g to judge them would be
n, exhorts them to keep
ntly in readiness for it.
presents to them the hap-
of a faithful steward, en-
d with the care of the
hold during his master's
ce, when his master return-
ome should witness and
d his fidelity. And he
them what must be the
f an unfaithful servant,
his master should come
ectedly and take an ac-
of his conduct. If the re-
of this master to his ser-
represents the relation of
. to his disciples, Christ
udge the world not as a

mere agent of another, but as a
proprietor securing his own
rights. And if we watch for
Christ's coming with such solicitude to gain approbation, as
is here inculcated, we shall hardly fail to regard him as Jehovah.

In the next chapter, from
verse 31st to the end, we find a
a decisive testimony that Christ
will judge the world for himself.
In this description of the judgment, the reason assigned for the
glorious reward of the righteous
is, that they had shown kindness
to Christ; for which kindness He,
as if indebted to them, would
make them a return. And when
the righteous express their surprise that Christ should represent himself as have experienced kindness from them, he
assures them, that since they
had done it to one of the least of
his brethren, they had done it
unto him. But the wicked are
condemned for having refused
to show kindness to Christ, since
they had not done it to one of
the least of his brethren And
this different treatment of Christ,
is the only ground here stated
of the acceptance of the righteous and the condemnation of
the wicked. The expressions
of the Judge, *Inasmuch as ye
have done it to one of the least
of these, my brethren, ye have
done it unto me*, and, *Inasmuch
as ye did it not to one of the
least of these, ye did it not to me*,
forcibly impress the idea, that
Christ will judge the world on
his own account; and not as the
mere constituted deputy of
another.

In various addresses to the
people, Christ represented himself as the Lord of all, in a sense
conformable to the foregoing.

representations of the judgment. He asked them, *Why call ye me Lord, Lord, and do not the things which I say?* Thus, even in his humiliation, he did not hesitate to reprove the ungodliness of his hearers, on this ground above all others, because it was a breach of their duty to himself. This is a clear proof, that the exaltation of Christ after his crucifixion was only declarative; except with respect to his human nature.

We may notice several other expressions implying, that Christ is the Supreme Lord. *If ye love me*, said he, *keep my commandments. He that keepeth my commandments, he it is that loveth me. If a man love me, he will keep my word.* Love to Christ is therefore the great principle of obedience to the divine will. This must be on the ground, that *to love the Lord our God, with all the heart, and with all the soul, and with all the strength, and with all the mind, is the first and great command.*

Christ died to recover sinful men to his service. They were as sheep that had gone astray; but those who have truly repented are returned to *the Great Shepherd and Bishop of their souls.* Christ is the true Shepherd, whose the sheep are, in in the most proper sense; and because they were his, he laid down his life for them. He died for all, that they which live *might not henceforth live to themselves,* but to the glory of him *who died for them and rose again.* They might still have a regard to their own interest and pleasure; but instead of living supremely to themselves, they would thenceforth live su-

premely to the glory of Christ. To bring them to this, was Christ's object in submitting to the death of the cross. All this implies that he is the Great Shepherd and Bishop of souls, from whom they had wandered, and to whom all that believe are returned.

Agreeably to the foregoing views of the character of Christ, we find that he forgave sins in his own name, as remitting offences committed against himself. In Luke vii, from verse 36th to the end, we have a striking example. In this passage, Christ compares himself to a creditor, and the Pharisee and the woman to his two debtors. The little love the Pharisee showed to Christ, is illustrated by the small degree of gratitude that debtor must feel to whom only a small debt was forgiven; the great love manifested by the woman, is illustrated by the great degree of gratitude the other debtor must feel for the remission of his large debt.

Paul gives a similar view of his obligations for pardon to the mercy of Christ. In 1 Tim. i, 16, he thus writes: *Howbeit, for this cause I obtained mercy, that in me first, (the chief of sinners) Jesus Christ might shew forth all long-suffering for a pattern to them, which should hereafter believe on him to life everlasting.* Thus Paul was indebted for his salvation to the long-suffering of Christ. And the principal object of Christ, in this mercy to Paul, was, that in all future generations sinners might be encouraged to hope, that through the same patient spirit of Christ there is room for them to receive pardon. All therefore, who

lieved in Christ, have
o his sovereign mercy
1 their sins, as commit-
:diately against himself.
'ars from Matt. xv, 21—
iat sense Christ sustain-
stituted character. To
of the importunity of
nitish woman, whose
was possessed with a
he disciples desired
grant her request. He
o them, that he was not
:pt to the lost sheep of
e of Israel. At length
an came up to him. and
red him, saying, *Lord,*
He told her, it was *not
ike the children's bread
it to dogs;* upon which
ed, *Truth, Lord, yet the
of the crumbs which fall
r master's table.* Then
swered, and said unto
oman, *great is thy faith;
thee even as thou wilt.*
rist might bear the con-
:haracter of a servant,
be an Almighty Sove-
H. S.

For the Panoplist.

R FROM A CLERGYMAN
S SISTER, ON HEARING
AD HOPEFULLY EXPERI-
RELIGION.

dear sister, did I ad-
1 with such feelings, as
de. Heretofore, when
to you has been the
my heart has been
ied with grief. I have
a thoughtless wander-
wildered child, walking
ear over dangerous pits,
roaching that precipice,
ruined souls plunge in-
gulf of sorrow and des-
X.

pair. I saw you treading on en-
chanted ground, and feared you
would not wake from your pleasing, though perplexing, dream,
before it would be too late. With
these views and feelings, I most
joyfully discover in you every
sign of serious consideration.
The mention you made of a pious book, just before I left you
in December, gave me more
satisfaction than all your sprightliness and gaity ever gave me
before. Your letter added to
my joy. O! my sister, how blessed is the soul, which relin-
quishes the vanities of the world
and finds rest in Jesus. What
thanks are due to the grace of
God, when he stops the mad career of a sinner, reveals Christ
in his soul, and guides him in
the steps of that holy One, who
is the perfect and infinitely amiable pattern for believers. Destitute of the image of Christ, we
are destitute of all real beauty.
Nothing else deserves the name
of beauty, compared with Christian holiness; and this never appears to so much advantage, as
in youth. How lovely is that
young person, who devotes the
sprightliness and activity of his
mind to God. How amiable religion, when accompanied by
the ardor of youthful affection.
How delightful the thought of a
lovely youth attending to the
one thing needful, and, amid all
the tempting pleasures and
countless dangers of life, looking up to the God of all grace,
and finding refuge there.

On this pleasing topic I might
long dwell; but the tenderness,
which I feel towards you,
prompts me to present the subject in a less delightful point of
light. I must not forbear tel-

47

ling you, my sister, that your present condition excites some concern, as well as much pleasure. I hope in the infinite mercy of God respecting you, and I regard the present state of your mind with gratitude But I know too much of the deceitfulness of the heart, not to feel some degree of anxiety. It is not an anxiety, which would discourage or depress you. No. I long that you may be filled with pure consolation, and holy confidence. But every one ought to know the dangers to which he is exposed. What means inspiration, when it speaks of *a goodness*, which is like *the morning cloud and early dew?* What does our Savior mean, when, in the parable of the sower, he says, a part of the seeds fell on stony places where they had not much earth; and they quickly sprang up, because they had no deepness of earth; and when the sun was up they were scorched; and because *they had no root they withered away?*

Our religion will meet with some trials in this life; and these trials often prove the emptiness of many pretensions to piety. The course of providence frequently makes it known, that those, who were esteemed hopeful Christians, are strangers to religion. But there is a more solemn thought: *We must all stand before the Judgment-seat of Christ.* There is an all-revealing day at hand which will display our characters. For the present, we may deceive others and ourselves. But the light of the last day will discover the deception; the veil of hypocrisy will then fall off, and the real

character appear. It will be of no ultimate advantage to pass for Christians, unless we are so in reality.

These are the warnings, and solemn alarms, which the Scriptures contain, and which ardent friendship now suggests to you. Far, far from my heart is the intention to give you pain, or to lessen your joy. My design is to do you a kindness. If your religion is real, it will bear examination. The more it is tried, the more plainly will the precious gold appear. If your religion be not saving, what can friendship do more friendly, than to help you to see it thus in season

Let the foundation of piety be laid deep. There is a repentance, which needeth not to be repented of. There is a faith, which unites the soul to Christ. There is a change of heart, which prepares for entrance into the kingdom of God Religion is a reality. It will last. Nothing on earth is so durable. 'Tis the only flower, which bears an unfading bloom. Endeavor, my dear friend, to form clear ideas of the nature of saving religion, as distinguished from all counterfeits. Let the word of God be your daily study, and your constant guide.

Let the house of God be your delight, and the friends of God your dear companions; and let your heart prize the THRONE OF GRACE above all other privileges and joys. Yield yourself unto God; be employed for him wholly, and forever. Walk in his ways, and he will give you his consolations.

I commend you, dear sister, to him, who can rescue you from

can carry you in the
mercy through this
s, and prepare you
:ct purity and bliss

For the Panoplist.

:en led to believe, that
iy b· done by publishing,
me, *hints and plans for*
The Apostle, writing to
says, *Let us consider one
avoke unto love and to
To do good, and to com-
ret not* Should your ex-
ue every month contain
on this subject, it is be-
l be much more exten-
In this way, many valua-
: be presented to the pub-
uld otherwise be lost to
here shall we find a char-
volent institution, which
roposed by an individual'
great encouragement for
e means of doing good,
possible to put them in
uld the following sugges-
iy of a place in the Pan-
e liberty to insert them.

Φιλος.

DO GOOD. NO. I.

ently been observed,
f long standing are
y overcome. If this
of the greatest im-
t children and youth
ire correct habits.
ess of society un-
depends much up-
t. It is a trite but
"What is bred in
·s long in the flesh "
is duly sensible how
ds upon their exer-
espect to the future
nduct of their chil-
e of education, very
in any which has
lly practised, would

ery incident, which

comes within the notice of children, contributes to form their
characters. If they are brought
up in idleness and vice, they
will have a strong propensity to
continue in them. If they acquire habits of industry, and are
inured to virtuous actions, there
is great reason to hope, that *these*
will continue. Many subjects
might be mentioned under this
head; but one must suffice at
present; viz.

*Children should early be accus-
tomed to give something in charity, or for benevolent purposes.*
There are many calls for charity, which are calculated to gladden the hearts of all, who are
truly benevolent. They *remember the words of the Lord Jesus,
how he said, It is more blessed to
give than to receive.* They rejoice whenever they have it in
their power to impart some of
their earthly substance, to supply the, wants of the destitute.
Beside the pleasure which may
be derived from giving food to
the hungry, and clothing to the
naked, Divine Providence is
now giving opportunity to the
benevolent, to send the bread
and water of life to those who
are ready to perish.

Missionary and Bible Societies have been formed; and numbers of all denominations of
Christians unite with effect to
spread the Gospel to the ends of
the earth. Much has already
been given, and the hearts of
thousands and millions have
greatly rejoiced in view of what
has been done. These benefac-
tions will continue and increase,
until *the earth shall be full of the
knowledge of the Lord, as the
waters cover the sea.* Those
who are in the habit of favoring

benevolent designs, it is presumed, know some of the pleasures of giving. Great numbers of such are parents, and would gladly impart these means of happiness to their children. *This can be done,* without diminishing their own happiness in the least; and at the same time more good would be produced with the same sum of money. Should they make their children the almoners of a part of what they have to spare, and in the mean time explain to them for what purpose it was given, would not the little ones rejoice to put it into the treasury of the Lord with their own hands?

The example of Elkanah, 1 Sam. i, 4, is worthy to be imitated by every head of a family. *And when the time was that Elkanah offered, he* GAVE *to Peninnah his* WIFE, *and* TO ALL HER SONS *and* HER DAUGHTERS, POR- TIONS. If parents would seek out objects of charity,—and frequently send their children to relieve them, might not their children in this way be taught to inquire for the abodes of distress; and thus grow up in a belief, that it is their duty to do something for the benefit of their fellow-men? Should a parent furnish his child of three or four years old with only a few cents at a time, for charitable purposes; and should these donations be frequent, and increase as his resources might increase, would not the child be more inclined to liberality, and of course more happy, than if he had always been taught to hold with an iron grasp every thing that pertained to himself? Acts of benevolence would become agreeable to him, and he would

dispense blessings to the full extent of his means.

Contemplate such a person just entering upon active life, with an ample fortune daily increasing by economy and good management. Behold him like pious Job of old, *delivering the poor that cry, and the fatherless, and him that hath none to help him. The blessing of many ready to perish comes upon him; and he causes the widow's heart to sing for joy.* Behold him *putting on righteousness, and it clothes him, and his judgment is as a robe and a diadem* He is *eyes to the blind, and feet to the lame.* He is *a father to the poor, and the cause which he knows not he searches out. The candle of the Lord shines upon his head, and by his light he walks through darkness. When the ear hears him, then it blesses him; and when the eye sees him, it gives witness to him. His glory is fresh in him; and his bow is renewed in his hand.* His life is peaceful, his death triumphant, and his eternity blessed.

I seem to hear parents, in different parts of the world, exclaim, "O that our children, and our children's children to the latest generation, may possess such a character." Let all, who would entail so rich a blessing upon posterity, be careful to give children a religious education, and make use of their influence, wherever their lot may be cast by Divine Providence, to promote so desirable an object. Let children be accustomed, while very young, to search out, and as far as they can, to relieve the distresses of their fellow-creatures.

REVIEWS.

*A Sermon preached at
n, at the Annual Elec-
May 25, 1814, before his
llency Caleb Strong, Esq.
rnor, his Honor Wil-
Phillips, Esq. Lieuten-
Governor, the Honorable
cil, and the Legislature of
achusetts. By Jesse
:ston, D. D. President
wdoin College.* Boston:
ed by request of the Leg-
ire.

r occasions is a minister
iospel called to discharge
important duty, than to
to the assembled legisla-
a free people. To a re-
mind the annual return
lay when the newly elect-
esentatives of the people
pon their duties, brings
many interesting consid-
l. The stupendous ma-
f civil government, the
ent ends which it is de-
to answer, the blessings
rty under the protection
and efficient laws, the
which invests the char-
an upright and disinter-
uler, the majesty of a nu-
people, as exhibited in
sons of their chief mag-
and of those who fill the
departments of the gov-
it;—these and many other
s crowd upon the mind,
it alternately with sub-
d tender emotions. It is
to be desired, that all
ers should feel, as some
do, the real dignity and
ibility of their stations,
rd the rights and morals
a community as Ma

chusetts, containing three quarters of a million of persons, is indeed a weighty concern. Instead of rushing forward with
eagerness into places of power
and honor;—instead of considering elevation to office as a personal aggrandizement;—a wise
man will enter upon the duties
of such a station with diffidence
and anxiety. With feelings
somewhat analogous to these
will a judicious preacher sit
down to compose an election
sermon. A desire to be the instrument of making a salutary
and lasting impression on the
consciences of men, whose influence is closely connected with
the state of public morals, may
well excite in the mind a more
than ordinary concern. A desire
to make the best possible use
of an important opportunity to
do good; an opportunity which
will never be repeated to the
same individual;—is not less
easily distinguished from a desire of obtaining reputation, than
from criminal negligence. The
preacher, on the present occasion, appears entirely absorbed
in the attempt to promote the
welfare of society by urging upon his audience the paramount
claims of God, as the Governor
of the world. The great principles, inculcated in this sermon, would be applicable in any
state of society; but are pecu!i-
arly so in a country, where the
connexion between the rulers
and the people is so intimate as
in ours.

The text is Isa. xxxiii, 6.
*Wisdom and knowledge shall be
nes, and*

strength of salvation; the fear of the Lord is his treasure. After describing the connexion in which this passage stands, and citing Bishop Lowth's translation of it, Dr. A. gives the following brief and satisfactory explanation of the prophet's meaning:

"The terms, *wisdom and fear of God,* as frequently used in Scripture, are synonymous. *The fear of the Lord, that is wisdom.* But, as both occur in our text, it is rational to conclude, that, by the latter, is signified an ability to accomplish desirable ends, by a judicious choice and arrangement of means. This ability, though often found in connexion with knowledge and piety, is not to be confounded with either. The *fear of God* directs men to aim at the purest and noblest ends. For the accomplishment of these, *wisdom* makes a selection from those various means, which *knowledge* has provided.

"The doctrine, inculcated by our text is, therefore, that *the permanent prosperity of a nation is best secured by a union of knowledge, wisdom, and the fear of God.*" pp. 3, 4.

The greater part of this sermon is occupied in shewing, by appealing to reason and revelation, by referring to history and addressing the conscience, that the durable prosperity and good government of a nation must be ultimately sought for, in the religious education of children, in upholding the public morals by the preaching of the Gospel, and in preserving a solemn conviction, in the minds of both rulers and people, of responsibility to God. We do not mean, that these topics are every where prominent; (for the preacher spent some time in describing the benefits of science, the nature and design of civil society, &c.) but that the topics above-mentioned were held perpetually in view as the great points

to be established. The following arguments to prove the intimate connexion between the moral character of a people and that of their rulers, are judicious and worthy of particular attention:

"*Fourthly*—as an enlightened people will know how to value their rights, they will place those in office, who, by their ability, knowledge, and integrity, are entitled to such distinction. To obtain their suffrages, it will not be enough, that a man professes his attachment to order, religion, or liberty. He must have more solid ground, on which to establish his claims to public favor. In knowledge and wisdom is doubtless implied a spirit of discernment. To enjoy the confidence of a wise people, there must therefore be a consistency of character, a uniform regard to moral principle and the public good. They will clearly perceive, that the civil interests of millions cannot be secure in the hands of men, who, in the more confined circle of common intercourse, are selfish, rapacious, or aspiring.

"An enlightened regard to self interest, and a religious sense of responsibility, will, in this case, lead to the same practical result. In exercising the right of freemen, the man of religion experiences no conflict between his duty and his inclination. Towards the dishonest, profane, ambitious and profligate, he feels

"*The strong antipathy of good to bad*"

He has no wish to behold, arrayed in the robes of office, men, whose largest views do not extend beyond the limits of mortal life, and whose deportment and conversation indicate neither love nor reverence for the Author of their being.

"In very popular governments, where the elective franchise is widely extended, it is, doubtless, impossible, that candidates for public office should be personally known to all, whose suffrages they receive. How generally soever knowledge is diffused, all the members of a large state cannot be brought within the sphere of mutual observation. In this case, resort must be had to the best sources of information. But it should not be forgotten, that a portion of the same intelligence and virtue, required in rulers, is necessary in giving information concerning candidates. An honest and well-informed freeman will rely on none but honest and well-informed witnesses.

"*Fifthly*—a nation, distinguished by a union of wisdom, knowledge, and the

...ol, is morally certain of having
...ument well administered, not
the reason just assigned, but be-
tone of morals, existing in such
will operate as a powerful re-
f, by any casualty or deep dis-
n, persons of yielding virtue
: placed in office.

o opinion constitutes a tribunal,
r men, and, least of all, those,
in pursuit of popular favor, will
set at defiance. It is scarcely
that a people, truly wise and
should have a government badly
...red. Whenever the majority
...mnity complain of their rulers,
...dietly utter reproaches against
es, for having placed their des-
...se hands of men, with whom it
...e. If their reproaches are long
..., it is good proof that their own
...hibit no very striking contrast
morals of those, whose profligacy
...lemn. In popular overruments,
es and vices of rulers must flour-
...ither with those of the people."

... are particularly pleased
... he high testimony which
. bears to the wisdom of
...rly rulers of New-Eng-
...articularly as it is becom-
...hionable, in some degree
..., to depreciate their char-
...and undervalue their pat-
...:ertions.

...lustrate and exemplify these re-
...e need only refer to the early
...four own country. Those illus-
...n, who, under God, directed the
...stinies of New England, were di-
...d for the character, of which we
...n speaking. They were equally
...ble for their love of liberty, and
...tired of anarchy and misrule.
...old, without complaint, forego
...lgencies and elegancies of life;
...uld look unappalled on a vast,
...unfrequented ocean; they could
...rnselves and families, in a wil-
...endered hideous by every danger;
...ld submit, with invincible forti-
...toils and privations,—but their
...nds could not endure the spirit of
...religious bondage. How well
...derstood both the rights of
...le, and the rights of government,
...from the following words of one
...chief magistrates.* "There is a

* *Governor Winthrop.*

liberty of corrupt nature, which is inconsistent with authority, impatient of restraint, and the grand enemy of truth and
peace, and all the ordinances of God are
bent against it. But there is a civil, moral, federal liberty, which consists in every
one's enjoying his property, and having the
benefit of the laws of his country, a liberty
for that only, which is just and good; for
this liberty you are to stand for your
lives.'" pp. 12, 13.

Again; after urging the duty
of family instruction, the preacher adduces the example of our
forefathers:

"In view of this subject, I am irresistibly led to contemplate the primitive
character of New England. In relation
to those, who, by planting civilization and
religion on these shores, transmitted to
us this fair inheritance, the language of
inspiration may be well used, *when thou
wentest after me in the wilderness, in a
l nd, that is not sown, Israel was holiness to the Lord, and the first fruits of his
increase.* In almost every dwelling was
there both an altar and a church. *Then began men to call on the name of the Lord.*
The child was early engaged in the worship of *Jehovah,* to whom he had been
consecrated by a Christian ordinance.
From the lips of maternal piety and love,
he imbibed the lessons of heavenly wisdom. By a father's authority, guided
and softened by the spirit of religion, his
aberrations were reclaimed, and virtuous habits were aided and confirmed. It
was a scene, which angels delighted to
witness. The Bible, the Sabbath, and
the sanctuary, were objects not only of
veneration, but of affection. Together with
the love of truth and probity, they formed
a strong attachment to rational freedom; a character, remarkable for solidity,
decision, and independence. They knew
both how to appreciate their rights and to
defend them. They knew what was expected from children, of whose parents it
could be emphatically said, that they
"feared God, and feared nothing else."'
p. 20.

From the address to the Governor we select the latter part,
as an admirable specimen of
ministerial fidelity, the app...
priateness and solemn...
which made a deep i...
upon the audie...

"In the midst of those scenes and duties, which are connected with an office so highly responsible; while there are a thousand interests to regard, and a thousand temptations to resist; while, on the one hand, there are solicitations to repel, and, on the other, provocations to pass by and forgive, your Excellency, perhaps, needs not to be reminded, that there is scarcely a poor h an among your constituents, whose situation, in regard to spiritual improvement, is less favorable, than your own. We implore for your Excellency a large supply of the spirit of Jesus Christ, that, when all human beings shall appear, as trembling suppliants, before the Divine Tribunal, it may be your glory, not that you have been frequently called to preside over a free state, but that, by divine grace, you have been enabled to *do justly, love mercy, and walk humbly with God.*" pp. 24, 25.

We close our long quotations from this able discourse, by presenting our readers with nearly the whole address to the Council, Senate, and House of Representatives. After briefly mentioning the present war as an awful calamity, Dr. A. proceeds.

"Wherever may exist the immediate *occasion* of our unhappy condition, the ultimate *cause* is to be sought in our national character. The spirit of vice has diffused a deadly contagion throughout every state in the union. The infection is not unknown in this northern extremity, once so pre-eminently the abode both of private and of public virtue. The holy Sabbaths of God are extensively violated by men of all conditions in life, and of all political creeds. As temptations to this sin have been recently multiplied, the evil has become enormous and intolerable. The habitual profanation of sacred things, but especially of the divine name and attributes, is as general as it is impious and demoralizing. The demon of intemperance is stalking through our country, wasting our property, consuming our health, and destroying our best hopes, both from objects of earth, and from those beyond the skies. The morals of men hang loosely about them, and are too frequently thrown off whenever an assault is made by individual or party interest.

"On this subject, I make a respectful, but solemn appeal to the honored legislators of the Commonwealth. Do you believe, that any state, community, or nation can be powerful, tranquil, and permanently happy, if their morals are extensively depraved? Would not the most alarming depravation of morals result from a general disbelief of the Christian religion? Would the happiness of families, would property or life be secure in a nation of Deists? If Christianity is the most powerful guardian of morals, are you not, as civilians, bound to give it your support and patronage? Do you, in the last, question whether the institution of the Sabbath has an extensive influence in bringing to the view of men their dependence on God, the extent and purity of his law, the soul's immortality, and a day of judgment? Is it doubtful, whether that reverent regard, with which this day was treated by our ancestors, was nearly connected with those habits of integrity, industry, sobriety, and moderation, for which they were so remarkable? Have not the general profanation of God's name, and the inconsiderate use of that language, in which he has been pleased to express the sanctions of his law, a direct tendency to impair the influence of those sanctions, and to dissipate the fears of profligate men?

"Probably there was never a time, that we became a nation, when the crime of perjury had become so frequent, as at present. This is the legitimate offspring of other sins, to which we have been long accustomed; and to those, who are acquainted with the human character, it can produce but little surprise. When the witness, the complainant, or the accused adds to his promise of uttering nothing but the truth, these words, *so help me God*, he does, indeed, imprecate on himself the divine anger, if his testimony should be designedly false. But imprecations of a similar import, he has used, perhaps, a thousand times, without feeling his responsibility, or realizing the solemnity of an oath. That individual, therefore, especially if placed in a commanding station, who swears profanely, or violates the Sabbath, does much towards demolishing the foundations, on which civil society is supported. He breaks up the fountains of the great deep; the waters will rush out from their caverns, and overflow the earth. Whatever may be the immediate authors of our present sufferings, certain it is, that in order to our obtaining the blessings of permanent and solid prosperity, a reformation must be effected in our national character.

"The Greeks, with good reason, inveighed against the ambition of Philip. Nor with less reason were the patriots of Rome alarmed at the daring measures of

But neither did Philip nor Cæsar a yoke on the necks of a free peo-, both cases, the people were en-y their passions, and by the un-ed depravity of the heart. Liber-not immolated either at Chæronea ppi. She had been long declining; se places only witnessed her dy-gies It is the immutable pur-God, that a people, destitute of rinciple, shall be neither free nor

We may, therefore, consider Je-speaking to us, as he once spake l. *Put away the evil of your from before mine eyes. Cease to and learn to do well. Them, or me, I will honor: and they, pise me, shall be lightly esteem-*

naking this appeal to the vener-rdians of the state, I do not sug-idea of multiplying laws for the sion of those vices, which have entioned. If the laws, now exist-re executed, the evil would soon ressed. If they can be executed, not, it is evident, where rest the ibility and the guilt. But, if our character has so degenerated, gistrates would not be supported ating the laws; if the torrent is y and rapid, as to overwhelm the horits, then is immediate refor-our only hope. Considering the s, which compose this legislative the talents, wealth, and character, embraces, its influence, if con-d on a particular object, would be ly powerful. There is scarcely a plantation in the Commonwealth, not here represented. That you opularity and influence in your ve towns and districts, is evident e places of honor, which you now You are, therefore, the persons to in this work of reform. You may ionably do much. And, permit say, that when God gives means ity, there is something, which he ire us to give in return; I mean unt of the manner, in which we m. Nothing, at present, is better ood, than systematical operation. litical contentions have taught us y this art to high perfection. re be the same union of zeal and ts suppress vice, and to revive its, the spirit, and piety of our ers, which is discovered in bearing r interest, and your names will er recorded, as the honored in-ats of perpetuating the union, and ving the salvation and glory of untry." pp. 25—29.

have been seldom more y impressed with the dig-. X.

nity and importance of the Christian ministry, than while hearing the preceding paragraphs delivered. The audience generally were deeply attentive; the persons, to whom the preacher addressed himself, received his expostulations, apparently at least, as it became them to receive a message from God; and there is reason to believe, that so seasonable a testimony to the truth has not been ineffectual. Let the people bear in mind their duties, as they are here brought into view; let every true friend of his country accomplish his full share in producing a national reformation; and let him never think of contributing to place in office men who *swear profanely*, or *violate the Sabbath*, remembering that every such man, to use the words of Dr. Appleton, *"does much towards demolishing the foundations on which civil society is supported"*

LXV. *Proposals for establishing a Retreat for the Insane, to be conducted by George Parkman, M. D. Boston: John Eliot. 1814.*

THE institution described in this pamphlet has been projected, as we are informed, solely by the gentleman whose name appears on the title-page; and under whose superintendence it is expected to commence its beneficent operations. The description of the "Retreat" is briefly as follows:

"A Retreat for Insane persons is to be established on one of the most delightful and retired spots, near Boston.

"Application for admission into it may be made immediately to Dr. Parkman.

"No time will be lost in making preparations for the accommodation of each.

applicant, as his or her circumstances may require.

"Accommodations will be made for those patients, for whom the occasional or constant residence of a friend or attendant with them is advisable.

"Expenses will be proportioned to each patient's pecuniary situation, and to his demands on the Institution. The expenses will not exceed those in similar establishments.

"The object of the Institution has been a subject of the particular attention of the Physician from the commencement of his professional pursuits. He has visited most of the establishments for the Insane of Our Country, of the British empire, of France, Italy and Switzerland; and he has formed such connexion with them, as will give him early information of improvements, which shall be adopted in them." p. 3.

Dr. Parkman proceeds to give a somewhat more particular account of the intended institution, and adds a description of the manner in which the insane should be treated. We do not consider ourselves as qualified to judge on such

a subject; but all that is here said appears to us in the highest degree reasonable. The zeal with which Dr P. engages in this benevolent enterprise may be considered, not only as proof that he possesses humane feelings and a strong desire to mitigate the sufferings of his fellow men, but also as a pledge of his success.

'The institution has not the means of extending its influence to objects of charity; but will be ready to second the views of the charitable. The superintendent, as is stated, at the close of the pamphlet, is encouraged by the support and advice of his professional fathers; and the Trustees of the Massachusetts General Hospital have expressed their warmest approbation of this plan, and their best wishes for its success.'

RELIGIOUS INTELLIGENCE.

A Narrative of the state of religion within the bounds of the General Assembly of the Presbyterian Church; and of the General Association of Connecticut, of Massachusetts, and of the General Convention of Vermont, during the last year.

IN reviewing the dealings of Divine Providence towards their churches the past year, the General Assembly have abundant testimony, that the King of Zion is the guardian of his people. Every glance discovers the finger of God. In those congregations that are favored with the institutions of the Gospel, the Assembly are happy to find a respectful, and general attention to the preached word. Though in a few places, there has been a partial suspension of ministerial labors, arising from the unhappy state of some congregations on our frontiers; and in others, some defection in the regard which has been heretofore paid to the duties of the Sanctuary, yet there has been, on the whole, an increased attention to the means of grace.

There is a state between that stupidity, which casts a gloom around every prospect, and that excitement, which gilds every prospect with hope, that characterizes many of our congregations. In these churches, there is no general out-pouring of the Spirit of grace; but there is that anxiety to hear the preached word, that solicitude to frequent public and private associations for prayer, together with some instances of conviction, and more of solemnity, which we venture to hail as the earnest of better days.

In many of our congregations, these days of hope have already issued in seasons of refreshing and joy. The same Savior that took away the hard and stony hearts of the Jews in Babylon, and that shed forth his Holy Spirit on the day of Pentecost, is giving before our eyes, signal exhibitions of his amiable sovereignty, and irresistible grace. In many places, the people of God have been roused from their lethargy; affected with clear views of divine things; and animated with ardent desires to promote the interest of the Redeemer's kingdom, and to see it promot-

ie world. The attention of the
.ess has been powerfully arrested.
les have been awakened to a sense
sinfulness, their danger, and their
d many a stout hearted rebel has
ought to bow before the feet of a
l Savior. The Congregations
e been eminently favored with
iusions of mercy are in the towns
sey and Homer, within the Pres-
d Onondaga; in Utica, Whitesb...d
d Latchfield, within the Presbyte-
neum, and in Hebron, within the
ery of Columbia. In several con-
us within the bounds of the Jer-
sbytery, in addition to the glean-
in earlier harvest, there have been
er of extensive revivals. Newa-
nee, Morristown, Bloomfield,
Newark, Elizabethtown and
lout Farms, have b en highly fa-
'tied. In Hanover, South Hano-
Springfield particularly, the *right
the Lord has been* truly *exalted,*
the course of the past winter.
..sting our eyes toward this favor-
et of country where there have
ee extensive revivals in eleven
we remember with thankfulness
n of the right hand of the Most
nd render praise to him *whose
nul neth f...ver* In Princeton
r g-ton, within the bounds of the
unswick Presbytery, we have also
llege to state, that there is an inattention to religion. We are ex-
y happy to hear that God is draw-
ear n..e of our principal Semina-
..arning; and we indulge the hope,
will again visit in mercy, this in-
istitution. We have reason to beat vital piety is evidently rising in
e in some parts of Virginia. In
nd, Petersburgh, Fredericks-
and particularly Norfolk, there
en considerable effusions of the
hough o general revivals. New
s have been established, encourag-
tions to them have been made;
he present time, the prospect is
y animating In the counties of
arle, Culpepper and Madison, ve y
able attention has been excited by
as of Missionaries.—In the con-
as of Hawfields and Crossroads,
he bounds of the Presbytery of
there has also been some unusual
ess. In the Presbytery of Weston, the pr v h use of malignant
has been followed by deep search-
heart and anxious cries for mercy.
long the blacks in the Presbytery
nony), we are rejoiced to learn
much solemnity, and great engag-
n divine things—In some of the
atiiened place ,, the attention to re-

ligion seems to be at present on the decline, and in others it is still advancing
The whole scene is enough to gladden the
heart. The risen Redeemer still has the
work of salvation in his own hands, and
turn th the hearts of the children of men,
whithersoever he will, as the rivers of
water are turned.

The subjects of these revivals have been
chiefly from among the youth—from the
children of believing parents, and in some
places, particularly from the youth who
have paid punctual and respectful regard
to catechetical instruction. The general
character of the work has been such as
usually marks the genuine operations of
the Holy Spirit Though not without
great power of feeling, the subjects have
been free from the appearance of extrav-
gance. The seasons of worship have been
sacredly still, rather than tumultuously
violent. The speechless agony of multitudes who have been brought to see their
sinfulness and their danger, has been more
the effect of truth bearing down upon the
conscience, than that transient and violent emotion, excited by natural fear, and
cherished by animal feeling. They have
been deeply impressed with a sense of
the infinite majesty and holiness of God,—
of the spirituality, extent, and obligation
of the divine law, the exceeding sinfulness
of sin,—the total depravity of the human
heart,—the necessity of regeneration by
the Almighty power of the Holy Spirit—
of justification, *not by works, but free y
by the grace of God, through the redemption that is in Christ Jesus*—the indispensable necessity of an interest in atoning blood, and of that *holiness without
which no man shall see the Lord.*

The General Assembly are gratified to
learn that praying societies, established for
the special purpose of imploring the effusion of the Holy Spirit upon the churches, charitable institutions for the rert of
poor and pious young men for the Gospel
ministry, and for sending the Gospel to
the heathen—and societies for the religious instruction of the children in the
suburbs of our cities, have increased in
number and are widely extending their
influence Nor can they regard, with too
much gratitude, the heavenly ardor o
many pious families, whose weekly associations for prayer, and daily exertions in
the distribution of Bibles among the poor,
show us what it is to imitate the example
of him who *went about doing good*

The Assembly feel no small satisfaction,
in stating the increase of united and vigorous efforts in some portions of country
within their limits, for the advancement
of morals A solicitude upon this subject
is beginning to be felt. The indispensable necessity of embodying the influence

plicant, as his or her circumstances may require.

"Accommodations will be made for those patients, for whom the occasional or constant residence of a friend or attendant with them is advisable

"Expenses will be proportioned to each patient's pecuniary situation, and to his demands on the Institution. The expenses will not exceed those in similar establishments.

"The object of the Institution has been a subject of the particular attention of the Physician from the commencement of his professional pursuits. He has visited most of the establishments for the Insane of Our Country, of the British empire, of France, Italy and Switzerland; and he has formed such connexion with them, as will give him early information of improvements, which shall be adopted in them." p. 3.

Dr. Parkman proceeds to give a somewhat more particular account of the intended institution, and adds a description of the manner in which the insane should be treated. We do not consider ourselves as qualified to judge on such a subject; but all that is here said appears to us in the highest degree reasonable. The zeal with which Dr P. engages in this benevolent enterprise may be considered, not only as proof that he possesses humane feelings and a strong desire to mitigate the sufferings of his fellow men, but also as a pledge of his success.

'The institution has not the means of extending its influence to objects of charity; but will be ready to second the views of the charitable. The superintendent, as is stated, at the close of the pamphlet, is encouraged by the support and advice of his professional fathers; and the Trustees of the Massachusetts General Hospital have expressed their warmest approbation of this plan, and their best wishes for its success.'

RELIGIOUS INTELLIGENCE.

A Narrative of the state of religion within the bounds of the General Assembly of the Presbyterian Church; and of the General Association of Connecticut, of Massachusetts, and of the General Convention of Vermont, during the last year.

In reviewing the dealings of Divine Providence towards their churches the past year, the General Assembly have abundant testimony, that the King of Zion is the guardian of his people. Every glance discovers the finger of God. In those congregations that are favored with the institutions of the Gospel, the Assembly are happy to find a respectful, and general attention to the preached word. Though in a few places, there has been a partial suspension of ministerial labors, arising from the unhappy state of some congregations on our frontiers; and in others, some defection in the regard which has been heretofore paid to the duties of the Sanctuary, yet there has been, on the whole, an increased attention to the means of grace.

There is a state between that stupidity, which casts a gloom around every prospect, and that excitement, which gilds every prospect with hope, that characterizes many of our congregations. In these churches, there is no general out-pouring of the Spirit of grace; but there is that anxiety to hear the preached word, that solicitude to frequent public and private associations for prayer, together with some instances of conviction, and more of solemnity, which we venture to hail as the earnest of better days.

In many of our congregations, these days of hope have already issued in seasons of refreshing and joy. The same Savior that took away the hard and stony hearts of the Jews in Babylon, and that shed forth his Holy Spirit on the day of Pentecost, is giving before our eyes, signal exhibitions of his amiable sovereignty, and irresistible grace. In many places, the people of God have been roused from their lethargy; affected with clear views of divine things; and animated with ardent desires to promote the interest of the Redeemer's kingdom, and to see it promot-

world The attention of the [...] has been powerfully arrested. [...] have been awakened to a sense [...] fulness, their danger, and their [...] many a stout hearted rebel has [...] ht to bow before the feet of a Savior. The Congregations [...] been eminently favoured with [...] ons of mercy are in the towns and Homer, within the Presbytonolaga; in Utica, White bor ateafield, within the Presbytery [...] ida, and in Hebron, within the [...] of Columbia In several con [...] within the bounds of the Jersey, in addition to the gleaner [...] harvest, there have been of extensive revivals New-[...], Morristown, Bloomfield, Newark, Elizabethtown and it Farms, have been highly fa[...]ed In Hanover, South Hano-ringfield particularly, the *right Lord has been truly exalted,* course of the past winter. [...]ing our eyes toward this favor of country where there have extensive revivals in eleven remember with thankfulness *of the right hand of the Most* render praise to him *whose* [...] *eth forever* In Princeton g-ton, within the bounds of the [...] es Presbytery, we have also e to state, that there is an in-[...] ention to religion. We are ex [...] appy to hear that God is draw [...] o e of our principal Semina-nag, and we indulge the hope, [...]a visit in mercy, this fa-t tion We have reason to be-vital p ety is evidently rising in [...] some parts of Virginia In [...] Petersburgh, Fredericks-[...]d particularly Norfolk, there [...] considerable effusions of the [...]h o gen eral revivals. New [...]ave been established, encourag-[...]s to them have been made; present time, the prospect is mination In the counties of Culpepper and Madison, very [...]e attention has been excited by of Missionaries.—In the con-o. Hawkfields and Crossroads, [...]unds of the Presbytery of ere has also been some unusual [...] In the Presbytery of West [...] the prevalence of malignant [...] been followed by deep search-rt and anxious cries for mercy. g the blacks in the Presbytery [...]y, we are rejoiced to learn [...]ch solemnity, and great enga[...]-divine things—In some of the used places the attention to re-

ligion seems to be at present on the de-cline, and in others it is still advancing The whole scene is enough to gladden th heart. The risen Redeemer still has the work of salvation in his own hands, and turn th the hearts of the children of men, whithersoever he will, as the rivers of water are turned.

The subjects of these revivals have been chiefly from among the youth—from the children of believing parents, and in some places, particularly from the youth who have paid punctual and respectful regard to catechetical instruction The general character of the work has been such as usually marks the genuine operations of the Holy Spirit Though not without great power of feeling, the subjects have been free from the appearance of extrava-gance. The seasons of worship have been sacredly still, rather than tumultuously violent. The speechless agony of multi-tudes who have been brought to see their sinfulness and their danger, has been more the effect of truth bearing down upon the conscience, than that transient and vio-lent emotion, excited by natural fear, and cherished by animal feeling. They have been deeply impressed with a sense of the infinite majesty and holiness of God.—of the spirituality, extent, and obligation of the divine law, the exceeding sinfulness of sin,—the total depravity of the human heart,—the necessity of regeneration by the Almighty power of the Holy Spirit—of justification, *not by works, but free'y by the grace of God, through the rede p-tion that is in Christ Jesus*—the indis-pensable necessity of an interest in atoning blood, and of that *holiness without which no man shall see the Lord.*

The General Assembly are gratified to learn that praying societies, established for the special purpose of imploring the e fusion of the Holy Spirit upon the church-es, charitable institutions for the aid of poor and pious young men for the Gospel ministry, and for sending the Gospel to the heathen—and societies for the relig-ious instruction of the children in the suburbs of our cities, have increased in number and are widely extending their influence Nor can they regard, with too much gratitude, the heavenly ardor of many pious families, whose weekly asso-ciations for prayer, and daily exertions in the distribution of Bibles among the poor show us what it is to imitate the example of him who *went about doing good*

The Assembly feel no small satisfaction, in stating the increase of united and vig-orous efforts in some portion of country within their limits, for the advancement of morals A solicitude upon this subject is beginning to be felt. The indispensa-ble necessity of embodying the influence

applicant, as his or her circumstances may require.

"Accommodations will be made for those patients, for whom the occasional or constant residence of a friend or attendant with them is advisable.

"Expenses will be proportioned to each patient's pecuniary situation, and to his demands on the Institution. The expenses will not exceed those in similar establishments.

"The object of the Institution has been a subject of the particular attention of the Physician from the commencement of his professional pursuits. He has visited most of the establishments for the Insane of Our Country, of the British empire, of France, Italy and Switzerland; and he has formed such connexion with them, as will give him early information of improvements, which shall be adopted in them." p. 3.

Dr. Parkman proceeds to give a somewhat more particular account of the intended institution, and adds a description of the manner in which the insane should be treated. We do not consider ourselves as qualified to judge on such a subject; but all that is here said appears to us in the highest degree reasonable. The zeal with which Dr. P. engages in this benevolent enterprise may be considered, not only as proof that he possesses humane feelings and a strong desire to mitigate the sufferings of his fellow men, but also as a pledge of his success.

'The institution has not the means of extending its influence to objects of charity; but will be ready to second the views of the charitable. The superintendent, as is stated, at the close of the pamphlet, is encouraged by the support and advice of his professional fathers; and the Trustees of the Massachusetts General Hospital have expressed their warmest approbation of this plan, and their best wishes for its success.'

RELIGIOUS INTELLIGENCE.

A Narrative of the state of religion within the bounds of the General Assembly of the Presbyterian Church; and of the General Association of Connecticut, of Massachusetts, and of the General Convention of Vermont, during the last year.

IN reviewing the dealings of Divine Providence towards their churches the past year, the General Assembly have abundant testimony, that the King of Zion is the guardian of his people. Every glance discovers the finger of God. In those congregations that are favored with the institutions of the Gospel, the Assembly are happy to find a respectful, and general attention to the preached word. Though in a few places, there has been a partial suspension of ministerial labors, arising from the unhappy state of some congregations on our frontiers; and in others, some defection in the regard which has been heretofore paid to the duties of the Sanctuary, yet there has been, on the whole, an increased attention to the means of grace.

There is a state between that stupidity, which casts a gloom around every prospect, and that excitement, which gilds every prospect with hope, that characterizes many of our congregations. In these churches, there is no general out-pouring of the Spirit of grace; but there is that anxiety to hear the preached word, that solicitude to frequent public and private associations for prayer, together with some instances of conviction, and more of solemnity, which we venture to hail as the earnest of better days.

In many of our congregations, these days of hope have already issued in seasons of refreshing and joy. The same Savior that took away the hard and stony hearts of the Jews in Babylon, and that shed forth his Holy Spirit on the day of Pentecost, is giving before our eyes, signal exhibitions of his amiable sovereignty, and irresistible grace. In many places, the people of God have been roused from their lethargy; affected with clear views of divine things; and animated with ardent desires to promote the interest of the Redeemer's kingdom, and to see it promot-

e world. The attention of the
ess has been powerfully arrested.
ies have been awakened to a sense
sinfulness, their danger, and their
d many a stout hearted rebel has
ught to bow before the feet of a
Savior. The Congregations
e been eminently favored with
usions of mercy are in the towns
ey and Homer, within the Pres-
t Onondaga; in Utica, Whitesbor-
d Litchfield, within the Presbyte-
neida, and in Hebron, within the
ery of Columbia In several coun-
ns within the bounds of the Jer-
sbytery, in addition to the glean-
n earlier harvest, there have been
er of extensive revivals. Newar-
ace, Morristown, Bloomfield,
Newark, Elizabethtown and
bout Farms, have been highly fa-
God In Hanover, South Hano-
Springfield particularly, the *right*
the Lord has been truly *exalted,*
he course of the past winter.
asting our eyes toward this favor-
ot of country where there have
ree extensive revivals in eleven
ve remember with thankfulness
s of the right hand of the Most
nd *tender praise to him whose*
endureth forever In Princeton
ington, within the bounds of the
unswick Presbytery, we have also
ilege to state, that there is an inattention to religion. We are ex-
y happy to hear that God is draw-
ear one of our principal Semina-
rarning; and we indulge the hope,
will again visit in mercy, this institution We have reason to be-
it vital piety is evidently rising in
e in some parts of Virginia. In
nd, Petersburgh, Fredericks-
and particularly Norfolk, there
en considerable effusions of the
hough no general revivals. New
s have been established, encourag-
tions to them have been made;
he present time, the prospect is
y animating In the counties of
irle, Culpepper and Madison, very
able attention has been excited by
ns of Missionaries.—In the coun-
ns of Hawfields and Crossroads,
he bounds of the Presbytery of
there has also been some unusual
ess. In the Presbytery of West
on, the prevalence of malignant
as been followed by deep search-
ieart and anxious cries for mercy.
ong the blacks in the Presbytery
ony, we are rejoiced to learn
much solemnity, and great engag-
n divine things—In some of the
attached places, the attention to re-

ligion seems to be at present on the decline, and in others it is still advancing
The whole scene is enough to gladden the
heart. The risen Redeemer still has the
work of salvation in his own hands, and
turn th the hearts of the children of men,
whithersoever he will, as the rivers of
water are turned.
The subjects of these revivals have been
chiefly from among the youth—from the
children of believing parents, and in some
places, particularly from the youth who
have paid punctual and respectful regard
to catechetical instruction. The general
character of the work has been such as
usually marks the genuine operations of
the Holy Spirit. Though not without
great power of feeling, the subjects have
been free from the appearance of extrava-
gance. The seasons of worship have been
sacredly still, rather than tumultuously
violent. The speechless agony of multitudes who have been brought to see their
sinfulness and their danger, has been more
the effect of truth bearing down upon the
conscience, than that transient and violent emotion, excited by natural fear, and
cherished by animal feeling. They have
been deeply impressed with a sense of
the infinite majesty and holiness of God.—
of the spirituality, extent, and obligation
of the divine law, the exceeding sinfulness
of sin,—the total depravity of the human
heart,—the necessity of regeneration by
the Almighty power of the Holy Spirit—
of justification, *not by works, but free'n*
by the grace of God, through the redemp-
tion that is in Christ Jesus—the indispensable necessity of an interest in atton-
ing blood, and of that *holiness without*
which no man shall see the Lord.
The General Assembly are gratified to
learn that praying societies, establ hed fo
the special purpose of imploring the effusion of the Holy Spirit upon the churches; charitable institutions for the aid of
poor and pious young men for the Gospel
ministry, and for sending the Gospel to
the heathen—and societies for the religious instruction of the children in th
suburbs of our cities, have increased in
number and are widely extending their
influence. Nor can they regard, with too
much gratitude, the heavenly ardor of
many pious families, whose weekly associations for prayer, and daily exertions in
the distribution of Bibles among the poor,
show us what it is to imitate the example
of him who *went about doing good.*
The Assembly feel no small satisfaction,
in stating the increase of united and vigorous efforts in some portion of country
within their limits, for the advancement
of morals. A solicitude upon this subject
is beginning to be felt. The indispensable necessity of embodying the influence

of the land in favor of religion and morality is beginning to be felt *deeply;* and we cannot but hope that such a combination will be formed, and cannot but believe that it will be greatly successful.

During the year past, Bible Societies have greatly increased in number and utility. Few districts of our country are now without them. Their influence is widely extensive, and incalculably beneficial. Experience has proved that no human exertions are so effectual to harmonize Christians, to excite religious-zeal, to suppress vice and immorality, and to diffuse light and knowledge, as the gratuitous distribution of the Word of Life.*

The Assembly rejoice, to have it in their power to state, that the Great Head of the Church, has vouchsafed a special blessing, on the Missionary efforts of the past year. Forty Missionaries have been employed the last year, whose journals afford the most pleasing testimony of the beneficial result of their labors. Several new churches have been organized, and more have been put into a forming state. Many new churches are growing up in the western parts of Tennessee, a Missionary Society has lately been formed in that State. The call for Missionary exertion is loud; and the services of our Missionaries have been received with emotions of gratitude and joy.

In taking a view of the state of religion within the bounds of the Assembly, an interesting object which arrests the attention, is the infant Theological Seminary, lately established at Princeton. From this Seminary it is hoped, that many able and faithful laborers will go forth to reap the whitening harvest. The state of this Seminary is at once promising and critical.

* *A circumstance of peculiar interest to the church, occurred lately in one of the Western towns of Virginia. "A pious young man was employed to sell on the day of election, Bibles for the Bible Society; who having disposed of them, sent for an additional quantity. The person who applied for them is a pure descendant of him who "as a prince had power with God and with men and prevailed." But he is converted to the doctrine of the cross; is a been baptized in the name of our crucified but risen Master; is a member of Messiah's church militant, lives in the faith and hope of eternal death and life in Jesus," and adorns the doctrines of God our Saviour. Behold then, a Jew, carrying on the presence of a vast assembly of citizens Messiah's Bibles, and exerting himself to increase the dispersion of the word of life. The Jew laden with that Gospel which his Fathers rejected!*

It is under the immediate superintendence and instruction of two able Professors, who devote their whole time, laboriously to the education of the youth committed to their charge. The number of the youth has already been as great as twenty-four; and if the means of supporting the establishment shall be furnished, there is the most flattering prospect that it will become a fruitful nursery for the church. But unless these means shall be furnished speedily and liberally, every prospect will be clouded, and the raised expectations of many of the friends of Zion utterly disappointed. The Directors of that Seminary have reported a statement of the assistance which has been furnished by benevolent associations of females, to such of the Theological students as need pecuniary aid, which has surprised, gratified, and exceedingly rejoiced their fathers and brethren in the church. Let them proceed, and abound in these works of pious benevolence, so worthy of them, and so ornamental to our holy religion; and let all of both sexes, who witness their Liberality, resolve to *go and do likewise.*

In this review we rejoice. *Who is a God like unto our God, that passeth by the transgressions of the remnant of his heritage, and will not retain his anger for ever, because he delighteth in mercy!*

But we have this pleasing prospect. We turn with grief from these scenes of verdure and delight, to that extensive waste, where no verdure animates; that barren heath, on which there is no dew, nor rain from the Lord. Between three and four hundred of our congregations are destitute of the stated ministrations of a preached Gospel. Thousands in this land of vision are destroyed for lack of knowledge,—thousands suffering a famine, not a famine of bread, nor a thirst for water, but of hearing the word of the Lord. And even in the midst of Gospel privileges, we behold very many and very large portions of our Church in a state of deplorable stupidity. The same rain and sunshine that ripen the wheat for the garner of the Great Husbandman, appear to be ripening the tares for the unquenchable flame. We have also too much evidence of awful declension among many of the professed followers of Jesus Christ. In very many of our congregations, the past year has been a season of chilling indifference towards Divine things. Seasons when the people of God were animated with fervent zeal for the promotion of the Divine glory, have given way to seasons, when the pitiable attachment to earth, the pursuit of things vanities that cannot profit, unhappy and

dissensions, have superseded,
it eradicated the once tender so-
r the accomplishment of God's
designs in favor of his people.
all we speak of that criminal
ce toward the cause, for which
of Bethlehem was bathed in
Son of God crimsoned with
erusalem is almost forgotten.
ir heritage lies desolate. The
e maxims, and the policy, of
l, begin in some instances, to
ately interwoven with the dis-
d policy of the church.—The
and the strongest bands of
some churches, begin to be
That noxious weed, the spirit of
ile it embitters the sweetness,
ns the life of vital godliness, is
g the vigor of Christian exer-
nnected with these foreboding
s, there is a melancholy preva-
vice and immorality. Profane
, intemperance, Sabbath break-
other immoralities, exist in ma-
to an alarming degree, threaten-
the foundation of our religious
institutions
our brethren in the New Eng-
es we have received very inter-
formation. From the General
on of Connecticut we learn,
erous revivals of religion have
ice in that state the past year;
rly in the city of Hartford, in the
tion of East Hartford, Orford,
field, Simsbury, North Coven-
hfield, Milton and South Farms.
evivals have, under God, been
d, and promoted by the preach-
great doctrines of the Reforma-
some instances, this work of
ace has been slowly progressive;
, sudden and powerful; but in all,
eep, and apparently genuine
oral influence of this work of
s been eminently salutary, and
manifested, in unusual, and gen-
itude for the suppression of vice,
promotion of morality
the General Association of Mas-
s Proper we learn, that the
truth, in opposition to Socinian
n errors, is on the whole advanc-
igh not rapidly. A number of
of religion have taken place in
e, particularly in the towns of
er, Lee, Long Meadow and
dge Some favorable appearan-
xhibited at Falmouth, and in sev-
es, in the western part of the
The number of students in the
ical seminary at Andover, is
ty. The greater part of the
members of Williams College,
ssors of religion Spirited and

persevering efforts are likewise here making for the reformation of morals.

From the General Convention of the
state of Vermont we hear some things to
deplore, and some, that are matter of
rejoicing. In those places that are adjacent to the seat of war there has been
an awful defection from good morals, and
a lamentable increase of bold and daring
vices. A few towns have been favored
with special out-pourings of the Divine
Spirit, particularly Bridport and Pawlet.
Of the members of Middlebury College
we are happy to learn there are about
fifty who have it in view to devote themselves to the work of the ministry.

On the whole, the Assembly cannot
but feel that the cause of religion and
morality has been signally advanced the
past year. Notwithstanding all the sin
and wretchedness of our world, the past
year has been a year of joy to our churches. The Lord seems to have come out
of his place to *redeem Zion with judgment, and her converts with righteousness.* While, with one hand, he is *pull-
ing down strong holds, and casting
down imaginations;* with the other, he
is raising Jerusalem from the dust, and
clothing her with the garments of
strength and salvation The same voice
that is proclaiming *the day of vengeance
of our God,* is also proclaiming the *acceptable year of the Lord* The *night is
far spent, the day is at hand* The
darkness is *past.* Already is the command gone forth to the tribes of the wilderness and the islands of the sea, *Arise,
shine, O Zion! for thy light is come,
and the glory of the Lord is risen upon
thee, and the Gentiles shall come to thy
light, and kings to the brightness of thy
rising*—It is too late a period, Christians,
to sit down, and fold your arms in the
gloom of discouragement and inactivity.
Yes, it is too late a period —The mountains of ignorance and idolatry *will* welcome the feet of them that publish good
tidings; the wilderness of this Western
world *will* blossom as the rose; the altars
of the East *will* be overturned; the images
of Moloch *will* be broken down, and the
only question is, whether the work shall
be performed, and the reward enjoyed
by others, or by you? O brethren, our
hearts beat high with hope *Will the
Lord cast off forever? Will his anger
smoke against the sheep of his pasture?
Arise, O God! plead thine own cause!
Amen.*

Published by order of the General
Assembly.

Attest,
JACOB J. JANEWAY, *Stated Clerk.*
Philadelphia, May, 1814.

PETITION IN REFERENCE TO THE SABBATH.

The following petition has been prepared by a Committee of the General Association of Massachusetts, with a view to have it generally circulated for subscription and forwarded to Congress.

The Subscribers, inhabitants of the town of   in the Commonwealth of Massachusetts, beg leave with due submission and deference, to express our feelings and desires to the Congress of the United States, relative to the accustomed transportation and opening of the mail on the Christian Sabbath.

BELIEVING in the divine authority of the Christian religion, and its importance to man; that it points out the path to immortal blessedness, and will infallibly enrich with this blessedness all who cordially embrace, and conscientiously practise it; that, in all its influences upon the hearts and lives of men, it forms them, not only to be at agreement in their spiritual concerns, and to move forward, as brethren, in pursuit of the prize of their high calling, but to be the best members of civil society, that it ought therefore to be cherished by the national policy, as the highest interest of our country, and its salutary precepts carried into practice by all descriptions of its inhabitants; believing the Sabbath to be a perpetual institution of this religion, and that it is to be sanctified by an intermission of those secular employments which are proper to the other days of the week, that we are to expect tokens of the divine favor or displeasure towards the nation, as the Sabbath is, or is not, generally sanctified; and that, as the manners of the people verge towards its extinction, religion will be trodden under foot, virtue will languish, vice will triumph, and the public miseries will be multiplied; we notice with deep concern, the very extensive and increasing profanation of this holy day.

Though it is not proper for us to enter into a minute discussion of the subject of the Sabbath, the Honorable Congress will permit us to express the high esteem in which we hold it.

We consider the Sabbath, not as a burden imposed, but as a blessing conferred; not as a superfluous restraint, but a relief mercifully granted from the pressure of care and toil. It is an institution in this view propitious, not only to man, but to the laboring brutes. It provides the means, and affords excellent periodical opportunities, for the diffusion of Christian knowledge, for the correction of evil propensities and habits over which the laws of the land can have no control, for the public

and impressive inculcation of those virtues which adorn society, and for the promotion of that kingdom which is not meat and drink, but righteousness, and peace, and joy in the Holy Ghost. It gives the best opportunity for that reasonable worship of God, which he has required, which the wise and the pious have always held to be a first duty, and which, surely, a Christian government ought not to embarrass, but, to the utmost, countenance and encourage. The Sabbath with us is most estimable, as a type of the holy, eternal rest of heaven; and a standing sign of God's constant, gracious presence, as their covenant God, with those who piously observe it. We believe that we owe it to our posterity, to ourselves, to our country, and to our God, to guard the sanctity of the Sabbath. The present moment is one of special interest in regard to the subject. Our own legislature, at their last session, sent abroad a recommendation to the friends of religion and order in this Commonwealth to unite their exertions to maintain the authority of the laws respecting the due observation of this day. We are ready to obey the impulse of this recommendation, and are, in fact, coalescing with many others in this, and adjoining states, to carry into effect these salutary laws.

Under these impressions and for these reasons the transportation and opening of the mail on the Lord's day, is to us a matter of painful consideration; and it must be perceived, that, if continued, it will operate as a powerful, and indeed insurmountable check to the attainment of our object. In every moral view it is an evil of pernicious influence. It is, in many cases interruptive of the worship the pious would render to the Almighty Governor of the world. It diverts the attention of multitudes, especially in commercial and post towns, from the proper objects of the Sabbath. It becomes an authoritative example under the sanction of which individuals go from bad to worse, and we think has a tendency, directly and powerfully, to spread insubordination, to relax all other restraints, and to sink the nation into ignorance and barbarism. It is a species of secular business which we are credibly informed is not permitted in the greatest commercial city in Europe, and which we cannot consider as indispensible to the national interest, as the government is in the practice of employing expresses on special emergencies.

We therefore respectfully entreat the legislatures of the nation, to whom we are to look as guardians of public order and the public morals, to interpose and effectuate, in their wisdom, a radical and thorough reform in this practice;—and as in duty bound shall ever pray.

OF NEIGHBOURING CHURCHES

at number we published several ecclesiastical documents, on the ... of the union and government ... rches. The Convention of Congregational Ministers, took up the same ... in 1773, and unanimously adopted an address to the churches, ... supports the same opinions, as expressed in the ancient documents above referred to. The commencement of our revolutionary struggle probably interrupted their ... course. This address, which ... lately published by the General Association of Massachusetts, closes the following paragraphs.

... vident from the preceding quotation, that the venerable fathers of ... urches, agree in opinion, that ... of more than ordinary weight ... ortance, and those of common ... ent ought not to be transacted ... advice of council. And many of ... express in asserting, that the ... n of an elder, or pastor, is a matter of weight and importance, as to ... the counsel and advice of neighbouring churches. We do not find, on the ... ful enquiry, a single instance ... congregational church from the ... tlement of the country to the ... day, which has deposed or dismissed a teaching elder, or pastor, without advice of a council of neighbouring churches, except when a dismission ... effected by the mutual consent ... der and church. And, even in ..., it appears from what has been ... duced, that such discussion is ...; and contrary to the constitution of these churches.

... cannot forbear, on this occasion, ... ness and gentleness of Christ, ... to advise the churches of our ... us Christ in this land, attentively ... the noble and truly Christian ... in which our fathers have placed ... to preserve that union, which ... so much cherish, as our truest ... and glory, and which is so necessary to preserve the ... of the mind ... the privileges of the fraternity, ... which we ... ... to ... and as a ... of this, ... churches ... ... more ... of each other ... and ... ... them ... ... to consider ... of light ... ... or ready to oppose ... ... our best ... recommended this ...

... as a Gospel institution for conveying light and peace to the church; and what fatal consequences inattention to, and much more a contempt of, such an institution is likely to produce.

"From the same considerations, we trust, the churches will be ever ready to afford their assistance and counsel to sister churches, in all seasons of darkness and perplexity, and to act on such occasions with deliberation, impartiality, and unanimity, considering how much the honor of Christ, and the peace and welfare of his churches may depend on their results."

MISSIONS OF THE UNITED BRETHREN.

The following abridgment of the periodical accounts of the Moravian Missions is taken from the Christian Observer, and continued from Panoplist, vol. ix, p. 369. These accounts are very interesting, as almost every paragraph furnishes matter of reflection on the benign and glorious effects of Christianity, when plainly preached, even among the rudest and most uncivilized portions of the human race. ED. PAN.

JUNE 20, 1810. "Two Hottentot soldiers arrived from the camp, with their wives and children, and asked leave to reside here. We spoke with them on the following day, and asked them whether they would not do much better to go and live at the farmer's as they might then live as they pleased, and according to their own lusts, which they must avoid, if they lived on our land, for we were obliged to send all those away again, who would live here in the commission of actual sin. Coert Bootman, one of them, said 'We should not have come hither, if we had not wished to give ourselves up to Jesus. This is a settlement like Gnadenthal, and the doctrines taught there are taught here too. I am sick of serving sin, it is high time that I should care for my soul.'

23d. "Seven more men arrived with their families, in all 22 persons. The men had belonged to the Hottentot regiment. As we had many days of rainy weather, and the poor people with their small children had been day and night without cover, our first concern was, to distribute them among the inhabitants for lodgings, and we were pleased to perceive the willingness with which they were received.

30th. "We went to inspect our cornfield, and saw with thankfulness that the eleven sacks we had sowed promise an abundant produce. Several of our Hottentots were busy in their fields, ploughing and sowing, and we were much pleased to perceive an increase of diligence in agricultural pursuits so that they may hope to be relieved from the want they formerly felt, when they were obliged to travel many miles in search of corn, and brought themselves into great trouble, by running into debt for it.

Aug. 1. "Adrian, a very self righteous Hottentot, said: 'My heart is so disturbed, that I can neither eat nor drink.' He was advised to turn to Jesus, as a contrite sinner, and to seek mercy and the pardon of his sins from Him. He answered: 'I do every thing in my power; I pray to God when I get up in the morning, and when I lie down at night, and often in the middle of the night when I awake. I can do no more, and yet I always continue the same.' We told him his error was in depending upon his own doings, and advised him to give up his self-righteousness."

Dec. 31. "During the past year 10 persons have been confirmed and admitted to the holy communion; 16 adults and 5 children have been baptised; 2 communicants and 2 baptised Hottentots have removed here from Gnadenthal."

"The congregation consists at the close of 1810, of 12 communicants; 19 baptised adults; 6 baptised children; 17 candidates for baptism; in all 54 persons, 28 more than at the close of last year. There live on our land, in 36 dwellings, 47 men, 49 women, and 62 children: in all, 158 persons.

Gnadenthal, Aug. 17, 1810. "If a Caffre is ill, and so weak, that his recovery is despaired of, his companions remove him from the kraal into the open fields, lay him down on the ground, surround him with bushes, kindle a small fire in the neighborhood, and leave him, saying: 'If you get well, you will return to us again.' If the patient, thus forsaken, dies, they abandon his remains to the wild beasts, and remove into another part of the country. The widow or widower of the deceased throw away their clothes, cut off their hair, and shun all human society, till it may be supposed the remains of their relatives are entirely gone into corruption. They all avoid the sight of death, and are much afraid of a death-bed."

Dec. 31. "Many strangers and friends, who intended to celebrate the close of the year with us, began to assemble early in the morning, and the number was so great in the evening, that the church was much too small to contain them; many were therefore obliged to listen on the outside. Notwithstanding the crowd, among whom were families from Cape-town, Stellenbosch, and Swellendam, the silence and decorum which prevailed in the Church was truly edifying. All join-

ed with us in bowing the knee to Jesus, and our dear people praised the Lord with heart and voice for all the good which He had done us in the past year. No less than 36 waggons stood in our yard, exclusive of a considerable number near the houses of the Hottentots, yet not a single profane word was heard; all seemed disposed to keep the holy solemnity with gladness of heart and the voice of joy and praise.

"The following alterations have taken place in our Hottentot congregation: Births, 33; new-comers, 33 men, 36 women, and 51 children; in all, 110. Admitted as candidates for baptism, 66; baptised, 92; admitted as candidates for the communion, 44; confirmed and admitted to the communion, 41; received into the congregation, 10; married, 8 pair; departed this life, 27; removed to Gruenekloof, 4. The congregation consists, at the close of 1810, of 132 communicants; 58 candidates for the communion; 109 baptised adults; 219 baptised children; 116 candidates for baptism: in all 684 persons, 46 more than at the close of last year. Our settlement is found to contain, in 213 habitations, 245 men, 265 women, and 454 children: in all, 964 persons; 97 more than last year.

1811. *Jan.* 22. "Anna Mary Magrita departed this life. Her father had been baptised by our late brother G. Schmidt, and used frequently to speak to her of our Savior. He entreated her not to remove far from Bavianskloof, assuring her, that teachers would again come to the Hottentots, and make a settlement there. She was so firmly fixed in this idea, that she expected them year after year to arrive on the spot; great, therefore, was her joy, and that of her husband, when the first three brethren came to renew the mission.* They immediately joined them, and were the first whom they baptised. She lived in communion with the Lord, was active in His service, as an assistant among her country-women, and proved the efficacy of the Gospel by her exemplary walk and conversation. Of late she suffered much from bodily infirmities, but was perfectly resigned to the will of God her Redeemer, to whom, shortly before her departure, she was recommended in prayer. Having taken an affectionate leave of her children and grandchildren, and made the necessary arrangements respecting her little property, she fell asleep in Jesus."

May 25, Brother Kohrhammer was seized with a disorder of the chest, to

* *How much does this remind us of a Simeon and an Anna waiting for the consolation of Israel!*

e was subject; bu. it now attacked
violently, that he was soon con-
th.t it would be the means of his
re.

.he evening of the 1st of June he
the holy communion with his
d his cheerful countenance testi-
he state of his mind.

the 2d, he sent for all the Euro-
sthren and sisters, and took an af-
te leave of them. His departing
as commended to the Lord in fer-
ayer During the whole of his
e maintained his unshaken resig-
a the will of his heavenly Father,
I so graciously led him from the
his youth He once expressed
as follows: 'I know that I am a
nner, and have often erred from
t way; but my Savior has forgiven
y faults, and atoned for my trans-
s. Be not concerned on my ac-
Kohrhammer goes home to his
as a pardoned sinner. I have no
towards any one; and there is
to prevent my approaching my
vith confidence. He is mine and
.' On the 6th, in the morning,
ed the Lord to receive our brother
realms of peace He was in his 66th
nd has now obtained the victory,

crown of his faith. May the
omfort his dear widow, who has
in a worthy and a beloved husband,
who are deprived of a faithful com-
and kind friend. He was a diligent
ascientious laborer in the Lord's
d; the extension of the kingdom of
re particularly among the Hotten-
s the desire of his heart. and great
his joy, to join at the throne of the
with the perfected spirits of many
ots also in everlasting praise and
ving.

the morning of the 17th, to
hat the communicant sister, Beata
, had departed this life She was
l follower of Jesus, notwithstand-
numerous trials to which she was
, particularly from the unprinci-
navior of her unworthy husband,
en deserved to be sent away from
lement, but was suffered to re-
t of compassion to his wif and
us family. She often poured forth
plaints on this subject in fervent

The day before her departure,
t for one of the missionaries, whom
ressed thus. 'I have troubled you
to come to me, but my cough pre-
ne saying more, than that I am
and wish soon to be at rest.' This
us granted her, and she obtained
release from a state of sorrow
ction."

l. "A woman came to us, and
.. X.

requested leave to live in the settlement.
She was extremely eager in her application, and said that her only motive was,
to hear and believe the word of God. Her
native place was in the snow mountains,
on the Caffre frontier. She was informed, that we wished her well to consider
what she professed, as we required of all
those people who asked leave to live here,
that their behavior should be, in every
respect, correct, and that they should
leave off all their old heathenish customs,
otherwise we should immediately send
them away. On the contrary, if she lived
at a farm, she would enjoy more l berty,
and might live as she pleased. She answered with earnestness: 'No, baas,* I
seek not to have liberty to sin, as I might
in other places: I only desire to have that
liberty which Jesus allows.' We assured
her, how much we wished, that she also
might be truly converted to Jesus, and
that, therefore, we should permit her to
live upon our land, on trial."

July 21. "Eighteen persons were baptised, and four young people received into
the congregation. Nothing gives our
Hottentots so much pleasure, as when
they see children, born and baptised in
the settlement, growing up in the fear of
the Lord, and solemnly received as members of the congregation."

August 1. "In the evening-meeting,
brother Kuester delivered a cordial salutation from brother Matthew Wied and the
Christian Negroes in St Croix. He had
written to every one of the missionaries
here. Our Hottentots were highly gratified by the remembrance of their Black
brethren and sisters in the West-Indies,
and begged to salute them and their
teachers. When we asked them, whether we should add, that they all wished to
live unto Jesus alone in this world, they
answered with an unanimous and powerful affirmative, in a very striking and affecting manner. On the 2d, several came
and dictated letters to the Negro congregations in St Croix.

August 17. "We had a particular solemnity as usual in our church, in commemoration of the great awakening among
the little girls in the congregation at
Herrnhut in the year 1727. Brother
Kuester read to a large number of them,
assembled at the church, an account of
that memorable event, and asked them
whether they also would covenant together, to live alone unto the Lord in this
world? They answered, with many tears,
that they earnestly desired it, and each
gave him her hand to confirm her promise. It was a truly affecting sight, to see
mothers coming forward with their little
children in arms, helping them to stretch-

* *Master.*

out their hands and begging that they might join in the same covenant. After they left the church, the little girls went of their own accord, to the top of a neighboring eminence, spoke some time with each other, of their wish to live to our Savior, and then offered up their child-like prayers to Him, that he would accept of their hearts, and grant them the forgiveness of all their sins in his precious blood. They then sat down in a circle, and sang many verses with cheerful voices. On their return, they visited us, which gave again opportunities of profitable conversation. In the afternoon they repeated their walk, and concluded the day with hymns of praise. To serve the children of both sexes, is our delightful duty; and we pray our Savior, that he would direct them by his Spirit, unto himself. There is a great number of children living at Gnadenthal, all attention is paid to their schools, and instruction in the Christian doctrines: and we have the pleasure to see good fruit, especially among the girls."

September 18 "A Hottentot captain, called Moses, left us, after an agreeable visit of two days. His kraal, or village, is in the neighborhood of Swellendam He is likewise captain of the Hottentots on the Schlangen, or Serpent's River. Some years ago, he lived here, and we entertained good hopes of his conversion, but he was obliged to return and reassume his station as captain. In his kraal there are several persons who formerly lived at Gnadenthal, and among them a woman who had learnt to read at our school. She has taught several children in that place, and we therefore gave the captain some spelling-books and Testaments, to give to such as might distinguish themselves by their diligence, for which he was very thankful. He was much affected at taking leave, and said 'Dear teachers, do not forget me! I am sinful in soul and body, and have many wicked thoughts, but God knows that I do not like to be a slave to sin. I still feel a love to Jesus and to you, and pray that teachers may soon come to my kraal' This his wish has been lately fulfilled, some English and Dutch missionaries having settled there.

23 "Joseph Velentyn departed this life. He must have been about 100 years old. When the late brother George Schmidt was here, he had already attained to the age of manhood, and was one of the first who came from a distant place to live with the Brethren in 1792 Brother Kohrhammer baptised him in 1800, and in 1808 he became a communicant. He was a man of exemplary character, loved the Lord Jesus Christ in sincerity, and knew himself as a helpless creature, depending entirely upon his grace."

December 31. Our congregation consists, at the close of the year, of 769 members, of whom 223 are communicants; 113 baptised, but not yet partakers of the Lord's supper; 69 candidates for the communion, and 106 for baptism; and 255 baptised children. In 208 houses in this settlement, dwell 993 persons: 31 more than at the close of 1810. In the year past 141 persons have been baptised, 47 admitted to the communion, 16 received into the congregation, 62 new people came to live on our land, and 30 departed this life. Think of us often, dear brethren and sisters and friends, when you make intercession before the Throne of Grace."

By letters from the Cape, dated in May 1812, it appears, that the missions there were in a progressive state. At Gnadenthal, 81 had been baptised since the 1st of January, and 53 became candidates for baptism: at Grueneklooof, 21 had been baptised, and 22 admitted candidates for baptism.

SURINAM.

By accounts from Surinam, it appears, that the mission among the free Negroes at Bambey had been on the decline, owing to the discontent with the government, which prevailed among them; but it had been resolved to persevere. The writer adds; "I have been on a visit to Sommelsdyk, and found the affairs of the mission among the slaves more promising than I expected. The new director of Fairfield estate is well disposed, and grants full liberty to preach the Gospel to the negroes. The poor people are very thankful for it, and enjoy, under him, a time of rest which they hope to improve for their spiritual benefit. They shed tears at taking leave, and promised to cleave to the Lord with their whole heart"

An attempt is about to be made to reestablish the mission among the Arawack Indians on the Corentyn which had been broken up in consequence of the dissolute and refractory conduct of some among them A missionary and his wife paid them a visit towards the close of 1810."

"They found the former settlement at Hope on the Corentyn quite forsaken, and overgrown with wild bushes About an hour's walk further up, on the Berbice side of the river, they met with a considerable number of baptised Indians, who formerly lived at Hope, and had made a settlement there Brother Langballe was received by them with great cordiality, and staid with them three weeks Every day he held a meeting with them, and after reading a portion out of the four Evangelists, especially those parts that relate to our Lord's sufferings and death, he

...h them on the necessity of true
n, and faith in him, as the only
They always listened with great
, and apparent devotion. Several
declared their sorrow at having
er now residing among them,
earnest desire, not only to be in-
...in with opportunities of hearing
of God, but to live in conformity
or the present, brother Langballe
no more than make a regulation
... b which they should meet,
one of them who had learnt to
he school at Hope, read to them
: New Testament. He en...
...m to turn anew their whole
Jesus, and to for sa e all heathen-
ees, and help to b... each other
faith He t... t... ith has
visited the o her baptised, who
ersed on the Z p... and Me-
vers Many of the e poor peo-
led the loss of their teachers, and
d their sincere wish that mission-
ght again come and dwell among

rding to the best information
Langballe could procure from
om he visited, he found that of
er inhabitants at Hope, he
, 197 persons were still living
elf had spoken with 77 of the

May the Lord in mercy, grant
o our endeavors, and by his own
d grace, collect again the poor
sheep of this once favored flock,
may yet obtain a rich harvest from
wreck, and other Indian tribes of
nerica He is able to remove all
, and to give his servants ability
ss, notwithstanding their weak-

our missionaries who passed
England on their way to Suri-
December 1811, two are particu-
ed to assist in the re-establish-
the Arawack missions; and we
t but that all, who rejoice in the
of Christ's kingdom, will unite
yers, that these renewed exer-
d the laborers employed in this
art of the Lord's vineyard, may
ed and blessed by him with

llowing is an extract of a letter
inam, dated Dec. 27, 1811.
are all at present in good health.
governor is arrived, and shows
dness and favor, for which we are
kful. The blessing of the Lord
ded us in our outward concerns,
ave not suffered any want. But
ater importance to us, is the pro-
the work of His spirit among the
by which our labors have not

been unfruitful. We have just celebrated
the Christmas holidays with our congregation very happily. Four adults were baptised on this occasion. The number of
those who have attained to this favor, in
the year 1811, is 48. Twenty-three persons have become partakers of the Lord's
supper, 17 have departed this life in
peace, rejoicing in their Savior. After all
the changes that have occurred in this
year, by decease, exclusion, addition and
re-admission, the negro congregation, at
Paramaribo, consists of 456 persons exclusive of 39 candidates for baptism, and
new people. The number of communicants is 362."

The same missionary then writes on the
4th March, 1812:

"Our present governor, Major-general
Bonham, is a man whom we highly respect, and who indeed establishes the credit and character of the British nation, actively promoting every measure for the
benefit of the colony. He has assured us
of his good will and protection, and given
us every advice and recommendation
needful for the prosecution of this business," (viz. the re-establishment of the
mission in the Corentyn) "which seems to
begin under very favorable external appearances. I have also the best hopes, that the
brethren appointed to this service, will be
blessed and supported by the Lord in their
labors. A year or more will be required
to learn the language sufficiently to speak
and preach to the Indians, and direct those
poor straying sheep, who belonged to
Hoop congregation, back to the fold. I
feel a great love for the Arawacks, and
was exceedingly grieved when, in 1808,
a combination of untoward circumstances
made the suspension of the mission absolutely necessary."

At Paramaribo, there is a pleasing prospect, and the work of the Lord is powerfully made manifest in our negro-congre-
gation, for our comfort and encouragement. He has also preserved us from
heavy sickness, though each feels more or
less something of the effects of this un-
healthy climate. But we are greatly refreshed, when we perceive that our Savior
blesses our feeble endeavors to promote
his cause among the negro slaves in this
place and its neighborhood.

"The number of new people has increased this year, more than at any former period, and our hearts are filled with
humble joy and thankfulness, whenever
we meet in the presence of our Savior, and
receive renewed assurances, that the
word of his cross, which we preach in
weakness, is accompanied with power and
the demonstration of the Spirit in the
hearts of our h...

GREENLAND.

The communication with the missionary settlements in Greenland has been greatly interrupted by the Danish war, and in consequence of this interruption, they have suffered severely from the want of provisions and other necessaries. By permission of the English government, their wants have been at length supplied. The following are extracts of the few letters that have been received from this quarter since the beginning of 1810.

"*New Herrnhut, May* 16, 1810. We are often much perplexed, when we consider that all intercourse between Europe and this country seems at an end. We measure, as it were, every mouthful we eat, to make our provisions last as long as possible. May God soon send us relief! All the brethren and sisters, however, are preserved by his mercy in good health, and both we and our Greenland congregations have got well through last winter, though at Newherrnhut the latter have suffered some want of oil to light and warm their houses. They had, however, enough to eat, and could even spare us a little, to make out. We feel most the want of linen, and other articles of clothing."

July 21, 1810. "All our fellow-missionaries in the other two settlements were well, according to the latest accounts received in June and July. The work of God our Savior proceeds and prospers; his presence is with us, and he blesses our feeble testimony of his atoning death and passion."

May 22, 1811. "You may easily suppose, that by this time our situation is very trying and deplorable, no ships having arrived in Greenland last year. We have therefore not received any provisions whatever from Europe, nor does it appear as if we should obtain any relief this year, and if not there is little prospect for us left, but that we must die with famine and distress of mind; for no European can subsist on what the Greenlanders eat, without bread. The consequences soon appear in a dysentery, which carries the patient off in a short time."

"Notwithstanding all distress experienced from without, it pleases the Lord to lay his blessing upon our labors, and he carries on this work uninterruptedly. I might here quote many encouraging proofs of his mercy, and many instances of his powerful grace in the hearts of many of our people, which fill us with joy and astonishment, but my time is too short. We enjoy the love and confidence of the Greenlanders. They frequently brought us a supply of food last year, for which, however, we were not able to make them

equal compensation; but they were always satisfied with little or nothing."

August 20, 1812. "Where shall I find words to express myself, and to declare our gratitude? At length you have succeeded, dearest brethren, in sending us provisions and other necessary articles of subsistence! The ship Freden has safely arrived here, on the 16th of this month"

"Present our warmest acknowledgments to all our dear friends and benefactors. May the Lord reward you all for your great kindness to us. We have now a supply of provision for two years. We were in great want of clothes, those you sent were therefore very welcome. You have kindly considered all our wants. Tell the brethren of the elders' conference of the Unity, that they need not mourn over us any longer, for that we shall feel no want for two years to come. We now mean soon to celebrate the Lord's supper with our people, and our hearts overflow with thanks to our Savior for all his mercies towards us."

ST. CROIX.

The accounts from this island are confined to notices respecting several negro converts, who have departed this life. They are all very interesting, but we can only insert the following, which we select in order to exemplify the absurdity of those charges of Obeah, or witchcraft, that are so common in the West Indies. "The death of Cicero was followed by that of one of our communicants, who for some years had not been a partaker, being accused by the negroes of witchcraft. About three months ago one of the missionaries hearing that she was very ill, went to see her, and turned the conversation upon the above-mentioned accusation. She answered 'Some years ago, I was so silly, that when persons were sick on the plantation, and I was asked my opinion about their recovery, I would often say, I believe this person is going to die, and that person to recover. And as my predictions frequently happened to prove true, I came under such persuasion, that I could make people well or sick, as I pleased, and was a witch. But it is a most grievous trial to me, not to enjoy the love and fellowship of my brethren and sisters on that account.' She added, that under these circumstances, our Savior was her only comfort. The missionary hereupon called all the Christian negroes on the plantation together, after their dinner, and succeeded in convincing them, that the above accusation was groundless. The poor patient was so affected at this, that she burst out into loud weeping, and all present assured her of their love, and

in owned her as a sister.
in to recover, after having
l to her bed nine months;
ble to work a little; but sud-
relapse, and departed this
to the report of our negroes,
nd happily, calling on the
Lord to her latest breath."

ST THOMAS.

"I have again," one of the
rites, "arrived in St Thom-
roes received us with the
pressions of joy " "I must
; concerning the distribution
a Testaments, which l was
ry out with me, with a view
o those Spaniards who come
'orto Rico. As the worthy
reign Bible Society has been
ce that trust in me, I am
I may hope to have fulfilled
entions already. I had a rich
performing this act of benev-

I presented to the dark
ards this valuable gift from
Their gloomy countenances,
ral seem to indicate a dispo-
or all the wrathful passions,
lship and confidence, bright-
an expression of gratitude,
teais gave farther evidence,
lared their regard and love
factors in the warmest terms.
do not belong to me. they
due to that benevolent bo-
oin I beg you to transfer
lly rewarded by what I have
blessing for my own soul, on

I endeavored to give them
unt of the Bible Society, and
ir labors; which was to put,
o the hands of every man, to
could procure access, the
ed, that he might read and
himself Many wished to
hole Bible in their own lan-
ie worthy Society should feel
se d more to this island for
rpose, I should esteem it the
to be the distributor."

ANTIGUA.

Dec. 30, 1811. "In answer
made by the legislature, we
the number of baptised ne-
jing to our congregations in
St John's, 3646; at Grace-
grace bay, 790, adults, baptis-
in the three settlements,
amens, 1,046, besides the

tion-stone for a new chapel
much ceremony at Grace-
'and, on the 19th of Novem-
peaking of the contributions

of the negroes to this work, the missionaries observe. "Notwithstanding the negroes have suffered much, as well last
year by tempests, as in this, through the
long drought, they have nevertheless,
with great willingness, brought in their
mite, and insisted on its being accepted,
and when refused, on account of their poverty, many cried bitterly. Some of them,
being in want of every necessary clothing,
lame and helpless, and destitute of every
comfort in life, exclaimed, 'The Lord Jesus enabled me to get that money, that I
might give it to the church: do pray take
it '"

BARBADOES.

May 30, 1812. "I am sorry that I cannot give you a more pleasing account of
success attending this mission, though
the power of God has not ceased to be
made manifest in it. We fervently entreat the Lord, that He would also remember Barbadoes in mercy, and cause
the showers of His grace to descend and
fructify this poor barren soil, and we will
still hope, that, in His own time, He will
help us to call sinners to repentance with
such effect, that the number of His saved
ones may be increased Nor are we without some encouraging proofs of the power
of the word of the Cross. In the last
year we baptised five adults and four
children."

After giving an account of the unnatural darkness produced at Barbadoes, by the
volcano, which took place at St. Vin-
cents, and which reminded me, says one
of the missionaries, "of that awful darkness when all nature seemed to shudder,
and the sun to hide its face, at the expiration of the Son of God on the cross," he
thus proceeds:

We looked upon to our Almighty Father and Savior, in this state of awful uncertainty, and he filled our hearts with
peace. At seven o'clock, our whole family was called together into our hall, and
during a solemn feeling of our helplessness,
we exhorted each other to faith and trust
in God our Redeemer, offered up fervent prayer for ourselves and our fellow-
men, and were richly comforted by a
sense of His Divine presence. This in-
explicable and utter darkness continued
till about half past twelve o'clock About
one a little light from the sun's rays appeared, to the great comfort of every human being in the island. About three
o'clock many negroes, from far and near,
assembled together in our church, forming a large congregation, to whom a discourse was delivered on the Scripture
text for that day: 'The works of His
hands are verity and judgments, all
His commandments are sure.' Ps. cxi,

Long night—dark night—with heavy sway,
Hangs frowning o'er their homes of clay,
The pale—pale stars, that break the gloom,
Glance coldly on their living tomb

Ah! what can cheer that lonely spot,
Or bind the suff'rer to his lot?
The hand that spread those frigid skies,
And gave the polar storm to rise;
The Hand that stretch'd that frozen plain
And shew'd to man his drear domain;
Gave to enhance the scanty store,
An humble mind that ask'd no more.

And yet a better boon than this
In later times He gave,
A warning voice—a call to bliss—
A hope beyond the grave;
A page whose lustre shines to bless
The lone retreat of wretchedness.

The Indian reads,—his pray'rs arise
To Him who hears a sinner's cries;
Sounds soft as music seem to roll,
Strong lights are kindled in his soul,
While deep repentance, watchful care,
And grateful love are rising there,
And tears stand trembling in his eye
That Christ the Lord, for him should die.

Now when the storm more feebly blows,
And cold plants creep thro' wasted snows;
When Summer lifts its fleeting wings,
With ardor to his task he springs,
Blesses the hand that gilds the scene,
And kindly spreads a sky serene.

Nor wintry storms to him are drear,
Though hoarse they thunder in his ear,
Who, in his humble cell at rest,
Feels peace divine inspire his breast,
And sees fair Hope, in heavn'ly bloom,
Descend to share his clay-built room.

Thus to his silent grave he goes,
And meekly sinks to long repose,
In firm belief at last to hear
The strong Archangel rend the sphere,
A trump proclaim the day of doom,
A hand break up his ice-bound tomb,
And bear him where no pain shall come,
Nor winter shroud the scene with gloom;
No withering plant, no flinty soil,
Nor want be found, nor fruitless toil,
No lamp emit a glimm'ring ray,
No setting sun forsake the day;
But light shall beam before unknown
From Him who sits upon the throne,
And joy, and peace, and love shall cheer
The child of wintry realms severe,
Who, ransom'd by his Savior's blood,
Has found a mansion with his God.

    March 27, 1814.

NOTICE.

The Alumni of Yale College are respectfully invited to meet at the State House In New Haven, on Thursday of commencement week, at 9 o'clock, A. M. for the purpose of conferring together on the practicability and duty of making a respectable charity foundation for the education of indigent young men, who give promise of future usefulness to their country and the church of Christ. The design is, that funds subscribed for this object shall be held by the Corporation of Yale College, under statutes imposed by the donors; and that an association shall be formed, from among the Alumni in the first instance, for the purpose of making a systematic attempt to procure funds adequate to the object, by voluntary contributions of the members, and by other fair and honorable methods.

There are two reasons for calling a meeting of the Alumni, which have prompted this notice. 1. All, who have received the benefit of an education at Yale College, are under peculiar obligations to promote and extend the usefulness of that highly honored institution. 2 An application to a particular class of the community is more likely to be effectual, than a general application to the public.

TO CORRESPONDENTS.

The unknown writer of the biographical notice of the Rev William Graves, is requested to disclose his name to us, or to certify us in some other way of the accuracy of the notice refered to. This request is made, not because we have any doubts as to the fidelity of the account, but because we must comply with an invariable rule, (which we have repeatedly stated, though some of our correspondents seem yet unapprized of it,) that in regard to all biographical notices, and all statements of facts not generally known, we must either be made acquainted with the character of the writer, or be able in some other way to ascertain the accuracy of his statements.

Φιλος will see that we have inserted his first number of *Hints to do good* The second may be expected next month. The delay in this and many other cases, must be attributed to our inability to publish approved communications, so fast as they come to hand This fact need not induce any one who holds the pen of a ready writer, to desist from his labors; for it is very desirable, that an editor of a periodical work should always have a considerable number of valuable papers on hand

No correspondent is warranted to conclude, that his communication is rejected, from the mere fact that it does not appear immediately.

THE

PANOPLIST,

AND

ISSIONARY MAGAZINE.

SEPTEMBER, 1814.   VOL. X.

MISCELLANEOUS.

EDUCATION OF CHIL-
DREN.

IT is very frequently
t habits of obedience
ous behavior are, at
it day, less observable
n than they were in
f our fathers. Allow-
ld be made, no doubt,
neration which we are
to things which are
best side of which is
stained in recollection,
orst forgotten; but still
ned to think, that we,
ow on the stage, have
laxed, in respect of ed-
om the judicious pre-
our ancestors. The
being austere has car-
ry far towards the op-
reme. Lest we should
id, we have become too
It is the fashion of the
e lenient, loose, licen-
parents, out of mere
ffection, as they would
ust give their children
ion of that indulgence,
ry allow themselves.
not so much my inten-
patiate on the extent
l, as to point out a few
its existence, and to
ome means for its re-

ot and foundation of
.

misconduct in children is human depravity; depravity in the
parent, and depravity in the
child. This ought never to be
overlooked, nor forgotten, in any
of our systems of education; but
should be perpetually kept in
view. Corrupt ourselves, we
look with a more favorable eye
upon the faults of our children,
and feel a reluctance in conveying a censure to them, which
will recoil upon ourselves. Men
cannot readily abhor their own
resemblance; they will regard
it with tenderness, if not with
complacency; they will palliate
what they cannot entirely excuse,
and but feebly rebuke what they
dare not wholly pass over without notice. This is on the supposition that the evil is *really*,
though dimly seen; but this is
not one half of the mischief.
Human depravity renders the
subject of it blind, and callous;
it makes him insensible of the
disorder which is upon him, and
deliriously fond of his dangerous
condition It is a mad disease
which allows its victim but few
lucid intervals; and the glimps-
es which he then has at his
true situation, serve only, in general, to bring on a recurrence of
his disorder. Others, too, languish around him under the
pressure of the same complaint;

but their example does not abate his own malady, but rather adds to its violence. Such being the case, how shall the parent correct the child for a fault, which he is not perceived to possess; or which, if perceived, is lightly estimated, and possibly approved? Even the best of parents have very inadequate conceptions of the extensive evil of sin; and those conceptions, inadequate as they are, are rendered still more vague and feeble, when applied to the tender objects of parental affection. The parent, indeed, sees his child conducting amiss; but then it is only a weakness deserving commiseration, rather than censure; a momentary impulse which could not be avoided, and which will readily cease with the occasion which produced it. But this infantile weakness, inconsiderable as it is deemed, soon becomes gigantic, and bids defiance to the puny efforts which may afterwards be made for its coercion. The truth is, the parent cannot, or will not, believe, that *his* child, *his* offspring, *his* darling, is naturally dead in trespasses and sins; that *his* nature is corrupt, and the imagination of *his* heart is evil, and that only, and continually. He does not consider with what abhorrence God beholds those actions which he himself looks upon with so much indulgence. He does not consider with what abhorrence God beholds *his* criminal indifference to the growing sinfulness of his offspring; nor the dreadful impiety of treating those sins as trifling imbecilities, which the Most High declares worthy of eternal punishment. Did the parent look upon sin as exceedingly sinful, he would

not regard with indifference, and even with complacence, those strong indications of it, which every child exhibits, as soon as it begins to express its feelings at all.

But are children indeed so depraved from the birth; are they naturally so corrupt; that the parent's regarding their little foibles, and occasional sallies of harmless passion without any very strong disapprobation, is to be accounted sinful, and as affording evidence of his own depravity? Such, and similar, questions are often asked, and they amount to pretty strong evidence that the person, who asks them, is himself very far gone in depravity; or at the least has been a very inattentive observer of his children's temper and disposition. We often hear parents calling their children "harmless creatures," "pretty innocents," and other fond and endearing names which *figuratively* denote the same thing, such as "little doves," "harmless birds," with a thousand other equivalent appellations; and, I confess, I never hear them without trembling, lest those, their unfledged offspring, should prove birds of evil omen, if not birds of prey, fitted to be taken themselves at last in the snare of the fowler. Take an infant yet unable to walk, and offend him. With every natural member of annoyance, which he is able to exert, he will give you proof palpable and positive, that he has other attributes than those which are purely innoxious. No sooner does a child begin to take notice of objects so as to be pleased with them, than he covets them; and no sooner does he covet, than he endeavors, by all

in his power, to possess
ot by gentle methods, but
e. Completely selfish
lits no opposite rights,
.inis. His object is to
himself; and every thing
sition to this is assaulted
)lence, and the interfer-
others is treated with
nt resentment. Persons
mes wonder, that infants
come into the world, and
e a great length of time,
nd helpless, while the
of other creatures are
mmediately. or within a
ort period of time, strong
tive. But surely a little
on would teach us the
ss of God in this particu-
Vere infants from the
dowed with strength and
like the young of some
, the most fatal effects
follow. Give the child
ngth of manhood without
ought from the violence
verseness of his temper;
vould willingly be his
or his attendants? In such
instead of the present
measures of restraint,
uld be compelled, for
wn safety, to resort to
nd fetters, and to invent
cthods of coercion in or-
educe him to obedience.
aroxisms of rage at some
intment in his pleasures,
e hesitate, do you think,
your life, were you the
of his exasperation; or,
in this attempt, would he
to lay violent hands on
, or to do some other act
ul import? Did you nev-
a child in some fit of pas-
ho wanted nothing but
ver to make such scenes
And from what can such

a disposition proceed, except
from the most deep-rooted depravity? But this, you reply, is
an extreme case, and cannot
prove a generally depraved disposition, Does he not at other
times sport and play; is he not
pleased with my caresses; is he
not attached to those by whom
he is fed, and by whom he is
fondled? Undoubtedly; and the
depravity of his temper is, for
this very reason, the more conspicuous. On these very objects of his affection that is, objects of affection, so long as they
please him, it is, that on turning
the tables, he will vent the utmost of his resentment. Offend
him, and all past attachments
and good offices are forgotten;
his impotence, and not his gratitude, will prove his own restraint, and your protection.
Offer him food which he does
not want, or when he is sullen;
will he be pleased with it, or will
he thank you? Caress him when
he is angry; will he return you
his caresses, before he has gained his object, or until he has forgotten the cause of his anger?
When he plays, is it to gratify
another, or *himself?* Will he
give up his play things before
he is tired of them, in order
that another may play with them?
Or will he scruple to demand,
and forcibly to take, another's
play things, whether the latter
has done with them or not? To
prove a child's depravity, it cannot be necessary to show, that
he is constantly in a passion, that
he is every moment a fury,
which nothing can withstand.
Nor can any argument against
his depravity be derived from
the fact, that he often plays, and
sports, and prattles. Were he

incapable of pleasure, and of expressing it, he would not be human. · His depravity is always ready to manifest itself, whenever there is an occasion to draw it forth; and when there is no such occasion the disposition is as really there, as if it were in exercise.

If, then, both parents and children are depraved, it becomes important that the former should be well aware, that this moral distemper is upon them, They should not deceive themselves in a matter of so much moment. The *fact* will remain unaltered, whatever credit they may please to attach to it; nor is their responsibility diminished, because they do not choose to open their eyes to conviction   True wisdom would teach them to adapt themselves to the real state of things; to foresee the evil, and guard against it. Let the parent be convinced, that he has in him a disposition to that which is evil, and which, if not corrected, will lead him to ruin; he will then the more readily believe that his children possess the same disposition, and will feel the more strongly their need of his parental guidance. Let him once obtain the mastery over this disposition in himself, he will then the better understand how to apply proper correctives to the same malady in his children. Let him be very cautious how he indulges himself in the very common fault of discrediting every thing which impeaches the innocence of his children; of imagining *his* children to be faultless.   Let him take the fact as it is; let him believe, feel, and acknowledge, that even *his* offspring, *his* darlings, are nat-

urally ·perverse; that they are by nature just as bad as the children of other people; that they are possessed of the same natural temper, have the same malignant passions, and that *their* faults are viewed with no greater complacency by the eye of Him, who can never be a respecter of persons.

Some parents from a false affection for their children, have always some sort of excuse ready at hand for every error which they commit. The child is sick, is fatigued, is affrighted, is abused, is grieved, or is something else, which is sure to have no harm in it, whenever he manifests any ill humor. Though he should rave and storm like a maniac, still human corruption has no hand it; some commonplace apology is made in his behalf; and the child, half smothered with caresses, is pronounced sweet-tempered as a lamb. Exactly in proportion as he is ill-natured, he is indulged; and the more indulgence he receives, the more he demands; till at length it becomes a question of no doubtful solution, which governs, the parent or the child? But let it be remembered, that every palliation of a fault gives countenance to it—is a premium set upon iniquity; and that no parent can offer such a premium and be guiltless. To his guidance and care are committed the interests of an immortal soul; he is deeply responsible for the trust. If he allows and fosters that which God abhors; if he calls that innocent and good, which God pronounces evil; and justifies that which God condemns, he opposes the divine constitution of right and wrong,

ipeaches the veracity of
it High. In such a con-
y, whose decision shall
In such an issue, whose
ihall be maintained?
o thwart and control the
tions of children is cruel
kind. Yet in what does
ielty consist. To be cru-
) inflict unnecessary pain.
fer a benefit, is to be kind.
children possess disposi-
iat lead them into sin, it
cannot be cruel to check
ispositions, or give them
and better direction. It
strange that Christian
should deem it cruel and
, to refuse their children
assres of sin; for to this
ulgence of their perverse
oward tempers actually
is. *They,* certainly, ought
that all children, their
icluded in the number,
aturally corrupt passions
ipensities; that such pas-
id propensities, without
it, will certainly lead to
l sin conducts to endless
They, certainly, ought to
that the Most High re-
hatever tends to sin with
ihorrence, and that sin is
ominable thing which his
tes. How then can *they*
rith such complacency,
ie regards with indigna-
ir deem that as cruel,
saves their children from
ect of His displeasure?
ey deem it an act of un-
ss to teach their children
if obedience, both to Di-
id parental authority; and
i purpose to give them
of self-denial in the ways
or even to *compel* them to
io do evil, and to learn to
i? Is it an act of unkind-

ness to attempt to save a soul
from death? Yet such, let it be
remembered, is the natural tendency of parental discipline
when properly directed. I do
not say that it will of itself infallibly produce this desirable effect; but certain it is, that it
tends that way, and that it serves
to prevent their progress in the
opposite course, which leads to
the chambers of death. Here,
then, are powerful motives to
attempt the proper government
of children; motives which all
parents, and especially Christian
parents, ought most sensibly to
feel. Yet strange as it may
seem, many, who call themselves
Christians, are, in these matters,
as greatly delinquent, as the
mere people of the world; as
prone to complain of the cruelty
of enforcing their commands on
their offspring, and equally indulgent to their wayward caprices.
Some, who make no pretensions
to religion, often excel this class
of persons, in correct and wholesome discipline; more effectually restrain their children from
evil courses; better accustom
them to useful habits; and with
more scrupulosity bar the avenues to sin and ruin. But Christianity, if rightly understood and
applied, ought to insure, and
will insure, a better education,
than mere morality, or a mere
sense of propriety, can ever
produce. When those, therefore, who are styled Christians,
fail to train up their children to
virtuous and useful habits, it is
very apparent that they neglect
their trust, and poorly employ
the talents committed to their
keeping. They wound the cause
of religion, and lead the ungodly to say, if not actually to be-

lieve, that religion tends to licentiousness, and presents less imposing motives to obedience, than the maxims of mere human prudence and invention.

But to insure, as far as may be, the proper behavior of his children, let every parent make it his inflexible determination, that he will be obeyed—*invariably* obeyed. An uniform adherence to this resolution will save him from a multitude of difficulties, and produce incalculable good The sum and substance of good government is to *be obeyed;* not now and then, when the humor suits; but always, and *invariably.* The child should know on what it has to depend, and should not be lost in uncertain conjectures, whether you really *intend* to be obeyed; whether you merely *propose* obedience, or actually *command* it. If you do not mean to enforce obedience, it ought not to be commanded; if you mean to command it, it ought to be enforced. The connexion between *your* command, and *his* obedience, should be as certain as that between cause and effect; the one should be the unfailing consequent of the other. It is hardly necessary to say, that your commands should respect things lawful and proper to be done; for surely unlawful commands have very little to do with good government. Your commands may indeed respect things previously indifferent; but the moment you command them they lose that character, and become positive duties, the performance of which is as indispensable, as your authority to enjoin them was proper and unquestionable. But you will ask, am I to whip

and torture my children for every little infraction of my orders, and play the tyrant in order to enforce their obedience? A hard case surely—but one of your own making. Habitual obedience has no need of such severities; it is yielded readily, and as a matter of course. Nothing short of very obstinate and habitual disobedience can bring matters to such extremities. Parents, who govern well, never suffer their children to arrive at such a pass, that nothing short of torture will coerce them. They commence the business in season, and enforce obedience by gentler methods; they master the disease at its first appearance, and so avoid the necessity of desperate remedies. A moderate, but equable, regimen afterwards succeeds; such as is calculated to prevent relapses, and to invigorate the system. It is worthy of observation that parents, who govern badly, usually correct their children most; and how should it be otherwise? If children are not taught to obey habitually, how can obedience be expected from them occasionally, without resort to compulsory measures. The child that is accustomed to disobey in nine cases out of ten, will always remember that the chance of escaping punishment is in his favor, and nothing short of actual smarting will suffice to convince him that obedience is really demanded. The truth is, children always learn to obey, at first, from a sense of necessity, not from a sense of moral duty. If they consider this necessity to be uniform, their obedience will be so; if the necessity be only occasional, such also will be their obedience. Hence it hap-

it those parents who suf-
children to disobey them
y with impunity, find
res really obliged to re-
:vere methods, in order
:e their commands.

no friend to frequent
re punishment; I neither
it necessary, nor an evi-
proper discipline. But
1 wholly from correction,
in some extraordinary
hen probably both par-
:hild are extremely ex-
d, affords surely no proof
le parental affection. It
wever, prove one point,
parental *tenderness*, so
:tolled, can be dispensed
hen the gratification of
ssions comes into com-
while it affords little
 of any great progress
t of self-government.
ys one, I too am of opin-
it does no good to chas-
ldren perpetually: the
ings, as they grow in
ll grow in discretion, and
remselves soon learn to
 improper habits, and to
correctly. I never use
, when they arrive at a
ge, I endeavor to *rea-*
1 into their duty My
are too tender to suffer
lren to be put to unne-
pain.
very *sensitive* parent
rmit me to ask him one
uestions. Is it out of
to *yourself*, or to your
save *yourself* or *him*,
in, that you never chas-
? Is it not more from a
 your own feelings, than
od, that you are so very
in a plain case of duty?
1 willing to have the
of doing your duty to

your children? Have you not
some whim, some prejudice,
some conceit, of which you are,
in reality, more tender, than you
are of your children's welfare?
To be frank, my own opinion is,
that almost all the excuses which
parents make to cover their
neglect of training up their children to obedience, have their origin in sheer selfishness; in their
own self-gratification and caprice, more than in any real tenderness towards those objects of
their indulgence; and that they
in fact prefer their own humors
to their children's welfare.

But what says Divine truth on
the subject of correcting children? The Spirit of inspiration,
surely has given no improper directions on this topic; nor can
their Heavenly Parent be supposed to have a less tender and
suitable regard to his children,
than have their earthly ones.
By consulting the Scriptures, we
shall find that those parents do
not best consult their children's
welfare, who withhold correction
from them, when they forsake
their duty *He that spareth his
rod, hateth his son; but he that
loveth him, chasteneth him betimes.* He begins in season,
and repeats the chastening so
often as there is occasion; and
this, instead of showing that he
has no affection for his son,
proves that he loves him. *Foolishness is bound in the heart of a
child; but the rod of correction
shall drive it from him. Withhold not correction from the
child, for if thou beatest him with
a rod, he shall not die.* A very
different sentiment from one often peevishly intimated—*shall I
kill my child to make him obey
me?* It is believed, however, that

few children *die in that way.—
The rod and reproof give wisdom;
but a child left to himself, bringeth his mother to shame.* Another sentiment altogether opposed to one very prevalent among
parents, that discipline makes a
child dumpish and stupid, impairs his mental faculties, and
oppresses his animal spirits. But
it seems that the plainest declarations of Scripture are to pass
for nothing, provided our criminal negligence can find a covering.   Many affect to believe
that a child left to himself will
bring his parents to honor; will
grow up a man of spirit, superi-
or to low and vulgar prejudices.
The experience of all ages, however, proves them to be mistak-
en, and that in this case, as well
as in others, *God is true*, and
men, when opposed to him, *are
liars.*   So true is it that *a
child left to himself bringeth his
mother*, in other words, *his parents* to shame; that such a child
always carries with him the
badge of his own and their disgrace. His want of subordination
betrays itself in every successive stage of life; at home and
abroad; in his boyish pastimes,
and in the pursuits of manhood;
in private, and in public relations.   How common is it to remark, that such an one shows
his *bringing up;* that he betrays
his *breeding;* that he learned his
bad habits *at home;* and to conclude with saying, it is no wonder, for his parents always *indulged him.*   Such remarks are
not made directly to the parents
themselves; *they*, in the mean
while, are congratulating themselves secretly, and perhaps
publicly, on their superior wisdom in managing, or rather *not*

managing their children; idoliz-
ing them in imagination, at the
expense of their fellows.   No
fault is told a person with more
reluctance, than that he fails in
family government; hence he
commonly continues ignorant of
his mistake, till some flagrant
misconduct convinces him of it,
and he is usually brought to
shame at a time, and in a manner, which he had least expected, and while priding himself,
that his children thus left to
themselves would bring him to
honor.   Again, it is commanded; *Chasten thy son while there
is hope, and let not thy soul spare
for his crying.*   That is, defer
not this duty until it shall be too
late, nor let false compassion
keep you from its performance.
It is here worthy of remark, that
an Apostle teaches Christians to
infer, from the chastisements
which they receive, that they
are the children of God, in the
same manner, and for the same
reason, as they would infer, that
a child which received correction from an earthly parent, was
not illegitimate. *If ye endure
chastening, God dealeth with you
as with sons: for what son is he
whom the father chasteneth not.
But if ye be without chastisement,
whereof all are partakers, then
are ye bastards, and not sons.*
But how many children are
there among us at this day, who
from the want of proper chastisement, are more like illegitimate than aknowledged sons;
who grow up as untutored as
do those unfortunate beings
alluded to, cast off from the
birth, unaknowledged, groping
into manhood without a guide,
and without a helper! Need parents to be exhorted to rescue

ielves and their children
the imputation of such dis-
?

it be admitted, then, that
en ought to be trained to
ence, and, if necessary, to
e chastisement: at what
iall parental authority be
ed for this purpose? I an-
there is little danger of its
exerted too soon; the dan-
altogether on the other
I know not that a child
:ver injured by commenc-
he habit of obedience too
;; very many have been ru-
by neglecting it till too
A child will learn either
:y, or disobey; there is no
e ground. If he learns the
you have your desire, and
iubsequent task to contin-
: habit will be comparative-
it. First impressions ought
good; they are easiest
and usually strong and
ig. But if the child first
res the habit of disobeying,
iave then not only to teach
new habit afterwards, but
ilso an old one to oblíter-
nd you need not be told
iuch easier it is to estab-
han to destroy, a habit. If
ild is taught to obey, and
s of no way to avoid it, he
obey of course, and do it
ully. If you compel him
iow and then to listen to
:ommands, and suffer him
ir times to do as he pleas-
will obey you only from
ilsion, and never from hab-
t in beginning to establish
iuthority over him, it is ad-
e that your first commands
i be of the negative kind.
: him *not to do* a thing,
: than *to do it.* You can
easily compel him to *de-*
L. X.

iist from an action, than to perform one; and in that way you establish your authority to the full
as well, for you teach him to obey,
and that is the whole which you
have in view. When once taught
to obey your negative commands,
he will readily submit to such as
are positive. I have known parents spend more time, use severer measures, and put their
children to more pain, in endeavoring to procure their submission to one single positive
command, and give up the point
at last, than would have been necessary to secure their obedience
for life, had the business been
undertaken in season, and conducted properly afterwards. It
is unnecessary, perhaps impossible, to assign any precise age,
at which this work of obedience
is to be commenced. It is sufficient to say, that as soon as a
child is old enough to form
wishes that ought not to be gratified, to be malignant, obstinate
and turbulent, if he is crossed in
obtaining them, it is time to deny him the gratification of his
desires, and to restrain his resentment which may in consequence ensue. If he is old
enough to be spiteful, and vindictive, when you interfere with
the objects which he covets, it is
time that you teach him self-denial, and reduce him to a better
temper. Here begin; here interpose your parental authority;
accustom him to be denied, and
to take it patiently; habituate him
to submit *his* will to *yours,* and
to take pleasure in gratifying
you, as well as *himself.* My own
opinion is, that by the time a
child is two years old, the important work of securing his obedience may and ought to be as-

complished; oftentimes still earlier; and that the business is better and more effectually done then, than at a later period It was the advice of the late President Witherspoon, that sagacious observer of human nature and truly great man, to begin with the infant, as soon as he should manifest a fondness for a play thing, and, before he should obstinately covet it, to take it from him, and so gradually habituate him to self-denial, and to his parent's authority. It was his opinion that in this way, the child might be taught the habit of obedience without punishment, and without a contest. I have known the experiment to be made in part, and so far with entire success. But on this particular topic, and the subject of education generally, I cannot do so well as to refer my readers to the author himself in his "Letters on Education;" a work which every parent ought to read, and which contains more practical good sense on the subject in hand, than I remember to have seen in any other book, the Bible excepted.

Many parents will not hesitate to acknowledge themselves culpable in neglecting the proper discipline of their children. The task, they say, is difficult, and one to which they are not equal; their will is good, but their resolution feeble. Having said this, they seem to feel as if they had disburdened their consciences by so frank a confession, and then very quietly pursue the same path which they had previously trodden. But in such a case, something more is required than empty confessions of allowed faults, to remedy the mischief

which they have occasioned. If they have erred, this furnishes no reason for continuing the error, but a very strong one for relinquishing it Nor is proper discipline so difficult a task as it is represented The real difficulties lie on the other side; the object of discipline is to avoid, not to create them. Who meets with most difficulties; the parent that has his children under due subordination, or he that suffers them to live without any control? But allow the task to be as difficult as it is represented; are you unwilling to encounter a few obstacles for the sake of your children? Had you rather ruin them by your neglect, than promote their best interests at the expense of a pittance of your present ease? Is a plain and obvious duty to be abandoned, because some trifling obstacle may oppose its fulfilment? The truth is, great numbers of our countrymen have gone very far in the neglect of parental discipline, and are more willing to acknowledge or palliate the fault, than they are to renounce it. Every one can *talk* on the subject, as it happens to strike his humor at the moment; can condemn, or justify himself as circumstances vary, or the occasion suits him. But without serious pains to produce a reformation, the evil has taken too deep root to be easily eradicated. The united efforts of all, who rightly estimate the importance of obedience to parents, are necessary to arrest the progress of the mischief complained of, and to restore us to that better course, which our fathers took in training up their children for public and private usefulness. In the number of those against

, the Apostle tells us, the
of God is revealed from
:n, are the *disobedient to*
s, and such as are *without*
il affection. At the pres-
y too many can be found
nswer to this description.
iltitude of parents daily
bute to the revelation of
rath, by their neglect in
ting their children to obe-
:; herein manifesting their
·int of proper natural af-
i, and teaching them also
me impiety. Had we our
:, with which generation
l we wish to have our lot;
uch an one as lived fifty
ago, or such, as from pres-
prospects, without a spe-
iterposition of Providence,
: to be on the stage of ac-
t the end of half a century
ne? May our efforts be
and such be the blessing
ant upon them, that fu-
generations may account
elves happy in being de-
:d from those, who put a
·alue on faithful parental
line, and filial obedience.

CRISPUS.

For the Panoplist.

DVICE OF A FATHER.

owing is a copy of a written ad-
iven by a father in the county of
is ter, (Mass.) to his daughter, on
aving his house in consequence of
iarriage. If you should think it
ated to do good, please to give
Place in your valuable publication,
blige   A CONSTANT READER.

beloved daughter A——
u are about to leave your
's house expecting never
:o return except on occa-
visits, I have thought

proper to give you a word of
advice.

You have formed new and interesting connexions for life.
As you retire from your parents,
let virtue and religion, humility
and the fear of God, be your constant companions. Forget not
seriously to read and study the
Bible I have given you. You will
find in that Sacred Book every
thing, which is necessary to direct your steps, to guide you in
difficulty, and console you in
trouble. As you pass through
this uncertain and troublesome
world, remember there is a divine over-ruling hand that guides
and directs all things. If you
put your trust in Him that ruleth, you will be safe; but if you
place confidence in your own
wisdom and strength, or in vain
man, in whom is no help, you
must fail, and meet with sad disappointment and sorrow. Endeavor to act well your part in life.
Be kind to all with whom you
have connexions, or dealings.
Remember to do all that in you
lies to assist and comfort the afflicted widow, your mother-in
law. Let her always have occasion to speak well of you, and to
mention your kindness to her:
And by no means forget your
own parents, especially your afflicted mother, who will be able
to visit you but seldom. Be kind
to the poor, that may be around
you; and be ever ready to afford
them help as their wants and
your abilities call for and allow.
Never turn away your face from
the distressed; but be always
ready to afford them relief, so
far as Providence may give you
the means. Strive, in coopera-
tion with your husband, to lay
up some of the good things o

this world for old age, if you
may be spared to that period.
But remember, *One thing is
needful.* Remember the Sabbath day to keep it holy. Seriously and constantly attend on
public worship, so far as circumstances will permit. Though
you are now young, remember
that you were born to die, and
that you *may die soon* Strive, I
intreat you, to be prepared for
that solemn event. Be penitent
and believing. Be reconciled to
God, submissive and devoted to
the Savior. Forget not the advice of your father. Perhaps
this may be the last opportunity*
I shall have to counsel you.
Think on these things. And
finally, God bless you, my
daughter. Farewell.

April 8, 1813.

ON THE IMPORTANCE OF BEING ACQUAINTED WITH THE EVIDENCES OF THE CHRISTIAN RELIGION.

To the Editor of the Panoplist.
Sir,
SHOULD you think the following thoughts
calculated to promote the interest of
the Redeemer's kingdom, you are requested to give them a place in your
useful publication.

IT is often asked by the friends
of Zion, "Why has the Gospel
so little influence on multitudes
to whom it is preached?" In
answer to this inquiry various
reasons have been given. I beg
leave to suggest one, which is
seldom mentioned; viz. Igno-

* Probably it was the last opportunity,
unless on a death bed for the writer sick-
ened and died, in a few months after the
above was written, in the midst of his
days, and greatly lamented.

rance of the evidences on which
this religion is founded.

In our enlightened country,
which has ever enjoyed the Gospel—a land of Bibles and Sabbaths.—it seems to be taken for
granted, that every person believes the truth of revelation,
who does not openly acknowledge
himself an infidel. But by a few
moments' reflection on this subject, we must all be convinced of
the contrary.

That Mahomedanism should
be handed down from generation
to generation; that parents
should bequeath, and children
inherit it, without ever examining whether it be true, or false,
or even once suspecting its au-
thenticity, is not strange; for this
religion exactly coincides with
the propensities of man's depraved nature. It fosters some
of the strongest and worst passions of the human heart. But
Christianity has a tendency directly the reverse. It arrays itself against every darling sin; it
strikes a death blow at all our
inordinate desires. Hence arises
our opposition to the religion it
inculcates. We are hostile to
Christianity, because it opposes
our vicious inclinations The
religion of the Bible and a wicked heart are very bitter enemies.
The sinner therefore will naturally be led to doubt the truth of
this religion, unless he has such
evidence as will bring to his
mind irresistible conviction.
This evidence indeed exists;
but unhappily he is ignorant of
it. It is true he has lived in a
Christian land all his days, *known
the holy Scriptures from his
youth,* and has heard the Gospel preached from Sabbath to

Many things which
d hears are calculat-
e the belief, that the
true. But, on the
he finds much which
zible;—it is above his
sion; and the great ad-
:ing every ready to
vary souls, and lend-
uence to help on the
in, the practical unbe-
igth reasons himself
lative belief, that the
f Scripture are incon-
i themselves, and con-
ason; and that there-
innot be true. It may
not become a confirm-
at once, perhaps not
'e; but he has many
·king in his mind,
: the fowls of the air,
rable of the sower,
the good seed of the
fe, lest he should be-
ie saved. The means
·e ineffectual. Though
iuch on the subject of
t has little or no ef-
life. It is like build-
indy foundation. Un-
lermines the super-
*He needs to be taught
the first principles of
of God.*
re undoubtedly many,
i much occupied with
:ss and pleasures of
they have never felt
iety to know whether
on be true or false.
· leave to ask every
a serious reflecting
i has not yet cordially
Christianity, whether
remarks do not har-
·ith his own feelings;
iey do not form a mir-
iich he discovers his
ess? Judging from my

own experience, I should be led
to conclude, that all of the above
description might safely give
this question an affirmative answer. And I know not that it
will be a breach of charity to
account, on the same principle,
for that numerous class of lukewarm professors,—those diseas-
ed members, which, as it were,
sicken the whole body of the
Christian church. For I am
inclined to believe, that in many
cases, the secret working of unbelief is one great cause why
such persons do not come forward boldly, and with zeal defend
the cause, which they have professedly espoused.

They are not indeed absolutely certain that Christianity is a
system of falsehood; and if it be
they do not see any danger in
professing it. If it be true, it is
of the highest moment; they
choose therefore to be on the
safer side.

Let me appeal to those, also,
who are now the sincere disciples of Christ, whether, while
they were asleep in sin, secret
infidelity was not the fatal opiate
which deadened the sensibility
of their hearts; and whether a
sincere conviction that the Bible
was the word of God did not
first, and most of all, disturb their
security?

The grand object of all religious instruction is the conviction, conversion, and salvation of
men's souls; and to discover in
what manner this can best be accomplished should be the study
of every Christian. To assist our
inquiries, let us consider for a
moment the course pursued by
the Apostles.

Our Lord, after his resurrection, commissioned his Apostles

to *go into all the world, and preach the Gospel to every creature.* They obeyed and went forth. Their object was the salvation of men's souls. The same glorious object should engage every Christian, in some way or other, at this day.

The Jews already believed the Old Testament Scriptures. When the Apostles preached to the Jews, therefore, they labored to convince them, from these Scriptures, that Jesus was the Messiah foretold by the prophets—the Son of God—the Savior of the world. And what was the effect? Sometimes, it is true, they closed their ears, and shut their eyes against the light; but, in many cases, *the word of God was quick, and powerful, and proved a savor of life unto life to them.* Sometimes the Holy Ghost descended in a miraculous manner, as on the day of Pentecost. The Jews were unable to resist the force of the Apostle's reasoning. It brought conviction to their consciences. *They were pricked in their hearts and said unto Peter, and to the rest of the Apostles, men and brethren, what shall we do!* Their hearts were now prepared, by the influences of the Spirit, to comply with the direction, which was immediately given, *to repent,* &c. whereas had the Apostle given the same direction previously, before he had reasoned with them, and convinced them out of their Scriptures that Jesus was the Messiah, we have no reason to suppose, that the day of Pentecost would have been remarkable for the conversion of three thousand souls.

When the Apostles preached among the Gentiles, they first

endeavored to turn them their idolatrous worship to the living God. When saw the whole city of A given to idolatry, worshi they knew not what, he them, *Whom ye ignorantly ship, him declare I unto* and then went on to expla nature of the Supreme Be the worship he requires very judiciously labored t cite their attention, and re their prejudices, by instru them out of their own poet

And now I would ask reader, who believes with that there are many among who are unacquainted wil evidences of our religion, w er there is not the same r for using means to instruct persons, and open their mi conviction, as there was t form the unenlightened i days of the Apostles? Igno is surely the same wherev be found; whether among Hindoos, or Christians.

It is not to be expected, our public teachers of rel should employ a great porti their time in inculcating mere rudiments of Christi They are to labor, not only the conversion of sinners. for the edification of the s They must *feed the churc* God. But is it not true tha seldom hear a single disco on this subject? Suffer me, tl fore to suggest to those w business it is to watch for s *whether they would not rightly divide the word of* should they take up this ject, in a concise, and fam manner, and bring togethe a few discourses, the prin evidences of the Christian

These sermons might be
·ed occasionally, as cir-
inces should render most
ient. And to complete
.tem, it might be well to
the example of the Apos-
1ose labors were so re-
bly blessed on the day of
:ost, by a pungent exhor-
to their hearers to repent
lieve.
ile the primary object of
discourses would be to
ce those, who, through cri-
negligence, are deplora-
porant on this all-impor-
1bject, they would at the
time have a tendency to
't and animate such as
Jready been taught, and
rate the faith of others,
belief of the Gospel is
d rather on 'a *witness in
fves*' than on any out-
vidences. These sermons
excite attention by their
y; for, as has just been re-
d, we seldom hear any
on the subject; and there
:h reason to believe, that
the blessing of God they
produce a happy effect on
wavering persons.
som:thing still further is
ary to be done; for though
be possible to heal a dan-
i malady, it is much safer
rd against its attacks —Let
en, uien, be early instructed
evidences of the Christian
Though suc.i have a nat-
erverseness of temper, yet
heads have not been filled
lelusive speculations, nor
minds darkened by words
it knowledge, and perveri-
th the sophistical reason-
infidel objectors. Their
are open to conviction,
ould be stored with argu-

ments, that in future life they
may be able to withstand gainsayers; and, should the Spirit
of grace afterwards operate on
their minds, *be ready to give an
answer to every man that asketh
them a reason of the hope that is
in them.*

The principal evidences of our
religion are plain and simple,
and may be comprehended in
very early life; and among all
our catechisms I should be glad
to see one comprising these evidences, adapted to the capacities
of children. Let this be introduced into our schools; let children be taught it, as they are, or
ought to be, the Assembly's catechism. They could learn it
with as much ease, and probably
understand it much better.
Would it not likewise be an excellent practice to introduce
something of this kind, as an
occasional study, into higher
schools, academies, and colleges?

I am persuaded, that this is a
subject of importance; ' and
should ministers of the Gospel,
and those who have the care of
children and youth, be of the
same opinion, and act accordingly, there is reason to believe that
some of the present generation,
and multitudes who are now
just coming forth into active life,
would hereafter rise up and call
them blessed. LAOS.

ORIGINAL LETTER FROM GOV-
ERNOR BELCHER TO PRESI-
DENT EDWARDS.

My good Friend,
SIR—I am still to humble myself and ask forgiveness, while I
mention the receipt of yours of

the 22nd of November last. Indeed, the difficult situation of the affairs of this province has latterly pretty much drawn my attention, and broken in upon the regularity of my more private correspondence, which I now renew with you to my great pleasure and satisfaction. ·

Alas, Sir, when I consider how miserable and worthless a creature I am, and how unworthy of that respect you would fain wish I might lay some claim to; I say when I consider these things, I prostrate myself before that God, who searcheth the heart and trieth the reins of the children of men, and cry out, *God be merciful to me a sinner!* And yet, if I know my own heart, if God will please to honor me, in the station wherein he has placed me, with being instrumental in bringing some revenue of glory to his great name, I am sure it will give me the greatest joy in life, and comfort in death.

As I have heard nothing for a long time from two of the best friends and favorers of the Indian congregation of Housatonnot, (Mr. Isaac Hollis and Capt. Coram,) I am afraid they are dead; and if so, this with the death of the late worthy Mr. Sergeant, draws a gloomy prospect over that excellent design of carrying the Gospel into those regions, where there is no vision, but the people are daily perishing

Our infant College meets with unkindness and opposition from such as have no taste for learning, and too great a contempt for the religion of the blessed Jesus: and yet we have reason to praise a gracious and bountiful God, that while clouds and discouragements have been hovering over this little seminary, the day-spring from on high seems to visit it, by finding out ways and means for its support. A gentleman that died lately, in the colony of Pennsylvania, has left to our College his whole estate after his wife's decease, (who is between 60 and 70,) and this donation is judged to be at least five hundred pounds sterling; and by a lottery, it has lately gained about nine hundred pounds sterling more. The President has at present, I think, 29 pupils, and several of them very promising. The commencement is to be the last Wednesday of the next month, when I understand a number intend to offer themselves for admittance. Thus far, through the tender mercy of our God, we are creeping along.

I am truly grieved and sorry to repeat to you, that I observe more and more among the people, in these parts, an indifference and coldness in all religious matters; and to talk with them of regeneration, or of the new creature, they wonder with Nicodemus and say, *Can a man enter the second time into his mother's womb, and be born?* I fear multitudes in these parts are destroyed for lack of knowledge: but I hope the rising College in New Jersey will not only be a nursery for the best human learning; but that, by the favor of heaven, it may, in times to come, be a *river, the streams whereof shall make glad the city of our God.* While God is pleased to spare life and opportunity, nothing in my power shall be wanting to promote the pros-

and establishment of this
y And if God shall vouch-
bless this undertaking, I
ill concerned will humbly
orth his praise, saying,
to us, O Lord, not unto
unto thy name give glory,
y mercy and thy truth's
Amen and Amen.

ank you, Sir, very kindly,
pleasing account you give
some tokens for good. As
revival of religion in Eng-
have advices of the same
from the learned and pi-
Dr Doddridge, and from
ear Mr. Whitefield, to
I refer in postscript. For
things *our souls should*
fy the Lord, while we hum-
joice in God our Savior.
I now, dear Sir, I come to
elancholy affair of the dif-
e between yourself and the
h and people of Northamp-
Mr. President Burr visited
it week, and told me that
atter was actually come to
aration between you and
people; for which I am ex-
ngly sorry, and heartily
God to support you under
ere a trial, and to pour out
you an uncommon meas-

ure of divine wisdom and grace
in this extraordinary event of
his Providence, that in the end
his glory may be best displayed
and comfort arise to your soul:
For it is easy with God to bring
order out of confusion and light
out of darkness. *But it shall*
come to pass that at evening time
it shall be light—Yet have I not
seen the righteous forsaken, nor
his seed begging bread. The sal-
vation of the righteous is of the
Lord, he is their strength in the
time of trouble. But the Sacred
Oracles, from Genesis to the
Revelation, are so full of promises and comforts, and with
which you are so well acquainted, that I ask pardon and modestly forbear mentioning any
thing more than that I wish
you, and Mrs. Edwards, and
your offspring, the blessings of
that covenant, which *is ordered*
in all things and sure.

When you bow yourself at the
throne of grace, you will re-
member, Rev. and worthy Sir
your hearty friend and servant,
J. BELCHER.
Burlington, N. J.
Aug. 20, 1750.
Mr. Edwards.

RELIGIOUS COMMUNICATIONS.

THOUGHTS ON ECCL. V, 1.

To the Editor of the Panoplist.

ollowing thoughts shall appear wor-
f a place in your useful publication,
are at liberty to insert them.

thy foot when thou goest
the house of God; and be
re ready to hear, than to
e the sacrifice of fools.

public worship of God is a
institution. The employ-
.. X.

ment is solemn; and the temple
or house dedicated to this sublime service must of course be
a solemn place. The *anointing*,
or dedication, of the tabernacle
in the wilderness, (see Ex. xl,)
and the dedication of the temple
at Jerusalem, (see 1 Kings viii,)
afford abundant evidence, that
the house of God, or the place
dedicated to the worship of God,
must be filled with solemnity.
In view of this truth the wise
man uttered the exhortation,

which stands at the head of this paper. It is not my design to attend particularly to the phraseology of the wise man, when he says, *Keep thy foot*. The leading sentiment conveyed by these words, is evidently, *Keep thyself;* that is, be serious and solemn, remembering that thou art about to enter into the more immediate presence of a holy God. He then says; *Be more ready to hear, than to give the sacrifice of fools*. These words naturally lead to some thoughts, respecting the feelings and conduct of those, who, as *hearers*, attend the public worship of God.

1. It becomes every one to *feel*, that he is personally and deeply interested. Every one has an immortal soul to be saved or lost. Every one is accountable to God for the use of all his time and talents. And of course every one is personally and deeply interested in the great duties of public worship. Let it be remembered, that the house of God is not a *theatre;* and that those, who assemble there, are not mere *spectators*. Far from it. They are all interested. And as each one must hereafter give account of himself to God, it follows that all are *alike* interested. Every one ought then to *feel*, that he is interested. And feeling this, he ought to conduct with that solemnity and reverence, which become the house of God, and the followers of Jesus Christ.

2. It becomes every one, on entering the house of God, to dismiss all worldly cares, and to indulge no worldly thoughts. The pure sublime worship of that holy Being has no connex-

ion with the cares and ❚❚ this world. To indulge ❚ thoughts, or to conver❚❚ near the house of God❚❚ business, or the pleasure❚ politics of this world, ❚❚ person for religious wo❚❚ diverts his attention fro❚ ious subjects: it destr❚ fervor and almost the ❚❚ of devotion in his heart. ❚ renders the religious ❚❚ of the day unprofitable ❚❚ teresting to him; and, wh❚ finitely more dreadful, is ❚ gether offensive to that❚ whom he professes to w❚ If men converse on the b❚ or the politics of this wo❚ fore they enter the house❚ will not their thoughts ❚ ployed in meditating ❚❚ subjects, while *in* this ho❚ so, Christ, were he ❚ would say, as he once di❚ money-changers, *Make* ❚ *Father's house an house ❚ chandize*.

3. It becomes every one that *God* is there. The ❚ of which the wise man ❚ and in which they are ass❚ is *His house*, dedicated ❚ secrated to His worship. ❚ He has graciously conde❚ ed to record His name❚ He has manifested Him ❚ His own children: and ❚ there: there as the object ❚ only proper object of re❚ worship; there as a Comfo❚ His own children; there ❚ their prayers, and accep❚ praises; and there as a V❚ to take cognizance of ❚ thought and every action❚ truly is a solemn conside❚ Were it felt, were it re❚ that God is there, the t❚ would be sufficient of it

one solemn and at-
ut, alas, how little is
realized, by a large
of those who go to
f God. If we may
e actions of no small
of them, we must say,
not feel that God is
·y do not feel, that
irit, and that those,
to Him, must wor-
spirit and in truth.
fore do not realize
He is there, whether
nt and sinful crea-
rare of it or not.
mes each one to at-
solemnity *to every*
blic worship. To
to God is as solemn
ghtful. And to sing
a on a thoughtless
but solemn mockery
. To remain heed-
uninterested, during
g part of divine ser-
s a criminal want of
. How sinful must
o remain thoughtless
ent in the time of
d yet how shameful-
and indifferent are
as, during that sol-
of public worship.
looking around to
coming in; some are
he dress of others;
e impatiently waiting
closing sentence. All
rly inco-sistent with
on. Such persons
rshippers: they are
ators. They act as
speaker were the
son interested in the
of this duty. And
mitate them by look-
on others, in the
otion, they would be
at the indecency and
of his conduct. It

is a truth, that such persons pay
more deference to the speaker, *as
a speaker*, in sermon time, than
they do to Jehovah, as the object
of worship, in the hour of devotion. But these things ought
not so to be.

5. Every one should be *more
ready to hear*, than to see or to
be seen. To go to the house
of God merely to see others, or to
be seen by them, is to give the
sacrifice of fools. It is, no less
than to prostitute the time appropriated to the worship of
God to mere sport and pastime,
and to convert the house of God
into a place of amusement. *It
pleased God by the foolishness of
preaching*, says an Apostle, *to
save them that believe*. The
same Apostle says, *Faith cometh
by hearing, and hearing by the
word of God*. The design of
preaching is not only to edify and
establish saints, and to comfort
mourners in Zion; but to warn
and reprove sinners, to convince
gainsayers, and to detect hypocrites. If, then, those who *go
to the house of God* do not hear;
if they are not *more ready* to hear
His word, than to see or to be
seen, they lose all the benefit
of preaching; they cast contempt
on this divine institution. To
them, if they continue thus stupid and indifferent, the preacher is a savor, not *of life unto life,
but of death unto death.* Reader,
is not this a just statement of
the subject? And if so, is it not
an affecting, alarming thought?
Ought you not, whoever you
are, or whatever may be your
situation or profession in life,
to take heed to yourself, to
keep your foot when you go
to the house of God? Be persuaded to remember, that you
are personally and deeply intere

ested; that it becomes you to dismiss worldly cares, and to abandon vain conversation; to *feel* that God is there; to attend with due solemnity to every part of public worship; and to be more ready to hear the word of God, to pray to Him and to praise His name, than to see your fellow creatures, or be seen by them. Should these broken hints tend to solemnize or awaken one individual, and make him more attentive to the worship of God in His house, the writer will have great occasion to rejoice.   JUVENTUS.

AN ATTEMPT TO SHOW HOW CHRISTIANS MAY DERIVE MOST ADVANTAGE FROM ILL-TREATMENT IN THE WORLD, AND TO AFFORD THEM CONSOLATION UNDER IT.

ENEMIES are instruments in the hand of Providence, to instruct, to prove, and to discipline the followers of Christ. Much depends, therefore, on the conduct of Christians under ill-treatment. They should be solicitous to manifest, exercise and improve the Christian temper; and they should guard against dejection and discouragement. To afford them assistance in these duties, is the object of this paper.

1. When persons defame, or any way injure us, let us consider the Providence of God, and examine ourselves. Nothing takes place without the holy and wise permission, and controlling direction of Him, without whose notice *not a sparrow falls to the ground, and by whom the very hairs of our head are all numbered.* Why does he suffer us to be reproached, defamed, or otherwise injured? There is a cause, why God permits this. We may not deserve it from those, who are the agents; but do we not deserve this correction from God? He corrects us not without cause; and he corrects us for our benefit. Let us, then, at such a time, with close self-examination, make inquiries similar to these.

Do I not, in some way or other, dishonor the name of God? Am I as careful as I ought to be, to promote his glory among men? Instead of seeking his honor, as I should do, have I not been seeking my own honor? If so, how just and suitable is his correction in leaving me to be censured and defamed. He hath said, *Them that honor me, I will honor; and they that despise me shall be lightly esteemed.*

We should also inquire. Do I not unjustly censure others; or in some other way injure their good name? Have I been sufficiently tender of my neighbor's reputation? Have I been careful not to raise, or circulate, false reports to the disadvantage of others; or do I make exact representations, when my duty calls me to speak of their ill conduct? If I have offended in these things; how proper a correction is similar treatment from others *With what measure ye mete, it shall be measured to you again.*

We may also ask ourselves, whether we have not been too ambitious to obtain the praises of men; or too much afraid of their censures? If so, how fit it is, and what a mercy it is, that we should be humbled and made sensible of our sin, by their ill opinion and calumny.

reproached and defam-
hould review our lan-
id conduct in different
; and conscientiously
e the habits and tenor of
versation and actions.

are keen sighted, and
old faults in us, which
aped our own observa-
s an old saying; "Malice
l informer; though it be
lge." By the tongue of
. and slander we may be
of those things in our-
vhich ought to be re-
When accused of faults
y others, though we may
;uilty particularly as al-
:t us inquire, whether
ot in some degree guil-
)ugh their accusations
, we may be guilty of
ns akin to those, with
re are reproached. At
should be more eminent,
are, for the virtues op-
the sins, of which we
sed.

should also inquire,
we have avoided, us we
he *appearance* of evil?
netimes has all the bad
n others, which the real
d have It is therefore im-
not only that our conduct
ot be, but that it should
ar to be, reprehensible.
es of other kinds should
ind us of the holy Prov-
t God, and excite us to
nination. Have we not
mpt, pride, neglect, or
ig else, given some
ion, which led to them?
e not by imprudence or
isconduct afforded the
of their being done?
|uiries we should make,
nay discover and correct
s and imprudences. But

if, in all such respects, our conscience acquits us; the injuries
we receive may remind us of some
of our past sins, and make us
more humble and penitent. For.
in how many instances and ways
have we done injury to others;
to their souls if not to their persons, property, or reputation?
Perhaps we may recollect some
wrong we have done, for which
reparation is an incumbent, but
hitherto neglected, duty. Would
we have others make compensation, as far as it is in their power
for injuries done to us? Then let
us *go and do likewise.*

When we hear of our having
been reproached or defamed, or
when we receive any ill-treatment, we should pay special attention to our hearts, and observe
what tempers and feelings are
excited in them. This is a favorable time to acquire farther
knowledge of our hearts, and to
discover those evil dispositions
in us, which ought to be corrected. These let us immediately
check, considering their repugnance to the commands of God,
and their evil tendency. Let
us repent of the sinful tempers thus discovered, bewailing them before God, and
praying with devout fervor for
their extirpation from our
breasts. On such occasions, we
should endeavor to lay the axe
at the root of pride, selfishness,
revenge, and all malevolent feelings.

The time when we receive injuries, and the time when we
are flattered, or receive approbation and applause, should be embraced as special seasons for the
acquisition of self-knowledge,
and the reformation of what we
find amiss. But this is too sel-

dom done. Our weak minds are at such times absorbed by other considerations; and too much agitated, or too much pleased and elated. If, however, we cannot remember to embrace such opportunities, while present, for this important purpose; let us afterwards recollect, as much as we can, our feelings and the effects which injury and praise had upon us, and make a wise use of our recollections for the knowledge and amendment of our hearts.

If defamation and other injuries lead us to careful self-examination, they may be instrumental in making us better acquainted with ourselves; in detecting, and bringing us to correct, many faults or sins, which otherwise we should not have observed; and in making us more humble, watchful, and holy. Thus abuses may be good monitors, and instruct us how to speak and live better. "The dirt of reproaches," said one of the martyrs, "is only to scour you, and make you bright, that a high shelf in heaven may be assigned to you."

Let us make such use of the aspersions of our enemies, that they may serve to take away our rust and dross, to render us wiser and better, and to brighten our future crown and glory. Let us adore the mercy of our God, that through his gracious assistance it is practicable to make all our trials and calamities in this world the means of improving our character, and of preparing us for his heavenly kingdom;— *that all things work together for good to them that love him, to them who are the called according to his purpose.*

2. When persons defame us, or in any other way act an unfriendly part towards us, we should make it a point to pray for them very particularly, until we fully forgive them, cordially love them, and desire, and feel a disposition to promote, their real good. This is the time to consider, and to comply with the import of the following passages. *Love your enemies; bless them that curse you; do good to them that hate you; and pray for them which despitefully use you, and persecute you; that ye may be the children of your Father, who is in heaven; for he maketh his sun to rise on the evil and on the good, and sendeth rain on the just and on the unjust. For if ye love them, which love you, what reward have ye? Do not even the publicans the same? Recompense no man evil for evil. Dearly beloved, avenge not yourselves; but rather give place unto wrath. Be not overcome of evil; but overcome evil with good.* It would seem, from the temper too generally manifested, that it is forgotten by many professed Christians, that these duties are inculcated in our Bibles, and were prominently exemplified by our blessed Redeemer. Mankind are prone to take revenge; to return injury for injury; and to justify themselves in doing so. Who has not felt in himself this disposition of our corrupt, fallen nature? It is no easy matter for us to forego retaliation, when within our power; and not only to subdue the very desire of revenge, but to repay love for hatred, and good for evil; and to intercede with God sincerely for those, who are not well disposed towards us, and who are doing, or have done us injury. But al-

these duties are difficult,
e not impracticable; and
t the true Christian en-
to imitate his Divine Sa-
id to obey his commands
respect? Will not he, who
his own unworthiness;
:ed he himself has of for-
is, of often repeated for-
is from God, forgive his
men their trespasses?
it he, who *feels* how much
ndebted to the grace of
id whose heart is touched
ie love of Christ, show
[of a merciful temper? He
ie will. Yet there may
quently a long struggle
irrupt nature; and that the
lence of a pious heart
umph, much watchfulness
iyer are necessary.
:n you receive injuries,
ire, observe well your
and let *first impressions*,
f *resentments*, be speedily
d. It is ever easiest
ming sins at the begin-
Suffer them awhile, and
re stronger, and you are
r. Safety and duty there-
quire you to check the
iotions of wounded pride
[fishness; their first excite-
to revenge, or to any in-
ice of malevolence. That
iay do this, do not allow
iinds to dwell on the
s and injuries, which you
received; but turn your
its immediately to your
iwoithiness and need of
:ness, to the precepts of
ispel, and to the example
meek and lowly Jesus;
inder on these things. On
occasions, also, pray ear-
lor divine grace to enable
> fulfil your duty. This,
irayer for those who have

injured us, is the best way to
bring ourselves to feel and speak
and conduct towards them as we
ought.

This is not the duty of an
hour. Such are the evil propensities of our hearts, that continued watchfulness and prayer
are requisite. When we have
received ill-treatment, we should
set a special guard upon our
lips. It becomes Christians to
speak as well as truth will permit, of those who speak evil of
them, or otherwise oppose and
injure them. They should not
unnecessarily speak of the sins,
of which they know their enemies to be guilty, lest they find
a satisfaction in doing it, inconsistent with that universal benevolence which they ought to feel.
Much less should Christians ever repay their enemies in their
own coin, by returning railing
for railing, slander for slander,
evil for evil. Yet, alas, through
their negligence of remaining
sins, they too often do this in
some measure. Is it not much
too common for Christians to
manifest something of a wrong
spirit in their conversation;—to
say many things, which do not
proceed from love; and to show
something of contempt, of sneer,
or of ill will, in their looks and
demeanor, in reference to those,
who differ from them in sentiments, who oppose them, or who
slander and injure them? Surely,
fellow Christians, *these things
ought not so to be.* Ought we
not to bear the infirmities of the
weak? Ought we not to pity
those, whom we deem to be in
darkness and error? Ought we
not to be grieved for those, who
oppose us because we are engaged in a good cause, or who

are bringing guilt and misery on themselves by calumniating and abusing us? Ought we not to commiserate their case, to pray for them, and in every possible way to seek their good? Most certainly, then, we ought to repress all improper feelings towards them, and to refrain from all improper airs, representations, and expressions in relation to them. To enable us to do this, in such circumstances as frequently exist, the most earnest vigilence and prayer are requisite Let us then most conscientiously watch, and sincerely pray, when evil tongues assail us, or enemies oppose and injure us, that we speak not unadvisedly with our lips; that we be not excited to retaliation; that our temper be not soured and embittered; but that the ill-treatment of enemies may be the occasion of softening and meliorating our hearts; and that we may be enabled to forgive them, to love them, and to bless them.

If we are provoked by our enemies, so as to recompense evil for evil; and *their* sins are the occasion of making *us* more sinful, they do an essential injury to our souls. But if we recompense them good for evil, and make their sins the means of our own spiritual improvement; however ill *their* intentions may be, the temporal injuries, we receive from them, will in the end be eternal benefits.

I would not, however, hold out our own advantage, as the sole motive; a regard to God's glory and commandments, and benevolence to our enemies themselves, ought to be still more influential motives in our hearts. We should forgive others, *as*

God for Christ's sake hath forgiven us. Having had *ten thousand talents* forgiven us, can we forbear to forgive our fellow sinners *a few pence?* We should, also, by forgiveness, meekness, kindness, and prayer, endeavor to overcome evil with good, and to win the guilty unto Christ. *For he, that converteth a sinner from the error of his way, shall save a soul from death, and shall hide a multitude of sins.* Right behavior to the unfriendly is most happily calculated, through the grace of God, to convince, soften, win, and save them.

3. We should be careful not to speak often, nor to take great notice, of the ill-treatment, which we receive. To be continually reflecting on the abuses and injuries we receive, and to be frequently conversing about them, will have a bad effect on our hearts. In this way they will be to us the occasion of sin. We should take no public notice of the injuries and calumnies of our enemies, nor attempt to vindicate ourselves, unless such a vindication is a plain and imperious duty.

When defamed and injured, we should be more anxious to conduct well, to become better, and to display and recommend the spirit of the Gospel, than to vindicate ourselves. We should not often regard affronts, misrepresentations, and slanders, except for our own improvement. To learn from them the characters of men; to derive from them matter for meditation and prayer; and to make them the occasion of becoming better acquainted with ourselves, and of cultivating holy tempers and affections, are objects for which we may take notice of them. But we should not busy ourselves in inquiring what persons say or think of us; nor should we appear to take much notice of unfriendly, and slanderous remarks, which come to our knowledge. To be jealous of the speech of people, and to be easily moved by it, is injurious to our peace and usefulness. The sneers, cavils, misrepresentations, and ridicule of the foes of virtue and religion are generally best frustrated by neglect. The less the "squibs of the tongue" are regarded, the less injury they do, and the sooner they are forgotten. You cannot much more gratify evil minded railers and defamers, than to take notice of their slanders and abuses, and to appear solicitous in consequence of them. It gives them an importance, which they would not otherwise attain. It shows, that you feel disturbed and wounded, which is a gratification to the slanderer, and an encouragement to proceed. One of the ancients, being told that a certain person *privately* reproached him, replied; "Say nothing, or he will proceed to do it *publicly* also." Why should an innocent and useful person regard the cavils and defamations of the wicked? "Let the sun," observes a writer, "say nothing, but only *shine on*, when owls or snails complain of him." The best way to silence most censures and slanders, is to despise them, or to contradict them only by greater piety and innocence.

This is generally more mortifying to the guilty, than any retaliation in our power would be; and, what is of much greater importance, it is calculated to lead

them to reflection, to convince them of their faults, and to bring them to repentance. Whereas retaliation, upbraidings, or much notice, has a tendency to arouse their pride and prejudices, and to render them obstinate and permanent enemies.

Much notice of defamations and censures often defeats its own purpose. *A lying tongue is but for a moment.* Most falsehoods and misrepresentations will soon be forgotten by those who hear them, if they are not kept in remembrance by recriminations. We ought not generally to trouble ourselves about refuting slanders and misrepresentations, otherwise than by greater piety and goodness, unless the glory of God and the interests of virtue and religion unquestionably require it; which is seldom the case with persons in private life; and less frequently with persons in a public station, than they are apt to imagine. Rather let us so serve the Lord and seek his glory, that his cause may be ours; and then trust the vindication of our good name to his Providence.

There are many other benefits, beside those, that have been mentioned, which Christians may derive from ill treatment, and from enemies. They may teach us to be more sensible of human depravity, and more to admire the example of Christ under the manifold abuses and sufferings, which he endured, and the immensity of his love. They may teach us to seek worldly enjoyments less; to reduce earthly expectations; and to raise our affections and hopes more to Heaven. They call us to exercise patience; to lament the prevalence and evils of sin; and to praise God for his mercy to us;—for the continuance, protection and enlargement of his Church, and for all his goodness to our guilty race. But I shall not enlarge on these topics, lest this communication be tedious.

As the pious are often grieved and afflicted by opposition and ill-treatment. and sometimes disheartened, and therefore need support and encouragement, let us,

4. Consider some sources of encouragement and consolation.

The benefits, which they may derive from ill-treatment in the world, should console and encourage them As we have already seen, it may assist them in the acquisition of self-knowledge, humility, patience, and a meek forgiving temper; which are of vast utility and importance. It may make them more vigilant, circumspect, and holy; and it gives them an opportunity by a right temper and deportment towards their enemies, to copy some of the sublimest virtues of the Savior, and thus to convince others of the power and excellence of the Christian religion, and recommend it to them. The meekness and patience of pious Christians under provocations and injuries, their forgiveness of enemies, and their kindness to them, have always had powerful efficacy in convincing sinners and alluring them to take up their cross and to follow Christ.

Ill-treatment in the world also shows Christians, that here is not their rest, and that they ought not not to place their affections on earthly objects; and it in a manner compels them to look more to the things, which

are unseen and eternal. It trims them and makes them brighter and more useful lights here; and it increases their treasure in Heaven, as it contributes in various ways to their final advantage.

The considerations of these things should reconcile the righteous to the scourgings of evil tongues. and to all the abuse received from their enemies; and make them solicitous, rather to derive as much advantage as possible from them, than about their present ease and reputation. When reviled, slandered, and persecuted for Christ's sake, let them rejoice and be exceedingly glad; for great is their reward in heaven.

The unparalleled indignities and sufferings, which the blessed Jesus himself endured; the persecution of the ancient prophets, and of the Apostles and primitive Christians, by those, who rejected their messages, hated their reproofs and opposed their religion, and the ill-treatment of pious and good men by the ungodly in every age, afford consolation to those, who are persecuted, reviled, and have all manner of evil spoken of them falsely for Christ's sake. *For so persecuted they the prophets, which were before you*, said our Savior to his disciples for their encouragement. Conformity in this respect to the great Head of the Church, and to holy and pious men, who have lived before us, must have great influence in reconciling us to the ill will and abuses of the world, when obedience to God brings them upon us.

Because our Lord conversed familiarly with sinners, as a

physician with the sick, he was accused of being *a friend of publicans and sinners*, an approver and partaker of their wickedness. He was reproachfully called *a wine-bibber*; probably because he miraculously turned water into wine at a wedding. As he delivered from the power of demons, those who were possessed and afflicted by them; he was accused of being in confederacy with the powers of darkness. He was meek and peaceable; he disavowed all pretensions to an earthly kingdom, and inculcated submission to rulers; yet he was accused, as *a mover of sedition* He went about doing good, and was without sin. No person could bring any explicit and supported charge against him; yet he was *numbered with transgressors*, and crucified with malefactors. Thus we see, that perfect innocence, and the highest excellence, afford no shelter from ill tongues; nor, in many circumstances, from the hand of violence. An evil eye will see matter for censure and misrepresentation in the best conversation and life. If perfect goodness, and the most meritorious actions, be thus distorted and calumniated; what have the best of the disciples of Christ to expect? They are often imprudent and faulty, and have many imperfections, which give a plausibility to the defamations of their adversaries. It should be remembered, that we deserve our sufferings, and that those of Christ were wholly undeserved.

The ancient prophets were hated, persecuted, and accounted the troubles of Israel. The primitive Christians were considered and treated, as *the offscouring of all things. Yea, and all that will live godly in Christ Jesus, shall suffer persecution;* if not the persecution of the sword, the persecution of the tongue, from some quarter or other. Persecution, strictly so called, blessed be God, is not the characteristic of the present age. But if we are in any measure faithful to our Savior; can we expect the cordial approbation of the world? If we are not *conformed to the world*, will not our exemplary and holy singularity, as it conveys a reproof of the evil conversation and practices of the irreligious, excite their contempt and hatred, or lead them to smite us with the tongue? Is this age so refined; has human nature at length become so improved; that a Christian can now be faithful in showing his disapprobation of sin, faithful in opposing all iniquity, and zealous in every good work, and not be an object of the envy, the displeasure, or the reproaches of the wicked? It is true, that there has been a great and favorable change in the opinions and practices of men respecting persecution; and there is a less bigoted attachment to unessential articles of faith and modes of worship, at the present day, than there has been in some periods: but are those, who are not the cordial disciples of Christ, any more in love with true religion? Has darkness more communion with light, than formerly; or is there more concord between Christ and Belial? No, mankind are naturally and essentially the same in every age; and the true disciples of Christ must still be *a peculiar people*,

In proportion to their fidelity to Christ, they will now often meet the gross opposition and scurrility of the openly profane and vicious; and they must expect, that the fashionable world and formal professors will sometimes represent their religion as bigotry, superstition, and enthusiasm, and endeavor by sneers, ridicule, and subtle insinuations, to blacken their name, and to obscure their example. It is a thing of course, that they, who do evil, hate, oppose, and malign those, who, by their virtue and piety, are burning and shining lights; especially if placed near themselves. Such lights disturb and irritate the wicked by showing them the horrid contrast which they form.

If we are decidedly holy and pious, we may often have occasion to consider the ill-treatment of the prophets, and apostles, and of our Lord, for our consolation and encouragement. But let us remember to look to Christ for another purpose;—for grace to imitate his example. *Because Christ suffered for us, leaving us an example, that we should follow his steps;—who, when he was reviled, reviled not again; when he suffered he threatened not, but committed himself to him, that judgeth righteously.* When on the cross, he prayed for his implacable murderers. If we suffer for our goodness and piety with meekness and with prayer for our enemies, we resemble our Redeemer. A pious man, who endured great indignities, remarked cheerfully, "what ado here is, to make a poor sinner like his Savior!" If we resemble our Lord in meekness, peaceableness, resignation, benevo-

lence, forbearance, and piety; then if we suffer with him, we may have the consolation, that we shall also reign with him. *Great will be our reward in Heaven.*

Considering the illustrious company, and considering the *end,* who would not rather suffer with Christ and his followers, than triumph with the wicked, or enjoy *the pleasures of sin for a season? It is enough for the disciple that he be as his Master, and the servant as his Lord. If they have called the Master of the house Beelzebub, how much more shall they call them of his household?* Will not, therefore, the benefits, the reward in heaven, and conformity to Christ, prophets and apostles, afford us sufficient consolation with the comforts of the Holy Spirit, when defamed, opposed, and injured by the wicked? Let no pious man therefore faint in the day of adversity, or be discouraged in the service of God. Let us seek the approbation of God more than the praises of men, and *be steadfast, immoveable, always abounding in the work of the Lord. Watch ye; stand fast in the faith; quit you like men; be strong. Let all your things be done with charity.*

Some will perhaps call the humble firmness, the holy elevation and the indefatigable perseverance of a zealous Christian, pride. But pride never elevates men above the world. If pride despise the opinions of men in some instances, still it idolizes fame; it is ever selfish; it is resentful; it loves to have its consequence felt and acknowledged. Only the humble can cheerfully obey God, rejoice in his will, and live above

les and frowns of earth.
humility which enabled
ised Jesus to be content-
his poor accommoda-
) despise the baits of the
o tread under foot the
f life, to bear patiently the
of the wicked, and to be
signed to his Father's
Let us learn of him, who
ek and lowly in heart.

is the world, that we
expect tribulation in it.
ongues cannot be silent.
tleness and kindness ean
em; do not unnecessarily
ate them; give them no
n to speak reproachfully;
not your peace of mind
on the speeches of the
y. Let them not gall, pro-
r discourage you. Only
rticularly careful, that
ll manner of evil is spok-
you, it may be spoken
for Christ's sake. Then
ay trust and rejoice in
d; and in anticipation of
ce and glory of heaven.
rill the pious be, where
cked will forever cease
oubling.

e endeavor, on all occa-
o be faithful and to mani-
spirit of Christ, we must
pect coldness, censures,
peeches, and rash judg-
from some, of whom we
better things, and whom
still believe to be pious,
under prejudices and
es. The zeal of some
ans is too fiery, bitter, and
lminate; the prudence of
s too much allied to luke-
ess and the fear of man.
who take the happy mean
n these two classes, will
y be censured by both,
regarded with jealousy.

But let none of these things deter us from the firm and resolute, yet gentle and affectionate,
discharge of duty.

Finally, let all of us, who profess to be disciples and followers of Christ, endeavor to derive
all possible advantages from the
ill-treatment we receive in the
world, and to persevere in our
duty without remissness or discouragement. Thus we may
make great improvement in self
knowledge, and in the Christian
temper and practice; and we
may do great good to many, and
adorn and recommend genuine
religion. Thus also we may do
much to prevent divisions, contentions, and animosities. How
often revenge perpetuates a
quarrel, which forgiveness might
easily and speedily heal. How
many, and how extensive, are
the evils which infest, not only
society in general, but the
churches of God; which might
be prevented, would all, who
call themselves Christians, study
to know and subdue the evil
tempers of their own hearts; to
love, forgive, and pray for their
enemies; to be meek, humble,
and peaceable; to bear ill-treatment with the spirit of Christ;
and to overcome evil with good.
Let us, my brethren, deeply and
seriously consider the importance of these things; and may
God direct and enable us by his
Spirit, to glorify him by a right
temper and conduct in every
situation.   R. W.

HINTS TO DO GOOD.   NO. II.

BIBLE Societies are formed in
almost every country of the
Christian world; and many, who
are rich, cast in much to pro-

mote the circulation of the Holy Scriptures. Cannot some more effectual way be devised, than has been devised hitherto, in which the poor may unite and help forward this great and good work? There are numbers among the poorer class, in almost every town. who are as desirous of doing good, as their more wealthy neighbors. Why should not their benevolent feelings be gratified, and an opportunity be given them to bring their offering, even if it were no more than one mite.

The Savior noticed with approbation the poor widow who cast but a single farthing into the treasury of the Lord; and an inspired Apostle hath informed us, *If there be first a willing mind, it is accepted according to that a man hath. and not according to that he hath not.* Let every one give, then, according to his ability. *He that giveth let him do with simplicity; he that showeth mercy, with cheerfulness. But this I say, He which soweth sparingly shall reap also sparingly; and he which soweth bountifully shall reap also bountifully. Every man as he purposeth in his heart, so let him give, not grudgingly, or of necessity; for God loveth the cheerful giver. And God is able to make all grace abound towards you; that ye, always having all sufficiency in all things, may abound to every good work. As it is written, He hath dispersed abroad; he hath given to the poor; his righteousness remaineth forever. Now he that ministereth seed to the sower, both minister bread for your food, and multiply your seed sown, and increase the fruits of your righteousness: Being enriched in eve-*

ry thing, to all bountifulness, which causeth through us thanksgiving to God." *

I beg leave to introduce a quotation from Scott's commentary upon these words. "The Apostle would not prescribe the proportion, (says he) which every one ought to give; nor would he write as one that aimed to extort money from them; but this he said, that God would measure to them. according to the measure which they used towards their poor brethren. Money given in charity, seems to unbelief and selfishness to be finally thrown away; but in fact, when given from proper principles, it is seed sown, and the only part of a man's substance from which a *valuable increase* can be expected. The Lord would without fail in one way or other make up to the givers what they expended in this good work; for he was able to make every gift of his free favor to abound to them; and so having a sufficiency of all things desirable for themselves and families, and being enlarged in faith and love, they might have both a willing mind, and ability for every good work. Thus the character and blessedness mentioned by the Psalmist would be verified in them; and their acts of kindness to the poor, from love to Christ, would be accepted works of righteousness for which the benefit would remain with them forever.

"Many an intended good work has been neglected or rendered useless by delay: it is therefore proper to exhort men to be prompt in doing what they have shown a willingness to engage

---

* Rom. xii. 8; 2 Cor. viii. 12. and ix. 6–11.

7orks of piety and charity
flow spontaneously from
ititude and benevolence of
:ving heart, and not re-
extorting by importunity.
avors of covetousness, and
puts those, who forward
designs, to the painful
ity of laboring to draw
from those, who ought to
)ut are reluctant to part
. Yet the main benefit of
act of charity for the
sake will redound to the
He sows his good seed
uitful soil, and his bounti-
s to man will assure him
Lord's bountifulness to
Whatever expenses there-
.re retrenched, or from
ver fund it is deducted, we
I not grudge, or be sparing
seed. It is spiritual pol-
us to spend less on every
f indulgence, and to lay by
r our families, that we may
more to the needy for
's sake: for this will be
ecured and most produc-
Even persons in *moderate*
stances may sow *much* of
ed; if by various little sav-
ind self-denials, they will
idy to spare something to
: their distressed brethren;
is they *will do* if their faith
re abound.

iere are a few *who scatter
et increase,* but there are
ire, even among those who
2lous for evangelical doc-
. who *withhold more than
t, and it tendeth to poverty.*
:an easily give us enough
; and enough to disperse;
ve may have more, sow
and reap more. and so *in-
the fruits of our right-
ss,* that, being enriched in
thing unto all bountiful-

ness, we may be happy in ourselves, blessings to others, and
instruments of promoting his
glory.*"

The plan which I would propose,—that all persons of every denomination may unite together in doing good, is to have
Bible Societies formed in every
town throughout the United
States, and subscription papers
circulated among all classes of
people. Such societies might
be under the direction of committees, whose duty it should be
to collect, and pay over to a common treasurer, such sums of
money as might be subscribed,
and likewise to make inquiries
concerning those who were in
need of assistance from the society. Should such societies be
formed, would not the poorer
classes feel more interested to
procure Bibles for themselves,
and make inquiries among their
neighbors to ascertain who were
destitute. If there were any,
who should wish to join such societies, who could pay but a
small part of what a Bible would
cost, let it be accepted, and if on
inquiry it should be found that
these persons were destitute of
the Bible, let them be supplied

---

* It is earnestly recommended, to every
one who can have access to Dr. Scott's
Notes, and Practical Observations, upon
the 8th and 9th chapters of the 2 Cor.
to read them with careful attention, and
also consult his marginal references.
There, indeed, is a feast of fat things. If
other readers gain half the pleasure from
the perusal, which the writer of this paper has experienced, they will be abundantly rewarded for their trouble. Would
not these two chapters with the marginal
references, and Scott's commentary upon
them, make a very useful tract, to be
printed by Religious Tract Societies, for
distribution? The subject is submitted to
the consideration of the committees of such
societies.

from the funds of the society. In this way a number of poor families might have the word of life put into their hands, who will otherwise remain without it. Another important benefit resulting from this method, would be, that persons in indigent circumstances would more highly prize the Bible which should cost them something, than if they could possess it *gratis.*

It may perhaps be said, that the sums of money collected in this way would generally be very small; and it would not be best to subject a committee to the trouble of collecting such trifling sums, as would be frequently contributed by the poor. To this it may be answered, that all great sums are made up of small items, and a large part of the expenses of government are ultimately paid by the poor in small sums. Let us turn our attention for a moment to the subject, and inquire what would be the result should each individual contribute only one cent in a year. According to the last census, the number of inhabitants in the United States, and their territorial governments, was 7,239,514. A tax of one cent upon each individual would produce a sum of 72,305 dollars and 14 cents. This sum, according to the cost of Bibles to Bible Societies, would procure 115,680 Bibles, which might be distributed to the poor. Surely this would make no contemptible figure in the reports of these general Bible Societies. But where is the individual who cannot give one cent or even six cents in a year. These minor contributions need not prevent a single dollar being given by the opulent. Indeed, I believe, should such societies become general, probably many times more would be given by the rich, than is given at present. Let an annual Report be published, stating the sums contributed and the number of Bibles distributed in each town; and, in a few years, there would no doubt be an astonishing change in the moral state of society for the better; and almost all classes of people would be so interested to promote the common cause, that there would not be a single cottage where human beings could be found without a Bible. This may seem a chimera; but it will surely take place in its time. It is a great and good work, to be engaged in spreading the Holy Scriptures, and let none who have entered the field retreat or be dismayed at the enemies which appear: To those, who have done little or nothing, a door is now opened, and they are invited, *to come up to the help of the Lord, to the help of the Lord against the mighty.* I shall close the present number in the words of Moses to the children of Israel. *This is the thing which the Lord commanded, saying, take ye from among you, an offering unto the Lord: whosoever is of a willing heart, let him bring it, an offering of the Lord; gold, and silver, and brass, and blue, and purple, and scarlet and fine linen.*

Φιλος.

RELIGIOUS INTELLIGENCE.

BAPTIST MISSION IN INDIA.

From the Christian Observer.

5th Number of the Periodical Accounts of the Baptist Missionary Society, brings down the history of the Mission to the close of the year 1812, has just reached us. It is prefaced by some observations of the Committee which serve to a comprehensive view of its progress to the close of the year 1809. At that time there were six stations, containing 11 members; at the close of 1812 were twelve stations, and about 500 members. The main part of what has been done in Calcutta, has been done in these years. By circulating the Scriptures in native languages, by preaching, and establishment of a large school, on Lancaster's model, a strong impression has been made on that city. During this period, not less than 160 persons have been baptized at Calcutta and Serampore: a mission has been planted in Orissa, the seat of Juggernauth, where not only have scriptures, in the language of the country, been liberally distributed, even within the precincts of the temple, but the gospel has been diligently preached, a church formed of between thirty and forty members:—the church in Jessore increased from thirty to eighty members:—the Gospel has been preached and churches formed at Bheerbhoom, Agra, Patna, and Dacca—the word of God has been introduced into the Mahratta country, where many are reading it with different effect:—and three new stations been occupied, viz. Columbo, Chittagong, and Bombay.

The state of the *translations* at the end of 1812, was as follows: 1. In Bengalee, New Testament had gone through editions, and was ready for a fourth; second edition of the Old Testament printed to the fourth chapter of Leviticus. 2. In Sungskrit, New Testament printed; Old Testament printed to 2d Samuel, and translated to 2d Chronicles. 3. Orissa, New Testament printed, and approved by Orissa Pundits; Old Testament, the Hagiographa and the Prophets, and the Historical Books to 1st Samuel, printed. 4. In Telinga, New Testament translated, Matthew in the press. 5. Kurnata, New Testament translated—Matthew revised. 6. In Mahratta, Testament printed, and in circulation—Old Testament printed to Numbers.

7. In Hindoosthanee, New Testament, second edition in the press; Old Testament printed to Exodus. 8. Shikh, New Testament, translated and printed to Luke vii. 9. In Burman, types cast, a volume of Scripture extracts printed, and the translation prepared to Luke xviii. 10. In Chinese, New Testament translated; Old Testament translated to 1st Samuel v, and Gospel of St. John printing. 11. In Cashmire, New Testament, translated to Rom. ii. 12. Assam, New Testament, translated to John vi. Besides which the translation of the Scriptures into the Pushtoo or Affghan, the Nepala, the Brij Basha, the Bilochee, and the Maldivian were commencing. Important improvements had been made in casting types and manufacturing paper, and the younger branches of the family were so educated, as to be able to carry on the translations.

"The feeling excited by the disaster at Serampore, not only produced a prompt and very liberal contribution for the reparation of the loss, but probably increased the interest which the Christian part of the nation felt in the question, Shall Christianity have free course in India? That interest certainly was great, and of great importance. The temperate but decided way in which the sense of the country was expressed, as well as the respectful manner in which it was treated by the Government and the Legislature, call for our grateful acknowledgments both to them, and to Him who disposes the hearts of all for the accomplishment of his purposes."—"Finally the Committee observe, and we are anxious to second their pious admonit'on, "while solicitous for the success of Christ's kingdom in other lands, let us not forget our native country, and while the souls of our fellow-sinners are dear to us, let us not be unmindful of our own. It is too possible that a zeal may be kindled for a public object, while at the same time things of a personal nature are neglected. Surely it would be a grievous thing, if while busy here and there about converting the heathen, we lose our own souls!"

We proceed to make some extracts from the Periodical Accounts themselves.

"*Serampore and Calcutta.*—Fifty-nine have been added to this church, the greater part of whom are natives of India of various religions." "The Scriptures and Scripture tracts in various languages have been largely distributed by the members of the church among their neighbors, their servants, and the strangers from various parts of India." "Several of the younger members of the church have applied to the study of the Bengalee, Nagree, and Persian characters, to enable them to read the New Testament to their servants and neighbors." "The Benevolent Institution for the instruction of poor children, has been this year extended to girls, who, with the boys in a distinct apartment, amount to upwards of 300." "A building, during this year, has been erected near the chapel, which will contain 800 children."

The impression made on the neighborhood by the conduct of the Missionaries, and the quiet manner in which they are heard by the natives, will appear by the following account of one of their excursions: "On January 26, in the evening, the brethren Marshman and Ward went to Ishra. The people in the bazar kindly accommodated them with seats; and nearly fifty sat down around them, to whom they read and expounded the Ten Commandments, asking the people which of them they thought evil or unjust. They answered, 'None: they were all good.' The tree then, said they, must be good from whence the e branches come; and proceeded to shew them how every man by nature was averse from these righteous commandments, and of course from the God who gave them; which state of mind must be a state of wickedness, and of the utmost danger. They then shewed them how Jesus Christ came into the world to deliver men both from the guilt and the dominion of sin; and that their errand into this country was wholly to bring a message of love, to make known these glad tidings to them, and beg them to come to Christ and share the blessings which they themselves enjoyed, appealing to them whether, in the twelve years that they had resided near them, any thing had appeared in their conduct which could lead them to deem them enemies instead of friends! They answered, 'No,' and seemed extremely attentive to the discourse."

Feb 23, 1812. "In the afternoon," observes one of the Missionaries, "I renewed my visit to the once hardened prisoners in the house of correction. The women here are but little interested; but the men, both old and young, Hindoos and Mussulmans, when I compared their conduct towards God to that of the prodigal, and set forth his long-suffering and mercy through the Son of his love, were so affected that both they and myself found it a painful task to part. They followed me as far as they could, and when we parted it was with tears. One of the seapoys on the guard, a Hindoo, thanked man, told me with tears, too, that though I had spoken in Bengalee the words had pierced his heart. During

my address an inquisitive Hindoo interrupted me by asking where our Lord Jesus Christ, the new Savior that I declared unto them, had been for so long time, that he had only now heard of him? I told him that the Savior I preached was no new Savior, but the only one appointed of God, even that God against whom we had sinned; and that to him alone all the ends of the earth are exhorted to look and be saved. If he then said he be a Savior for all the world, how is it that the Europeans who appear to have had him revealed to them, did not all this time make him known to us? I told him, this did not lessen the truth of my assertion; for that all the Europeans whom he saw in India were not Christians."

March 11. The Missionaries having heard that at Chagda, about 24 miles from Serampore, a large concourse of people would be assembled, sent thither Jonathan Carey, with the native converts Deepchund and Vikoontha. They arrived there the next morning at seven. "Here," the itinerants observed, "a spectacle was exhibited which we seldom witness. The river, which at this place is about three quarters of a mile wide, was covered with men, women, and children, nearly to the middle of the stream. In one place was a Brahmun and his train of followers, dipping themselves with the greatest devotion in the sacred stream; in another, a mother was even dragging her shivering child into the river; in another, a Gooroo instructing his disciples in the rites and ceremonies practised on these occasions; in short every one, from the grey head to the youth scarcely versed in idolatrous ceremonies, rich and poor, Brahmuns and Shoodrus, all seemed intent on the same object. The immense crowds which thronged the shore seemed like a forest of heads. Some had travelled journeys of several days; some had come from Chittagong, others from Orissa, and from other parts of the country not less than a hundred miles distant. About seven in the morning we went out, and Deepchund began to speak to the people; but so great was the press that we were obliged to climb a boat which lay on the shore with its bottom upwards; from which place we declared to them the inefficacy of the act they were then performing to remove their sins, and pointed them to the Lamb of God. The people listened with the greatest attention. After preaching for more than an hour, we brought from our own boat a number of Scripture-tracts, but we were again obliged to ascend the boat, where the people followed us clambering up the sides till the boat itself was covered with the crowd, all eager to obtain books. Thinking our situation unsafe, on account of the pressure of the crowd, we retired to our own boat; but there also the people followed us for books; some up to their necks in water; some even swam to the boat, and having obtained pamphlets swam again to the shore. After resting a few minutes, we landed a little way higher up, and ascending a small hillock, where a large number soon surrounded us, we again declared the truths of the Gospel. A young Brahmun, who said he was acquainted with Mr. Carey, raised a shout among the people, crying out Hanbal,* which was soon vociferated by the whole crowd, so that all our efforts to be heard were ineffectual. The noise having in some measure subsided, we resumed our discourse. At length, Vikoont'ha discovered some people from his native village, whom he addressed for more than an hour; after which, a Brahmun, whose house lay at the entrance into the town of Chagla, entreated us to come and explain this new doctrine. We went, and hither a crowd followed us, to whom we explained our message. During the discourse a lewd Brahmun came up, and, insulting us, said, that if we would bestow upon him the means of gratifying his lewd desires, he would become our disciple. Upon this, the Brahmun who had invited us took up the matter, upbraided him for uttering such vile sentiments, and continued disputing with him for a considerable time. I was glad to observe, that the people seemed to exult at his being put to shame. Having unanimously driven him away, they entreated us to proceed. After preaching for a long time, we distributed a number of tracts, which the people received with the greatest eagerness. From hence we went to the market, and from thence to a place where two robbers were hung in chains: here the people's attention was drawn off from our discourse, by a number of lewd fellows; and night coming on, we returned to the boat. In our way, we beheld a most gratifying spectacle: a number of people were sitting under a tree, growing close to an old temple in ruins, dedicated to Shiva; and in the midst of them, a Brahmun who had obtained a pamphlet, was explaining its contents to the attentive crowd. I could not help stopping to contemplate this scene for a moment—one of these images of the divinity, with a poita hung round his neck, and who had just been bathing with the rest of the people in the sacred stream, and from whose lips nothing had ever proceeded but the praises of the gods at the very door of the temple

* *A sort of Huzza! or—Great is Diana of the Ephesians.*

too, within whose walls he perhaps had been accustomed to pay his idolatrous adorations, and from which very likely he had all his life received his maintenance—this man became an unwitting teacher of the Gospel! This sight was so new and so cheering, that it compensated for all our trouble. Returning through the bazar, we saw a man, who had been disappointed in obtaining a pamphlet, buying a book of a boy who had received it from us gratis. On the whole, considering the vast concourse of people, we have reason to bless God for what was done; some thousands of Scripture-tracts were distributed, many of them to people who had come more than ten days' journey, and who will carry them back into their own country; so that though they went to Chagla to worship a river, they may have found Him who is the pearl of great price; and perhaps others also may become inclined to read these pamphlets, and may be converted. Night coming on, and all our stores being exhausted, we took our leave, and arrived at Serampore on Friday night where we learned that the printing-office had been consumed two days before.

(To be continued.)

DONATIONS TO SUPPORT FOREIGN MISSIONS AND TRANSLATIONS.

Aug. 23, 1814. From the Foreign Mission Society in the Eastern District of New Haven County, by the Rev. Matthew Noyes, the Treasurer, $100 00

From the Bible Society of Tioga, for the translations, by Mr. T. Dwight, jun. 89

From the Ladies' Cent Society of East Haven, 23—32 00

From a female friend, by the Rev. Micah Stone of Brookfield, 2 00

23. From the Foreign Mission Society of Norwich and the Vicinity, by Hezekiah Perkins, Esq. the Treasurer, viz. for the translations, $246

For missions, 14—260 00

25. From a female in the S. parish of Andover, for the translations, by the Rev. Justin Edwards, 4 00

26. From a friend to missions, for the translations, 5 00

27. From the Female Foreign Mission Society of New London, by Mrs. Charlotte Wolcott, the Treasurer, 82 00

From a female friend of Missions in .... for the ....ington, 5 00

.... $100 0

Brought forward $490 06

30. From the Foreign Mission Society of Salem and the Vicinity, by Mr. John Jenks, the Treasurer,   59 00

31. From the Foreign Mission Society of Boston and the Vicinity, the balance on hand at this date,   51 10

From the Foreign Mission Society of Newark and the Vicinity, by William Walkee, Esq. the Treasurer,   354 19

A part of the clear profits of the Panoplist, vol v, new series,   236 34

From Mr Solomon Goodell, of Jamaica, Vermont, to the permanent fund.*   1,000 00

          $2,190 69

---

* *This donation by Mr. Goodell was first mentioned in the Panoplist for Feb. 1812, in a note. It was soon after secured to be paid with interest from March 30, 1812; but as the business was conducted by a member of the Board, who lives at no great distance from Mr. Goodell, and who has the papers in his possession, the sum has never been formally entered on the books of the Treasury until now. The donations from Mr. Goodell to the Board may be found in the following numbers of the Panoplist; viz.*

Feb 1812 For the current expenses of the Board, $50 00
July, 1812.   Do.   Do.   126 00
March, 1813.   Do.   Do.   123 90
July, 1813.   Do.   Do.   200 10

          $500 00

Additional donation at the same time,   14 00
Jan 1814. To aid in translating the Scriptures into the languages of Asia,   465 00
June, 1814 To the permanent fund to be applied to the diffusion of a knowledge of the Scriptures in the East,   198 00
July, 1814 To aid in the distribution of the Scriptures in India,   100 00

          1,277 00

To which is to be added the donation entered above to the permanent fund which was secured in March 1812,   1,000 00

          $2,277 00

Besides this, Mr. Goodell has paid two years' interest on his donation of $1,000

Mr. Editor,

IF you think the following will be a mean of exciting others to form similar Societies, you will oblige one of your constant readers by inserting it in your useful publication. The Society formed under the following Constitution is not large; but it has increased much beyond the most sanguine expectations of its first projectors, and there is a probability that it will still increase. The members appear to be animated with zeal for the spread of the Gospel. The Society heard with pleasure the address of the American Board of Commissioners, published in the Panoplist for October, 1813. If Foreign Mission Societies were formed in every town in this state, to cast in their mite to the Board, would not piety be thereby promoted in our land? Would not the Board receive a large accession of pecuniary aid from those little streams? And would they not be enabled more extensively to send out Missionaries, and the Holy Bible to the poor heathens, who are perishing for lack of vision? Are not souls precious! Christians! can you withhold your mite, when such a door is open? Have you forgot the exhortation, *To do good, and to communicate?*† Have you the Spirit of Christ?† Can you tell what may be done, till experiment be made?   L. B.

Plympton, March 29, A. D. 1814.

A NUMBER of persons in the town of Plympton and its vicinity, having been impressed with the danger of those, who sit in darkness and in the region and shadow of death, and of the duty of doing what within them lies to spread in the world the knowledge of Christ, have agreed to form themselves into a Society to assist in promoting Foreign Missions.

We consider ourselves invited to this by the leadings of Divine Providence in opening the door for the establishment of the Christian Religion in the heathen world. What has already been done by the churches in this country through the channels, which are now opened, affords us the fullest assurance, that what is given will be faithfully and religiously appropriated to the object we now have in view. This Society shall be called by the name of the *The Aiding Foreign Mission Society of Plympton and its Vicinity.*

We agree to adopt and maintain the

---

* Heb xiii, 16.
† Rom xii, 9; Matt. xviii, 11; Luke xv, 43.

Articles as the basis of this

CONSTITUTION.

I. *Officers.*

e shall be a President, Secreta-
urer, and Committee, chosen

duty of the President. shall be
re order, and make known busi-
ll meetings of the society.

Secretary shall record all pro-
f the society, and manage their
dence, by receiving and trans-
l communications to and from
y.

Treasurer shall receive the
ons, donations and contributions
he society, and faithfully trans-
same to the Treasurer of the
Board of Commissioners for For-
ions; or to the persons qualified
oard to receive it, and produce
instrument certifying the sum
remitted by this society.

Committee shall use all Chris-
tions in their power to obtain
s, donations, or contributions,
iety, and audit the Treasurer's
and lay them annually before
y.

II. *Membership.*

persons, who believe the Chris-
on, sustain good moral charac-
desire to promote the kingdom
may be admitted into this soci-
te; having been previously pro-
three months.

y person received into this soil, at the time of his admission,
he Treasury of the society, the
e dollar at least, and one dollar
or before each successive annual
while he continues a member of
y.

person wishing to withdraw his
from this society, shall certify
Treasurer, who shall record his
er which, he shall not be consid-
mber; provided he pay his ar-
if any be due.

the Meetings of the Society.

society shall meet annually on
Monday of April, at one o'clock,
vhich time such religious exer-
l be performed, as the society
previously determined.

re shall be Quarterly Meetings;
and places of holding them to
ined by vote of the society at
ual meeting. At which times,
d religious conversation, calcu-
gage each other in the work of
shall be attended to.

y meeting shall be opened and
prayer.

hall be no alteration of this Constitution, without the votes of two thirds
of the members present; the proposed alteration having been notified at a previous
meeting.

At the formation of the Society, March
29, 1814, the following persons were chos-
en officers for the current year, viz.

The Rev. ELIJAH DEXTER,
    Pres. and Treas.
LEWIS BRADFORD, *Sec.*
Lt. DANIEL SOULE,
LEMUEL COBB,   } *Committee.*
CEPHAS BUMPUS,

CHURCH MISSIONARY SOCIETY.

ON the 7th of January a meeting of this
Society was held at Freemason's Hall, the
Right Hon. Lord Gambier in the chair, for
the purpose of addressing four Missionaries who were designated to stations in
the East;

1st. The Rev. Thomas Norton and the
Rev. W. Greenwood, who having been
educated in the Society's Seminary and
admitted to Holy Orders, are now serving curacies. When their engagements
are fulfilled, they will embark for the isl-
and of Ceylon, to act as Missionaries of
the Society.

2d. The Rev. John Christian Schnarre,
and the Rev. Charles Theophilus Ewald
Rhenius, who having studied some years
in the Missionary Seminary at Berlin,
were ordained in that city by the Counsellor of the Consistory, the Rev. Jacobus
Hecker; and having since passed about fifteen months in this country in preparation
for their future labors, were appointed as
Missionaries to Tranquebar.

Our readers are already apprised of
the benevolent and extensive plans of Dr.
John, and of the pecuniary aid rendered to
them by the Calcutta Corresponding Committee of the Society. Mrs. Schnarre and
Rhenius having been destined by the Committee to enter into the fields of labor
which he has presented in the peninsula
of India, their attention was directed to the
studies suitable to that destination, in the
confidence that the Court of Directors of
the East India Company would grant them
their license to proceed to India for the
furtherance of plans so wisely conceived,
and put in practice with so much benefit
to the natives. This confidence was not
disappointed. The Court granted, with
the utmost readiness, the request of the
Committee; and these Missionaries are
now on their passage to India, on board
the Marquis of Huntly, Capt. M'Leod.

On this occasion there were present
1500 or 1600 members and their friends

The Secretary of the Society delivered
the Instructions of the Committee to the

Missionaries, and the Rev. William Dealtry, Rector of Clapham, in the unavoidable absence, through indisposition, of the Rev. Dr. Claudius Buchanan, delivered an Address to them, drawn up by Dr. Buchanan, at the request of the Committee.

From the Christian Observer.

BRITISH AND FOREIGN BIBLE SOCIETY.

SOME select Extracts from the Correspondence of this Society since the publication of the Ninth Annual Report have been printed and circulated. We propose to give the substance of them.

1 From Copenhagen we learn, that the resolution of the Committee to print 5000 additional copies of the Icelandic New Testament was on the point of being executed. "This generosity," it is observed, "towards the poor Icelanders, could not have been applied to more deserving objects. Their assiduity in reading the Scriptures when they have access to them, and the veneration in which they hold their contents, give the fullest anticipatory assurances that the grand object the committee have in view will be attained in that island." It was intended shortly to send a number of Bibles and Testaments to Norway, where the want of the Scriptures was greatly felt. A farmer, eager to possess the Bible, had offered a cow at the next market town for one, but in vain. There were none for sale, and those who possessed a Bible would not sell it for any price.

2 From Zurich we learn, that the "Bible Institution prospers wonderfully."

3. A Bible Society has been formed at Kanapa in Esthonia, under the patronage of the Dean. In that district, Mr. Paterson states, that among 106,000 inhabitants, 200 Testaments are not to be found. Thousands had never seen a New Testament, and many pastors had it not in the vernacular tongue; although there are great numbers of very pious people, and among the rest, 11,000 persons connected with the United Brethren, in this district. An edition of 10,000 Testaments was to be forthwith printed.

Another Bible Society, to be called the Courland Bible Society, has been formed at Mitau in Courland, with the full concurrence of the principal clergy, and under the patronage of Count Meden, President of the Consistory. The meeting for this purpose took place in the hall belonging to the nobles, where persons of all ranks assembled. The business was opened by Count Lieven. "The subscription," says Mr. Paterson, "I hear, will amount to about 3000 rubles; a sum, con-

sidering what this province has suffered by the calamities of war, more than double whatever could have been expected from the first meeting of the Society, but a fire is kindled by the Lord in the Russian empire which warms every heart, and inflames them with zeal to follow the example of their much beloved monarch."

A third society has been formed at Riga, through the instrumentality of the same indefatigable servant of Christ, Mr. Paterson, in which the Consistory and some noblemen took the chief lead. Mr. Paterson expects great things from this Society, which, after that of St. Petersburgh, he thinks will be the first on the Continent. A fourth Society has been formed at Dorpat, and a fifth at Reval, still under the same kind of patronage. The Society at this place are about to print a large edition of the New Testament, and Mr. Paterson adds, "the translation in the Revalian dialect, is supposed to be one of the best in Europe."

After completing these great objects, Mr. Paterson returned to Petersburgh on the 23d of July, when he found that on "the same day on which the Society was formed in Reval a Bible Society had been established in Moscow. At the first meeting, the Bishop and a number of his clergy were present, and subscribed largely. The Bishop publicly thanked Mr. Pinkerton for the part he had taken in the business. This Society will prove of great importance to the cause in Russia. There are now seven Bible Societies in the Russian empire, including that at Abo in Finland."

A peasant, living beyond Moscow, had written to prince Galitzin, the President of the Petersburgh Society, begging a large folio Bible to read to his family and neighbors, and sending five rubles to pay for its carriage. Another peasant offered to subscribe 20 rubles yearly, and presented the Society with some leather for binding the Bibles.

ORDINATION.

ORDAINED, at Dennis, Barnstable co. Mass. on the 27th ult. the Rev. Joseph HAVEN. Sermon by the Rev. Dr. Ware, from 1 Cor. xiii, 9. *We know in part.*

AUXILIARY BIBLE SOCIETY OF NEWARK (N. J.) AND ITS VICINITY.

AGREEABLY to previous notice in the public paper, and from the pulpit in the several congregations of this place, a number of the YOUNG MEN from the town and its neighborhood met on Thursday, the 20th

e last, and formed themselves into
y by the name of *"The Auxiliary
Society of Newark and its Vicinity."*
design of the institution is to raise
o be exclusively appropriated to
nate the sacred Scriptures among
who are destitute.

r the adoption of a constitution, the
gs of the Society were continued
urnment on Thursdays the 7th and
stant, and the following persons
as officers for the ensuing year,

v. Mr. Jones, *Pres.*
v. Mr. Cumming, 1st *Vice Pres.*
v. Mr. Robinson, 2d *Vice Pres.*
nry Mills, 3d *Vice Pres.*
illiam Ward, *Sec.*
oses Lyon *Assistant Sec.*
mes Crane, *Treas.*

e Directors were appointed, in each
five religious congregations
Society at present consists of up-
of ONE HUNDRED members. The
g have been appointed a commit-
receive donations, viz.
v. Lewis P. Bayard,
v. David Jones,
r. William Tuttle,
William Lee,
William Ward
Society deem it unnecessary on
casion to make any appeal to the
of the Christian public. The object
Institution is *Charity*—charity of
st exalted kind. The aid of the
s now solicited, and to the benevo-
nd no other argument is necessary,
be assured of the well attested fact,
st multitudes of poor in our own
ble the millions in heathen
re destitute of that sacred volume
hat gives life and immortality to light—
ich one all powerful influences,
here diffuses the sublime hope of
.

SOCIETY AT FREDERICKSBURG, VIR.

ns of the Fredericksburg Bible So-
stablished May 5th, 1814.

ALFRED B WILSON, *Pres.*
RYS DAY, Esq. *Vice Pres.*
AWSON C. Mc GUIRE, *Cor. Sec.*
AW F. GRAY, Esq. *Rec Sec.*
HENDERSON, Esq. *Treas.*

Hedgman, John Mack, Robert
James Vass, David Briggs, Lau-
Battaile, Charles Tacket, Timothy
Robert Lewis, Andrew Glassell,
H. Shinker, Benjamin H. Hall,
ray, Hugh Mercer, John Scott,
Directors.

SOCIETY FOR THE SUPPRESSION OF VICE.

A SOCIETY with this designation has for
twelve years past existed in London, and
several branches have extended themselves into different parts of the British
empire. In our eighth volume, p 571, we
published part of an abstract of one of
their reports. We now publish the remainder of that abstract, as peculiarly interesting at the present time, on account of the
exertions now making among us to enforce the observance of the Sabbath.

"The Committee have assisted," says
the abstract, "in establishing similar societies at Newcastle upon Tyne, Liverpool,
and Stowmarket; and also at Oxford, under the patronage of the Vice Chancellor.
"The following extract of a letter from
Stowmarket will illustrate the benefits derived from the institution of societies of
this description: I received your much esteemed favor, in answer to mine of the
9th February, and immediately after began my proceedings nearly in the following
manner. It was my intention to have
sent a private notice to each person, but
having only one of each sort, I called on
them, read the printed one to them, and
left a written copy, allowing them two
more Sundays. By some I was much
abused, and by others welcomed. After
the expiration of the two Sundays allowed,
many were informed that they should be
still supplied with goods on a Sunday; I
therefore deemed it necessary to have it
regularly cried, (that all those who should
henceforth, &c.) which was done on the
21st ult. in every part of the town; and
the next day being Sunday, I had the satisfaction to see every shop closed, and the
town wear a quite different aspect. The
printed papers really conduced to effect
my purpose; and had it not been for the aid
of the Society for the Suppression of Vice,
I should have found much trouble even in
compulsory measures. This is one more,
amongst the many evils suppressed by that
excellent institution, whose aid is here
gratefully acknowledged by, &c. ""

If zeal and boldness have done so much
in effecting a reformation, even in places
where all the shops were kept open on the
Sabbath, how much would the same qualities do in this country, where the Sabbath is still regarded with more veneration by the mass of the people, than in any
part of England.

PROFANATION OF THE LORD'S DAY.

THE Tything-men of the towns of Beverly, Hamilton, Manchester, Ipswich, Reading, Andover, Bradford, Wilmington, and

Tewksbury in Massachusetts, and Concord and Salem in New-Hampshire, amounting to forty persons in all, have given public notice in the newspapers of their intention to execute the laws with respect to the Lord's Day.

LITERARY INTELLIGENCE.

NEW WORKS.

An Historical Sketch of Charlestown, in the county of Middlesex and Commonwealth of Massachusetts, read to an assembly of citizens at the opening of Washington Hall, Nov. 16, 1813. By Josiah Bartlett, M. D. Boston: John Elliot 1814.

The burden and heat of the day borne by the Jewish Church: A Sermon preached at Shelburne, before the Auxiliary Society for Foreign Missions, at their annual meeting, Oct. 12, 1813. By Joshua Spaulding, A. M. Pastor of the Church in Buckland. Boston: S. T. Armstrong. 1814.

OBITUARY.

Died, in North Carolina, ALEXANDER DIXON, Esq. leaving $12,000 for the education of poor children in Dublin County.

At Hudson, (N. Y.) the Rev. HENRY JENKS, A. M. aged 27, pastor of the Baptist church in that place.

At Boston, on the 12th ult., the only son of Mr. Constant Hopkins, aged 4 years, of the hydrophobia.

At Delhi, (N. Y.) JAMES GRAHAM, executed for the murder of *Hugh Cameron* and *Alexander M'Gullaway.*

At Bath, Maine, on the 12th ult. THREE CHILDREN of Mr. *John Pursley,* aged from 8 to 12, suffocated and burnt to death, in his house, which was consumed very suddenly by fire.

At Wilkesbarre, Penn. JOHN DIXON, a U. S. soldier, whose death was occasioned by the brutality of a serjeant. Verdict of the inquest, *Wilful Murder.*

At New Haven, on the 26th ult, Mr. BARNEY CARROLL, stone-mason, burnt to death in the house where he lodged, which was suddenly consumed by fire.

At Salem, the Hon BENJAMIN GOODHUE, Esq. aged 66, formerly a Senator in Congress from Massachusetts.

At Newburyport, the Hon. ENOCH TITCOMB, Esq aged 62.

In London, on the 6th of August 1812, Jacob Mix, a Jew, and native of Elbing in Polish Prussia.

He embraced the Christian faith upwards of twelve months before his death, and was publicly baptized by the Rev. Dr. Nichol, at the Jews' chapel, on the 20th of May, 1812. From the time he professed the Christian religion, he was diligent in attending the means of grace at the Jews' Chapel. Having received a German Bible from the London Society, he was observed to be constantly and seriously engaged in perusing it; and from the plain and unequivocal declarations he made of his faith in the Messiah, there is good ground to believe that the Scriptures were accompanied with the blessing of the Holy Spirit.

He had been, in one moment, reduced from very affluent circumstances to poverty, by the incursion of the French. From the natural independence of his mind, he applied himself diligently, at the age of forty three, to learn the business of a tailor; but grief was rapidly undermining his constitution. He gradually became weaker, and, soon after his baptism, was so reduced as to be confined to his room. During his illness he often expressed the greatest solicitude about his family, who arrived in England only five weeks before his death, and to whom he earnestly and repeatedly recommended the Christian religion. Fearing he might not live to see them, and being deeply concerned for their eternal interests, he had, before their arrival, made a will, appointing the Rev. Thomas Fry, the Rev. J. S. C. F. Frey, and Joseph Fox, Esq. guardians of his five children, with full power to secure their instruction in the Christian religion. When his family arrived, he committed his wife and children to the London Society, expressing the greatest resignation, and declaring the satisfaction it would give him to see them baptized. He was sensible to the last, and his conversations evinced that he built his hopes on that Foundation which God has laid in Zion.

He was interred in the German burying ground, Ayliff Street, Goodman's Fields, attended by the Committee of the London Society for promoting Christianity among the Jews, and the children under its patronage. The Rev Dr. Schwabe addressed a numerous and attentive audience in the German language, and spoke to the children in English; and the Rev Mr. Frey concluded with an address in English. This account was printed by desire of the committee of the above named Society.

We are often led to adore the Providence and electing love of God, in making temporal afflictions the means of everlasting good. Unless this Jew had been suddenly reduced to poverty, he would not, in all probability, have been brought to hear the truth, much less to embrace it.

N. B. As our number for July contained half a sheet more than usual, this contains half a sheet less.

THE
PANOPLIST,
AND
MISSIONARY MAGAZINE.

| 10. | OCTOBER, 1814. | VOL. X. |

RELIGIOUS COMMUNICATIONS.

to Editor of the Panoplist.

ttremely happy to learn, from
es of the General Assembly of
rterian Church, and of the Gen-
istions of Connecticut and Mas-
, that it was resolved, at the
is of these venerable bodies, to
titioning Congress, to put a stop
ying and opening of the mail,
Sabbath. The plan of circulat-
of the general petition for sig-
among all denominations of Chris-
ighout the United States, is, I
y judicious. It is calculated to
id ascertain the strength of the
le of this country, and to bring
s and wishes, in regard to the
e of the Christian Sabbath, fairly
: national legislature. Anxious
I this noble and patriotic design,
proper means in my power, I
induced to depart a little from
ir order of the discussion on
ave entered, and to send you a
ares, which I had intended to
other place, upon the existing
s of the Post Office Depart-
you think an early insertion of
b likely to promote, in any de-
great and good object in view,
t your service.   Z. X Y.

HE SABBATH. NO. IV.

*ying the Mail upon the
     Sabbath.*

i be made to appear, that
ular transportation and
of the mail, upon the
ay, interferes, unavoida-
extensively, with the ap-
e duties of holy time;
the practice cannot be
X.

justified by the plea of necessity;
it will, I trust, be admitted, (nay
more than *admitted*,) by all who
have any regard for the Sabbath,
that it is a practice, which ought
to be discontinued. Does the
practice, then, interfere with the
religious duties of the sacred
rest? This is the first point to be
considered; and surely, there
can be no room for doubt, where
conclusive facts present themselves,

"Thick as the leaves, that strow the
     brooks,
In Vallombrosa."

It will be seen, at a glance,
that in a country so extensive as
ours, and one which is every where
intersected by post-roads, it requires a very great number of
drivers and carriers to transport
the mails. All these persons
have souls to be saved or lost.
The law of God binds them,
equally with others, to keep the
Sabbath holy. It is their indispensable duty to make it a day of
rest from worldly employments,
and to spend it in the "public and
private exercises of God's worship." But the existing regulations of the General Post-Office
render such an observance of the
Sabbath, by them, impracticable.
They are required to be on the
road, when they should be in the

house of God, in their families, or their closets.

Thus freed from the restraints, and deprived of the blessings of the Lord's day, they gradually lose whatever reverence they previously had for its sacred hours, and divine requirements. The consequences are such as might be expected. The Sabbath being soon forgotten by them, other divine institutions are of course disregarded, and they are placed at a remove, almost hopeless, from the kingdom of heaven. How many persons are employed every Sabbath, as mail-carriers, in this extensive country, I know not. The number must certainly be great. Probably from ten to fifteen hundred. And ought not their services to be dispensed with, if possible? I am sure, that the answer of Christian benevolence must be in the affirmative.*

* As we conceive this subject to be incalculably important, our readers will pardon us for adding, by way of note, a few remarks on some of the topics, discussed by our respected correspondent.

We must premise, that no salutary effect can be expected to be produced, by this discussion, upon the mind of any person, who does not regard religion with seriousness, and man as an immortal being, whose future destiny is to be fixed by the character which he forms in this life. Infidels and scoffers are beyond the reach of the most powerful and decisive arguments on this subject. But we make a confident appeal to every person, who meditates with sacred awe upon the value of the human soul,—to every person, who believes, that *without holiness no man shall see the Lord*, and that with the observance of the Sabbath are intimately connected all the ordinary means of grace and salvation. No such person will deem it a light thing, that a thousand or fifteen hundred men are statedly employed in such a manner, as to separate them utterly from public worship, and to transform them into heathens. We are of opinion, that not a single employment, which is tolerated among us in time of

But mail-carriers are not the only persons, who are prevented from sanctifying the Sabbath, by

peace, is so perfectly hostile to every thing of a serious nature, as is the employment of driving stage-coaches on the Sabbath, which is an inevitable consequence of carrying the mail on that day. Let a young man be engaged one year in this employment, and it is almost certain, that he will be an inveterate Sabbath-breaker through life, and that his soul will be lost for ever. We say *almost* certain; for God may interpose and rescue such a man from eternal death. Neither the word of God, however, nor his Providence, authorize any expectation that he will thus interpose. Quite the reverse.

We insist not here, on the vastly greater number of persons, who are employed on the Sabbath in driving other carriages than those in which the mail is conveyed, and who would not be thus employed, were it not for the customary travelling of mail-stages on that day. Let us suppose all other travelling on the Sabbath prevented, and all the inhabitants, except mail-carriers, in the happy possession of the Sabbath, and its various means of spiritual improvement. In that case, would it not be thought a great evil, that several hundreds of persons should be so employed, as to be removed from hearing God's word, from the ordinary means of grace, and the offers of salvation? Would not the whole country be filled with lamentations, on account of so melancholy a seclusion from the common blessing of Christianity? Is the evil less now, when the multitudes involved in it are immensely greater, than in the case supposed? and when its magnitude is concealed by the extent and authority of bad example? Would it be thought a small matter, that a thousand or fifteen hundred men should be subjected to all the horrors of Algerine captivity without hope of deliverance? Would a humane man consent, that so many individuals should be exposed to imminent danger of such captivity, for the purpose of furnishing him, and others like him, with papers and letters a day earlier than he would otherwise receive them? But how trifling an evil is Algerine captivity compared to an eternal confinement in the great prison of despair.

Nor is the evil to be lightly estimated because it may be voluntarily incurred? How many of the sufferings of this life are brought upon men by their voluntary misconduct? Yet no man thinks lightly of these sufferings on this account. Men are too ready, it is true, to trifle with their

e now under consider-
the postmasters, who
ed to open the mail on
re subjected to such
ons, as must be very
a serious mind, and
dicial to religious im-
.. By the arrival of
during the hours of
rship, many are pre-
m waiting upon God
se. And where this is
se, how painful must it
se post-masters, who
roper regard for the
, to be interrupted by
l of the mail, when
ne Scriptures, or, per-
ne midst of family or
er, and compelled to
attention, for hours
o letters, newspapers,
ills. How much also,
ses, are their families
by the arrival and de-
stages, and the noise
which they occasion.*
the evils complained
ere. For the sake of
assengers on the Sab-
impunity, stage-coach-
ployed, even on those
ere the mail might be
with convenience on
. The consequence is,

that all the stage-houses are
subjected to more or less disturbance every Sabbath. Some-
body must be in waiting. Horses
must be changed. Passengers
must be accommodated. The
whole company of Sabbath-breakers must breakfast at one inn,
and dine at another. Have inn-
keepers no souls? Have they no
religious duties to perform? Is
it not exceedingly to be lamented, that they should be subjected
to all these interruptions on the
Sabbath, in consequence of the
transportation of the mails on
that day?*

Let another thing be considered. The mail-stages cannot
travel, without making a great
deal of disturbance. It is no uncommon thing, where they pass
near houses of public worship,
for the voice of the speaker to
be wholly confused by their rat-
tling, while the eyes of half the
congregation are turned to the
doors and windows. Thousands
and thousands of families, are
much disturbed by the same
means.

Further; the multiplied profanations of the Sabbath, which
are occasioned by this practice,
ought not to be left out of the
general estimate. A stranger,
who happens to spend the Lord's
day in one of our large commercial towns, has his attention arrested by crowds of people passing by his lodgings. His first

---

ests, and to squander away
ut is this a reason why they
outraged to do so? We should
, that the disposition of men
eir souls should make every
mmunity cautious how any
tolerated, which have an
gency in strengthening this
position.
rger towns, each post-master
n two to six clerks, who are
re or less, on the Sabbath, in
business of the office. In
, it is believed the business
post-office is little less on the
n on any other day of the

* Passengers in the stage, on many
routs in the United States, are compelled
either to travel on the Sabbath, or to stop
on the road three or four days. Such a
delay cannot usually be suffered without
extreme inconvenience. But if no stages
travelled on the Sabbath, every passenger in the stage could so arrange his journey, as to suffer no inconvenience.

thought is, that they must be going to public worship; but he soon recollects, that it is not the proper hour, and perceives, that they are pressing not into the church, but the coffee-house and the post-office. He inquires the cause of all this eager bustle, and is told, that the mail is expected, or that it has just arrived. But are the people of your city in the habit of thronging the post-office on the Sabbath? O yes, nothing is more common. Hundreds go thither directly from the churches. Whenever the mail arrives, people must and will go, to inquire for letters and to hear the news. The stranger, if he is a man of piety, answers with a sigh, *These things ought not so to be.*

We need not inquire as to the rest, it being perfectly obvious what must follow. If newspapers and letters are taken out, they will be read; and, in nine instances out of ten, their contents will more or less engross the thoughts for the rest of the day. Nor is this all: many of the letters demand, or are thought to demand, immediate answers. Writing these answers occupies much of that time, which God claims as his peculiar property. By the fluctuations of our own and of foreign markets, new fields of speculation are opened, on which hundreds are eager to enter. Nor must the Sabbath be permitted to prevent, or to interfere with, the requisite calculations. All these evils, and many more, are directly occasioned every Sabbath, in a single town, by the arrival and opening of the mail.

Now let the reader stop a moment, and consider how many large commercial towns there are in the United States, besides a vast number of smaller ones, where the mails are opened on the Lord's day; and of course how many thousands of people, of all ranks, are induced to profane the day, in the manner just mentioned. Let him consider, likewise, that where the mail is merely carried through a place, without being opened, many are in the habit of collecting at the stage-house, to glean whatever news they can, from the driver and passengers. Then let him say, whether a practice, which is productive of so much evil, ought not to be discontinued.

There is one other point of view, in which this subject deserves to be seriously contemplated. Merely seeing the mail-stages pass every Sabbath, tends exceedingly to make the young think lightly of that sacred institution; to embolden transgressors, and to increase the difficulty of executing the laws. It is extremely natural for children to suppose, that what is sanctioned by high authority must be right. They soon learn that the mail is carried by such authority. Their first deduction is, that there can be no harm in the practice. Their second, that travelling for other purposes, cannot be very criminal. And thus their reverence for the Lord's day is gradually weakened, and, in many cases, ultimately destroyed. The mail-stages being filled with passengers, and permitted to go on, others think they have as good a right to travel in their private carriages, and the pressure becomes so great, that

few efforts to stop the
, magistrates and inform-
.ers are discouraged.

are the evils of trans-
the mail upon the Sab-
It takes off carriers and
.sters from the religious
if the day; interrupts pub-
ship; disturbs thousands
lies on the post-roads; in-
nen of business and curi-
profane the sacred rest
r ways; injures the rising
ion by bad example;
hens the hands of Sab-
:akers, and weakens those
istrates.*

:w of all these evils, I ask
ntly, whether any thing
f the plea of absolute ne-
and that plea well sup-
can justify the practice
consideration? To the
n of necessity, then, let
r call the reader's atten-

the public interest require
sportation and opening of
il, on the Sabbath, either
of peace or war?
necessary in time of peace?
tat purpose? To facilitate
linary operations of gov-
it? Surely the public in-
could not often suffer,

inroads which are made and
upon the Sabbath, by the arrival
ul and the keeping open of post-
re astonishingly great. It is prin-
ving to this cause, that there is
iversation in regard to the news
ty, on the Sabbath, than on any
r of the week. Great multitudes
ge towns are entirely engrossed,
ie whole Lord's day, by the news
r business. We do not believe
in the power of man to invent
r practice, which shall aim so di-
io powerfully, and so constantly,
bversion of the Sabbath, and shall
me time excite so little alarm, as
tice of carrying the mail on that
it is now tolerated in the United

by the short delay which the law
of the Sabbath requires; and when
there is danger of public injury,
how easily might it be prevented, by sending off an express.
The expense of sending expresses cannot be urged as an
objection, because, in fact it
would bear no proportion to the
additional expense incurred by
the regular transportation of the
mail on the Sabbath. The public good, then, does not require
the latter, in time of peace.

2 Does it in time of war? Here
something more plausible may
be urged, in the affirmative. It
may be said, that when a country
is invaded, or threatened with
invasion; when important military operations are going on, at
many different points, the orders
of government, especially in the
war-department, must become
very numerous; that these require the utmost despatch, as
well as the official returns from
commanding officers, to the head
of that department; and that to
keep up these necessary communications, the transportation of
the mail upon the Sabbath is
unavoidable.

Now, I readily admit, that in
time of war it may be necessary
to transmit despatches, on the
Lord's day. But is there, permit me to ask, no way of doing
this, without keeping all the
mails constantly going? How easily might expresses be kept in readiness, at the seat of government;
and what hinders, but that similar arrangements might be made,
in each of the military districts?
Such arrangements would not
only supersede the necessity of
transporting the mails, in the
manner complained of, but would
produce a very considerable sav-

ing of expense. Nearly a seventh part of what it now costs to carry the mail, would be saved in the first instance, by letting that establishment lie still on the Sabbath; and it is presumed, that not more than one seventh part of this saving, would be requisite to pay all the necessary expresses.

But conclusive as this view of the subject is, why should I rest the question here, when every body knows, that expresses are now employed by the government, on those very routs, where the mails are most expeditiously carried? This fact destroys at once the plea of necessity, so far as the *public* is concerned. If, then, it is still urged, it must be on the ground, not of public, but private interest. And here, undoubtedly, we are to look for the mighty necessity, so earnestly pleaded. It is to accommodate the merchants, and other men of business, who have agents and correspondents in different parts of the country, that the mails must be kept constantly in motion. But what claim have they to this indulgence? What claim, I should rather have said, have they upon the public, which makes it necessary that a practice, most pernicious to the community, most destructive to themselves, should be continued. Is their business more important to them, than that of the farmer, or the mechanic, is to to him? Must many hundreds of men, acting under the head of the post-office department, be deprived of the rest and all the blessings of holy time, to advance the imagined private interests of a part of the community? Must the Sabbath, the main

pillar of our moral and religious institutions, be thus gradually undermined? Must the great interests of the nation be sacrificed, out of complaisance to the unreasonable wishes of a small part of its population? Surely, the most craving speculator alive will not say this.

And what is gained after all, by writing and receiving letters on the Sabbath? Was any man a loser, in the long run, by keeping that sacred day holy? Let it be remembered, that obedience to the commandments of the Lord, has the promise of the life that now is, and of that which is to come. Men may seem to be gainers for a time by doing their own work on the Lord's day, but this *making haste to be rich* undoubtedly *will not leave them innocent*, and probably will tend to poverty.*

* We have often been surprised to observe on what slender arguments the defence of the most pernicious practices is occasionally rested. Duelling, gambling, the theatre, and especially war and its consequences, are often defended by their respective advocates, in a train of reasoning, which betrays a union of childish imbecility and inveterate profligacy. In a similar manner, the most outrageous violations of the Sabbath are too frequently palliated, and even defended. The only arguments of a private nature, which we have ever heard used in favor of carrying the mail on the Sabbath, are these two. 1. The interest of merchants requires, that they should have early notice of the state of the markets, &c. 2. Cases of sickness, &c. &c. may occur, in which relatives and friends would be glad to receive early intelligence from each other. As to the first argument, it would be worse than ridiculous to pretend, that merchants are, or ought to be, exempted from the general law of the Sabbath But so far as merchants are to profit by the arrival of the mail on the Sabbath, so far are they acting as if exempted from a wise general law, which was given for the benefit of all mankind. Besides, to assert that merchants derive even an apparent benefit from the opera-

a of necessity, then,
rting and opening the
e Sabbath, cannot be
on any ground. The
ught therefore to be

ail on the Sabbath, is alto-
varranted assumption. Sup-
ierchants of Boston, for in-
eive intelligence from their
orrespondents on Monday
ad of Sabbath morning. Is
gence is new on Monday, as
been on the Sabbath? Let
be perfectly removed from
siness, as it was intended to
ly morning succeed Satur-
as to all worldly purposes,
ay morning succeeds Mon-
and no inconvenience will

But why need we argue?
tible facts, prove, that the
sessity of conveying the mail
th is perfectly imaginary.
1801, or 1802, if we are cor-
ed, the mail was not convey-
bbath, through any part of
; perhaps not through any
nited States. Did the com-
uffer? Further; within these
t, during a great part of the
as been no southern mail at
onsequently none at Salem,
, Portsmouth, &c. &c. on
/as this arrangement deem-
ible grievance? Far from it.
as said about news on Mon-
wer was; We have no mail
here the complaint ended.
ry time, when the commer-
l the political world kept on
courses without a Monday's
I have been strenuously con-
absolute necessity required
f the mail on the Sabbath.
change the mail-day from
o Monday? Indeed, that is
can answer.

this subject, it is proper to
to our certain knowledge,
mail-carriers would be gladly
carrying the mail on the
stage proprietors, on a cer-
:10 miles, were accustomed
mail through the whole dis-
a week, viz. from Monday
ednesday evening, and from
rning to Saturday evening.
ment permitted drivers, post-
inn-keepers to rest on the
t last, for a reason which is
ate, as we could easily show
er to go into particulars a
rude, so that the stage now
Monday morning to Wednes-

discontinued. Let every Christian patriot; let all who have the best interests of the nation at heart, exert their whole influence in favor of the general petition, which is to be presented next winter to the National Legislature. This is no party question. The object aimed at, in the petition, is one, in which the whole body of the people are deeply interested. Let Christians of different denominations vie with each other, in giving the petition currency and swelling the list of subscribers. Attempts at reformation are apt to fail for want of union and perseverance. Every man, who is likely to favor the object, must have the petition presented to him for sub-

day evening, and from Friday morning to Sabbath evening; leaving a day of rest indeed, *but changing it from the Sabbath to Thursday!* When this change was proposed, every stage-proprietor on the whole rout remonstrated against it; yet all were compelled to agree to it, or not have their contracts renewed; so that now the stage travels every Sabbath 70 miles at each end of the rout, making 140 miles out of 210, contrary to the wishes of the stage-proprietors, drivers, post-masters and inn-keepers, and, we have a right to presume, of the passengers also. Let it be added, that passengers on a part of this rout must proceed on the Sabbath, or be left on Saturday evening without any means of advancing on their journey, till the ensuing Wednesday; and even then they could not be admitted if the stage should be full.

As to the argument that friends may be sick, or in trouble at a distance, and intelligence may be desired from them on the Sabbath; it is a sufficient reply, that the proposed advantage is so small and so contingent, as to bear no sort of proportion to the magnitude of the evil in question. According to this argument, it would be the duty of thousands in a populous city to send for their letters, and read them, on the Sabbath, on account of the probability that some one out of a thousand would receive a letter containing something of the kind supposed. A demand so extravagant as this cannot be considered as reaching further consideration.

scription. To this end, let the business be done systematically, by entrusting it to some thorough person, or persons, in every town, who will engage to see to it effectually. Let this course be adopted every where, and it can hardly be doubted, I think, that the voice of the people will be so strong and decisive, as to induce Congress to take the subject into their serious consideration, and pass a law to remedy the evil.

Will it be said, by any body, that such an application as is contemplated would be disrespectful to the national legislature? How so? I never heard of its being deemed improper, to petition Congress on subjects of minor importance; how then can it be, in a case which involves the highest and best interests, of the present, and of succeeding, generations? The intended petition does not imply even a virtual condemnation of any former legislative act; for I am well assured, that no law exists, which requires, or in express terms permits, the evil complained of. Carrying and opening the mails on the Sabbath, is a mere regulation of the Post-master General.

Let not the timid and faithless suggest, that the application, however well supported, will be ineffectual. It is not to be believed, until the trial shall have been fairly made, that the great council of our nation, will hastily reject so reasonable a request, especially when made by the great body of the wise and good, from one end of the United States to the other. Even if Congress were known to be hostile to the application, a suppo-

sition which I am far from making, it would be very unbecoming in those, who believe that all hearts are in the hand of the Lord, to despair of success. Let us do our duty and cheerfully leave the event with God. Let us bestow our labor, and *in due season we shall reap, if we faint not.*

For the Panoplist.

ON MINISTERIAL FELLOWSHIP.

IT is proper that we should remind the reader, that we are not to be considered as approving every opinion expressed in all the articles which we publish. We think the following paper will be useful, though we do not precisely agree with the writer in every particular. ED.

IT is extremely desirable, that intimate union should subsist among all the servants of the Prince of Peace. But the state of things in our country is such, that when a faithful man has entered the ministry, he finds it difficult to regulate his exchanges of labors, and other acts of fellowship, in such a manner as to satisfy his own conscience, maintain uniformly the cause of truth, commend himself to the people of his charge, and preserve that intercourse with other ministers, which custom and propriety seem to require. The principal cause of this difficulty is, that many professed teachers of the Gospel, though not openly heretical or immoral, keep back part of the truth, and preach the remainder in such a manner as to render it without effect. With such persons some faithful men do not exchange ministerial labors, and have but little ministerial intercourse; and they are consequently censured for their want of charity, and accused of inconsistency. Other faithful men do exchange with them, and thus grieve many of God's children, and strengthen, however unintentionally, the hands of the enemy against those who are more firm and decided.

A belief that the subject has been too long neglected induces me to offer a few thoughts upon it to the public. It is a subject of great and increasing interest to our churches.

I propose,

I. To describe several *different kinds of ministers.*

II. To offer some *rules of ministerial intercourse or fellowship.*

I shall, in the first place, attempt to describe several different kinds of ministers. I would not judge another man's servants; much less the servants of the Most High God. I would not unnecessarily proclaim the failings of ministers I would not wantonly expose the nakedness of the land of Israel, and cause the uncircumcised to rejoice. I shall endeavor to speak on this subject, as the cause of truth demands, with meekness and fear.

It should be lamented, but cannot be denied, that there is a great diversity of character among those, who have been regularly ordained to the work of the ministry in the Congregational churches.

1. There are some unhappy instances (though I trust but very few) of men, who are known to be immoral in their lives; whose conduct has brought great reproach upon the Christian name and ministry; who,

nevertheless, are not regularly ejected from office. They retain their standing through the favor of particular friends; perhaps of a party among their people; or through the fears of others, who, though dissatisfied, yet neglect to support the discipline of the church. I cannot forbear here to notice the great defect, which seems to exist in our plan of church government in this particular; and to express the hope, that the evil here mentioned, will, among others, convince us of the necessity of adopting a different course

2. There are men of regular standing in the ministry, who avow error, and preach it. I mean, that they expressly deny some of the leading and fundamental truths of the sacred oracles, and instead of these, preach their own preconceived opinions, and the delusive inventions of others. Here, again, there is no regular and united separation of the churches from those who live in error.

3. There are some ministers, whose conduct cannot be proved to be immoral, but is in a great measure inconsistent with the Gospel; who are *conformed to this world;* who are generally considered as men of the world; whose lives are such as not to reprove, but strengthen, the wicked.

4. Others are unexceptionable in their external conduct, and their preaching is not directly heretical; but is, in its effect, subversive of the Gospel. I refer to those, who do not preach the doctrines of grace, nor yet explicitly deny them. They advance some opinions consistent with the Gospel, and many

which are not. They declaim, in general terms, upon the excellency of religion, but explain nothing They inveigh earnestly against sin, but not in such a manner as to show their hearers that *they* are guilty, or in danger. They preach salvation by Christ, as a Teacher and Exemplar, while they forget that he bled for lost sinners. They sometimes declare a doctrinal truth, and hinder all its effect by an erroneous application.

5. A fifth class may comprehend those, who are orthodox in sentiment, and regular in their lives; but who give no evidence of a *spiritual mind*. They can preach upon doctrines; but say nothing upon experience, and the life of God in the soul. In their hands the truth appears to be a collection of speculative facts, arranged and connected with mathematical precision, but it does not resemble the words of Christ, which are spirit and life.

6. I bless God I may still add, that there are many, who preach the truth as it is in Jesus; who understand the things whereof they affirm; whose lives in a good degree manifest the power of godliness; and who commend themselves to every man's conscience in the sight of God.

I shall not consume time in adducing evidence of the accuracy of these statements. Every man of information can testify, that the foregoing varieties of character are found among ministers, as they appear to human view.

I proceed to inquire, secondly, whether some rules may not be adopted, for the regulation of fellowship with different kinds of ministers.

The advocates of liberality will scarcely contend, that all who are found in the sacred office should be received, by a faithful man, into full and perfect fellowship. The most strenuous advocate of unvarying truth, having the spirit of Christ, will object to any measure tending unnecessarily to increase divisions and strifes. I should only be anxious to know what our Lord will have us to do, and to do it in his spirit. No separation should be made on account of private or personal injuries, party animosities, or trifling differences of opinion. Such considerations should yield to the interests of the Redeemer, and not disturb our unity in him. In case of a necessary separation, it should be made in the spirit of meekness, forbearance, and love. The party to whom fellowship is denied, should be informed of the objections of the other; and all evangelical means should be used to convince him of his error.

Ministerial intercourse may be divided into three kinds. In the first, I merely *acknowledge official character*, without any special connexion with the minister. Thus I address a man by his proper title, and recognise his ministerial character, in the common intercourse of life. I acknowledge, that his official acts, such as preaching, administering the ordinances, and assisting in ordinations, are valid. In the second sort of intercourse, I acknowledge his official character by *acting with him*, in cases not altogether voluntary on my part, or in a duty to which I have been called by others. Of this kind is the act of sitting with him in councils. Associations of ministers, are of two kinds. If the association, with which I am connected, meet on the broad principle of merely acknowledging each other as ministers regularly ordained, I may voluntarily unite with them, and shall exercise this second sort of intercourse. But if they have any special bond of union, containing articles of faith or specified principles for mutual assent, and I should voluntarily unite with them, I should express a stricter intercourse. In the third degree, I exchange labors, or by some other action *voluntarily engage another minister* to perform pastoral duties for me; thus conveying my own opinion and approbation of his principles and conduct, and expressing the most perfect and intimate ministerial fellowship. It is clearly right and proper, that, in all cases where the course of duty is doubtful, and our professed brethren are concerned, we should be careful to listen to the calls of candor and forbearance.

I now proceed to state some rules, which seem calculated to direct my own conduct in this matter.

1. We must admit all the regular ministers, whom I have described, to some degree of intercourse. This rule is justified by our Lord's direction to his disciples and the multitude, concerning the regular officers in the Jewish church, who were not faithful and of good character. *The Scribes and the Pharisees sit in Moses' seat. All, therefore, whatsoever they bid*

you observe, *that observe and do; but do ye not after their works; for they say and do not.* This amounts to a direction to respect the office, the institution of God; though we cannot approve and reverence the man. We regard the same rule, in respect to private brethren. We commune with professed Christians in the same church, though they may give us no evidence of piety. If they become immoral or heretical, we must regard them as brethren, and not reject them, except in a regular and evangelical way. So all professed ministers of Christ, who have had a regular induction to the office, must be acknowledged as such, until they are regularly silenced. This rule will not be disputed; for so far as my information extends, no man administers the ordinance of baptism a second time to one, who has received it even from an immoral or heretical minister, still retaining his standing in the church.[*]

2. A faithful minister should withhold intercourse, in the second and third degrees, from ministers who are known to be immoral or heretical. He should refuse to sit with them in councils and associations, or to interchange labors with them. Thus far he can and ought to come out from them, and be separate; marking and avoiding those, who cause offences contrary to sound doctrine, and keeping his garments from being polluted with their iniquities. He does not in

[*] The General Assembly of the Presbyterian Church have lately decided, that baptism, administered by a Unitarian, is not valid. **Ed.**

this case, (as he would, if he denied their official acts,) take upon himself the office of condemning and excommunicating them. He only acts for himself, and withdraws from those, whose doctrine and life are known to be contrary to the Gospel He exercises the private right of withdrawing from those, who are not disciplined as they should be, by the proper authority.

3. A faithful minister may withhold the strictest degree of fellowship from those, *who live after the fashion and course of this world*, although they cannot be charged with gross immoralities. Their lives hinder the Gospel, and bring reproach upon religion. My voluntary connexion with them would increase the evil effect Perhaps, however, a faithful minister would not be authorized to refuse sitting with such an one, in a council or association.

4. With ministers of the fifth and sixth classes an evangelical minister may hold the highest degree of communion. If the neighboring ministers are moral, exemplary, and orthodox, without spirituality, his connexion with them will be less agreeable, than with those who drink into the same spirit; whose hearts glow with the love of Christ. But with both he may doubtless live on terms of intimacy, and fulfil his duty to Christ and the people over whom the Holy Ghost has made him an overseer, by admitting them to his pulpit O that all who are called ambassadors of Christ would mind and speak the same things, and strive together for *the faith* of the Gospel. Then

would they all find, as many now do, how pleasant it is for brethren to dwell and labor together in unity.

It only remains to inquire what rule should regulate ministerial intercourse with those, who are unexceptionable in their lives, and do not expressly avow and advocate a system of error; but whose preaching is in its effects subversive of the truth.

5. A servant of Christ may exercise to men of this class, (the fourth as above) two kinds of intercourse; but must withhold the third. In other words, he may acknowledge their official character, and unite with them in councils and associations, but not in exchange of labors and other acts of strict fellowship.

As this is the principal object of inquiry, and probably the only disputed point on this subject, (except among those who find no heresy in the world,) my remarks will be more particular.

All will admit, that to such men we should extend the first degree of intercourse.

Some deem it inconsistent to decline exchanges and yet unite in councils and associations. I believe it is not inconsistent, and will assign my reasons.

If an association has a special bond of union, it would be improper for me to unite with them, and for each individual to unite with me, unless we could all assent to the principles of union; and after union upon special principles, I ought to have fellowship with every member, so far as those principles require. But if neighboring ministers associate on the simple

at each acknowl-
others as regular
sters, I may come
em, and make no
ions of fellowship,
no higher degree
I should meet one
house of a friend,
place, and address
le. If strict fellow-
implied in associa-
ssociate, yet not be
n refusing to ex-
terial labors
jection to meeting
the same princi-
d there to perform
ch I am called   I
e in calling others
is duty. The min-
se supposed, is not
aracter, as that I
onsidered by the
niving at manifest
cr heresy, if I
h him on the occa-
not understood to
probation of all the
he council, in ev-
sitting with them.
another service.
to it in connexion
men, merely ac-
that they are in the
fice; and, if it is
ny religious opin-
ent from theirs, I
othing by doing it.
h good; I may pre-
k whereas, if I had
g, I should have
self from the op-

anging labors with
r inviting him to
e people of my
ltogether volunta-
to a service; it is
to see, that he is
qualified for that service. If I
have reason to believe he will
subvert the truth, it is clearly
my duty not to invite him to
preach.

The importance of this subject constrains me to add something more upon the character
of the preachers here intended.
I mean to include in this class
all those, who do not preach the
essential truths of the Gospel. A
man may not *deny* these truths,
and yet neglect to preach them;
or he may so intermix truth with
error, as to lead his hearers in
the way to death and hell. There
are some, who preach the truth
substantially but indistinctly   I
would extend the hand of strict
fellowship to all such as appear
to be advocates of the grace of
God to sinners through Christ
our Lord; and who preach so
much truth, as that their preaching tends, on the whole, to lead
their hearers in the way of
life. It is evident that our Lord
would not send an ambassador,
who did not in the midst of all
his infirmities and mistakes deliver that truth, which is able to
save the soul. He will be so explicit, as that his people will be
able to learn, essentially, what
the Lord their God has said.
He will not give such an uncertain sound with the trumpet, as
that no one shall understand how
to prepare himself for the battle. He will not address rebels
as if they were obedient subjects; nor leave a trembling inquiring sinner in doubt concerning the author and the way of
pardon, righteousness and life.
He who fails in thus commend-
ing himself to men as the servant
of Christ, cannot surely be fully

accredited by the faithful servants of their Lord. Our principal cause of complaint with respect to some ministers is, that they omit some important truths, while they preach others, thus shunning to declare the *whole counsel of God;* that they give very general, vague, and inadequate views of the doctrines they *do* preach; that when they exhibit an important truth, they totally pervert it by a misapplication; that they mingle the truth, when they exhibit it at all, with much carnal reasoning and heathen morality. A few examples will illustrate my meaning. Some have called upon their hearers to believe in Christ, and have represented him as the Savior of the world, who yet never speak of the excellence of his nature, and the glories of his person, as the true God manifest in the flesh; thus passing over, though not expressly denying, the mystery of godliness. Some have told sinners they must be saved by the righteousness of Christ, and have yet directed them to trust in their own righteousness. They have passed over, if not directly denied, the great doctrine of regeneration by special divine influence. They totally obscure the bright effulgent glory of the divine justice, and of God's holy law, by saying that the law is good, but exceedingly strict; and that God is not so hard a master as to require or expect a perfect obedience and conformity from his frail, ignorant unfortunate creatures, especially under the Gospel dispensation, and since Christ has kindly alleviated the burden we were not able to bear, appeased

the anger of God, and brought down the divine demands to suit our fallen state and character. They often destroy the good effect of all the truth they have taught, or rather give it a very pernicious effect, by forgetting that most of their hearers are, and all have been, rebels against God, and dead in trespasses and sins. This is, indeed, with many the grand failure. Forgetting that the human heart is totally corrupt, or expressly asserting the contrary, and extolling its supposed virtues, they do not preach even the *truth* of God's word, as messengers of his grace to guilty men. They do not humble the sinner at the feet of a Savior of sovereign mercy. They do not call upon rebels to submit; but rather upon obedient subjects to persevere in well doing, and perhaps to amend a few things which may be amiss. They do not lay open the deceits of a wicked heart; but, by a perverted application of the promises, quiet the fears of the impenitent, and cry peace to those who are not humble and contrite. They make no distinctions. They confound the outward morality and the amiable instincts of sinners with the evangelical obedience of the children of God. They confound the sorrows of the world, which worketh death, as in Judas and Ahab, with the godly sorrow, which is unto life. They confound speculative with transforming faith; thus bringing the devil himself, (if their principle were carried to its full length,) within the intent of the promise, *He that believeth shall be saved.*

man who preaches thus,
view, preaches another
l. He deludes those whom
s sent to alarm. He han-
ie word of God deceitful-
hides his instructions; he
s his character and office;
erts the service which he
sed to undertake; he be-
he trust his Master repos-
him; he joins the Lord's
ous subjects, flatters them
he hope of His favor, and
ts His word to the base
se of sanctioning both the
on and the deception. He
o all this, and yet not deny,
/ and expressly, one doc-
of the living oracles, when
in general terms.

h being my view of the
t, can I lend, ought I to
my voluntary aid in this
of delusion and death? Can
ly *bid him God speed*, and
ie *partaker of his evil*
' Can I open my pulpit to
and invite him to come
lude those precious souls,
I am bound to feed with
edge and understanding?
I introduce him, with a
certainty that he will ad-
sentiments pleasing to
litent men, and so much
ore calculated for recep-
ecause they are connected
ome portions of the truth;
dangerous to unwary souls,
direct and flagrant attacks
e doctrines according to
ess? Shall I invite him to
h in my stead those things
I could never preach my-
hough tortures and racks
l compel me? I desire to
cused. I will regard the
he sustains. I will not
to unite with him in those

duties to which others may have
called us both. I will not assume the office of his Judge and
mine in determining his final
state. I will admonish him as a
brother; I will bear testimony
against his conduct or principles, so far as I think it my
duty, in the spirit of meekness;
I will, God giving me grace,
pray for his conversion and salvation. But I cannot freely request him to disseminate destructive principles, and perver-
sions of the Gospel.

I confess that when I confer
with flesh and blood, when I
value the friendship and favor
of men, when I am in spirit conformed to this world, I find many vain reasonings, calculations,
and suggestions, on this subject.
But when I go into the sanctuary; when I can realize the worth
of souls, their awfully dangerous
and critical state, and the precious value of time and opportunity to *pluck them as brands
from the burning;* when I can
regard supremely the glory and
honor of God in the prevalence
of his truth, I am confirmed beyond a doubt in the course of
duty. And it is not improper to
add, that I am grieved to the
heart with the conduct of some
of my brethren, who themselves
preach and love the truth, and
yet, by exchanges, countenance
and encourage those, *who daub
with untempered mortar.* I trust
it is done through the power of
custom, and from want of satisfaction respecting the call of
duty in so difficult a case; and I
therefore intreat them to review
the subject with ardent prayer,
and close attention to the Scriptures.

It may be proper briefly to reply to the most common and plausible arguments in favor of exchanges with men of the above character.

It is said, we may do good to people, to whom we should have no access unless by exchanging labors with their ministers. But we should not do evil, even that good may come. It seems but poor policy to poison a hundred, for the chance of curing one or two, or even an equal number. Neither is he a faithful shepherd, who, from tender regard to his neighbor's flock, goes to look after them, leaving his own to the attacks of wolves, and even inviting one to guard them in his absence.

It is said, we *may* preach erroneously ourselves, and our own people ought to have the opportunity to hear others, that they may prove all opinions, and then judge. We reply, that we are unfit for the sacred trust, if we have any doubt of the certainty of the truths of the Gospel; and Satan will take all care to furnish our people with a sufficient variety of delusive hopes and plausible lies, without our connivance.

It is said, that in this way we withhold that fellowship which we professed, when we received ordination from men of this description; when we accepted the right hand from them, and gave them ours. I reply, that a candidate is not supposed to know, and very rarely does in fact know, the particular religious opinions of all the members of the council by whom he is ordained. He is bound to presume, till he has good reason to believe the contrary, that the professed servants of Christ are his real servants. Supposing this charitable presumption to prove erroneous, how can be be bound to receive and treat the known subverters of the Gospel as its true friends?

It is said, that to exclude a man from perfect fellowship by declining exchanges, is arrogant, an assumption of authority; that it is uncharitable and censorious. If so, then did Paul transgress exceedingly and frequently. To name only one instance. Would he have exchanged labors with the *angel from heaven,* whom he would lay under the anathema of Jehovah, for *preaching another Gospel?* And what was that other Gospel, which was not another? i. e. which was no Gospel at all? A deviation from the truth, which the liberal preachers of the present time would deem very trifling indeed, and no cause of the least separation, or even of admonition.

No, let us contend *earnestly for the faith once delivered to the saints,* and endeavor to be pure from the blood of all men, by preaching the truth, and guarding their minds against error. Thus let us wait for that blessed day, when *the watchmen shall see eye to eye, and when the Lord shall bring again Zion.*

AZRO.

MISCELLANEOUS.

VALEDICTORY ADDRESS.

AFTER the annual examination of the students in the Theological Seminary at Andover, one of the members of the class then about to leave the institution delivers a valedictory address. The style and sentiment of these addresses have uniformly been such as to strengthen the favorable impression made by the examination, and to do credit to the institution. At the close of the late examination, Mr. THOMAS H. GALLAUDET, of Hartford, Conn. performed this part of the anniversary solemnities. We applied for a copy of his address, and are gratified in being able to lay it before our readers. ED.

IT is very grateful to those, who are just leaving this seminary, thus to have an opportunity of bidding all connected with it an affectionate farewell. As we exchange this peaceful retreat for the busy and momentous scenes of untried action, we cannot but look, with a melancholy pleasure, on the countenances of friends, whom many of us now see for the last time. Their united presence awakens a thousand associations in our minds, and fills the past, the present and the future, with the deepest interest.

If we retrace the "lines" of life, which have "fallen to us" so pleasantly for three years past, here are those venerable men through whose generosity and guardianship we have received from Heaven our "goodly heritage." If we review the steps we have trod, however few and feeble, in pursuit of religious truth and of those gifts and graces which the sacred office requires, here are those faithful instructors who have opened to

us the fields of their own knowledge, guided us in our various researches, and labored, by their prayers and counsels, to direct us in the path of usefulness and duty. Here, too, are our fellow-students, whose Christian friendship and converse have smoothed the occasional difficulties of our way, and from whom we are soon to be separated, to wander in a mazy world, and to labor in whatever part of the vineyard our common Master may see fit to place us.

If separation is ever painful, and the expression of sorrow becoming, then might we be indulged, at this time, in giving vent to our feelings.—But we forbear,—and choose rather to shed a more cheerful aspect on the scene, by considering, that we are drawing nearer the goal to which our eye has been long directed; that we are about to pursue a course which, though arduous, is delightful; and that those, whose kind offices we are soon to lose, will still accompany us with their prayers, that we may "run" with fidelity and "patience the race that is set before us." We will forget, then, "those things which are behind, and reaching forth unto those things which are before, press toward the mark, for the prize of the high calling of God in Christ Jesus." Our emotions shall be those of a serene and joyful gratitude for the advantages which we have so liberally enjoyed at this seminary, and for the hope we may venture to entertain, though "with fear and trembling," of being made, in some humble degree, the useful instruments of promoting the cause of the Redeemer. While we thus acknowledge the goodness of God, and recognize Him alone as the author of all our blessings, we are not unmindful how much we owe to those who have been the generous stewards of his bounty. And they will pardon us, if we take this public opportunity of presenting to them our united thanks, for the liberality which founded, and the care which has fostered, this seminary, in the benefits of which we have so richly participated.

Respected Founders, Benefactors and Guardians,

We have learned from the history of the institution, whose sixth anniversary is this day celebrated, what were the motives which led to its establishment, and what are the objects it was designed to accomplish; motives and objects commensurate with all that is of real interest in this life, and of awful import in the future. For what is the *end of our being?* Something above this low vale, in which we grope, of fleeting and shadowy images. Something beyond the dazzling top of worldly grandeur, to which, for ages, the ardent eye of genius, and the step of panting ambition have been directed. Something, which he sees not, whose gaze is bounded by the horizon of this earthy ball, however proud may be the eminence on which he stands, however keen the glance and extensive the scope of his intellectual vision. Something which was hid from the "wise and prudent" of heathen antiquity, save where its few and scattered rays penetrated their moral midnight, through the medium of traditionary revelation. On us revelation beams in meridian splendor. The Gospel has shed the clear light of eternity on what would else have remained dark and gloomy. It has shown us whither our path through this life leads. It has extended our sphere of vision into the boundless regions of futurity, and invested every thing here below with a sublime dignity and importance, by linking it, most indissolubly, to the eternal destiny which awaits us. It has taught us, that the *great end of our being* is to promote the glory of God and the welfare of the Redeemer's kingdom, and that man's truest happiness is to devote to these objects the best affections of his heart, and the most earnest labors of his hands. Many there are, who are wise to obey this heavenly monitor, according to the humble measure of their talents, and the limited sphere of their exertions. But to a few only is given the exalted pleasure of bearing a conspicuous part in this cause of God; of contributing from their substance the ample resources which it requires, or of promoting by their influence and guiding by their wisdom its grand and comprehensive movements. *Of this class are Buchanan and Wilberforce;* men, who discern a meaning in the aspect of human affairs, which eludes the wisdom of this world; and standing on a higher eminence than they occupy, who compose the cabinets of kings and wield the destinies of empire,—and looking beyond the narrow maxims of state-policy and the petty interests of rival nations,--observe in the progress of human events the silent though sure advance of the Redeemer's cause to its final victory and triumph. These are the men whose hearts glow, and whose hands toil, in the business of doing good, upon a scale worthy of their own character, and of the cause in which they are engaged.

With such spirits did you associate, Respected Founders, Benefactors and Guardians, and for such objects, in the establishment of this seminary. For without assigning to your generous exertions the precise rank which they hold among the various noble projects of Christian benevolence, which have, of late years, engrossed the attention and called forth the efforts of the friends of Zion, we may venture so far to "magnify" our expected "office," as to say, that without a *faithful and learned ministry*, no sober hopes can be indulged of extending the sway of the Redeemer's kingdom. To furnish such a ministry has been the object of your beneficence. Future generations in our own country, nay, in these regions of the east, which now sit in darkness, will have reason to embalm your names in their memory, and thank the Giver of "every good and perfect gift" for having sent them, through your instrumentality, the words of eternal life.—*Embalm your names in their memory!* Alas! we may yet have to perform this melancholy duty, as we now cherish the grateful remembrance of those who were originally associated with you in this pious undertaking. The generous Norris and his *consort*, the ven-

erable Abbot have left you; and she,[*] too, the ornament of her sex, whose graces adorned with their milder lustre the splendor of your united benevolence. They *rest from their labors, and their works do follow them.* We have heard the history of their prayers and efforts, together with yours, for the establishment and prosperity of this seminary. We will ever retain the recollection of this goodness. And, as we have access to the throne of grace, we will pray Almighty God, that your path like theirs, may *shine more and more unto the perfect day;* that the sun of your declining years may sit cloudless and serene; and that the morning may at length beam upon you of a glorious and happy resurrection. Respected Founders, Benefactors and Guardians, we bid you an affectionate farewell.

Reverend Professors,

Through your hands we have more immediately received the benefits of this seminary. We owe you many thanks for the paternal solicitude, with which you have watched over us, and for the kind manner in which you have encouraged us, at all times, to resort to you for counsel and advice. And while there throbs in our hearts one pulse of

[*] The reader, who is acquainted with the origin and progress of the Theological Seminary, need not be informed, that the late Madam *Phebe Phillips*, relict of the late Hon. *Samuel Phillips*, is here alluded to. The pious liberality of that excellent lady endeared her name to many Christians who never saw her; and her amiable manners, hospitality, kindness, sincerity, and active benevolence, made a deep and lasting impression on all, who were intimately acquainted with her. For a more particular account of Mrs. Phillips, see the Panoplist for January 1813, p. 35. E.

manly independence; while we continue to claim the unalienable rights of conscience, and to cherish a sober though generous freedom of inquiry in pursuit of religious truth, we will never forget the candor, the condescension, the affability, we had almost said the familiarity, with which you have guided our investigations. Here we have been free from the fetters which dogmatical wisdom imposes. Here we have been encouraged to form our opinions from the *pure word of God*, and, without reserve, to suggest doubts, to propose difficulties, and to offer, fearless of censure, our own views and illustrations of whatever subject has engrossed our attention. You have exercised no dominion over our faith but that of truth. You have thus enabled us to settle our opinions on an immoveable basis; not like the sandy foundation, for ever shifting, trembling, and ready to fall, of *his* belief, who relies on *mere human authority*, and who, therefore, has always reason to suspect the influence of prejudice on his mind, and to fear lest his sentiments change just as fast as he finds an oracle, which he may deem wiser than his former one. Still, we would ever bear in mind, what you have so often inculcated upon us, that mere human attainments and soundness of religious doctrine are worth nothing without fervent piety and an ardent love for the souls of men; that the work in which we hope to engage is one of awful responsibility; that the wisdom of God enlightening our minds, and his grace purifying our hearts can alone qualify us for it; and that nothing but

his "strength made perfect in our weakness" can carry us through its important and arduous duties.—We solicit, dear Sirs, the continuance of your prayers, that we may "be strong in the grace which is in Christ Jesus," and "faithful unto the death" in his service. May you long continue to adorn the station which you now fill, and to be made the happy instruments, under God, of training up a succession of faithful workmen for those extensive fields of spiritual labor which, we trust, are growing whiter and whiter unto the harvest. Reverend Professors, we bid you an affectionate farewell.

And now, what shall we say to you, beloved brethren, whom we leave behind.—Our minds love to linger on the many peaceful and happy hours we have spent with you within these sacred walls. In this "pavilion" of security, while others have been stunned with "the confused noise" of the "battle of the warrior," and seen "garments rolled in blood," we have heard at a distance "the noise of the seas, the noise of their waves, and the tumult of the people." Our employment has been the delightful one of "inclining the ear unto wisdom, and applying the heart to understanding;" of "searching for the hid treasures" of that divine knowledge, into which "angels desire to look." Surely we have reason to say, "Blessed be the Lord; for he hath shewed us his marvellous kindness in a strong city." We are soon to leave you, perhaps no more to see you on this side the grave. Will you suffer us to urge upon you, it is our last expression of

), the solemn duty of
ing yourselves, with
le soul, and strength
to the service of the
:. Alas! we have to
r own great deficiency
pect. And, believe us,
ı come to tɪead in our
eps, no pang will be
an the recollection of
ted by indolence, or
by a worldly spirit; no
n will be sweeter than
ːk upon hours devoted
"Gird up," then, "the
ʻour minds." Where
ɔitered, do ye "so run
ɪy obtain." And hav-
t a good fight," having
your course," having
faith," may you at last
at "crown of righteous-
h the Lord, the right-
e, shall give—at that
ı all that love his ap-
When you surround
ultar, where we have
ɪingled our devotions
ɪ, may we have a re-
:e in your prayers, that
ʻhether called to labor
ɪ or in a foreign land,
ure hardness as good
ɪf Jesus Christ," and
ɛngth the unspeakable
ʻ being admitted, with
hose mansions of rest,
ɛre will be no more
ʋith sin, and where
ı meet shall meet to
ore forever. Beloved
we bid you an affec-
ʻewell.

you farewell, too, all
of this seminary, who
day encouraged and
ɪs by your presence.
you join us in the last
y we have of publicly
expressing our wishes for the
prosperity of this establishment,
by responding the petition of its
venerable founders, when they
consecrated it to God;—"devoutly imploring the Father of lights
richly to endue with wisdom
from above all his servants the
visitors and trustees of this seminary, and with spiritual understanding the professors therein; that, being illuminated by the
Holy Spirit, their doctrine may
drop as the rain, and that their
pupils may become trees of renown in the courts of our God,
whereby he may be glorified.".

ANECDOTE.

THE following statement, which
is made on the authority of the
person who is the subject of it,
is thought to exhibit no uncommon case, and to give a fair representation of the depraved
heart of man.

The person in question lived
as a mere man of the world,
careful in a good degree about
any thing which would destroy
his character among men; but,
until about thirty-seven years of
age, he appeared to be totally
void of any religious principle,
and with respect to any thing
like religious practice he was
but little removed from a mere
infidel. About eight years ago
he became a hopeful subject of
converting grace, and has ever
since supported a fair religious
character. After this change,
he often endeavored to recollect
what he previously believed on
the subject of religion; but could
not recollect any thing which deserved the name of belief. He

had tried to be a Universalist;—he had tried to be a Deist;—he had tried to believe that there is no future state; that this world is man's all; and that the sum of human happiness is to make the most of this world, without reference to a Supreme being or a future state. There was but one thing in which he could recollect that he was uniform, and that was, *in hating the peculiar truths of the Gospel.*

WHAT IS IDOLATRY?

From Saurin's Sermons, vol. i, p. 368.

"To consider a creature as the cause of human felicity, is to pay him the homage of adoration, and to commit idolatry. The avaricious man is an idolater; the ambitious man is an idolater; the voluptuous man is an idolater: and to render to a creature the homage of fear is also idolatry; for supreme fear is as much due to God alone as supreme hope. He, who fears war, and doth not fear the God who sends war, is an idolater. He, who fears the plague, and doth not fear the God who sends the plague, is an idolater.

"It is idolatry, in public or in private adversities, to have recourse to second causes, to little subordinate deities, so as to neglect to appease the wrath of the Supreme God. To consult the wise, to assemble a council, to man fleets, to raise armies, to build forts, to elevate ramparts, and not consider the succor of heaven, which alone is capable of giving success to all such means, is to be guilty of idolatry."

PART OF AN ORIGINAL LETTER FROM GOV. BELCHER TO PRESIDENT EDWARDS.

Dear Mr. Edwards.
    Sir,
    "ALTHOUGH I am often obliged to begin my letters by way of apology for answering your good and very kind letters so unduly, and so much out of course. yet I have great dependence on your candor and goodness, when I mention the date of your last favor of Nov. 14, 1750, which I received about three months after its date.
    I am sure I want no love, respect, or affection, for Mr. Edwards, but, although this is a small government, yet the perplexities of it are not so, and those, with my private affairs, I sometimes think too much engross me: *Verbum sapienti sat est;* and so I will go on.
    In answer to all you say, I am quite ashamed and tremble when I think what a mistaken opinion you have of me, who am so worthless a worm. Yet I greatly thank you that it sets before me this lesson, to prostrate myself at the footstool of sovereign grace, that I may be honored with being made though one of the least instruments in advancing the kingdom of the blessed God, our Savior, in this world.
    If I know my own heart I think I am not ashamed of the cross of Christ: God grant I may never be a shame to it. I am always longing to say, as St. Peter to his Master, *Lord Jesus, thou knowest all things; thou knowest that I love thee.* Amen and Amen.
    As cold waters are to a thirsty

do the intelligences you
e rejoice my heart, and
my bowels; inasmuch as
Jesus seems to be casting
assionate eye upon the
:ople in our western bor-
id is setting himself up a
lighten the Gentiles, as
the glory of his people

re an account from my
in England, as also from
of the generous disposi-
some of the royal family,
as among other well-dis-
Christians, to bring for-
he civilizing and Chris-
g of our Indian neigh-
your parts, for which
raise and honor are due
icious and merciful God.
e the difference you men-
:ween Col. W— and Mr.
made up; for how can it
between good Christians;
dare they, as they ought,
ur Lord's most excellent

And since I have got to
ridge, let me rejoice ex-
;ly and congratulate you,
d has lifted up the light
ountenance upon you, in
omfortable settlement at
ce; where, in the strength
ist, may you go on con-
; and to conquer, and be
strument, in the hand of
eat Head of the Church,
ng down the strong holds
nd Satan, and more espe-
of taking off the scales
ie eyes of the benighted
, who have been so long
chains by the prince of
ss: and may you have
rophies from them to add
crown of joy, in the great
the appearance of your
nd Master: Amen.

I thank you, Sir, for the printed account you sent me of what
passed in the council at Northampton, on your affair. Had I
been one of the messengers, I
must have been among the number of protesters.

Alas, Sir, what a variety of
scenes does God draw for the
prospect of his dearest children
in this world. The mysteries of
his kingdom of providence and
grace are what we cannot dive
into: for his ways are unsearchable, and past finding out. But
our Savior said to his disciples,
though you do not now know,
you shall know hereafter. Whoever may be so infinitely happy,
as to become a subject in God's
kingdom of glory, will not see
things as in a glass darkly; but
all will be plain as face to face.
It is then certainly our duty to
be always in a state of perfect
submission and holy resignation
to Divine Providence; and, for
my own part, I rest in faith, that
in your removal to the place
where you now are, God will
best of all answer the ends of his
own glory.

We are much obliged to you
for the kind concern you express
towards the welfare of our infant
College; and I am sorry to tell
you, that Mr. Pemberton's designed voyage to Great-Britain
is entirely laid aside, as his people make so great an opposition
to his going. And this is a frown
of Providence upon our little
seminary; but, more especially
so since Mr. President Burr has
lately received letters from Scotland, that gave a most probable
prospect of our obtaining a handsome bounty from the Kirk of
Scotland, were some suitable

Chamber appertaining to said College; and that the Recording Secretary transmit a copy of this vote to the President.

Voted, That the Prudential Committee be directed to prepare and publish the annual report of the Board, including such parts of the Report of the Prudential Committee as they shall judge most useful, an abstract of the Treasurer's accounts, a statement of donations, and such other information as they shall deem proper and expedient.

The Rev. Dr. Lyman closed the session with prayer.

The preceding account is compiled from the original minutes of the Recording Secretary, with the omission of such particulars as might be uninteresting to readers generally.

REPORT OF THE PRUDENTIAL COMMITTEE.

BRETHREN,

THE last annual Report of your Committee left our missionaries in the East, on the mighty waters, uncertain where they should land, and still more doubtful where they should abide. During the year great solicitude has been felt for them; but at length that solicitude is considerably relieved. For a long season they were held in anxious suspense, painfully fluctuating between fear and hope; but at length that suspense appears to have come nearly to an end. Our last letters from them were received by the way of England about ten days ago; the latest date from Mr. Newell being the 20th of last December, at Columbo, in the Island of Ceylon; and from Messrs. Hall and Nott, the 23d of the same month, at Bombay. The principal facts and circumstances, related in their several communications, your Committee will report in order.

Messrs. Hall and Nott, as reported at our last anniversary, left Calcutta on the 20th of November, 1812, under circumstances not very pleasant, and embarked for Bombay, expecting to touch at Ceylon, and doubtful whether they should proceed any further. It appears, however, that they touched not at Ceylon, but at Pondicherry, where they staid about five weeks. The reason of this they probably assigned in a letter written at Pondicherry, to which in a subsequent letter they refer, but which has not been received. They arrived at Bombay on the 11th of February, 1813, about eleven weeks after leaving Calcutta. On their arrival, they immediately found that intelligence concerning them, forwarded from Calcutta, had reached Bombay; intelligence, disadvantageous to them, and accompanied with an expression of the will of the supreme government, that they should be sent to England. They were permitted to submit to Sir Evan Nepean, governor of Bombay, a very respectful and judicious memorial; which, together with accompanying documents, declared the views with which they came to India*—made known the patronage and instructions

* See Appendix A.

under which they had been sent forth—gave a narrative of their proceedings at Calcutta—explained the misunderstanding which had arisen between them and the supreme government there, and the reasons of their departing thence for Bombay, under circumstances so liable to misconstruction—referred their case to the well known clemency and candor of the Governor, and implored his favor and protection. Their memorial was very kindly received and considered; and every thing relating to their object and their proceedings appeared to the Governor in so satisfactory a light, that he not only allowed them to remain for the present at Bombay, but assured them of his disposition to render them every favor in his power; and even took upon himself the trouble to write a private letter in their behalf to Lord Minto, the governor general at Calcutta, with a view to remove the unfavorable impressions respecting them, which had been made on his Lordship's mind, either by misrepresentations or unexplained circumstances, and to obtain permission for them to reside at Bombay, or to go, unmolested, in pursuit of their object elsewhere. Thus encouraged, the two brethren sat down to the study of the Mahratta language, under the tuition of a Brahmin; in the hope of having the satisfaction, in due time, of preaching in that language to the natives at Bombay, and in the extensive and populous regions, in which the language is vernacular.

Sir Evan Nepean's letter appears to have been successful in satisfying the governor general's mind in regard to the character and proceedings of the two missionaries. The war, however, between the United States and Great Britain, intelligence of which had been received in India, gave rise to new difficulties. On the 25th of June the brethren were informed, by Dr. Taylor, a gentleman from whom they received many friendly offices, that the Governor, Sir Evan Nepean, had expressed his fears that, on account of the war, he should be under the necessity of sending them to England; though, as they state in their journal, "the Governor expressed to Dr. Taylor his firm confidence in their integrity, and the excellency of the character of those gentlemen by whom they were patronized."

On the 18th of August, by the advice of a Mr. Money, another gentleman to whom they were indebted for many offices of kindness, they drew up another memorial to the Governor, which was to be presented along with certain documents of a purport to shew decisively, that their mission had no connexion with the war. Mr. Money, they say, "urged us to do this immediately, as he had observed our names down at the marine office as passengers to England on the Caarmarthen, which was to have sailed about this time, but having sprung a leak will be detained a month or two." From this memorial, that something of the spirit and feelings of the brethren may be perceived and felt, the following passages are extracted:—

"Right Honorable Sir,

"When we consider that both English and American Christians are interested in our success—that already much time and money have been expended in our enterprise, and that much more must be expended if we are sent from this place;—that we must then be in perfect uncertainty, whether we shall ever be allowed to preach to the destitute the unsearchable riches of Christ;—and especially when we consider the command of that ascending Lord, in whom we all hope, and whom we would obey;—we feel justified, we feel compelled, by motives which we dare not resist, to intreat your Excellency's favor. To ourselves it cannot but be supposed, that to fail in our object must be in the highest degree trying. Our feelings are deeply interested, it may well be supposed, in our object, to which we have been looking for so many years—for which we have left our country, our prospects, and our dearest friends—to which we are conscientiously, and, by the help of God, unalterably devoted—in which the hearts of Christians are universally engaged, without distinction of country, and which, we cannot doubt, is under the favorable eye of our Lord and Master."

"Your Excellency's well known desire for promoting Christian knowledge, and the certainty that we should be in future as really under the direction and at the disposal of your Excellency, as at the present moment, encourage us in requesting that we may be allowed to remain, at least till it may be learned whether there will be a speedy termination of the unhappy war."

On the next day they write, "Having prepared the preceding memorial, we went with it to Mr. Money, being desirous to forward it as soon as possible, on account of a report which we last evening heard, that we were to go to England on the Sir Godfrey Webster, to sail on Sabbath next. At breakfast with Mr. Money, we saw the superintendant of embarkation, who told us, that he had, by order of the Governor, yesterday settled every arrangement for our going in the Sir Godfrey Webster, and that every pains had been taken to make us comfortable, and that we had been provided for suitably to our ministerial character. We were much distressed by this intelligence, and especially as we were entirely unprepared for such a voyage. Mr. Money immediately waited on the Governor, to tell him our unprepared state, and to hand him the above petition. On his return he informed us, that the Governor's orders from Bengal were such, that he would be unable to allow us to remain; but, as he was unwilling to put us to any inconvenience, he would allow us to stay until the sailing of the Caarmarthen, which is to be in about six weeks. We then waited on the Governor ourselves, and expressed our thanks for his kindness now, and on former occasions. He told us, that he had supposed us prepared on the ground of what he had told Dr. Taylor; and endeavored to justify the Supreme Government in sending us away on account of the war. He declared his perfect confidence that we were innocent and harmless men, whose weapons of warfare were not carnal but spiritual. He likewise told us that he had succeeded in removing the unfavorable impressions which had been made on the mind of the Governor General, to effect which he had written to Lord Minto a private letter. Thus it pleases the Lord to deal with us. We have never been covered with so thick a cloud."

Things remained in this posture until about the middle of September. At that time the brethren received from Calcutta the letters which about ten months before had been sent out for them from this country by the Alligator; and which, say they, "afforded us a pleasure which we cannot describe." With the advice of particular friends, they submitted to the Governor's inspection the official letter to them from the Corresponding Secretary, accompanied with a note in which they say; "We extremely regret that the accompanying letter did not come to hand at an earlier period.— Though received at so late an hour, we should not feel that we were faithful to our Patrons, to a numerous body of Christian friends, and to the Savior's cause, were we not to beg the liberty of presenting it to your Excellency for perusal. Its general tenor, and particularly the information which it gives of the appointment of a Committee at Calcutta to co-operate in our mission, seems to us fully to declare, that our Society is simply engaged in the great work, dear to English and American Christians, of spreading Christian knowledge and Christian hopes. The gentlemen, whom we now understand to constitute the Committee, are the Rev. Dr. Carey, the Rev. Mr. Thomason, Chaplain, and George Udny, Esq. the latter two in the place of Dr. Brown, and J. H Harrington, Esq. To this Committee we yesterday made known our unhappy situation; and we beg leave to express our desire to your Excellency, that our departure from this Presidency may be so long delayed, as to give them an opportunity of acquainting the Governor General with their relation to us, and of removing, if possible, the objections to our stay arising from the unhappy war."

The next day after this note was delivered, they write in their journal, "Mr. Nott waited on the Governor this morning at his request. He mentioned, that he felt greatly embarrassed on account of yesterday's letter to him;—that he wished to do all in his power for us; that he would think on the subject, and give an answer in two or three days. He did not hesitate in saying, that were he left to himself, he could not send us away."

The Committee of Agency for our affairs in India, appointed by the Prudential Committee, as this Board will recollect, were the Hon. John H. Harington, Esq. and Drs. Carey and Brown. But when our communications arrived at Calcutta, Dr. Brown was dead, and Judge Harington was absent. Under these circumstances, Dr. Carey thought fit to appoint the Rev. Thomas Thomason* in the place of Dr. Brown, and they unitedly requested George Udny, Esq.† to act in the place of Mr. Harington. Intelligence

---

* The Prudential Committee, before receiving this communication, had appointed the Rev. Mr. Thomason to supply the vacancy occasioned by the death of the Rev. Dr. Brown.

† George Udny, Esq. has been for many years a member of the Supreme Council in the Bengal Government, and has been uniformly favorable to the diffusion of Christianity in India. The Supreme Council consists of four members with the Governor General at their head.

of this arrangement was duly communicated to the two brethren at
Bombay; and they, perceiving the advantage which it offered them,
immediately addressed the letter, referred to in the above cited note
to Governor Nepean, to the Committee at Calcutta, for the purpose
of engaging their good offices with the Governor-General in their
behalf.

About five days after this, the two brethren received letters from
Mr. Newell at Columbo, and from the Rev. Mr. Thomson, Chaplain
at Madras, from which the following extracts are given. Mr.
Newell, under date of Aug. 18th, 1813, writes, "I have had repeated
assurances from the Hon. and Rev. Mr. Twistleton, senior Chaplain, and Mr. Brisset the other Chaplain, the Governor's brother-
in-law, that as many of my friends as choose to come here shall be
safe, and have liberty to go to any part of the Island." Mr. Thomson, under date of Sept. 7th, writes, "You have, I believe, received
notice from Mr. Newell, that you will be welcomed at Ceylon. I
am warranted by letters from the Hon. and Rev. Mr. Twistleton, to
confirm it. I think you should lose no time in submitting this to
the Governor, Sir Evan Nepean, and requesting leave to retire
thither, instead of being sent to England."

Accordingly, after prayerful consideration, Messrs. Hall and
Nott, on the 22d Sept. submitted the communications from Messrs.
Thomson and Newell to the Governor, accompanied with a memorial, in which they say, "After having read them, we beg your Excellency to regard with a favorable eye the pure, peaceful, inoffensive, Christian character of our mission, proved incontestably by our
instructions, by our letters, and by the appointment of a Committee
of British gentlemen of the clergy and laity to co-operate in the
mission, which we have had the happiness of making known to
your Excellency; and to bestow an indulgent consideration on our
present distressing situation, which must be aggravated in a severe
degree, if we are sent across the seas to a foreign land, divided
from our own by an unhappy war, the commencement of which we
have sincerely deprecated, and for the conclusion of which we
earnestly pray."—"It is still our highest wish to remain here, and
render ourselves useful as instructors of youth and preachers of
the Gospel, under the protection of your Excellency's government,
where the spiritual miseries of thousands call so loudly for the
blessings of Christianity, where there are so many facilities for diffusing those blessings, and from which we cannot be sent without
so much grief to numerous Christians, and so much discouragement to others, who are desiring to leave their own country, and go
to preach Christ in Pagan lands. It is only therefore in the last
resort, and with the hope of preventing the entire defeat of our
pious attempt, that we implore your Excellency's sanction to
remove ourselves from this place to Ceylon, where we have such
assurances of a favorable reception, where we cannot but be under
the superintending eye of a British government, and where, we
trust, our conduct will be unobjectionable to his Excellency Governor Brownrigg."

In their journal, Oct. 2, the brethren write, "Mr. Money having, at our request, conferred with the Governor concerning our petition, received this day from his Excellency a note nearly as follows: find myself awkwardly situated relative to the two Missionaries whom I wish to serve. On the 20th of August I wrote to Lord Minto, and I ought to have received his Lordship's answer some days since, and am now in daily expectation of it. I told his Lordship, that I understood he had changed his plan concerning missionaries, and allowed one in similar circumstances to remain in Bengal; and that now there was time for him to shew the same favor to Messrs. Hall and Nott; but that if I should receive no new commands from his Lordship, I should send them to England by the next ships. I had thought of another plan for them, which was, that in case Captain Digby should arrive in season, I should request him to give them a passage in the Cornwallis, which, as that ship will stop at Ceylon, would give Governor Brownrigg an opportunity to take such measures relative to them as he might judge proper." Nine days afterwards they write, "This day dined with the Governor. He added nothing to what he had said in Mr. Money's note. He repeated that he must send us in one of these ships, unless something new should take place." And five days after this, that is, on the 16th of October, they say, "This afternoon we received a note from our friend W. T. Money Esq. informing us, that the Governor had failed in his application to Captain Digby. He says, 'Sir Evan sincerely regrets his ill success. I am sure he felt, and does now feel, much interest for you—Under these auspicious circumstances, nothing now remains, but to prepare for your departure in the Caarmarthen.'"

The Caarmarthen was, at this time, on the eve of sailing, and there remained to Messrs. Hall and Nott scarcely a gleam of hope that they should avoid being sent to England. On the 18th of October, however, they had information of a vessel going to Cochin; learned that she would give them a passage, if they could be ready to go on board in about four or five hours; and understood, that from Cochin she would shortly convey them to Columbo in Ceylon. The time for deliberation was short. They concluded to go; and accordingly, taking some of their most necessary things, they embarked; leaving Mrs. Nott with her child, and some notes hastily written to acquaint their friends at Bombay with the fact and the reasons of their departure. On the 30th of the same month they arrived at Cochin, where they were very kindly received, and during their stay very generously entertained, by Mr. Pearson, magistrate of the place.

On the 5th of November they write in their journal. "For five days we have been laboriously employed in travelling among, and inquiring about, the Jews and Christians. We have visited the College at Valipoli and several Catholic churches; Candenade, the see of the late Syrian Bishop, and the synagogues of the Jews at Cochin. We have carefully committed to paper what information we could obtain, having been kindly furnished with such facilities the place affords."

The vessel, which had conveyed them to Cochin, could not, as they had expected, convey them thence to Columbo. While waiting and seeking for a passage, and just as one seemed to be presenting itself, an order arrived from Bombay, requiring them to be sent back to that place. They accordingly returned, after an absence of almost a month. With their private departure from Bombay Sir Evan Nepean was not well pleased; as it might, from the favor which he had shewn them, subject him to censure from the General Government, for imputed connivance or delinquency. In a respectful and able memorial to him, however, after their return, they justified the procedure on the broad principle, that the authority of the Lord Jesus, under which they had been sent forth to preach the Gospel to the heathen, was paramount to any civil authority, which would frustrate, or counteract their mission;* and the Governor at length was so far satisfied, as to allow them to leave the ship in which they had been brought back to Bombay, and which for several days after their arrival they were not allowed to leave, and, free from all duress, to occupy a house provided for their accommodation in the city Still he considered himself as required by the Supreme Government to send them to England; and as under particular obligations, from assurances which he had given the Governor General, to send them by the earliest regular conveyance.

On their return into the city, the two brethren were received by their worthy friends there with great joy, and with expressions and tokens of undiminished affection, confidence, and respect. Very soon afterwards, on the 10th of Dec. they received; from the Rev. Mr. Thomason of Calcutta, the last of three letters.† bearing date Oct. 8th, and 13th, and Nov. 19th, 1813, in answer to theirs of Sept. 15th, addressed to our agents at Calcutta. In these letters, Mr. Thomason, with strong expressions of Christian affection, and of desire to promote the great object of their mission, related to them the measures which he and his colleagues in the agency had taken in their behalf with the Government, and the success with which those measures had been attended. "The last letter, in particular," say the brethren, "filled us with joy and thanksgiving to God. We immediately sent a copy of it to brother Newell, and to Mr. Money on the Gauts. Our friends advise to wait a day or two in hopes of something more full from Calcutta; and if nothing should come, to lay them before the Governor." Accordingly, on the 13th of December, they sent to the Governor the following note, enclosing the two last letters from Mr. Thomason.

　　　"Right Honorable Sir,
"Having always been convinced that the resolution to send us from this country emanated solely from the orders of the Supreme Government, and not from the disposition of your Excellency, which we know to be friendly to the evangelical object of our mission;

* See Appendix B　　　　　　　　　　　† See Appendix C.

and having received letters from Calcutta, evincing a change of sentiments in the late Governor General, and the conviction of Lord Moira the present Governor General, "that our intentions are to do good, and that no conceivable public injury can arise from our staying," and that his Lordship "spoke very decidedly about our being allowed to stay;" we beg to submit to the perusal of your Excellency two letters, dated 13th Oct. and 19th ult. addressed to us by the Rev. Thomas Thomason, a most respectable minister of the Church of England, resident at Calcutta. We trust that your Excellency will consider these letters as containing decisive evidence of the favorable inclinations of Lords Minto and Moira in regard to our present circumstances, and future views: and that with this proof of the light in which our mission is now regarded by the supreme British authority in India, your Excellency will have no difficulty in permitting us to remain in this place.

"It is with inexpressible satisfaction that we are enabled, by a kind and overruling Providence, to present these communications to your Excellency, at this very interesting moment.

We have the honor to be, &c. &c.

"Bombay, Dec. 13, 1813."

On the 16th Dec. their friend Mr. Money informed the two brethren, "that he had just been with the Governor, who mentioned, that no orders having been received from Calcutta concerning their stay, and he being still under the positive orders of the supreme Government to send them away, he must now send them." And on the 20th, R. T. Goodwin, Esq. the senior magistrate of police, officially notified them, "that a passage was to be provided for them to England on board the Charles Mills."

The Charles Mills was then under orders to sail on the 22d of the same month, only two days after this note was given. At this critical moment they drew up a memorial to the Governor, as their last appeal:* a memorial, which they considered as a private communication, addressed to his Excellency, not as a Governor only, but as a man, and a Christian; which was written with the feelings and the solemnity of the occasion; and which, as they are careful to note, they viewed as of a confidential nature, but that the worthy Governor was pleased himself to give it publicity. It appears to have been generously received by the Governor, according to his accustomed goodness, and to have had its desired effect.

On the next day after sending this letter, the brethren write in their journal, "We continued our preparations —By two o'clock, (same day) our things were packed and labelled; by three the Coolies (porters) were all here; the things were all carried below; the boats were engaged to carry them on board ship, and the carpenter to go and fasten them. The friend, who had charge of the things, then went to the Captain for orders to have them received on board. The Captain went to the pay office for the money for our passage; the money was refused, and it was reported, that we were

* See Appendix D

not to go. The friend returned with this information, and the things were all put into a room below, and the coolies dismissed. About five, Mr. Goodwin, the senior magistrate of police, called upon us to say, that our letter had been communicated to the Council; and that upon examination, it had been found, that no orders of any kind had been received from Bengal, of a later date than the 19th of November, and that the government would allow us to remain, until they should receive further orders from Bengal concerning us. This intelligence at this decisive moment has filled us with great joy; and given us great hopes, that we shall yet be allowed to remain at Bombay. How wonderful and how merciful are God's dealings with us!"

The next morning, 22d Dec. they received the following official note.

"*To the Rev. Gordon Hall, and the Rev. Samuel Nott, American Missionaries.*

"Gentlemen,

"I am directed by the Right Honorable, the Governor in Council, to acquaint you, that under the expectation of receiving some further instructions from the Supreme Government respecting you, he has determined to defer the carrying the directions he has received into execution, until such instructions shall arrive.

"I am, gentlemen, your obedient servant,

W. NEWNHAM, Sec. to Government."

"*Bombay Castle, Dee. 21,* 1813.

Our last letters from these brethren appear to have been forwarded to England, by the same ship, in which they themselves expected to have been conveyed thither, and which sailed from Bombay on the 23d of December. Later than this date we have no intelligence from them. From the facts and circumstances now communicated, however, your Committee derive a pleasing confidence, that our mission may obtain an establishment at Bombay: and they are persuaded that this whole Board, and the Christian public extensively, will unite with them in adoring the goodness of the Lord, so remarkably displayed in the signal interpositions of his providence in behalf of our missionaries. Under Providence, grateful acknowledgments are due to the Right Honorable Sir Evan Nepean for the candor, magnanimity, and kindness, exhibited in his treatment of the missionaries, so creditable to his character, as a magistrate, and a Christian. Nor can the Committee forbear to express their high sense of the admirable spirit and conduct, shewn by the missionaries themselves, in the circumstances of severe trial in which they have been called to act. The evidence here exhibited of their firmness, their perseverance, their wisdom, and their devotedness to the great object of their mission, cannot fail to raise them in the estimation and affection of this Board, and to secure to them the confidence and favor of the Christian public.

On the 24th of Feb. 1813, Mr. Newell embarked at the Mauritius on board a Portuguese brig, bound to Bombay, but destined to touch at Point de Galle in the Island of Ceylon. At the latter place he expected to meet one or both of the other brethren; but on his arrival he learned that they were both gone to Bombay. Supposing, however, that they would not be allowed to remain there, he thought it best for him to stay in Ceylon, where he was assured of the protection and favor of Governor Brownrigg, and other principal officers of the government. He immediately despatched a letter to the brethren at Bombay; and by the return of the mail he received an answer from them, from which he learned, that, though their situation at Bombay was quite precarious, yet they·had considerable hope that they should be allowed to establish themselves there, and thought it advisable for him to direct his studies with a view to that place. Accordingly, as soon as he could make arrangements for the purpose, he commenced the study of the Sangskrit, Hindoostanee, and Persian languages; and quietly pursued this study until some time in November, when, from information received from the brethren at Bombay, he felt himself compelled to give up all hope of the establishment of the mission at that place. From the time of his arrival in Ceylon, however, till the date of his last letter, he preached in English constantly once, twice, or three times a week, to English and half-cast people; of whom, he says, "there are thousands in and about Columbo, who stand in need of instruction, as much as the heathen," and among whom he hoped his labors would not be in vain. At the date of his last letter, Mr. Newell supposed that his brethren were actually on their passage to England, and that he was left alone. "Stript," says he, "of all my domestic enjoyments, by the death of my wife and child, and separated from all my dear missionary associates, I find myself a solitary pilgrim in the midst of a heathen land. My heart is sometimes quite overwhelmed with grief. But my prevailing desire is, and my determination, to try to do something for the wretched heathen around me. My conviction of the duty and practicability of evangelizing the heathen has not been diminished, but greatly increased, by all that I have witnessed in this part of the world." Thus circumstanced, he was undetermined in regard to the field in which to fix his mission; whether to remain in Ceylon, or attempt an establishment at Bussora at the head of the Persian Gulf. The reasons which weighed in his mind for the one and for the other, he states at large, and in a manner which indicates much attention and reflection.* His trials, though different from those of his brethren, have been not less painful; and appear to have been sustained in a manner not less creditable to the character of a Christian missionary. He must have been greatly rejoiced to learn, as he doubtless did in a short time, that his brethren had not been sent to England, as he supposed; and if they have been permitted to remain at Bombay, he has probably joined them there, to the great joy of them all.

Messrs. Richards and Warren, who, at the time of our last annual meeting, were, as then reported, in very eligible situations a·

* See Appendix E

Philadelphia, have just completed their respective periods of engagement there; and. so far as appears, very much to their own satisfaction, and to the satisfaction of those with whose patronage and friendly offices they have been favored.

Soon after our last annual meeting, Messrs. Benjamin C. Meigs, Burr Baldwin, Horatio Bardwell, and Daniel Poor, were admitted by the Prudential Committee, as Candidates for our missionary service; and since, after such a period and measure of trial as the Committee judged suitable, they have all, excepting Mr. Baldwin, been formally received as Missionaries, to be under the patronage and direction of this Board. Mr. Baldwin has been prevented from being thus received, by feeble health, which the Committee greatly lament, and from which they devoutly hope he will ere long be recovered.

Messrs. Richards, Warren, Meigs, Bardwell, and Poor, will hold themselves in readiness to go forth to the heathen with the glad tidings of salvation, as soon as Providence shall open the door for their being sent. At present the door at every point seems to be closed by the war; but this Board and the friends of Christian missions will not cease to pray, that the war may soon be terminated; nor are the Committee without hope, that, should it continue, some way will nevertheless be found out for the conveyance of the waiting missionaries to their destined fields of labor.

From three other young gentlemen, one now a practising physician of distinguished promise, another a student at the Theological Seminary at Princeton, and the other a student at the Theological Seminary at Andover, the Committee have received very pleasing communications, expressing their desire to be engaged in the missionary service, under the direction of this Board. But upon these applications, as they are yet quite recent, no decisive act has been passed.

It will appear, by the statements which the Treasurer will furnish, that the liberality of the Christian public toward this Board is continued and extended. New associations are formed for the purpose of contributing their aid. The number of pious persons, who are becoming acquainted with the wants and the miseries of the heathen world, and who are desirous of uniting their efforts to remove these wants and alleviate these miseries, is evidently on the increase Your Committee have reason to believe, that should Providence soon prepare the way for the establishment of missionary stations in different pagan countries, an adequate number of pious, able, devoted servants of Christ would offer themselves as heralds of the Gospel to the heathen, and the means would not be withheld of supporting them in their most laborious, as well as most benevolent, undertaking. It is a pleasing thought, and one which may be indulged without presumption, that the Redeemer will graciously bestow upon Christians in America the honor of becoming joyful instruments in promoting his cause, and advancing the progress of the millennium, not only within our own borders, but extensively also in foreign lands. How noble will be the dis-

n, should we be known as a people, to the inhabitants of dis-
ntinents and islands, not as covetous of territory,—not as am-
of poli ical dominion,—not as engrossed by commerce and
ved up by the cupidity of avarice;—but as the liberal dis-
s of unsearchable riches, as cheerfully and zealously impart-
others God's unmerited bounty to ourselves.

le regarding the subject in this point of light, your Commit-
mot refrain from expressing their joy, that this glorious
as been begun;—that it has been formally and systematically
l upon by Christians in this country;—that missionaries, in
ployment of this Board, have been engaged on the shores of
a preparing to preach to the people in their own languages;—
: Scriptures, in the common tongues of the countries, have
urchased and distributed, as a free will offering to God, from
lorable women, our *young men and maidens,* our *old men and*
s.

ght to be thankfully noticed, that many enlightened persons
a;—men of enlarged views and great acquaintance with the
—dignified magistrates and persons of professional emi-
—have most unequivocally and earnestly expressed their
ion of the necessity of missionaries, and their sense of the
ible condition of the people in a moral point of view. Per-
this description have joyfully hailed the co-operation of
ca, in the great work of evangelizing mankind, as a most de-
event. They have expressed an anxious wish, that our ef-
sy be greatly and indefinitely increased. The limits of this
, already too long perhaps, will not allow your Committee to
all the facts on the authority of which these assertions are
Many such facts have appeared, in the course of the pre-
narration, and the accompanying documents

evident also from every page of the correspondence of the
iaries, that notwithstanding all their discouragements and
cities, they have been more and more convinced, by all that
ive seen and heard, not only of the practicability and duty of
ting missions, but of its being their particular duty, as it is
tly their highest pleasure, to consider themselves as unalter-
voted to this work. They are also convinced, as their re-
discussions of this topic abundantly prove, that whatever
the design of Providence in regard to themselves or their
t, it is the duty of Christians to take it for granted, that the
f missions will prevail, and to resolve, that by the help of
nd with all reverential submission to his holy dispensations,
prevail.

agents of this Board in London have remitted to Calcutta,
earliest opportunities, the avails of our several remittances
t. We had calculated, that our missionaries would have re-
our first remittance at an earlier date than that of their last
us this remittance was sent from London by the earliest
ships of 1813. It could not, we think, be much longer de-
But, through the kindness of friends whom Providence had
up for them in every place they had visited, there was little

danger that our brethren would be put to serious inconvenience by any accidental delay of remittances.

At the conclusion of their Report, the Committee would direct their respectful attention to the Christian public. They need not solicit, what will be granted of course and without solicitation, a candid perusal of this their annual communication, and of the papers which will follow it. All who have contributed to send the blessings of the Gospel to the heathen;—all who love the prosperity of Zion, will feel a deep interest in the history of our infant mission, and, we doubt not, will perceive the necessity of continued and persevering exertions. The object in view is so transcendantly important, as not to admit of any halting or hesitation in the pursuit, while any prospect of success remains. Such a prospect will remain, we are persuaded, without suffering even a temporary eclipse, till the Gospel shall shed its benign influence on every land. With thankful acknowledgment of the many favors shewn by the Christian public to this object, and of the many prayers offered in its behalf, the Committee would animate their fathers and brethren, as well as themselves, with the exhortation, *Be not weary in well-doing; for in due season we shall reap, if we faint not.*

New Haven, Sept. 15, 1814.

APPENDIX (A.)

[On the day after their arrival at Bombay, Messrs. Hall and Nott, after taking suitable advice, put into the hands of Mr. Money, a gentleman of that place, the following petition to his Excellency, the Governor.]

To the Right Honorable Sir Evan Nepean, Governor of Bombay, &c.

Right Honorable Sir,

The Undersigned, lately arrived from America by way of Bengal, beg leave to state to your Excellency, that having been ordained to the Gospel Ministry, they have come to this country with a desire of being useful, by translating the Scriptures, by aiding in the education of children, and ultimately by making known the Gospel to some who are now ignorant of it.

Humbly trusting that these objects will meet with your Excellency's approbation, they most earnestly beg, that they may be allowed to pursue them. At the same time, they cherish the hope, that should they be permitted to remain in the country, an orderly and prudent conduct will show, that your Excellency's indulgence has not been misplaced.

They are happy indeed, Right Honorable Sir, in thus presenting the advancement of our holy religion to a Christian Governor;—one, too, who has given so many proofs of a desire for the diffusion of the Scriptures, and the promotion of happiness among mankind.

They have the honor to be, with the highest respect,
Right Honorable Sir, your most obedient
and most humble servants,

Bombay, Feb.
12, 1813.

GORDON HALL.
SAMUEL NOTT.

[On visiting the police office, the same day on which the preceding petition was forwarded, the missionaries were told, that they would not be permitted to remain, and that unfavorable impressions concerning them had been made upon the mind of this government. They found themselves charged with having broken their word, in not going from Calcutta to the Isle of France; and with having concealed themselves at Calcutta, while the police officers were in search of them to put them on board ship for England. For the purpose of refuting these charges, and explaining their conduct, they drew up and presented, by his Excellency's permission, the following memorial.]

Bombay, Feb. 18, 1813.

To the Right Honorable Sir Evan Nepean, Governor of Bombay, &c.

Right Honorable Sir,

We have heard with the deepest concern, that your Excellency has received from Bengal intelligence deeply injurious to our character as men, as Christians, and especially as Ministers of the Gospel. Our concern is the more distressing, when we consider our solemn responsibility to the great Head of the Church, and the high importance that the missionary character should stand without reproach; especially in a region like this, where the forfeiting of that character must be attended with circumstances so truly deplorable. We beg, therefore, your Excellency's indulgent consideration of the following statement of our conduct.

When we left America, as your Excellency will perceive by our letter of instructions, a copy of which we take the liberty of sending herewith, our destination was not precisely fixed; but was left for our subsequent decision. On arriving at Calcutta, our first object was to obtain such information as would enable us to decide with discretion. But from representations made to us at that time, we were induced to believe, that we should not be allowed to remain in the Honorable Company's dominions. An order from government, received about a week after our arrival, which order included Messrs. Johns, Lawson, and May, three English missionaries, and Mr. Rice, an American, increased our fears. We doubted whether we should be allowed to leave the Honorable Company's dominions for any place east of the Cape of Good Hope; and, if for any, supposed it would be for the Isle of France alone. With these views we presented the petition marked No. 1.[*]

When this petition was handed, Mr Martin[†] objected to the presenting of it; and said, that the order of government was positive for our return to America,—that we must depart upon our own ship, but that she might carry us whither she liked.

In the course of a week from this, we received an answer from government, stating, that our assurances of going to the Isle of France were accepted; but that we must expect to be at the disposal of the government of that island.

After this, we continued in the expectation of going to the Isle of France, for about two months. We were endeavoring to obtain a passage, when we were taken sick. As soon as we recovered we renewed our endeavors, engaged our passage on the ship

---

[*] See No. 1. at the close of this Memorial.
[†] Mr. Martin was the chief magistrate of police.

Adele, and paid for it as early as the 17th of September, at which time we were expecting the Adele to sail in a few days, though she did not till about the middle of the following month.

During our delay at Calcutta, the causes of which we have now explained, we were led by observation to believe, that our fears had been premature: for we found Missionaries, who had been ordered away no less positively than ourselves, nevertheless residing quietly in Bengal; and we ascertained the same to be true of others in India. We therefore began to hope, that, had we pursued a different plan, we might have been allowed to go to the place, which our inquiries should incline us to choose. Several reasons at length inducing us to desire to go to Ceylon, rather than to the Isle of France, we prepared the annexed petition, No. 2;* but, lest we should presume too much on the indulgence of government, we at the same time pursued our arrangements, intending, should that petition be rejected, to proceed, according to our original plan, to the Isle of France. The petition, when delivered at the Police, was carried by the clerk to Mr. Martin, who was on the opposite side of the room, and who replied, through the same clerk, 'that it was unnecessary to present that petition, and that he would give us a pass at any time.' The question was asked by Mr Hall, 'Should we go to Ceylon, instead of the Isle of France, would that be equally acceptable to government?' and was answered in the affirmative.

The petition was withdrawn; and we did all in our power to obtain a passage for Ceylon. But before we could obtain one, we were summoned to the Police, and our reasons were demanded for not having gone to the Isle of France. Our reply was, that we had been endeavoring to go thither, till we had learnt from the Police, that a pass might be obtained equally well for Ceylon; and that we were then seeking for an opportunity to depart for that island. We did not at this, or at any other time, say, at the Police, nor to any person whomsoever, that our delay of going to the Isle of France was for want of opportunities. Nor could we have said this without obviously appearing to many, who well knew our proceedings, to be totally destitute of every principle of honor and religion.

Notwithstanding all our efforts, we found no opportunity of going to Ceylon; nor could we hope for one, we were told, earlier than the January fleet. In the mean time, it had been suggested to us, that Mr. Martin would probably give a general pass from Bengal, without specifying any particular place. We supposed, from what he had said respecting his giving a pass, that a pass from him, and not a formal permission from government, was a regular departure. Whether such a pass could be obtained we did indeed doubt; but we were encouraged to make the attempt in the confidence, that to fail could not injure us, and that, should we succeed,

* See No. 2, at the close of this Memorial.

In the voice of the police we should have the voice of government; particularly as the police had been the only organ of government to us.

Our application succeeded; and on the faith of our passes "to depart on the ship Commerce, capt. Arbuthnot," we proceeded to make our arrangements; esteeming it a great favor that we had obtained permission to depart, though it gave us no right of remaining in the place to which we intended to go.   Our friends expressed their happiness at our success;—among whom were some, in whose judgment we thought it safe to confide.

The passes now in the hands of R. T. Goodwin, Esq.,[*] were obtained on the 10th of November, with the expectation that the ship would sail in four or five days.   On Saturday the 13th, a part of our baggage was put on board   On Tuesday morning, the 16th, we paid our passage to the captain's agent, and, in the afternoon of the same day, we were unexpectedly summoned to attend at the Police, which we did the next morning with Messrs Rice and Judson, who had received a like summons.   We then received a communication from government, stating, that on account of our having failed to go to the Isle of France, we were considered as having forfeited all claim to the further indulgence of government; and directing the Police to correspond with the Marine Board, concerning the provision for our departure for England, on the fleet under despatch.   The fleet, we were informed, was to sail within five days, which would allow no more than three days to prepare for a voyage to England.

After reading the order, Mr. Nott mentioned to Mr. Martin his circumstances, and asked, whether the order of government would interfere with his previous arrangements, and prevent his departing according to his pass?   The reply was "Certainly; the order of government is positive."   Mr. Martin then mentioned the opportunities there had been of going to the Isle of France, which had been neglected; and added that he had always told him, that he would have to go to the Isle of France or England.   Neither of us, however, had heard our going to England mentioned before.

We were directed by the person who went with us from the Police, to give information should we change our place of residence; and were also advised by him to write to Mr. Martin concerning our families, as they had not been noticed in the orders of government.   This advice, however, we did not follow, as we immediately formed the plan of making the annexed address to the Right Honorable the Governor General.

Concluding from the unexpected orders, that, if we applied, we should not perhaps be permitted to proceed to Bombay, we resolved to attempt to obtain liberty to go to Point de Galle, where the captain was so obliging us to promise to put us on shore. With these views we prepared the petition, No. 8 †

---

[*] Mr. Goodwin is chief magistrate of police at Bombay.
† See No. 8, at the close of this Memorial.

After this paper had received the approbation of some of our friends, we went on Thursday morning to Barrackpore, for the purpose of presenting it to his Lordship. The Hon. Mr. Elliot, his Lordship's private secretary, upon reading the first sentence observed, that as it related to an order in council, his Lordship would not receive it in his private capacity. We mentioned the urgency of the case, and requested him on that account to deliver it; but he refused, and advised us to hand it to the secretary to whose department it belonged. We left him without his probably knowing who we were, and returned to Calcutta.

Having found upon inquiry, that the meeting of the council was postponed till after the time appointed for the sailing of the fleet, we did not hand our petition to the secretary, according to the Hon. Mr. Elliot's advice; but resolved to embrace the doubtful but only alternative of embarking on the Commerce, according to our previous arrangements and our passports, should we find, that the captain had reported us to the police as his passengers and obtained the port-clearance for his ship. Upon inquiry we found that he had not. We therefore delayed our embarkation till Friday noon, when the captain showed us his certificate, (which he can doubtless now show,) that he had reported us to the police, agreeably to the orders of the Governor General in Council; and likewise told us, that the ship was cleared out at the custom-house, and would probably sail the next day. We then completed our arrangements and went on board the same day. Till we went on board we were either at our known place of abode, or moving publicly about Calcutta on our necessary business. We did not give information of our going on board to the Police, because our having obtained a pass, and the captain's having reported us on that very day as his passengers, furnished them, we supposed, with sufficient means of knowing where we were.

Though both the captain and the agent had told us, that the ship would sail the next day, yet she remained at her moorings till Monday morning, when we proceeded down the river. We imputed our not being sent for to the intention, and not to the ignorance, of the Police.

On this statement of the circumstances of our leaving Calcutta we beg leave to remark, that we did diligently endeavor to obtain an audience from government till it appeared that no audience could be obtained before too late an hour;—that considering our passes, and particularly the captain's report to the police, which was made after the same police had communicated the orders of government to us, we did consider ourselves as acting with regularity, and presumed, when we found ourselves suffered to proceed, that the police, as we were now manifestly on the point of leaving Bengal, were not disposed to carry their inquiries any further.

Though we had not succeeded in presenting the above-mentioned petition to Lord Minto, we still intended to stop at Ceylon, supposing that a fresh departure from that island might be more favorable to our reception in Bombay, than to arrive directly from Bengal. But as Bombay continued to be the place of our desire;—as the government of Bengal had suffered us to proceed, while considering us, as we supposed, bound to Bombay;—as we met with a long and unexpected delay on the coast;—and as our funds were low, we concluded to proceed directly to this place.

We beg leave to express our fears, that some appearance of inconsistency in us may have arisen from a mistaken connexion of us with our two brethren;* from whom we lived at considerable distance apart; with whose plans we were unconnected; and from whose business at the Police ours was generally distinct and different. Your Excellency will readily perceive, that such a connexion, though the conduct of each, severally, might be explained, would give an appearance of inconsistency to both.

The above we declare to be a full statement of our conduct, in relation to the government of Bengal; the truth of which is known to many of our friends, with whom our conversations have been frequent and particular. That we have acted with integrity, we have the testimony of our own consciences. That we have guided our affairs with discretion, we will not say. But if the above statement exhibit indiscretions, we hope they will appear to be such as have arisen, not from rashness and obstinacy, but from an honest zeal in what we considered as laudable objects, and from the ignorance of strangers in a strange land. Above all, we hope, Right Honorable Sir, that our intentions will appear to have been good, and our conduct such as not to have cast a deserved reproach upon our holy religion, nor to have destroyed our character as ministers of Jesus, in the interests of whose church we believe your Excellency to feel deeply concerned.

Having said these necessary things, respecting our characters and conduct, we beg your Excellency's further indulgence, while we submit at large the objects we desire to pursue in this place.

Our great and general object is the diffusion of Christian knowledge and Christian morals. In attempting this, we should consider our first step to be the acquisition of the language of the country, which, in a tolerable degree, we suppose, must occupy the greatest part of our time for two or three years. During this time we should hope to be useful, by the instruction of schools composed either of European or half-cast children,† or by teaching the English language to the natives themselves. While engaged in the acquisition of the language, we should hope to be useful in our intercourse with the people, particularly the lower classes; giving religious instruction to such as should be inclined to receive it; and, finally, should we be allowed to remain, it would be our intention to do all in our power to forward the translation of the Scriptures into the Mahratta language; and, perhaps, should our lives be spared, into the Guzerattee likewise; with the hope that by our feeble endeavors some might be induced to embrace them as the word of

* Messrs. Rice and Judson. Ed.

† Our readers may not all be informed, that half-cast children are those, one of whose parents is a European, the other a Hindoo. Ed.

life, and become partakers of the unsearchable riches of **Christ,** which are such an inestimable blessing to Christian countries.

This statement we cheerfully submit to your Excellency, hoping that our conduct has not forfeited, and that our object claims, your Excellency's indulgence; and that we shall not be under the painful necessity of relinquishing an object, in which so many Christian friends are so deeply interested.

With sentiments of the highest respect,

Right Honorable Sir,

We are your Excellency's most obedient,

and most humble servants,

GORDON HALL,
SAMUEL NOTT.

No. I.†

To the Honorable the Governor General, in Council.

WE, the Undersigned, passengers lately arrived on board the American ship Harmony, having received an order to depart out of the country on board the same ship, beg leave to state, that agreeably to our intention, stated at the Police on our arrival, of leaving the Company's dominions, we request liberty to depart, by the earliest opportunity, for the Isle of France; and therefore that the Harmony may not be refused a clearance on our account.

LUTHER RICE,
GORDON HALL,
SAMUEL NOTT.

Calcutta, Aug. 21, 1812.

No. II.

To the Right Honorable Lord Minto,† Governor General, in Council.

THE Undersigned, having been detained by sickness and other causes from going to the Isle of France, as permitted about two months ago, and now wishing to depart to Ceylon, beg permission to pass out of the Honorable Company's dominions to that island.

GORDON HALL,
SAMUEL NOTT.

Calcutta, Oct. 17, 1812.

No. III.

To the Right Honorable Gilbert Lord Minto, Governor General.

THE Undersigned, having read at the Police the orders respecting their going to England, wherein they are said to have forfeited all claim to the further indulgence of government, by not having gone to the Isle of France, beg leave to solicit your Lordship's attention to the causes of their delay, and to their present circumstances.

As early as the middle of September, and as soon as they had recovered from the sickness into which they fell on their arrival, they engaged their passage on the ship Adele, bound to the Isle of France, which was to sail in the course of that month, but was detained till sometime after the date of the enclosed petition.‡

* *This petition was published in the Panoplist for Jan* 1813, p 373; *but as it is short, it is republished here for the sake of preserving the connexion.*

† *Lord Minto administered the government of Bengal for six years. His term of office expired sometime in 1813, and he sailed for England probably in December last. Late English papers mention his death soon after he reached home, aged 54, about the year 1788, then Sir Gilbert Elliot, he was an active member of the British House of Commons. He is succeeded, in the government of the Company's dominions, by Lord Moira, known as Lord Rawdon in the American revolutionary war.*

ED. PAN

tion received during this delay led them to wish to go to Ceylon; and two
its date they conveyed the enclosed petition to C. F. Martin, Esq. to be
to government; intending to proceed immediately to the Isle of France, if
on should be denied. They were informed by Mr. Martin, that it was unto present that petition, and that he would give them a pass at any time.
ly the petition was withdrawn, the design of going to the Isle of France re-
L and they endeavored to find an opportunity to go to Ceylon. Not finding
est of a ship going directly to Ceylon, they made application on the 10th
e Police for a pass to depart on the ship Commerce, which pass was grant-
and on the faith of it, they have paid their passage, put part of their baggage
and are expecting daily that the ship will sail.

that had been said on presenting the enclosed petition at the Police, and
ng obtained the pass, they supposed they might innocently and safely make
ugements for departure. The arrangements are made; the ship is ready
own the river, and convey them to Point de Galle, where she would leave

mbly beg of your Lordship, that in consideration of our present circum-
he order of government may not be carried into effect on us, and that we
eed from the very serious inconvenience of a voyage to England.

Your Lordship's
most obedient and most
humble servants,
GORDON HALL,
SAMUEL NOTT.

utta, *November* 18, 1812.

PECUNIARY ACCOUNTS OF THE BOARD.

rican *Board of Commissioners for Foreign Missions in account current
with Jeremiah Evarts, their Treasurer, Dr.*

paid from Sept. 1, 1813, to August 31, 1814, in conformity to orders of the
d of the Prudential Committee, from No. 53, to No. 79, inclusive, for ex-
curred in the prosecution of the objects of the Board $7,071 62
es by counterfeit bills received in donations, 6 00—$7,077 62
ance carried to the credit of new account, Sept. 1, 1814, 13,467 53

$20,545 15

Contra Cr.

ance brought to the credit of new account, Sept. 1, 1813, as ap-
the Auditor's certificate of Sept. 11, 1813, $8,077 59
h received in donations, between Sept. 1, 1813, and August 31,
usive, viz. as published in the Panoplist for

September, 1813, (part I) p. 238,	$1,527 58	
——— (part II) p. 285,	173 25	
October, (part I) p. 329,	127 25	
——— (part II) p. 379,	381 97	
November, (part I) p. 425,	440 06	
——— (part II) p. 478,	126 00	
December, (part I) p. 528,	220 55	
January, 1814, vol. x, p. 44,	1,841 23	
February, p. 90,	277 74	
March, p. 139,	803 74	
April, p. 187,	1,175 27	
May, p. 236,	590 92	
June, p. 286,	1,340 73	
July, p. 332,	627 00	
August, p. 390,	164 95	
September, p. 427,	2,190 69	—12,008 91

h received as income of stock and interest on notes, during the
ending August 31, 1814, 458 63

$20,545 15

A STATEMENT OF THE EXPENDITURES OF THE BOARD FROM SEPT 1, 1813, TO AUG. 31, 1814, INCLUSIVE.*

Oct. 8, 1813. Paid for 100*l.* sterling exchange, at 15 per cent discount, the avails of which to be remitted to Calcutta and expended under the direction of the Committee of the Board at that place, in forwarding the translation and publication of the Holy Scriptures in the vernacular tongues of Asia, - - - - $577 78

March 15, 1814. Paid for 250*l.* sterling, exchange, at 8 per cent. discount to be remitted on the same account, - - 1,022 22

July 23. Paid for 385*l.* 14*s.* 3*d.* at 12 1-2 per cent. discount, to be remitted on the same account, - - - - 1,500 00—$2,099 00

Sept. 17, 1813. Paid for 100*l.* exchange, at 14 per cent. discount, the avails of which to be remitted from London to Calcutta, for the payment of the salaries and extraordinary expenses of the missionaries, - - - - $582 22

June 22, 1814. Paid for 250*l.* exchange, at 9 1-2 per cent. discount, for the same purpose, - - - 1,095 55

Also for 39*l.* 4*s.* 5*d.* at 11 per cent. discount, for the same purpose, - - - - 155 16

July 23. Paid for 55*l.* 16*s.* 6*d.* exchange, at 14 per cent. discount, for the same purpose, - - - 213 33

27. Paid for 10*l.* exchange, at 14 per cent. discount for the same purpose †, - - - 38 22

Aug. 3. Paid for 278*l.* 2*s.* exchange, at 12 per cent. discount, for the same purpose, - - - 1,087 69—2,332 24

Dec. 10, 1813. Paid toward the expenses of Messrs. James Richards, jun. and Edward Warren, while obtaining their medical education at Philadelphia, - - - 145 50

April 18, 1814. Paid to Mr. Burr Baldwin, on account of the expenses of his education with a view to employment as a missionary, - - - 100 00

Paid at different times for books purchased for the Board, including a copy of Rees's Cyclopædia for the use of our missionaries, - - - 225 93

Travelling expenses of the members of the Board in attending the annual meeting at Boston, Sept 15, 1813, - - - 224 87

Other contingent expenses of said meeting, - - 56 91

Expense of printing 1,500 copies of the Report of the Board, embracing the various documents laid before them at their annual meeting, - - - $93 15

All other printing during the year, including blank stationary, and copies of the exercises of the annual meeting, - 20 35——113 50

Toward necessary expenses in prosecuting the suit for Mrs. Norris's legacy of 30,000, - - - 35 51

Contingent expenses of the missionaries before they sailed from Salem, 12 09

Cash paid by the Prudential Committee in travelling expenses, in attending meetings on the business of the Board, and refunded to them, 24 25

Paid by the Corresponding Secretary for a press for the seal of the Board, - - - $4 00

For postage and stationary, - - - 4 40——8 40

Paid by the Treasurer for postage, - - - 20 55

For a stamp for a draft, - - - 75

For a trunk to be deposited at one of the banks containing the property of the Board, - - - 4 00

For stationary, - - - 50——25 81

Sexton's bill for services at the annual meeting, - 4 00

Postage paid by a member of the Board, - - 1 75

Paid for brokerage in purchasing exchange, - - 7 10

Carried forward $5,075

* It is thought better to publish these expenses in this way, than to enter them at full length under their respective dates.

† This bill was a donation to the Board, and of course was charged to it at the current rate of exchange for small gifts.

Brought forward $6,767 56

by counterfeit bills received in donations, - - $6 00
nt on uncurrent bills, - - - - - - - 4 06——10 00
mce to the Treasurer for his services during the year preceding
al meeting, in Sept. 1813, - - - - - - 300 00
                                                         ————————
                                                         $7,077 62

THE AUDITOR'S CERTIFICATE.

New Haven, Sept 16, 1814.
tifies that I have examined the accounts of the Treasurer of the American
Commissioners for Foreign Missions, for the year ending the 31st of August,
I have found the same correctly cast, and well vouched, and that the balance
en Thousand Four Hundred and Sixty Seven Dollars, and fifty three cents,
bank stock, and cash remains in the Treasury; which sum is accounted for in
Balance, dated August 31, 1814. DE LAUZUN DAFOREST, *Auditor.*
57 53.

Trial Balance above mentioned the particulars, which compose the following
· given
's on interest, - - - - - - - - - $6,765 67
k stock, - - - - - - - - - - 3,150 00
's not on interest, - - - - - - - - 287 81
aft on demand, - - - - - - - - 354 19
ted at the New England, Hartford, and Eagle Banks, - 2,614 56
hands of the Prudential Committee to meet contingent expenses, 295 30
                                                         ————————
                                                         $13,467 53

IONS TO SUPPORT FOR-
MISSIONS AND TO AID
RANSLATING THE SCRIP-
S.

, 1814 From a lady,
ev. Jonathan Burr of
b $1 50
om Mrs. Lois Par-
f Hatfield, by the
Lyman, $5 00
he Rev. David H.
, of Tunbridge,
, 50 00
a female friend of
n Goshen, Mass. 1 00——56 00
the Female Foreign
Society of Wethers-
n. by Miss Nancy
he Treasurer, 62 00
rom the Female Be-
Society in New Ca-
Mrs Sarah Bonney,
surer, 35 00
rom Mrs. Rowe, of
on, Con. by the Rev.
rter, 5 00
Dr Jacob Porter, of
, Mass. 2 00
Mr. Edward and Mrs.
ker, of Farmington,
each, 10 00

Carried forward, $171 50

Brought forward, $171 50
From the Foreign Missiona-
ry Society of Springfield and
the neighboring towns, by the
Hon. George Bliss, Esq. the
Treasurer, 82 00
A collection after the Rev.
Mr. Richards's Sermon before
the Board, 126 76
16. From the Female
Cent Society in Shore-
ham, Ver. by the Rev.
President Davis, $24 58
From Elisha Sheldon,
Esq. of Sheldon, Ver. 10 00——34 58
From the Female Cent So-
ciety in Uxbridge, Mass. by
the Rev. Dr. Worcester, half
to missions and half to trans-
Lations, 10 00
From individuals in North
Salem, N. Y. remitted by Mr.
Herman Daggett to the Rev.
Dr. Dwight, viz:
From Herman Daggett, $10
Artemas Weed, 5
Hannah Ambler, 5
Solomon M. Smith, 1
Philetus Phillips, 5
Sidney Stratton, 1
Matthew Smith, 5
A friend to missions, 2——34 00

Carried forward, $479 44

Brought forward, $459 44

19. From the Hon. Elias Boudinot, Esq of Burlington, N. J.   37 75

21. From the Foreign Mission Society of the North Association of Hartford County, by Mr. P. W. Gallaudet, the Treasurer, paid to Mr. Henry Hudson,   38 50

23. From the Female Cent Society in Stoddard, N. H. by the Rev. Isaac Robinson,   14 15

From a female friend of Missions in Foxborough, Mass.   1 50

28. From individuals in Plainfield, Mass. by Mr James Richards, jun.   19 25

From pupils in Miss Hills's School at Andover,   6 01

Oct. 1. From a few ladies in Goffstown, N. H. remitted by Mrs Elizabeth M'Farland to the Rev. Dr Morse,   10 09

From Clarissa Hoyt, of South Salem, N. Y. by the Rev Jacob Burbank,   1 00

4—5. From the Foreign Mission Society of New London and the Vicinity, by Mr Reuben Langdon, the Treasurer,   123 00

5. From Mrs. Hannah Jackson, of Boston, deceased, paid by her husband, Mr. William Jackson, in conformity to her request,   30 00

6. From individuals in Paris, Oneida county, N Y remitted to the Rev. Dr Lyman by Dr. Elnathan Judd, viz.

Elnathan Judd,	$5
Chauncey Burritt,	3
Philip Taylor,	15
Adam Simmons,	5
Benjamin Simmons,	2
Aaron Simmons,	4
Isaac Scofield,	2
Andrew Pierce,	1
Elijah Dressen,	2
Eliphalet Steele,	10
A friend to foreign missions,	5 —54 00

7 From a female in Dudley, Mass by Mr. S. T. Armstrong,   5 00

10 From the Rev William R. Weeks, by the Rev. Dr. Morse,   20 00

1. From the Female Cent Society in Gorham, Maine, by the Rev Mr. Hilliard, remitted to Mr Duren,   25 00

Carried forward, $844 69

Brought forward, $844 69

22. From the Westfield Female Foreign Mission Society, by the Rev. Dr. Morse,   11 50

$856 19

N. B. The donation of *one hundred and ninety eight dollars,* which was entered in the Panoplist for June last, and noticed again in the Panoplist for September, as given to *the permanent fund,* was intended by Mr. Goodell to be given *for immediate use,* and has been thus applied in late remittances to India. The occasion of the mistake was a misapprehension of the terms in which the donation was communicated. The donations of the Rev. Eliphalet Lyman, ($40,) and of the three persons immediately following, ($3 50,) entered in the Panoplist for June, were also not intended by the donors to be devoted to the permanent fund. This mistake was occasioned in the same manner as the other. Donors are respectfully informed, that should any future mistake occur, in regard to the application of their donations, it will be readily corrected.

Among the donations above referred to, for *Mrs. Prudence Clark,* read *Mrs Prudence Church.*

OBITUARY.

DIED, at Montague, Mass. HENRY WELLS, M. D. and M. M S an eminent physician.

At Paris, the Duke of MASSA, grand judge and minister of justice under the reign of Bonaparte.

At Williamsburg, (N. Y.) Col. JOHN B CAMPBELL, of the 11th U. S. regiment, of a wound received in the battle of July 5th.

In Tyrrel county, N. C. Col. JOHN CLAYTON, inhumanly murdered by some lurking villains near his house, in consequence, it is supposed, of his inflexible execution of the duties of a magistrate.

TO CORRESPONDENTS.

WE regret that we have been compelled to omit several articles prepared for this number; particularly Mrs Simpkins's list of donations to the Cent Institution, the annual report of the Fragment Society, and several obituary notices. We regret, also, that we could not present, at one view, the principal communications from the missionaries from this country in Asia. They will be found in future numbers.

THE

PANOPLIST,

AND

IISSIONARY MAGAZINE.

| 1. | NOVEMBER, 1814. | VOL. X. |

RELIGIOUS COMMUNICATIONS.

For the Panoplist.

HE SABBATH. NO. V.

ctification of the Sabbath.

3atter myself, it has been
that the Sabbath is a di-
titution, and of universal
petual obligation, it be-
:xtremely interesting to
*How is the Sabbath to
ified? What duties are
? What thoughts, words,
ons are forbidden?* The
these inquiries must be
I to a future number, as
ill scarcely be room, in
sent, for even a concise
id view of the appropri-
:s of holy time.
first clause of the fourth
idment, *Remember the
day to keep it holy*, com-
s every thing that God
uired. It contains two
requisitions. The first
we *remember the Sabbath*
as, that men should ever
o sacred, so benevolent
ution! And yet who does
w, how many sorts of
s, how many amuse-
ind pleasures, are every
almost, permitted to in-
upon the first hours of
le! If the Sabbath is not
ered;, if, in other words,

X.

its arrival is not anticipated; if
the necessary arrangements are
not made, to enter upon its religious duties, as soon as it commences, there is little probability, that it will prove either a
pleasant or a profitable season to
the soul.

Those who *remember* the Sabbath, according to the spirit of
the commandment, frequently
carry their thoughts forward to
it, while engaged in the cares
and business of the week. Especially, when it draws near, do
they strive to banish worldly
concerns from their minds, well
knowing, that it requires time to
prepare for that exclusive attention to religion, which the law of
the Sabbath most reasonably demands. Fully aware, at the same
time, of their own weakness, and
ever mindful of the dark and unknown deceitfulness of the heart,
they apply, in earnest prayer to
God, for the quickening influences of his Spirit, to fit them for
an early and joyful entrance upon that weekly rest, which is a
lively type of eternal rest in
heaven. Always on their guard
against anger, envy, and other
sinful passions, they are more
especially so towards the close
of the week, deeply sensible,
how necessary the humble and

61

forgiving spirit of the Gospel is to the sanctification of the Lord's day.

Remembering the Sabbath implies, also, such a previous arrangement of secular affairs, that they may not encroach upon the beginning of holy time. So far is the conscientious observer of this divine institution, from making his calculations to labor harder and later on Saturday than usual, that he endeavors to favor himself and others, as much as he can, that neither he, nor they, may be unfitted, by extreme fatigue, for private and public religious duties. Is he a husbandman, he will not, if he can avoid it, undertake, even in harvest time, more work than can be accomplished in season. If he regards Saturday evening as holy, he will calculate to keep it so; and to this end, will, if possible, return from the field and have his family together, before the setting of the sun. His hired laborers he will dismiss at an early hour, that they too may be with their families, when the Sabbath begins. Nor will they, if conscientious and pious, loiter in idle company, or waste the evening in noisy and sinful mirth. Is he, who *remembers* the Sabbath, a mechanic, his journeymen and apprentices will have liberty to leave their work, in due season. His shop will be shut early, and the noise of the hammer will cease. Is he a merchant, his arrangements will indicate the approach of the sacred rest, before it actually arrives. Every thing will be put in its place;—his accounts will be adjusted, and his customers, knowing his habits, will voluntarily retire. He will

shut up his counting-room, and, leaving his books, merchandise, and cares behind, will go to his house, collecting his thoughts, and meditating upon the requirements and blessings of God's holy day.

Does the business of such a person, as I am describing, call him from home on Saturday, he delays not; but, if possible, returns early. Does he ride, or walk abroad for amusement in the afternoon, he waits not to be told, that the least trespass upon holy time would be wholly inexcusable. In planning and prosecuting journies, he does not, like many of his neighbors, leave home on Friday, or Saturday, with the express view of getting out of the town, or state, so as to travel without interruption upon the Lord's day. Nor does he trespass upon its sacred hours, when far from home, and exposed only to the sight of strangers; but, taking his conscience along with him, and remembering that God is every where, he has the same regard to his commandments, when a hundred, or a thousand miles from home, as if he were exposed to the scrutinizing eyes of all his acquaintance. Reader, is this thy character? Dost thou thus *remember* the Sabbath day?

The second requisition of the law is, that we *keep the Sabbath holy*. Here, the whole duty turns upon the meaning of the word *holy*. Till we know the exact import of this word, we cannot be certain, what is required, or forbidden in the law. The Divine Oracles are, in this case, our only guide. To what the Holy Ghost teacheth let us then appeal. In turning over the sa-dred pages, with reference to this subject, it will be found, that many things are denominated *holy*, on account of their being set apart for religious purposes. Thus, to give a few examples, the oil, with which the tabernacle and its furniture were anointed, in the wilderness, was *holy* oil. Exod. xxx, 25. The crown worn by the high priest. was a *holy* crown Exod. xxix, 6. The tenth part of the annual produce of Canaan was *holy.* Lev. xxvii, 30. The ark was *holy* 2 Chron. xxxv, 3. The temple at Jerusalem was a *holy* building, and so were the vessels belonging to it. 1 Chron. xxii, 19, and xxix, 3. The first fruits of the ground were *holy,* Ezek. xlviii, 14. Now it is obvious, that the things above mentioned were considered as *holy* because they were *sanctified*, or set apart for the service of God. Thus we read, *I will sanctify the tabernacle and the altar. All the firstling males thou shalt sanctify. I have chosen and sanctified this house in the temple. All the vessels have we prepared and sanctified.* The tabernacle, then, was *holy*, because it was dedicated exclusively to the worship of the one living and true God. The tythes were *holy*, because they were appointed to be appropriated solely to the support of religion. The temple was *holy*, because it was set apart from every other use, and dedicated to the honor and worship of Jehovah. The vessels of the temple were *holy*, because they were devoted to religious uses, and might on no pretence whatever be put to any other use. The first fruits were *holy*, because they were separated in the same manner; and

accordingly, the people were expressly forbidden to sell them.

But, not to enlarge, it is most evidently in the same sense, that the weekly Sabbath is called *holy.* It is because God himself has been pleased to sanctify it, or set it apart as a day of holy rest and religious worship, that it is a holy day. As, therefore, it would have been a profanation of the vessels of the temple to have put them to any common use. so it is a profanation of the Sabbath, to spend any part of it, in those "worldly employments and recreations, which are lawful on other days." If we would keep the Sabbath holy, then, we must abstain from labor, and every thing of the kind; must spend the day in public and private exercises of God's worship, not contenting ourselves with the forms of religion; not wasting any part of the sacred rest in sloth; but employing the whole of it in those lively exercises of worship, by which the heart is made better, and the soul is gradually prepared for the heavenly rest.

The preceding observations might serve for a very brief and general answer to the inquiry before us. But a subject of such practical moment, as the sanctification of the Sabbath, demands a more particular investigation. I shall therefore proceed to specify some of the regular and appropriate duties of holy time. These duties are religious meditation, prayer, self-examination, reading the Scriptures and other religious books, attending public worship, religious conversation, and the pious instruction of children.

1. A part of every Lord's day

should be spent in religious meditation. With this the Sabbath should invariably be commenced. It is essential to prepare the mind for the pleasant and acceptable performance of other religious duties. It is by early and serious meditation upon the perfections of God, and the holiness of his law; upon our own sinfulness, obligations, and dependence; and upon the astonishing work of redemption, which the Christian Sabbath commemorates, that the affections are enlivened, worldly cares are excluded, and the soul is warmed with true devotion. Meditation should also be intermingled with all the duties of the Sabbath. It should precede every prayer. It should follow the reading of every passage of Scripture. It should, in part at least, fill up the intervals of public worship. It should be employed upon every sermon. When we enter our closets, a solemn pause should precede our addresses to God; during which our thoughts should be absorbed in contemplating *His* greatness and holiness;—*our* guilt and nothingness. In the same manner, should a few moments be spent in deep and solemn meditation, before engaging in family prayer. After we have heard, or read a sermon, it is meditation that fixes the truth in the memory. It is this, which converts warnings and invitations, doctrines and precepts, reproofs and promises into spiritual nourishment. This is one of the means, by which, under the culture of the Holy Spirit, God's children grow wiser and wiser;—wax stronger and stronger. *I have more understanding*, saith the Psalmist, *than all my teachers, for thy testimonies are my meditation.*

When the Sabbath draws to a close, it is very much by solemn meditation upon all that we have read and heard; upon our shortcomings in duty; upon the mercy of God in permitting us to enjoy a day of sacred rest; and upon our renewed obligations to serve him in newness of life, that we are to prepare for the duties and trials, of the succeeding week.

2. Nearly allied to religious meditation is prayer. The latter of these, indeed, as well as the former, is a *daily* duty. Till we cease to need our daily bread, as well as every other good and perfect gift, that cometh down from the Father of lights, we cannot, without the blackest ingratitude, neglect to offer Him our daily prayers. But it is obvious, from the very nature of the Sabbath, that it should be a day of *special* prayer. Some Christians have made it a point, to call their families together, before the setting of the sun on Saturday evening, that they might unitedly implore the presence and blessing of God, at the very commencement of holy time: An excellent practice, worthy to be universally adopted. Certain it is, that, in entering upon the Sabbath, we ought to lift up our hearts to God, for the assistance of the Holy Spirit, that we may perform every duty to his acceptance, and enjoy some lively anticipations of eternal rest.

Do we sincerely desire to sanctify the Lord's day? then we must be instant and fervent in prayer. Retiring to our closets, when it begins, we must shut out the world, and commune with the

our spirits, in earnest
ons, for that prepara-
rt, which he requires.
pray over every por-
e Scriptures that we
before and after the
We must pray when
n at night, and when
n the morning. When
rom our beds again
families and closets
ar devotions. Again
er precede and follow
g of God's holy word.
be particular and fer-
r supplications for the
of the Divine Spirit to
minds in a praying
y moment, so that, in
ls of other duties, our
s, petitions, and thanks-
ay ascend, spontane-
e throne of grace. It
ly be necessary to add,
r must precede, ac-
and follow, our medi-
n the sermons which
nd the religious books
read;—that the eve-
ice of the family must
nitted;—that the Sab-
be ended, as it was
h prayer.

e portion of every
, should be spent in
nation. As the care-
experienced mariner
s use of the quadrant
ad to ascertain where
hould we endeavor to
piritual reckoning, by
and deliberate use of
ures, in the way of
nation. Once a week
means often enough.
and to commune, every
ur own hearts; to ex-
temper of our minds;

and to scrutinize the motives by
which we are actuated. But
these duties are more especially
binding, I think, on the Sabbath.
If some persons, in defiance of
God's law, avail themselves of
the leisure, which the sacred
rest affords, to adjust their accounts and post their books, how
much more should we regularly
embrace so favorable an opportunity to inquire, how matters
stand between God and our souls.

Let us, then, make it an invariable rule to call ourselves to a
strict account, on Saturday evening, in regard to the manner in
which we have spent the preceding week, interrogating ourselves, as in the Divine presence,
what we have done to advance the
interests of true religion; what
preparations we have made for
the Sabbath, and for heaven; and
what sins of thought, word, and
deed, we have been guilty of.
On the morning of the Lord's
day let us resume the scrutiny,
going over all the circumstances
of our guilt, on purpose to make
way for deep and sincere repentance. Let serious self-examination form the personal application of every portion of Scripture that we read, and of the
public discourses which we
hear. Particularly, when the
Sabbath is drawing to a close,
let us inquire, how we have
spent it; what vain thoughts we
have indulged; what formality
has attended our worship; what
instruction we have gained; what
communion we have enjoyed
with the Father and the Son, and
whether or not we have made
any progress in the divine life.

Z. X. Y.

Stockbridge, Dec. 1, 1757.
Rev. and dear Sir,

YESTERDAY I received your two letters of the 12th and 17th of November; but I neither saw nor heard any thing of Mr. Hill. I thank you for your concern that I may be useful in the world. I lately wrote you a letter informing you of our choice of a council to sit here on the 21st of this month, and inclosed in it a letter missive to Mr. Brinsmade, who is one of the council. I hope you have received it. Don't fail of letting me see you here; for I never wanted to see you more.

As to the question you ask about Christ's argument, in John x, 34, 35, 36. I observe,

First, that it is not all princes of the earth that are called Gods in the Old Testament; but only the princes of Israel that ruled over God's people. The princes that are called Gods, in that 82nd psalm, are, in the same sentence, distinguished from the princes of the nations of the world *I have said, Ye are Gods; but ye shall die like men, and fall like one of the princes.*

Secondly; The reason why these princes of Israel were called *Gods*, was, that they, the rulers and judges of God's Israel, were figures of Him, who is the true King of the Jews and Prince of God's people, who is to rule over the house of Jacob forever, the Prince and Savior of God's church, or spiritual Israel, gathered from all nations of the earth; who is God indeed. The throne of Israel, or of God's people,

properly belonged to Christ. He only was the proper heir to that crown; and therefore the princes of Israel are said to sit *upon the throne of the Lord,* 1 Chron. xxix, 23; and the kingdom of Israel under kings of the house of David, is called *the kingdom of the Lord,* 2 Chron. xiii, 8. And because Christ took the throne as the Antitype of these kings therefore he is said to sit upon their throne, Luke i, 32. Thus the princes of Israel are called Gods, in this 82nd psalm, and sons of God, and all of them *children of the Most High,* being appointed types and remarkable representations of the true Son of God, and in him of the true God. They were called Gods and sons of God, in the same manner as the Levitical sacrifices were called an atonement for sin, and in the same manner as the manna was called the *bread of heaven* and *angels' food.* These things represented, and by special divine designation were figures of, the true atonement, and of Him, who was truly *angel's food;* and in the same sense as Saul, the person especially pointed at in the 82nd psalm, is called the *Lord's anointed,* or Messiah, as it is in the original, or Christ, which are the same. And it is to be observed, that these typical Gods, and judges of Israel, are distinguished from the true God and true Judge of God's people, (who was to come as their Antitype,) in the next sentence, Ps. lxxxii, 8 *Arise, O God, thou JUDGE of the earth, for thou shalt inherit all nations.* This is a wish for the coming of Christ that king that should reign in righteousness and judge uprightly, who was to inherit the Gentiles as well as the Jews. And the words, as they stand in connexion with the two preceding verses, import thus much: "As to you, the temporal princes and judges of Israel, you are called Gods and sons of God, being exalted to the place of kings, judges and - saviors of God's people, the kingdom and heritage of Christ But you shall die like men and fall like other princes; whereby it appears that you are truly no Gods, nor is any one of you the true Son of God which your injustice and oppression likewise show. But O that He, who is truly God, the true and just Judge and Savior (who is to be King over Gentiles as well as Jews,) would come and reign."

It is to be observed, that when it is said in this verse, *Arise, O God*, the word *God* is *Elohim*, the same that is used verse 6th, *I have said, Ye are Gods.*

Thirdly; As to those words of Christ, John x, 35, *If he called them Gods, UNTO WHOM THE WORD OF GOD CAME*, I suppose, that by the word of God coming to these princes of Israel is meant their being set forth by special and express divine designation to be types or figurative signification of God's mind. Those things which God had appointed to be types to signify his mind were a visible word. Types are called the word of the Lord, as in Zech xi, 10, 11, and iv, 4, 5, 6. The word of God came to the princes of Israel, both as they by God's ordering became subjects of a typical representation of divine things, which was a visible word of God, and also as

this was done by express divine designation, as they were marked out to this end by an express audible and legible word, as in Ex. xxii, 28, and Ps. lxxxii, 1. And, besides, the person they were appointed types of, was Christ, who is called the word of God Thus the word of God came to Jacob as a type of Christ; 1 Kings xviii, 31. *And Elijah took twelve stones, according to the number of the tribes of the sons of Jacob, UNTO WHOM THE WORD OF THE LORD, CAME, saying, ISRAEL shall be thy name.* The word Israel is *Prince of God* Jacob being by that express designation appointed as a type of Christ, (who is called by the name of Israel, Isaiah xlix, 3,) the true Prince of God, in his wrestling with God to save himself and his family from destruction by Esau, who came against him, and obtaining the blessing for himself and his seed. Now, Fourthly; Christ's argument lies in these words, *the Scripture cannot be broken.* That word of God, by which they are called Gods as types of Him, who is truly God, must be verified; as they cannot be thus called unless the Antitype be truly God. They are so called as types of the Messiah, or of the *anointed One*, which is the same, or the *sanctified* or *Holy One*, or Him that was to be *sent.* See Dan. ix, 24 25; Ps lxxxix, 19, 20, and xvi, 10, and John ix, 7. But it was on this account, that the types or images of the Messiah were called Gods, because He, whom they represented, was God indeed. If He were not God, the word, by which they were called Gods, could not be verified; as the word, by which the legal sacrifices were called an atonement and are said to atone for sin, was true in no other sense than as they had relation to the sacrifice of Christ, the true atonement. If Christ's sacrifice had not truly atoned for sin, the word, that called a representation of it an atonement, could not be verified. So, if Jesus Christ had not been the true *bread from heaven,* and *angel's food indeed,* the Scripture, that called the type of him *the bread of Heaven* and *angel's food,* would not have been verified, but would have been broken.

These, Sir, are my thoughts on John x, 34, &c.

I am yours
most affectionately,
J. EDWARDS.

P. S. Dec. 5.
Sir,
The opportunity for conveyance of my letters to ministers to be of the council, your way, not being very good, I have sent other letters desiring you to take the care of conveying them with all possible care and speed.

Mr. Bellamy.

LETTER TO A YOUNG FRIEND.

Boston, April 1, 1814.
My dear young Friend,
PERMIT one, who is desirous of your best good, to write a few lines on a subject, which has at times occupied your thoughts, and perhaps excited some resolutions in favor of a holy life.

You are just about to enter the busy world, having passed through the helpless state of infancy and childhood 'into the interesting period of youth. It is

probable your expectations of worldly happiness are great. You are pressing forward amid the throng in pursuit of happiness, eagerly seeking it in the acquisition of riches, honors, and pleasures.—A youthful imagination, naturally warm and glowing, attaches much more enjoyment to those scenes of life, which are yet untried, than experience will realize.

Riches you may think indispensably requisite to secure against the wants incident to frail human nature. Property is no doubt valuable, as it supplies us with necessary food and raiment and convenient accommodations, while residing in the present mutable state. To a benevolent mind it is also valuable, as it enables us to communicate happiness to others;—to extend the means of mental improvement, and of support to the sons and daughters of adversity. When judiciously applied it causes the widow's heart to leap for joy, decks with smiles the face of aged want, and dries up the tear of the orphan. Many a houseless stranger has been sheltered from the severity of inclement seasons, and had his life not only protracted, but rendered comfortable and useful. Many poor children have found an asylum, where they may dwell safely, secure from the guilt and ruin to which their helpless condition exposed them, and where they may receive instruction that fits them for present usefulness, and prepares them, through grace, for future happiness. Riches thus employed may prove inestimable blessings to their possessors.

But, my friend, pause, and inquire: are they generally thus employed? Alas, daily observation and experience evince the lamentable truth, that they are often *kept for the owners thereof to their hurt.* Some use them for the gratification of their sensual appetites, and debase the rational part of our nature. Others spend them to decorate their frail bodies. Some waste them in riotous living; while others sordidly hoard them up till *their rust is a witness against the possessor.*

O, my friend, what a miserable account must such persons give, at the day of final retribution! Wealth is a talent committed to us, and shall we *hide it in a napkin,* while multitudes are *perishing for lack of knowledge,* and others are suffering for daily sustenance?

What is there in honor that demands our anxious regard? It is fleeting as the passing zephyr; unsatisfying in its nature, and uncertain in its duration, and at best is but an imaginary good.

To be esteemed by the virtuous is desirable; to seek such persons for our intimates is wise, and calculated to promote our respectability and usefulness. But to be anxious for popular applause is foolish and criminal, and will prove prejudicial to our best interests. We shall be tempted to sacrifice truth and act inconsistently with the dictates of our own consciences. We shall incur the displeasure of our best friends, and the indignation of Him. *who ruleth over all, and is blessed for ever.* We may servilely flatter the great to succeed in a favorite project; and, after all our efforts, may be disappointed in

the attainment of either a real or supposed advantage. We may pant after some distinguished station in society, not sufficiently realizing the weight and responsibility attached to it, nor duly considering whether we are qualified to fill it. To preserve an unsullied reputation, so far as this can be done by discharging every duty, is incumbent on us; but to be desirous of vain applause will certainly be destructive of present and future peace. *Seek not the praise of men, but the honor that cometh of God only.* Would you possess lasting honor, *pursue the path of holiness,* and you will hereafter be approved before an assembled universe, and receive a *crown of glory which fadeth not away.*

What are the pleasures of the world, for which some are ready to sacrifice every thing truly valuable and even life itself? How many precious hours are devoted to prepare for such enjoyments? No expense is esteemed too great for ornaments and dress. Music, dancing, and cards, alternately lend their aid to dissipate reflection.—But all the retinue of pleasures cannot afford you a peaceful thought to cheer your dying hours. Then will you look in vain for comfort to your splendid equipage; to your costly furniture, and circles of pleasure. These will not avail you in the trying, closing, solemn scene!

No, my friend, there is no refuge at that gloomy period but religion; not the mere external religion of nominal professors; but *the religion of the heart, the religion of the blessed Jesus.* This will bestow riches, which are satisfying and durable. Yes, it will make you an heir of glory; and you will finally, through the merits of the Savior, be received *into everlasting habitations.* Having obtained the pardon of sin, and an interest in Christ, you will have that peace, *which the world cannot give,* and of which it can never deprive you. The pleasures resulting from this source, are spiritual, refined, and never fail. Through eternity you will continually progress in likeness to God, in love, joy, and peace. Sorrow, sighing, and death, will never interrupt the tranquillity of the holy soul. The true Christian has joys in reserve, which *eye hath not seen, nor ear heard, nor the heart of man conceived,* in this state of imperfection. He will be permitted to see the glorious person of his Savior, and to unite with the millions of the redeemed, in ascribing praises to Him, who gave himself a ransom for the sins of our perishing race. One hour's communion, in secret prayer with his heaven y Father, is more precious to the Christian, than whole years of sensual delights. One glimpse of his Divine Savior will reconcile him to the loss of all created good. One foretaste of heaven, at the foot of the cross, is inconceivably valuable in his estimation. His outward condition may be poor and despicable; yet he would not for ten thousand worlds exchange situations with the prosperous unbeliever. *Possessing the favor of God, he has enough.* The love of Christ infinitely transcends every other good.

Sometimes, through the prevalence of corruption and the strength of temptation, he is left to wander from his Father's house; but ere long he is enabled, through Divine mercy, to return, and to confess his guilt with shame and remorse. He meets again the beloved of his soul; peace ensues; and he is animated in the Christian course.

Now, my friend, seriously consider and compare the different states of the worldling and of the pious. Ask your own heart, which you prefer; a short life of pleasure on earth, or an eternity of blessedness in heaven? Do you wish to have God for your Father; the blessed Jesus for your Savior, Counsellor, and Friend; the Holy Spirit for your Teacher, Guide, and Sanctifier; Christians for your companions; and holy Angels for your associates; or *the friendship of the world,* which the Scriptures assure us *is enmity with God? Love not the world, nor the things of the world. If any man love the world, the love of the Father is not in him. Ye cannot serve God and Mammon.*

That you my dear friend, may choose and pursue the path of truth and holiness, is the fervent unceasing prayer of your
affectionate   MYRA.

For the Panoplist.

THOUGHTS ON ACTS ix, 11.

Behold, he prayeth.

IN the context is presented one of the most interesting scenes, which men are ever called to witness. A *wicked* man is alarmed. A man of distinguished *natural* and *acquired* talents is brought to tremble in view of the spirituality, purity, and extent of the divine law. A great and learned *Jew*, whose heart, according to the description he afterwards gave of it, was *enmity against God*, and that enmity was grown into such madness against the Christians, as led him to seek their entire extirpation from the earth, by means the most unjustifiable and malevolent;—a *Pharisee* of the Pharisees, who was filled with strong and deep-rooted prejudices against Christianity;—gives up all for Christ and his religion; *counts all things but loss for Christ.*

Of this man it is said, *Behold, he prayeth.* But what is the meaning of the inspired historian? Did Saul never pray before? Could a *Jewish Pharisee*, who was working his passage to heaven, who considered himself *as touching the law blameless*, who lived *in all good conscience*, and was a *Pharisee after the straitest sect;* could such a man refrain from prayer? The sect to which he belonged were remarkable for their long and public prayers. And no doubt Saul of Tarsus was distinguished for *his* learned, long, and apparently fervent, prayers. The meaning cannot be, that he never offered any sort or form of prayer till now; no doubt he was constant and able in that exercise. Still it is written of him, *Behold, he prayeth.* To this portion of holy writ there is attached important meaning. And what is it? Doubtless it is this; He never, till now, offered a *holy, acceptable, prayer.* Till now, his heart was never right with God. All his former sacrifices were full of blemishes; they were corrupt,

forbidden things. His *mouth spake*, out of the abundance of his totally wicked heart, which was as incapable of sending forth holy affections, as a corrupt fountain is of sending forth sweet streams, or as a salt fountain is of sending forth fresh water. While he was *in the flesh*, and he always had been till now, he possessed a *carnal mind*, which he himself afterwards declared to be *enmity against God, and not subject to his law; neither indeed could it be.* Whence he draws the following conclusion, and it is a very rational one; *They that are in the flesh cannot please God.* Saul of Tarsus was, to use the plain language of our Savior, *a child of the devil;*—did his works, and was exceedingly industrious to perform the drudgery, which that infernal tyrant set him about. He was *exceeding mad, and persecuted the saints even to strange cities.*

A question may here arise, How could he then *live in all good conscience towards God?* Because his conscience, being misinformed, did not accuse him. With such a conscience, *he verily thought he ought to do many things contrary to the name of Jesus of Nazareth.* Had his conscience been duly enlightened, he would have found it harder than he did, *to kick against the pricks. When the commandment came, sin revived, and he died;* and no sooner was he born again, than he began to pray a holy prayer. He began, like a new born child, to enter upon a spiritual life. For the first time he cried to God aright. The prayer of the boasting Pharisee is changed for that of the humble.

publican. Instead of applying
o the chief priests for employment, he now submissively, and
with the ardor of a Christian,
cries to his Divine Savior, *Lord,
what wilt thou have me to do?*
So changed is the man, that his
prayer, instead of *going out of
feigned lips*, proceeds from a
broken and contrite heart, which
before he never knew. Having
learned the way to the throne of
grace, the Spirit of inspiration
introduces the thought with the
note of admiration, *Behold. Behold*, (it is worthy of very particular attention,) *he prayeth.*

EPSILON.

P. S. Should these plain
thoughts be admitted, it is probable, Mr. Editor, that some de-
ductions from the above exposition and remarks will be communicated. They are at your
disposal.

For the Panoplist.

DIRECTIONS FOR HEARING THE
GOSPEL.

IN this country we are highly
privileged, not only with the
written word of God, but with
a stated dispensation of it by
ministers of the Gospel. It is
of great importance, that we
make a good use of this privilege. Our eternal all depends
upon it. It will be to us either
a *savor of death unto death*, or,
a *savor of life unto life*. If we
give diligent attention to it, and
hear it aright, happy will be our
condition. But if we refuse to
give a listening ear, and harden
our hearts against the motives
of the Gospel, we shall suffer

great loss, and finally be cast into
outer darkness.

Though such is the necessity
of spiritual improvement, we
find, by observation, that but few
really profit by the preached
word. Many wholly neglect it;
and those, who do not, are often
not much the wiser. Some are
careless and inattentive, and go
to the house of God as they
would go to the theatre, or some
other place of amusement, and
not as to a place of spiritual instruction and worship. There
are others more attentive, who
yet complain of not profiting by
what they hear.

To remedy this evil I would
recommend the observance of
the following rules which I have
found profitable to myself.

1. Before going to hear the
word preached, endeavor to
prepare your mind for its reception. The ground must be prepared, or it will be in vain to
sow the seed. Lay aside the
world with all its concerns and
cares. Remember that you are
to hear for your life. Remember that the preaching of the
word is appointed by God for
the salvation of souls;—that you
have a soul to be saved; and
that if saved at all, it will probably
be saved by the ordinary means
of grace. The age of miracles
is over. You have no reason to
expect a voice from heaven, or
a revelation in any other miraculous way. The written word
is divine revelation; and the
preaching of it, when faithfully
performed, is of the same use to
us now, as a direct revelation
was to the patriarchs.

2. To such a preparation add
fervent prayer, that God would

mnize your mind, and give
a teachable disposition. Im-
e him that his Spirit may fill
' mind, and guard you from
insuitable thoughts.

Remember that all the re-
ous privileges you enjoy are
free grace; and that God
ld have dealt justly with
had you been placed in
rant idolatry like the Hindoo,
) a wretched delusion like
Muhometan. Remember
you are a poor perishing
er, unless saved by divine
:e. Remember that if you
not profited by the word,
· condemnation will be the
iter, as was the case with
ernaum and the other cities
hich our Lord did his mighty
ks, because they remained
nbelief, in the splendor of so
ious a light. Go to the
:e of God humbled under
) views, if you wish to profit.
ery careful, that you are not
ad up with a conceit of your
:rstanding, righteousness, or
on in the church or civil so-
r. Such a conceit will effec-
y hinder your obtaining any
l.

Cultivate a devotional spir-
by joining heartily in the
ers and praises of the con-
:ation. Shut out all wander-
thoughts in the performance
hese duties Be sensible
you have to do with a heart-
ching God, who will detect
ypocrisy. By entering with
t into these duties you will
he better prepared to hear
proht.

During the preaching of the
l give your undivided atten-
to it. Store it up in your
iory as much as possible.
ould be of service to you in

recollecting what you have
heard, if, during the delivery of
a discourse, you would note the
heads of it, and fix them in your
memory. By remembering them,
you will remember more easily
the illustrations of them.

6 When you have returned
from the house of worship,
retire as soon as convenient,
recollect as much of what you
have heard as you can, and compare it with the Scriptures.
Christ directed the Jews to
search the Scriptures. The
Bereans are called noble for
comparing daily the doctrines,
which the Apostles preached,
with the Scriptures. By so doing you will find what has b en
said agreeable to the will of
God; what you are to believe,
and what to practise.

7. Look to God for a blessing
on what you have heard. Let
not this be done in a general
manner only; but be particular,
and introduce much of the sermon into your prayer. A great
advantage will arise from this.
If by the sermon you have been
convinced of sin. confess that
sin freely, and humbly implore
pardon for it.

8. Converse on what you
have heard, as you have opportunity. Different persons will
naturally retain different parts
of the same discourse. By sta-
ing these to each other, they will
all profit by each other's observations.

9 Be particular in attending
punctually on the preaching of
the word. Let not trifling difficulties keep you away. You
know not which portion of his
word God will bless. Attend
upon the whole, if possible.

10. Carry what you hear on

the Sabbath into the week, and conform your conduct to it. There is no part of the word but what is capable of a practical inference, which you may easily draw, if so disposed. Be careful that you make application to to yourself and not to your neighbor, which is very easy and natural, but very unprofitable.

11. Avoid a criticising spirit in hearing, and conversing about sermons. Many apparently well-meaning people indulge a secret vanity and pride in such criticisms, rob themselves of profit in hearing, and often, we have reason to fear, do much injury to the cause of Christ.

These directions, if diligently attended to, will have a tendency to remedy the great evil of not profiting in hearing the word. He that goes to hear with a humble, teachable, prayerful spirit, hears with attention, and afterwards prays over and reduces to practice what he hears, will, I trust, be blessed of God, and find that it was good for him to hear. He will find his mind enlarged, his soul fed, his strength renewed, and his joys increased.   A. D.

A SHORT SERMON. NO. IV.

1 COR. vi, 20.
—*Glorify God in your body, and in your spirit, which are God's.*

THIS precept, addressed to Christians, is introduced by the apostle as an inference from the doctrine of redemption; and enforced by the exalted motives, which a just view of that doctrine is calculated to inspire.

Writing to the Corinthian verts, and through them lievers of every age and try, he saith; *What! know that your body is the te the Holy Ghost, which is i which ye have of God? A are not your own; for bought with a price; the glorify God in your body, your spirit, which are God*

Let as many, then, as to be Christians, and as wish to be Christians, in what is the true import o apostolic exhortation, and to the interesting conside by which it is enforced.

To glorify God, as this is used by the inspired w denotes that disposition an duct in man, by which C honored;—by which his m reverenced, his laws obey praise proclaimed;—by in a word, his will is d earth, as in heaven. To God *with*, or *in, the bod spirit*, therefore, is to cons to his service all the powe faculties with which we a dowed. It is to regard h thority and will, in all ou poses and employments. in substance, obedience— ual, unreserved, universal ence to him, who made a deemed us.

Our text, thus expo furnishes a criterion of Ch character;—a standard fo examination;—a rule, by we may regulate our co in life. By it we may ly try any particular cust habit, to which we are a ed;—any special employm which we occasionally eng any peculiar manner of priating our time;—any

, are neither expressly
landed nor forbidden in the
:ures;—but more especial-
at whole class of actions,
are usually denominated
ments, in all their varieties
rms. It is true, that the
ss estec m these things, as
rs of indifference in a mor-
int of view;—as acts, for
they are not accountable;
ther good nor bad, neither
us nor vicious, neither sin-
ir holy. But they are not
ewed by Him, who hath
that he *will bring every
into judgment with every
thing*. They are not so
d by those, who have de-
themselves sincerely and
ut reserve to his service;
esire and endeavor to glo-
lod with their bodies and
s who, *whether they eat or
or whatever they do*, act
the influence of the same
ar principle of obedience
Divine will, aiming to do
the glory of God. To such
is every custom, every
every practice, every ap-
lation of time, every em-
ent of talents. becomes a
r of importance, and fur-
a case for the decision of
ence. In their estimation,
ly those things, which are
ely prescribed and pre-
defined in the Scriptures,
l the actions of our lives,
orally good or evil. They
ler no business, in which
ngage, nor any acts which
erform, to be of an entirely
rent character. For us ev-
iluntary act has its motive,
ject, and its probable ef-
so has it the property of
good or evil, according to
otive, this object, and this
le effect.

If, then, the Christian should
glorify God with his body and
spirit, we may readily and safely
try the character of those actions, which are neither expressly commanded nor forbidden—
we may be furnished with an unerring standard, by which we may
at once regulate our conduct,
with reference to those things
which are usually denominated
matters of indifference. For example; fix in your mind some
particular practice, if you please
some amusement, which you
wish to try by this test. Now to
learn whether, as a Christian,
you can consistently perform this
act, consider whether you can
propose any rational object. any
good end, any beneficial effect.
Will it be useful to yourself or
others? Will it promote your
health? Will it enlarge your
mind? Will it improve your
temper? Will it render you
more pious or benevolent? In a
word, will it either enable or
dispose you to do more good?
Can you, with a view to this
utility, before you enter upon
the act in question, consistently
retire into your closet and ask a
blessing upon it? Can you, at the
close of the transaction, contemplate it with satisfaction, and
give thanks unto God through
our Lord Jesus Christ, for the
privilege of rational enjoyment
and actual improvement; for the
good you have thus been enabled
to acquire or to do? By these
and similar inquiries we may
learn, whether any questionable
practice is proper for a Christian, and consistent with that
self-dedication, which our text
enjoins.

Let none, who profess to be
Christians, excuse themselves
from attending to this casualty

with the plea, that the rule proposed is rigid and austere. For it is certainly the rule of the Gospel, and therefore the only safe rule for Christians. We are expressly commanded, *whether we eat or drink, or whatever we do, to do all to the glory of God.* And, with the same universal application to the past, we are directed to give thanks unto God always, *for all things, through our Lord Jesus Christ.*

Christians, make this rule, I beseech you, the test of all your conduct; of the appropriation of your time; of the employment of your property; of every practice, in which you engage, and every action, which you perform. The thoughtless and vain may assume some different standard of moral conduct; but whatever it may be, it will probably prove a snare to their souls. You may stop short in your inquiries concerning a particular practice, by saying, "It is the fashion; it is a common practice; it has existed for ages; great men, and even good men, have sanctioned it by their example." All these are dangerous and delusive standards. Do you make general custom your rule of action? The command of Heaven is, *Thou shalt not follow a multitude to do evil.* Do you allege the authority of great men, to justify your practice? Great men are not always good; nay, the Scripture saith, *Not many wise, not many mighty, not many noble are called.* Do you appeal, for your justification, to the example of those, who have been esteemed good men—pious and benevolent? Here too, to say the least, you fix on a very imperfect criterion. For we may be deceived, by the mere semblance of goodness; we may account those good who are mere hypocrites and formalists in worship, and selfish time servers in morality. Beside, if the example of really good men in this imperfect state, were to be made the standard of action, we might select from the falls of one, and the foibles of another, an example for every vanity; yea, for every crime under heaven. No; the truth is, that there is no universal test and safe criterion of conduct, but the one furnished by our text; and the man, who shrinks from an investigation of his character by this standard, and refuses to regulate his practice according to this rule, has not devoted himself without reserve to the service of God; whatever he may profess, he is not a Christian; his religion is vain; his faith is dead; he is yet in his sins; his hope will be finally cut off and perish.

Once more, therefore, let me exhort all, who pretend to be Christians, to bring their characters, their habits, their practices, their employments, yea, all their pursuits, to this standard. Be not deceived, I intreat you, by the delusive standards of the thoughtless, and the fallacious glosses of the crafty. Let not the unmeaning epithets of *innocent amusements,* and *harmless recreations,* draw you into those practices, which you cannot justify; which your hearts condemn; which, you are persuaded, will not glorify your God and Redeemer. Remember the woe pronounced upon those, *who call evil good, and good evil.* Forget not that you are accountable creatures, and that every action will be brought into judgment, with every secret thing. Recollect that you are not your own; that you are bought with a price; that you are therefore bound to glorify God in your body and spirit, which are God's. *Finally, my beloved brethren, be ye steadfast, unmoveable, always abounding in the work of the Lord. Whether you eat or drink, or whatever you do, do all to the glory of God. Amen.*

MISCELLANEOUS.

LIFE OF NELSON.

To the Editor of the Panoplist.

Sir,

I send for publication, if you think proper, a few remarks on the Life of Nelson, as an antidote to the fascinating but pernicious influence of such a character upon the minds of young men.

L.

HORATIO NELSON, the son of a clergyman, entered the navy in a ship commanded by his uncle; and, though of a feeble constitution, rose by his own merit to be the greatest admiral of whom England has ever boasted. Till he fought himself into notice, he often experienced, as he conceived, great neglect and injustice; and repeatedly resolved to abandon the service for ever. From this resolution he was dissuaded by his friends; and he determined that he would have a gazette of his own, which should tell the world his deeds, without dependence on the caprice of any man.

He was engaged in about one hundred and twenty battles, and lost, in the service of his country, an eye and his right arm. Among the victories gained by him was one under the command of Lord St. Vincent, of which his Lordship took the honor, and Nelson was scarcely named.

The battle of the Nile, the battle of Copenhagen, and the battle of Trafalgar;—three as splendid victories as were ever won upon the sea;—brought as much honor to Nelson, and as much solid benefit to his country, as were ever the result of naval skill and bravery in any British admiral. He possessed a mind of the first order;—quick, clear, comprehensive, of great decision and much correctness. He saw intuitively in every emergency what was proper to be done; decided instantly; and executed his decisions with an ardor of mind—a promptitude and courage, which nothing could resist. Such ardor, decision, and boldness, in a mind less intuitively correct, would have been rashness. But Nelson was not rash; he saw all that could be done up to the very point of rashness; and decided upon the highest practicable achievement, with as much precision, coolness, and confidence, as he could have done, if his soul had not been on fire. He seldom failed in any attempt, which he planned, and in which he commanded It is to the above traits in his character, that all his victories are to be ascribed. These traits constituted his greatness. His mind illumined a vast circumference, within which all things lay exposed to perfect view. While others reconnoitred, he saw by a blaze of intuition. While others deliberated, he decided. While they loitered to wait for the coincidence of circumstances, he compelled circumstances to his aid and conquered. *I came, saw, and conquered,* is the laconic language, which Nelson might have employed as well as Cæsar, in giving the account of his victories.

In the above view of his character, and so far as a mere military character can with propriety be admired, I have never been more gratified with the character of any man. In his whole course, no painful disappointments intervene to excite unavailing regret. No opportunity is lost. Wherever Nelson is, all is done that you expect; all that you can desire, so far as it depends on him. Few such minds are found; for a few only are enough to save or to destroy nations, as they are made by Heaven the instruments of salvation, or the ministers of divine anger. Pitt and Nelson were instruments of salvation; while Bonaparte alone was sufficient to execute the wrath of God upon guilty nations.

Nelson's natural disposition was affectionate and amiable: his moral character was in some respects good, in others very defective. His honesty was inflexible. Money was not indeed his object; but if it had been, there is reason to believe he never would have stooped to knavish practices to obtain it. He was not envious. Though glory was the supreme object of his desire, he sought it not by diminishing the lustre of another's

name, but by surpassing him in illustrious actions. He was also patriotic and incorruptible. But he was guilty of profaneness; a sin which no greatness, and no lustre of glory, can cancel or hide.

He was incontinent. Horatia Nelson, a child about five years old at the time of his death, was supposed to be his daughter by an illicit connexion. He suffered his affections to be diverted from an affectionate wife, and became attached to infatuation to Lady Hamilton, a woman of great accomplishments, and of a mind, as to vigor, not unlike his own. He separated from his wife, on account of his alienated affections, and spent all his time on land in the society of Lady Hamilton. His biographer suspects, that there was no criminal intercourse. But had he been a Christian, this inspired interrogation, *Can a man take fire in his bosom and his clothes not be burned?* might have led him to suspect, that such unlawful ardent affection did not content itself with professions, and mere acts of courtesy. It has been rumored, that Nelson was a pious man; and it is with deep regret I am obliged to say, that no evidence appears of the fact; but much to the contrary. The most that can be said is, that he was a believer in Revelation, and in the particular providence of God; that he offered up prayers to Him before battle, and returned thanks after victory; and, on some occasions, used the *language* of resignation to his will. But it is manifest to demonstration, that his supreme object was glory—personal glory;—that his great moral principle was patriotism.

ve of his country more than
ve of God, and the love of
ry as identified with him-
and as the means of pro-
g *his* glory. Dissolve that
ation, and leave out his su-
s hatred of the French;—let
ly guarantee be his real
o God or real benevolence
n, and in the tempest of
n and temptation he would
been like a ship without
r, rudder, or compass, driv-
out of fierce winds His
character is also incom-
e with piety, and there is
his whole life, in none of
rayers, any recorded con-
n of sin, any apparent sense
n, or any penitential feel-
There is no recognition
e atonement, no mention
of the name of the Savior,
o allusion, from which it
l be inferred, that he had
heard of a Savior. His
was by no means, even in
rance, the death of a good
Not a word do we hear in
slemn moment about par-
or mercy, or heaven. "I
lone my duty," he exclaim-
en, by which it is too obvi-
s meant his duty to his king
suntry as a good subject,
than to God as an account-
reature. His mind is oc-
d with thoughts of Lady
lton, his daughter, and the
y which was deciding in
vor; and from the pinnacle
rldly fame, in the full blaze
restrial glory, he went to
nent to receive his eternal
ation according to the
done in the body. The
icy of his example, and of
ography, will be doubtless
ite in the breast of thous-
the throbbings of ambi-
o inspire the same kind of

patriotism which he felt, and to
exalt and perpetuate the prow-
ess of the British navy. As,
however, he uniformly disobey-
ed the orders of his superiors,
when he judged the good of the
nation demanded it, and always
judged correctly, and covered
himself with glory by doing so,
in consequence of his peculiar
intuition and decision, I should
imagine the example would be
dangerous, and, if imitated, extensively ruinous, when attempted by minds less infallible than
his own. The moral tendency of
the life of Nelson is, on the
whole, to make heroes and patriots of the Roman school, but
not of the school of Christ; and
to render moral character itself
a trifling consideration, the want
of which may be compensated by
greatness of intellect, and splendid achievements, and worldly
glory. Should any youthful
bosom be inflamed by such un-
hallowed fire in reading his life,
it is a providential favor that we
have from his own lips a disclosure, which ought in a moment
to extinguish it.

"There is no true happiness
in this life, and in my present
state I could quit it with a smile.
Believe me, my only wish is, to
sink with honor into the grave;
and when that shall please God, I
shall meet death with a smile.
Not that I am insensible to the
honor my king and country have
heaped upon me; so much more
than any officer could desire.
Yet am I ready to quit this world
of trouble, and envy none but
those of the estate six feet by
two."*

This was written soon after
the battle of the Nile.

* Vol. ii, p. 49

For the Panoplist.

ON THE KNOWLEDGE OF THE HEART.

THE ancient philosophers, who made critical observations upon the powers and pursuits of man, pronounced it to be his most uncommon acquirement to become acquainted with himself. Hence arose that admired precept of antiquity, "*Man, know thyself;*" and hence the enlarged aphorism of a Christian poet,

"Man, know thyself: all wisdom centres there."

We may penetrate into the characters of those who surround us; we may learn the habits dispositions, and languages of foreign nations; we may become acquainted with all the properties of the globe that we inhabit, —the course of its rivers, the height of its mountains,—the treasures that are concealed in its secret caverns; we may gain a knowledge of the deeds of blood that in past and present ages have stained its surface; we may follow science, as she soars to the heavens, find the places of the stars, call them by their names, compute their distances, magnitude and periods of rotation; yet, if we span the whole circle of the universe, we may return, and find mysteries in the little empire within, to perplex our researches, and baffle our keenest penetration. We have heard and felt much of the *monitor within;* but whoever attempts to trace his actions to their first spring, and his designs to their real source, will be convinced that he has also an *advocate within.* When this advocate

perceives the eye of the mind turned inward, it strengthens itself to repel the pursuit; but if it finds indications of a resolute search, it casts obstacles in the way; it spreads a veil over what is sought to be investigated; softens errors into virtues; presents crimes as inadvertences; endeavors to pervert the firmness of reason, the judge, and to silence the voice of conscience, the accuser. All this results from the natural selfishness of the human heart; it assumes as many shapes, as fancy can devise; it flies from reproof, and *will not come to the light, lest its deeds should be reproved.* Its object is to keep the soul ignorant of herself, to deceive her into compliance; to force her into submission. But both our duty and happiness require, that this dominion should be broken, and the first step towards it, is to think humbly of ourselves. We are beings who have received much, and are accountable for it; who are placed in a state of trial, with a law of rectitude before us; who are subject to many afflictions, liable to many errors, bearing within us much which needs to be regulated, reformed, or taken away, and bound to an eternal destination of happiness or misery. What is there in this description to awaken pride, or to justify vanity? Every thing around excites us to watchfulness; every thing within to humility. We should esteem it a great unhappiness to have a friend, whose real sentiments were sedulously concealed from us, and whose character we could not decypher; how much more uncomfortable and dangerous to remain ignorant of our own character.

Self-knowledge, though not the growth of an hour, or matured by a few experiments, is attainable by perseverance, and brings an ample recompense for the toil. It is necessary to self-control; for we must become acquainted with our prevailing errors, and their probable sources, before we can be successful in reforming them. Must not the physician understand the disease, before he applies the remedy? The soul from a knowledge of its most vulnerable parts, knows better where to station its strongest guards; how to arouse its slumbering energies to some difficult virtue; and how to quell the mutinous passions, till, like some wise monarch who has reduced his realm to submission, it at length wields an undisputed sceptre, and tranquilly exercises its legitimate powers.

Self-knowledge is necessary to mental and spiritual improvement. Hence arises its great importance to the young, whose principal care ought to be to improve. He, who wishes to acquire knowledge, must be convinced that he possesses little; and, if he candidly observes his own deficiences, the limited nature of his attainments, and the imperfect use he makes of those attainments, he will feel inclined to that humble and teachable disposition, which is the beginning of all true wisdom. It is the attempt of vanity to repress this conviction; to make the mind contented with superficial knowledge, or to inflate it with the pride of showy accomplishments; because the sway of vanity, like

that of all despotic governments, is built upon the ignorance and the weakness of the subject.

Self-knowledge is favorable to the virtue of candor. When we perceive errors and imperfections in others, this teaches us that we are also chargeable with the same; and when we feel inclined to condemn some more prominent failure, this points within our own hearts to the same sources of frailty, and teaches us, that in the same circumstances our own conduct might have been equally censurable. This represses the spirit of calumny and detraction, those poisons of human kindness. This repeats with new feeling the injunction of our Savior; *Judge not, that ye be not judged;* and, from the conviction that we ourselves are *compassed with infirmity,* excites that charitable temper, which, to borrow the inimitable illustration of Scripture, *beareth all things, vaunteth not itself, thinketh no evil.*

Self-knowledge is favorable to our own enjoyment. Most of the repining and discontentment of mankind arise from their cherishing too high an opinion of themselves. This leads them to expect much deference, and to be angry if they do not receive it; to fancy slights, ill treatment, or partiality, where none were intended; and to be vindictive, when they meet with real injuries. But self-knowledge teaches us not to expect more attention than we really deserve; not to overrate our talents, nor place ourselves in situations where we are unqualified to perform a suitable part. Thus it preserves us ↑ much unhappiness and disgrace, leads us to be grateful for small instances of kindness, and to be patient under misrepresentations and injuries. For if these actions which 'are despised among men,' have arisen from pure and disinterested motives, it teaches us to extract from those very motives, a pleasure which human applause could never have bestowed. Do I proceed too far when I assert, that self-knowledge is necessary to our acceptance with heaven? It is the parent of humility; and with this we must be clothed, before we can hope for the divine favor.

If a high opinion of our own merits makes us disgusting to our fellow-creatures, how sinful must it cause us to appear in the sight of One, who sees all our hidden imperfections, whose eye pierces every disguise by which we deceive others, and possibly delude ourselves, and in whose sight our greatest follies and errors are more excusable than our pride. The assurances of his favor are given only to those of a humble and contrite heart. He has promised to bring down *the loftiness of man, to scorn the scorners, but to give grace unto the lowly.*

Self-knowledge is favorable to the promotion of piety. It has already been exhibited as the parent of humility,—and without humility there can be no piety. He, who cultivates an acquaintance with his own heart, will perceive that the frequency of his sins demands constant watchfulness, and that his strongest resolutions often betray their trust; he will feel the necessity of goodness, and his own inability to keep its law perfectly. A

deep feeling of these wants and weaknesses will teach him the necessity of divine assistance, and his dependence upon God; and will increase the fervency of his petitions, that "what is dark he would illumine, what is low, raise and support." Thus a knowledge of the heart is a powerful preparative for the reception and operation of that Spirit, *who leadeth into all truth.* Neither let us suppose, that self-knowledge, though of difficult acquirement, will be a source of mental reproach and mortification only. If it brings latent errors to light, and thus gives pain to the spirit, the pain is salutary, and bears with it a sure remedy, the desire of reformation. But self-knowledge will not always act the part of an accuser; it will sometimes point out disinterested motives, and virtuous actions, and present you the exquisite reward of conscious rectitude. Let us then strive to gain a knowledge of our own hearts, and to scrutinize carefully the actions of our lives.

"'Tis greatly wise to talk with our past hours,
"And ask them what report they bore to heaven."　　　Young.

Let us then erect a tribunal within, before which the deeds of every day shall pass in nightly review. Let us give it power to censure folly, to encourage goodness, and to penetrate into those hidden motives, which elude the eyes of our fellow men. We shall find ourselves animated to virtue by the approbation of our consciences, and deterred from transgression by the assurance of meeting, in the silence of our apartment, an image of the last tribunal.　　March 26, 1814.

For the Panoplist.

EFFORTS TO PROMOTE THE OBSERVANCE OF THE LORD'S DAY.

Mr. Editor,

I HAVE been highly gratified with the exertions of the Legislature of Massachusetts, and of individuals, for promoting the due observation of the Lord's day. I cannot but view them as a day-star, casting a ray of hope on our benighted country. Although various associations have been formed, and much has been done towards the accomplishment of this benevolent object; yet with nothing have I been more pleased, than with what has been done by the Middlesex Convention.

Their proceedings, both at their first meeting in Burlington, at their adjourned meeting in Concord, with the report of their committee; the laws of Massachusetts, for promoting the due observation of the Lord's day; and the very able report of the Legislature upon the subject; copious and minute directions to Tythingmen, and others, how to proceed in executing the laws, and an address to the public, have lately been published, in a cheap and convenient form.

This interesting pamphlet is sold, at No. 50, Cornhill, Boston, at the very low price of $3 a hundred. It is worthy of the serious perusal of all who regard the Sabbath, or the welfare of their country: and I cannot but hope, that all the charitably disposed will interest themselves, in its extensive circulation. It would, no doubt, greatly promote the cause of piety and good morals, especially among the children and youth, if a copy of it could go into every family in the Commonwealth.

The profanation of the Sabbath is one of the enormous sins of our country, and we shall groan under the judgments of heaven until it be removed.

JUNIUS.

RELIGIOUS INTELLIGENCE.

APPENDIX (B.) TO THE REPORT OF THE PRUDENTIAL COMMITTEE TO THE AMERICAN BOARD OF COMMISSIONERS FOR FOREIGN MISSIONS.

[When the missionaries were brought back to Bombay, they heard that they had been considered as prisoners of war, and were charged with having violated a parole. This charge they refute in the first part of the following memorial. The refutation proved to be unnecessary, as the Governor explicitly declared, after reading it, that he had never considered them as prisoners of war, nor as bound by a parole. They were judicious, however, in meeting a charge of so serious a nature, and which they had reason to suppose had received some sanction from persons in authority. It had even been surmised in Bombay, that they were political spies.

The concluding part of the memorial will speak to the understanding, the conscience, and the feelings, of every reader.]

Copy of a Letter to the Right Honorable, the Governor, dated Bombay Harbor, on board the Honorable. Company's Cruiser Ternate, Dec. 4, 1813.

To the Right Honorable Sir Evan Nepean, Baronet, Governor, &c. &c. &c. of Bombay.

Right Honorable Sir,

It has pleased a wise and holy Providence to return us to this place, and in circumstances on many accounts extremely unpleasant. But we have learnt with peculiar distress, that your Excellency, besides having felt officially obliged to interrupt our voyage, on which we were well advanced towards the Island of Ceylon, has conceived our conduct to have been inconsistent with the duties of our profession, and with the obligations arising from the indulgence and attentions, which we had the honor to receive from your Excellency, during our stay in Bombay.

Did the present case concern ourselves merely, and were the consequences depending on its decision to fall on us alone, we are happy in the belief, that your Excellency is not one of those ungracious rulers, who condemn without allowing the accused to be heard in his own defence. But with how much greater confidence ought we to hope and pray for an indulgent and attentive hearing, while we stand so highly impeached as the ministers of Jesus—the living God If we have departed from the path of Christian simplicity and innocence;—if we have prostituted the confidence, inspired by our sacred office, to the base purpose of deception;—if, under the cover of zeal for God, we have dared to engage in the infamous designs of political intrigue, we have wounded our Savior, in the house of his friends;—we have brought an awful scandal on the Christian name, and done what tends to destroy all confidence in the Missionary character, and to delay that period, which is the object of Christian hope, when the heathen shall all be gathered unto Christ.

As these mournful consequences must follow necessarily upon our guilt, we should be uncharitable indeed to believe, that your Excellency, whose standing is so high, not only in the political but in the religious world, and whose decision on the subject is of such great importance, would not, like ourselves, earnestly desire that our characters, if possible, should stand without reproach.

Whether we can say any thing to remove, or even extenuate, our imputed crime and guilt, is not for us to decide. It is the prerogative of Him, who has seen all that we have done, and before whom our conduct is sealed up for judgment and eternity. We do, however, hope, that after having read what we now desire to offer, your Excellency will at least believe we have acted with Christian honesty, integrity, and zeal, though our zeal should still seem to have been inordinate, and our measures indiscreet.

We have understood, that we are charged with having violated the obligations of a parole—obligations so universally held sacred, and which so materially mitigate the calamities of war. We confess, that, we are in a great measure ignorant of the laws of nations; and are sensible, that ever since we have been in the country, we have been exposed to numerous though involuntary errors in those painful transactions relative to Government, which, as ministers of peace, we had little reason to expect If we have violated the obligations of parole, we have certainly done it through ignorance; though we did not act without careful consideration.

We had been warned, as your Excellency has seen, by our Reverend and beloved Patrons at home, and we were disposed most entirely ourselves, to be particularly cautious in our conduct, on account of the unhappy war in which our country is engaged We felt therefore under peculiar obligations to examine the subject according to our ability; and it appears to us in the following light.

We were originally ordered to leave the country, long before any intelligence of the war had arrived in India; and the same orders included unimpeached and well recommended English Missionaries, in precisely the same terms as ourselves: for both which reasons we could not consider these orders as having any relation to our national character, and much less as making us prisoners of war, or afterwards to be exercised upon us as such.

On our arrival at Bombay, we were informed by R. T Goodwin, Esq. the chief magistrate of Police, that Government would not allow us to remain in the country, on account of orders which had been received from Bengal. These orders must have left Calcutta before any intelligence of the war had reached that place, having then but just arrived overland at Bombay Mr. Goodwin's communication to us therefore did not, as we conceive, regard us as prisoners of war; nor did he intimate, that we were to be considered as such. He directed us to procure ourselves a passage to England, and to give him information of our place of residence. We replied, that we had not the means of procuring ourselves a passage to England. We certainly did not suppose that what passed at this time amounted, either to an express, or an implied, parole; that we had laid ourselves under any of the obligations, or that we were to enjoy any of the peculiar privileges, of a parole. Nor did we suppose, that the liberty, with which we left the office, resulted from any thing which had been transacted there; much less from any peculiar confidence reposed in us, as we were then under severe censure.

We had other reasons for supposing we were entirely free from the obligations of a parole. We did indeed think, that no one could consider us to be under such obligations, while we did not enjoy the provision usually made for prisoners of war;—while we were defraying expenses exceeding our means, and while expecting to be sent to a land of strangers, without the prospect of a provision there.

Besides, we have been led frequently to inquire, whether peaceably behaved gentlemen, being found in a civilized state, at the commencement of a war between that state and their own, are usually considered as prisoners of war.—We were uniformly answered "*No*"—And from the nature of the case, as well as numerous facts, we supposed "No" the only rational answer

But we certainly had a higher reason for believing that we were not to be considered as prisoners of war. We had declared our-selves—and our declaration had received the confidence of your Excellency, and of the Governor General—to be the Ambassadors of the Prince of Peace, employed in his service, and devoted to that alone. We knew that we were parties in no war, and we believed that we were the friends of all men. We thought we could not be considered as prisoners of war, while adhering to the peaceable maxims of our Divine Lord—the common Redeemer—the God of England and America, before whom both nations, and all nations, are as one.

Shortly after our arrival in Bombay, we presented to your Excellency a statement of our proceedings in Bengal, and of the ob-ject of our Mission; accompanied by the official instructions under which we were to act. The liberality and kindness, with which your Excellency was pleased to view these documents, exacted our gratitude, and animated our hearts. Distressing as our circumstan-ces had been, and conscious as we were of the integrity of our hearts, and the sacredness of our object we received your Excell-ency's favor as a signal blessing from Heaven; we indulged the most pleasing hopes; *we thanked God, and took courage*

The attention your Excellency was pleased to bestow upon our subsequent addresses, we thankfully acknowledge. The indulgent confidence with which you viewed us, and the kind attentions which we continually received, were flattering to our hearts, and increas-ed our desire of doing that, and that only, which should be agreea-ble to you. But while they attached our hearts, we should have mistaken their intention, had we considered them as shown for our personal merits, and not as the effusions of a pious and liberal mind, and to us as ministers of the Gospel, for our work's sake.

While, however, in all our requests to your Excellency, we so-licited what we thought would be for the honor of Christ, we never had occasion to ask for a greater degree of personal liberty, than we at first enjoyed. From the time of our first visit to the Police, we were not aware that any additional liberty was granted, any new restrictions, added, any old one removed, any pledge required, or that any act of our own laid us under any restraining obligation, not to be found in the nature of our character as Christians, or our office as ministers of the Gospel. We were not aware of any other difference made in our relation to Government, than that which arose from an orderly and Christian conduct, and from those high and unsolicited attentions, which were never due to us as men, but only to the ministerial character, which we hope was unsullied be-fore we left Bombay.

Your Excellency will allow us to express our honest belief, that the liberty we had, when we left Bombay, was the same that was given us before we had made any communications to you, or had received those kind attentions which we most thankfully acknowl-edge. We of course felt ourselves under obligation to act, not as American prisoners on parole, but as Missionaries of Jesus, and to regulate ourselves by the inspired directions and holy examples, which are to guide the ministers of the cross.

n thus considering ourselves, we felt indeed as having in general
as the sanction of your Excellency; whom we had understood
ay, that we were not prisoners of war, but harmless, inoffensive
i, whose weapons of warfare were not carnal but spiritual.

Ve have observed, that we felt under obligation to regulate
elves by the inspired directions and holy examples of the Bi-
If we know our own hearts, these, and these alone, influenced
minds, not with the delusive force of novelty, but with the
nanence of a conviction settled by meditation, and unaltered in
midst of delay and trials, and the darkest prospects.

ong before we were ordained to the Gospel Ministry, it became
i us a solemn inquiry, in what part of the world it was the will
Christ we should preach his Gospel. In Christian countries
saw thousands of ministers, innumerable Bibles and other re-
•us books, to guide immortal souls to everlasting life.

Ve looked upon the heathen, and alas! though so many ages had
sed away, three-fourths of the inhabitants of the globe had not
n told, that Jesus *had tasted death for every man.* We saw them,
wing their fathers in successive millions to eternal death. The
r was overwhelming—the convictions of our own duty were
lear as noon, and our desire was ardent to bear to the dying
hen, *the glad tidings of great joy*—to declare to them Him
i had said, *look unto me and be ye saved, all the ends of the earth;*
who, after he had brought from the grave the body crucified
men, said, *Go—teach all nations—He that believeth shall be
d, and he that believeth not shall be damned.*

ffected and convinced as we were, though fastened to our coun-
y the strongest ties;—though we had aged parents to comfort,
beloved friends to enjoy;—though urged by affectionate congre-
ons to stay and preach the Gospel to them;—we were compel-
to leave all and come to this land, with the prospect of no tem-
il advantage, but with the prospect, the certainty, of much tem-
l loss, and even of suffering too, should our lot be cast under
athen government, as the experience of all ages warned us
xpect. We were determined, as we thought, to deliver our
sage at the hazard of every personal convenience or suffering,
ting in God who guides the ways of all men, and willing to
e his allotments.

ight Honorable Sir, thus we were devoted to a work of which
are, and ever shall be, infinitely unworthy;—devoted for reasons
ch can never lose their force, but whose weight in our own case
been increasing by all the preparations we had made, and by all
information we had acquired. Before we left Bombay we had
it more than a year in different parts of India;—had conversed
i many gentlemen, clergy and laity, on the subject of Missions;
d learnt much of the language, manners and customs of the
ole; and had become more deeply impressed with their wretch-
ss, and the duty of publishing to them the blessings of the
pel. While we enjoyed these advantages, we trusted we had
ined a valuable degree of preparation for a prudent and useful

management of a Christian Mission; which made it more than ever our duty to preach to the heathen.

We were standing on heathen ground. We were surrounded by immortal beings, polluted by idolatry, dead in sin, and exposed to hell. There was not one messenger to a million, among all the idolaters of India, to preach Jesus to them There was enough before our eyes to convince us, that the command of Christ to teach all nations had not been thoroughly fulfilled; and we knew that it had never been revoked. We had for years been preparing; and we had come to this country for no other purpose than to obey this command. But now we were called upon to relinquish the purpose which had been so long conceived—to abandon the work for which we had been so long preparing—and to depart, not only from the particular field which we had entered, but from the heathen altogether.—We were commanded by a government we reverenced, a government exalted, as an enlightened and a Christian government, among the nations of the earth—a government, under which Christian people have been active beyond a parallel in modern ages, in their efforts for the universal diffusion of Christian knowledge;—and, what was peculiarly distressing, your Excellency had considered it your official duty to execute upon us orders, which would remove us from this *field white already to the harvest.*'

Thus situated, what could we? as Ministers of Christ, what ought we to have done? The miseries of the heathen were before us. The command of Christ remained in full force. We had hoped, and prayed, and waited—till almost the day on which the orders for our going were to be executed, our work defeated, and our prospect of preaching to the heathen destroyed. We ask again what could we? We appeal to your own Christian feelings, what ought we to have done? That the Gospel should be preached to these heathen we knew was according to the will of Christ. If by any means we could do this, though we had been forbidden, we thought, (we say it with all possible deference,) that we ought to obey God rather than man.

There did seem to be a way authorized by the Holy Scriptures, which, though doubtful in its issue, furnished, we thought, considerable prospect of success. It was to escape and reach Ceylon, where we had been assured of protection and encouragement. Paul and Barnabas escaped from Thessalonica; and again Paul was let down in a basket by the wall of Damascus, while he knew that the highest civil authority of the city was waiting to apprehend him.

We stand far behind apostles, those venerable Messengers of the Lord; but though so far behind them, yet, as Ministers of the same Lord, we feel bound in duty to plead their example, especially when we consider ourselves, if prevented from doing our work in one city, under a command of our Lord *to flee to another.* This we attempted, but without success; and for this attempt we now stand so highly impeached.

Amidst the distress which unavoidably results from the imputation of guilt, it affords us consolation to reflect, that until we left

Bombay, our character, by a fair testimony, both here and at Calcutta, stood unimpeached.

If this single act does really bring guilt upon our souls; if it does justly destroy the confidence previously reposed in our characters; how can we justify Apostles and others, of whom the world was not worthy, who in like manner fled from city to city rather than abandon their work?

Such, Right Honorable Sir, is the statement which we have thought it our duty to submit to your serious consideration. We should be happy indeed, should it remove from our characters the imputation of guilt. Confident as we are of none other than the best intentions, we most earnestly hope, and anxiously desire, it may, and pray that the time may not be distant, when we shall be freed from the painful duty of vindicating ourselves, and when we shall enter with joy and thanksgiving upon that work, for which we are literally strangers and pilgrims, and have no certain dwelling place. But the matter rests with God. On Him we will endeavor quietly and patiently to wait;—to Him we will look to bear us through our present trials—to publish his own Gospel to the dying Heathen, and to honor his dishonored Son among all nations.

We have the honor to be, Right Honorable Sir,
With the highest respect, your Excellency's
Most obedient and most humble servants,
GORDON HALL,
SAMUEL NOTT.

APPENDIX (C.)

[Letters from the Rev. Thomas Thomason of Calcutta, addressed to one of the missionaries at Bombay, the last of which was received Dec. 10, 1813.]

My dear Sir,   Oct. 8, 1813.
I HAVE been favored by your two letters, and to save the post of this evening write in haste to say, that Mr. Udny seems to think that some attempt may be made with Earl Moira to interest him in your favor; but how, or of what nature, he has not intimated. I am now going to wait upon him. No time will be lost in doing what can be done; nor, if any thing is to be done effectually, ought a moment to be thrown away. You shall hear as soon as any thing may be concluded.

We are deeply concerned in all your motions, and shall feel most happy and thankful to God, if any thing should arise favorable to all our desires. It will be from *Him.* Vain is the help of man.
Yours affectionately,   THOMAS THOMASON.

My dear Sir,   Oct. 13, 1813.
IT has been no easy matter to know how to proceed in our business. At first we determined on an address to Lord Moira, to be signed by Mr. Udny, Dr. Carey, and myself. After preparing the letter we demurred about the expediency of addressing Lord Moira, on so delicate a business, so soon after his entering on the gov-

ernment, especially as we had to plead, not for Missionaries merely, but for *American* Missionaries; and moreover to urge a *revocation of a government order*, even while Lord Minto, the Ex-Governor General, was upon the spot.

On the whole, we thought it best to apply first to Lord Minto; and this morning I have had a long interview with him. I showed him a copy of your last letter, and also of the letter of the Board of Commissioners for Foreign Missions, appointing us to act in India. This I did in order to explain why we interested ourselves individually in this matter.

His Lordship was very gracious—professed the highest opinion of your intentions—but could not give a decided answer without consulting with his late colleagues in council. For his own part, however, he seemed to think, that Sir Evan Nepean could judge as well as they could; and that the business might be left to him to act as he thought proper

I told him, that we petitioned only for a relaxation of the order, which *bound* Sir Evan Nepean to send you away. He said he would inform me, as soon as he had had an opportunity of conversing with the council. If they can be persuaded to relax in their views of the subject, the way will be cleared for Lord Moira to act without any indelicacy to his predecessor.

Thus the matter rests. It may be several days before you hear the result. But as there is a hope that it may be favorable, I hope you may obtain *permission to stay until you hear again.*

But we look above Councils and Governors in this matter. We have a gracious Head, who is not unmindful of his Church. To Him let us commit the matter in faith and prayer.

Yours affectionately,

THOMAS THOMASON.

My dear Sir,   Nov. 19, 1813.

AFTER much delay I have at length received a favorable intimation from government, which grants all that you requested. Lord Minto was long in giving me his judgment of the case. So I wrote again, enclosing in my letter a copy of a letter from a Mr. Erskine of Bombay to his friend Dr. Hare. A copy was at the same time sent to Lord Moira by Dr. Hare. In that letter Mr. Erskine spoke very candidly and kindly of you both. No answer, however, was sent by Lord Minto to this second communication; but *he called* upon me, and said, that he thought I should find no difficulty in obtaining the permission of this government. Our address to Lord Moira, signed by Mr. Udny, Dr. Carey, and myself, was accordingly sent in without delay.

Yesterday I had an audience of Lord Moira. He spoke very decidedly about your being allowed to stay; and expressed his conviction that you meant to do good, and that no conceivable public injury could arise from your staying. But, he added, your letter will come before Council in a day or two, and will be publicly answered.

. Thus the matter stands. In a short time I hope to write again. Meanwhile, Sir Evan Nepean may be assured, that the government here has a friendly disposition towards you. May this arrive in time to prevent any decisive steps for your leaving India; and may you be abundantly blessed in all your plans and labors.

I have the inexpressible satisfaction to observe, that Lord Moira has come out with every laudable desire to do all the good he can, and with the determination to extend the efficient aid of government in forwarding plans of general instruction and improvement. I am now preparing the materials of a very extended plan of operations, which, in the course of a month, I hope to submit to him. You shall hear from me on the subject more at large, if nothing unforeseen prevent me from writing.

My kindest regards to your colleague, and to Dr. Taylor, to whom I am in arrears, and hope to write shortly.

Yours affectionately,

THOMAS THOMASON.

APPENDIX (D.)

To the Right Honorable Sir Evan Nepean, Governor, &c. &c.

Right Honorable Sir,

WE understand that the final arrangements for our being transported to England are now made. At this decisive moment, we beg to submit to your Excellency the following considerations.

That exercise of civil authority, which, in a manner so conspicuous and determined, is about to prohibit two ministers of Christ from preaching his Gospel in India, can be of no ordinary consequence; especially at the present moment, when the Christian public, in England and America, are waiting with pious solicitude to hear how the religion of the Bible is welcomed and encouraged among the Pagans of this country. Our case has had so full and conspicuous a trial, that its final decision may serve as a specimen, by which the friends of religion may learn what is likely to befal, in India, those evangelical missions, which they are laboring to support by their prayers, and by their substance.

Had the decision been favorable to missions, it would have encouraged the hearts of thousands to increase their exertions for the enlargement of the Redeemer's kingdom; it would have brought thanksgivings to God and blessings to the Heathen. But if the decision must be unfavorable, it will tend to deject the hearts of Christians; it will cast a new cloud of darkness over this heathen land, and discourage many from attempting to rescue the poor Pagans from the doom which awaits idolaters. This momentous decision, Right Honor ble Sir, rests with you.

Now we would solemnly appeal to your Excellency's conscience and ask: Does not your Excellency believe, that it is the will of Christ that his Gospel should be preached to these Heathens? Do you not believe, that we have given a creditable testimony that we are ministers of Christ, and have come to this country to preach his Gospel? and would not prohibiting us from preaching to the Heathen here be a known resistance to his will? If your Excellency finally exerts civil authority to compel us from this heathen land, what can it be but a decided opposition to the spread of the Gospel among those immortal beings, whom God has placed under your Excellency's government?* What can it be but a fresh instance of that persecution against the Church of Christ, and that opposition to the prevalence of true religion, which have so often provoked the indignation of God, and stamped with sin and guilt the history of every age? Can you, Right Honorable Sir, make it appear to be otherwise to your own conscience—to that Christian public who must be judges in this case—but especially can you justify such an exercise of power to your God and final Judge?

Your Excellency has been pleased to say, that it is your duty to send us to England, because you have received positive orders from the Supreme Government to do so. But, Right Honorable Sir, ———— ———— ———— ————

———— ———— ———— ———— ————

———— ———— ———— ————

were it even admitted, that whatever is ordered by a superior authority is right to be done, would not our case stand thus: Several months ago, your Excellency received from the Supreme Government positive orders to send us to England; but repeatedly expressed a deep regret that you were obliged to execute such orders upon us. But a few days since we had the happiness to present to your Excellency such communications from Bengal, as were acknowledged to evince such a change in the mind of Lord Minto, as that he was willing we should remain in the country, and that Lord Moira was also favorable to our staying. May not your Excellency therefore presume, that notwithstanding the previous orders of the Supreme Government, it has since become their pleasure that we should remain in the country?

Besides, those communications further state, that the subject was soon to come before the Council for a formal decision. But delays are so liable to occur in such cases, that at this moment a reasonable time has hardly elapsed for the arrival of an official decision, though we have reason to expect it daily.

Under such circumstances, could your Excellency be judged unfaithful to your trust, should you at least suspend our departure until a further time were allowed for official communications to be received from Bengal? By so doing could you be thought to take upon yourself an unjustifiable responsibility; especially when it is considered what a discussion the spreading of the Gospel in India has undergone in England, and how great is the probability, that

* It is manifest, from the whole history of this business, that this question, and the succeeding one, were meant to apply to the system of measures adopted by the East India Company and the Bengal government, and not to Sir Evan Nepean in his individual capacity; for he appears to have been favorably disposed toward the missionaries

nething decidedly in its favor will soon be announced in this untry? —— —— —— —— ——

[t is our ardent wish, that your Excellency would compare, most riously, such an exercise of civil authority upon us with the genil spirit and tenor of our Savior's commands We most earnestintreat you not to send us away from these Heathens. We intreat u by the high probability, that an official permission from the ipreme Government for us to remain here will shortly be receiv; and that something more general, and to the same effect, will on arrive from England. We intreat you by the time and money ready expended on our Mission, and by the Christian hopes and ayers attending it, not utterly to defeat its pious obj. ct by send; us from the country. We intreat you by the spiritual mise>s of the Heathen, who are daily perishing before your eyes, and der your Excellency's government, not to prevent us from eaching Christ to them. 'We intreat you by the blood of Jesus, iich he shed to redeem them:—As Ministers of *Him*, who has all wer in Heaven and on earth, and who with his farewell and as:nding voice commanded his Ministers to *go and teach all nations,* e intreat you not to prohibit us from teaching these Heathens. y all the principles of our holy religion, by which you hope to i saved, we intreat you not to hinder us from preaching the same iligion to these perishing idolaters. By all the solemnities of the dgment-day, when your Excellency must meet your Heathen objects before God's tribunal, we intreat you not to hinder us from eaching to them that Gospel, which is able to prepare them as ell as you for that awful day. —— —— —— —— ——

7e intreat your Excellency not to oppose the prayers and efforts the Church, by sending back those whom the Church has sent rth, in the name of the Lord, to preach his Gospel among the eathen; and we earnestly beseech Almighty God to prevent such i act, and now and ever to guide your Excellency in that way, hich shall be most pleasing in his sight. —— —— —— —— ——

We have the honor to be,
Right Honorable Sir,
Your Excellency's
most obedient and most humble servants,
GORDON HALL,
SAMUEL NOIT.

Bombay, Dec. 20, 1813.

APPENDIX (E.)

[Extracts of a letter from Mr. Newell to the Corresponding Secretary, dated Combo, Ceylon, Dec. 20, 1813. This letter is very copious, and, lest preceding letters ould have miscarried, contains many facts which had before been communicated. he introduction of the letter, and the comparison of Jaffna and Bussora, as missiony stations, are selected to accompany the Report of the Prudential Committee. ther miscellaneous parts of the letter may hereafter be selected for the Panoplist.]

Rev. and dear Sir,

NEARLY two years have elapsed, since you sent us forth to carry the glad tidings of salvation to the perishing heathens in the east. Our Christian friends in America will perhaps expect, that before this time we have chosen our station, arrived at the field of our labors, commenced the study of the language or languages of the place, and made considerable progress in our work. It would be no less pleasing to me, than to you and them, to be able to communicate such intelligence. But I rejoice, dear Sir, to see, by your report for the last year, that you are prepared, and that you have endeavored to prepare the minds of the Christian public, to hear of our disappointments. It has pleased God, in his inscrutable wisdom, to call us, in the very outset, to pass through the depths of affliction, and to experience the disappointment of our dearest hopes. Perhaps God intends by these trials to humble us; to purify our hearts from pride and ambition; to crucify us to the world, and make us more sensible of our dependence on his grace, that we may be better prepared to serve him, in the kingdom of his Son, among the heathen. If tribulation work in us *patience*, and patience *experience*, and experience *hope*, we shall have reason to bless God that we have been so early and so deeply afflicted. Pray for us, fathers and brethren, that the things which have befallen us in Asia may turn out *for the furtherance of the Gospel* of Christ; that as *the sufferings of Christ abound in us, so our consolation may abound* by Christ, that we may be able *to comfort them, who are in any trouble, by the comfort wherewith we ourselves are comforted of God.*

[* At the time of Mr. Newell's writing this letter, he took it to be certain beyond a doubt, that Messrs Hall and Nott had been sent from Bombay to England, and that the British government over the dominions of the East India Company was inveterately opposed to missions. He does not appear to have been informed of the great exertions, which had been made in England, to open India to the preachers of the Gospel. He considered himself as obliged to act alone, at least till he could be joined by fellow-laborers from this country. In this state of things, he looked around for the best place to establish an infant mission. His views on that subject are as follows—

I have also written to our Committee at Calcutta for advice. I am wavering between two places, Ceylon, and Bussora at the head of the Persian gulf. They both have their advantages and disadvantages. I will give you a summary of my reasoning with respect to each.

The reasons for establishing our mission at Ceylon are these:

1. The country is the king's, and his majesty's government is friendly to missions. His Excellency General Browntigg, the present Governor of Ceylon, has been pleased lately to say, that he is authorized by the Secretary of State, (Eng.) to encourage the efforts of all respectable ministers.* Sir Alexander Johnstone, the

---

* This is an exceedingly important fact. Mr N also states, in another part of his letter, that Gov. Browntigg had interceded with Sir Evan Nepean in behalf of

-chaplains, the Hon. and Rev. Mr. Twisleton and the Rev. Mr. Bisset, and indeed every influential character in the place, is favorably disposed.

2. There is here a very considerable scope for missionary exertions. The population of the island is variously estimated, from a million and a half to three millions. It is probably somewhere between these limits.

3. There are very great facilities for evangelizing this people. There are but two languages spoken in the island, so that when a missionary has acquired these, he may preach to several millions of people. The natives can read and write. The whole of the Bible has been translated into the Tamul, the language spoken in the north of the island, and the New Testament into the Cingalese,* which is spoken in the south and the interior. There are, at the lowest computation, 200,000 native Christians, as they are called, but who are totally ignorant of Christianity. "They have no objection to the Christian religion," says Mr Twisleton, "but for their amusement are apt to attend the Budhist festivals." Under the head of facilities may be reckoned the schools. There are about 100 already in operation, and the government is establishing others in every part of the island. Here we should be perfectly secure, under the protection of the British government, from all those dangers to which we should be exposed in the Burman country.

4. There are but two missionaries in the whole island, Mr. Errhardt, a German, from the London Society, and Mr. Chater, from the Baptist Society, the same that was four years in the Burman country. Mr. Vos, who was sent hither by the London Society, has left the place, and gone to the Cape, where he is settled in a Dutch church. Mr. Palm, another of the missionaries from the London Society, has left Jaffna, where he resided eight years, and has been appointed by government to the Dutch church here in Colombo, so that he ceases to act as a missionary. Mr. E. has not yet acquired the Cingalese language; nor has Mr. C. yet had time to acquire it, so that there is not at this time one missionary on the island, who can speak to the people in their own tongue.

5. Mr. Chater has told me, that Mr. Talfrey, (who has been engaged in translating the New Testament into Cingalese,) has re-

missionaries, and that Sir Alexander Johnstone, Chief Justice, had also written to Bombay in their favor. These kind applications either had not reached the Bombay government, at the date of our last letters from that place, or the applications, if received, had not been made known to our missionaries. The Christian public in this country may draw a favorable conclusion, as to the importance of this mission, when they consider, that the Governor of Bombay, the Governor and Chief Justice of Ceylon, and a member of the Supreme Council of Bengal, together with a considerable number of very respectable gentlemen, chaplains, missionaries, physicians, and other of different religious denominations, at Calcutta, Madras, Colombo, and Bombay, places many hundred miles from each other, not only *desired* that our missionaries might fix themselves within the British dominions in Asia, but exerted a *gratuitous and active influence* to promote such an event. Ed.

* This translation is thought to be so imperfect, as that a new version is necessary. This appears by the fifth topic of this discussion.

peatedly expressed a desire, that I would apply myself to the study of Cingalese, and qualify myself to carry on the translation. Mr. C. has also expressed the same wish. There seems to be no jealousy on this point. Mr. C. himself wishes me to stay here. He is somewhat advanced in the acquisition of the Cingalese, having been here a year and a half, and it is his intention to engage in the business of translation; but he wishes that more than one may be engaged in the work.

6. If we take our station at Jaffna, where the Tamul language is spoken, we have an immense field before us; for the same language is spoken just across the channel, on the neighboring continent, by seven or eight millions of people. The intercourse between the island and continent is nearly as easy and frequent, as if they were contiguous. Besides, on the little island of Ramisseram, between Ceylon and the continent, is one of the most famous Hindoo temples, that is to be found in all India. Sir Alexander Johnstone recommended this place to me, as a missionary station, on account of the crowds of pilgrims, who resort to this temple from all parts of the continent. The Brahmins here are said to have the power of restoring *cast*, when it is lost, a prerogative which is not claimed by the priests of any other temple in India. I visited this place in September, on my way to Jaffna, upon the recommendation of Sir Alexander. The result of my inquiries was a conviction that much good might be done here by distributing tracts, and portions of the Scriptures, among the pilgrims who would carry them to the various parts of the continent from which they came, and thus divine instruction would be conveyed to many places, where no European missionary might go for a hundred years to come. *We* cannot be allowed to settle on the continent at present, perhaps never. But a station at Jaffna is in fact the same thing, as one any where in the south of India. Our personal labors can extend but a little way around us, wherever we fix our station. There are a hundred and twenty thousand natives in Jaffna, and this is more than we can instruct ourselves. We might establish an institution for the religious education of youth, to raise up and qualify the natives themselves for schoolmasters, catechists, and itinerating missionaries; and if Christianity be once firmly established in Jaffna, it must from its nature spread into the adjoining continent. Then, if some of us learn the Cingalese language too, we may prepare and send forth missionaries in that language also, to carry the Gospel up into the Candian country in the interior of the island. These are the principal arguments for establishing our mission here.

[Mr. Newell briefly enumerates his objections to a mission any where in the British dominions; which objections we hope are now obviated by the favorable issue of the decision of the British Parliament on the subject.]

I will enumerate particularly my reasons for a mission to Bussora, on the Euphrates, near the Persian gulf.

1. Bussora is a commercial town, the great emporium of western

ia, through which the merchandise of the east is distributed to
rsia. Arabia, and Turkey. It is situated on the confines of these
ee extensive countries, and the Persian, Arabic, and Turkish
guages are, I believe, all spoken there.

I In the whole of western Asia, containing a population of forty
fifty millions, there is not one protestant missionary. The Ka-
s mission. (which is certainly a most important one,) is, I believe,
hin the limits of Europe.* The Turkish and Tartar languages
the proper sphere of this mission; the Arabic and Persian,
t of a mission to Bussora.

I It is an object of primary importance to procure correct trans-
ons of the whole Bible into Persian and Arabic. The Arabic
ne was said by the late Rev. Mr. Martyn to be of more impor-
ce than three fourths of all the translations now in hand. This
ntleman had undertaken to superintend the translation of the
riptures into these two languages, with the assistance of N. Sa-
, the converted Arabian, and Mirza Fitrut, a learned Persian.
·. M. died in December last, on a tour through Persia and Ara-
, having only completed the New Testament in both languages.
hether any other person in Bengal will take up the work, and
ish it, I do not know. I have written to ascertain. But even if
: Bible were completed in both languages, it would be of little
:, until some person would go and carry it to them, and say to
: people, *Hear the word of the Lord.*

i. There are numerous bodies of Christians, of different sects,
ittered through these countries, who have sunk into the grossest
rkness for want of instruction, but who would gladly receive the
ole. These Christians might be made instrumental in diffusing
: light around them, but would never take the lead in such a
rk. How many ages did the Syrian Churches of Travancore
e in the midst of an idolatrous people without ever thinking of
ring them the Bible, or even of translating it into the vulgar
igue for their own use. But no sooner was the thing proposed
Dr. Buchanan, than the Syrian bishop himself sat down to the
rk, and the Malayalim Gospels have already been published. It
highly probable that in the Syrian and Armenian churches in
ise western regions, men may be found qualified and disposed
assist in spreading the light around them.

i. The Persians and Arabians rank as high in the scale of in-
lect, as any people in the world; and, if truly converted, would
:ome very useful to the cause of Christianity.

i. There are several considerations, which, at the present time,
:m to furnish a high degree of probability, that the Gospel may
spread through these hitherto benighted regions. In the first
ce, the mussulmans are a kind of heretical Christians. They
ifess to believe in one God; in Moses and his law, David and his
lms, Jesus and his Gospel; though they say these books have

---

* Karass is in Russian Asia. Ed.

been corrupted by the Christians. And besides, the Persians profess so lax a system of Mahometanism, that they are considered by some other mussulmans as a kind of heretics. It is certain that Christians are, and ever have been, tolerated in Persia. When I was in Bengal, Mr Sabastiani, a Catholic missionary, arrived there, who had been ten or twenty years in Persia, and reported that the Christians in that country were numerous. The story, which Dr. Buchanan has related, of Nadir Shah's attempt to get the Gospels translated into Persian, is a proof that they are not very scrupulous about admitting new religions into the country. When the late Mr. Martyn was last year at Shiraz, the seat of the Persian court, he wrote, that "the men of Shiraz had offered to assist him in translating the Bible into Persian."

All these circumstances seem to indicate the dawn of Gospel day on those regions where the star, which led to Bethlehem, first appeared. Especially the progress of *Wahhahbe*, the Arabian conqueror, seems to portend the speedy downfal of the Mahometan power. The creed of this adventurer is simply this; *There is no other God but God.* He denies the divine mission of Mahomet, and the authority of the Koran, and destroys all the monuments of Mahometan superstition, which fall into his hands. He is said to show more favor to Christians than to mussulmans; but he sets himself up as a prophet, or rather pretends to a divine commission.

But after all it must be confessed, a mission to these parts would be attended with considerable hazard. If the Gospel should spread, and be embraced by persons of consequence, persecution would most probably follow. Already the streets of Bucharia have been stained with the blood of a martyred Christian In that bigoted city, Abdallah, the noble Arabian convert, witnessed a good confession, and, in the presence of a wondering crowd, laid down his life for the name of the Lord Jesus But Abdullah was a nobleman, and filled an office of the highest dignity in the Persian court. The common people, I believe, are not persecuted for changing their religion. But shall we wait till Persia and Arabia *are willing* to change their religion before we offer them the Gospel. Great and discouraging difficulties lie in our way, wherever we would attempt to propagate the Christian religion. In China Mr. Morrison is translating and publishing the Scriptures, in opposition to an *imperial edict*, which renders him every moment liable to be seized and put to death.

Finally, a mission to western Asia would be all our own; and it would be free from the objections which I stated to establishing our mission in British India We should be in the neighborhood of Mesopotamia, Syria, Palestine, and Egypt, those interesting theatres, on which the most wonderful and important events, recorded in sacred history, took place. There are Christian churches in all these countries. Might we not, by giving them the Bible, of which they have long been destitute, rekindle their zeal, and lift up in the midst of them *a great light*, that will dart its cheering beams far into the regions of thick darkness, by which they are surrounded.

When I think of these things, I long to be on my way towards Jerusalem. But, dear Sir, I stand alone; I have no missionary associate to advise with, and I am afraid to rely on my own judgment. What would I not give to be one half hour with you. We could settle the business at once. Could I know that it would meet the approbation of the Society at home. I think I should be decided.

A consideration of minor importance, which makes me desirous of engaging in the mission, is, I have been at very considerable expense in procuring Persian and Arabic books, and have devoted several months to the study of the Persian language. This I did with a view to Bombay, which I must now give up.

I am sorry that I cannot say to you in this letter precisely what I intend to do. I fear our disappointments and delays will prove a severe trial to the faith and patience of our Christian friends But you will be able to inform them that nothing has befallen us but what is common to similar attempts in the first outset. The Baptist mission, which is now so flourishing, was severely tried for a time. They got no permanent establishment for six or seven years after the first missionaries came out. In two instances, where they have attempted to plant new missions, their missionaries have spent four or five years, and many thousands of rupees, and after all have abandoned the attempt and gone to other places. The same discouragements have been experienced by some of the missionaries of the London Society.

In the mean time, I hope I am not altogether useless. I have preached in English constantly, once, twice, or three times a week since my arrival in Ceylon. There are thousands of half-cast people, in and about Colombo, who stand in need of instruction as much as the heathens, and who understand the English language. Mr. Chater has a place of worship here, in which we preach alternately twice a week. We also keep the monthly prayer meeting, and a private prayer meeting every Monday evening. While I was at Jaffna, I (with the permission of Mr. Twisleton, senior chaplain) performed divine service in the fort for the few civil and military officers and soldiers there, as they have no chaplain at that station. For this month past, since I have been obliged to give up the hope of going to Bombay, I have laid aside the study of the eastern languages, until I am determined where I am to labor; and I am at present reviewing my Greek and Hebrew, with the study of critical works on the Bible.

[Mr. N specifies the letters which he had previously written, and observes in reference to the probability that the letter he was then writing would be examined at the London post-office, "The worst thing I have to say, [relative to national affairs] is, that I am under the greatest obligations to his majesty's government, and that I do most deeply lament the existence of the present unhappy war between the two countries." He proceeds thus]

I have deposited in the letter-box at Galle two parcels directed to you. One contains two printed documents, Mr. Bisset's sermon before the Colombo Bible Society, and a specimen of the eastern translations now in the mission-press at Serampore. The other is a manuscript of six sheets of letter paper, containing extracts from Mrs. Newell's letters and diary, and an account of her sickness and death. In this communication you will find much information respecting our affairs, which I have not repeated in my letters to you. I shall enclose in this a letter to Mrs. Atwood, which I wrote some time ago. All these are left open for your perusal. The letter and the manuscript, when you have read them, I wish you to send to my dear mother, Mrs. Atwood. I received letters by the Alligator—did not get them till the first of November. Your official letter, and that of Mr. Evarts, the brethren Hall and Nott have. I have not seen them. The books are at Calcutta. We have received no order from the Committee at Calcutta respecting supplies, but expect one soon. The Rev. Mr. Brown is dead, and Mr. Harington is absent. The Rev. Mr. Thomason, (a good man,) has taken the place of Mr. Brown, and G. Udny, Esq. (another good man,) the place of Mr. Harington.

[Mr. N. gives a statement of his pecuniary affairs, adds several articles of intelligence, and concludes as follows:]

I expect another opportunity of sending letters in about a month, and shall write again at that time, and mention such things as do not occur to me now. I hope then to be more particular, respecting my future prospects. This letter must serve for all my friends, for this time. The brethren Hall and Nott, I trust, will immediately return from England, and join me. Some more will probably come out with brother Rice.

Rev. and dear Sir, I am your servant for Jesus' sake,

SAMUEL NEWELL.

DONATIONS TO SUPPORT FOREIGN MISSIONS AND THE TRANSLATIONS OF THE SCRIPTURES.

Oct 26, 1814 From the following persons by Mr. P W. Gallaudet, of Hartford, viz by Messrs P W. Gleason, and Co $3
A female friend of missions in East Hartford, by do. 5
do   do   do. 5
Julia Bronson, 2
The Rev. Gideon Burt of Long Meadow, Mass towards the translations, 30 $45 00
27 From several young men in Townsend, by Mr. Cushing Wilder, 10 26
31 From a Society of Females in Hingham, by Mrs. Ruth Wilder, 12 00
Nov. 2. From the Female Foreign Mission Society in

Cornish, (N H) by H. R. the Treasurer,* 14 90
From a female, the avails of cloth which had been received for bed-curtains,† 11 50

* *This donation was enclosed in a letter containing the following sentence "With gratitude to the American Board of Commissioners for Foreign Missions for having engaged in the great work of evangelizing the heathen, and affording others an opportunity of assisting in the same design, a second donation from the Female Foreign Mission Society in Cornish is committed to their disposal"*

† *This donation was from a female who, unable to furnish the means of be*

4. From a lady, by Mr. Artemas Woodward, ... 1 00

5. From Miss Nancy Blanchard, of Weymouth, by Mr. S. T. Armstrong, ... 2 50

From a friend, by the Rev. Dr. Morse,* 10 00

8. From Q. by the Rev. Dr. Worcester, for the translations, ... 6 00

11. From a female friend of missions in Shenango county, (N. Y.) by the Rev. Reuben Hurd, ... 10 00

17. From a friend of foreign missions in Braintree, by the Rev. R. S. Storrs, ... 4 00

13. From the Female Charitable Society in Montville, (Con.) by General Huntington of New London, ... 72 50

25. From two females in Boylston, (Mass.) by the Rev. Dr. Austin, for the translations, ... 4 00

23. From the Foreign Mission Society of Northampton and the neighboring towns, by Josiah Dwight, Esq. the Treasurer, ... 558 62

30. From a female of Rupert, (Ver.) by Mr. R. C. Morse, ... 1 00

$763 28

---

restored. I hope you will then get our Magazines, which contain an immense mass of information, always increasing.

Some of our friends have lately visited France, that almost heathen country. Mr. S asked at more than 50 bookshops and stalls, for a Bible, in any language. Not one could he obtain! This is a fact.

I have just been informed, that Napoleon had an intention of suppressing the Catholic Religion as soon as he could, and substituting Unitarianism, under the new title of *Napoleonism.* He had read a book published by a protestant minister in defence of himself as a *Socinian,* with which he was so pleased, that he determined to adopt it, and use all his influence to make it the religion of France. This he intended, because he had observed that Moses, Confucius, Jesus Christ, and Mahomet, lived in the minds of their followers more than political or military men only. Determined, therefore, to live for ages in the hearts of *Napoleonists,* he fixed on this plan.‡

But He, that sits on the throne of heaven, has laughed at the tyrant, and hurled him from his throne, no longer able to oppose the kingdom of Christ our Lord. To Him, our best and unchangeable friend, I heartily commend you.

I am, dear Sir,

Your affectionate brother,

*** ***

London, June 15, 1814.

Dear Sir,

I REGRET, that through your pressure of business, and mine, and the war, we correspond so little. I hope to do better; but my business increases, and something, alas, is every day omitted.

I hope you will receive with this our last Report,† by Mr. Osgood. We now print eight pages of our Magazine separately, so as to send by post to our friends in England, and we can send them to you monthly, when peace is

---

CHARITY LIBRARIES.

SOME of our readers may recollect, that in the number for January last, we published a communication on *Charity Libraries;* and that, in our notices to correspondents, we requested a copy of the constitution of such libraries for publication, either in whole, or in an abridged form. A copy of it was sent us not long after; an abridgement of which we now publish.

Art. 1. THIS Library belongs to the

---

pious liberality in any other way, sold cloth which had been intended for a suit of bed-curtains, and remitted the avails as above. Her letter evinced a most commendable disposition to deny herself for the sake of promoting the cause of her Savior.

* See notice of Mr. AMOS WARREN, in the Obituary of this number.

† The Report of the Missionary Society.

‡ The project here stated may be thought so extravagant as to appear incredible. For several years, however, previous to the downfal of Bonaparte, it was suspected by many intelligent men, that he intended to establish a new religion. From the character of several publications, which issued from the Parisian press under the auspices of the French government, it was supposed that the new religion would be a modification of Mahometanism; as that religion is more favorable than any other to a military despotism.

——— Missionary Society,* and is to be continued in this settlement, for the benefit of subscribers, so long as they shall make a good use of it, and the missionary society shall not think it may be more needed, and more useful, in some other destitute settlement

2. Any head of a family, by subscribing this constitution, and these laws, may, with his family, enjoy the benefit of the Library

3. The officers shall be a librarian, and two assistants, who shall continue in office till others shall be appointed.

4. The officers shall be appointed from among the subscribers by a missionary, who will consult the wishes and the interests of the people

5. It shall be the duty of the librarian to keep the books with care, to give them out to subscribers according to the laws; to set down in a book kept for that purpose, the number of the volume, and the time when drawn and returned, &c &c.

6. It shall be the duty of the assistants, to aid the librarian, as he may need, in performing the duties of his office; to see that the subscribers observe the laws, particularly article 9th; and with the librarian, to make report to the inspecting missionary

8. The books, belonging to this Library shall not be drawn on the Sabbath; but, on any other day, a subscriber shall have a right to draw one book at a time, and no more; provided always, that he shall not have two bound books in his possession at once

9. The subscribers shall refrain from labor and business on the Sabbath, they shall not indulge themselves in the habit of visiting on that day, or of receiving visits, except in cases of sickness, or for religious conversation and prayer; they shall refrain from amusements and sports, such as hunting and fishing on the Sabbath, and oppose and bear testimony against all these vices and practices in others. They shall also restrain their children and families from these practices, and take them to the worship of God, as often as they can conveniently, and particularly to hear the preaching, and attend to the instruction of missionaries, whenever they shall be sent among them

Moreover the subscribers shall refrain from profane swearing, and the intemperate use of ardent spirits, and use their

* It would be observed, that, when the missionary societies agree to Charter Libraries, they engage to send a missionary, at least once a year, to the place to which is established each of the congregations, to inspect the Library, and to make report concerning it.

endeavors to prevent, or suppress these vices in others.

10. Any subscriber, who shall violate the laws, and persist in the violation, may be suspended from drawing books, when the officers shall judge best; and if he shall not make satisfaction so as to be restored to his privilege, when the missionary inspects the Library, his name may be erased from the book, and then he shall have no more right in the Library till he makes satisfaction.

We have been informed, on the most respectable authority, that Libraries, established according to the preceding plan, have had a very beneficial tendency; and that they are found to be powerful aids of missionaries. Ed.

FRAGMENT SOCIETY.

The Fragment Society of Boston held their annual meeting on the second Monday in October. In making their yearly Report, "The Directors present their renewed congratulations to the subscribers on the arrival of their second anniversary. In contemplating the success which has attended this Society since its institution, they would feel lively emotions of gratitude toward Him, who alone can *prosper the work of their hands* To the intervention of his blessing must it be ascribed, that at such a time as this, when some of our most respectable citizens are more or less subjected to the inconveniences of privation or want, the resources of this little association have not been diminished, and it is sincerely hoped, that nothing but the imperious demands of necessity will hereafter induce any to withhold that charity, of which the poor feel the additional need, by a more than equal participation with the rich in the sufferings of the times

"In executing the trust committed to them, they have been anxious to discriminate between real and pretended want, and have made it their constant aim, so to dispense your alms, as to soothe the niceties and mitigate the sufferings of indigent merit, and not to encourage idleness or discontent And though their means of usefulness have been limited, they indulge the humble belief that through this Society, streams of comfort have been diffused into the abodes of sorrow, and cheered the hearts of their miserable occupants

"The Directors thankfully acknowledge many liberal donations of clothing and materials:—the amount received the past year, in subscriptions and donations, being *twelve hundred and fifty-two dol-*

lars, fifty-five cents. About *five hundred* families have been assisted by the distribution of various articles of clothing, including in the whole *twenty eight hundred* garments. They have likewise contributed much to the comfort of the sick, by lending necessary garments, which have generally been received with gratitude, used with care, and returned in a decent and cleanly state. *Forty-nine* families have been assisted in this way. They have distributed among the children of the Charity-Schools much comfortable clothing, and in the course of the last winter lent them a number of great-coats for the purpose of enabling them to appear decent at church. The children, in their turn, have employed much of their time in sewing for the Society, and have made many articles in a very neat manner."

The Society solicit further encouragement. Donations in money or clothing will be gratefully received.

CORBAN SOCIETY.

FROM the Report of the Directors of this Society, it appears, that during the year preceding the annual meeting in September last, they had assisted twenty one young gentlemen in obtaining their education for the Christian ministry. They had been able to afford more or less assistance to every applicant; and had given articles of clothing, which cost $251:79, beside $59, in money. Several members of the Society added materially to the value of the articles of clothing, by their own personal labor; thus saving a considerable expense to the Society. The receipts during the past year were $286:25. The balance on hand is about $270, of which $200 is devoted to form a permanent fund.

At the close of their Report, the Directors say, "Considering the importance of the object embraced by this Society, and the continual succession of persons, who are benefited by its charity, the Directors feel it to be their duty to recommend to the members to increase their exertions in obtaining annual subscriptions, that their funds may afford a more extensive and ample supply."

"As our Heavenly Father," they add, "has condescended to employ us feeble instruments in his service, let us by our gratitude for his past favors, and by the purity of our motives in future, secure to ourselves his gracious benediction."

CENT INSTITUTION.

Money received by Mrs. Simpkins.
July 29, 1813. Received by the Rev.

Mr Rockwood from Ladies in Westborough, $23 50
Oct. 4. By George Russell from ladies in Kingston, 2 21
6. By Paul Bayley from ladies in Newbury, 15 50
15. By the Rev. Mr. Wadsworth from ladies in Danvers, 7 75
29. By the Rev. Mr. Homer from ladies in the east parish of Newton, 40 00
Jan. 13, 1814. By Rebecca Holmes from ladies in Kingston, 2 77
May 25. By the Rev. Mr. Barker from ladies in the first parish of Middleborough, 9 00
26 By Mr. Stow from ladies in Marlborough, 5 22
By the Rev. Elisha Rockwood from Cent Society in Weston, 9 25
30. By a female Cent Society in the Rev. Mr. Codman's Parish in Dorchester, 20 00
June 4. By Mr. B. Pond, from Mrs. Cleaveland's Cent Society in Wrentham, 10 82
18. By the Rev. Freegrace Reynold's, from Cent Society, Wilmington, 16 79
By Mrs. Whitney from ladies in Lunenburg for Bibles, 12 80
July 15. By Paul Bailey from ladies in Newbury Newtown, 17 25
From ladies in Boston, 48 64

$241 50

MISSIONARIES TO INDIA.

IT appears from magazines received by late arrivals, that four missionaries have already been set apart for the work in India, by the Church Missionary Society; viz. the Rev. Thomas Norton and the Rev. William Greenwood, destined as missionaries to Ceylon, and the Rev. John Christian Schnarre and the Rev. Charles Theophilus Ewald Rhenius, about to sail as missionaries to Tranquebar. An address was delivered to them, on the 7th of January last, at Freemason's Hall, London, by the Rev. Dr. Buchanan, at a special general meeting of the Church Missionary Society.

This Society publishes a small monthly magazine, entitled the Missionary Register, copies of which are distributed gratis to small associations of persons, who make regular contributions to the Society.

FOREIGN ABSTRACT

The Ladies Auxiliary Bible Society of Dublin was formed two or three years ago. Viscountess Lorton is patroness, and three countesses, one viscountess, and twelve other distinguished ladies vice-patronesses

The Report of the Youth Bible Society contains the following anecdote. "An old man, (upwards of seventy-five years of age,) who is assisted to a maintenance by the parish, has, within the last fifteen months, learnt to read his Bible in his native (the Welsh) language, through the persevering efforts of a religiously disposed workman, who lodges in his cottage; and now rejoices in the privileges he enjoys, at this late period of his life, considering it as one of the greatest blessings of his earthly existence. His wife (aged 72) is now learning her letters, in the hope of more fully partaking in the benefits arising from the perusal of the Scriptures for herself; and, on a late occasion, emphatically expressed her strong preference for a participation in this privilege, by holding out her hat with an air of enthusiasm, and exclaiming; 'Yes, I would rather that I could read than to have this hat full of silver and gold.'"

The English Government have caused a distribution of books to be made in the navy, in the following proportions: one copy of the New Testament, two common prayer-books, and two Psalters to a mess of 8 men, and one Bible to every two men.

The British National Society for promoting the education of the Poor, within a few months after its institution, received subscriptions and donations to the amount of $175,000.

The Society for the relief of widows and children of medical men in London and the Vicinity, has a capital of above $55,000.

The Society in London for enforcing the observance of the Lord's Day prosecuted to conviction 440 persons, in the course of the year 1812. Some bills of indictment were withdrawn, on the parties acknowledging their error, and engaging to reform.

For repairing the loss sustained by the burning of the printing office at Serampore, above $28,000 was raised by contributions in England and Scotland.

OBSERVANCE OF THE SABBATH.

A CORRESPONDENT, whose communication appears in this number, has taken notice of the Middlesex Convention, which met for the purpose of devising and adopting measures for the due observation of the Lord's day. The pamphlet, which contains the doings of this convention, is one of the most interesting documents which have appeared on this subject.

The convention met Sept. 5, 1814, at Burlington. Joseph Locke, Esq. was called to the chair, and the Rev. Jacob Coggin, chosen Scribe. The meeting was opened with prayer by the Rev. Mr. Ripley, of Concord. A number of suitable resolutions were adopted, and a central committee appointed consisting of the following gentlemen; viz. the Rev. Mr. Ripley, of Concord, the Rev. Mr. Stearns, of Bedford, the Rev. Mr. Allen, of Chelmsford, Joseph Locke, Esq. of Billerica, the Rev. Mr. Chickering, of Woburn, the Rev. Mr. Coggin, of Tewksbury, and the Rev. Mr. Edwards, of Andover.

The convention was adjourned to meet at Concord, on the 26th of October; at which time gentlemen from thirteen towns convened. Dr. Isaac Hurd was called to the chair, Joseph Locke, Esq. being absent. The Rev. Mr. Litchfield, of Carlisle, opened the meeting with prayer. The central committee presented a very able and impressive Report, which, with several spirited resolutions, was unanimously adopted. The central committee were directed to prepare and publish the pamphlet, (of which these notices are an abstract,) and the following gentlemen were added to their number: Samuel Hoar, Esq. of Concord, Dr. Rufus Wyman of Chelmsford, Benjamin Rhey, Esq. of Marlborough, and Jeremiah Evarts, of Charlestown. The convention now stands adjourned to meet at Concord, on the last Wednesday of January next.

The pamphlet is closed by an address written with great vigor, and which must, if circulated and read as it ought to be, produce a decisive effect. Let all who reverence the Sabbath, awake to this subject. They have already slumbered too long. Now is the time for exertion. The beneficial effect of the first attempts entirely surpasses the hopes of the most sanguine. To faint or falter now, would be shameful cowardice.

INSTALLATION.

INSTALLED, at New Hartford, (N Y) on the 19th ult. the Rev. NOAH COE. The Rev. Samuel F. Snowden preached from 2 Cor. vi, 1.

REPORT OF THE DIRECTORS TO THE TWENTIETH GENERAL MEETING OF THE MISSIONARY SOCIETY, MAY 12, 1814.

By the kindness of the Rev. Thaddeus Osgood, who has returned from England to Quebec, we have lately receiv-

ed a variety of religious intelligence. The most important article, however, is the following Report, which, as it contains a late official account of the state of all the missions under the direction of the great English Missionary Society, is peculiarly worthy of an attentive perusal. ED. PAN

Christian Friends,

To those of you who recollect the first meeting of this Society, in the memorable month of September, 1795, who can trace its gradual progress from year to year, and who now contemplate the number of missionaries employed in various parts of the world, and the happy success of their labors, together with the flourishing state and extensive usefulness of other institutions which spring from this, the present occasion must afford a high degree of sacred delight, approaching perhaps to the felicity of the heavenly world, where the conversion of sinners on earth, and the enlargement of the Mediator's kingdom, contribute to the joys of the redeemed

Which of us, at the first commencement of the Society, could have ventured to hope that in less than twenty years so general a movement of the Christian church would be effected; that so many hundred thousands of languid professors would have been roused from their supine and torpid state; that with so much union of spirit, so much ardor of desire, so much energy of exertion, so much liberality and benevolence, they would concur in sending the heralds of the Gospel, and the Scriptures of truth, to the remotest nations of the earth. This hath God done! His be the glory! be our's the joy!

The Directors for the past year will now complete their duty, by laying before you a brief account of their proceedings during that period, with the present state of the several missions under your patronage.

OTAHEITE.

The Directors commence their Report with a pleasure they never before enjoyed—the pleasure of stating, that after the patient labors of fifteen years, enlivened only by some faint rays of hope, those labors were not entirely fruitless, your faithful missionaries at Otaheite feel themselves rewarded for all their toil by the conversion of King Pomarre to the faith of the Gospel. They did indeed derive some solace from the belief, that a few individuals, feeling in their departing moments the need of that salvation which they had too long neglected, cast their dying eyes to the cross, and expired in hope of eternal life by Jesus Christ They faithfully persisted for many a long

year; having received of the Lord, and of the Society, this ministry, they fainted not; and after they were driven from the scene of their labors by civil war, they readily returned at the invitation of the king, and with pleasure renewed their work. In the course of a few months after their return, their hearts were cheered with the pleasing appearance of the effects of divine grace on the heart of the king. The Directors first received the welcome information by a letter dated October 21, 1812, which however did not arrive till October 1813. On the 18th of July, 1812, Pomarre declared to the Missionaries his full conviction of the truth of the Gospel, as the result of deliberate consideration; his determination to worship Jehovah as the only living and true God, and his desire to make a public profession of his faith, by being baptised. The missionaries, greatly rejoiced, assured him that they would not cease to pray for him, but thought it prudent to defer his baptism till he should have received further instruction, and until, by a careful observation of his conduct, they should be fully satisfied as to the reality of his conversion. In this advice he calmly acquiesced, but was earnestly desirous of immediately building a convenient house for divine worship; this however was deferred for a while, until the peace of the island should be fully established.

Subsequent letters seem to afford increasing evidence of Pomarre's sincerity The missionaries state, that when at a distance from them, and amidst very important engagements, he regularly observed the Lord's day; that he labored to persuade his relations to embrace Christianity; that he has entirely abandoned his idols; that he entertains very clear and consistent views of the principal doctrines of the Gospel, and, above all, that he expresses the most deep contrition on account of his former vicious life, and a most humbling sense of his native depravity. We trust therefore we may indulge the pleasing hope, that Pomarre is become a real Christian, and, if so, that his influence and example will at least induce his subjects to hear more attentively, and examine more carefully, the great truths proposed to them by our missionaries.

One of the brethren, in a letter dated New South Wales, in June 1813, says, "I shall only add, respecting him, that supposing him to be a real convert, of which there is every rational evidence, and there can be no reasonable doubt, he is, not to say *the greatest*, (which I think I might venture to say) but *one of the greatest* miracles of grace ever exhibited on the stage of this world To God's holy and glorious name be all the praise."

But Pomarre appears not to be the only fruit of our brethren's labors. "There
are others," say they, "whom the Lord
is drawing to himself from among this
people, there is one man in particular of
whom we entertain good hopes, we have
little doubt that his heart is changed by
divine grace, but we do not like hastily to
baptize any. One of our domestics, who
departed this life the other day, we hope
died in a safe state, he cried for pardoning mercy through Christ as long as he
was able." Other circumstances, they observe, are encouraging; but they add,
"We wish still to keep to the maxim we
have hitherto (perhaps too rigidly) adhered to—to say too little about such
things, rather than too much."

While the Society rejoice in this
pleasing intelligence, they cannot but feel
pain in reflecting upon the serious loss
which this mission has sustained by the
death of several of the pious females.

Mrs Henry died July 28, 1812. She
was a most valuable woman, patient and
resigned under all privations and hardships. Her natural disposition was amiable, her piety unaffected, and her love for
the poor heathen unfeigned. She died
after a tedious illness, worn out in the
service of the mission

Mrs. Davies was also an excellent woman, she unexpectedly departed on the 4th
of September, 1812, her infant followed
her to the grave three weeks after.

Mrs. Hayward also, after suffering
much from a complication of disorders,
departed October 4, 1812. She was
greatly supported in the prospect of
death by the precious promises of the
Gospel

These valuable women are doubtless
gone to receive the gratuitous reward of
those labors and sufferings which they
voluntarily encountered, that they might
advance the kingdom of Christ in the
world, and their memory is blessed

The missionaries had come to a determination, agreeably to our directions, to
separate and form a mission on another
of the Society Islands, and they had fixed
upon Reaotea, as the largest or most
central of the group, but the melancholy
losses they had sustained rendered it necessary to defer the execution of their
plan, especially as they were about to
build a vessel of about fifty or sixty tons,
as strenuously recommended to them by
his excellency Governor Macquarie and
the Rev Mr Marsden, to both of whom
the Society is much indebted for their
kind attention to the missionaries

It is with great satisfaction we learn,
that the obstacles which appeared to be
in the way of establishing a mission in the
Island of New Zealand, were likely to be
removed; a young chief of that country,
who had resided for two years at Port
Jackson, having returned to it, and introduced agriculture and other arts of civilized life, and who was likely to become a
true friend to the missionaries who may
hereafter go thither.

(To be continued)

LITERARY INTELLIGENCE.

NEW WORKS.

The Panoplist Review of Two Pamphlets, which were published on the subject of the Ecclesiastical Controversy in
Dorchester. Boston: S. T. Armstrong
1814. pp. 46 Price 25 cents

A Sermon delivered before the Maine
Missionary Society, at their annual meeting, in Gorham, June 22, 1814 By Francis Brown, Pastor of a church in North
Yarmouth Hallowell N. Cheever.

A Sermon occasioned by the death of
Mr. William Coombs, and delivered June
12, 1814. By Daniel Dana, A. M Pastor
of the first Presbyterian Church in Newburyport. Newburyport E Little and Co.

A Sermon preached before the North
Church and Society in Salem, Oct. 16,
1814, on the death of their pastor, th-
Rev. Thomas Barnard, D. D who died
Oct. 1, 1814, in the 67th year of his age
By the Rev John Prince, L. L. D. Pastor
of the First Church in Salem. Salem;
Thomas C. Cushing. pp. 32

An Oration pronounced before the
Knox and Warren branches of the Washington Benevolent Society, at Amherst,
on the celebration of the Anniversary of
the Declaration of Independence, July 4,
1814 By Noah Webster, Esq. Northampton, William Butler.

NEW EDITION.

Biblia Hebraica, secundum ultimam ex-
itionem Jos Athiæ, a Johanne Leusden
denuo recognitam, recensita variisque no-
tis Latinis illustrata ab Everardo vand r
Hooght, V D M Editio prima Ameri-
cana, sine punctis Masorethicis. Philadel-
phiæ Cura et impensis Thomæ Dobson
edita ex aedibus lapideis Typis Gulel
mi Fry 1814 Price 14 dollars in boards

WORKS PROPOSED.

Messrs Hale and Hosmer, of Hartford,
propose to publish The Catechism of
nature, by the Rev John Calvin Translated by the Rev E. Waterman. Author
of the Life of Calvin Price 50 cents in
marble

ars. H. and H. propose also to pub-
subscription, Dr. Lardner's Cred
of the Gospel History, Truth of
anity, and Jewish and Heathen
onies. The Rev. Mr. Yates, of
Hartford, is to superintend the
s editor. It is to be published in 8
$2 each, in boards.

OBITUARY.

, at Alexandria, (Louisiana,) on
2nd of August last, JOHN C M.
air, Esq. Counsellor at Law, aged

West Cambridge, Mass Mr. HEN-
JNSON, aged 20 He was gradu-
Harvard College in 1813

Milford. Con. on the 21st ult. a
a lady, a passenger in the stage, by
She went into the kitchen, took
afe, and drew it across her throat;
effecting her purpose, she instant-
ged it into her bosom, and soon ex-

Burlington. Vt. Major EBENEZER
, of the 6th regiment U. S. infan-

Gloucester, Mass. Mrs. NANCY C.
r, aged 36. The genuine piety,
hence, and distinguished talent of
ly, made her extensively useful,
ed her to all who knew her, and
her death a subject of general la-
son in the circle of her acquain-
She has left an aged mother, and
than children to lament her d par-
It is probable that a more extend-
ant of this lady will appear in the
ist.

alem, Mass. on the 1st inst Rev.
BARNARD, D D pastor of the
Church, aged 66, in an apoplectic

Townsend, Vt the Hon. SAMUEL
KER, Esq. aged 70

Wiscasset, JAMES PEARINGTON,
representative of Gardiner in the
l Court.

ngland, ANTHONY J P. MOLLOY,
tain in the royal navy. He was
captain in Earl Howe's victory of
1794, and commanded the Cæsar,
ship p

Philadelphia, the Hon. JOHN MIL-
sq M C aged 56.

pringfield, Mass. a child of Mr.
Chapin, by its clothes taking fire
day preceding

Brighton, Eng on the 5th of Au-
t, his Excellency FRANCIS JAMES
s, Esq. aged 44. He had been

Ambassador to Turkey, Spain, Prussia,
Austria, France, Denmark, and the United States.

On the 17th ult. at his father's house in
Andover, the Rev. JOHN LOVEJOY AB-
BOT, pastor of the First Church in Bos-
ton, aged 27.

At St Louis, Missouri Territory, Brig.
Gen BENJAMIN HOWARD, of U. S. army,
and late Governor of that territory.

At Charleston, S. C. the Rev. JAMES D.
SIMMONS, an Episcopal clergyman.

At Attleborough, Mass. Rev. JAMES
READ, pastor of a Baptist church in that
town.

At Charlestown, Mass. Sept. 13th,
Mr. AMOS WARREN, merchant, aged
25, after a short and sudden illness. The
death of this young man is deeply lamented by his friends and intimate acquaintances, as a painful event to themselves and a real loss to the community.
From early youth he had been thoughtful on subjects of religion; and about four
years ago, after much deliberation and a
diligent examination of his spiritual state,
he made a public profession of his faith in
Christ. His conduct was consistent with
his profession, and, by a life of piety and
virtue, he seemed preparing for more extensive usefulness in the church and the
world. But the Great Disposer of events
removed him suddenly, and with little
warning to the world of spirits. His surviving friends have reason to believe, that
death was a welcome messenger to him,
and that he is numbered among those,
whose sins have been washed away by the
blood of Christ.

Among his papers was found, after his
decease, a letter to his pastor, the Rev.
Dr. Morse, written for the purpose of enclosing a donation, in aid of the mission-
ry cause, as from an unknown person.
This donation is published in the present
number of the Panoplist, as from a *friend.*
The letter was written just before the
writer was taken ill, and was one of the
last actions of his life. It contains the
following sentences, which indicate a pious and benevolent disposition. After
alluding to the distinguishing privileges
which we enjoy, and the uncertainty of
life and the enjoyment of earthly posses-
sions, the writer adds:

"These reflections, a conviction of past
neglect, and the thoughts of the vast
numbers, both in our own country and in
Asia, destitute of the means of grace, have
induced me to make this small contribution, to be appropriated for the advancement of the religious cause, in any way
you think best: hoping, that in future I

may be enabled by the smiles of Providence on my worldly concerns, and disposed by God's grace, to make much larger; and that all who have the interest of the Redeemer's kingdom at heart may be excited to do likewise."

The following elegy, written by a friend, has appeared in the public papers.

WHEN modest merit and intrinsic worth,
For climes congenial leave this barren earth;
When youthful virtue, in its op'ning bloom,
Untimely sinks a victim to the tomb;
Friendship would fain her last sad honors pay,
And wake the plaintive dirge and chant the mournful lay.

Friendship and Love this wasting world survive,
In other realms, 'mid happier scenes to thrive;
In vain the grave, that forces friends to part,
Would chase their memory from the faithful heart;
The faithful heart still mounts on fancy's wings,
And back to earth the dear departed object brings.

He whose short pilgrimage has ceas'd below,
Was meek to learn what duty bade him know;
Was wise to shun whate'er to vice inclin'd,
For bless'd religion sanctified his mind;
No vot'ry he, at pleasure's glitt'ring shrine—
Low bent his youthful knee before the throne divine.

While thoughtless myriads throng the road of life,
Eager to grasp its flow'rs, and share its strife,
He seem'd a lonely traveller, in a way
Narrow, but leading to celestial day;
Where fruits and flowers immortal fragrance shed,
And crowns of joy await the pious pilgrim's head.

Though cold the sod, dear youth, that wraps thy clay,
Thus lowly once the world's great Savior lay;
Sweet be thy slumbers, and thy rest serene,
Till the last trump shall wake the glorious scene;
Till He whose voice bade Lazarus "arise,"
Shall rouse his slumbering saints, and call them to the skies.

TO CORRESPONDENTS.

The Complaint of the Non-Donors is ingeniously drawn up by our correspondent, D. Perhaps sarcasms may provoke this class of persons to more decided hostility.

The metrical version of Habakkuk iii, was duly received from our correspondent A D. We thank him sincerely for his communication; but he must permit us to say, that an attempt to exhibit this incomparably sublime passage, in the form of a regular stanza, or indeed in any metrical form, is an extremely hazardous experiment. Scarcely one poet in an age could hope to succeed, in such a manner as to satisfy either himself, or his readers. The smaller pieces, forwarded by the same correspondent, have the faults common to most of the rhymes, which are sent to us, on religious subjects. They appear to have been hastily written; and the thoughts are most obvious in themselves, and expressed in too careless a manner.

The private experience of A SINCERE FRIEND TO THE HEATHEN contains many excellent things, and appears to be the history of a pious mind. There are passages, however, which appear so liable to misconstruction, or objection, that we think it best to decline publishing the piece. With the communication was enclosed a ten dollar bill for the support of foreign missions, which was mentioned in the Panoplist for June last, p. 287.

The paper of F. containing MOTIVES FOR MAGISTRATES AND RULERS, is the production of a sensible, reflecting, mind; but the subject is discussed in too abstruse a manner to be perused with interest by the mass of readers

THE
PANOPLIST,
AND
MISSIONARY MAGAZINE.

| No. 12. | DECEMBER, 1814. | VOL. X. |

REVIEWS.

LXVI. *Christian Mourning: A Sermon occasioned by the death of Mrs. Isabella Graham: and preached on the evening of Subbath, the 14th Aug. 1814. By J. M. MASON, D.D.* New York; Whiting and Watson. pp. 50.

THERE are but a few men, whose occasional sermons are fitted to produce any considerable effect, beyond the narrow limits of personal influence. Dr. Mason justly ranks high among the select few. The originality of his manner of discussing a subject, the weight of his matter, the vivacity of his illustrations, the conclusiveness of his reasoning, and the pungency of his applications, are obvious characteristics of his compositions generally. Of these characteristics the sermon before us contains many admirable specimens; a considerable part of which we intend to lay before our readers in copious extracts.

While reading this sermon, once and again, we have felt a deep regret, that our countrymen are so very slow and reluctant to purchase valuable pamphlets. Of the mass of pamphlets we are not speaking. They are generally very insignificant things, printed from local or personal considerations, or from mere civility to the orator or preacher. It is not expected that they should ever sell. But there are pamphlets, (the sermon before us is one of them.) which deserve to be generally known and read; and of which, instead of a few hundred copies, many thousand ought to be importunately called for. We could enumerate half a dozen pamphlets, printed in this country within a few years, concerning which it may be confidently asserted. that hundreds of thousands of each would be greedily purchased, if as many persons were desirous of promoting their best interests, as are willing to inflame the passions and corrupt the heart by patronizing and perusing calumny, misrepresentation, and falsehood, in a large proportion of our newspapers. No one will be surprised, that, in the present state of the world, the friends of virtue should be considered as the minority; but it may very justly excite astonishment, that in this minority there should be so much apathy, so much timidity, so much pusillanimity, and so little active, courageous, persevering exertion.

The only plausible excuse,

which we have ever heard assigned for not purchasing valuable pamphlets, is that they are sold at too high a price. Without stopping to consider whether they are thus sold or not, and without denying that this alleged excuse may have had some influence, we are perfectly sure that it has never had the influence ascribed to it. The following are our reasons:

First, men are not apt to forego a great enjoyment, merely because it costs rather more than they imagine it ought to cost. The truth of this assertion is observable in ten thousand instances, and must be obvious to every considerate man.

Secondly, the expense of procuring the pamphlets, which are fitted for all classes of readers, and deserve a universal circulation, would be extremely small. Probably one dollar a year, would purchase all the pamphlets of this character, which have been published in this country for ten years past. The clergyman would need to expend two or three dollars, perhaps, in this way, annually, and the politician eight or ten. In this estimate, we reckon occasional pamphlets only, and not magazines

Thirdly, whenever pamphlets have been printed for charitable distribution; and sold at cost, or for less than cost,—for so small a price, indeed, that nobody thought of complaining in that respect—they have not been purchased with any more avidity than in other cases. The fact is, however we may attempt to conceal it, that we are not a *reading people.* Newspapers are read to be sure; but the mass of the community read nothing else.

Many good men,—many real Christians, keep themselves in a state of shameful ignorance, and mental imbecility, because they do not read and reflect, and act, in reference to the great duties of their profession; especially the duties to which the present state of the world calls their attention.

The text of the sermon now under consideration, is 1 Thess. iv, 13, 14. *I would not have you to be ignorant, brethren, concerning them which are asleep; that ye sorrow not, even as others which have no hope. For if we believe that Jesus died and rose again, even so them also, which sleep in Jesus, will God bring with him.*

After remarking, that the cardinal doctrine of Christianity 'is the justification of a sinner, through faith in a Savior, who himself fell a victim to his enemies,' and that 'the cardinal fact of Christianity is the resurrection from the dead of the same crucified Savior,' the preacher observes,

"Against this great fact the *children of disobedience,* from the Pharisees of Jerusalem down to the scoffers of New York, have levelled their batteries. One assails its proof; another, its reasonableness; all, its truth. When Paul asserted it before an audience of Athenian philosophers, "some mocked"—a short method of refuting the Gospel; and likely, from its convenience, to continue in favor and in fashion." p. 6.

Dr. M. then gives a rapid glance at the progress of Christianity, and the state of the early converts from Paganism. The first part of the discourse is occupied in urging this general topic, that we ought "so to cherish the knowledge of the Gospel, as that our hearts shall not be depressed, by the death of believers, but that there shall be an immeasurable' distance between our grief and the grief of unbelievers." The following description of death is not less just than forcible.

"Death is, in itself, a most serious and distressful event. It is nature's supreme evil, the abhorrence of God's creation—a monster from whose touch and sight every living thing recoils. So that to shrink from its ravages upon ourselves or upon those whom we love, is not an argument of weakness, but an act of obedience to the first law of being—a tribute to the value of that life which is our Maker's gift.

"The disregard which some of old affected to whatever goes by the name of evil; the insensibility of others who yield up their souls to the power of fatalism; and the artificial gayety which has, occasionally, played the comedian about the dying bed of *philosophy, falsely so called,* are outrages upon decency and nature. Death destroys both action and enjoyment—mocks at wisdom, strength, and beauty—disarranges our plans—robs us of our treasures—desolates our bosoms—breaks our heart-strings—blasts our hope. Death extinguishes the glow of kindness—abolishes the most tender relations of man—severs him from all that he knows and loves—subjects him to an ordeal which thousands of millions have passed, but none can explain; and which will be as new to the last who gives up the ghost, as it was to murdered Abel—flings him, in fine, without any avail from the experience of others, into a state of untried being. No wonder that nature trembles before it. Reason justifies the fear. Religion never makes light of it: and he who does, instead of ranking with heroes, can hardly deserve to rank with a brute." pp. 10, 11.

Scarcely any trait in the human character more strikingly exhibits the depravity and stupidity of man, than the prevalent disposition to treat death with levity. This subject, so interesting to all, and so solemn in all the circumstances which relate to it, is still a standing topic of sport and jesting with multitudes of thoughtless men. But it is, chiefly in reference to the field of battle, that a stupid, senseless, profane disregard of death and its consequences, is honored with the appellation of heroism. A man may prove by the irresistible evidence of his habitual conduct, that he is destitute of all good principles;—he may be a tyrannical and unfaithful husband, an improvident and unkind parent, a disorderly and quarrelsome member of society, a profane and dissolute wretch, abhorred by all his acquaintance, a nuisance and a burden to the community; with these qualities he may enlist in an army, without the ability or the inclination to judge of the merits of the cause; very probably, indeed, the cause may have no merits, but infinite demerits; he may there lead a life of intoxication, idleness, and profaneness, till called out to battle; at that solemn period, when exposed to instant death, he may make a jest of death, of heaven and hell, of Christ and salvation, and may engage in the work of slaughter with hatred, revenge, and a desire of glory, (three passions from which it is difficult to select the worst,) all striving for the mastery; and, after performing the actions of a fiend with a fiend-like disposition, for a while, he may be snatched from the world, in a moment, with malice in his heart and blasphemy on his lips, and summoned to give his final account to a God of holiness and peace. Yet, with all this evidence of worthlessness and depravity, his character may be blazoned forth to the world as that of a patriot, a hero, a martyr, and his fellow worms may most impudently and presumptuously undertake to give him a passport to heaven. How odious and detestable must all such conduct appear in the view of angels and glorified spirits, but especially in the view of God. It seems to us that Christian nations, and even Christians themselves, have been deeply guilty in making light of death, when it takes place on the field of battle. Men who would disapprove of cock-fighting, as a cruel amusement, not suitable for a Christian, or even a gentleman, have not hesitated to speak in terms of warm approbation of bravery in the field, when the only conceivable merit was that of imitating the fury and obstinacy of such animals, as will die by inches rather than yield. Of all deaths, excepting only those occasioned by suicide, and sometimes those occasioned by duelling, the deaths which take place on the field of battle ought surely to be regarded with pain, anxiety, and even terror, by every good man Instead of saying, "We have gained a glorious victory. The enemy left a thousand on the field, though he succeeded in removing his wounded: It was a hard fought battle, and it is feared our loss was not greatly inferior: Our brave fellows advanced to the charge in the most gallant style, and covered themselves with glory," the good man ought to say, "We have indeed melancholy tidings: Nearly two thousand immortal beings have been violently *driven away in their wickedness:* They gave no evidence of goodness; and, there is every reason to fear, that, from the indulgence of malice and revenge here, they are gone to dwell with malice, revenge, and despair, forever:

There may have been exceptions among them; but the characters of most are too legibly written in blood to be the subject of mistake" Such *ought* to be the language of a good man; and we cannot but think that many good men, who have been led astray by the erroneous maxims of a wicked world, and who have been accustomed to speak of war and fighting in such a manner as to encourage the warlike spirit, will one day repent of their sin and folly.

It is most astonishing, that Christians should have been led to adopt so utter a perversion of the most obvious principles of religion and morality, as is implied by their falling into the current, and adding the sanction of their authority to the warlike spirit. Surely running a man through the body, or blowing out his brains, is no very decisive proof of virtue; but, one would think, something like a proof of the contrary. How is it, then, that this act, unexplained by any circumstance, except that the warrior is employed under national authority, should be considered as highly meritorious? Perhaps on a more thorough search it will be found, that some latent virtue lurks under this covering of violence and blood. Make the trial. Search thoroughly. Pass through the camp; and, as you go from tent to tent, you will be convinced, that the *mouths* of a soldiery are full of cursing and bitterness. Follow the ranks into the field of carnage. Amid the thunders of artillery, the shouts of victory, and the groans of the dying, hear the confused mingling of oaths and imprecations.

the indications of all
passions. After this
i, speak conscientious-
y, whether devils incar-
i cast a deeper shade
scene; whether they
form worse actions in
manner; whether any
evidence of depravity
given within the same

How preposterous
, how monstrous, how
a trifling with reason,
e, and common sense,
it virtuous, which bears
ble stamp of extreme
ss. "What!" it will be
you wish us all to be-
akers?" We *do* wish
to become Christians;
) conceive that it would
uit the character of
s, never to make light
and never to engage
ny farther than can be
er the guidance of the
iod, with supreme love
and perfect love to all
ecially to our enemies.
stians had borne a loud,
unvarying testimony
he warlike spirit;—if
looked at it themselves,
e others look at it, as
d with the meek, peace-
evolent, holy instruc-
examples of Christ and
eminent servants; who
ow much such a testi-
uld have accomplished
keeping down those
se inordinate desires,
godly passions, from
ne *wars and fightings*

me will come, we hope
at hand, when this sub-
he regarded in a differ-
er from that, in which
sually been regarded,

even by real Christians; when
the glory of the warrior shall
suffer a total and everlasting
eclipse; when a man shall no
sooner think of boasting that
his ancestors were great military commanders, than that they
were enterprising captains in
the slave trade; and when many
a chieftain, who lived in splendor, decorated with the badges
of martial honor, applauded by
admiring senates, idolized by deluded millions, and praised without limits by cotemporary poets
and historians, will find his station, (a station from which he
will never be displaced,) at the
head of petty thieves and murderers. But let us return from
the digression, to which we were
led by the last sentence quoted
above.

Dr. M. proceeds to describe
the melancholy condition of the
heathen, in relation to the subject of death, by enlarging upon
the following particulars: 1.
"They *know* nothing, whatever
they might conjecture, of the
state of departed man." 2. 'With
the resurrection of the body they
were absolutely unacquainted.'
A part of what is said here we
quote, not for its eloquence
merely, but for the valuable
truths which it contains, and
which ought to be held in perpetual remembrance.

"Such was Paganism bending over the
remains of a deceased friend. Such, too,
was Judaism, after it had rejected *the hope
of Israel, and the Saviour thereof.* Such
are still the millions, whether of Gentiles
or Jews, who know not God.

"And wherein have unbelievers among
ourselves the pre-eminence? What have
they to gild their evening hour, to bind
up their aching head, to soothe their laboring heart? What living hope descends
from heaven to shine on the sinking features, whisper peace to the retiring spirit,

and announce to the sad surrounding relatives that all is well? There is none! Astonishment, dismay, melancholy boding, are the *portion of their cup.* Sit down, ye unhappy, in the desolation of grief. Consolation heard the voice of your weeping: she hastened to your door, but started back affrighted; her commission extends not to *your* house of mourning; ye have no hope!

"But, Christians, believers in the Lord Jesus, *your* condition is widely different, and so must be your carriage. You, too, must resign, many of you have already resigned, some of you very recently, your believing friends to the stroke of death. You must feel, have felt, the pang of separation. You are not forbidden to mourn. The smitten heart will bleed; the workings of nature must have vent. It is right. Tears were not made that they should never be shed: nor the passion of grief implanted only to be stifled. God's gifts to us in the persons of those whom he animates with his love, beautifies with his image, and honors with his communion, are too precious to be relinquished without emotion. It would be a strange way of glorifying him for the best of his earthly blessings, to behave, when they are removed, as if they were not worth one thought. Nor could there be a fouler stain upon the religion of the cross, than a tendency to extinguish affections calculated, in a peculiar manner, to lessen the evils of our miserable world. No! the *grace which bringeth salvation* does not destroy, but restore, the man. All that belongs to him, excepting sin and its effects, she acknowledges, regulates, exalts. Jesus, the perfection of moral beauty, Jesus himself wept at the tomb of his friend. He has dignified as well as vindicated, by his example, the most sacred of our social feelings. And if we, sharing his sympathy, weep at the tomb of those who are not less his friends than our own, instead of falling beneath the level of profane fortitude, we rise up to the grandeur of fellowship with the *man of sorrows.*" pp. 14—16.

In the second part of the discourse, are exhibited "the grounds of our consolation with respect to departed saints." The mere enumeration of topics would give a very inadequate view of this discussion To the infidel, who objects that the resurrection of the dead is incredible, the following paragraph is recommended:

"But how are these transformations to be effected? How? By that same *power* which *calleth things that be not as though they were.* God shall bring his risen ones with Jesus Christ. This is our short answer. I cannot open my ears to the objections of unbelief. We are upon too high ground to stoop to the cavilier who marshals his ignorance and imbecility against the knowledge and might of God. Let him puzzle himself with his theories about personal identity—Let him talk about one part of the body interred in Asia, another in Africa, and a third in Europe—Let him ask as many questions as he can devise about limbs devoured by ravenous animals, and become, by nutrition, part of their bodies; which bodies again have passed, by the same process, into the flesh of other animals; and these in their turn, consumed by man, and incorporated with the substance of a new human body—Let him ask such questions, and ten thousand like them. Has he done? *Dost thou not therefore err, not knowing the Scriptures, nor the power of God?* It will be time enough to plead thy difficulties, when God shall commit to thee the raising of the dead. For us it is sufficient that he, who rears up the living blade from the rotted grain, will be at no loss to rear up an incorruptible from a corrupted body, through what forms and varieties soever it may have passed." pp. 25, 26.

The character of Mrs. Graham, which occupies twenty pages, is admirably drawn. We shall select several passages which will doubtless be read with universal interest.

"ISABELLA MARSHALL, known to us as MRS GRAHAM, received, from nature, qualities which in circumstances favorable to their developement, do not allow the possessor to pass through life unnoticed and inefficient.

"An intellect strong, prompt, and inquisitive—a temper open, generous, cheerful, ardent—a heart replete with tenderness, and alive to every social affection, and every benevolent impulse—a spirit at once enterprising and persevering The whole crowned with that rare and inestimable endowment, good sense, were materials which required only skilful management to fit her for adorning and dignifying any female station. With that sort of cultivation which the world most admires, and those opportunities which attend upon rank and fortune, she will

in the circles of the great,
iting the esteem of the good.
ot fallen among the literary
of the continent, she might
in the sphere of the Vol-
effands, and the other *esprits*
is. She might have been as
, as dismal in private, and as
her end, as any the most
among them for their wit
e. But God had destined her
cenes and services—scenes
greatness turns away appal-
nces which all the cohorts of
re unable to perform. She
epared by poverty, bereave-
rief, to pity and to succour
e bereaved, and the grieving.
of widowhood were to teach
rt of the widow—her babes,
their father, to open the
er compassion to the father-
han—and the consolations of
'uge and strength, her very
in trouble, to make her a
consolation to them who were
the valley of the shadow of

her betimes for the future
of his providence, the Lord
heart of this "chosen vessel"
youth. The spirit of prayer
r infant lips; and taught her,
a her memory could go, to
er heart" before God. She
hed her eleventh year, when
a bush in the retirement of
ul there devoted herself to
faith in the Redeemer. The
her education, thoughtless
, the love of dress, and the
ol, as she has herself record-
or a while the warmth of her
obbed her bosom of its peace.
cious Lord revisited her with
and bound her to himself in
ng covenant, which she sealed
table about the 17th year of
pp. 29—31.

. was left a widow in
, and provided for her-
er children by educat-
g females in Edinburgh.
ive years ago she open-
ol for the education of
lies in New York. We
lp quoting the descrip-

irits, freethinkers. *Dr. M.*
us for translating a phrase,
ever well known to literary
not be understood by plain
erally.

tion of her government, and of
all good government,—a description, which fills us with sad-
ness, when we consider what sort
of government has too commonly afflicted mankind.

"In governing her little empire, she
acted upon those principles which are the
basis of all good government on every
scale and under every modification—to
be *reasonable*, to be *firm*, and to be *uniform*. Her authority was both tempered
and strengthened by condescension. It
commanded respect while it conciliated
affection. Her word was law, but it was
the law of kindness. It spoke to the conscience, but it spoke to the heart; and
obedience bowed with the knee of love."
pp. 34, 35.

After Mrs. G. retired from the
business of education, she was
still actively employed in doing
good.

"Admonished, at length, by the infirmities of age; and importuned by her
friends, this venerable matron retired to
private life. But it was impossible for
her to be idle. Her leisure only gave a
new direction to her activity. With no
less alacrity than she had displayed in the
education of youth, did she now embark
in the relief of misery. Her benevolence
was unbounded, but it was discreet.
There are charities which increase the
wretchedness they are designed to diminish; which, from some fatal defect in their
application, bribe to iniquity while they
are relieving want; and make food, and
raiment, and clothing to warm into life
the most poisonous seeds of vice. But
the charities of our departed friend were
of another order. They selected the
fittest objects—the widow—the fatherless
—the orphan—the untaught child—and
the ignorant adult. They combined intellectual and moral benefit with the communication of physical comfort. In her
house originated the *Society for the relief
of Poor Widows with small Children.*
Large, indeed, is this branch of the family of affliction; and largely did it share in
her sympathy and succour. When at the
head of the noble association just named,
she made it her business to see with her
own eyes the objects of their care; and to
give, by her personal presence and efforts, the strongest impulse to their humane system. From morning till night
has she gone from abode to abode of these

destitute, who are too commonly unpitied by the great, despised by the proud, and forgotten by the gay. She has gone to sit beside them on their humble seat, hearing their simple and sorrowful story—sharing their homely meal—ascertaining the condition of their children—stirring them up to diligence, to economy, to neatness, to order—putting them in the way of obtaining suitable employment for themselves, and suitable places for their children—distributing among them the word of God, and little tracts calculated to familiarize its first principles to their understanding—cherishing them in sickness—admonishing them in health—instructing, reproving, exhorting, consoling—sanctifying the whole with fervent prayer. Many a sobbing heart and streaming eye is this evening embalming her memory in the house of the widow.

Little, if any, less is the debt due to her from that invaluable charity the *Orphan Asylum*. It speaks its own praise, and that praise is hers. Scores of orphans redeemed from filth, from ignorance, from wretchedness, from crime—clothed, fed, instructed—trained, in cleanliness, to habits of industry—early imbued with the knowledge and fear of God—gradually preparing for respectability, usefulness, and happiness—is a spectacle for angels. Their infantine gayety, their healthful sport, their cherub-faces, mark the contrast between their present and former condition; and recal, very tenderly, the scenes in which they used to cluster round their patron-mother, hang on her gracious words, and receive her benediction.

"Brethren, I am not dealing in romance, but in sober fact. The night would be too short for a full enumeration of her worthy deeds. Suffice it to say, that they ended but with her life. The Sabbath previous to her last sickness occupied her with a recent institution—*A Sunday School for Ignorant Adults;* and the evening preceding the touch of death found her at the side of a faithful domestic, administering consolation to his wounded spirit.

"Such active benevolence could hardly be detected in company with a niggardly temper. Wishes which cost nothing, pity which expires on the lips—*Be ye warmed, and be ye clothed,* from a cold heart and an unyielding gripe, never imprinted their disgraceful brand upon ISABELLA GRAHAM. What she urged upon others she exemplified in herself. She kept a purse for God. Here, in obedience to his command, she deposited *the first fruits of all her increase;* and they were sacred to his service, as, in his providence, he should call for them. No shuffling pre-

tences, no pitiful evasions, when a fair demand was made upon the hallowed store; and no frigid affectation in determining the quality of the demand. A sense of duty was the prompter, candor the interpreter, and good sense the judge. Her disbursements were proportioned to the value of the object; and were ready at a moment's warning, to the very last farthing.* How pungent a reproof to those ladies of opulence and fashion, who sacrifice so largely to their dissipation or their vanity, that they have nothing left for months without toil, and limbs without raiment! How far does it throw back into the shade those men of prosperous enterprise and gilded state, who, in the hope of some additional lucre, have thousands and ten thousands at their beck; but who, when asked for decent contributions to what they themselves acknowledge to be all important, turn away with this hollow excuse, "I cannot afford it!" Above all, how should her example redden the faces of many who profess to belong to Christ; to have received gratuitously from him, what he procured for them at the expense of his own blood, *an inheritance incorruptible, and undefiled, and that fadeth not away;* and yet, in the midst of abundance which he has lavished upon them, when the question is about relieving his suffering members, or promoting the glory of his kingdom, are sour, reluctant, mean! Are *these* the *Christians?* Can it be that they have committed their bodies, their souls, their eternal hope, to a Savior whose thousand promises on this very point of *honoring* him *with their substance,* have less influence upon their hearts and their hands than the word of any honest man? Remember the deceased, and hang your heads—Remember her, and tremble—Remember her, and *bring forth fruits meet for repentance.*" pp. 36—40.

To the diffusive charity of Mrs. G. we would direct the peculiar attention of our readers. As they read, let them consider, that it is undoubtedly their duty, as it was her duty and her pleasure, *'to keep a purse for God; to deposit in this purse the first fruits of all their increase; that their disbursements from this sa-*

* *The author knew her, when in moderate circumstances, to give, unsolicited, Fifty pounds at once, out of that sacred purse, to a single most worthy purpose*

cred deposit should be proportioned to the value of the objects; and that they should be always ready at a moment's warning.' How different a description this, from such a one as truth would draw of the character and conduct of most professed Christians.

We must copy another long passage before we close. It is replete with solid instruction, as it exhibits the proper uses to be made of the heart-cheering example of this venerable matron. For the affecting account of her last hours on earth, we refer to the sermon.

"From this review allow me, brethren, to urge the *value of private exertions in promoting general good.*

"In pursuing his *gratifications*, man is apt to look upon himself as a being of great importance. In fulfilling his *duties*, to account himself as nothing. Both are extravagancies which it will be his wisdom and happiness to correct. He is neither supreme in worth, nor useless in action. Let him not say, "I am but one: My voice will be drowned in the universal din; my weight is lighter than a feather in the public scale. It is better for me to mind my own affairs, and leave these higher attempts to more competent hands." This is the language, not of reason and modesty, but of sloth, of selfishness, and of pride. The amount of it is, I cannot do every thing, "therefore I will do nothing"—But you can do much. Act well your part according to your faculties, your station, and your means.—The result will be honorable to yourself, delightful to your friends, and beneficial to the world. I advise not to gigantic aims, to enormous enterprise. The world has seen but one Newton and one Howard. Nothing is required of you but to make the most of the opportunities within your reach. Read the example of Mrs. Graham. Here was a woman—a widow—a stranger in a strange land—without fortune—with no friends but such as her letters of introduction and her worth should acquire—and with a family of daughters dependent upon her for their subsistence. Surely if any one has a clear title or immunity from the obligation to carry her aims beyond the domestic circle, it is this widow, it is this stranger. Yet within

a few years this stranger, this widow, with no means but her excellent sense, her benevolent heart, and her *persevering will* to do good, awakens the charities of a populous city, and gives to them an impulse, a direction, and an efficacy, unknown before! What might not be done by *men;* by men of talent, of standing, of wealth, of leisure! How speedily, under their well-directed beneficence, might a whole country change its physical, intellectual, and moral aspect, and assume, comparatively speaking, the face of another Eden—a second garden of God? Why then do they not diffuse, thus extensively, the seeds of knowledge, of virtue, and of bliss? I ask not for their pretences; they are as old as the lust of lucre; and are refuted by the example which we have been contemplating—I ask for the true reason, for the inspiring principle, of their conduct. It is this—let them look to it when God shall call them to account for the abuse of their time, their talents, their station, their *unrighteous mammon*.—It is this: They believe not *the words of the Lord Jesus, how he said,* IT IS MORE BLESSED TO GIVE THAN TO RECEIVE. They labor under no want but one—they want *the heart!* The bountiful God add this to the other gifts which he has bestowed upon them! I turn to the other sex.

"That venerable mother in Israel, who has exchanged the service of God on earth for his service in heaven, has left a legacy to her sisters—she has left the example of her faith and patience; she has left her prayers, she has left the monument of her Christian deeds: and by these she *being dead yet speaketh.* Matrons! has she left her *moral* also? Are there none among you to hear her voice from the tomb, *Go and do thou likewise?* None whom affluence permits, endowments qualify, and piety prompts, to aim at her distinction by treading in her steps? Maidens! Are there none among *you,* who would wish to array yourselves hereafter in the honors of this *virtuous woman?* Your hearts have dismissed their wonted warmth and generosity, if they do not throb as the reverend vision rises before you—Then prepare yourselves now, by seeking and serving the God of her youth. You cannot be too early *adorned with the robes of righteousness and the garments of salvation* in which she was wedded, in her morning of life, to Jesus the king of glory. That same grace which shed its radiance around her shall shed it on you also to shine in the *beauty of holiness;* and the fragrance of those virtues which it shall create, develope, and ennoble, will be *the smell of a field which the Lord hath blessed.*" pp 15—48

We fully agree with the preacher, (indeed it has long been a favorite opinion of ours.) that this country contains men of sufficient 'talent, wealth, standing, and leisure, to produce, by a well-directed beneficence, a change in its physical, intellectual, and moral aspect,—to transform it into another Eden, a second garden of God.' We agree with him, also, that the great reason why this transformation does not take place, 'is the want of the *heart*.' There are other reasons, however, among which are these: The *minds* of some men are more contracted than their *hearts*. They are real Christians; but as to all the duties of Christian beneficence, of that enlarged liberality, which the Gospel requires, they are babes, mere helpless babes, unable to speak or act. Again, the practice of beneficence, on the proper scale, has never yet been so firmly established, as to carry the mass of the people in a strong current. Many would cheerfully give, and act, on a large scale, if they saw it to be the fashion. We say *cheerfully*. They have the heart to do so: They see the need of doing so: But when they look around them, and see what others do, their feelings are damped by the multitude of negative, or niggardly, examples. We have witnessed many instances of these chilling effects. Such are the low and inadequate views of many, who would fain be thought friendly to charitable exertions, that they depress the views and feelings of others who think more justly. The fact is, that all beneficent efforts, on the proper scale, appear so extravagant to the mass of mankind, as

that the few, who are disposed to make them, run a great hazard of being considered as absolutely beside themselves. It is time, however, that these few should pay less deference to the opinions of others, than they are accustomed to do. When they go on with independence and firmness, others will be disposed to follow.

As to the ability of this country, we can prove, to our own complete satisfaction, that, all things considered, no people upon earth are so able, according to their numbers, to make great exertions in doing good, as the people of the northern and central parts of the United States.

LXVII. *Christian India; or an Appeal on behalf of* 900.000 *Christians in India, who want the Bible. A Sermon preached at Calcutta, on Tuesday, Jan. 1, 1811, for promoting the objects of the British and Foreign Bible Society. By* HENRY MARTYN, *B. D. Fellow of St. John's College, Cambridge, and Chaplain to the Honorable East India Company in Bengal.* Published by request, with a list of Benefactors. Calcutta; P. Ferris. 1811. pp. 47.

MANY of our readers know, that the Rev. Henry Martyn, having received the highest honors of one of the great English universities, went to Bengal as a chaplain to the East India Company; that he was there associated with the Rev. David Brown, and other excellent men, in attempting to diffuse the blessings of Christianity throughout the populous regions of Asia; that he was la-riously engaged in translating the Scriptures into the Arabic and Persian languages, when he undertook a journey overland to Europe; that after visiting the capital of Persia, he proceeded westward, and, exhausted by hard study, and debilitated by the climate, yielded up his life in Asiatic Turkey. He was an eminent servant of Christ, and as such his memory is greatly honored.

A copy of the sermon before us was sent from India by the American missionaries. It is just such a production as we should expect from such a person. The style unites the simplicity of a child with the vigor of an able man; and the sound sense every where apparent indicates, that the author had lived in habits of reflection, and that, for a man of his years, he had uncommon claims to the character of a Christian sage.

The text is, Gal. vi, 10. *As we have therefore opportunity, let us do good unto all men, especially unto them who are of the household of faith.*

After exploding the unmeaning infidel doctrine of universal philanthrophy, the author proceeds thus:

"From these observations it will be seen, how properly the Apostle has qualified the precept of universal beneficence. *As we have opportunity,* let us do good unto all men. With equal accuracy is the great Christian precept expressed, *Love thy neighbor as thyself;* since it directs to that which is really practicable in the theory of universal benevolence, and to no more. For who is our *neighbor?* every one that comes within the sphere of our action, our observation, our knowledge. All beyond are as though they were not. If there be any thing of which we form no idea, we cannot be affected with love or hatred to it.

"It may be here allowed us to remark,

that human systems of morality, constructed on a plan apparently more large and liberal than that of the Gospel, deserve very little attention: for what is really to the purpose in them was found in the Gospel long before. All the rest is most probably crude, imposes only upon inexperience, and is so far from arguing any superiority of mind, that the love of such theories rather proves a mediocrity of intellectual power.

"For all extremes, while they have a grandeur which captivates, are simple; on which account minds of a narrow span comprehend them easily. Hence it is, that the young and weak are pleased with romances, where the coincidences are exact, and the events extravagant. Hence also arise many of those struggles in states, which keep the world in perpetual agitation. For the commonalty, who will neither reason themselves, nor profit by the experience of others, are ever hurrying to extremes. Dissatisfied with monarchical government, they rush at once to anarchy. Weary of this, they go all the way back again to slavery. Thus weak man is like the restless ocean, which is but for a moment at its proper level, or like the tremulous needle, which requires time and a steady hand, before it lies true. The same species of imbecility is apparent in all our intercourse with each other. Disliking one or two parts of a person's character, we condemn him altogether; for the sake of as many good qualities, we bestow upon him unqualified praise.

"To avoid extremes is the part of wisdom. A child can lay his hand on the ends of things, but to find the middle requires reasoning. The wise will check the precipitation of the foolish, will except against sweeping changes, and, considering that nothing on earth is so bad, but there is some good in it, and nothing human so good, but it has something bad in it, will perceive, that to destroy a whole system, because some parts are out of order, is the way to leave us no good at all, and that to construct new ones without noticing the possibilities of things, and the state of imperfection in which we are, is only to waste time, and make room for disappointment.

"Happy are we in the possession of that Book of Wisdom, which marks its superiority to the flimsy productions of visionaries, by adapting itself to the circumstances of real life, and pointing out a certain and intelligible method of attaining perfection." pp. 5—8.

The word *neighbor* is sufficiently explained, in the parable

of the good Samaritan, by an unerring Expositor. It comprehends every person within the
sphere of our influence, when
beneficent action is concerned, and every person within
the circle of our knowledge, so
far as benevolent feelings are
in question. It is common, even
since the days of the man *who
fell among thieves*, to restrict the
word *neighbor* to local proximity, or national limits. Such a
restriction is contrary to the very
genius of Christianity. When
called upon to do good to any
part of the human race, the question is not *how near* to us the
proposed objects of our bounty
happen to live; but do they live
within the sphere of our action?
Is it practicable to do them good?
When the comparison is made
between different claims upon
our beneficence, the question is
not, which class of claimants are
placed *the nearest* to us, but to
which class we can probably *do
the most good*, all things considered. A man may live in the
same street with us, and yet it
may be impossible to come into
contact with him, in such a manner as to do him good; and yet it
may be very possible to do good
to those who live on the banks
of the Ganges, or in the centre
of Africa   There may be an
insuperable barrier between two
persons, who are very near each
other, in a local point of view,
and at the same time a perfect
freedom of access to others who
live at the antipodes. Though
local proximity is *one* important
consideration, in all charitable
enterprises, there are many others scarcely less important. *As
we have opportunity*, is the only
scriptural limit to beneficent action.

We are far from denying, that
certain relations in life impose
peculiar obligations; but the
principal reason for this may be,
that the very fact of sustaining
these relations implies peculiar
opportunities of doing good.

The following illustration of the
duty of giving money to charitable objects is well expressed.
Let the reader ask himself, as
he proceeds, whether he does
all that he can.

"Against the possibility of assisting any
but their friends, some will plead their
penury. The stream of their bounty is
too scantily supplied to flow beyond the
limits of their own ground. Be it so.
May it refresh and fertilize all within.
God neither requires impossibilities, nor
loves disorder. On the contrary, he would
have us adhere to his own arrangements,
and, if we cannot do all that we would, is
satisfied if we do all that we can.

"To those, who really have no opportunity, we do not speak, to the rest we
do. Your wealth is itself an opportunity,
and unless, from the desire of aggran-
dizing your families, you prefer to let it ac-
cumulate at home, you have it in your
power to bless many around you." pp. 9, 10.

The advantages of associations
for benevolent purposes are very
clearly as well as very briefly
stated in the following sentences:

"The intelligent Christian will perceive
the advantage which accrues from the
combination of strength, and gladly embrace the opportunity of acting in con-
junction with others. For the power of associated bodies is incalculably greater than
the aggregate of the powers of the component parts, because wisdom and strength
are brought together in them." p. 12.

It is an axiom in natural philosophy, that the whole is equal
to the sum of all its parts. Let
it ever be remembered as an axiom in moral philosophy, not
less certain than the other; that
the whole of an associated body
is immensely greater than the
sum of its component parts

om is enough to silence
mon inquiry on this sub-
hat need of Societies?
y not each man dispense
rity for himself? The
posal of these questions
iat charitable enterprises
omparatively in their in-
he time will come, when
will think of asking,
d of charitable societies,
a than he would think of
g, What need is there of
ernment?

lartyn, in the latter part
srmon, enumerates the
classes of natives in In-
make more or less of a
m of Christianity. Vast-
eater part have nothing
itianity but the name;
have more knowledge;
rs still are, as there is
son to hope, true believe-
ie different classes are
d by Mr. M. as follows.
Portuguese, 50,000
tians of Tanjore, 12,000
uans on the Mal-
coast, of whom
fourths are Ro-
Catholics, and the
yrian Christians, 200,000
Cingalese Chris-
(of whom about
re Roman Cath-
) amounting in
hole to above 600,000
artyn, while urging the
ion of the Bible as the
jan of raising up native
s, observes, "it has al-
:n so in every country;
e *first called and direct-*
missionary, and after a
went on by themselves.
decision of a man every
petent to decide, be re-
vith the consideration,
merits.

The closing paragraph of this
excellent sermon is as follows:

"Imagine the sad situation of a sick or
dying Christian, who has just heard e-
nough of eternity to be afraid of death and
not enough of a Saviour to look beyond it
with hope: He cannot call for a Bible to
look for something to support him, or ask
his wife or child to read him a consolatory
chapter. The Bible, alas! is a treasure,
which they never had the happiness to
possess. O pity their distress, you that
have hearts to feel for the miseries of
your fellow-creatures; you that have discernment to see, that a wounded spirit is
far more agonizing than any earth-begot-
ten woes; you that know that you too must
one day die, O give unto him what may
comfort him in a dying hour. The Lord
who loves our brethren, who gave his life
for them and for you, who gave you the
Bible before them, and now wills that they
should receive it from you; He will reward you. They cannot recompense you :
but you shall be recompensed at the resurrection of the just. The King himself
will say unto you, *inasmuch as ye have
done it unto one of the least of these my
brethren, ye have done it unto me.*"

In the year 1810, a subscription was opened at Calcutta for
the promotion of the objects of
the British and Foreign Bible
Society, but principally for the
distribution of the Scriptures in
the Tamul language. To satisfy the natural curiosity of our
readers we copy a list of those
donations, which were not less
than 200 rupees each, expressing
the value of the donations in dollars. The names of several of
the donors are well known in this
country.

His Excellency Lieut. Gen. Hewett, com-
mander in chief, &c. &c. £900
John Lumsden, Esq. of the Su-
preme Council, - - 96
Sir John Royds, Knight, do. 96
Sir William Burroughs, Bart. do. 96
James Alexander, Esq. - 96
—— Baring, Esq. - - 96
R. M. Bird, Esq. - - 96
Rev. David Brown, - - 96
———
Carried forward, £1,632

Brought forward,	$1,632
Lieut. Col. Peter Carey,	96
Rev. D. Corrie,	96
C. R. Crommelin, Esq.	96
R. Downie, Esq.	154
Sir John D'Oyly,	96
A Friend, by the Rev. D. B.	96
J. H. Harington, Esq.	96
A Lady, by the Rev. T. T.	238
Rev. H. Martyn,	96
Rev. J. Parson,	444
Maj. Thomas Penson,	240
R. C. Plowden, Esq.	190
J. Richardson, Esq.	480
Mrs. Richardson,	96
Rev. T. Thomason,	96
Rev. M. Thompson, of Madras,	96
J. Thornhill, Esq.	240
George Udny, Esq.	144
From eighty five other donors, in sums less than 200 rupees each,	$1,835
	$4,477

We remark with pleasure, that the name of every Episcopal clergyman in that part of India, so far as our knowledge extends, is to be found in the preceding list of donations.

LXVIII. *An Address to the Rev. Eustace Carey, Jan. 19, 1814, on his designation as a Christian Missionary to India. By* ROBERT HALL, M A. Leicester; [Eng] Thomas Combe. pp. 49.

THE character of Mr. Hall has been several years established, and is now universally pronounced to be that of an able and eloquent writer, a truly great man, and a consistent and catholic Christian. All his productions bear the stamp of greatness and dignity; and the sublimity of his eloquence has certainly not been surpassed in modern times. The Eclectic Reviewers have declared, that they know not where to find a parallel, in any oration ancient or modern, to the close of his *Fast Sermon,* preached in 1803.

Mr. H. modestly styles this address "a few hints of advice," and not "a regular charge," which he did not judge himself equal to; but we are free to affirm, that we have never seen so much wisdom on this subject embodied within so small a compass.

The first qualification for a missionary is, in Mr. Hall's opinion, "a decided predilection for the office;" the second, "singular self-devotement;" the third, "the spirit of faith," by which he intends, "not merely that cordial belief of the truth, which is essential to a Christian; but that unshaken persuasion of the promises of God respecting the triumph and enlargement of his kingdom, which is sufficient to denominate its possessor *strong in faith.*"

After enlarging on these topics, Mr. H. seems naturally to fall into a series of great and affecting considerations, on the motives which should influence a missionary, the wretched state of the heathen world, and the benign influence of Christianity. The flame of eloquence is steady and pure, but kindles into uncommon brightness when the character of Paul is brought into view.

We proceed to give several quotations for the gratification and instruction of our readers.

"It is impossible that the mind of a missionary should be too much impressed with the beauty, glory, and grandeur of the kingdom of Christ, as it is unfolded in the oracles of the Old and New Testament; nor with the certainty of the final accomplishment of those oracles, founded on the faithfulness and omnipotence of their Author. To those parts of Scrip-

fore his attention should be especially directed, in which the Holy Ghost employs and exhausts, so to speak, the whole force and splendor of inspiration in depicting the future reign of the Messiah, together with that astonishing spectacle of dignity, purity, and peace, which his church will exhibit, when *having the glory of God,* her bounds shall be commensurate with those of the habitable globe, when every object on which the eye shall rest, will remind the spectator of the commencement of a new age, in which *the tabernacle of God is with men, and he dwells among them.* His spirit should be imbued with that sweet and tender awe, which such anticipations will infallibly produce, whence will spring a generous contempt of the world, and an ardor bordering on impatience to be employed, though in the humblest sphere, as the instrument of accelerating such a period. For compared to this destiny in reserve for the children of men, compared to this glory, invisible at present, and hid behind the clouds which envelope this dark and troubled scene, the brightest day that has hitherto shone upon the world, is midnight, and the highest splendors that have invested it, the shadow of death." pp. 9, 10.

We have repeatedly expressed the opinion, that nothing was easier, or more natural, considering the state of the human heart, than for Christian nations to relapse into idolatry. Without the continued influence of the Holy Spirit, the descent from true religion to idolatry would be rapid and inevitable, either by the road of superstition on the one hand, or latitudinarianism and infidelity, on the other. Both these roads terminate in the same place, and are of about equal length. Reason alone will never preserve men, much less reclaim them, from idolatry.

"For a nation to *change* their gods, is represented by the highest authority as an event almost unparalleled; and if it be so difficult to induce them to change the *mode* of their idolatry, how much more to persuade them to abandon it altogether. Idolatry is not to be looked upon as a mere speculative error respecting the object of worship, of little or no practical efficacy. Its hold upon the mind of a fallen creature is most tenacious, its ope-

ration most extensive. It is a corrupt practical institution, involving a whole system of sentiments and manners which perfectly moulds and transforms its votaries. It modifies human nature, in every aspect under which it can be contemplated, being intimately blended and incorporated with all its perceptions of good and evil, with all its infirmities, passions, and fears. In a country like India, where it has been established for ages, its ramifications are so extended as to come into contact with every mode, and every incident of life. Scarce a day, or an hour passes with an Hindoo, in which by the abstinences it enjoins, and the ceremonies it prescribes, he is not reminded of his religion. It meets him at every turn, presses like the atmosphere on all sides, and holds him by a thousand invisible chains. By incessantly admonishing him of something which he must do, or something which he must forbear, it becomes the strongest of his active habits; while the multiplicity of objects of worship, distinguished by an infinite variety in their character and exploits, is sufficient to fill the whole sphere of his imagination. In the indolent repose which his constitution and climate incline him to indulge, he suffers his fancy to wander without limit, amidst scenes of voluptuous enjoyment, or objects of terror and dismay; while revolving the history of his gods, he conceives himself absorbed in holy contemplations. There is not a vicious passion he can be disposed to cherish, not a crime he can be tempted to commit, for which he may not find a sanction and an example in the legends of his gods. Though the system of polytheism established in India, considered in an argumentative light is beneath contempt, being destitute of the least shadow of proof, as well as of all coherence in its principles; yet viewed as an instrument of establishing a despotic empire over the mind, nothing, it must be acknowledged, was ever more artfully contrived; not to mention the distinction of casts which is obviously adapted to fix and perpetuate every other institution. That the true religion should degenerate into idolatry is easily to be accounted for from the known principles of human nature, because such deterioration is aided by its corruption, flatters its strongest propensities, and artfully adapts itself to whatever is feeble, sensitive, and voluptuous in the character of the species.

...... *Facilis descensus averni.*

"As it is easy to descend from an elevation which it is difficult to climb, to fall from the adoration of the Supreme Being to the worship of idols, demands no effort. Idolatry is strongly intrenched in the corruptions, and fortified by the weakness of human nature. Hence we find all nations have sunk into it in succession, frequently in opposition to the strongest remonstrances of inspired prophets; while we have no example in the history of the world, of a single city, family, or individual who has renounced it, through the mere operation of unassisted reason: such is the fatal propensity of mankind to that enormity. It is the vail of the covering, cast over all flesh, which nothing but the effulgence of Revelation has pierced. The true religion satisfies and enlarges the reason, but militates against the inclinations of men. Resting on a few sublime truths addressed to the understanding and conscience, affording a few distinct images to the fancy, and no indulgence to the passions, it can only be planted and preserved by a continual efflux from its Divine Author, of whose spirituality and elevation it so largely partakes." pp. 11—14.

"In India, Satan maintains an almost undisputed empire, and the powers of darkness, secure of their dominion, riot and revel at their pleasure, sporting themselves with the misery of their vassals, whom they incessantly agitate with delusive hopes and fantastic terrors, leading them captive at their will, while few efforts have been made to despoil them of their usurped authority. Partial invasions have been attempted, and a few captives disenthralled, but the strength and sinews of empire remain entire, and that dense and palpable darkness which invests it, has scarcely felt the impression of a few feeble and scattered rays. In India you will witness the predominance of a system which provides for the worship of gods many, and of lords many, while it excludes the adoration of the Supreme Being, legitimates cruelty, polygamy, and lust, debases the standard of morals, oppresses with ceremonies, those whom it deprives of instruction, and suggests no solid hope of happiness beyond the grave.

"You will witness with indignation that monstrous alliance betwixt impurity and devotion, obscenity and religion, which characterises the popular idolatry of all ages, and which, in opposition to the palliating sophistry of infidels, sufficiently evinces it to be what the Scriptures assert —the worship of devils, not of God." pp. 27, 28.

The manner of preaching to the heathen, which Mr. H. prescribes, is as follows:

"In recommending the principles of Christianity to a Pagan nation, I would by no means advise the adoption of a refined and circuitous course of instruction, commencing with an argumentative exposition of the principles of natural religion, and from thence advancing to the peculiar doctrines of revelation: nor would I advise you to devote much time to an elaborate confutation of the Hindoo or Mahometan systems. The former of these methods would be far too subtle and intricate for popular use; the latter calculated to irritate. Great practical effects on the populace are never produced by profound argumentation; and every thing which tends to irritation and disgust should be carefully avoided. Let your instruction be in the form of a *testimony:* let it, with respect to the mode of exhibiting it, though not to the spirit of the teacher, be *dogmatic. Testify* repentance towards God, and faith in our Lord Jesus Christ." pp. 32, 33.

"After reminding them of their state as guilty and polluted creatures, which the ceremonies of their religion teach them to confess, exhibit to the inhabitants of Hindostan, the cross of Christ as their only refuge. Acquaint them with his incarnation, his character as the Son of God and the Son of man, his offices, and the design of his appearance; not with the air of a disputer of this world, but of him who is conscious to himself of his possessing the medicine of life, the treasure of immortality, which he is anxious to impart to guilty men. Insist fearlessly on the futility and vanity of all human methods of expiation, on the impotence of idols, and the command of God to *all men every where to repent, inasmuch as he has appointed a day in which he will judge the world in righteousness* Display the sufferings of Christ like one who was an eye witness of those sufferings, and hold up the blood, the precious blood of atonement, as issuing warm from the cross It is a peculiar excellence of the Gospel, that in its wonderful adaptation to the state and condition of mankind as fallen creatures, it bears intrinsic marks of its divinity, and is supported not less by internal than by external evidence. By a powerful appeal to the conscience, by a faithful delineation of man in his grandeur, and in his weakness, in his original capacity for happiness, and his present misery and guilt, present this branch of its evidence in all its force seize on every occasion those features of Christianity which render it interesting, and by awakening the fears, and exciting the hopes of your hearers, endeavor to annihilate every other object, and make it appear what it really is, the pearl of great price, the sovereign balm, the cure of every ill, the antidote of death, the precursor of immortality. In such a ministry, fear not to give loose to all the ardor of your soul, to call into action every emotion and every faculty which can exalt or adorn it. You will find ample scope for all its force and tenderness, and should you be called to pour your life as a libation on the offering of the Gentiles, you will only have the more occasion to exult and rejoice." pp. 33—35.

Few men will deny, after reading the following paragraph, that great dignity belongs to the character of a missionary.

"If to survey mankind in different situations, and under the influence of opposite institutions, civil and religious, tends to elevate the mind above vulgar prejudice, by none is this advantage more eminently possessed than by Christian Missionaries. In addition to the advantages usually anticipated from foreign travel, their attention is directly turned to man in the most interesting light in which he can be viewed. An intelligent Missionary, in consequence of daily conversing with the natives on the most momentous subjects, and at the most affecting moments, has opportunities of becoming acquainted, not merely with the surface of manners, but with the interior of the character, which can rarely fall to the lot of any other person; besides that Christianity, it may be justly affirmed, is the best decypherer of the human heart, and is that alone which can solve its contradictions and explain its anomalies. Hence it may be fairly expected, nor will the expectation disappoint us, that an experienced Missionary, possessed of the talent and habit of observation will, in every country, deserve to be classed amongst the most enlightened of its inhabitants. "Few things more powerfully tend to enlarge the mind than conversing with great objects, and engaging in great pursuits. That the object you are pursuing is entitled to that appellation, will not be questioned by him who reflects on the infinite advantages derived from Christianity to every nation and clime where it has prevailed in its purity, and that the prodigious superiority which Europe possesses over Asia and Africa, is chiefly to be ascribed to this cause. It is the possession of a religion which comprehends the seeds of endless improvement, which maintains an incessant struggle with whatever is barbarous, selfish, or inhuman, which by unveiling futurity, clothes morality with the sanction of a Divine law, and harmonizes utility and virtue in every combina-

tion of events, and in every stage of existence; a religion which by affording the most just and sublime conceptions of the Deity, and of the moral relations of man, has given birth at once to the loftiest speculation, and the most child-like humility, uniting the inhabitants of the globe into one family, and in the bonds of a common salvation; it is this religion which rising upon us like a finer sun, has quickened moral vegetation, and replenished Europe with talents, virtues and exploits, which in spite of its physical disadvantages, have rendered it a paradise, the delight and wonder of the world. An attempt to propagate this religion among the natives of Hindostan, may perhaps be stigmatized as visionary and romantic, but to enter the lists of controversy with those who would deny it to be great and noble, would be a degradation to reason." pp. 40—42.

At this place Mr. H. inserts a note, in which he inflicts merited chastisement upon a writer in the Edinburgh Review, who is understood to be the Rev. Sydney Smith, a Socinian of the lowest class, and yet a minister of the English Church. Every intelligent reader of the Edinburgh Review must be surprised, at the extreme ignorance of religion, which is characteristic of many articles in that publication. The note here inserted is as follows:

"It is impossible to read the strictures of the Edinburgh Review on Missions, in an article which appeared under that title, without surprise and indignation, that such sentiments could find admission in a work which possesses such just claims to literary merit. The anonymous writer of the article alluded to, with the levity of a buffoon, joined to a heart of iron, and a face of brass, has more than insinuated that the Christianity attempted to be promoted in India by the Missionaries at Serampore, would, were it adopted, prove a serious injury to the natives, and that they are much happier and more virtuous under their present institutions. The system of religion, be it remembered, which these men have attempted to introduce, and which this *Christian Reviewer* loads with abuse, is precisely the same in its doctrinal articles with that of the Church of England, to which he has subscribed, ex animo no doubt, his unfeigned assent and consent. It may be hoped that at a time when the Church of England is evincing a spirit of moderation, and forbearance, and can boast of so many prelates and dignitaries, distinguished for their piety and learning, no clergyman for the future will be allowed to degrade himself in a similar manner, without the most indignant rebuke. It may possibly gratify certain spirits to see the dissenters and methodists vilified and abused, but they will do well to remember, that the indulgence of a profane and scoffing humor must be ultimately injurious not only to Christianity, but to any Christian community whatever; and that to stab religion through the sides of fanaticism, is a stale artifice of infidels, by which the simplest can no longer be deceived. I sincerely hope the Conductors of the Edinburgh Review have long been ashamed of the article in question. When I compare the intellectual power displayed in some articles of that publication with the extreme ignorance of religion evinced in others, I know not how better to characterize it than in the language of Virgil, in speaking of Polyphemus,—

"Monstrum horrendum, informe, ingens, *cui lumen ad-mptum.*" pp. 42, 43.

It is often said, especially by men who call themselves liberal Christians, that we must first civilize the heathen, and afterwards Christianize them. This favorite dogma is, indeed, very easily refuted, but was never more happily refuted than in the first of the following paragraphs; for if even Christianity itself cannot civilize, unless when inculcated for an infinitely higher purpose, how evident it is, that no inferior agent can produce so great an effect:

"In the views of the most enlightened statesmen, compared to those of a Christian minister, there is a littleness and limitation, which is not to be imputed in one case as a moral imperfection, nor in the other as a personal merit; the difference arising purely from the disparity of the subjects upon which they respectively speculate. Should you be asked on your arrival in India, as it is very probable you will, what there is in Christianity which renders it so inestimable in your eyes, that you judged it fit to undertake so long, dangerous, and expensive a voyage, for the purpose of imparting it,—you will answer without hesitation, it is the power of God to salvation; nor will any view of it short of this, or the inculcation of it for any inferior purpose, enable it to produce even those moralizing and civilizing effects it is so powerfully adapted to accomplish. Christianity will civilize, it is true, but it is only when it is allowed to develope the energies by which it sanctifies. Christianity will inconceivably meliorate the present condition of being,—who doubts it? Its universal prevalence, not in name but in reality, will convert this world into a semi-paradisiacal state; but it is only while it is permitted to prepare its inhabitants for a better. Let her be urged to forget her celestial origin and destiny, to forget that "she came from God, and returns to God," and whether she is employed by the artful and enterprising, as the instrument of establishing a spiritual empire and dominion over mankind, or by the philanthropist, as the means of promoting their civilization and improvement, she resents the foul indignity, claps her wings, and takes her flight, leaving nothing but a base and sanctimonious hypocrisy in her room.

"Preach it then, my dear brother, with a constant recollection that such is its character and aim. Preach it with a perpetual view to eternity; and with the simplicity and affection with which you would address your dearest friends, were they assembled round your dying bed. While others are ambitious to form the citizen of earth, be it yours to train him for heaven, to raise up the temple of God from among the ancient desolations, to contribute your part towards the formation and perfection of that eternal society, which will flourish in inviolable purity and order when all human associations shall be dissolved, and the princes of this world shall come to nought. In the pursuit of these objects, let it be your ambition to tread in the footsteps of a Brainerd and a Swartz, I may add, of your excellent relative, with whom we are happy in perceiving you to possess a congeniality of character, not less than an affinity of blood.

"But should you succeed beyond your utmost hope, expect not to escape the ridicule of the ungodly, or the censure of the world; but be content to sustain that sort of reputation, and run that sort of career invariably allotted to the Christian Missionary; where agreeable to the experience of St. Paul, obscurity and notoriety, admiration and scorn, sorrows and consolations, attachments the most tender, and opposition the most violent, are interchangeably mingled." pp. 44—46.

The close of this admirable address is in the same noble, unaffected strain;

"I need not remind you that as the society under whose auspices you are now proceeding to India, have on no occasion employed a Missionary in whom they reposed more confidence, or of whom they formed more raised expectations; if you should become vain, worldly, sensual, indolent, and consequently useless, ours will not be an ordinary disappointment; we shall have fallen from a great hope. You will be sensible of the indispensable necessity of not interfering with the politics of India, nor of giving the smallest ground of umbrage and distrust to the constituted authorities, to whom it will be your duty not less than your interest to pay on all occasions, in return for the protection they will yield, the most respectful deference.

"Let me also recommend you to listen to the advice, and be guided by the suggestions, as far as your conscience will permit, of your Fathers in the Mission, and of Dr. Carey in particular, whose wisdom and experience, to say nothing of his relationship to you, entitle him to reverential attention. You are now about to be removed from us, who it is probable shall see your face no more; but you will not be removed from the communion of saints, which no seas can divide, no distance impair, in which we shall often meet at a throne of grace, whence fervent prayers will ascend to the Father of mercies, that he may keep you under his holy protection, and cause the richest of his blessings to descend on the head of him who was separate from his brethren." pp. 48, 49.

We are happy to state that a cheap edition of this address has just been republished by S. T. Armstrong, with an appendix containing an extract from Mr. Chalmers's sermon, which is the subject of the following article.

LXIX. *The Two Great Instruments appointed for the Propagation of the Gospel; and the duty of the Christian Public to keep them both in vigorous operation: A Sermon preached before the Dundee Missionary Society, on Monday, Oct. 26,* 1812. *By the Rev. Thomas Chalmers, Kilmany.* London; printed and distributed as a tract by the Missionary Society. pp. 24. 12mo.

In the last volume of the Panoplist, p. 420, we inserted a speech delivered by Mr. Chalmers, at the formation of a Bible Society. Few articles which have appeared in our pages, perhaps none, ever received more unqualified approbation. From the tract before us, it is evident, that the author is not less able, or less disposed, to plead the cause of the Missionary Society than of Bible Societies.

The text is Rom. x, 17. *Faith cometh by hearing, and hearing by the word of God.*

The doctrine of subordinate agency, under the control of the Almighty Agent, is well stated in the introduction to the discourse.

"As all is suspended upon God; and as he reigns with as supreme a dominion in the heart of man as in the world around us, there is no doubt that every affection of this heart—the remorse which embitters it, the terror which appals it, the faith which restores it,—the love which inflames it,—there can be no doubt, I say, that all is the work of God. However great the diversity of operations, it is He that worketh all in all; and the apostle Paul expressly ascribes the faith of a human soul to the operation of his hand, when he prays, in behalf of the Thessalonians, that God would fulfil in them all the good pleasure of his goodness, and the work of faith with power.

"But, on the other hand, it is evident, that throughout the wide extent of nature and of providence, though it be God alone that worketh, yet he worketh by instruments; and that, without any wish to question or to impair his sovereignty, it is an established habit of language to ascribe that to the instrument which is solely and exclusively due to the Omnipotent himself. We say that it is rain which makes the grass to grow: it is God, in fact, who makes the grass to grow; and he does it by the instrumentality of rain. Yet we do not say that there is any impiety in this mode of expression: nor does it imply that we in thought transfer that to the instrument which is due only to Him in whose hand the instrument is: it is a mere habit of language; and the apostle himself has fallen into the use of it. None were more impressed than he with the pious sentiment that all depends upon God and cometh from God; yet he does not overlook the instrumentality of a preacher; and tells the Romans, in the words of my text, that faith cometh by hearing, and hearing by the word of God.

"If, in that extraordinary age when the Author of Nature broke in upon the constancy of its operations, and asserted by miracles his own mighty power to subdue and to control it—if, in such an age, one of his own inspired messengers does not overlook the use and agency of instruments, surely it would ill become us to overlook them. It is right that we should carry about with us, at all times and in all places, a sentiment of piety; but it must not be piety of our own forging,—it must be the prescribed piety of revelation; we have no right to sit in indolence, and wait for the immediate agency of Heaven, if God has told us that it is by the co-operation of human beings that the end is to be accomplished, and if he orders that co-operation; we are not merely to acquiesce in the sentiment that it is God who does the thing, but we must acquiesce in his manner of doing it; and if that be by instruments, nothing remains for us but submissively to concur and obediently to go along with it." pp. 1—3.

The preacher establishes the following points beyond debate; viz. that the two great instruments of propagating the Gospel are mentioned in the text; that in no age of the Church does it appear that one of these instruments has superseded the other; that neither instrument can ever safely be dispensed with; and that there is an equal duty binding on Christians to keep both instruments in operation.

On the efficacy of the *preaching* of the Gospel we cite the following sentences:

"I do not speak of his ministrations from house to house; I speak of his ministrations from the pulpit, whence it is of-

ten the high prerogative of a single man to make the word of God bear with energy and effect upon the consciences of hundreds. And he can do more than this; he can spread around him his own piety; he can kindle the fine ardors of sentiment and sincerity among his hearers; he can pour out all his tenderness and all his anxiety upon them; by the power and urgency of a living voice, he can touch the hearts of his people; and, with the blessing of God upon his endeavors, he can pull down the indolence and the security and the strong holds of corruption within them. The worth of the man can give a mighty energy to the words of the minister; and, what with the example of the one, and the stirring eloquence of the other, I hold an active, a pure, and a zealous ministry, spread over the face of the country, and laboring in its districts and parishes, to be one great palladium of Christianity in the land." pp. 9, 10.

Since the institution of Bible Societies, it has become common to represent the distribution of the Bible, both in Christian and Heathen countries, as the exclusive instrument of extending the influence of the Gospel. Such an opinion is totally unsupported by Scripture and by fact. It is not only unsupported, but is a very dangerous opinion; an opinion, which, however undesignedly, charges God foolishly for having instituted a perpetual Christian ministry. The great *immediate* instrument in the conversion of sinners, is undoubtedly *the preached Gospel;* but that this instrument may be used to the best possible effect, it is necessary that *the written Gospel* should be universally diffused. This is so plain a case, that we really know not how to argue it. We challenge the world to produce a single instance of a flourishing religious community, in which the Gospel has not been stately preached. We challenge the world to give a plausible scheme for the propagation of

pel among the heathen,
for the preservation of
g ourselves, without the
ation of preachers; un-
deed, miracles be resort-
And on the presumption
racles are to be exerted,
te as probable, that they
exerted without Bibles,
out preachers.
e are persons who object
ing missionaries to the
, who yet think very fa-
of sending them Bibles.
very statement of such a
evinces the most entire
ce of the whole subject.
ll you send Bibles with-
issionaries? This simple
never could be answer-
on this we might rest the
But we will descend to
ars. There are heathens
waters of the Missouri.
ible would be a boon
. You wish to send
it must go without mis-
s. Very well. You will
we suppose, by the wes-
aders. For a suitable
sation they will deliver
nber of boxes of Bibles
banks of the Missouri.
. In what language will
d the Bible? in English,
French, Greek, or He-
.h! the Bible must be
ed into the languages of
ves! Indeed it must; and
all translate it? Shall this
s be committed to these
orthy western traders?
all the people of Sumat-
ve their Scriptures from
ds of our supercargoes,
y pepper, for a week or
a time, on their shores?
all the Scriptures be
ed for the Burmans. by
a-captain, who happens

to touch at Rangoon? No, you
will say, the translation of the
Scriptures is a work of years, a
work of unremitted strenuous
labor. In order to be qualified
for it, a man must reside long
with the natives; must become
acquainted with all their habits,
customs, and modes of speech;
must feel a deep interest in his
work; must live under the influence of a strong desire for the
conversion, sanctification, and
salvation of the heathen; must
be freed, as far as possible, from
worldly embarrassments; must
abandon worldly projects; must
be accustomed to speak with the
natives on religious subjects; and
must occasionally make experiments by preaching from his
translation, to ascertain whether
he has conveyed the true meaning of the original. Who shall
do all this but a missionary? It
must be admitted, then, that
missionaries are absolutely necessary to translate the Scriptures; and that you cannot advance a step towards the conversion of the heathen without
them This is enough for our
present purpose; for many years
must elapse, (we earnestly pray
that it may not be centuries,) before the Scriptures will be translated into every language.

If our argument needed confirmation, we should say, *Look
at India.* How many years have
the most enlightened nations of
Europe had colonies in Asia, and
who ever thought of translations
till missionaries led the way?

But suppose the Scriptures to
be translated with perfect accuracy; suppose an indefinite number of copies to be printed and
ready for distribution; we still
utterly deny that missionaries

would be superseded; nay, we should urge this very fact as a reason why their number should be indefinitely increased. What course would an inquisitive heathen pursue, when the Bible was put into his hands, and be became anxious concerning his spiritual state? Doubtless he would be desirous to find a spiritual instructor. This is the natural consequence in Christian countries, and the same motives will operate in every country. They, who object to sending missionaries to the heathen, ought, if they would be consistent, to object to preaching the Gospel at all.

It is perfectly proper, however, and in many instances wise, for individuals, who make donations for the purpose of diffusing Christian knowledge, to designate the objects to which their donations shall be applied. This they will do according to their views of present exigency; and thus, under a superintending Providence, both objects will be provided for.

Mr. Chalmers has pleaded the cause of missions most efficaciously, by bringing forward the Bible Society as a witness in favor of her elder sister, the Missionary Society. Indeed, more than half the transactions of the Bible Society are an indirect, but highly honorable, encomium on the cause of missions. But hear this illustrious witness and encomiast, as adduced by Mr. Chalmers:

"They are sister societies. I have not time to detail the operations of either; for these I refer you to their Reports which are published every year, and are accessible to all of you: but, to satisfy you, I shall select a few particulars, from a source which you will deem pure and unexceptionable: I shall give the testimony of one

Society to the usefulness of the other; and from the Reports of the Bible Society, I shall present you with arguments why, whatever extent and efficiency be given to the one, the other is not to be abandoned.

"The very second in the list of donations by the Bible Society is "To the Mohawk Nations, two thousand copies of the Gospel of St. John." But who prepared the Indians of Upper Canada for such a present?—They were missionaries. There are missionaries now laboring amongst them employed by our Society; and had it not been for the previous exertions of human agents, this field of usefulness would have been withheld from the Bible Society altogether.

"Another donation is "To India, to be applied to the translation of the Scriptures into the Oriental languages, one thousand pounds;" this has been swelled by farther donations to the princely sum of seventeen thousand pounds. It is in aid of the noble undertaking of translating the Scriptures into the fifteen languages of India. But who set it a-going?—A Missionary Society. Who showed that it was practicable?—The human agents sent out by that Society. Who are accomplished for presiding over the different translations? —The same human agents, who have lived for years among the natives, and have braved resistance and death in the noble enterprise. Who formed a Christian population eager to receive these versions the moment they have issued from the press, and who have already absorbed whole editions of the New Testament!— The same answer,—missionaries. Our own Society can lay claim to part of this population: they have formed native schools, and have added to the number of native Christians.

"The next two donations I offer to your attention are, first, "For circulation in the West India Islands and the Spanish Main, one hundred Bibles and nine hundred Testaments in various languages;" second, "To negro congregations of Christians in Antigua, &c. five hundred Bibles and one thousand Testaments." Why is there any usefulness in this donation!— Because missionaries have gone before it. Do these copies really circulate! Yes, they do, among the negroes whom these intrepid men have christianized under the scowl of jealousy;—whom they have taught to look up to the Savior as their friend, and to heaven as their asylum,—and who, for the home they have been so cruelly torn from, have held out rest to their oppressed but believing spirits in the mansions which Christ has gone to prepare for them.

"The next example shall comprise sev-

s. "First, To the Hottentot
Bavian's kloof and Grune
ith Africa, so many Bibles
nts; second, To the Rever-
der Kemp, at Bethelsdorp,
for the Christian Hottentots,
teh Testaments and twelve
s third, to the Reverend Mr.
brange River, South Africa,
Testaments, and Twelve
s; fourth, To the Reverend
t, in the Namaequa country,
, fifty Dutch Testaments and
h Bibles; fifth, To the Rev.
r, Graaff Reinet, South Af-
dred Dutch Testaments and
Bibles." Now, what names
intries are these?—They are
itrics which the Missionary
w cultivating, and the names
aborers sent out and main-
m. The Bibles and Testa-
sent out in behalf of the
eds whom our Society had
eclaimed from heathenism:
iety is enabled to scatter the
such profusion, because the
had prepared the ground for
Nor are the labors of these
n confined to the business of
: they are at this moment
s, and industry, and civiliz-
: natives: they are raising a
stade to the moral eye amid
as around them;—they are
and virtue, and intelligence,
ng savages of Africa; and ex-
ing the wildest of nature's
comforts and the decencies
f life. O, ye orators and
who make the civilization of
our dream! look to Christian
if you want to see the men
ilze it: you may deck the
the praises of your unsub-
ence; but these are the men
complish the business! They
ting every earthly comfort
n the cause; while you sit in
y, and pour upon their holy
the cruelty of your scorn!"
at draw to a close; and shall
e donation more to your no-
idence of the close alliance in
t betwixt the Bible and Mis-
ties—those two great fellow-
ie vineyard of Christian be-
"For the Esquimaux Indians,
d copies of St Matthew's
ir vernacular tongues'" Who
Indians a written language!

ect the *Edinburgh Review-*
ure, Who is meant here?
ED. PAN.

Who translated a Gospel into their vernacular tongue? By what unaccountable
process has it been brought about, that
we now meet with readers and Christians
among these furred barbarians of the
north?—The answer is the same,—All
done by the exertions of Missionaries:
And had it not been for them, the Bible-
Society would no more have thought at
present of a translation into the language
of Labrador, than they would have thought
of a translation into any of the languages
of unexplored Africa.

"The two Societies go hand in hand.
The one plows while the other sows: and
let no opposition be instituted betwixt
their claims on the generosity of the public. Let the advocates of each strain to
the uttermost. The statement I have already given proves that there is a vast
quantity of unbroken ground in the country for subscriptions to both; and how, by
the accumulation of littles, which no individual will ever feel or regret, a vast sum
is still in reserve for the operations of these
Christian philanthropists. They are at
this moment shedding a glory over the
land far beyond what the tumults or the
triumphs of victory can bestow: their
deeds are peaceful, but they are illustrious; and they are accomplishing a grandeur and a more decisive step in the history of the species, than even he who in the
mighty career of a sweeping and successful ambition has scattered its old establishments into nothing. I have only to look
forward a few years, and I see *him* in his
sepulchre; and a few years more, and all
the dynasties he has formed give way to
some new change in the vain and restless
politics of the world. But the men with
whom I contrast him have a more unper-
ishable object in contemplation: I see the
sublime character of eternity stamped upon their proceedings! The frailties of
earthly politics do not attach to them; for
they are the instruments of God,—they
are carrying on the high administration of
Heaven,—they are hastening the fulfilment of prophecies uttered in a far distant
antiquity: *Many are going to and fro,
and knowledge is increased: For my
thoughts are not your thoughts, neither
are your ways my ways, saith the Lord;
for as the heavens are higher than the
earth, so are my ways higher than your
ways and my thoughts than your thoughts.
For as the rain cometh down and the snow
from heaven, and returneth not thither,
but watereth the earth, and maketh it
bring forth and bud, that it may give seed
to the sower and bread to the eater,—so
shall my word be that goeth forth out of
my mouth. It shall not return unto me
void; but it shall accomplish that which*

I please, and it shall prosper in the thing whereto I sent it.

"I stand here as the advocate for the Missionary Society—for the men who are now going to and fro and increasing knowledge, and are preparing ground in so many different quarters of the world for the good seed of the word of God. I have already urged upon you the plea of their usefulness: I have now to urge upon you the plea of their necessities. They have exerted themselves not only according to their power, but beyond their power: they are in debt to their Treasurer. Their embarrassments are their glory; and it is your part to save them from these embarrassments, lest they should become their disgrace." pp. 15—20.

The following address to the rich is well worthy of their perusal; particularly the rule of their beneficence, *Give only what you can spare:*

"We do not ask any to impoverish or exhaust themselves: We assail the rich with no more urgency than the poor; for we say to both alike—*Give only what you can spare.* We hold the question of alms-giving to depend not on what has been already given, but on what superfluity of wealth you are still in possession of. We know that to this question very different answers will be given, according to the principles and views and temper of the individual to whom it is applied, nor are we eager to pursue the question into all its applications: We do not want the offerings of an extorted charity; we barely state the merits of the cause, and leave the impression with your own hearts, my friends and fellow Christians. But when I take a view of society, and see the profusion and the splendor that surround me,—when I see magnificence in every room that I enter, and luxury on every table that is set before me,—when I see the many thousand articles where retrenchment is possible, and any one of which would purchase for its owner the credit of unexampled liberality,—when I see the sons and the daughters of fortune swimming down the full tide of enjoyment; and am told, that out of all this extravagance there is not a fragment to spare for sending the light of Christianity into the negro's hut, or pouring it abroad over the wide and dreary wilderness of paganism;—surely, surely, you will agree with me in thinking, that we have now sunk down into the age of frivolity and of little men. Think of this, my brethren,—that upon what a single individual has with-

held out of that which he ought to have given, the sublime march of a human soul from time to a happy eternity may have been arrested. Seize upon this conception in all its magnitude; and tell me, if, when put by the side of the sordid plea and the proud or angry refusal, all the gayeties of wealth, and all its painted insignificance, do not wither into nothing." pp. 22, 23.

LXX — *A Summary of the Evidences of Natural and Revealed Religion, designed for Young Persons. By A. Clarke. A.M. Preceptor of Salem Street Academy, Boston.* Boston; S. T. Armstrong; 1814.

It is a fact well known to those, who are conversant with modern publications, that Infidelity, in the course of the last half century, has marshalled all its forces, and exerted all its strength and ingenuity, to undermine the foundations of religion. For this purpose it has labored to pervert all the principles of sound learning and correct logic. With this object in view, it has distorted facts and invented fables;—has substituted bold conjecture for careful inquiry and sober criticism;—has, in a word, exhausted the stores of superficial learning, unsanctified reason, and profane wit. Metaphysical subtilty and licentious ridicule have each in their turn been employed in attempts to abolish the beautiful fabric of principles, hopes, and morals, which Christianity has erected in the world. The poison of infidelity has been distributed in every form, which promised to deceive and destroy. Books of natural philosophy, of history, of travels, of romance, &c. have been written with the sole design of propagating licentious opinions. The beauties of style and the enchantments of fiction have thus been employed to catch the attention, conceal the danger, and decoy the unwary to their destruction

It is true, that antidotes to this moral poison, in most of its forms, have been provided. The friends of religion and human happiness have not been idle. We have elaborate treatises on the evidences of Christianity, calculated for men of literature and leisure. We have smaller works, also, in abundance, for those, who have less time and ability for deep research and thorough investigation. Our colleges are furnished with volumes on the subject, suitable for young men, while engaged in a course of liberal education; and even in our best academies the evidences of Christianity are studied. Still, however, there is a class of the community who have been left almost without a weapon of defence against the insidious attacks of the great enemy. We mean that class of persons, who go directly from our minor academies and common schools to the active employments of life. Let it not be said, that such persons are free from danger. They meet with infidel objections in all their walks, and in a thousand forms. They find them at our taverns, in our streets, and even in some of our public journals. We believe too, that it would be discovered upon inquiry, that infidelity is more prevalent, at the present moment, with men of this description, than with

any other portion of the community

To prevent this evil, every boy in our schools should be furnished with a general view of the evidences of natural and revealed religion, before he enters upon the stage of active life. The Summary before us, we think well calculated to give such a view, and worthy of a distinguished place among our school-books. It is a pamphlet of twenty four duodecimo pages, written in a catechetical form. The author has for several years been an approved instructor of youth; and, as he informs us in the preface of this little book, he originally compiled it for the youth immediately under his care. We think the compilation well made; and are gratified with its publication for the use of others. It is certainly a very rich compend of the evidences of natural and revealed religion. The plan is judiciously formed and ably executed. There is indeed a small inadvertency, which should be corrected, in the answer to the question, "What evidence is there of a Divine Providence in the government of the world?" We think too, that the answer to the first question on the fourteenth page is rather more extensive, than the question demands, or truth will justify. With these two unimportant exceptions, we cheerfully recommend the work to the public; especially to parents, instructors of children, and school-committees.

MISCELLANEOUS.

SPEECH OF BARON ROSENBLAD.

The following speech is truly admirable. Happy would it be for mankind, if reason generally possessed the religious knowledge and the pious zeal, manifest in this document. The reader will perceive that it has been the fashion to present the hearer with "dry moral portraits" from the pulpit, in Sweden, as well as in other parts of Christendom.   ED. PAN.

The Speech of His Excellency Baron Rosenblad, one of the Lords of the Kingdom of Sweden, Minister of State, Knight and Commander Grand Cross of all His Majesty's Orders, &c. &c. &c.—when he took the Chair as President of the Evangelical Society, in the Committee, which met at Stockholm, on the 5th of October, 1813.

Gentlemen,

WITH sentiments of the sincerest gratitude, I now undertake the confidential office with which your choice has honored me. I am aware of my deficiencies; and they could not fail to occasion me great anxiety, even so as to make me very doubtful whether I ought to accept this place among you, when I consider that I succeed that venerable and revered character, whose great age has induced him to withdraw from a Presidency which he has held from the commencement of this Society, and which, under the blessing and favor of Almighty God, he has filled, with great advantage to the diffusion of Gospel Light, as well as with much satisfaction to all the Members of the Institution.

But, Gentlemen, I have considered your call as the finger of Providence, pointed by that unerring Hand, which, unseen, directs the conduct of mortals, and always with a view to lead them nearer to himself. The principal part of my life has been occupied in my extensive and laborious official engagements; and the unceasing care I have been obliged to exercise in order to accomplish their many important duties, has not seldom awakened in me the painful reflection, that but a small portion of my time had been alike laboriously devoted to advancing the cause of religion. But now, although in the autumn of life, a gracious Providence has been pleased to open to me a new field, and so favored me with an opportunity of correcting my past neglect: placing me, through its kind guidance, within this not only more exalted, but also more peaceful sphere of action; in order that I may do my part in furthering and supporting the important objects of this Society. To do so is my resolution; nay, the very desire of my heart: but I feel my own incapacity for such a solemn work, and rest all my hopes of success upon assistance from our Lord and Savior Jesus Christ—yes, upon him alone, who has assured us, that he will not quench the smallest spark of grace: and truly we may all encourage ourselves in the certainty of his Almighty aid, if we follow the light of his Holy Spirit, and have a single eye and a firm purpose to promote his glory, and to communicate to our fellow-men a knowledge of salvation by faith in His atonement.

We have outlived the awful period when the doctrine of the Atonement of Christ was shrouded in darkness. Mournful was the lot of those who confessed His name. For almost an entire century, did infidelity, with unblushing front, deride the revealed Will of God, and either openly or secretly undermine the sacred foundations of the Gospel doctrine. The deleterious poison, having worked its way among what are called the most enlightened nations of Europe, and established its influence in their higher circles, soon spread abroad among the mass of the people; and rolled on in fearful torrents of iniquity, carrying with it a sweeping destruction wherever it went—We have truly the most abundant cause for thankfulness to a gracious God, for having preserved our native land from such scenes of desolation. We dare not, however, deny, that even among us were found an increased indifference to the Word of God; and with many, a bold contempt of it. Not a few were ashamed to confess the name of Jesus; and have we not ourselves had to endure long discourses upon religion, in the course of which we hardly heard that blessed name mentioned, before which, however, every knee shall bow, "whether it be upon earth or under the earth?" But the promises of God are fulfilling; for "heaven and earth shall pass away, but my words shall not pass away." (Luke xxi, 33.) And "Upon this rock will I build my Church, and the gates of hell shall not prevail

against *her*." Gospel light is dawning again on those nations where the shadow of death sat almost enthroned, and barriers are raising against "the abomination of desolation."

In a certain country, most powerful because of its veneration for religion, and consequently for the laws; where, as a result, the welfare of the public and individuals rests on the surest foundation; a Society was established, and in times too, while the whirlwinds of desolation were yet laying waste the earth; the aim and glorious object of which Society embrace a distribution of God's Holy Word and Gospel Light through the whole habitable globe. That revered Society, which has also held forth its friendly and generous hand to our Swedish Evangelical Institution, has found in its zeal and liberality a success which so utterly exceeds the power of all human effort, as evidently to proclaim—that the finger of God is in it: His guardian care is therein distinctly unveiled.

Warned and roused from their indifference by what they have experienced of the horrible effects of infidelity, several other nations have also bestirred themselves, and followed the glorious path struck out by the beforementioned honored Society. And we, among others, cannot help being exceedingly thankful to God, that what is called the "New Philosophy," begins to be treated with contempt in our native land, and the minds of men have taken a favorable turn towards better things.

Under the protection of a Government affectionately attentive to the preaching of the pure

Gospel of Christ, measures are now actively adopted for improving both the character of preaching and the mode of education; and we have often the happiness to find, that the best gifts of eloquence are no longer wasted upon dry moral portraits, but suitably exerted to honor the Giver, by ascribing glory to the name of Jesus and his atonement.

Gentlemen, you are reaping the comfort of that delightful reflection, that from the first moment which gave existence to your Society, you have been co-workers with Him who alone can bless the works of our hands, and the meditations of our heart. You have sent forth among high and low, thousands and ten thousands of instructive Religious Tracts, but what is infinitely better—the Holy Scriptures, that fountain of all true light, which shews us the way to everlasting salvation. We know that these precious donations have brought forth much fruit, and been received with gratitude throughout the land: which cannot but be very pleasing tidings to you, and afford you a mighty encouragement to persevere in well-doing.

Eternal Savior of the world! strengthen and support the desire thyself hast graciously awakened in this Society: that all the Members of it may work as one man; and, with full purpose of heart, spread abroad that heavenly knowledge, which records thy atonement, thy suffering, and thy death. Grant success and thy richest blessing to all we shall do towards promoting this great end. We place all our reliance on Thee; and rest our hope of a gracious answer to our supplications, upon on that wonderful love which brought Thee into the world to save sinners.

I AM NOT ASHAMED OF THE GOSPEL—Rom. i, 16.

THE writer of this article, having lately heard from the pulpit, in a discourse from the above cited text, a sentiment substantially like the following—that *to be ashamed of one's religious opinions, seriously formed in the belief that they were according to the Scripture, whether RIGHT or WRONG, is to be ashamed of the Gospel*—has been led to inquire, whether this position could fairly be grafted on the text; or, indeed, whether it could be supported by Scripture at all? and whether such a shame as is there described might not more properly be considered as *the being ashamed of one's opinions*, than of the Gospel? And, however inconsistent it might make the holder of such opinions appear, whether it could ever approach to that class of feelings which would belong to one, who is ashamed of *the truth as it is in Jesus?*

It was said further, however, that this set of opinions being *really considered to be the Gospel by the person professing them*, to be ashamed of them, would, *to that person*, constitute the crime of *being ashamed of the Gospel.* But it is apprehended, that much fallacy is concealed in so vague a sentiment. *There is a way which seemeth right unto a man;*

eeming to be right could
a man so, in any measure,
would *the end thereof be the
of death?* Can a man's er-
is opinions of the Gos-
er constitute the Gospel
ist? If so, will not error
uth be blended in one un-
;uishable mass?

writer would further ob-
that he has noticed many
ofessors of religion, not
ting some of the clergy,
o not openly avow their
entiments. They would
to be ashamed of their
opinions, lest the declara-
them might injure their
arity But the writer has
en in the habit of consid-
such persons, as being, in
spect, *ashamed of the Gos-
A late venerable Doctor of
ty, who was known to be a
rsalist for several years be-
is death, was either afraid
amed to preach that sys-
a more obscure case might
luced of a lay Universalist,
was been heard to assert,
e was led into his system
Holy Spirit, who, never-
s. when called to assist in
rdination of an orthodox
er (for he was in regular
h-standing,) though the
late was examined respect-
s belief in the doctrine of
l punishment, made no ob-
n, but readily took an ac-
art in the ordination. And
a writer, whatever absurdi-
might have discovered in
cases, the last of which ap-
to be directly in point, had
considered them as con-
ing the apostolic declara-
the text, viz. that in these
nces of their favorite sen-
s, the parties were *asham-
he Gospel.*

If the writer is in an error in
this matter, he requests that
some person will have the goodness to set him right, for the
benefit of other inquirers, as well
as himself. The truth is precious.[*]   Q.

Oct. 1814.

QUESTIONS INTIMATELY CON-
NECTED WITH CHRISTIAN
PRACTICE, RESPECTFULLY
PROPOSED FOR DISCUSSION
AND SOLUTION.

1. CAN that be denominated a
field of wheat, which exhibits a
visible proportion of *tares* to the
wheat. as 11 to 1, or 21 to 3?

2. Is the *power* of executing
Christ's law of *discipline*, in a
church, necessary to constitute
it a church of Christ?

3. Is the *open avowal* of any
acknowledged *heresy*, in a church
member, (suppose it to be Uni-
versalism or Unitarianism) a
proper subject for church discipline?

4. Is the *habitual omission* of
any plain *practical duty*, (such as
family prayer, for instance,) a
proper subject for church discipline?

5. Ought a faithful minister
of the Gospel to proceed in the
stated administration of ordinances to his church, without *administering personal admonition*. In
case a large majority of it should
obviously appear to be men of the
world, and a considerable number unsound in sentiment and
negligent of family worship?

6. What is the nature of the
fellowship, and the extent of the

[*] Enclosed is a bill of six dollars, which
is presented as a small tribute in aid of
the translations, by one whose *heart's desire and prayer to God for the Heathen,
is, that they may be saved.*

covenant-obligations, which true saints ought to exercise towards mere professors in the same church?

7. Did Christ, during his stay on earth, always commune with the Jewish church? and was his conduct in that respect designed for our imitation?   X.

CHRONOLOGICAL TABLE

OF REMARKABLE EVENTS, WHICH TOOK PLACE IN THE YEAR 1813.

The publication of a chronological table in the Panoplist has been objected to, on the ground that political and other secular affairs are introduced. But we cannot believe, that the objection will be persevered in, especially by any person who will take the trouble to reflect upon it. Ignorance of the great political events, which are changing the face of the world, is not commanded as a Christian duty. Facts only are intended to be stated, and those without any coloring whatever, and in as brief a manner as possible. Unless we thought such a table to be of real utility, we certainly should not be at the trouble to compile it.   **ED.**

Jan. 2. The President of the U. S. signs a law for the increase of the navy; and another for cancelling the bonds, given by merchants under the non-importation law.

6. The Russians enter Konigsberg, and take 8000 prisoners.

9. The Prince Regent of G. B. issues his manifesto, stating the causes of war against U. S.

10 The French Conservative Senate boast, that they have 300,000 regular forces in the interior of France and Italy. They advise to send 100,000 of the newly raised conscripts to the armies, and to raise 200,000 more. Not long after this, they call out 430,000 additional conscripts.

18. Platoff and his Cossacs invest Dantzic.

22. The Spanish Cortes abolish the Inquisition, 94 votes to 43. The decree to take effect from Feb. 3.

Gen Winchester is attacked by the British and Indians at the river Raisin. His detachment is entirely cut off. American loss in killed and missing 396; prisoners 536.

25. Bonaparte signs an agreement with the Pope.

26. A loan bill passed the H R. 75 to 38, for $16,000,000.

30. The thermometer at Boston 4 below 0; at Salem 10; at Portsmouth 11; at Portland 16.

Feb. 1. Louis XVIII issues a proclamation to the French people.

The British government publishes an order in council, permitting the sale of vessels by belligerents to neutrals.

4. Chesapeake bay blockaded by the British.

7 A party of Americans cross the St. Lawrence from Ogdensburg, and take about 50 prisoners.

8 The Russians enter Warsaw.

10 Votes counted and declared for President and Vice President of the U. S. Mr Madison had 128 votes, and Mr. Clinton 89, for President; Mr, Gerry had 131 and Mr Ingersol 86, for V. P.

16. Bonaparte makes a speech to his Senate, in which he professes a desire of peace, but insists upon the same arrogant terms as before

18. The British House of Commons, after having the diplomatic intercourse between the two nations for the last three years laid before them, unanimously resolve to support the ministry in the American war.

21. Ogdensburgh taken by the British. American loss, 20 killed.

25 The American sloop of war Hornet, 16 guns, Capt Lawrence, took the British brig Peacock, 19 guns, after a battle of 15 minutes. The British captain, Peak, was killed British loss 8 killed, 27 wounded; American loss, 1 killed, 2 wounded. The Peacock sunk before all her crew could be taken out.

March 3. Expiration of the 12th Congress.

4. The Russians enter Berlin.

5 The Pope's nuncio in Spain issues an ecclesiastical order forbidding the publication of the decree, which abolished the Inquisition.

6. Swedish manifesto published, assigning the reasons for engaging in the war against France A treaty of peace between Russia and Prussia about the same time.

10. The Russians enter Hamburgh.

16. Wittgenstein, the Russian general, issues a spirited proclamation, calling upon the Germans to join him in the great work of national deliverance

20. The British land at Cuxhaven, and the people of Hanover declare in favor of their old government.

27. The Prussian manifesto against France published.

30. The American ports, New York, Charleston, (S. C.) &c. declared in a state of blockade.

During this month Leipsic was the head-quarters of Bonaparte's army, and Hanau, on the Rhine, the head quarters of his army of observation.

April 1. Bonaparte introduces his wife into the council of state, and makes her provisionally Empress Regent.

2. The Russian general Tettenborn cuts off the whole French detachment under Morand at Luneburg.

4. A Russian division enters Leipsic.

5. Wittgenstein defeats Beauharnois near Magdeburg. French loss 3,000.

13. Suchet defeated near Valencia by Sir John Murray. French loss, 2,500. Loss of the allies, 600.

15. Bonaparte leaves Paris for his armies;—arrives at Mayence in two days.

27. The American army under Gen. Dearborn takes Little York, the seat of the British government in Upper Canada. Gen. Pike killed, and 100 others, by the explosion of a mine.

30. The Russian, Prussian, and French armies were forming near each other. French head quarters at Naumberg The Elbe nearly the line of demarcation

May 1—5. Gen. Harrison was besieged six days in Fort Meigs, by the British and Indians. Loss during the seige 81 killed, and 186 wounded. At the same time Gen. Clay's detachment was taken by the British almost entire. American loss 50 killed and 600 prisoners. British loss not known.

1—2. The battle of Lutzen, between Bonaparte and the Allies Loss supposed to be nearly equal, about 15,000 on each side The allies held the field of battle, but were obliged immediately after to retreat and cross the Elbe.

6—8. The British sent 15 barges with troops from their squadron in the Chesapeake, and burnt Havre de Grace, Georgetown, and Fredericktown, in Maryland

8. Messrs. Bayard and Gallatin sailed for St. Petersburgh, to negotiate a peace with G. B under the mediation of Russia.

10. The French army enters Dresden, which the month before had been the head quarters of the Russian army.

19—21 The battles of Konigswartha, Bautzen, and Wurtzchen; usually called the battle of Bautzen; between Bonaparte at the head of his great army, and the Emperor of Russia and King of Prussia with their united forces. The loss nearly equal; about 20,000 on each side The allies obliged to retreat.

24 Congress meets

25. The President of the U. S. sends his message to Congress.

27. The American army under Gen. Dearborn, having some time before left Little York, landed in U. C near Newark with little resistance. The British blew up their magazines at Fort George, and abandoned it.

28. The British took 100 American dragoons.

An armistice agreed upon between Bonaparte and the allies, not to expire till July 26, unless with six days notice

29. The British landed at Sacket's harbor, and caused the Americans to burn all the military and naval stores.

31. The French left Madrid for the 4th and last time.

June 1. The U S. frigate Chesapeake taken by the British frigate Shannon, Capt. Broke, after a short action. Capt. Lawrence of the Chesapeake mortally wounded early in the battle. American loss 47 killed, 98 wounded; British loss 27 killed, 58 wounded.

2. The U. S. frigates United States and Macedonian chased into New London by a British squadron.

The Growler and Eagle, American sloops, taken by the British on Lake Champlain.

4. The armistice between the French and the allies in Germany completely adjusted. The French occupy all Saxony, the allies all Prussia.

6. An American detachment surprised in U. C. and Generals Chandler and Winder and about 150 men taken prisoners.

12. The French evacuated Burgos, and blew up the citadel.

14—15. Lord Wellington in rapid pursuit of the retreating French.

16. A violent tornado at Philadelphia and the vicinity.

21. The allied army in Spain under Lord Wellington obtains a decisive victory over King Joseph and Gen. Jourdan. All the French artillery, 151 pieces, military chest, 415 waggons, and many prisoners were taken. Loss of the allies, 5,000; of the French 20,000.

22. The British attack Craney Island, in the Chesapeake, and are repulsed with considerable loss.

25. The British take Hampton, (Vir.).

A detachment of 570 men under Col. Boerstler taken by surprise and destroyed about 15 miles from Fort George, by a small detachment of British and Indians.

26. Joseph Bonaparte enters France with the remnant of his army.

July 6. Death of Granville Sharp, an illustrious benefactor of mankind.

8. The land-tax bill passed H. R. 97 to 70.

19. H. R. refused to consider a resolution approving the conduct of the President of the U. S. respecting the diplomatic intercourse with the French government.

21. The Royal assent was given to an act of Parliament renewing the East India Company's charter, in which there was a provision for permitting Christian missionaries to go to India and reside there.

23. Marshal Soult, having been sent to command the French armies on the Spanish frontier, issues a vaunting proclamation.

24. A loan bill passed H. R. for $7,500,000.

25. The British attempt to take St. Sebastian's by storm, and are repulsed with the loss of nearly 1,000.

28—30. A series of severe battles between Marshal Soult and Lord Wellington, the result of which was, that the French army was again driven back into France.

30. Saragossa surrendered to the Spaniards.

Aug. 2. The British attack an American fort at Lower Sandusky, and are repulsed with great loss.

9. Two American schooners, the Scourge and Hamilton, sunk in a gale of wind on Lake Ontario; 70 persons drowned.

10. Two other schooners, the Julia and Growler, taken on Lake Ontario by the British.

The allies in Germany give notice that the armistice will cease, and hostilities commence on the 16th.

11. Austria declared war against France, and joined the allies with all her forces.

14. The U. S. brig Argus taken by the British brig Pelican, after a battle of 45 minutes. Capt. Allen of the Argus mortally wounded. The Argus threw 456 pounds of metal at a broadside;—the Pelican 536. The Pelican had 116 men, the Argus 127.

17. Hostilities commenced between the French and Allies, along the whole line from the vicinity of Hamburgh to Dresden.

20. The manifesto of France against Austria published.

21. Bonaparte in person attacks the allied centre under Blucher, on the Bobr, and compels it to retire. Bonaparte took with him 110,000 men.

22. He repeats the attack with the same result. Blucher retires behind the Katzbach.

A gale at Charleston, S. C. which destroyed much property.

23. Bonaparte returns to Dresden, leaving M'Donald's corps to withstand Blucher.

24. A violent and destructive hurricane at Turk's Island.

25. Blucher utterly defeats M'Donald's corps, taking 15,000 prisoners and 100 cannon.

26. The allied Austrians and Russians, under Swartzenberg, advanced upon Dresden 140,000 strong.

27. A battle under the walls of Dresden. The allies repulsed with loss. Moreau mortally wounded. This battle was fought in a tremendous storm of wind and rain. Bonaparte commanded the French in person.

30. A French corps of 15,000 under Vandamme, which had pursued the allies into the Bohemian passes, was there overwhelmed and compelled to surrender, with 60 pieces of cannon.

The Creek and Chootaw Indians attacked the fort on the Tensaw, took it by storm, and put to death in the fort and vicinity 247 Americans.

31. St. Sebastian's taken from the French by storm. British loss about 2,400.

At the same time, the French under Soult attacked the Spanish lines on the Bidassoa, and were several times repulsed.

In this month the British Parliament passed a new bill for the relief of insolvent debtors, with benevolent provisions.

Sept. 1. A strict blockade of the ports south of the Chesapeake declared by Sir J. B. Warren.

3. The U. S. brig Enterprise, Lieut. Burrows, mounting 16 guns, took the British brig Boxer, Capt. Blythe, mounting 18 guns, after a battle of 45 minutes. Both commanders killed. American loss 9. British loss 45.

6. The battle of Dennewitz, in which the French, 70,000 strong under Ney, were defeated by Bernadotte. The French loss, in this wing of the grand army, on this and a few preceding days, was about 20,000 and 50 pieces of cannon.

10. The American squadron on Lake Erie, under Com. Perry, captured a superior British squadron, under Com. Barclay, consisting of 2 ships, 2 brigs, 1 sloop, and 1 schooner.

13. The allied forces advance from Bohemia into Saxony.

19 *Te Deum* sung by public authority in Paris, on account of the victory on the 27th ult. at Dresden.

23. The Americans under Gen. Harrison advance into U. Canada.

27. Gen. Harrison enters Malden.

28 A partial engagement between the hostile squadrons on Lake Ontario. No vessels lost on either side.

Detroit evacuated by the British and entered by the Americans.

30. Czernicheff with his Russian cavalry entered Cassel, the capital of Westphalia, far in the rear of the French army.

A battle between the Royalists and Revolutionists of Venezuela;—the former defeated.

Oct. 3. The Prussians under Blucher defeat the French under Bertrand.

4. Bernadotte crosses the Elbe at Dessau, and establishes a bridge at Achen.

5. Bonaparte leaves Dresden with his main army, and concentres his forces toward Leipsic.

Com. Chauncey takes 5 small vessels, and destroys 2, on Lake Ontario; British prisoners 308.

Gen. Harrison defeats the British under Gen. Proctor, near Moravian town U. C. American loss very small, nearly all the British force taken prisoners.

7. A part of Lord Wellington's army enters France, after a severe action on the Bidassoa

11. Bernadotte's and Blucher's forces post themselves behind the Saale, in the rear of Bonaparte's army. Bonaparte then makes a feint towards Berlin, crosses the Elbe at Dessau, and destroys Bernadotte's bridge at Achen. Bernadotte re-establishes his bridges at Dessau and Achen, and recrosses the Elbe with part of his army.

13 Bonaparte concentres his armies near Leipsic, and the allies press upon him on the north, the east, and the south.

The Russians enter Bremen.

16 The first great battle of Leipsic, between Bonaparte's concentred forces, and the armies of Russia, Prussia, Austria, and Sweden with the allied sovereigns at their head. On the south-east the battle was nearly equal. Murat led a tremendous charge of cavalry, which broke the allied ranks for a while; but at night the allied line was in the same place as in the morning. On the east and north east Bernadotte and Blucher gained considerable advantages; but the battle was far from being decisive. About half a million of men were engaged, drawn from almost every country in Europe, and under the control of a greater number of experienced military commanders than ever before directed in a single battle.

17. The Sabbath—The French and allied forces in a state of the most active and anxious preparation for resuming the battle the next day.

18. The second battle of Leipsic;—one of the greatest which was ever fought, and one which decided the campaign against Bonaparte, and was a signal token of his approaching downfal. The Saxons and Westphalians deserted his standard by regiments in the midst of battle, and turned their arms against him. His loss was full 60,000 on this single day. Some judgment of this battle may be formed by the declaration of Bonaparte that he discharged 220,000 cannon balls at the enemy in two days, and that he had not enough left for two hours' use. In the succeeding night he began his retreat across the Elster by a single bridge.

19. Bernadotte's troops entered Leipsic by storm, two hours after Bonaparte had left it;—20,000 French prisoners taken this day. The bridge over the Elster blown up in the midst of the French retreat. Prince Poniatowski drowned in the Elster Many French generals taken; some escape on foot, after swimming the Elster

21. The remnant of Bonaparte's army reached Erfurt.

26. An affair of outposts between the Americans under Gen. Hampton, and the British forces just within the boundaries of Lower Canada. The American detachment returned.

30. Bonaparte is met at Hanau by the Bavarians under Wrede. He cuts his way through them with the loss of many thousands.

31. Pamplona surrendered to the Spaniards.

Nov. 4. The British ministry send a proposal to America to negotiate for peace, at Gottenburgh or London.

5. The Emperor of Russia has his head-quarters at Frankfort on the Maine.

6. Gen. Wilkinson, at the head of his invading army, issues a proclamation to the inhabitants of L. C.

7. About 300 Creek Indians slain in battle by the Americans under Gen. Jackson.

9. Bonaparte arrives at Paris.

The allied sovereigns at Frankfort, declare to a French functionary, that they are willing to make peace with Bonaparte, on the basis that France shall be confined within her ancient limits; Holland, Germany, Switzerland, Italy, and Spain, being taken out of French control.

10. Marshal Wellington attacked Marshal Soult, and wrested from him the first line of defences before Bayonne.

11. Dresden surrendered to the allies. The garrison, with St. Cyr at their head, amounted to 15,000.

A battle between a part of Gen. Wilkinson's army and a British detachment, at Cornwall in Canada. The Americans retire, and give up the expedition to Montreal.

13. A violent and destructive gale at Halifax.

14. Holland rose and asserted its liberties.

Bonaparte made a speech to his Senate, in which he said, "A year ago all Europe was with us; now all Europe is against us."

18. More Creek Indians killed, above 60 in number.

20. A formal proclamation in Holland, in the name of the Prince of Orange.

29. The Antossee town, belonging to the Creek Indians, and containing 400 houses, burnt, and 200 Indians killed.

Dec. 1. The allied sovereigns publish to the world, that they are willing to make peace with Bonaparte, on terms honorable to France, and allowing her to retain larger dominions than under her kings.

Dantzic is surrendered to the allies.

The Prince of Orange lands at Schevelling in Holland after an exile of 19 years.

6. Congress meets.

7. The President of the U. S. sends his message to Congress.

9. The President sends a message to Congress, recommending an embargo.

10. Bonaparte makes a speech to his Senate, in which he says he has acceded to the terms proposed by the allies.

11. Fort George evacuated by the American army. Newark in U. C. burnt by order of Gen. M'Clure, and his forces withdrawn to the American side of the river.

Bonaparte made a hasty treaty with Ferdinand VII, and released him from captivity.

11—14. Severe but indecisive battles between Soult and Wellington near Bayonne.

17. An embargo law passed, 85 to 57 in H. R. 20 to 14 in Senate.

19. Fort Niagara, on the American side, taken by surprise by the British

21. The allied armies enter the Swiss territories, and issue their proclamations.

22. A great fire in Portsmouth, (N. H.) the work of some incendiary.

23. The French Conservative Senate publish a report in which peace is urged.

Bonaparte sends Commissioners Extraordinary, with despotic powers, into all the departments of France.

30. The British cross at Black Rock, and burn Buffaloe and other villages on the Niagara frontier, in retaliation for the burning of Newark.

Despatches by the Bramble reached government, bringing overtures for peace.

Bonaparte issues a proclamation calling vehemently upon France to repel invasion, and declaring that he no longer contemplates retaining the conquests which he had made.

RELIGIOUS INTELLIGENCE.

REPORT OF THE DIRECTORS TO THE TWEN-
TIETH GENERAL MEETING OF THE MIS-
SIONARY SOCIETY MAY, 14, 1814.

(Continued from p. 526.)

AFRICA.

DURING the past year, the communications from Africa have been peculiarly interesting.' Our dear brother, Mr. Campbell, agreeably to the proposed object of his mission, has visited the various missionary stations in distant parts of South Africa; has suggested many excellent regulations for their improvement; and has fixed upon several new places, in which missionary settlements may probably be established. A minute account of his journies would fill a volume; and such a volume we trust he will supply after his return to England, which is shortly expected:* a very slight sketch is all that can be admitted into this report.

After a careful examination of official papers relating to the missionaries, with which he was indulged, and obtaining passports from his Excellency the Governor, Sir John Cradock, to the Landrosts of the districts through which he was to pass, he left Cape Town on the 21st of February, 1813, accompanied by Mr. Hammes (a valuable friend and agent of our Society,) his son, Mr. Bartlett, a catechist, and several Christian Hottentots and others belonging to Bethelsdorp. In a fortnight he reached the Drosdy of George, the inhabitants of which are desirous of having a missionary settled among them. Mr. Campbell promised that Mr. Pacalt should be sent to them for a time, to be succeeded by Mr. Wimmer.

Mr. Campbell reached Bethelsdorp on the 20th of March, and was received by Mr. Read and all the missionary brethren with the most cordial affection, and by the Hottentots with the liveliest expressions of joy.

He witnessed a greater degree of civilization than he was led to expect from the reports in circulation, on his arrival in South Africa. He found at Bethelsdorp, natives exercising the businesses of smiths, carpenters, sawyers, basket-makers, turn-

* *Mr. Campbell arrived in London, May the 7th, and gave the Society a full account of his mission on the 12th. It was thought proper, however, to give this concise statement of his proceedings, as well as of the several settlements.*

ers, &c. He saw cultivated fields, extending two miles in length; on both sides of a river; their cattle had increased from two hundred and eighteen to two thousand two hundred and six; from three hundred to four hundred calves were produced in a year, not more than fifty of which were in that space of time allowed to be slaughtered. The blessed effects of religion were displayed in benevolent institutions formed among them: they had a fund for the support of the poor and sick, which amounted to two hundred and fifty rix dllars; they proposed to build a house for the reception of part of their poor. They had also a common fund for the purpose o improving the settlement, amounting to one hundred and thirty dollars and about thirty head of cattle; and they contributed, dur ng the last twelve months, seventy rix dollars in aid of this Society.

Such are the precious fruits of the seed sown among them by Dr Van der Kemp, Messrs. Read, Ulbricht, Wimmer, and other faithful missionaries'—Such are the powerful effects of divine truth among the most degraded of our species, in their civilization, as well as in the more important concerns of religion. Thus, we see a Christian church; cultivated fields and gardens; useful manufactories; an hospital; and an Auxiliary Missionary Society among *Hottentots!* Who now will doubt whether the Gospel ought to be preached to uncivilized nations'

It is peculiarly pleasing to find that the Lord has raised up several native preachers from among the converted Hottentots, who preach to their countrymen with great acceptance and usefulness.' One of these preached at Plettenberg's Bay with great success.

From Bethelsdorp Mr. Campbell proceeded through a wild country almost uninhabited, on the borders of Caffreland, in order to fix upon two spots eligible for missionary settlements, in ZUURVELD, near the Great Fish River, the Government having kindly promised to give sufficient portions of land for that purpose. Two suitable places were accordingly fixed upon, where the land being good, a part of the people now at Bethelsdorp might settle, and to which some of the cattle might occasionally be sent for the sake of better pasture. Here it was agreed that Mr. Ulbricht, aided by Mr. Bartlett, should assist in forming a settlement.

Mr. Campbell next travelled in a north-westerly direction to Graaf Reinet, where Mr. Kicherer resides, and had the pleasure of witnessing the happy effects of his labors; here also he met with John, Mary, and Martha, the Hottentots who visited England in the year 1803.

Here Mr. C. continued about a week, and was favored with an interview with a Mr. Burchel, a botanical traveller in South Africa, who had just returned from an excursion very far north, and who was the first European who had penetrated to that part of Africa from Graaf Reinet. After receiving from him the most valuable directions and cautions, and accompanied by the native who had been his guide, he commenced his journey to the Orange River, about the 10th of May; Mr Kicherer, and other friends accompanying him a week's journey, as far as the limits of the colony, preaching, wherever they had opportunity, to the boors and the heathen, some of whom, alas! had never heard of a God, nor had they a word in their language whereby to denote him. He crossed the wild Boschemen's country until he reached the Orange River, and after travelling about one hundred miles along its banks to the eastward, he found a ford which he safely crossed; he describes the river as wider than the Thames at Loudon Bridge.

On the next day he reached Klaar Water, the Missionary settlement which has long been under the care of the Brethren Anderson, Kramer, and Janz. Here he remained but a few days, and left it, accompanied by Messrs. Anderson, Kok, and Hendrick, in order to explore a large and populous city which had been described to him.

After travelling ten days in the direction N N E they arrived at the city of LATAKKOO, which contains about 1500 houses, neatly built, and about 8000 inhabitants. After waiting ten days for the King Mateebee, who was absent on a jackal-hunt, Mr. Campbell was introduced to him at sunset, and at the very time of the monthly missionary prayer-meeting, when our friend requested leave to send missionaries to his people, to acquaint them with the religion of Jesus Christ. After stating several objections to that measure, which Mr. C was enabled to answer to his complete satisfaction, the king gave him this laconic answer—'Send them, and I will be a father to them.' This conference was repeated publicly, at the request of the king, on the next day, in the presence of his subjects, and the same liberty to send missionaries openly granted.

Here Mr Campbell obtained the important information, that there were twenty tribes of people north of Latakkoo, who all speak the same language, and who

are reported to be still more civilized. The hope of being able, at a future day, to visit these people by able and faithful missionaries, and to diffuse among them the knowledge of our Savior, so agitated with joy the heart of our zealous brother, that for several successive nights he could scarcely sleep. May the cheering prospect ere long be realized! Our Brother Read had similar impressions, regarding the immense field that is now opened to British Christians.

From Latakkoo Mr. Campbell travelled *eastward*, and in five days reached a large Coranna town called *Mulapeetze*, where he understood that no white man had been seen before; to this place also he obtained leave from the chief and majority of the inhabitants to send Missionaries.

Travelling southward from thence, he went in search of the *Mulaluren River*, and discovered a kraal, situated in a most beautiful valley, where *Mukoon*, the chief of all the Boschemen in that part of Africa, resided, he appeared to be a man of talents, and though he had never before seen a European, he consented to Mr Campbell's proposal of sending missions there also.

From thence, Mr. C. travelled along the *Mulaluren* River to its junction with the Great Orange River, which he discovered was composed of four smaller rivers, the *Mulaluren*, the *Yellow* River, and two others which he named, in compliment to his respected friends, the Governor and Secretary at the Cape, the *Cradock* and the *Alexander*. This geographical discovery has since afforded great pleasure to gentlemen of science at the Cape.

Mr Campbell and his friends then returned to Klaar Water, after a circular tour of six weeks; and Mr C continued about a fortnight there to arrange the affairs of that settlement.

Our enterprising brother then proceeded on a route entirely new, directly across the continent of Africa, westward, pursuing nearly the course of the Great Orange River, and on the 13th of September, reached Little Namaqualand, on the western coast, where he had the pleasure of meeting the Missionary Brethren Albrecht, Schmelen, and Ebner, laboring in their usual manner.

From hence Mr Campbell despatched Mr Schmelen towards the mouth of the Great River, distant about ten days journey, to ascertain, if possible, whether supplies could be obtained by sea from the Cape. Should this be found practicable, it would be found of inestimable advantage to all the settlers on the banks of that ver, and save the great labor and xpense of long journies by land to a Cape Town.

[...]lution was desired after explor[...] country, especially the coast of [...]aqualand, to penetrate, if pos[...] the Damara country, to obtain [...] concerning its inhabitants, and [...] beyond them, known to Euro[...] by name. His journey, it is says Mr Campbell, "will open tensive fields of usefulness as will [...] and liberality of the benevo[...]be;" but he adds a sentiment, in re are certain that the whole So[...]ll heartily concur—"that Britai[...] ns only require the fields to be [...] open before them"—their an[...] tributions will follow of course.

circumstance, among the many [...] and deliverances which Mr. [...]ell experienced, must not be omit[...] the midst of that desolate wilder[...]rough which he passed, an attack night made on his company by a [...] wild Boschemen, who killed one Hottentots, and carried off all their hich were more than one hundred. [...] the brethren in a situation, the [...] horror of which we can scarcely [...], for had not their oxen been re[...], their total destruction seemed [...]. In their trouble they called [...]od, put themselves into the best [...] defence they could, and sent a Hottentots in pursuit of the plun[...] most happily they overtook them Boschemen fled, and the cattle rought back before morning. Such [...]able deliverance demands the [...] gratitude of the whole society.

[...] a journey of nine months, replete [...]ngers, discoveries, and mercies, [...] brother returned to the Cape in [...]health than when he set out; for [...] then the state of his health, that [...]ely expected to return.

[...]loses that interesting letter from his part of the report is extracted, [...] most earnest request that six or missionaries may immediately be [...] Africa to supply the stations pro[...] The Directors have not yet been [...] accomplish this, but have been preparatory measures for the pur[...]nd are in hope of soon obtaining missionaries both in Britain and [...] and.

Directors need not enlarge on this [...]ing intelligence: every member of [...]ety feels its importance, and will [...] rejoice in the prospect of a wide [...] of the blessings of the Gospel, [...]concomitant blessings of civilized [...] social happiness.

NAMAQUA COUNTRY.

IT will be recollected, that about the close of the year 1810, Mr. and Mrs. Albrecht, (with many of their people) being under the most painful apprehensions from the threatened invasion of Africaner, a notorious plunderer, left the settlement at Warm Bath, in the Great Namaqua Country, removing what they could of their property, and hiding the rest in the earth;* after several painful removals Mr. and Mrs. Albrecht reached Cape Town, in order to procure the assistance of the Governor. It will also be recollected, that having settled their affairs there, they again journied northward, hoping, if practicable, to resume their labors at the Warm Bath. After sustaining extreme hardships and difficulties for three months, in the wilderness, they reached Silver Fountain, the residence of the friendly Captain Kok. There, it will be remembered, that our most excellent female missionary Mrs. Albrecht, terminated her pilgrimage, and departed to her eternal rest, April 13, 1812.

Sometime after this event, Mr. Albrecht, accompanied by Mr. Schmelen, paid a visit to the Namaquas, south of the Orange River, and preached the Gospel in various places, in some of which deep impressions appeared to have been made. Some of their people wished them to return to Warm Bath, but they were convinced, that on account of the sterility of the country, they would soon be under the necessity of dispersing; they were also under apprehensions of a renewed attack from Africaner; they determined, there fore, on residing for the present at least at Kamiesberg, as being nearer the colony, and because the Orange River would prove a kind of barrier to them from their enemies. Here also they would have nearly the same people to instruct as had formerly lived at the Bath. The ground however is barren and unfit for agriculture; but there are several springs of water The number of persons residing at this station, were, according to the last

* *In August 1812, some of the brethren visited this spot, attended by twelve armed men: they found the place almost without inhabitants: they examined the place where Messrs. Albrecht and Sade n jadin had buried part of their goods, a few of which they found, but the greater part had been carried off. The houses and church were burnt down, a few walls only were standing. Thus a place in which the Lord had greatly blessed his word was become a heap of ruins, and an habitation of lions. The country around was almost deserted.*

accounts, about five hundred, besides the bastard Hottentots at the neighboring krall of Bysondermeid, who amounted to one hundred and forty-five, including men, women, and children. Others had left the country in consequence of the depredations of Africaner. The loss sustained at the Warm Bath, and the expense occasioned by the long journies of the missionaries, is very considerable; in which is included a great number of sheep and goats; besides eighteen oxen, which could not proceed on their journey, and others stolen and slaughtered by the Boschemen

The present station of the brethren Albrecht, Schmelen, Helm, and Ebner, is about three days journey from their former residence at the Warm Bath. When Mr. Campbell was at this place, he wrote a conciliatory letter to Africaner, and sent him some presents, thus returning good for evil, and not without hope that the brethren would be permitted to return to their former residence, to which the people were much attached.

KLAAR WATER, NEAR THE ORANGE RIVER.

The Directors regretted in their last Report, that they had heard nothing of Mr. Anderson, at the Orange River, for a long time: during the past year, however, they have received several letters from him.

Mr. Anderson, who had been a very long season at the Cape, set off, (with his wife and youngest child) on the 19th of June 1811. At Tulbagh, (formerly called Roodesand) they were joined by Mr. Kramer, his wife, and child They were alarmed, on the road with repeated reports of enemies, who were lying in wait to attack them; they were frequently much perplexed, not knowing what to do; they persisted, however, on their journey without any molestation, and, by the good providence of God, arrived safely at Klaar Water, on the 20th of September, late in the evening. On the next morning, a public meeting was held to offer up thanks to God for their preservation on their journey, and for his numerous favors bestowed upon Mr. Janz, who had continued at this station during the absence of Mr. Anderson.

Mr. Anderson complains much of the general lukewarmness of the people; there had been 1 tel; but few awakenings among them; but he expresses an earnest desire for a gracious revival. About three hundred persons generally attended the preaching of the word on the Lord's days, and the behavior of the people was, in general, decent and moral. In agriculture but slow progress was made, and the corn raised was insufficient for the subsistence of the people. Their cattle, however, are multiplied. One individual

in the settlement had 400 head of cattle, 1700 sheep, and 300 goats; others had 200 head of cattle, and several from 50 to 100, so that in the last year, the colony of the Cape had been supplied from Klaar Water with about 500 head of cattle; in return for which they brought back waggons, horses, and other articles. This progress in civilization is very cheering to the benevolent mind. The number of people in this settlement was, in August 1812, about seven hundred or eight hundred, including men, women, and children. Four persons had been baptised and received into communion in the course of the year.

For several years after the missionaries took up their residence among this people, they lived a wandering life, consequently were obliged to follow them from place to place, which was extremely inconvenient to the missionaries, and a great obstacle to the civilization and improvement of the people. However, at length, after many intreaties, the people resolved to take up a settled residence at Klaar Water, and two neighboring outposts. Since that time they have cultivated and sown a considerable portion of ground, planted several gardens, some of them have built houses of stones, and now begin to feel themselves at home.

SILVER FOUNTAIN.

Mr. and Mrs. Sass, after a most difficult and hazardous journey through the wilderness, in which they lost several of their oxen, and were without bread for nearly a month, reached, at length, the residence of Captain Kok. Their gratitude to God, and to him, was greater than they could express; they were filled with astonishment at the divine goodness, so that they wept tears of joy and thankfulness through the silent hours of the night. Here the people were so desirous of hearing the word, that they intreated him to preach to them twice every day, and on the Lord's day thrice. They built him a little hut to dwell in, urging him to reside among them as their teacher, till they should be able to remove to the neighborhood of Mr. Anderson, near the Orange River, where he might have two hundred hearers, and obtain a garden and ground for vegetables and corn. Mr. Sass promised to comply with their request, so agreeable to the Society at home. This plan was also approved by Mr. Albrecht, who arrived soon after, having been helped forward in his journey by the oxen sent to meet him by Captain Kok.

Many persons here received the word with joy, and several individuals appeared to be really converted to the Lord One person, of some influence, who had been an enemy, now fell under the power of the word, and rejoiced that her house and garden could afford any refreshment to the missionaries who instructed them. A farmer and his family, who came from a distance, begged leave to stay at Silver Fountain for the purpose of instruction. Several others removed to this place for the privilege of hearing the Gospel. The number of the people, in the beginning of the last year, (including old and young) was about 118.

Here we must mention, with the deepest concern, that Mrs Sass, (formerly Miss Gordon, a sister of Mr. Gordon, one of the Missionaries in India) was removed by death, after a very short illness, from her useful employment, as the helper of our brother Sass in his evangelical labours. This took place at the very time when Mr. Campbell called at Silver Fountain, on his long journey. "I think," says he, "she was as well suited to the missionary work, as any female in the world. We spent two pleasant days together, when she was in good health, but on the third she entered the realms of endless day, with the serenity of a martyr."

Messrs. Read and Wimmer were for a time at the Hooge Krall, the Drosdy of George, near Bota's Place, where they preached both to free persons and slaves, who heard them with great interest, and it is believed with no small profit, and most earnestly entreated that a missionary should come and reside among them. The brethren much approved of this measure, and Mr. Wimmer felt himself strongly inclined to reside among them. When the people of this krall were apprised of the approach of Mr. Campbell and his friends, they sent messengers to meet him, and about fifty of them came several miles to welcome him, expressing the greatest anxiety to know whether or not they might expect a missionary, and when one was promised by Mr. Campbell, they displayed the highest degree of satisfaction. "Could I," says Mr. Campbell, "have brought the great missionary assemblies in the month of May to this krall, to witness the scene that passed, I think they would have thrown in their gold by handfuls to aid the missionary funds." At present, Mr Pacalt, (whose ultimate destination is the island of Madagascar) is laboring with success among these Hottentots, till an opportunity shall occur for his reaching that island, when it is expected Mr Wimmer will succeed him at Hooge Krall.

The journal and letters of Mr Messer, at Brackeldaie, contain many pleasing instances of the power of divine grace on the hearts of the Hottentots, several of whom were slaves. Mr. Messer seems

to possess a true missionary spirit, and delights greatly in seizing every opportunity of doing good. He sometimes preached at five o'clock in the morning to the slaves, who went away from the meeting singing to their work. The arrival of Mr Campbell and Mr. Thom afforded great pleasure to Mr. Messer, who was exceedingly refreshed in spirit by their visit and prayers. Mr. Messer's engagement with Mr. Ross, among whose slaves, and others from the neighborhood, he had been laboring for twelve months, having terminated, it was judged necessary for him to remove to Bethelsdorp, to supply the place of some Missionaries who were on the eve of removing to other stations, where we trust his labors will be attended with the blessing of God.

CAPE.

FROM Mr Thom, at the Cape, many valuable communications have been received during the past year. He continues to preach three or four times a week to a considerable number of persons, chiefly the soldiers of the 93d regiment, (Sutherland Highlanders,) of whom he has frequently from two hundred to six hundred hearers. He speaks very highly of their moral conduct, their serious piety and their exemplary liberality. Among other charitable objects, they have contributed seven hundred rix dollars, (above one hundred pounds sterling) to the missionary cause. Seventy of these pious soldiers have been formed into a Christian church. The transient labors of the Brethren Read, Pritchett, Hands, Brain, and Thompson, while they were at the Cape, appear to have contributed to those pleasing results which Mr Thom has witnessed. But Mr. Thom's labors are not confined to the ministry of the Gospel; he has been instrumental in the formation of religious institutions, and in the distribution of the Scriptures, other books, and religious tracts; he has also under his care some young men, intended for the work of the ministry.

In the month of September last he administered the Lord's Supper to more than one hundred communicants, when about four hundred persons were spectators.

In the month of January, 1812, Captain Kok, with more than twenty Hottentots, paid a visit to the Cape, when a meeting was held for prayer and conference with them. Many questions were proposed by Mr. Thom, which were answered in a manner which proved that the instructions which had been given them by the Brethren Anderson, Janz, and Kramer at Klaar Water, had not been in vain. Those who have read the account of the

conference (published in the Evangelical
Magazine for July, 1813,) will rejoice to
find that the minds of Hottentots, enlightened by the Spirit of God, are well
able to see all the distinguishing doctrines
of the Gospel, and that their Christian
experience is exactly of the same kind
with that of their polished brethren in
Europe. It affords also strong encouragement to missionaries to proceed in
their labors of love among the heathen.

Mr Milne, a missionary to China, who
was present on this affecting occasion,
says, 'If some of you, my aged fathers,
who have long exercised faith in the
promises of God, and have long been
praying for their accomplishment, could
now see Ethiopia literally stretching out
her hands to God, I think you would be
almost ready to fall into the arms of death
with the song of Simeon in your mouths,
'*Lord, now lettest thou thy servant depart in peace.*' "

INDIA.

Whex this Society last assembled, every
member of it felt deeply interested in the
applications made to the Legislature,
(from all classes of pious men, and from
all parts of our country,) for permission
to send missionaries to India. The public feeling was never more warmly expressed. Nine hundred petitions (a number unequalled on any other occasion)
claimed liberty to preach the Gospel to
the millions of India. The Legislature
of our country, attentive to the public
voice, decided in favor of the petitioners,
and an Act for the purpose requested,
passed both houses of Parliament, and
received the royal assent on the 21st of
July, 1813.

This Society cannot forget how much
they owe to those honorable members of
both houses of Parliament, who readily
presented their petitions, and supported
them by their manly and pious eloquence
Their thanks are also due to his Majesty's Ministers, who, in the most polite
and obliging manner, listened to their
representations. The happy effect of this
act has already been experienced, and
liberty allowed for Missionaries to proceed to the East. The expenses attending this application to Parliament were
considerable, but the very great importance of the object, will, no doubt, fully
justify, in the opinion of the Society, the
contribution made for this purpose by the
Directors.

In our Report of the several East India
Missions we begin with

VIZAGAPATAM.

Here the Brethren Gordon and Prichett
continue to labor, both in the work of
translation and of instruction. Having
made a good proficiency in the Telinga
language, they can now declare to the
people in their own tongue, the wonderful works of God. They go frequently
into the villages around them, reading
and explaining portions of the word of
God, to which many pay an attentive regard, pressing close that they may more
exactly hear what is said. Sometimes
they have visited the idol temples, and
have prevailed upon some of the Bramins to listen to the Scriptures. On one
of these occasions, each of the Bramins
accepted a copy of one of the Gospels,
and promised to peruse it diligently; "and
thus," say the Missionaries, "will the
Gospel, for the first time, be conveyed to
what may be called the head-quarters of
superstition here."

It affords great satisfaction to learn that
the converted Bramin *Anundrayer* goes
on well, and takes delight in the instruction of his countrymen. Of another Bramin, Narasimooloo, they entertained good
hopes, and intended when they last wrote,
soon to baptise him. He also is employed
in reading the Scriptures to the natives,
in company with the Missionaries, who
explain the passage read. "This is the
way," say they, "by which the truth
must be propagated, and present appearances produce such hopes as repel the
force of the insinuations of many that our
views are chimerical."

Their visits to the native schools, sometimes afford a high degree of pleasure
When they entered one of these, they
found a number of children, repeating
aloud the first chapter of St Luke's Gospel, which they had begun to transcribe
upon their Palmyra Leaves. Thus they
perceived copies of the word of God
quickly multiplied, and that by the hands
of the heathen themselves. "O that this
practice," say they, "might be universally
adopted," in this pious wish we must all
cordially unite, and should the establishment of schools in India be rendered, as
we hope it will be, more general, this
method will we trust be diligently observed.

GANJAM.

Mr. Lee, who was at Vizagapatam, has
removed, with the consent of his brethren, and at the invitation of some friends
of religion, to Ganjam, a populous town
on the coast. Here he is surrounded not
only by a vast body of the natives, but
also by a multitude of Portuguese and
country-born people. When we last

heard from him, he was about to open a school for children of the latter description, and another for the natives, in which he would teach both English and Gentoo, and thereby have another opportunity of introducing and explaining the doctrines of the Gospel. The attendance of Europeans and others on public worship was encouraging. About one hundred persons attend twice on the Lord's day, and hear the word with seriousness, and he hopes with good effect. In the morning he reads the church service before the sermon. He wishes that more Missionaries may be sent to assist him.

TRAVANCORE.

MR. RINGELTAUBE still resides at Magilady, near Oodagherry, in Travancore, and continues his labors at several villages in that neighborhood. In the summer of 1812, he took a journey to the eastward, and at Negapatam was happy to meet with some of the fruits of Mr. Vos's ministry at that place. His successor has a flourishing school there. At Tranquebar he had a dangerous illness, from which, however, he was happily restored. In the month of October he reached his usual residence and resumed his labors. He visits twice a month his several congregations, and every evening addresses as many as are willing to attend. In some of these places, the people are irregular in their attendance, but at Eotamoly and Auticada they attend much better; at the latter place he thinks of enlarging the church. Pit alow and Covilvilly appear stationary; but a new congregation has sprung up at Ananda-nadan-culi-yirappa, where the people have erected a small church; upon the whole, there has been an increase in number; one hundred and forty-six have been baptised since he last wrote. The number of church members is about six hundred and seventy-seven. About sixty children are in the schools under his direction.

The Directors intend, if possible, to strengthen the hands of Mr. Ringeltaube, by sending another missionary to labor with him (in addition to the Catechists he already employs,) as they conceive there are many people in that quarter disposed to listen to the truth.

We are sorry to learn from Mr. Ringeltaube's journal, that many of the Syrian priests in that neighborhood are inclined to the Church of Rome, and more than a few congregations have joined it.

BELLARY.

SINCE our last Report, we have learned that Mr. Hands, at Bellary, had been alarmingly ill with the liver complaint; he was, however, mercifully recovered, and

after a journey to Vizagapatam and to Madras (to which he was advised,) returned to his station and resumed his labors, assisted by Mr. Taylor, a native of Madras, and one of the fruits of his ministry there; and who, on his recommendation, has been received as a missionary under the patronage of this Society.

On his long journey from Bellary to Vizagapatam, (more than five hundred miles,) wherever he halted, he usually endeavored to publish among those who knew the Canara language, the truth of the Gospel, which in general the people were so ready to hear, that they crowded the choultry, from the time he entered till he left it. He passed through some hundreds of towns and villages, in some of which he found congregations of Roman Catholics, especially near the Coromandel Coast; and in some of the villages, the greater part of the inhabitants were Christians of that communion; but, alas! too generally they were scarcely to be distinguished from their heathen neighbors. Many places he passed through seemed to be eligible stations for missionaries. The paucity of Bramins there, the ruinous state of their pagodas and religious houses, and the disregard now shewn to their once favored deities, afford encouragement to hope, that the time is not far distant when they shall hear and receive the truth of the Gospel.

In the last letter to the Directors received from Mr. Hands, he states, that his charity school was in a flourishing state; and that he had nearly forty boys in his native school. Some additions had been made to the church. He was engaged in correcting his translation of the Gospel of St. Matthew into the Canara language, the second time; and he hoped soon to send to the press both that and the Gospel of St. Luke

(To be continued.)

LONDON MISSIONARY SOCIETY.

The following account of the last meeting of this venerable society is taken from the Missionary Chronicle of June last.

The twentieth general meeting of the Missionary Society, held in London on the 11th, 12th, and 13th days of May, 1814. We have once more the pleasure of presenting to our readers an account of the proceedings of the Missionary Society at their Annual Meeting, and we rejoice to state that the same fervor of holy zeal which animated that great body on former occasions appears to burn with undiminished force, or rather to increase

Surry Chapel.

THE annual services commenced, as usual, at Surry Chapel, which was crowded early, and to excess. The prayers were read by the Rev. Rowland Hill. After which, previous to the sermon, the Rev. Nicholas Sloane, of Torneck, North Britain, offered extemporary prayer in the pulpit.

The Rev. C. F. A. Steinkopff, minister of the German Lutheran Church in the Savoy, London, preached on those appropriate words in the 13th chapter of St. Matthew's Gospel, verse 38th,—'The Field is the World.' This gave him occasion to describe the field of missionary labors. He directed the attention of his hearers—1. To its extent—2. To its need of cultivation—3. To the means necessary for its improvement, and—4. To the difficulties which this undertaking presents, as well as to its final success. Under the third head, relative to the means necessary to the improvement of this vast field, he specified—The dissemination of the Scriptures to the utmost possible extent— The sending of Missionaries to preach the Gospel in every part of the world—The increase of Missionary Societies, in number, activity, and harmonious co-operation —The establishment of schools in every heathen town and village—The offering up of prayer with tenfold fervor, from every Christian country, every Christian church, every Christian heart; and finally —More abundant contributions than ever must flow in from every quarter.

The Rev. John Campbell who visited the several missionary stations in South Africa, who had been nearly two years absent, but happily returned on the preceding Saturday, was requested by the Directors to gratify the audience with a short account of his journies. Universal joy pervaded the congregation, and every one heard with delight his account of several remarkable interpositions of Providence in his favor, in seasons of imminent danger. Multitudes of hearts were lifted up to God with gratitude for all the kindness he had shewn to his dear servant in his voyages and travels. But a full account of his proceedings was reserved for a future opportunity.

The Rev. Mr Griffin, of Portsea, was the mouth of the great congregation in presenting their tribute of heart-felt praise to God, in the concluding prayer.

Tabernacle

This large house of worship was filled at an earlier hour than usual, and to a degree which we think we never witnessed before. It was with extreme difficulty that the ministers could reach the pulpit. The Rev. George Townsend, of Rams-

gate, prayed before sermon; the Rev. T. Raffles, of Liverpool, preached from Acts xix, 23—27. 'And the same time there arose no small stir about that way.'

To prevent the total disappointment of a great number of persons who could not obtain admission, the Rev. W. Cooper of Dublin, preached in the yard before the Tabernacle, on Isaiah xix, 22. 'Look unto me and be ye saved, all the ends of the earth; for I am God, and there is none else.' The Rev. Mr. Ray, of Sudbury, prayed before the sermon; singing was omitted, lest the congregation within the walls should be disturbed. A collection was then made, which shewed that the audience was well pleased with what they had heard, and were unwilling that the funds of the Society should lose any thing by their want of accommodation. Thirty-two pounds were collected out of doors.

Meeting for Business.

The Annual Meetings of the Society for the transaction of business have, for several years past, been held in the Rev. Mr. Jones's Chapel, in Silver-Street, which, though very spacious, has latterly proved insufficient for the purpose. There was also reason to expect on this occasion a larger assembly than ever. Mr Hill, with his accustomed kindness to the Society, readily granted the use of Surry Chapel, on Thursday morning. A great congregation thronged the place long before the appointed hour, and notwithstanding a very numerous meeting of the Tract Society, at the City of London Tavern, which did not break up till about 10 o'clock. A convenient platform was placed before the pulpit, from which the speakers could be readily heard

William Shrubsole, Esq who was called to the Chair, congratulated the Society on the auspicious circumstances in which they were then met, on the overthrow of tyranny in Europe, and the prospect of universal peace, which tended so much to facilitate the operations of the Society, and on the seasonable return of our esteemed brother, Mr Campbell. The Rev. Dr Romeyn, of New York, commenced the service by prayer to God for his presence and blessing. After which, the Rev. Mr Platt read the Plan of the Society as formed at its commencement in 1795, together with that Fundamental Principle of the Society, agreed upon at the first anniversary, declarative of its liberal and comprehensive spirit, which, declining all distinctive names of sect and party, embraces Christians of various denominations.

The Annual Report of the Directors was next read by Mr. Burder, omitting, however, that part of it which related to Africa, as Mr. Campbell was expected to give a fuller account of the state of the missions than had previously been received. After that part of the Report which related to the Lascars had been read, the Secretary made a pause, to give the congregation an opportunity of hearing them read the Scriptures and sing the praises of God in their own language. One of the teachers prayed in the Bengalee tongue.

After the remaining part of the Report was read, Mr Campbell gave a very full and interesting, as well as entertaining, account of his journies in Africa, interspersing many particulars, anecdotes, and remarks which had not previously appeared in the public prints. It is impossible to express the delightful feelings of the great assembly on that occasion.— Wonder, joy, love, and thankfulness, were alternately excited, and every heart was drawn forth in lively desires to promote the Savior's reign throughout the world.

The Rev. Mr Bogue rose to move the acceptance of the Report. He remarked the great increase of the Annual Meetings for business, from small beginnings, when the Society used to meet at Haberdasher's Hall, to the number of a hundred or two, and now the largest places were insufficient for their accommodation. He referred to some of the first friends of the Society, particularly to the Rev. John Eyre, and to several of the missionaries, Cran, Desgranges, Brain, Thompson, and others, who have passed into eternity; but how many young men, and ministers, had come forward to fill up the ranks! He congratulated the Society on the success of their efforts in various places, and especially on Mr. Morrison's having, by the good hand of God upon him, completed the translation of the whole of the New Testament, into the language of China,— a language understood also in other populous countries around it,—a language which perhaps might be read by nearly half the inhabitants of the earth. This he considered as a work of unspeakable importance, and expressed a hope that the British and Foreign Bible Society would vote the printing of 20,000 copies of it, for the use of that immense population. He could not fail to advert to the state of France as a field of future labors, and especially to the French Prisoners, several of whom appeared to have received the word of God, preached to them by the Missionary Students and others, and several of them seem to have become real Christians He described a delightful scene which he witnessed on board one of the prison ships, where Mr. Perrot, accompanied by himself and others, administered the Lord's

Supper. Several have a strong desire to become missionaries to the heathen Great numbers of the prisoners had returned to their own country with the Bible and good books, which would be distributed through France Mr. Bogue considered this as the most delightful of all the anniversaries he had witnessed from the beginning, and hoped the impression would not be transient, but productive of much good to the persons present, and to the cause of God

Mr. J. Clapham of Leeds seconded the motion, and expressed his wish that the Report they had heard, might be very extensively diffused through Yorkshire, and all other parts of the United Kingdom, being persuaded that the information would gladden every heart, and essentially promote the interests of the Society.

The thanks of the Society were then voted to the Rev John Campbell, for the very important services he had performed to the Missionary Society, by his visit to South Africa. The motion was made by the Rev. Alexander Waugh, in a very neat and elegant speech, and seconded by the Rev Rowland Hill, in a truly pious and affecting manner. It is needless to say that the Resolution passed not only unanimously, but with a cordiality of Christian love and gratitude, which no words can express.

To save time, votes of thanks to the treasurer, Joseph Hardcastle, Esq. to the secretary, the Rev G. Burder, and to the late Directors, for their several services, were moved together, and passed with the usual unanimity. The motion was made by the Rev. Mr. Paterson, and seconded by the Rev. Mr Pinkerton, whose appearance on this occasion, after the long and hazardous journies they have taken in behalf of the cause of Christ, afforded great additional pleasure to the assembly The services they have been enabled to render to the interests of Christianity in Denmark, Sweden, Norway, Russia, &c. by promoting Bible Societies, and Tract Societies, &c. &c. in so many countries on the continent, rendered their presence and speeches truly gratifying.

The names of the new Directors proposed were read by the Rev. Mr Tracy, and their acceptance moved by Rev. Mr. Griffin, and seconded by Mr. Steven.

The thanks of the Society to those ministers and other friends who have made public collections, or otherwise contributed to the funds of the Society during the last year, were moved by William Alers, Esq. and seconded by Benjamin Neale, Esq. The latter gentlemen took occasion solemnly to pledge himself and his young friends to the Society, that they were determined, by the grace of God, never to desert the good cause, but to employ their utmost energies in its support, when the fathers of the Institution should sleep in the grave. Old and young were deeply affected. Mr. Bogue rose, and requested that if the young people of both sexes then present concurred in the pious resolution just stated by Mr. Neale, they would hold up their hands. The hands of multitudes of young people were instantly elevated, and tears of joy filled the eyes of the elder friends of the Institution, who rejoiced in hope that when they shall be removed from the stage of action, many others will rise up in their stead to promote with their whole hearts the same glorious cause. May they never forget the solemn engagement. High heaven has witnessed their vow; they have lifted up their hands to the Lord, and they cannot, must not, go back. Let this page remind them in years to come, that the vows of the Lord are upon them.

Thanks to the several Auxiliary Societies which have been formed in various parts of England, Scotland, and Ireland, in aid of the funds of the Society, were then moved by the Rev. Matthew Wilks, with his usual energy of sentiment and language, and seconded by the Rev. Mr. Jones, who in a very handsome manner stated his joy in the insufficiency of his own chapel, to contain the augmented number of its friends on this occasion, and his readiness, on that score alone, to relinquish the pleasure and honor he had derived from the former meetings of the Society at Silver Street.

A short hymn of praise to God concluded the services of Thursday Morning. It was a meeting that will not soon be forgotten. The vast assembly departed with emotions of joy and gratitude, regretting that they were obliged to separate, and could not prolong the delightful engagements of the day. It seems desirable that measures may hereafter be taken to secure more time for this branch of the Anniversary Services, which through the multiplicity of meetings, is crowded into a space too narrow. It may perhaps be necessary also to admit by tickets, into some parts at least of all the places of meeting, that the contributors to the Institution may be able to secure seats, of which hitherto many have been painfully deprived.

Tottenham Court Chapel.

This place also was early filled. The prayers of the Church were read by the Rev. Mr Geary. The Rev. Mr. Tyreman of the Isle of Wight, prayed in the pulpit, and the Rev. David M'Indoe, of Newcastle-upon-Tyne, preached on those words in Isaiah xl, 5.—*And the glory of the Lord shall be revealed, and all flesh shall see it together; for the mouth of the Lord hath spoken it.*

St. Leonard's Church, Shoreditch.

A great congregation assembled in this spacious Church, notwithstanding the morning was very rainy. Prayers were read by the Rev. Mr. Crosby, and a sermon preached by the Rev. William Gurney, Vicar of St. Clement Danes, London. This service was kindly undertaken at a very short notice, in consequence of the illness of the Rev. Mr. Whish, of Bristol, who was engaged to preach. That gentleman who had been in Devonshire on account of his health, and was travelling towards London, was taken so ill at Exeter, that he could not proceed on his journey, of which he informed Mr. G. requesting that he or some other clergyman would perform the expected service in his stead. Mr. Gurney complied, and preached on Habakkuk ii, 14, *For the earth shall be filled with the knowledge of the glory of the Lord, as the waters cover the sea.*

Sion Chapel.

An adjourned meeting of the Society was held at Sion Chapel in the afternoon, the Rev. John Hilliard in the chair; when the thanks of the Society were voted to the Rev. Mr. Gurney, for the readiness with which he consented to preach, at a very short notice, at Shoreditch Church. Thanks were also voted to the Rev. Messrs. Steinkopff, Raffles, and M'Indoe, for their excellent sermons, and that all the said gentlemen be requested to furnish the Society with copies for publication.

Sacramental Services.

The delightful engagements of the Missionary Anniversary terminated as usual in the celebration of that ordinance in which Christ exhibits his dying love to his people, and they shew forth their attachment to him and their affection to each other. Mr. Bogue presided; Mr. Hillyard prayed, Mr. Cooper, of Dublin, gave the introductory address; Mr. Bogue gave thanks for the bread and wine, &c., Mr. Gardner, of Barnstable, Mr. Cockin, of Halifax, and Mr. Wilks, gave exhortations; Mr J Hyatt concluded with prayer. It was a solemn and delightful meeting.

The Lord's Supper was administered at the same hour in Orange-street Chapel, for the accommodation of those who reside in the western part of the metropolis. This place was well filled, but not so crowded as to be rendered uncomfortable. The Rev Rowland Hill presided. Inter-

ressed were delivered during and
administration, by the Rev.
Roby, Bruce, Cobbin, and Dr.
and prayers offered by the Rev.
J. Townsend and Sla torie.
re so often intimated, when re-
e Missionary Anniversari s, that
eeting was the best, that we feel
how to express our opinion of
ing. We believe none will say
rior to any of the former. The
e was, at least, as great, and et
een greater. The love and zeal
on the occasion were not appar-
inished. We have heard, that
gment of many ministers, there
sible improvement in most parts
vices; and the presence of our
who had travelled thousands of
romote the cause of Christ, gave
l additional interest to the whole.
only say, our delight was inex-
great; and the persuasion that
oves of our endeavors, that he
lantly succeeded them already,
we shall see still greater things
e, fills our hearts with joy and
ess. He who opens, and no man
opened new and wide doors for
on of his Gospel; he has raised
portionable number of instru-
r the work; and he has replen-
funds of the Society to support
what more can be desired! Let
ward in the name of the Lord,
praying that the power of the
it may accompany his word; and
with holy gratitude, 'The Lord
s with us, the God of Jacob is
e.'

IONS FOR THE SUPPORT
ISSIONS AND FOR THE
SLATIONS OF THE SCRIP-
S.

114. From an elderly
orthington, (Mass..) by
ey Wilbur, $0 75
a Mr. Paul Roberts,
s Bridge, Nassau, (N.
r. S. T. Armstrong,   2 00
Society of Females in
, (Mass.) by Mr. E.
                               5 50
n a man, who, having
usly benefited himself
abors of missionaries,
contribute something
enefit of others,   2 00
m a Female Cent So-
estbrook, (Maine,) by
                       _____
Carried forward $10 25

Brought forward $10 25
the Rev. Mr. Hilliard, remitted
by Mr. Duren.*   ,52
21. From a female in Bangor,
(Maine,) by the Rev. H. Loomis,   5 00
From the following persons re-
mitted by Mrs. H. Dana, of Or-
ford, (N H.) viz.
  Ladies in Orford, $20
  Mrs. Payson, of Bath N. H. 2
  Mrs. E. B. Woodward, of
    Hanover,   2
  Mrs. Lydia Woodward, Ha-
    verhill,   2
  Mrs. Hannah Trotter, Brad-
    ford, (Ver.)   4—30 00
23. From the following persons†
in Prattsburgh, (N. Y.) viz.
                       _____
Carried forward $45 77

* This sum is part of a donation remitted in October, $45 of which came to
hand on the 15th of that month, and has
been published under that date, as from a
Female Cent Society in Gorham,
(Maine.) The mistake was occasioned
by the original memorandum having been
mislaid before it reached the Treasurer.

† These donations were enclosed in the
following letter to the Treasurer of the
Board:

"Sir,
    Many of the friends of relig-
ion in distant parts of the country, would
be glad to contribute to the support of
Foreign Missions, but are discouraged
on account of the difficulty of transmit-
ting small sums to the Treasurer of the
Society. Thus, many times, the widow's
mite is not given. To remedy that evil,
in this place, I have proposed to transmit,
from time to time, at my own expense,
whatever sums shall be entrusted to my
care for that purpose. I wish some person would take that trouble. upon himself
in every society. I now enclose you
twenty dollars, a part of which has been
received in that way. Yours affectionately,
    Prattsburgh, Steuben county,
        N. Y. Dec. 1, 1814.
    J. Evarts, Esq.

P. S. If you think it will be of any
service, you are at liberty to publish the
above letter, omitting the name."

N. B. From expressions in the letters
of several donors, it is evident, that the
present depreciated and fluctuating
state of the paper currency in general, is
a circumstance which prevents many donations, as the donors are doubtful wheth-

Brought forward $45 77
Mr. Joel Tuttle, $5
— Richard Hull,   5
— Henry G. Linsley,   1
— Robert Porter,   4
Mrs. Roxana Porter,   5—20 00
           —————
           $65 77.

or such bills as they should transmit, could be converted to the use of the Board without the loss of a considerable part of the sum intended to be given.

On this subject the Treasurer thinks it proper to state, that all bills, which are current in any part of the country, are gladly received, and receipts given for the nominal value. The bills not current at Boston, are at present either kept on hand, or deposited in banks where they are current: and will ultimately be disposed of on the best terms possible. It is probable, however, that the Board, by the assistance of its agents and friends in different parts of the country, will be able to dispose of all bills received, at a smaller discount than would ordinarily be the case with an individual.

NEW WORKS.

The fulness of the Godhead dwelling in Christ: illustrated in a Discourse delivered at Haverhill, (N. H.) on Lord's day, April 17, 1814. By Caleb Burge. A. M. Minister of the Gospel. Boston; John M'Kown.

Address of Elkanah Watson, Esq. delivered before the Berkshire Agricultural Society, in the Old Church in Pittsfield, Oct. 7, 1814, and published by the unanimous vote of the Society. Together with the Premiums awarded, and the proceedings of the Society on that day. Pittsfield; Phinehas Allen.

A Sermon delivered before the Massachusetts Society for the Suppression of Intemperance, at their annual meeting in Boston, May 27, 1814. By John T. Kirkland, D. D. President of the University at Cambridge. Boston; John Eliot.

Elements of Greek Grammar, taken chiefly from the Grammar of Casper Frederick Hachenberg. Adopted for use in Yale College. New Haven; O. Steele. $1,25. 1814.

POETRY.

MONODY ON THE DEATH OF MRS. NEWELL.

HEARD you the music in the breeze,
    By angels wafted to our shore?
Its tragic sounds of distant woe,
In mildly plaintive notes and low,
Across the land, and o'er the seas,
    The last sad sighs of mourning Asia bore.

Yet now she mourns no guilty taste,
    Of tree forbidden, or unlawful bliss,
Nor sees her Great Redeemer plac'd,
With thorn-wove wreath, insulting, grac'd,
    Where Roman soldiers laugh, or Jewish foes can hiss.
In darker times, in days of woe,
When guilt was high, and hope was low,
The barb'rous cross and bloody show,
Rent the long vail that shaded o'er,
The sacred mysteries before,
    Reveal'd a sanctuary too,
       Whose cherubs wait,
       To ope its gate,
And bid diviner streams of richer comfort flow.

High in the holy, happy throng,
    Redeem'd from pain, and cleans'd from guilt,
Our once dear Harriet tunes her song,
While golden harps the strains prolong,
    To Him whose precious blood was spilt.
How sweetly shall that praise ascend,
    How long its glowing numbers swell,
Its sweetness angels scarce transcend,
    Its length, nor time, nor tongue, can tell.

Yet hapless seem'd the fatal hour,
When low beneath the tyrant's power,
  Her lifeless form was laid;—
Well might their pleasure cease to flow,
Who knew such loss, who felt such woe,
  And saw such prospects fade.
  Say, then, ye sons of Asia's heathen land,
  Who hail'd her footsteps on your strand;
Just hail'd, and saw the victim of disease,
  Her pallid corse in shrouded robes array'd,
Whose active spirit welcom'd such release,
  From earthly cares and sins incumbent load,
  Wing'd its glad way to realms of day,
  The bosom of her Father and her God—
Say ye, how sad, benighted India, say,
  How deeply mournful was the day,
Which left your fairest hopes your promis'd rich delight,
  That glowing fancy sketch'd so bright,
To pine and wither in untimely shade?

          For you her tender heart
Could break the ties that bound her to her home;
  For you with kindred could she part,
    Though sharp the pang, though deep the smart—
From the sweet circle of her friendship too,
  Where all might wish her stay,
  Could tear herself away,
And bid a long adieu.
How strong must be the love,
That could such pity move;
How nearly must those fond affections rise,
  To those which rule beyond the skies,
Which e'er could prompt in foreign lands to roam;
  And when her lot was cast,
On the uncertain blast,
  Could raise her mind from fear
  Or danger ever near,
  Till safe in port at last
  The storm and tempest past,
From the wide wat'ry waste, and ocean's billowy foam.

          Yea, safe indeed she is,
From every storm and every tempest safe.
  A better haven than Hindostan gives,
  And fairer clime than where the Indian lives,
She reach'd at last, the seat of purer bliss,
Where no dull care corrodes, no rankling ill can chafe.

  Nor mourn, thou partner of her fondest love,
That thou art left thus pensive and alone;
  Nor weep that she, so soon, has fled above,
So soon her toils and cares become thine own.
The sweet remembrance of thy early joys,
  Shall still remain, and still thy bosom warm.
And Oh! what motives to exertion rise,
From that one thought that she, alas! has gone:
  Yes, when thy pleasures just began to dawn,
Thou saw'st her winged chariot mounting to the skies,
  By faith and hope, those heav'nly coursers, drawn—
    Ah! did the mantle of her holy zeal,
  And did that sympathy, which bade her feel,
Fall from her rapid, bounding flight on you?
  Then shall thy ardor prove as great, as true;
  Since the same errand still thy soul employs,
The will to conquer, and the heart reform.

  Yet other friends may claim a pitying tear,
Friends who

Though not to them the less their Harriet dear;
 But e'en these friends could bid a last farewell,
And see her leave a much-lov'd, native land;
 Could wipe away the tear-drops as they fell,
And bless the youthful hand.
And will they now, her safe departure mourn,
 Her happy voyage to a brighter clime;
Or sigh, that she has pass'd the bourne,
 Beyond the reach of danger and of time.

And Oh! that all, who once their Harriet knew,
 And all who from her life her virtues learn,
Might prove, that they possess a love as true,
 Taught in their lives, as in their hearts to burn.
Shall not Columbia's daughters strive to gain,
 That sacred zeal in virtue's high emprise,
Which leads o'er sorrows dark and troublous main,
 To brighter realms beyond the lower skies?
Remember, too, where distant Ganges rolls,
 'Mong countless millions silently along,
How many poor, how many starving souls,
 Surround its banks, or on its surface throng.
And shall they call, and shall their voice be heard;
 Heard and not answer'd, known but scorn'd by all?
Or rather shall new Harriets yet be rear'd,
 And to the world her virtues too recall?

Go, then, nor heed the dangers of the deep,
 To where Mauritius rears his snow-capt head,
There may you lonely vigils keep,
 In silent hours, to watch and weep,
 And as you tread your mournful round,
Along Port Louis' consecrated shore,
 Perhaps o'er Harriet's nameless mound,
With sighs respond old ocean's roar—
 While ebon groves, that nod along the steep,
Shall shade the humble mansion o' the dead.
There write her name, there bid her virtues blaze;
 By kindred love, and kindred zeal display'd:
Let every effort, every action prove,
 No praise you seek, that comes not from above;
And though, perchance, the tenor of your days,
 Be dark, and rough, and far unknown to fame;
Yet look for joys that never, never fade,
For such your Harriet's were, and ye should seek the same.　 בצלה,

---

TO CORRESPONDENTS.

The communications of R. W. are received.

No VI, *On the Sabbath*, will be inserted in our next.

The paper from *A Lay Congregationalist* is under consideration.

Several other communications will be attended to in their order.

We are obliged to postpone several articles of religious intelligence; among which is a notice of the exertions made, during the last summer, by Christians of the Baptist denomination in the United States, for the support of missions among the heathen.

The premiums offered to writers in the volume of the Panoplist, which is now closed, will be adjudged as soon as convenience will permit; and the adjudication will be made public soon after it is declared. It will then be stated, whether a similar offer will be made in reference to the next volume.

TO PATRONS.

Our Patrons are respectfully informed, that our work begins to feel the pressure of the war very severely. We have no reason to expect exemption from the general calamity; but we do hope that our subscribers will generally feel the necessity of not suffering a temporary pressure to injure our work permanently. If a general effort were made, by the agents and friends of the Panoplist, to obtain new subscribers to succeed others, who have been compelled to withdraw their names by the impoverishing effects of the war, the object would be accomplished.

9 780266 659877